JAVA

IN TWO SEMESTERS

Second Edition

Quentin Charatan & Aaron Kans

JAVA

IN TWO SEMESTERS
Second Edition

Quentin Charatan & Aaron Kans

The *McGraw·Hill* Companies

London Boston Burr Ridge, IL Dubuque, IA Madison, WI New York San Francisco St. Louis Bangkok Bogotá Caracas Kuala Lumpur Lisbon Madrid Mexico City Milan Montreal New Delhi Santiago Seoul Singapore Sydney Taipei Toronto

Java in Two Semesters, second edition
Quentin Charatan and Aaron Kans

ISBN-13 978-0-07-710889-2
ISBN-10 0077108892

 **Education**

QA 76.73.J38C5
(CHA)

0660 3328 4

Published by McGraw-Hill Education
Shoppenhangers Road
Maidenhead
Berkshire
SL6 2QL
Telephone: 44 (0) 1628 502 500
Fax: 44 (0) 1628 770 224
Website: www.mcgraw-hill.co.uk

British Library Cataloguing in Publication Data
A catalogue record for this book is available from the British Library

Library of Congress Cataloguing in Publication Data
The Library of Congress data for this book has been applied for from the Library of Congress

Development Editor: Karen Mosman
Marketing Manager: Alice Duijser
Production Editor: James Bishop

Text Design by HL Studios
Cover design by ego creative limited
Printed and bound in the United Kingdom by Bell and Bain Ltd, Glasgow

ISBN-13 978-0-07-710889-2
ISBN-10 0077108892

The **McGraw-Hill** Companies

Dedications

To my mother and father (AK)
To Katy, Jonny and Nick Mills (QC)

Brief Table of Contents

Detailed Table of Contents

Preface

This book is designed for university students taking a first module in software development or programming, followed by a second, more advanced module. The book uses Java as the vehicle for the teaching of programming concepts – design concepts are explained using the UML notation. The topic is taught from first principles and assumes no prior knowledge of the subject.

The book is organized so as to support two twelve-week, one-semester modules, which might typically comprise a two-hour lecture, a one-hour tutorial and a one- or two-hour laboratory session. The self-test questions at the end of each chapter ensure that the learning objectives for that chapter have been met, while the programming exercises that follow allow these learning objectives to be applied to complete programs. In addition to these exercises and questions, a case study is developed in each semester to illustrate the use of the techniques covered in the text to develop a non-trivial application. Lecturers who teach on modules that run for fewer than twelve weeks in a semester could treat these case studies as a self-directed student learning experience, rather than as taught topics.

The approach taken in this book is ideal for students entering university with no background in the subject matter, often coming from pre-degree courses in other disciplines, or perhaps returning to study after long periods away from formal education. It is the authors' experience that such students have enormous difficulties in grasping the fundamental programming concepts the first time round, and therefore require a simpler and gentler introduction to the subject than is presented in most standard texts.

The book takes an integrated approach to software development by covering such topics as basic design principles and standards, testing methodologies and HCI as well as looking at detailed implementation topics.

In the first semester, considerable time is spent concentrating on the fundamental programming concepts such as declarations of variables and basic control structures, methods and arrays, prior to introducing students to the concepts of classes and objects, inheritance, software quality, graphics and event-driven programming.

The second semester covers more advanced topics such as packages, interfaces, exceptions, two-dimensional arrays, collection classes from the Java Collections Framework, advanced graphics, file-handling techniques, the implementation of multi-threaded programs and network programming.

This second edition of the book contains significant modifications and additions to the first edition, and is based around the latest release of Java, namely Java 5.0. Selection and iteration are now covered in separate chapters in the first semester, which now also includes a new chapter dedicated to the implementation of methods. The Swing package is now used throughout the book for the development of graphical user interfaces. The second semester includes new chapters on the Java Collections Framework and network programming. The latest features of Java 5.0 have been incorporated throughout the book. These include the Scanner class for keyboard input, the enhanced **for** loop for iterating over collections, generics for type-safe collections and enumerated types. As well as these changes, the end of chapter questions and programming exercises have been significantly revised.

The accompanying CD contains a Java IDE, with instructions for installation and use, and the source code for many of the classes from the book.

We would like to thank our publisher, McGraw-Hill, for the encouragement and guidance that we have received throughout the production of this book. We also would like to thank David Hatter for his continual help and support over the years.

Additionally, we would like to thank especially the computing students of the University of East London for their thoughtful comments and feedback. For support and inspiration, special thanks are due once again to our families and friends.

Dr Quentin Charatan (q.h.charatan@uel.ac.uk)
Dr Aaron Kans (a.kans@uel.ac.uk)
London, UK, September 2005

Acknowledgements

We would also like to thank the following academics who reviewed the previous edition of the book and draft chapters from this new edition. Thank you for providing us with your thoughts and suggestions for the book.

Bob Lang, University of the West of England
Des Stephens, University of Luton
Michael Evans, University of Kingston
Ray Jones, London Metropolitan University
Stuart Allen, Cardiff University
Julie Dawson, University of the West of England

Trademarks

Java®, is a trademark of Sun Microsystems.

Microsoft Windows®, Interet Explorer®, Word for Windows®, Visual Basic®, and J++® are trademarks of Microsoft Corporation.

Netscape® is a trademark of Netscape Communications Corporation.

JCreator® is a trademark of Xinox Software.

UNIX® is a trademark of X/Open Company Ltd.

Macintosh® is a trademark of Apple Computer Inc.

Guided Tour

Learning Objectives

Each chapter opens with a set of learning objectives, summarizing what readers should learn from each chapter.

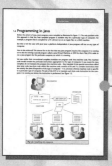

Key Terms

New terms and concepts in programming are highlighted throughout the chapter where they first appear, so they can be found quickly and easily.

Figures and Tables

Each chapter provides a number of illustrations, screenshots, figures and tables to help you to visualize the various models and concepts in Java programming

Programs

Throughout the text, the authors introduce a variety of programs. These are broken down step by step to show you how the code is written, how it works in practice when it is output, and demonstrate how to build your own programs using these techniques.

Self-Test Questions

These questions encourage you to review and apply the knowledge you have acquired from each chapter, testing your comprehension of new terminology, and acting as a useful revision tool of important concepts.

Programming Exercises

This end-of-chapter feature is the perfect way to practise the techniques you have been taught. By using the CD that accompanies this book, you can apply your knowledge to rewrite, design and create your own Java programs.

Case Study Chapters

The book includes three case study chapters that are designed to develop the programming skills you have acquired and apply them to a business problem or real-world situation.

Technology to enhance learning and teaching

Visit www.mcgraw-hill.co.uk/textbooks/charatan today

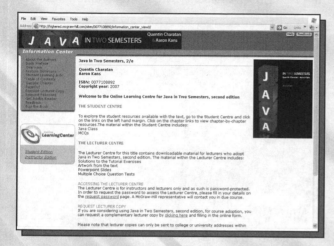

Online Learning Centre (OLC)

After completing each chapter, log on to the supporting Online Learning Centre website. Take advantage of the study tools offered to reinforce the material you have read in the text, and to develop your java programming skills in a fun and effective way.

Resources for students include:

+ Java Classes
+ Multiple Choice Questions

Also available for lecturers in a password protected area:

+ Solutions to the exercises
+ Artwork from the textbook
+ Powerpoint presentations
+ Multiple Choice Questions for use in assessments

Student CD-ROM

In the back cover of this book you will find a free CD-ROM. This CD contains a Java Integrated Development Environment (IDE) and Software Development Kit (SDK), with instructions for installation and use, and the source code for many of the classes from the book. Chapter One introduces these tools and explains how you use them to develop your Java programs.

For lecturers: Primis Content Centre

If you need to supplement your course with additional cases or content, create a personalised e-Book for your students. Visit www.primiscontentcenter.com or e-mail primis_euro@mcgraw-hill.com for more information.

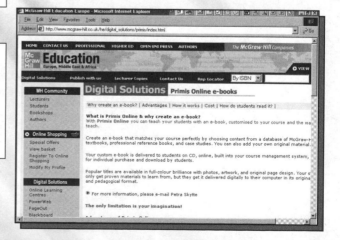

Study Skills

We publish guides to help you study, research, pass exams and write essays, all the way through your university studies.

Visit **www.openup.co.uk/ss/** to see the full selection and get £2 discount by entering promotional code **study** when buying online!

Computing Skills

If you'd like to brush up on your Computing skills, we have a range of titles covering MS Office applications such as Word, Excel, PowerPoint, Access and more.

Get a £2 discount off these titles by entering the promotional code **app** when ordering online at www.mcgraw-hill.co.uk/app

Semester One

CHAPTER: 01

The first step

J
A
V
A

Objectives:

By the end of this chapter you should be able to:

- *explain the meaning of the word **software**;*
- *explain how Java programs are compiled and run;*
- *write Java programs that display text on the screen;*
- *distinguish between the eight built-in **primitive types** of Java;*
- ***declare** and **assign** values to **variables**;*
- *create **constant** values with the keyword `final`;*
- *join messages and values in output commands by using the **concatenation** (+) operator;*
- *use the input methods of the `Scanner` class to get data from the keyboard;*
- *design the functionality of a method using **pseudocode**.*

1.1 Introduction

Like any student starting out on a first programming module, you will be itching to do just one thing – get started on your first program. We can well understand that, and you won't be disappointed, because you will be writing programs in this very first chapter. Designing and writing computer programs can be one of the most enjoyable and satisfying things you can do, although it can seem a little daunting at first because it is like nothing else you have ever done. But, with a bit of perseverance, you will not only start to get a real taste for it but you may well find yourself sitting up till two o'clock in the morning trying to solve a problem. And just when you have given up and you are dropping off to sleep, the answer pops into your head and you are at the computer again until you notice it is getting light outside! So if this is happening to you, then don't worry – it's normal!

However, before you start writing programs you need some background; this chapter therefore starts off with a few definitions, and then goes on to give you some general information about programming and programming languages, and how you go about writing and producing programs.

1.2 Software

A computer is not very useful unless we give it some instructions that tell it what to do. This set of instructions is called a **program**. The word **software** is the name given to a single program or a set of programs.

There are two main kinds of software. **Application software** is the name given to useful programs that a user might need; for example, word-processors, spreadsheets, accounts programs, games and so on. Such programs are often referred to simply as **applications**. **System software** is the name given to special programs that help the computer to do its job; for example, operating systems (such as UNIX or Windows, which help us to use the computer) and network software (which helps computers to communicate with each other).

Both application and system software are built by writing a set of instructions for the computer to obey. **Programming** is the task of writing these instructions. These instructions have to be written in a language specially designed for this purpose. These programming languages include C++, Visual Basic, Pascal and many more. The language we are going to use in this book is Java. Java is an example of one of the most recent advances in the development of programming languages – it is an **object-oriented** language. Right now, that phrase might not mean anything to you, but you will find out all about its meaning as we progress through this book.

1.3 Compiling programs

Like most modern programming languages, the Java language consist of instructions that look a bit like English. For example, words such as `while` and `if` are part of the Java language. The set of instructions written in a programming language is called the **program code** or **source code**.

Ultimately these instructions have to be translated into a language that can be understood by the computer. The computer understands only **binary** instructions – that means instructions written as a series of 0's and 1's. So, for example, the machine might understand 01100111 to mean `add`. The language of the computer is often referred to as **machine code**. A special piece of system software called a **compiler** translates the instructions written in a programming language into machine instructions consisting of 0's and 1's. This process is known as **compiling**. Figure 1.1 illustrates how this process works for most programming languages.

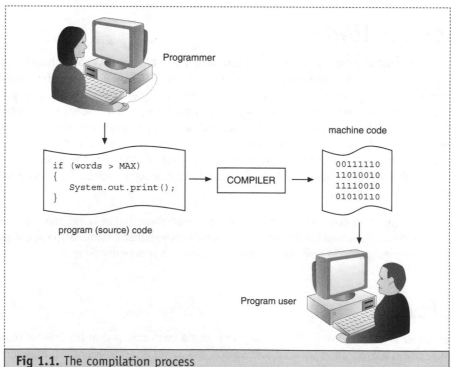

Fig 1.1. The compilation process

1.4 Programming in Java

Before the advent of Java, most programs were compiled as illustrated in figure 1.1. The only problem with this approach is that the final compiled program is suitable only for a particular type of computer. For example, a program that is compiled for a PC will not run on an Apple Mac or a UNIX machine.

But this is not the case with Java! Java is **platform-independent**. A Java program will run on any type of computer.

How is this achieved? The answer lies in the fact that any Java program requires the computer it is running on to also be running a special program called a **Java Virtual Machine**, or **JVM** for short. This JVM is able to run a Java program for the particular computer on which it is running.

We saw earlier that conventional compilers translate our program code into machine code. This machine code would contain the particular instructions appropriate to the type of computer it was meant for. Java compilers do not translate the program into machine code – they translate it into special instructions called **Java byte code.** Java byte code, which, like machine code, consists of 0's and 1's, contains instructions that are exactly the same irrespective of the type of computer – it is *universal*, whereas machine code is specific to a particular type of computer. The job of the JVM is to translate each byte code instruction for the computer it is running on, before the instruction is performed. See figure 1.2.

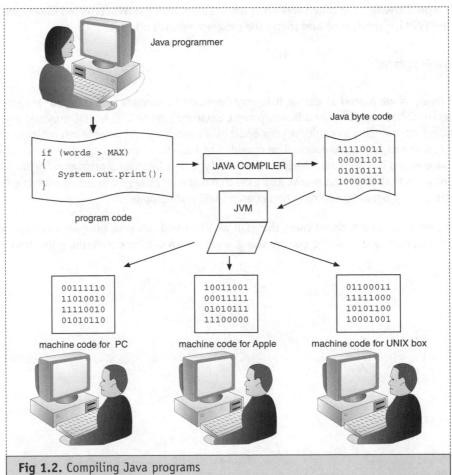

Fig 1.2. Compiling Java programs

There are various ways in which a JVM can be installed on a computer. In the case of some operating systems such as Linux and the Apple Mac OS, it comes packaged with the system. This is not the case with Windows, however, and one way to obtain a JVM is to download and install the Java **Software Development Kit (SDK)**, which is provided to the world free of charge from Sun Microsystems. This is obtained from the following website:

`java.sun.com`

We strongly recommend that you visit this site from time to time, because not only does it provide downloads such as the above, it also contains a wealth of information about the Java language.

In fact, to save you the trouble, we have provided this SDK for you on the accompanying CD – we have also provided a simple-to-use *Integrated Development Environment (IDE)*, the meaning of which we will explain in a moment. Before doing that however, we should explain that one way to compile and run your programs is from a command line in a console window. The source code that you write is in the form of a simple text file which has a `.java` extension. The compiler that comes as part of the SDK is called `javac.exe`, and to compile a file called, for example, `myProgram.java`, you would write at the command prompt:

javac myProgram.java

This would create a file called `myProgram.class`, which is the compiled file in Java byte code. The name of the JVM is `java.exe` and to run the program you would type:

java myProgram

However, as we hinted at earlier, it is very common to compile and run your programs by using a special program called an **Integrated Development Environment** or **IDE**. An IDE provides you with an easy-to-use window into which you can type your code; other windows will provide information about the files you are using; and a separate window will be provided to tell you of your errors. The reason that you are very likely to have errors in your code the first time you type it is because a programming language has a very strict set of rules that you must follow. Just as with natural languages, this set of rules is called the **syntax** of the language. A program containing syntax errors will not compile.

Not only does an IDE do all these things, it also lets you run your programs as soon as you have compiled them. Depending on the IDE you are using, your screen will look something like that in figure 1.3.

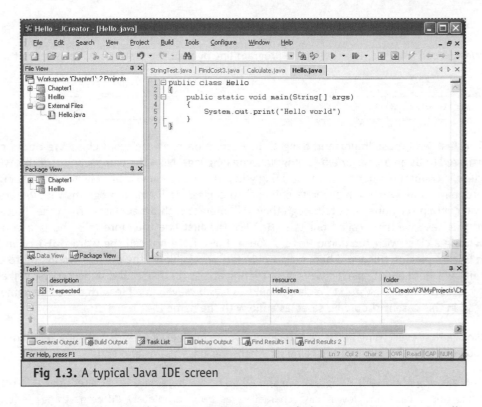

Fig 1.3. A typical Java IDE screen

Common IDEs include *Borland JBuilder*, *JCreator*, *NetBeans* and *BlueJ*. Instructions for installing and using the IDE provided with this book are contained on the disk.

1.5 Your first program

Now it is time to write your first program. Anyone who knows anything about programming will tell you that the first program that you write in a new language has always got to be a program that displays the words "Hello world" on the screen; so we will stick with tradition, and your first program will do exactly that!

When your program runs you will see the words "Hello world" displayed.[1] The type of window in which this is displayed will vary according to the particular operating system you are running, and the particular compiler you are using.

The code for the "Hello world" program is written out for you below as program 1.1.

Program 1.1

```
public class Hello
{
    public static void main(String[] args)
    {
        System.out.println("Hello world");
    }
}
```

---

[1] In some systems you might find that the words "Press any key to continue ..." are displayed immediately after the output.

1.5.1 Analysis of the "Hello world" program

We will consider the meaning of the program line by line. The first line, which we call the header, looks like this:

```
public class Hello
```

The first, and most important, thing to pay attention to is the word **class**. We noted earlier that Java is referred to as an *object-oriented* programming language. Now the true meaning of this will start to become clear in chapter 6 – but for the time being you just need to know that object-oriented languages require the program to be written in separate units called **classes**. The simple programs that we are starting off with will contain only one class (although they will interact with other classes from the "built-in" Java libraries); in this case we have called our class `Hello`. The first line therefore tells the Java compiler that we are writing a class with the name `Hello`. You will also have noticed the word **public** in front of the word **class**;[2] placing this word here makes our class accessible to the outside world and to other classes – so, until we learn about specific ways of restricting access (in the second semester) we will always include this word in the header. A **public** class should always be saved in a file with the same name as the class itself – so in this case it should be saved as a file with the name `Hello.java`.

Notice that everything in the class has to be contained between two curly brackets (known as **braces**) that look like this { }; these tell the compiler where the class begins and ends.

There is one important thing that we should point out here. Java is *case-sensitive* – in other words it interprets upper case and lower case characters as two completely different things – it is very important therefore to type the statements exactly as you see them here, paying attention to the case of the letters.

The next line that we come across (after the opening curly bracket) is this:

```
public static void main(String[] args)
```

This looks rather strange if you are not used to programming – but you will see that every application we write is going to contain one class with this line in it. In chapter 6 you will find out that this basic unit called a class is made up of, among other things, a number of **methods**. You will find out a lot more about methods in chapter 4, but for now it is good enough for you to know that a method contains a particular set of instructions that the computer must carry out. Our `Hello` class contains just one method and this line introduces that method. In fact it is a very special method called a `main` method. Applications in Java must always contain a class with a method called `main`: this is where the program begins. A program starts with the first instruction of `main`, then obeys each instruction in sequence (unless the instruction itself tells it to jump to some other place in the program). The program terminates when it has finished obeying the final instruction of `main`.

So this line that we see above introduces the `main` method; the program instructions are now written in a second set of curly brackets that show us where this `main` method begins and ends. At the moment we will not worry about the words **public static void** in front of `main`, and the bit in the brackets afterwards (`String[] args`) – we will just accept that they always have to be there; you will begin to understand their significance as you learn more about programming concepts.

---

[2] You will notice that we are using bold courier font for Java keywords.

Now, at last we can examine the really important bit – the line of code that represent the instruction, *display "Hello world" on the screen*. The line that does this looks like this:

```
System.out.println("Hello world");
```

This is the way we are always going to get stuff printed on a simple text screen; we use `System.out.println` (or sometimes `System.out.print`, as explained below) and put whatever we want to be displayed in the brackets. The `println` is short for "print line" by the way. You won't understand at this stage why it has to be in this precise form (with each word separated by a full stop, and the actual phrase in double quotes), but do make sure that you type it exactly as you see it here, with an upper case *S* at the beginning. Also, you should notice the semi-colon at the end of the statement. This is important; every Java instruction has to end with a semi-colon.

1.5.2 Adding comments to a program

When we write program code, we will often want to include some comments to help remind us what we were doing when we look at our code a few weeks later, or to help other people to understand what we have done.

Of course, we want the compiler to ignore these comments when the code is being compiled. There are two ways of doing this. For short comments we place two slashes (//) at the beginning of the line – everything after these slashes, up to the end of the line, is then ignored by the compiler.

For longer comments (that is, ones that run over more than a single line) we usually use another approach. The comment is enclosed between two special symbols; the opening symbol is a slash followed by a star (/*) and the closing symbol is a star followed by a slash (*/). Everything between these two symbols is ignored by the compiler. The program below shows examples of both types of comment; when you compile and run this program you will see that the comments have no effect on the code, and the output is exactly the same as that of the original program.

> **Program 1.1 – with added comments**
>
> ```
> // this is a short comment, so we use the first method
>
> public class Hello
> {
>     public static void main(String[] args)
>     {
>         System.out.println("Hello world");
>     }
>  /* this is the second method of including comments - it is more
>     convenient to use this method here, because the comment is longer and
>     goes over more than one line */
> }
> ```

In chapter 9 you will learn about a special tool called `Javadoc` for documenting your programs. In that chapter you will see that in order to use this tool you must comment your classes in the `Javadoc` style – as you will see, `Javadoc` comments must begin with /** and end with */.

1.6 Simple data types in Java

Program 1.1 is of course very simple indeed. One way in which this program is very limited is that it has no *data* to work on. All interesting programs will have to store data in order to give interesting results; what use would a calculator be without the numbers the user types in to add and multiply? For this reason, one of the first questions you should ask when learning any programming language is "what types of data does this language allow me to store in my programs?"

So we begin this topic by taking a look at the basic types available in the Java language. The types of value used within a program are referred to as **data types**. If you wish to record the *price* of a cinema ticket in a program, for example, this value would probably need to be kept in the form of a **real number** (a number with a decimal point in it). However, if you wished to record *how many* tickets have been sold you would probably need to keep this in the form of an **integer** (whole number). It is necessary to know whether suitable types exist in the programming language to keep these bits of data.

In Java there are a few simple data types that programmers can use. These simple types are often referred to as the **primitive types** of Java; they are also referred to as the **scalar types**, as they relate to a single piece of information (a single real number, a single character etc).

Table 1.1 lists the names of these types in the Java language, the kinds of value they represent, and the exact range of these values.

Table 1.1 The primitive types of Java		
Java type	**Allows for**	**Range of values**
`byte`	very small integers	-128 to 127
`short`	small integers	$-32\,768$ to 32 767
`int`	big integers	$-2\,147\,483\,648$ to 2 147 483 647
`long`	very big integers	$-9\,223\,372\,036\,854\,775\,808$ to 9 223 372 036 854 775 807
`float`	real numbers	$+/- \ 1.4 * 10^{-45}$ to $3.4 * 10^{38}$
`double`	very big real numbers	$+/- \ 4.9 * 10^{-324}$ to $1.8 * 10^{308}$
`char`	characters	Unicode character set
`boolean`	`true` or `false`	not applicable

As you can see, some kinds of data, namely integers and real numbers, can be kept as more than one Java type. For example, you can use both the `byte` type and the `short` type to keep integers in Java. However, while each numeric Java type allows for both positive and negative numbers, *the maximum size of numbers that can be stored varies from type to type.*

For example, the type `byte` can represent integers ranging only from -128 to 127, whereas the type `short` can represent integers ranging from $-32\,768$ to 32 767. Unlike some programming languages, these ranges are *fixed* no matter which Java compiler or operating system you are using.

The character type, `char`, is used to represent characters from a standard set of characters known as the **Unicode** character set. This contains nearly all the characters from most known languages. For the sake of simplicity, you can think of this type as representing any character that can be input from your keyboard.

Finally, the `boolean` type is used to keep only one of two possible values: `true` or `false`. This type can be useful when creating tests in programs. For example, the answer to the question "have I passed my exam?" will either be either *yes* or *no*. In Java a `boolean` type could be used to keep the answer to this question, with the value `true` being used to represent *yes* and the value `false` to represent *no*.

1.7 Declaring variables in Java

The data types listed in table 1.1 are used in programs to create named locations in the computer's memory that will contain values while a program is running. This process is known as **declaring**. These named locations are called **variables** because their values are allowed to *vary* over the life of the program.

For example, a program written to develop a computer game might need a piece of data to record the player's score as secret keys are found in a haunted house. The value held in this piece of data will vary as more keys are found. This piece of data would be referred to as a variable. To create a variable in your program you must:

> give that variable a name (of your choice);

> decide which data type in the language best reflects the kind of values you wish to store in the variable.

What name might you choose to record the score of the player in our computer game?

Although you can choose almost any name, such as *x*, it is best to pick a name that describes the purpose of the item of data; an ideal name would be *score*. You can choose any name for variables as long as:

> the name is not already a word in the Java language (such as `class`, `void`);

> the name has no spaces in it;

> the name does not include operators or mathematical symbols such as + and −;

> the name starts either with a letter, an underscore (_), or a dollar sign ($).

Although the name of a variable can begin with *any* letter, the convention in Java programs is to begin the name of a variable with a *lower case* letter.

Which data type in table 1.1 should you use if you wish to record a player's score? Well, since the score would always be a whole number, an integer type would be appropriate. There are four Java data types that can be used to hold integers (`byte`, `short`, `int` and `long`). As we said before, the only difference among these types is the range of values that they can keep. Unless there is specific reason to do otherwise, however, the `int` type is normally chosen to store integer values in Java programs. Similarly, when it comes to storing real numbers we will choose the `double` type rather than the `float` type.

Once the name and the type have been decided upon, the variable is **declared** as follows:

```
dataType variableName;
```

where `dataType` is the chosen primitive type and `variableName` is the chosen name of the variable. So, in the case of a player's score, the variable would be declared as follows:

```
int score;
```

Figure 1.4 illustrates the effect of this instruction on the computer's memory. As you can see, a small part of the computer's memory is set aside to store this item. You can think of this reserved space in memory as being a small box, big enough to hold an integer. The name of the box will be `score`.

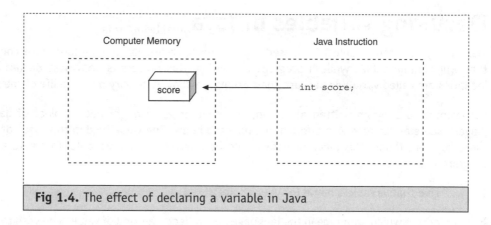

Fig 1.4. The effect of declaring a variable in Java

In this way, many variables can be declared in your programs. Let's assume that the player of a game can choose a difficulty level (A, B, or C); another variable could be declared in a similar way.

What name might you give this variable? An obvious choice would be *difficulty level* but remember names cannot have spaces in them. You could use an underscore to remove the space (*difficulty_level*) or start the second word with a capital letter to distinguish the two words (*difficultyLevel*). Both are well-established naming conventions in Java. Alternatively you could just shorten the name to, say, *level*; that is what we will do here.

Now, what data type in table 1.1 best represents the difficulty level? Since the levels are given as characters (A, B and C) the **char** type would be the obvious choice. At this point we have two variables declared: one to record the score and one to record the difficulty level.

```
int score;
char level;
```

Finally, several variables can be declared on a *single line* if they are *all of the same type*. For example, let's assume that there are ghosts in the house that hit out at the player; the number of times a player gets hit by a ghost can also be recorded. We can call this variable *hits*. Since the type of this variable is also an integer, it can be declared along with `score` in a single line as follows:

```
int score, hits;      // two variables declared at once
char level ;          // this has to be declared separately
```

Figure 1.5 illustrates the effect of these three declarations on the computer's memory.

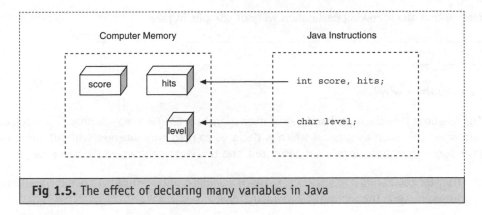

Fig 1.5. The effect of declaring many variables in Java

Notice that the character box, `level`, is half the size of the integer boxes `score` and `hits`. That is because, in Java, the **char** type requires half the space of the **int** type. You should also be aware that the **double** type in Java requires twice the space of the **int** type.

You're probably wondering: if declaring a variable is like creating a box in memory, how do I put values into this box? The answer is with assignments.

1.8 Assignments in Java

Assignments allow values to be put into variables. They are written in Java with the use of the equality symbol (=). In Java this symbol is known as the **assignment operator**. Simple assignments take the following form:

```
variableName = value;
```

For example, to put the value zero into the variable `score`, the following assignment statement could be used:

```
score = 0;
```

This is to be read as "*set* the value of `score` *to* zero" or alternatively as "`score` *becomes equal to* zero". Effectively, this puts the number zero into the box in memory we called `score`. If you wish, you may combine the assignment statement with a variable declaration to put an initial value into a variable as follows:

```
int score = 0;
```

This is equivalent to the two statements below:

```
int score;
score = 0;
```

Although in some circumstances Java will automatically put initial values into variables when they are declared, this is not always the case and it is better explicitly to initialize variables that require an initial value.

Notice that the following declaration will not compile in Java:

```
int score = 2.5 ;
```

Can you think why?

The reason is that the right-hand side of the assignment (2.5) is a *real* number. This value could not be placed into a variable such as score, which is declared to hold only integers, without some information loss. In Java, such information loss is not permitted, and this statement would therefore cause a compiler error.

You may be wondering if it is possible to place a whole number into a variable declared to hold real numbers. The answer is yes. The following is perfectly legal:

```
double someNumber = 1000;
```

Although the value on the right-hand side (1000) appears to be an integer, it can be placed into a variable of type **double** because this would result in no information loss. Once this number is put into the variable of type **double**, it will be treated as the real number 1000.0.

Clearly, you need to think carefully about the best data type to choose for a particular variable. For instance, if a variable is going to be used to hold whole numbers *or* real numbers, use the **double** type as it can cope with both. If the variable is only ever going to be used to hold whole numbers, however, then although the **double** type might be adequate, use the **int** type as it is specifically designed to hold whole numbers.

When assigning a value to a character variable, you must enclose the value in single quotes. For example, to set the initial difficulty level to A, the following assignment statement could be used:

```
char level = 'A';
```

Remember: you need to declare a variable only once. You can then assign values to it as many times as you like. For example, later on in the program the difficulty level might be changed to a different value as follows:

```
char level = 'A'; // initial difficulty level

// other Java instructions

level = 'B';          // difficulty level changed
```

1.9 Creating constants

There will be occasions where data items in a program have values *that do not change*. The following are examples of such items:

>   the maximum score in an exam (100);

>   the number of hours in a day (24);

>   the mathematical value of π (3.14176).

In these cases the values of the items do not vary. Values that remain constant throughout a program (as opposed to variable) should be named and declared as **constants**.

Constants are declared much like variables in Java except that they are preceded by the keyword **final**, and are always initialized to their fixed value. For example:

```
final int HOURS = 24;
```

Notice that the standard Java convention has been used here of naming constants in upper case. Any attempt to change this value later in the program will result in a compiler error. For example:

```
final int HOURS = 24;      // create constant
HOURS = 12;                // will not compile!
```

1.10 Arithmetic operators

Rather than just assign simple values (such as 24 and 2.5) to variables, it is often useful to carry out some kind of arithmetic in assignment statements. Java has the four familiar arithmetic operators, plus a remainder operator, for this purpose. These operators are listed in table 1.2.

Table 1.2 The arithmetic operators of Java	
Operation	Java operator
addition	+
subtraction	−
multiplication	*
division	/
remainder	%

You can use these operators in assignment statements, much like you might use a calculator. For example, consider the following instructions:

```
int x;
x = 10 + 25;
```

After these instructions the variable x would contain the value 35: the result of adding 10 to 25. Terms on the right-hand side of assignment operators (like $10 + 25$) that have to be *worked out* before they are assigned are referred to as **expressions**. These expressions can involve more than one operator.

Let's consider a calculation to work out the price of a product after a sales tax has been added. If the initial price of the product is 500 and the rate of sales tax is 17.5%, the following calculation could be used to calculate the total cost of the product:

```
double cost;
cost = 500 * (1 + 17.5/100);
```

After this calculation the final cost of the product would be 587.5.

By the way, in case you are wondering, the order in which expressions such as these are evaluated is the same as in arithmetic: terms in brackets are calculated first, followed by division, then multiplication, then addition and finally subtraction. This means that the term in the bracket

```
(1 + 17.5/100)
```

evaluates to 1.175, not 0.185, as the division is calculated before the addition. The final operator (%) in table 1.2 returns the remainder after *integer division* (this is often referred to as the **modulus**). Table 1.3 illustrates some examples of the use of this operator together with the values returned.

Table 1.3 Examples of the modulus operator in Java	
Expression	Value
29 % 9	2
6 % 8	6
40 % 40	0
10 % 2	0

As an illustration of the use of both the division operator and the modulus operator, consider the following example:

A large party of 30 people is going to attend a school reunion. The function room will be furnished with a number of tables, each of which seats four people.

To calculate how many tables of four are required, and how many people will be left over, the division and modulus operators could be used as follows:

```
int tablesOfFour, peopleLeftOver;
tablesOfFour = 30/4;                // number of tables
peopleLeftOver  = 30%4;             // number of people left over
```

After these instructions the value of `tablesOfFour` will be 7 (the result of dividing 30 by 4) and the value of `peopleLeftOver` will be 2 (the remainder after dividing 30 by 4). You may be wondering why the calculation for `tablesOfFour`

```
30/4
```

did not yield 7.5 but 7. The reason for this is that there are, in fact, two different in-built division routines in Java, one to calculate an integer answer and another to calculate the answer as a real number.

Rather than having two division operators, however, Java has a single division symbol (/) to represent *both* types of division. The division operator is said to be **overloaded**. This means that the same operator (in this case the division symbol) can behave in different ways. This makes life much easier for programmers as the decision about which routine to call is left to the Java language.

How does the Java compiler know which division routine we mean? Well, it looks at the values that are being divided. If *at least one value* is a real number (as in the product cost example), it assumes we mean the division routine that calculates an answer as a real number, otherwise it assumes we mean the division routine that calculates an answer as a whole number (as in the reunion example).[3]

1.11 Expressions in Java

So far, variable names have appeared only on the left-hand side of assignment statements. However, the expression on the right-hand side of an assignment statement can itself contain variable names. If this is the case then the name does not refer to *the location*, but to *the contents of the location*. For example, the assignment to calculate the cost of the product could have been re-written as follows:

```java
double price, tax, cost; // declare three variables
price = 500; // set price
tax = 17.5; // set tax rate
cost = price * (1 + tax/100); // calculate cost
```

Here, the variables `price` and `tax` that appear in the expression

```java
price * (1 + tax/100)
```

are taken to mean *the values contained in* `price` and `tax` respectively. This expression evaluates to 587.5 as before. Notice that although this price happens to be a whole number, it has been declared to be a **double** as generally prices are expressed as real numbers.

There is actually nothing to stop you using the name of the variable you are assigning to in the expression itself. This would just mean that the old value of the variable is being used to calculate its new value. Rather than creating a new variable, `cost`, to store the final cost of the product, the calculation could, for example, have updated *the original price* as follows:

```java
price = price * (1 + tax/100);
```

Now, only two variables are required, `price` and `tax`. Let's look at this assignment a bit more closely.

When reading this instruction, the `price` in the right-hand expression is to be read as the *old value* of `price`, whereas the `price` on the left-hand side is to be read as *the new value* of `price`.

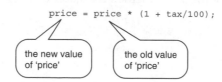

```java
price = price * (1 + tax/100);
```

the new value of 'price'

the old value of 'price'

---

[3] To force the use of one division routine over another, a technique known as **type casting** can be used. We will return to this technique in chapter 8.

You will find that one very common thing that we have to do in our programs is to increase (or increment) an integer by 1. For example, if a variable x has been declared as an `int`, then the instruction for incrementing x would be:

```
x = x + 1;
```

In fact, this is so common that there is a special shorthand for this instruction, namely:

```
x++;
```

The '++' is therefore known as the increment operator. Similarly there exists a decrement operator, '−−'. Thus:

```
x−−;
```

is shorthand for:

```
x = x - 1;
```

It is possible to use the increment and decrement operators in expressions. We will show you a couple of examples of this here, as you might easily come across them in other texts. However, we will not be using this technique in the remainder of this book, because we think it can sometimes be confusing for new programmers. If x and y are `int`s, the expression:

```
y = x++;
```

means assign the value of x to y, then increment x by 1.

However the expression:

```
y = ++x;
```

means increment x by 1, then assign this new value to y. The decrement operator can be used in the same way.

While we are on the subject of shortcuts, there is one more that you might come across in other places, but which, once again, we won't be using in this text:

```
y += x;
```

is shorthand for:

```
y = y + x;
```

The code fragments we have been writing so far in this chapter are, of course, not complete programs. As you already know, to create a program in Java you must write one or more classes. In program 1.2, we write a class, FindCost, where the main method calculates the price of the product.

Program 1.2

```
/* a program to calculate the cost of a product after a sales tax has
   been added */

public class FindCost
{
    public static void main(String[] args)
    {
        double price, tax;
        price = 500;
        tax = 17.5;
        price = price * (1 + tax/100);
    }
}
```

What would you see when you run this program? The answer is nothing! There is no instruction to display the result on to the screen. You have already seen how to display messages onto the screen. It is now time to take a closer look at the output command to see how you can also display results onto the screen.

1.12 Output in Java

As you have already seen when writing your first program, to output a message on to the screen in Java we use the following command:

```
System.out.println(message to be printed on screen);
```

For example, we have already seen:

```
System.out.println("Hello world");
```

This prints the message "Hello world" onto the screen. There is in fact an alternative form of the `System.out.println` statement, which uses `System.out.print`. As we said before, `println` is short for *print line* and the effect of this statement is to start a new line after displaying whatever is in the brackets. You can see the effect of this below – we have adapted program 1.1 by adding an additional line.

Program 1.1 – with an additional line

```
public class Hello
{
    public static void main(String[] args)
    {
        System.out.println("Hello world");       // notice the use of println
        System.out.println("Hello world again!");
    }
}
```

When we run this program, the output looks like this:

Hello world

Hello world again!

Now let's change the first `System.out.println` to `System.out.print`:

> **Program 1.1 – adapted to show the effect of using *print* instead of *println***
>
> ```java
> public class Hello
> {
>     public static void main(String[] args)
>     {
>         System.out.print("Hello world");        // notice the use of 'print'
>         System.out.println("Hello world again!");
>     }
> }
> ```

Now our output looks like this:

```
Hello worldHello world again!
```

You can see that the output following the `System.out.print` statement doesn't start on a new line, but follows straight on from the previous line.

If you want a blank line in the program, then you can simply use `println` with empty brackets:

```java
System.out.println();
```

Messages such as "`Hello world`" are in fact what we call **strings** (collections of characters). In Java, literal strings like this are always enclosed in speech marks. We shall look at strings again at the end of this chapter, and then in more detail in chapter 6. However, it is necessary to know how several strings can be printed on the screen using a single output command.

In Java, two strings can be joined together with the plus symbol (+). When using this symbol for this purpose it is known as the **concatenation operator**. For example, instead of printing the single string "Hello world", we could have joined two strings, "Hello" and "world", for output using the following command:

```java
System.out.println("Hello " + "World");
```

Note that spaces are printed by including them within the speech marks ("`Hello `"), not by adding spaces around the concatenation operator (which has no effect at all).

Java also allows any values or expressions of the primitive types that we showed you in table 1.1, to be printed on the screen using these output commands. It does this by implicitly converting each value/expression to a string before displaying it on the screen. In this way numbers, the value of variables, or the value of expressions can be displayed on the screen. For example, the square of 10 can be displayed on the screen as follows:

```java
System.out.print(10*10);
```

This instruction prints the number 100 on the screen. Since these values are converted into strings by Java they can be joined on to literal strings for output.

For example, let's return back to the party of 30 people attending their school reunion that we discussed in section 1.10. If each person is charged a fee of 7.50 for the evening, the total cost to the whole party could be displayed as follows:

```
System.out.print("cost = " + (30*7.5) );
```

Here the concatenation operator (+), is being used to join the string, `"cost = "`, on to the value of the expression, `(30*7.5)`. Notice that when expressions like `30*7.5` are used in output statements it is best to enclose them in brackets. This would result in the following output:

cost = 225.0

Bear these ideas in mind and look at program 1.3, where we have re-written program 1.2 so that the output is visible.

Program 1.3

```
/* a program to calculate and display the cost of a product after sales
   tax has been added */

public class FindCost2
{
  public static void main(String[] args)
  {
  double price, tax;
  price = 500;
  tax = 17.5;
  price = price * (1 + tax/100); // calculate cost
  // display results
  System.out.println("*** Product Price Check ***");
  System.out.println("Cost after tax = " + price);
  }
}
```

This program produces the following output:

*** Product Price Check ***

Cost after tax = 587.5

Although being able to see the result of the calculation is a definite improvement, this program is still very limited. The formatting of the output can certainly be improved, but we shall not deal with such issues until later on in the book. What does concern us now is that this program can only calculate the cost of products when the sales tax rate is 17.5% and the initial price is 500!

What is required is not to fix the rate of sales tax or the price of the product but, instead, to get the *user of your program* to *input* these values as the program runs.

1.13 Input in Java: the *Scanner* class

The latest release of Java, namely Java 5.0, provides a special class called `Scanner`, which makes it easy for us to write a program that obtains information that is typed in at the keyboard. `Scanner` is provided as part of what is known, in Java, as a **package**. A package is a collection of pre-compiled classes – lots more about that in chapter 13! The `Scanner` class is part of a package called `util`. Therefore, in order to make the `Scanner` class accessible to the compiler we have to tell it to look in the `util` package. We do this by placing the following line at the beginning of our program:

```
import java.util.*;
```

This asterisk means that all the classes in the particular package are made available to the compiler.

As long as the `Scanner` class is accessible, you can use all the input methods that have been defined in this class. We are going to show you how to do this now. Some of the code might look a bit mysterious to you at the moment, but don't worry about this right now. Just follow our instructions for the time being – after a few chapters, it will become clear to you exactly why we use the particular format and syntax that we are showing you.

Having imported the `util` package, you will need to write the following instruction in your program:

```
Scanner sc = new Scanner(System.in)
```

What we are doing here is creating an object, `sc`, of the `Scanner` class. Once again, the true meaning of the phrase *creating an object* will become clear in the next few chapters, so don't worry too much about it now. However, you should know that in Java `System.in` represents the keyboard, and by associating our `Scanner` object with `System.in`, we are telling it to get the input from the keyboard as opposed, say, to a file on disk, or a modem.

The `Scanner` class has several input methods, each one associated with a different input type, and once we have declared a `Scanner` object we can use these methods. Let's take some examples. Say we wanted a user to type in an integer at the keyboard, and we wanted this value to be assigned to an integer variable called x. We would use the `Scanner` method called `nextInt`; the instruction would look like this:

```
x = sc.nextInt();
```

In the case of a **double**, y, we would do this:

```
y = sc.nextDouble();
```

Notice that to access a method of a class you need to join the name of the method (`getInt` or `getDouble`) to the name of the object (`sc`) by using the full-stop. Also you must remember the brackets after the name of the method.

What about a character? Unfortunately this is a little bit more complicated, as there is no `nextChar` method provided. Assuming c had been declared as a character, we would have to do this:

```
c = sc.next().charAt(0);
```

You won't understand exactly why we use this format until chapter 6 – for now just accept it and use it when you need to. In fact, in chapter 6 we will simplify this whole process for you.

Let us return to the haunted house game to illustrate this. Rather than *assigning* a difficulty level as follows:

```
char level;
level = 'A';
```

you could take a more flexible approach by asking the user of your program to *input* a difficulty level while the program runs. Since `level` is declared to be a character variable, then, after declaring a `Scanner` object, `sc`, you would write this line of code:

```
level = sc.next().charAt(0);
```

Let us re-write program 1.3 so that the price of the product and the rate of sales tax are not fixed in the program, but are input from the keyboard. Since the type used to store the price and the tax is a **double**, the appropriate input method is `nextDouble`, as can be seen in program 1.4.

Program 1.4

```
import java.util.*; // in order to access the Scanner class

/* a program to input the initial price of a product and then calculate
   and display its cost after tax has been added */

public class FindCost3
{
    public static void main(String[] args )
    {
        Scanner sc = new Scanner(System.in); // create Scanner object
        double price, tax;
        System.out.println("*** Product Price Check ***");
        System.out.print("Enter initial price: "); // prompt for input
        price = sc.nextDouble(); // input method called
        System.out.print("Enter tax rate: "); // prompt for input
        tax = sc.nextDouble(); // input method called
        price = price * (1 + tax/100); // perform the calculation
        System.out.println("Cost after tax = " + price);
    }
}
```

Note that, by looking at this program code alone, there is no way to determine what the final price of the product will be, as the initial price and the tax rate will be determined *only when the program is run*.

Let's assume that we run the program and the user interacts with it as follows:[4]

*** Product Price Check ***

Enter initial price: **1000**

Enter tax rate: **12.5**

Cost after tax = 1125.0

You should notice the following points from this test run:

---

[4] We have used **bold italic** font to represent user input.

❯   whatever the price of the computer product and the rate of tax, this program could have evaluated the final price;

❯   entering numeric values with additional formatting information, such as currency symbols or the percentage symbol, is not permitted;

❯   after an input method is called, the cursor always moves to the next line.

The programs we are looking at now involve input commands, output commands and assignments. Clearly, the order in which you write these instructions affects the results of your programs. For example, if the instructions to calculate the final price and then display the results were reversed as follows:

```
System.out.println("Cost after tax = " + price);
price = price * (1 + tax/100);
```

The price that would be displayed would not be the price *after* tax but the price *before* tax! In order to avoid such mistakes it makes sense *to design your code* by sketching out your instructions before you type them in. We will look at ways of doing this in section 1.15.

1.14 Strings

So far all the data types you have used have been what we referred to as the primitive data types of Java – in other words the most simple types available in the language. It might have already occurred to you that it would be useful if we could construct rather more complex types – types that hold more than just one simple piece of information such as a type that records the time and the date, or a type that holds a lot of related information about a person. As we have hinted already, the way we do this in Java is by means of constructs known as classes and objects – but we won't be dealing with these concepts until we get to chapter 6. In the mean time, however, we will let you know about just one of these complex types, namely a `String`.

You have already seen that a string is a sequence of characters – like a name, a line of an address, a car registration number, or indeed any meaningless sequence of characters such as "h83hdu2&e£8". You can see at once how useful it will be for us to be able to use strings – this is why we are letting you do this even before you learn about classes and objects. When you declare a string you can do so in the same way as you have learnt to do with variables such as **int** or **char**. You should notice, however, that the `String` "type" (it is actually a *class*) has to start with a capital "S". For example:

```
String name;
```

You have already seen how to join strings together with the concatenation operator (the + sign); we should also tell you that Java allows you to use the normal assignment operator (=) with strings, so you can write statements like:

```
name = "Quentin";
```

In order to obtain a `String` from the keyboard, you should use the `next` method of `Scanner`. However, when you do this you should not enter strings that include spaces, as this will give you unexpected results.

We will show you in chapter 6 a way to get round this restriction, but until then you should refrain from entering strings with spaces when you run your programs.

Program 1.5 is an interesting little program that uses the Java `String` class. Some of you might also find it amusing (although others might not!).

Program 1.5

```java
import java.util.*;

public class StringTest
{
    public static void main(String[] args)
    {
        Scanner sc = new Scanner(System.in);
        String name; // declaration of a String
        int age;
        System.out.print("What is your name? ");
        name = sc.next(); // the 'next' method is for String input
        System.out.print("What is your age? ");
        age = sc.nextInt();
        System.out.println();
        System.out.println("Hello " + name);
        // now comes the joke!!
        System.out.println("When I was your age I was " + (age + 1));
    }
}
```

One thing to notice in this program is the way in which the + operator is used for two very different purposes. It is used with `Strings` for concatenation – for example:

`"Hello " + name`

It is also used with integers for addition for example:

`age + 1`

Notice that we have had to enclose this expression in brackets to avoid any confusion.

Here is a sample run from program 1.5:

What is your name? **Aaron**
What is your age? **15**

Hello Aaron
When I was your age I was 16

1.15 Program design

Designing a program is the task of considering exactly *how to build* the software, whereas writing the code (the task of *actually building* the software) is referred to as *implementation*. As programs get more complex, it is important to spend time on program design, before launching into program implementation.

As we have already said, Java programs consist of one or more classes, each with one or more methods. In later chapters we will introduce you to the use of diagrams to help design such classes. The programs we have considered so far, however, have only a single class and a single method (`main`), so a class diagram would not be very useful here! We will therefore return to this design technique as we develop larger programs involving many classes.

At a lower level, it is the instructions *within* a method that determine the *behaviour* of that method. If the behaviour of a method is complex, then it will also be worthwhile spending time on designing the instructions that make up the method. When you sketch out the code for your methods, you don't want to have to worry about the finer details of the Java compiler such as declaring variables, adding semi-colons and using the right brackets. Very often a general purpose "coding language" can be used for this purpose to convey the meaning of each instruction without worrying too much about a specific language syntax.

Code expressed in this way is often referred to as **pseudocode**. The following is an example of pseudocode that could have been developed for the `main` method of program 1.4:

```
BEGIN
   DISPLAY program title
   DISPLAY prompt for price
   ENTER price
   DISPLAY prompt for tax
   ENTER tax
   SET price TO price * (1 + tax/100)
   DISPLAY new price
END
```

Note that these pseudocode instructions are not intended to be typed in and compiled as they do not meet the syntax rules of any particular programming language. So, exactly how you write these instructions is up to you: there is no fixed syntax for them. However, each instruction conveys a well-understood programming concept and can easily be translated into a given programming language. Reading these instructions you should be able to see how each line would be coded in Java.

Wouldn't it be much easier to write your `main` method if you have pseudocode like this to follow? In future, when we present complex methods to you we will do so by presenting their logic using pseudocode.

Self-test questions

1 Explain the meaning of the word *software*.

2 Explain how Java programs are compiled and run, and how this differs from the way most other programs are compiled and run.

3 What would be the most appropriate Java data type to use for the following items of data?

> the maximum number of people allowed on a bus;

> the weight of a food item purchased in a supermarket;

> the grade awarded to a student (for example 'A', 'B' or 'C').

4 Explain which, if any, of the following lines would result in a compiler error:

```
int x = 75.5;
double y = 75;
```

5 Identify and correct the errors in the program below, which prompts for the user's age and then attempts to work out the year in which the user was born.

```
import java.util.*;

public class SomeProg
{
 public static void main (String[] args)
 {
    Scanner sc = new Scanner(System.in);
    final int YEAR;
    int age, bornIn;
    System.out.print(How old are you this year? );
    age = sc.nextDouble();
    bornIn = YEAR - age;
    System.out.println("I think you were born in " + BornIn);
 }
}
```

6 What would be the final output from the program below if the user entered the number 10?

```
import java.util.*;

public class Calculate
{
    public static void main(String[] args )
    {
        Scanner sc = new Scanner(System.in);
        int num1, num2;
        num2 = 6;
        System.out.print("Enter value ");
        num1 = sc.nextInt();
        num1 = num1 + 2;
        num2 = num1 / num2;
        System.out.println("result = " + num2);
    }
}
```

Programming exercises

1 Type, compile and run all the programs from this chapter.

2 Write a program that displays your name, address and telephone number, each on separate lines.

3 Adapt the above program to include a blank line between your address and telephone number.

4 A group of students has been told to get into teams of a specific size for their coursework. Design and implement a program that prompts for the number of students in the group and the size of the teams to be formed, and displays how many teams can be formed and how many students are left without a team.

5 Some while ago, the European Union decreed that all traders in the UK sell their goods by the kilo and not by the pound (1 kilo = 2.2 pounds). The following pseudocode has been arrived at in order to carry out this conversion:

```
BEGIN
  DISPLAY prompt for value in pounds
  ENTER value in pounds
  SET value to old value ÷ 2.2
  DISPLAY value in kilos
END
```

Implement this program, remembering to declare any variables that are necessary.

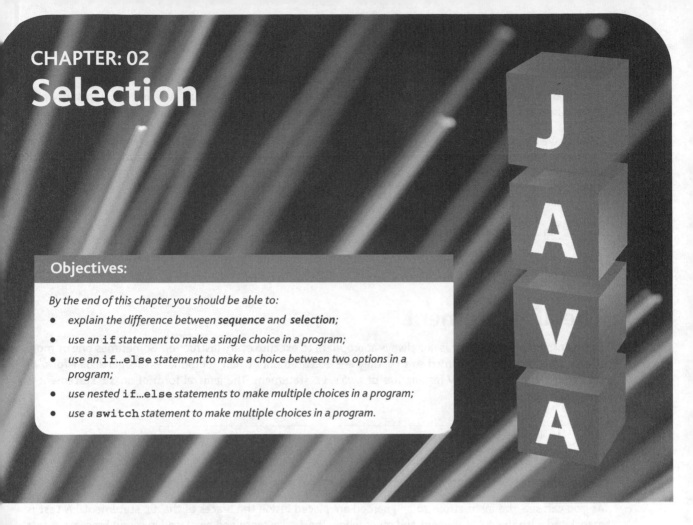

CHAPTER: 02

Selection

Objectives:

By the end of this chapter you should be able to:

- *explain the difference between **sequence** and **selection**;*
- *use an **if** statement to make a single choice in a program;*
- *use an **if...else** statement to make a choice between two options in a program;*
- *use nested **if...else** statements to make multiple choices in a program;*
- *use a **switch** statement to make multiple choices in a program.*

2.1 Introduction

One of the most rewarding aspects of writing and running a program is knowing that it is *you* who has control over the computer. But looking back at the programs you have already written, just how much control do you actually have? Certainly, it was you who decided upon which instructions to include in your programs but *the order in which these instructions were executed* was *not* under your control. These instructions were always executed in **sequence**, that is one after the other, from beginning to end. You will soon find that there are numerous instances when this order of execution is too restrictive and you will want to have much more control over the order in which instructions are executed.

2.2 Making choices

Very often you will want your programs to make *choices* among different courses of action. For example, a program processing requests for airline tickets could have the following choices to make:

> display the price of the seats requested;

> display a list of alternative flights;

> display a message saying that no flights are available to that destination.

A program that can make choices can behave *differently* each time it is run, whereas programs in which instructions are just executed in sequence behave the *same way* each time they are run.

As we have already mentioned, unless you indicate otherwise, program instructions are always executed in sequence. **Selection**, however, is a method of program control in which a choice can be made among which instructions to execute. In Java there are three forms of selection you can use:

> an `if` statement;

> an `if`…`else` statement;

> a `switch` statement.

2.3 The 'if' statement

During program execution it is not always appropriate to execute *every* instruction. Sometimes one or more instructions need to be guarded so that they are executed only when appropriate. This particular form of selection is implemented by making use of Java's `if` statement. The general form of an `if` statement is given as follows:

```
if ( /* a test goes here */)
{
    // instruction(s) to be guarded go here
}
```

As you can see, the instructions to be guarded are placed inside the braces of the `if` statement.[1] A **test** is associated with the `if` statement and must follow the `if` keyword and be placed in round brackets. A test is any expression that gives a `boolean` result of `true` or `false`. Examples of tests in everyday language are:

> this password is valid;

> there is an empty seat on the plane;

> the temperature in the laboratory is too high.

When the test gives a `boolean` result of `true` the instructions inside the braces of the `if` statement are executed. The program then continues by executing the instructions after the braces of the `if` statement as normal. If, however, the `if` test gives a `boolean` result of `false` the instructions inside the `if` braces are skipped and not executed.

For example, consider a temperature value that has been entered by the user as follows:

```
System.out.print("Enter a temperature value ");
double temperature = sc.nextDouble(); // using a Scanner object here
```

---

[1] Strictly speaking, as we shall discuss later, the braces can be omitted if only a single instruction is to be guarded by the `if` statement.

Let us now check if the temperature is below freezing point (0 degrees) and display an appropriate message if it is. Regardless of whether or not the temperature was freezing, we will then ask the user to enter another temperature. An **if** statement can be used to carry out this test:

```
if (temperature < 0) // test to check if temperature is below freezing
{
    // this line executed only when the test is true
    System.out.println("Temperature is below freezing");
}
// this line is outside the 'if' statement so is always executed
System.out.print("Enter another temperature value ");
```

Now, the message `"Temperature is below freezing"` is displayed only when the test (`temperature < 0`) returns a **boolean** result of **true**. When the test returns a **boolean** result of **false**, however, this message is skipped.

In this case there was only a single instruction inside the `if` statement. When there is only a single instruction associated with an **if** statement, the braces can be omitted if so desired as follows:

```
if (temperature < 0)
//  braces can be omitted if only 1 instruction within an 'if' statement
System.out.println("Temperature is below freezing");
// this instruction is outside the 'if' statement
System.out.print("Enter another temperature value ");
```

2.3.1 Comparison operators

In the example above, the "less than" operator ($<$) was used to check the value of the `temperature` variable. This operator is often referred to as a **comparison operator** as it is used to compare two values. Table 2.1 shows all the Java comparison operator symbols.

Table 2.1 The comparison operators of Java	
Operator	Meaning
==	equal to
!=	not equal to
<	less than
>	greater than
>=	greater than or equal to
<=	less than or equal to

Notice that these comparison operators are to be used with primitive values only (such as **int** and **double**) and not with strings (as strings are objects in Java, not primitives). We will come back to look at object comparison in chapter 6.

Since comparison operators give a **boolean** result of **true** or **false** they are often used in tests such as those we have been discussing. Note that a double equals ($==$) is used to check for equality in Java and not the single equals (=), which, as you know, is used for assignment. To use the single equals is a very common error! For example, to check whether or not an angle is a right angle or not the following test should be uused:

```
if (angle == 90)// note the use of the double equals
{
    System.out.println("This is a right angle");
}
```

2.3.2 Multiple instructions within an 'if' statement

You have seen how an **if** statement guarding a single instruction may or may not be implemented with braces around the instruction. When *more than one* instruction is to be guarded by an **if** statement, however, the instructions *must* be placed in braces. As an example, consider once again program 1.4 that calculates the cost of a product.

Reminder of Program 1.4

```
import java.util.*;

public class FindCost3
{
 public static void main(String [] args)
 {
    double price, tax;
    Scanner sc = new Scanner(System.in);
    System.out.println("*** Product Price Check ***");
    System.out.print("Enter initial price: ");
    price = sc.nextDouble();
    System.out.print("Enter tax rate: ");
    tax = sc.nextDouble();
    price = price * (1 + tax/100);
    System.out.println("Cost after tax = " + price);
 }
}
```

Now assume that a special promotion is in place for those products with an initial price over 100. For such products the company pays half the tax so, for the customer, the tax is effectively halved. Program 2.1 makes use of an **if** statement to apply this promotion, as well as informing the user that a tax discount has been applied. Take a look at it and then we will discuss it.

Program 2.1

```java
import java.util.*;

public class FindCostWithDiscount
{
 public static void main(String[] args )
 {
    double price, tax;
    Scanner sc = new Scanner(System.in);
    System.out.println("*** Product Price Check ***");
    System.out.print("Enter initial price: ");
    price = sc.nextDouble();
    System.out.print("Enter tax rate: ");
    tax = sc.nextDouble();
    // the following 'if' statement allows a selection to take place
    if (price > 100) // test the price to see if a discount applies
    {
       // these two instructions executed only when test is true
       System.out.println("Special Promotion: Your tax will be halved!");
       tax = tax * 0.5;
    }
    // the remaining instructions are always executed
    price = price * (1 + tax/100);
    System.out.println("Cost after tax = " + price);
 }
}
```

Now, the user is still always prompted to enter the initial price and tax as before:

```java
System.out.print("Enter initial price: ");
price = sc.nextDouble();
System.out.print("Enter tax rate: ");
tax = sc.nextDouble();
```

The next two instructions are then placed inside an `if` statement. This means they may not always be executed:

```java
if (price > 100)
{
    System.out.println("Special Promotion: Your tax will be halved!");
    tax = tax * 0.5;
}
```

Notice that if the braces were omitted in this case, only the *first* instruction would be taken to be inside the `if` statement – the second statement would not be guarded and so would *always* be executed!

With braces around both instructions, they will be executed only when the test (`price > 100`) returns a **boolean** result of **true**. So, for example, if the user had entered a price of 150 the tax discount would be applied; but if the user entered a price of 50 these instructions would not be executed and a tax discount would not be applied.

Regardless of whether or not the test was **true** and the instructions in the `if` statement executed, the program always continues with the remaining instructions:

```java
price = price * (1 + tax/100);
System.out.println("Cost after tax = " + price);
```

Here is a sample program run when the test returns a result of **false** and the discount is not applied:

```
*** Product Price Check ***

Enter initial price: 50

Enter tax rate: 10

Cost after tax = 55.0
```

In this case the program appears to behave in exactly the same way as the original program (program 1.4). Here, however, is a program run when the test returns a result of **true** and a discount does apply:

```
*** Product Price Check ***

Enter initial price: 1000

Enter tax rate: 10

Special Promotion: Your tax will be halved!

Cost after tax = 1050
```

2.4 The 'if...else' statement

Using the **if** statement in the way that we have done so far has allowed us to build the idea of a choice into our programs. In fact, the **if** statement made one of two choices before continuing with the remaining instructions in the program:

> execute the conditional instructions, or

> do not execute the conditional instructions.

The second option amounts to "do nothing". Rather than do nothing if the condition is **false**, an extended version of an **if** statement exists in Java to state an alternative course of action. This extended form of selection is the **if...else** statement. As the name implies, the instructions to be executed if the condition evaluates to **false** are preceded by the Java keyword **else** as follows:

```
if ( /* test goes here */ )
{
      // instruction(s) if test is true go here
}
else
{
      // instruction(s) if test is false go here
}
```

This is often referred to as a **double-branched** selection as there are two alternative groups of instructions, whereas a single **if** statement is often referred to as a **single-branched** selection. Program 2.2 illustrates the use of a double-branched selection.

Program 2.2

```java
import java.util.*;

public class DisplayResult
{
  public static void main(String[] args)
  {
    int mark;
    Scanner sc = new Scanner(System.in);
    System.out.println("What exam mark did you get? ");
    mark = sc.nextInt();
    if (mark >= 40)
    {
      // executed when test is true
      System.out.println("Congratulations, you passed");
    }
    else
    {
      // executed when test is false
      System.out.println("I'm sorry, but you failed");
    }
    System.out.println("Good luck with your other exams");
  }
}
```

Program 2.2 checks a student's exam mark and tells the student whether or not he or she has passed (gained a mark greater than or equal to 40), before displaying a good luck message on the screen. Let's examine this program a bit more closely.

Prior to the **if...else** statement the following lines are executed in sequence:

```java
int mark;
Scanner sc = new Scanner(System.in);
System.out.println("What exam mark did you get? ");
mark = sc.nextInt();
```

Then the following condition is tested as part of the **if...else** statement:

```java
(mark >= 40)
```

When this condition is **true** the following line is executed:

```java
System.out.print("Congratulations, you passed");
```

When the condition is **false**, however, the following line is executed *instead*:

```java
System.out.println("I'm sorry, but you failed");
```

Finally, whichever path was chosen the program continues by executing the last line:

```java
System.out.println("Good luck with your other exams");
```

The **if...else** form of control has allowed us to choose from two alternative courses of action. Here is a sample program run:

What exam mark did you get?

52

Congratulations, you passed

Good luck with your other exams

Here is another sample run where a different course of action is chosen.

What exam mark did you get?

35

I'm sorry, but you failed

Good luck with your other exams

2.5 Logical operators

As we've already pointed out, the test in an **if** statement is an expression that produces a **boolean** result of **true** or **false**. Often it is necessary to join two or more tests together to a create a single more complicated test.

As an example, consider a program that checks the temperature in a laboratory. Assume that, for the experiments in the laboratory to be successful, the temperature must remain between 5 and 12 degrees celsius. An **if** statement might be required as follows:

```
if (/* test to check if temperature is safe */)
{
      System.out.println ("SAFE");
}
else
{
      System.out.println("UNSAFE: RAISE ALARM!!");
}
```

The test should check if the temperature is safe. This involves combining two tests together

1   check that the temperature is greater than or equal to 5 (temperature>=5)

2   check that the temperature is less than or equal to 12 (temperature<=12)

Both of these tests need to evaluate to **true** in order for the temperature to be safe. When we require two tests to be true we use the following symbol to join the two tests :

&&

This symbol is read as "AND". So the correct test is:

```
if (temperature >= 5 && temperature <= 12)
```

Now, if the temperature were below 5 the first test would evaluate to **false** giving a final result of **false**. If the temperature were greater than 12 the second test would evaluate to **false** also giving an overall result of **false**. But when the temperature is between 5 and 12 both tests would evaluate to **true** and the final result would be **true** as required.

Notice that the two tests must be *completely* specified as each needs to return a **boolean** value of **true** or **false**. It would be wrong to try something like the following:

```
// wrong! second test does not mention 'temperature'!
if (temperature  >= 5 && <= 12)
```

This is wrong as the second test (<= 12) is not a legal **boolean** expression. Symbols that join tests together to form longer tests are known as **logical operators**. Table 2.2 lists the Java counterparts to the three common logical operators.

Table 2.2 The logical operators of Java	
Logical operator	Java counterpart
AND	&&
OR	||
NOT	!

Both the AND and OR operators join two tests together to give a final result. While the AND operator requires both tests to be **true** to give a result of **true**, the OR operator requires only that *at least one* of the tests be **true** to give a result of **true**. The NOT operator flips a value of **true** to **false** and a value of **false** to **true**. Table 2.3 gives some examples of the use of these logical operators:

Table 2.3 Logical operators: some examples		
Expression	Result	Explanation
10>5 && 10>7	**true**	Both tests are true
10>5 && 10>20	**false**	The second test is false
10>15 && 10>20	**false**	Both tests are false
10>5 || 10>7	**true**	At least one test is true (in this case both tests are true)
10>5 || 10>20	**true**	At least one test is true (in this case just one test is true)
10>15 || 10>20	**false**	Both tests are false
! (10 > 5)	**false**	Original test is true
! (10 > 15)	**true**	Original test is false

2.6 Nested 'if...else' statements

Instructions within **if** and **if...else** statements can themselves be *any* legal Java commands. In particular they could contain other **if** or **if...else** statements. This form of control is referred to as **nesting**. Nesting allows multiple choices to be processed.

As an example, consider program 2.4 below, which asks a student to enter his or her tutorial group (A, B, or C) and then displays on the screen the time of the software lab.

Program 2.4

```java
import java.util.*;

public class Timetable
{
   public static void main(String[] args)
   {
      char group; // to store the tutorial group
      Scanner sc = new Scanner(System.in);
      System.out.println("***Lab Times***"); // display header
      System.out.println("Enter your group (A,B,C)");
      group = sc.next().charAt(0);
      // check tutorial group and display appropriate time
      if (group == 'A')
      {
         System.out.print("10.00 a.m"); // lab time for group A
      }
      else
      {
         if (group == 'B')
         {
            System.out.print("1.00 p.m"); // lab time for group B
         }
         else
         {
            if (group == 'C')
            {
               System.out.print("11.00 a.m"); // lab time for group C
            }
            else
            {
               System.out.print("No such group"); // invalid group
            }
         }
      }
   }
}
```

As you can see, nesting can result in code with many braces that can become difficult to read. Of course, the tab spaces that are used are ignored by the compiler and are only there to make it easier for us to read the code. Such code can be made even easier to read by not including the braces associated with all the **else** branches.

```java
if (group == 'A')
{
        System.out.print("10.00 a.m");
}
else if (group == 'B')
{
        System.out.print("1.00 p.m");
}
else if(group == 'C')
{
        System.out.print("11.00 a.m");
}
else
{
        System.out.print("No such group");
}
```

This program is a little bit different from the ones before because it includes some basic **error checking**. That is, it does not *assume* that the user of this program will always type the *expected* values. If the wrong group (not A, B or C) is entered, an error message is displayed saying "*No such group*".

```
// valid groups checked above
else // if this 'else' is reached, group entered must be invalid
{
        System.out.print("No such group"); // error message
}
```

Error checking like this is a good habit to get into.

This use of nested selections is okay up to a point, but when the number of options becomes large the program can again look very untidy. Fortunately, this type of selection can also be implemented in Java with another form of control: a `switch` statement.

2.7 The 'switch' statement

Program 2.5 behaves in exactly the same way as program 2.4 but using a `switch` instead of a series of nested `if...else` statements allows a neater implementation. Take a look at it and then we'll discuss it.

Program 2.5

```
import java.util.*;

public class TimetableWithSwitch
{
  public static void main(String[] args)
  {
    char group;
    Scanner sc = new Scanner(System.in);
    System.out.println("***Lab Times***");
    System.out.println("Enter your group (A,B,C)");
    group = sc.next().charAt(0);
    switch(group) // beginning of switch
    {
      case 'A': System.out.print("10.00 a.m ");
                break;
      case 'B': System.out.print("1.00 p.m ");
                break;
      case 'C': System.out.print("11.00 a.m ");
                break;
      default:  System.out.print("No such group");
    } // end of switch
  }
}
```

As you can see, this looks a lot neater. The `switch` statement works in exactly the same way as a set of nested `if` statements, but is more compact and readable. A `switch` statement may be used when

> only one variable is being checked in each condition (in this case every condition involves checking the variable `group`);

> the check involves specific values of that variable (e.g. 'A', 'B') and not ranges (for example >=40).

As can be seen from the example above, the keyword **case** is used to precede a possible value of the variable that is being checked. There may be many **case** statements in a single **switch** statement. The general form of a **switch** statement in Java is given as follows:

```
switch(someVariable)
{
    case value1:  // instructions(s) to be executed
                  break;
    case value2:  // instructions(s) to be executed
                  break;
    // more  values to be tested can be added
    default: // instruction(s) for default case
}
```

where

>   `someVariable` is the name of the variable being tested. This variable is usually of type **int** or **char** but may also be of type **long**, **byte**, or **short**.

>   `value1`, `value2`, etc. are the possible values of that variable.

>   **break** is an optional command that forces the program to skip the rest of the **switch** statement.

>   **default** is an optional (last) case that can be thought of as an "otherwise" statement. It allows you to code instructions that deal with the possibility of none of the cases above being **true**.

The **break** statement is important because it means that once a matching case is found, the program can skip the rest of the cases below. If it is not added, not only will the instructions associated with the matching case be executed, but also, all the instructions associated with all the cases below it. Notice that the last set of instructions does not need a **break** statement as there are no other cases to skip.

There will be instances when a particular group of instructions is associated with more than one **case** option. As an example, consider program 2.5 again. Let's assume that both groups A and C have a lab at 10.00 a.m. The following **switch** statement would process this without grouping case 'A' and 'C' together:

```
// groups A and C have labs at the same time
switch(group)
{
    case 'A': System.out.print("10.00 a.m ");
              break;
    case 'B': System.out.print("1.00 p.m ");
              break;
    case 'C': System.out.print("10.00 a.m ");
              break;
    default:    System.out.print("No such group");
}
```

While this will work, both **case** 'A' and **case** 'C' have the same instruction associated with them:

```
System.out.print("10.00 a.m ");
```

Rather than repeating this instruction, the two **case** statements can be combined into one as follows:

```
// groups A and C have been processed together
switch(group)
{
        case 'A': case 'C': System.out.print("10.00 a.m ");
                            break;
        case 'B': System.out.print("1.00 p.m ");
                  break;
        default:  System.out.print("No such group");
}
```

In the example above a time of 10.00 a.m will be displayed when the group is either 'A' or 'C'. The example above combined two **case** statements, but there is no limit to how many such statements can be combined.

In the next chapter you will see how a **switch** statement can be particularly useful in developing menu based programs.

Self-test questions

1 Explain the difference between *sequence* and *selection*.

2 When would it be appropriate to use

> an **if** statement?

> an **if...else** statement?

> a **switch** statement?

3 Consider the following Java program, which is intended to display the cost of a cinema ticket. Part of the code has been replaced by a comment:

```
import java.util.*;

public class SelectionQ3
{
    public static void main(String[] args)
    {
        double price = 9.99;
        int age;
        Scanner sc = new Scanner(System.in);
        System.out.print("Enter your age: ");
        age = sc.nextInt();

        // code to reduce ticket price for children goes here

        System.out.println("Ticket price = " + price);
    }
}
```

Replace the comment so that children under the age of 14 get a reduced ticket price of 3.99.

4 Consider the following program:

```
import java.util.*;

public class SelectionQ4
{
    public static void main(String[] args)
    {
        int x;
        Scanner sc = new Scanner(System.in);
        System.out.print("Enter a number: ");
        x = sc.nextInt();
        if (x > 10)
        {
            System.out.println("Green");
            System.out.println("Blue");
        }
        System.out.println("Red");
    }
}
```

What would be the output from this program if

a) the user entered 10 when prompted?

b) the user entered 20 when prompted?

c) the braces used in the **if** statement are removed, and the user enters 20 when prompted?

5   Consider the following program:

```
import java.util.*;

public class SelectionQ5
{
        public static void main(String[] args)
        {
            int x;
            Scanner sc = new Scanner(System.in);
            System.out.print("Enter a number: ");
            x = sc.nextInt();
            if (x > 10)
            {
                    System.out.println("Green");
            }
            else
            {
                    System.out.println("Blue");
            }
            System.out.println("Red");
        }
}
```

What would be the output from this program if

a) the user entered 10 when prompted?

b) the user entered 20 when prompted?

6   Consider the following program:

```
import java.util.*;

public class SelectionQ6
{
        public static void main(String[] args)
        {
            int x;
            Scanner sc = new Scanner(System.in);
            System.out.print("Enter a number: ");
            x = sc.nextInt();
            switch (x)
            {
              case 1: case 2: System.out.println("Green"); break;
              case 3: case 4: case 5: System.out.println("Blue"); break;
              default: System.out.println("numbers 1-5 only");
            }
            System.out.println("Red");
        }
}
```

What would be the output from this program if

a) the user entered 1 when prompted?

b) the user entered 2 when prompted?

c) the user entered 3 when prompted?

d) the user entered 10 when prompted?

e) the `default` were removed from the `switch` statement and the user entered 10 when prompted?

Programming exercises

1   Design and implement a program that asks the user to enter two numbers and then guess at the sum of those two numbers. If the user guesses correctly a congratulatory message is displayed, otherwise a commiseration message is displayed along with the correct answer.

2   Implement program 2.2 which processed an exam mark and then adapt the program so that marks of 70 or above are awarded a distinction rather than a pass.

3   Write a program to take an order for a computer system. The basic system costs 375.99. The user then has to choose from a 38 cm screen (costing 75.99) or a 43 cm screen (costing 99.99).The following extras are optional.

Item	Price
DVD/CD Writer	65.99
Printer	125.00

The program should allow the user to select from these extras and then display the final cost of the order.

4   Consider a bank that offers four different types of account ('A', 'B', 'C' and 'X'). The following table illustrates the annual rate of interest offered for each type of account.

Account	Annual rate of interest
A	1.5%
B	2%
C	1.5%
X	5%

Design and implement a program that allows the user to enter an amount of money and a type of bank account, before displaying the amount of money that can be earned in one year as interest on that money for the given type of bank account. You should use the `switch` statement when implementing this program.

Hint: be careful to consider the case of the letters representing the bank accounts. You might want to restrict this to, say, just upper case. Or you could enhance your program by allowing the user to enter either lower case or upper case letters.

5 Consider the bank accounts discussed in exercise 4 again. Now assume that each type of bank account is associated with a minimum balance as given in the table below:

Account	Minimum balance
A	250
B	1000
C	250
X	5000

Adapt the `switch` statement of the program in exercise 5 above so that the interest is applied only if the amount of money entered satisfies the minimum balance requirement for the given account. If the amount of money is below the minimum balance for the given account an error message should be displayed.

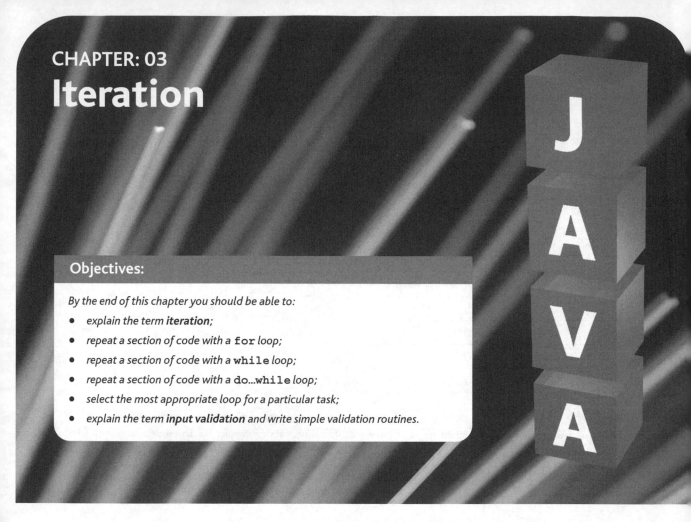

CHAPTER: 03

Iteration

Objectives:

By the end of this chapter you should be able to:

- *explain the term **iteration**;*
- *repeat a section of code with a* `for` *loop;*
- *repeat a section of code with a* `while` *loop;*
- *repeat a section of code with a* `do...while` *loop;*
- *select the most appropriate loop for a particular task;*
- *explain the term **input validation** and write simple validation routines.*

3.1 Introduction

So far we have considered sequence and selection as forms of program control. One of the advantages of using computers rather than humans to carry out tasks is that they can repeat those tasks over and over again without ever getting tired. With a computer we do not have to worry about mistakes creeping in because of fatigue, whereas humans would need a break to stop them becoming sloppy or careless when carrying out repetitive tasks over a long period of time. Neither sequence nor selection allows us to carry out this kind of control in our programs.

Iteration is the form of program control that allows us to instruct the computer to carry out a task over and over again by repeating a section of code. For this reason this form of control is often also referred to as **repetition**. The programming structure that is used to control this repetition is often called a **loop**. There are three types of loops in Java:

> `for` loop;

> `while` loop;

> `do...while` loop.

3.2 The 'for' loop

Consider a program that needs to display a square of stars (five by five) on the screen as follows:

```
*  *  *  *  *

*  *  *  *  *

*  *  *  *  *

*  *  *  *  *

*  *  *  *  *
```

This could be achieved with five output statements executed in sequence:

```
System.out.println("*****");
System.out.println("*****");
System.out.println("*****");
System.out.println("*****");
System.out.println("*****");
```

While this would work, all the program is really doing is executing the following instruction five times.

```
System.out.println("*****");
```

Writing out the same line many times is somewhat wasteful of our precious time as programmers. Imagine what would happen if we wanted a square 40 by 40!

Rather than write out this instruction five times we would prefer to write it out once and get the program to *repeat that same line* five times.

If we wish to repeat a section of code a fixed number of times (five in the example above) we would use Java's `for` loop.

The `for` loop is usually used in conjunction with a **counter**. A counter is just another variable (usually integer) that has to be created. We use it to keep track of how many times we have been through the loop so far. The loop works as follows:

1   the counter is set to some initial value (usually 0 or 1);

2   the counter is tested before each repetition of the loop. When the test returns a `boolean` value of `true` the loop repeats, when it returns a `boolean` value of `false` the loop ends;

3   after each repetition of the loop the value of the counter is changed (usually by adding 1 to it) so that eventually the test will stop the loop.

These three tasks are assembled as follows to construct the `for` loop:

```
for( /* start counter */ ; /* test counter */ ; /* change counter */)
{
      // instruction(s) to be repeated go here
}
```

We can construct a loop to display a square of stars consisting of five rows as follows:

```
for(int i = 1; i <= 5; i++)
{
     System.out.println("*****");
}
```

As with **if** statements, the braces can be omitted when only a single instruction is required in the loop – but for clarity we will always use braces with our loops. Notice that the loop counter 'i' is declared as well as initialized in the header of the loop. The counter is just like any other variable, and so can take any name – often though, simple names like 'i' and 'j' are chosen. Although it is possible to declare the counter prior to the loop, declaring it within the header restricts the use of this variable to the loop itself. This is often preferable.

The loop works in the following way. First the loop counter is set:

```
for(int i = 1; i <= 5; i++) // counter initialised to 1
{
     System.out.println("*****");
}
```

The counter is then tested to see if it is less than or equal to 5:

```
for(int i = 1; i <= 5; i++) // counter tested
{
     System.out.println("*****");
}
```

Since the counter was set to 1, this test is **true** and the body of the loop is entered. All the instructions within the braces of the loop are executed. In this case there is only one instruction to execute:

```
for(int i = 1; i <= 5; i++)
{
     System.out.println("*****"); // this line is executed
}
```

This line prints a row of stars on the screen. Once the instructions inside the braces are complete the loop returns to the beginning, where the counter is changed. In this case the counter is incremented:

```
for(int i = 1; i <= 5; i++) // counter is changed
{
     System.out.println("*****");
}
```

Notice that we have used the increment operator here. As you know, this is just a shorthand for

```
i = i+1
```

This assignment can be used in place of the increment operator, if so desired. After the increment, the counter now has the value of 2. The test is checked to see if the loop should repeat:

```
for(int i = 1; i <= 5; i++) // counter tested
{
        System.out.println("*****");
}
```

This test is still **true** as the counter is still not greater than 5. Since the test is **true** the body of the loop is entered again and another row of stars printed. This process of checking the test, entering the loop and changing the counter repeats until five rows of stars have been printed. At this point the counter is incremented as usual:

```
for(int i = 1; i <= 5; i++) // counter eventually equals 6
{
        System.out.println("*****");
}
```

Now when the test is checked it is **false** as the counter is greater than 5:

```
for(int i = 1; i <= 5; i++) // now test is false
{
        System.out.println("*****");
}
```

When the test of the **for** loop is **false** the loop stops. The instructions in the loop are skipped and the program continues with any instructions after the loop.

As you can see it is very straightforward to repeat a section of code many times. If, for example, we needed to print the row of stars 100 times instead of just five, how would you change the **for** loop? Well, all you would need to do would be to change the test as follows:

```
for(int i = 1; i <= 100; i++) // this loop repeats 100 times
{
        System.out.println("*****");
}
```

This is a very common way of using a **for** loop. Start the counter at 1 and add 1 to the counter each time the loop repeats. However, you may start your counter at any value and change the counter in any way you choose when constructing your **for** loops.

As an example, look at program 3.1 that prints out a countdown of the numbers from 10 down to 1.

Program 3.1

```
public class Countdown
{
  public static void main(String[] args)
  {
    System.out.println("***Numbers from 10 to 1***");
    for (int i=10; i>=1; i--)   // counter moving from 10 down to 1
    {
      System.out.println(i);
    }
  }
}
```

Here the counter starts at 10 and is reduced by 1 each time. Note the use of the loop counter inside the loop:

```
System.out.println(i); // counter 'i' used here
```

When you do this, however, be careful not to inadvertently *change* the loop counter within the loop body as this can throw the test of your **for** loop off track!

Finally, before moving on to look at another form of loop in Java, a reminder that the loop body can contain any number of instructions, including **if** statements, **switch** statements, or even another loop! In other words, you may nest loops just as you nested ifs. As an example of this, consider again the **for** loop we constructed to display a square of stars.

```
for(int i = 1; i <= 5; i++)
{
      System.out.println("*****");
}
```

The body of this loop has an instruction that displays five stars on the screen in a row. We could, if we had wanted, have displayed only a *single* star on the screen as follows:

```
System.out.print("*");
```

Now, to get the program to display five of these stars we could put this instruction within another loop. We will need to use another loop counter for this new loop – let's call this counter 'j'. The inner loop would look like this:

```
for (int j = 1; j<=5; j++)
{
      System.out.print("*");
}
```

We now need an instruction to move the cursor to a new line so that the next row of stars appears on the next line:

```
System.out.println();
```

This can be put together to give the following:

```
for(int i = 1; i <= 5; i++) // outer loop control
{
   for (int j = 1; j<=5; j++) // inner loop control
   {
       System.out.print("*");
   } // inner loop ends here
   System.out.println(); // necessary to start next row on a new line
} // outer loop ends here
```

Let's look at how the control in this program flows.

First the outer loop counter is set to 1:

```
for(int i = 1; i <= 5; i++) // outer loop counter initialised
{
    for (int j = 1; j<=5; j++)
    {
        System.out.print("*");
    }
    System.out.println();
}
```

The test of the outer loop is then checked:

```
for(int i = 1; i <= 5; i++) // outer loop counter tested
{
    for (int j = 1; j<=5; j++)
    {
        System.out.print("*");
    }
    System.out.println();
}
```

This test is found to be **true** so the instructions in the outer loop are executed.

The outer loop itself contains an inner **for** loop followed by a blank **println** statement. First the inner loop repeats five times.

```
for(int i = 1; i <= 5; i++)
{
    for (int j = 1; j<=5; j++) // this loop repeats 5 times
    {
        System.out.print("*");
    }
    System.out.println();
}
```

The inner loop prints five stars on the screen as follows:

* * * * *

After the inner loop stops, there is one more instruction to complete: the command to move the cursor to a new line:

```
for(int i = 1; i <= 5; i++)
{
    for (int j = 1; j<=5; j++)
    {
        System.out.print("*");
    }
    System.out.println(); // last instruction of outer loop
}
```

This completes one cycle of the outer loop so the program returns to the beginning of this loop and increments its counter:

```
for(int i = 1; i <= 5; i++) // counter moves to 2
{
    for (int j = 1; j<=5; j++)
    {
        System.out.print("*");
    }
    System.out.println();
}
```

The test of the outer loop is then checked and found to be **true** and the whole process repeats, printing out a square of five stars as before.

Although a **for** loop is used to repeat something a fixed number of times, you don't necessarily need to know this fixed number when you are writing the program. This fixed number could be a value given to you by the user of your program, for example. Program 3.2 asks the user to determine the size of the square of stars.

Program 3.2

```
import java.util.*;

public class DisplayStars
{
    public static void main(String[] args)
    {
        int num; // to hold user response
        Scanner sc = new Scanner(System.in);
        // prompt and get user response
        System.out.println("Size of square?");
        num = sc.nextInt();
        // display square
        for(int i = 1; i <= num; i++) // loop fixed to 'num'
        {
            for (int j = 1; j<=num; j++) // loop fixed to 'num'
            {
                System.out.print("*");
            }
            System.out.println();
        }
    }
}
```

In this program you cannot tell from the code exactly how many times the loops will iterate, but you can say that they will iterate *num* number of times – whatever the user may have entered for *num*. So in this sense the loop is still fixed. Here is a sample run of program 3.2:

```
Size of square?
8
* * * * * * * *

* * * * * * * *

* * * * * * * *

* * * * * * * *

* * * * * * * *

* * * * * * * *

* * * * * * * *

* * * * * * * *
```

3.3 The 'while' loop

As we have already said, much of the power of computers comes from the ability to ask them to carry out repetitive tasks, so iteration is a very important form of program control. The **for** loop is an often used construct to implement fixed repetitions.

Sometimes, however, a repetition is required that is *not fixed* and a **for** loop is not the best one to use in such a case. Consider the following scenarios, for example:

> a racing game that repeatedly moves a car around a track until the car crashes;

> a ticket issuing program that repeatedly offers tickets for sale until the user chooses to quit the program;

> a password checking program that does not let a user into an application until he or she enters the right password.

Each of the above cases involves repetition; however, the number of repetitions is not fixed but depends upon some condition. The **while** loop offers one type of non-fixed iteration. The syntax for constructing this loop in Java is as follows:

```
while ( /* test goes here */ )
{
        // instruction(s) to be repeated go here
}
```

As you can see, this loop is much simpler to construct than a **for** loop. As this loop is not repeating a fixed number of times, there is no need to create a counter to keep track of the number of repetitions.

When might this kind of loop be useful? The first example we will explore is the use of the **while** loop to check data that is input by the user. Checking input data for errors is referred to as **input validation**.

For example, look back at program 2.2 in the last chapter, which asked the user to enter an exam mark:

```
System.out.println("What exam mark did you get?");
mark = sc.nextInt();
if (mark >= 40)
// rest of code goes here
```

The mark that is entered should never be greater than 100 or less than 0. At the time we assumed that the user would enter the mark correctly. However, good programmers never make this assumption!

Before accepting the mark that is entered and moving on to the next stage of the program, it is good practice to check that the mark entered is indeed a valid one. If it is not, then the user will be allowed to enter the mark again. This will go on until the user enters a valid mark.

We can express this using pseudocode as follows:

```
DISPLAY prompt for mark
ENTER mark
KEEP REPEATING WHILE mark < 0 OR  mark > 100
BEGIN
     DISPLAY error message to user
     ENTER mark
END
// REST OF PROGRAM HERE
```

The design makes clear that an error message is to be displayed as long as the user enters an invalid mark. The user may enter an invalid mark many times so an iteration is required here.

However, the number of iterations is not fixed as it is impossible to say how many, if any, mistakes the user will make.

This sounds like a job for the `while` loop.

```
System.out.println("What exam mark did you get?");
mark = sc.nextInt();
while (mark < 0  || mark > 100) // check for invalid input
{
    // display error message and allow for re-input
    System.out.println("Invalid mark: Re-enter!");
    mark = sc.nextInt();
}
if (mark >= 40)
// rest of code goes here
```

Program 3.3 below shows the whole of the previous program rewritten to include the input validation. Notice how this works – we ask the user for the mark; if it is within the acceptable range, the `while` loop is not entered and we move past it to the other instructions. But if the mark entered is less than zero or greater than 100 we enter the loop, display an error message and ask the user to input the mark again. This continues until the mark is within the required range.

Program 3.3

```java
import java.util.*;

public class DisplayResult2
{
  public static void main(String[] args)
  {
    int mark;
    Scanner sc = new Scanner (System.in);
    System.out.println("What exam mark did you get?");
    mark = sc.nextInt();
    // input validation
    while (mark < 0 || mark > 100) // check if mark is invalid
    {
      // display error message
      System.out.println("Invalid mark: please re-enter");
      // mark must be re-entered
      mark = sc.nextInt();
    }
    // by this point loop is finished and mark will be valid
    if (mark >= 40)
    {
      System.out.println("Congratulations, you passed");
    }
    else
    {
      System.out.println("I'm sorry, but you failed");
    }
    System.out.println("Good luck with your other exams");
  }
}
```

Here is a sample program run:

```
What exam mark did you get?
101
Invalid mark: please re-enter
-10
Invalid mark: please re-enter
10
I'm sorry, but you failed
Good luck with your other exams
```

3.4 The 'do...while' loop

There is one more loop construct in Java that we need to tell you about: the do...while loop.

The do...while loop is another variable loop construct, but, unlike the while loop, the do...while loop has its test at the *end* of the loop rather than at the *beginning*.

The syntax of a do...while loop is given below:

```
do
{
     // instruction(s) to be repeated go here
} while ( /* test goes here */ ); // note the semi-colon at the end
```

You are probably wondering what difference it makes if the test is at the end or the beginning of the loop. Well, there is one subtle difference. If the test is at the end of the loop, the loop will iterate *at least once*. If the test is at the beginning of the loop, however, there is a possibility that the condition will be **false** to begin with, and the loop is never executed. A **while** loop therefore executes *zero or more times* whereas a **do...while** loop executes *one or more times*.

To make this a little clearer, look back at the **while** loop we just showed you for validating exam marks. If the user entered a valid mark initially (such as 66), the test to trap an invalid mark (mark <0 || mark > 100) would be **false** and the loop would be skipped altogether. A **do...while** loop would not be appropriate here as the possibility of never getting into the loop should be left open.

When would a **do...while** loop be suitable? Well, any time you wish to code a non-fixed loop that must execute at least once. Usually, this would be the case when the test can take place only *after* the loop has been entered.

To illustrate this, think about all the programs you have written so far. Once the program has done its job it terminates – if you want it to perform the same task again you have to go through the whole procedure of running that program again.

In many cases a better solution would be to put your whole program in a loop that keeps repeating until the user chooses to quit your program. This would involve asking the user each time if he or she would like to continue repeating your program, or to stop.

A **for** loop would not be the best loop to choose here as this is more useful when the number of repetitions can be predicted. A **while** loop would be difficult to use, as the test that checks the user's response to a question cannot be carried out at the beginning of the loop. The answer is to move the test to the end of the loop and use a **do...while** loop as follows:

```
char response; // variable to hold user response
do // place code in loop
{
     // program instructions go here
     System.out.println("another go (y/n)?");
     response = sc.next().charAt(0); // get user reply
}  while (response == 'y'); // this test must be at the end of the loop
```

For example, program 3.4 below amends program 1.4, which calculated the cost of a product, by allowing the user to repeat the program as often as he or she chooses.

Program 3.4

```java
import java.util.*;

public class FindCost4
{
 public static void main(String[] args )
  {
    double price, tax;
    char reply;
    Scanner sc = new Scanner(System.in);
    do
    {
      // these instructions as before
      System.out.println("*** Product Price Check ***");
      System.out.print("Enter initial price: ");
      price = sc.nextDouble();
      System.out.print("Enter tax rate: ");
      tax = sc.nextDouble();
      price = price * (1 + tax/100);
      System.out.println("Cost after tax = " + price);
      // now see if user wants another go
      System.out.println();
      System.out.print("Would you like to enter another product(y/n)?: ");
      reply = sc.next().charAt(0);
      System.out.println();
    } while (reply == 'y' || reply == 'Y');
  }
}
```

Notice the test of the **do...while** loop allows the user to enter either a lower case or an upper case 'Y' to continue running the program:

```java
while (reply == 'y' || reply == 'Y');
```

Here is sample program run:

*** Product Price Check ***

Enter initial price: **50**

Enter tax rate: **10**

Cost after tax = 55.0

Would you like to enter another product (y/n)?: **y**

*** Product Price Check ***

Enter initial price: **70**

Enter tax rate: **5**

Cost after tax = 73.5

Would you like to enter another product (y/n)?: **Y**

```
*** Product Price Check ***

Enter initial price: 200

Enter tax rate: 15

Cost after tax = 230.0


Would you like to enter another product (y/n)?: n
```

Another way to allow a program to be run repeatedly using a **do...while** loop is to include a *menu* of options within the loop (this was very common in the days before windows and mice). The options themselves are processed by a **switch** statement. One of the options in the menu list would be the option to quit and this option is checked in the **while** condition of the loop. Program 3.5 is a reworking of program 2.5 of the previous chapter using this technique.

Program 3.5

```java
import java.util.*;

public class TimetableWithLoop
{
   public static void main(String[] args)
   {
      char group, response;
      Scanner sc = new Scanner(System.in);
      System.out.println("***Lab Times***");
      do // put code in loop
      {
         // offer menu of options
         System.out.println(); // create a blank line
         System.out.println("[1] TIME FOR GROUP A");
         System.out.println("[2] TIME FOR GROUP B");
         System.out.println("[3] TIME FOR GROUP C");
         System.out.println("[4] QUIT PROGRAM");
         System.out.print("enter choice [1,2,3,4]: ");
         response = sc.next().charAt(0); // get response
         System.out.println(); // create a blank line
         switch(response)  // process response
         {
            case '1': System.out.println("10.00 a.m ");
                     break;
            case '2': System.out.println("1.00 p.m ");
                     break;
            case '3': System.out.println("11.00 a.m ");
                     break;
            case '4': System.out.println("Goodbye ");
                     break;
            default:  System.out.println("Options 1-4 only!");
         }
      } while (response != '4'); // test for Quit option
   }
}
```

Notice that the menu option is treated as a character here, rather than an integer. So option 1 would be entered as the character '1' rather than the number 1, for example. The advantage of treating the menu option as a character rather than a number is that an incorrect menu entry would not result in a program crash if the value entered was non-numeric. Here is a sample run of this program:

```
***Lab Times***

[1] TIME FOR GROUP A
[2] TIME FOR GROUP B
[3] TIME FOR GROUP C
[4] QUIT PROGRAM
enter choice [1,2,3,4]:  2


1.00 p.m


[1] TIME FOR GROUP A
[2] TIME FOR GROUP B
[3] TIME FOR GROUP C
[4] QUIT PROGRAM
enter choice [1,2,3,4]:  5


Options 1-4 only!


[1] TIME FOR GROUP A
[2] TIME FOR GROUP B
[3] TIME FOR GROUP C
[4] QUIT PROGRAM
enter choice [1,2,3,4]:  1
10.00 a.m


[1] TIME FOR GROUP A
[2] TIME FOR GROUP B
[3] TIME FOR GROUP C
[4] QUIT PROGRAM
enter choice [1,2,3,4]:  3


11.00 a.m
```

```
[1]  TIME  FOR  GROUP  A
[2]  TIME  FOR  GROUP  B
[3]  TIME  FOR  GROUP  C
[4]  QUIT  PROGRAM
enter  choice  [1,2,3,4]:    4


Goodbye
```

3.5 Picking the right loop

With three types of loop to choose from in Java, it can sometimes be difficult to decide upon the best one to use in each case. Here are some general guidelines that should help you:

> if the number of repetitions required can be determined prior to entering the loop – use a **for** loop;

> if the number of repetitions required cannot be determined prior to entering the loop, and you wish to allow for the possibility of zero repetitions – use a **while** loop;

> if the number of repetitions required cannot be determined before the loop, and you require at least one repetition of the loop – use a **do...while** loop.

The guidelines above will help you to pick the most appropriate loop construct to use in each case. However, it is possible to pick *any loop* to implement *any type of repetition*.

For example, program 3.1 used a **for** loop to display a countdown of numbers from 10 down to 1. The **for** loop is the most appropriate loop to use here as the number of repetitions can be determined. However, we could choose either a **while** or a **do...while** to implement this. Neither of these loops have a counter associated with them, so to use them to implement this task we will need to create our own loop counter prior to the loop. We will also need to modify the loop counter within the loop. Program 3.6 rewrites program 3.1 by using a **while** loop instead of the more obvious choice of a **for** loop.

Program 3.6

```java
public class CountdownUsingWhile
{
  public static void main(String[] args)
  {
    int i = 10; // declare and initialize a loop counter before loop
    System.out.println("***Numbers from 10 to 1***");
    while (i>=1)  // 'while' loop just consists of a test
    {
      System.out.println(i);
      i--; // modify the counter within the 'while' loop
    }
  }
}
```

When run, this program behaves in exactly the same way as program 3.1. Similarly, we could use a **for** loop to implement a repetition that may be more ideally suited to one of the other two loops. We do this by leaving the start condition of the counter, and the counter modifier blank. This just leaves the test, and so effectively reduces the **for** loop to a **while** loop. As an example, program 3.7 rewrites program 3.3 by using a **for** loop to check for valid exam marks, rather than the more obvious choice of a **while** loop.

Program 3.7

```java
import java.util.*;

public class DisplayResult3UsingFor
{
  public static void main(String[] args)
  {
    int mark;
    Scanner sc = new Scanner(System.in);
    System.out.println("What exam mark did you get?");
    mark = sc.nextInt();
    for (; mark < 0 || mark > 100; ) // just leave the test here
    {
      System.out.println("Invalid mark: please re-enter");
      mark = sc.nextInt();
    }
    if (mark >= 40)
    {
      System.out.println("Congratulations, you passed");
    }
    else
    {
      System.out.println("I'm sorry, but you failed");
    }
    System.out.println("Good luck with your other exams");
  }
}
```

Again, this program will behave in exactly the same way as the original program 3.3. Notice that when the **for** loop is reduced to containing just a test, semi-colons are still required to indicate that there is no start condition and no counter modification:

```java
// semi-colons either side of the test still required
for (; mark < 0 || mark > 100; )
```

While the loops can be used interchangeably in this way, each is designed for a specific purpose; so it is best to use the most appropriate loop for each situation.

Self-test questions

1 How does *iteration* differ from *selection*?

2 Consider the following program:

```java
import java.util.*;

public class IterationQ2
{
    public static void main(String[] args)
    {
        int num;
        Scanner sc = new Scanner(System.in);
        System.out.print("Enter a number ");
        num = sc.nextInt();
        for(int i= 1; i< num; i++)
        {
            System.out.println("YES");
            System.out.println("NO");
        }
        System.out.println("OK");
    }
}
```

a) What would be the output of this program if the user entered 5 when prompted?

b) What would be the output of this program if the user entered 0 when prompted?

3 What would be the output from the following program?

```java
public class IterationQ3
{
    public static void main(String[] args)
    {
        for(int i=1; i<=10; i++)
        {
            if (i%2 == 0)
            {
                System.out.println(i);
            }
        }
    }
}
```

4 Examine the program below that aims to allow a user to keep guessing a secret number. Part of the code has been replaced by a comment:

```java
import java.util.*;

public class IterationQ4
{
    public static void main(String[] args)
    {
        final int SECRET = 321;
```

```
        int num;
        Scanner sc = new Scanner(System.in);
        System.out.print("Enter a number ");
        num = sc.nextInt();
        do
        {
            System.out.println("Wrong number, try again");
            num = sc.nextInt();
        }   while (/* test to be completed */)
        System.out.println("Well done, right number");
    }
}
```

a) Why is a **do...while** loop not a good choice for this repetition?

b) Replace the **do...while** loop with a more appropriate loop construct.

c) Replace the comment with an appropriate test for this loop.

Programming exercises

1 Modify the program given in self-test question 3 above, so that the user enters a number and the program displays all the numbers from 1 up to the number entered. The program should identify which of these numbers are odd and which are even. For example, if the user entered 5 the program should display something like the following:

1 is odd

2 is even

3 is odd

4 is even

5 is odd

2 a) Using a **for** loop, write a program that displays a "6 times" multiplication table; the output should look like this:

```
    1 × 6 = 6
    2 × 6 = 12
    3 × 6 = 18
    4 × 6 = 24
    5 × 6 = 30
    6 × 6 = 36
```

```
      7 × 6 = 42

      8 × 6 = 48

      9 × 6 = 54

     10 × 6 = 60

     11 × 6 = 66

     12 × 6 = 72
```

b) Adapt the program so that instead of a "6 times" table, the user chooses which table is displayed.

c) Adapt the program further by replacing the **for** loop with a **while** loop.

3 Implement program 3.2 that allows the user to determine the size of a square of stars and then

   a) adapt it so that the user is allowed to enter a size only between 2 and 100;

   b) adapt the program further so that the user can choose whether or not to have another go.

4 Consider a vending machine that offers the following options:

```
[1] Get gum

[2] Get chocolate

[3] Get popcorn

[4] Get juice

[5] Display total sold so far

[6] Quit
```

Design and implement a program that continuously allows users to select from these options. When options 1–4 are selected an appropriate message is to be displayed acknowledging their choice. For example, when option 3 is selected the following message could be displayed:

```
Here is your popcorn
```

When option 5 is selected, the number of each type of item sold is displayed. For example:

```
3 items of gum sold

2 items of chocolate sold

6 items of popcorn sold

9 items of juice sold
```

When option 6 is chosen the program terminates. If an option other than 1–6 is entered an appropriate error message should be displayed, such as:

```
Error, options 1-6 only!
```

CHAPTER: 04

Implementing methods

J
A
V
A

Objectives:

By the end of this chapter you should be able to:

- *explain the meaning of the term **method**;*
- *declare and define methods;*
- ***call** a method;*
- *explain the meaning of the terms **actual parameters** and **formal parameters**;*
- *devise simple **algorithms** with the help of pseudocode;*
- *identify the **scope** of a particular variable;*
- *explain the meaning of the term **polymorphism**;*
- *declare and use **overloaded** methods.*

4.1 Introduction

As early as chapter 1 we were using the term **method**. There you found out that a method is a part of a class, and contains a particular set of instructions. So far all the classes you have written have contained just one method, the `main` method. In this chapter you will see how a class can contain not just a `main` method, but many other methods as well.

Normally a method will perform a single well-defined task. Examples of the many sorts of task that a method could perform could be to calculate the area of a circle, to display a particular message on the screen, to convert a temperature from Fahrenheit to Celsius, and many many more. In this chapter you will see how we can collect the instructions for performing these sorts of tasks together in a method.

You will also see how, once we have written a method, we can get it to perform its task within a program. When we do this we say that we are **calling** the method. When we call a method, what we are actually doing is telling the program to jump to a new place (where the method instructions are stored), carry out the set of instructions that it finds there, and, when it has finished (that is, when the method has terminated), to return and carry on where it left off.

So in this chapter you will learn how to write a method within a program, how to call a method from another part of the program and how to send information into a method and get information back.

4.2 Declaring and defining methods

Let's illustrate the idea of a method by thinking about a simple little program. The program prompts the user to enter his or her first name, family name and town – each time the prompt is displayed, it is followed by a message, consisting of a couple of lines, explaining that the information entered is confidential. This is shown below in program 4.1 – the program would obviously then go on to do other things with the information that has been entered, but we are not interested in that, so we have just replaced all the rest of the program with a comment.

Program 4.1

```java
import java.util.*;

public class DataEntry
{
  public static void main(String[] args)
  {
    Scanner sc = new Scanner(System.in);

    String firstName, familyName, town;

    // prompt for first name
    System.out.println("Please enter your first name");

    // display confidentiality message
    System.out.println("Please note that all information supplied is confidential");
    System.out.println("No personal details will be shared with any third party");

    // get first name from user
    firstName = sc.next();

    // prompt for family name
    System.out.println("Please enter your family name");

    // display confidentiality message
    System.out.println("Please note that all information supplied is confidential");
    System.out.println("No personal details will be shared with any third party");

    // get family name from user
    familyName = sc.next();

    // prompt for town
    System.out.println("Please enter your town");

    // display confidentiality message
    System.out.println("Please note that all information supplied is confidential");
    System.out.println("No personal details will be shared with any third party");

    // get town from user
    town = sc.next();

    // more code here
  }
}
```

You can see from the above program that we have had to type out the two lines that display the confidentiality message three times. It would be far less time-consuming if we could do this just once, then send the program off to wherever these instructions are stored, and then come back and carry on with what it was doing. You will probably have realized by now that we can indeed do this – by writing a *method*. The job of this particular method will be simply to display the confidentiality message on the screen – we need to give our method a name so that we can refer to it when required, so let's call it displayMessage. Here is how it is going to look:

```
private static void displayMessage()
{
    System.out.println("Please note that all information supplied is confidential");
    System.out.println("No personal details will be shared with any third party");
}
```

The body of this method, which is contained between the two curly brackets, contains the instructions that we want this method to perform, namely to display two lines of text on the screen. The first line, which declares the method, is called the method **header**, and consists of four words – let's look into each of these a bit more closely:

private

You will find out a lot more about the words **public** and **private** when we go into detail about classes and objects in later chapters. For now, it is enough for you to know that placing the word **private** in front of the method name means that the method cannot be accessed by any other class. Right now, of course, all the programs you have written have involved your writing one class only. However, you have already been using the methods of other classes such as the Scanner class. So you can see that when we have applications involving more than one class, it is perfectly possible to call a method from another class.

If you wanted the methods of your class to be used by other classes, you would declare your method as **public**. Here, however, we do not want to do this – the method in question is here purely to "help" the main method of this class, and so we declare it as **private**. A **private** method such as this, which is not accessible to other classes, is often referred to as a **helper** method.

static

You have seen this word in front of the main method many times now. However, we won't be explaining its meaning to you until chapter 7. For now, all you need to know is that in this case our method has to be **static**, because it is going to be called from another method (that is, the main method) that is also **static**. So until you understand the meaning of this term, you can take our word for it that you would not be able to compile your program if this method were not declared as **static**.

void

In the next section you will see that it is possible for a method to send back some information once it terminates. This particular method simply displays a message on the screen, so we don't require it to send back any information when it terminates. The word **void** indicates that the method does not send back any information.

displayMessage()

This is the name that we have chosen to give our method. You can see that the name is followed by a pair of empty brackets. Very soon you will learn that it is possible to send some information into a method – for example, some values that the method needs in order to perform a calculation. When we need to do that we list, in these brackets, the types of data that we are going to send in; here, however, as the method is doing nothing more that displaying a message on the screen we do not have to send in any data, and the brackets are left empty.

4.3 Calling a method

Now that we have declared and defined our method, we can make use of it. The idea is that we get the method to perform its instructions as and when we need it to do so – you have seen that this process is referred to as *calling* the method. To call a method in Java, we simply use its name, along with the following brackets, which in this case are empty. So in this case our method call, which will be placed at the point in the program where we need it, looks like this:

```
displayMessage();
```

Now we can rewrite program 4.1, replacing the appropriate lines of code with the simple message call. The whole program is shown below in program 4.2:

Program 4.2

```
import java.util.*;

public class DataEntry2
{
  public static void main(String[] args)
  {
    Scanner sc = new Scanner(System.in);

    String firstName, familyName, town;

    System.out.println("Please enter your first name");
    displayMessage(); // call displayMessage method
    firstName = sc.next();

    System.out.println("Please enter your family name");
    displayMessage(); // call displayMessage method
    familyName = sc.next();

    System.out.println("Please enter your town");
    displayMessage(); // call displayMessage method
    town = sc.next();

    // more code here
  }

  // the code for displayMessage method
  private static void displayMessage()
  {
    System.out.println("Please note that all information supplied is confidential");
    System.out.println("No personal details will be shared with any third party");
  }
}
```

You can see that the method itself is defined separately after the `main` method – although it could have come before it, since the order in which methods are presented doesn't matter to the compiler. When the program is run, however, it always starts with `main`.

We should emphasize again here that when one method calls another method, the first method effectively pauses at that point, and the program then carries out the instructions in the called method; when it has finished doing this, it returns to the original method, which then resumes. In most of the programs in this chapter it will be the `main` method that calls the other method. This doesn't have to be the case, however, and it is perfectly possible for any method to call another method – indeed, the called method could in turn call yet another method. This would result in a number of methods being "chained". When each method terminates, the control of the program would return to the method that called it.

You can see an example of a method being called by a method other than `main` in section 4.7.

4.4 Method input and output

We have already told you that it is possible to send some data into a method, and that a method can send data back to the method that called it. Now we will look into this in more detail.

In order to do this we will use as an example a program that we wrote in the very first chapter – program 1.4. Here is a reminder of that program:

A reminder of program 1.4

```java
import java.util.*;

/* a program to input the initial price of a product and then
   calculate and display its cost after tax has been added */

public class FindCost3
{
    public static void main(String[] args)
    {
        Scanner sc = new Scanner(System.in);
        double price, tax;
        System.out.println("*** Product Price Check ***");
        System.out.print("Enter initial price: ");
        price = sc.nextDouble();
        System.out.print("Enter tax rate: ");
        tax = sc.nextDouble();
        price = price * (1 + tax/100);
        System.out.println("Cost after tax = " + price);
    }
}
```

The line that calculates the new price, with the sales tax added, is this one:

```java
price = price * (1 + tax/100);
```

Let's create a method that performs this calculation – in a real application this would be very useful, because we might need to call this method at various points within the program, and, as you will see, each time we do so we could get it to do the calculation for different values of the price and the tax. Clearly we will need a way to send in these values to the method. But on top of that, we need to arrange for the method to tell us the result of adding the new tax – if it didn't do that, it wouldn't be much use!

The method is going to look like this:

```java
private static double addTax(double priceIn, double taxIn)
{
    return priceIn * (1 + taxIn/100);
}
```

First, take a careful look at the header. You are familiar with the first two words, **private static**, but look at the next one; this time, where we previously saw the word **void**, we now have the word **double**. As we have said, this method must send back – or **return** – a result, the new price of the item. So the type of data that the method is to return in this case is a **double**. In fact what we are doing here is declaring a method of *type* **double**. Thus, the *type* of a method refers to its *return* type. It is possible to declare methods of any type – **int**, **boolean**, **char** and so on. And we will see in later chapters that the return type could even be a class such as String.

After the type declaration, we have the name of the method, in this case addTax – and this time the brackets aren't empty. You can see that within these brackets we are declaring two variables, both of type **double**. The variables declared in this way are known as the **formal parameters** of the method. They are going to hold, respectively, the values of the price and the tax that are going to be sent in from the calling method (you will see how this is done in a moment). Of course, these variables could be given any name we choose, but we have called them priceIn and taxIn respectively. We will use this convention of adding the suffix In to variable names in the formal parameter list throughout this book.

Now we can turn our attention to the body of the method, which as you can see, in this case, consists of a single line:

```
return priceIn * (1 + taxIn/100);
```

The word **return** in a method serves two very important functions. First it ends the method – as soon as the program encounters this word, the method terminates, and control of the program jumps back to the calling method. The second function is that it sends back a value. In this case it sends back the result of the calculation:

priceIn * (1 + taxIn/100)

You should note that if the method is of type **void**, then there is no need to include a **return** instruction – the method simply terminates once the last instruction is executed.

Now we can discuss how we actually call this method and use its return value. The whole program appears below as program 4.3:

Program 4.3

```
import java.util.*;

/* we have adapted program 1.4 so that the new price is determined by
   calling a method that adds the sales tax */

public class FindCost5
{
    public static void main(String[] args )
    {
        Scanner sc = new Scanner(System.in);

        double price, tax;

        System.out.println("*** Product Price Check ***");

        System.out.print("Enter initial price: ");
        price = sc.nextDouble();

        System.out.print("Enter tax rate: ");
```

```
      tax = sc.nextDouble();

      price = addTax(price, tax); // call the addTax method

      System.out.println("Cost after tax = " + price);
   }

   private static double addTax(double priceIn, double taxIn)
   {
      return priceIn * (1 + taxIn/100);
   }
}
```

The line that calls the method is this one:

```
price = addTax(price, tax);
```

First, we will consider the items in brackets after the method name. As you might have expected, there are two items in the brackets – these are the *actual* values that we are sending into our method. They are therefore referred to as the **actual parameters** of the method. Their values are copied onto the formal parameters in the called method. This process, which is referred to as **passing** parameters, is illustrated in figure 4.1.

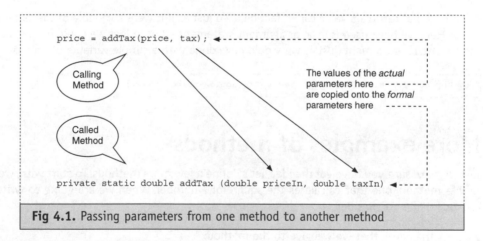

Fig 4.1. Passing parameters from one method to another method

You might have been wondering how the program knows which values in the actual parameter list are copied onto which variables in the formal parameter list. The answer to this is that it is the *order* that is important – you can see this from figure 4.1 – the value of price is copied onto `priceIn`; the value of tax is copied onto `taxIn`. Although the variable names have been conveniently chosen, the names themselves have nothing to do with which value is copied to which variable.

You might also be wondering what would happen if you tried to call the method with the wrong number of variables. For example:

```
price = addTax(price);
```

The answer is that you would get a compiler error, because there is no method called `addTax` that requires just one single variable to be passed into it.

You can see then that the actual parameter list must match the formal parameter list exactly. Now this is important not just in terms of the number of variables, but also in terms of the *types*. For example, using actual values this time instead of variable names, this method call would be perfectly acceptable:

```
price = addTax(187.65, 17.5);
```

However, this would cause a compiler error:

```
price = addTax(187.65, 'c');
```

The reason, of course, is that `addTax` requires two **double**s, not a **double** and a **char**.

We can now move on to looking at how we make use of the return value of a method.

The `addTax` method returns the result that we are interested in, namely the new price of the item. What we need to do is to assign this value to the variable `price`. As you have already seen we have done this in the same line in which we called the method:

```
price = addTax(price, tax);
```

A method that returns a value can in fact be used just as if it were a variable of the same type as the return value! Here we have used it in an assignment statement – but in fact we could have simply dropped it into the `println` statement, just as we would have done with a simple variable of type **double**:

```
System.out.println("Cost after tax = " + addTax(price, tax));
```

4.5 More examples of methods

Just to make sure you have got the idea, let's define a few more methods. To start with, we will create a very simple method, one that calculates the square of a number. When we are going to write a method, there are four things to consider:

>   the name that we will give to the method;

>   the inputs to the method (the formal parameters);

>   the output of the method (the return value);

>   the body of the method (the instructions that do the job required).

In the case of the method in question, the name `square` would seem like a sensible choice. We will define the method so that it will calculate the square of any number, so it should accept a single value of type **double**. Similarly, it will return a **double**.

The instructions will be very simple – just return the result of multiplying the number by itself. So here is our method:

```
private static double square(double numberIn)
{
    return numberIn * numberIn;
}
```

Remember that we can choose any names we want for the input parameters; here we have stuck with our convention of using the suffix `In` for formal parameters.

To use this method in another part of the program, such as the `main` method, is now very easy. Say, for example, we had declared and initialized two variables as follows:

```
double a = 2.5;
double b = 9.0;
```

Let's say we wanted to assign the square of `a` to a **double** variable `x` and the square of `b` to a **double** variable `y`. We could do this as follows:

```
x = square(a);
y = square(b);
```

After these instructions, `x` would hold the value 6.25 and `y` would hold the value 81.0.

For our next illustration we will choose a slightly more complicated example. We will define a function that we will call `max`; it will accept two integer values, and will return the bigger value of the two (of course, if they are equal, it can return the value of either one). It should be pretty clear that we will require two integer parameters, and that the method will return an integer. As far as the instructions are concerned, it should be clear that an **if...else** statement should do the job – if the first number is greater than the second, return the first number, if not return the second. Here is our method:

```
private static int max(int firstIn, int secondIn)
{
    if(firstIn > secondIn)
    {
        return firstIn;
    }
    else
    {
        return secondIn;
    }
}
```

You should note that in this example we have two **return** statements, each potentially returning a different value – the value that is actually returned is decided at run-time by the values of the variables `firstIn` and `secondIn`.

Working out how to write the instructions for this method was not too hard a job. In fact it was so simple, we didn't bother to design it with pseudocode. However, there will be many occasions in the future when the method has to carry out a much more complex task, and you will need to think through how to perform this task. A set of instructions for performing a job is known as an **algorithm** – common examples of algorithms in everyday life are recipes and DIY instructions. Much of a programmer's time is spent devising algorithms for particular tasks, and, as you saw in chapter 1, we can use pseudocode to help us design our algorithms. We will look at further examples as we progress through this chapter.

Let's develop one more method. There are many instances in our programming lives where we might need to test whether a number is even or odd. Let's provide a method that does this job for us. We will call our method `isEven`, and it will report on whether or not a particular number is an even number. The test will be performed on integers, so we will need a single parameter of type **int**. The return value is interesting – the method will tell us whether or not a number is even, so it will need to return a value of **true** if the number is even or **false** if it is not. So our return type is going to be **boolean**. The instructions are quite simple to devise – again, an **if...else** statement should certainly do the job. But how can we test whether a number is even or not? Well, an even number will give a remainder of zero when divided by 2. An odd number will not. So we can use the modulus operator here. Here is our method:

```
private static boolean isEven(int numberIn)
{
    if(numberIn % 2 == 0)
    {
        return true;
    }
    else
    {
        return false;
    }
}
```

Actually there is a slightly neater way we could have written this method. The expression:

```
numberIn % 2 == 0
```

will evaluate to either **true** or **false** – and we could therefore simply have returned the value of this expression and written our method like this:

```
private static boolean isEven(int numberIn)
{
        return (numberIn % 2 == 0);
}
```

It is interesting to note that the calling method couldn't care less how the called method is coded – all it needs is for it to do the calculation correctly, and return the desired value. This is something that will become very significant when we look at methods that call methods of other classes later in this semester.

Another point of interest is that a **boolean** method such as the one above can often be used as the test in a selection or loop. For example, assuming that the variable `number` has been declared as an **int**, we might easily need to write something like:

```
if(isEven(number) == true)
{
        // code here
}
```

In fact there is a very convenient and frequently used shorthand for this, which is as follows:

```
if(isEven(number))
{
        // code here
}
```

The same applies in a **for** loop or **while** loop, so that in general for a **boolean** expression:

    if(expression)

is equivalent to

                                    if(expression == true)

Similarly:

     while(expression)

is equivalent to

                                    while(expression == true)

To test for a **false** value we simply negate the expression with the *not* operator (!):

    if(!expression)

is equivalent to

                                    if(expression == false)

So, referring to the isEven method again, to test if a number is odd we would have:

```
if(!isEven(number))
{
      // code here
}
```

Before we leave this section, there is one thing we should make absolutely clear – a method cannot change the *original* value of a variable that was passed to it as a parameter. The reason for this is that all that is being passed to the method is a copy of whatever this variable contains. In other words, just a *value*. The method does not have access to the original variable. Whatever value is passed is copied to the parameter in the called method. We will illustrate this with a very simple program indeed – program 4.4 below:

Program 4.4

```
public class ParameterDemo
{
  public static void main(String[] args)
  {
    int x = 10;
    demoMethod(x);
    System.out.println(x);
  }

  public static void demoMethod(int xIn)
  {
    xIn = 25;
    System.out.println(xIn);
  }
}
```

You can see that in the `main` method we declare an integer, `x`, which is initialized to 10. We then call a method called `demoMethod`, with `x` as a parameter. The formal parameter of this method – `xIn` – will now of course hold the value 10. But the method then assigns the value of 25 to the parameter – it then displays the value on the screen.

The method ends there, and control returns to the `main` method. The final line of this method displays the value of `x`.

The output from this method is as follows:

25

10

This shows that the original value of `x` has not in any way been affected by what happened to `xIn` in `demoMethod`.

4.6 Variable scope

Looking back at program 4.3, it is possible that some of you asked yourselves the following questions: Why do we need to bother with all this stuff in the brackets? We've already declared a couple of variables called `price` and `tax` – why can't we just use them in the body of the method? Well, go ahead and try it – you will see that you get a compiler error telling you that these variables are not recognized!

How can this be? They have certainly been declared. The answer lies in the matter of *where* exactly these variables have been declared. In actual fact variables are only "visible" within the pair of curly brackets in which they have been declared – this means that if they are referred to in a part of the program outside these brackets, then you will get a compiler error. Variables that have been declared inside the brackets of a particular method are called **local** variables – so the variables `price` and `tax` are said to be *local* to the `main` method. We say the variables have a **scope** – this means that their visibility is limited to a particular part of the program. If `price` or `tax` were referred to in the `addtax` method, they would be out of scope.

Let's take another, rather simple, example. Look at program 4.5:

Program 4.5

```
public class ScopeTest
{
    public static void main(String[] args)
    {
        int x = 1;      // x is local to main
        int y = 2;      // y is local to main
        method1(x, y); // call method1
    }

    private static void method1(int xIn, int yIn)
    {
        int z;          // z is local to method1
        z = xIn + yIn;
        System.out.print(z);
    }
}
```

In this program the variables x and y are local to main. The variable z is local to method1. The variables xIn and yIn are the formal parameters of method1. This program will compile and run without a problem, because none of the variables is referred to in the wrong place.

Imagine, however, that we were to rewrite program 4.5 as program 4.6, below:

Program 4.6

```
// this program will give rise to two compiler errors

public class ScopeTest2
{
    public static void main(String[] args)
    {
        int x = 1;      // x is local to main
        int y = 2;      // y is local to main
        method1(x, y); // call method1
        System.out.print(z); /* this line will cause a compiler error as z
                                 is local to method1 */
    }

    private static void method1(int xIn, int yIn)
    {
        int z;         // z is local to method1
        z = x + y;     /* this line will cause a compiler error as x and y
                          are local to main */
        System.out.print(z);
    }
}
```

As the comments indicate, the lines in bold will give rise to compiler errors, as the variables referred to are out of scope.

It is interesting to note that, since a method is completely unaware of what has been declared inside any other method, you could declare variables with the same name inside different methods. The compiler would regard each variable as being completely different from any other variable in another method which simply had the same name. So, for example, if we had declared a *local* variable called x in method1, this would be perfectly ok – it would behave completely independently from the variable named x in main.

To understand why this is so, it helps to know a little about what goes on when the program is running. A part of the computer's memory called the stack is reserved for use by running programs. When a method is called, some space on the stack is used to store the values for that method's formal parameters and its local variables. That is why, whatever names we give them, they are local to their particular method. Once the method terminates, this part of the stack is no longer accessible, and the variables effectively no longer exist. And this might help you to understand even more clearly why the value of a variable passed as a parameter to a method cannot be changed by that method.

Before we move on, it will be helpful if we list the kinds of variables that a method can access:

> a method can access variables that have been declared as formal parameters;

> a method can access variables that have been declared locally – in other words that have been declared within the curly brackets of the method;

> as you will learn in chapter 7, a method has access to variables declared as *attributes of the class* (don't worry – you will understand what this means in good time!).

A method cannot access any other variables.

4.7 Method overloading

You have already encountered the term *overloading* in previous chapters, in connection with operators. You found out, for example, that the division operator (/) can be used for two distinct purposes – for division of integers, and for division of real numbers. The + operator, is not only used for addition, but also for concatenating two strings. So the same operator can behave differently depending on what it is operating on – operators can be overloaded.

Methods too can be overloaded. To illustrate, let's return to the `max` method of section 4.5. Here it is again:

```
private static int max(int firstIn, int secondIn)
{
    if(firstIn > secondIn)
    {
        return firstIn;
    }
    else
    {
        return secondIn;
    }
}
```

As you will recall, this method accepts two integers and returns the greater of the two. But what if we wanted to find the greatest of three integers? We would have to write a new method, which we have shown below. We are just showing you the header here – we will think about the actual instructions in a moment:

```
private static int max(int firstIn, int secondIn, int thirdIn)
{
    // code goes here
}
```

You can see that we have given this method the same name as before – but this time it has *three* parameters instead of two. And the really clever thing is that we can declare and call both methods within the same class. Both methods have the same name but the parameter list is different – and each one will *behave* differently. In our example, the original method compares two integers and returns the greater of the two; the second one, once we have worked out the algorithm for doing this, will sort through three integers and return the value of the one that is the greatest of the three. When two or more methods, distinguished by their parameter lists, have the same name but perform different functions we say that they are **overloaded**. Method overloading is actually one example of what is known as **polymorphism**. Polymorphism literally means *having many forms*, and it is an important feature of object-oriented programming languages. It refers, in general, to the phenomenon of having methods and operators with the same name performing different functions. You will come across other examples of polymorphism in later chapters.

Now, you might be asking yourself how, when we call an overloaded method, the program knows which one we mean. The answer of course depends on the actual parameters that accompany the method call – they are matched with the formal parameter list, and the appropriate method will be called. So, if we made this call somewhere in a program:

```
int x = max(3, 5);
```

then the first version of max would be called – the version that returns the bigger of two integers. This, of course, is because the method is being called with two integer parameters, matching this header:

```
private static int max(int firstIn, int secondIn)
```

However, if this call were made:

```
int x = max(3, 5, 10);
```

then it would be the second version that was called:

```
private static int max(int firstIn, int secondIn, int thirdIn)
```

One very important thing we have still to do is to devise the *algorithm* for this second version. Can you think of a way to do it? Have go at it before reading on.

One way to do it is to declare an integer variable, which we could call result, and start off by assigning to it the value of the first number. Then we can consider the next number. Is it greater than the current value of result? If it is, then we should assign this value to result instead of the original value. Now we can consider the third number – if this is larger than the current value of result, we assign its value to result. You should be able to see that result will end up having the value of the greatest of the three integers. It is helpful to express this as pseudocode:

```
SET result TO first number
IF second number > result
BEGIN
    SET result TO second number
END
IF third number > result
BEGIN
    SET result TO third number
END
RETURN result
```

Here is the code:

```
private static int max(int firstIn, int secondIn, int thirdIn)
{
    int result;
    result = firstIn;
    if(secondIn > result)
    {
        result = secondIn;
    }
    if(thirdIn > result)
    {
        result = thirdIn;
    }
    return result;
}
```

Program 4.7 illustrates how both versions of our `max` method can be used in the same program:

Program 4.7

```java
public class OverloadingDemo
{
  public static void main(String[] args)
  {
    int maxOfTwo, maxOfThree;
    maxOfTwo = max(2, 10);        // call the first version of max
    maxOfThree = max(-5, 5, 3);   // call the second version of max
    System.out.println(maxOfTwo);
    System.out.println(maxOfThree);
  }

  /* this version of max accepts two integers and returns the greater of
     the two */
  private static int max(int firstIn, int secondIn)
  {
      if(firstIn > secondIn)
      {
          return firstIn;
      }
      else
      {
          return secondIn;
      }
  }


  /* this version of max accepts three integers and returns the greatest
     of the three */
  private static int max(int firstIn, int secondIn, int thirdIn)
  {
      int result;
      result = firstIn;
      if(secondIn > result)
      {
          result = secondIn;
      }
      if(thirdIn > result)
      {
          result = thirdIn;
      }
      return result;
  }
}
```

As the first call to `max` in the `main` method has two parameters, it will call the first version of `max`; the second call, with its three parameters, will call the second version. Not surprisingly then the output from this program looks like this:

10

5

It might have occurred to you that we could have implemented the second version of `max` (that is the one that takes three parameters) in a different way. We could have started off by finding the maximum of the first two integers (using the first version of `max`), and then doing the same thing again, comparing the result of this with the third number.

This version is presented below – this is an example of how we can call a method not from the `main` method, but from another helper method.

```
private static int max(int firstIn, int secondIn, int thirdIn)
{
    int step1, result;
    step1 = max(firstIn, secondIn); // call the first version of max
    result = max(step1, thirdIn);  // call the first version of max again
    return result;
}
```

Some of you might be thinking that if we wanted similar methods to deal with lists of four, five, six, or even more numbers, it would be an awful lot of work to write a separate method for each one – and indeed it would! But don't worry – you will soon be ready for the next chapter, where you will find a much easier way to deal with situations like this.

4.7 Using helper methods in menu-driven programs

In chapter 3 we developed a program that presented the user with a menu of choices; we pointed out that this was a very common interface for programs before the days of graphics. Until we start working with graphics later in the semester, we will use this approach with some of our more complex programs. Take a look back at program 3.5. In this program, each **case** statement consisted of a single instruction (apart from the **break**), which simply displayed one line of text. Imagine, though, that we were to develop a more complex program in which each menu choice involved a lot of processing. The **switch** statement would start to get very messy, and the program could easily become very unwieldy. In this situation, confining each menu option to a particular method will make our program far more manageable.

Program 4.8 is an example of such a program. The program allows a user to process the sale of tickets for some event. The price of the tickets is built into the program; children are charged half-price. Four menu options are offered. The first allows the user to enter the number of tickets required and displays the total cost of these tickets. The second gets similar information from the user, but records the purchase of tickets by adding the cost to a running total. The third option displays this total, while the final one allows the user to quit the program.

Study it carefully, and then we will point out some of the interesting features.

Program 4.8

```java
import java.util.*;

/* This program demonstrates how helper methods can be used in a
   menu-driven program */

public class TicketVendor
{
  public static void main(String[] args)
  {

      /* The variables below are local to the main method; if the value of
         any of them is needed by a helper method, it must be passed in as
         a parameter */

      final double PRICE = 30; // the price of an adult ticket
      double total = 0; // the running total is initialized to zero
      double cost;
      char choice;
      do
      {
```

```
        Scanner sc = new Scanner(System.in);
        System.out.println("*** ACME TICKET VENDING SOFTWARE ***");
        System.out.println();
        System.out.println("1. Get cost of tickets");
        System.out.println("2. Record purchase of tickets");
        System.out.println("3. View total money received so far");
        System.out.println("4. Quit");
        System.out.println();
        System.out.println("Enter a number from 1 - 4");
        System.out.println();
        choice = sc.next().charAt(0);
        switch(choice)
        {
           case '1' : option1(PRICE);          // call method option1
                      break;
           case '2' : cost = option2(PRICE);   // call method option2
                      total = total + cost;    // add the cost to the total
                      break;
           case '3' : option3(total);          // call method option3
                      break;
           case '4' : break;
           default  : System.out.println("Enter only numbers from 1 - 4");
                      System.out.println();
        }
     } while(choice != '4');
}

// option1 calculates and displays the cost of tickets
private static void option1(double priceIn)
{
   Scanner sc = new Scanner(System.in);
   int adult, child;  // local variables
   double cost;       // local variable
   System.out.print("How many adult tickets are required? ");
   adult = sc.nextInt();
   System.out.print("How many child tickets are required? ");
   child = sc.nextInt();
   cost = adult * priceIn + 0.5 * child * priceIn; // calculate the cost
   System.out.println();
   System.out.println("The total cost of these tickets will be " + cost);
   System.out.println();
}

/* option2 returns the cost of tickets; this is added to the total in
   the main method */
private static double option2(double priceIn)
{
   Scanner sc = new Scanner(System.in);
   int adult, child; // local variables
   double cost;      // local variable
   System.out.print("How many adult tickets were purchased? ");
   adult = sc.nextInt();
   System.out.print("How many child tickets were purchased? ");
   child = sc.nextInt();
   cost = adult * priceIn + 0.5 * child * priceIn; // calculate the cost
   System.out.println();
   System.out.println("The amount received was " + cost);
   System.out.println();
   return cost; // return the cost of the tickets
}

// option3 displays the current total
private static void option3(double totalIn)
{
   System.out.println();
   System.out.pr"ntln("Total received " + totalIn);
   System.out.println();
}
}
```

There are no new programming techniques in this program; it is the *design* that is interesting. The comments are self-explanatory; so we draw your attention only to a few important points:

> Choosing menu option 1 causes the method `option1` to be called – the price of an adult ticket is sent in as a parameter.

> Choosing menu option 2 causes the method `option2` to be called. The price of a ticket is again sent in. The method returns the total cost, which is added to the running total once the method has terminated.

> Choosing menu option 3 causes the method `option3` to be called – the total so far is sent in as a parameter.

> Choosing option 4 causes the program to terminate – this happens because the body of the **while** loop executes only while `choice` is not equal to 4. If it is equal to 4, the loop is not executed and the program ends. The associated **case** statement consists simply of the instruction **break**, thus causing the program to jump out of the **switch** statement.

> You can see that we have had to declare a new `Scanner` object in each method – now that you understand the notion of variable *scope*, you should understand why we have had to do this.

Self-test questions

1 Explain the meaning of the term *method*.

2 Distinguish between *actual parameters* and *formal parameters*.

3 Explain the meaning of the term *polymorphism*.

4 What is meant by the term *method overloading*?

5 Consider the following program:

```
public class MethodsQ5
{
  public static void main(String[] args)
  {
    System.out.println(myMethod(3, 5));
    System.out.println(myMethod(3, 5, 10));
  }

  private static int myMethod(int firstIn, int secondIn, int thirdIn)
  {
    return firstIn + secondIn + thirdIn;
  }

  private static int myMethod(int firstIn, int secondIn)
  {
    return firstIn - secondIn;
  }
}
```

a) What would be displayed on the screen when this program was run?

b) Explain, giving reasons, the effect of adding either of the following lines into the `main` method:

i) `System.out.println(myMethod(3));`

ii) `System.out.println(myMethod(3, 5.7, 10));`

6 What would be displayed on the screen as a result of running the following program?

```
public class MethodsQ6
{
  public static void main(String[] args)
  {
    int x = 3;
    int y = 4;
    System.out.println(myMethod(x, y));
    System.out.println(y);
  }

  private static int myMethod(int firstIn, int secondIn)
  {
    int x = 10;
    int y;
    y = x + firstIn + secondIn;
```

```
      return y;
   }
 }
```

7 What would be displayed on the screen as a result of running the following program?

```
public class MethodsQ7
{
  public static void main(String[] args)
  {
    int x = 2;
    int y = 7;
    System.out.println(myMethod(x, y));
    System.out.println(y);
  }

  private static int myMethod(int a, int x)
  {
    int y = 20;
    return y - a - x;
  }
}
```

Programming exercises

1 a) Write a method that calculates the area of a circle, calculated by the formula πr^2 (you can use 3.142 for the value of π).

   b) Write a short program that makes use of the above method.

2 In chapter 1, programming exercise 5, you wrote a program that converted pounds to kilograms. Rewrite this program, so that the conversion takes place in a separate method.

3 a) Write a menu-driven program that provides three options:

   ❯ the first option allows the user to enter a temperature in Celsius and displays the corresponding Fahrenheit temperature;

   ❯ the second option allows the user to enter a temperature in Fahrenheit and displays the corresponding Celsius temperature;

   ❯ the third option allows the user to quit.

   The formulae that you need are as follows, where C represents a Celsius temperature and F a Fahrenheit temperature:

   $$F = \frac{9C}{5} + 32$$

$$C = \frac{5(F - 32)}{9}$$

b) Adapt the above program so that the user is not allowed to enter a temperature below absolute zero; this is $-273.15C$, or $-459.67F$.

CHAPTER: 05

Arrays

Objectives:

By the end of this chapter you should be able to:

- create **arrays** of primitive types;
- use loops to process arrays;
- use an enhanced **for** loop to process an array;
- use arrays as method inputs and outputs;
- develop routines for accessing and manipulating arrays.

5.1 Introduction

In previous chapters we have shown you how to create variables and store data in them. In each case the variables created could be used to hold a *single* item of data. How, though, would you deal with a situation in which you had to create and handle a very large number of data items?

An obvious approach would be just to declare as many variables as you need. Declaring a large number of variables is a nuisance but simple enough. For example, let's start to consider a very simple application that records seven temperature readings (one for each day of the week):

```
public class TemperatureReadings
{
    public static void main(String[] args)
    {
        // declare 7 variables to hold readings
        double temperature1, temperature2, temperature3, temperature4,
               temperature5, temperature6, temperature7;
        // more code will go here
    }
}
```

Here we have declared seven variables each of type **double** (as temperatures will be recorded as real numbers). So far so good. Now to write some code that allows the user to enter these temperatures. Getting one temperature is easy (assuming we have created a Scanner object sc):

```
System.out.println("max temperature for day 1 ?");
temperature1 = sc.nextDouble();
```

But how would you write the code to get the second temperature, the third temperature and all the remaining temperatures? Well, you could repeat the above pair of lines for each temperature entered, but surely you've got better things to do with your time!

Essentially you want to repeat the same pair of lines seven times. You already know that a `for` loop is useful when repeating lines of code a fixed number of times. Maybe you could try using a `for` loop here?

```
for (int i=1; i<=7; i++)
{
      // what goes here?
}
```

This looks like a neat solution, but the problem is that there is no obvious instruction we could write in the `for` loop that will allow a value to be entered into a *different* variable each time the loop repeats. As things stand there is no way around this, as each variable has a *distinct* name.

Ideally we would like each variable to be given the *same* name (`temperature`, say) so that we could use a loop here, but we would like some way of being able to distinguish between each successive variable. In fact, this is exactly what an **array** allows us to do.

5.2 Creating an array

An array is a special data type in Java that can be thought of as a *container* to store a *collection of items*. These items are sometimes referred to as the **elements** of the array. All the elements stored in a particular array must be of the *same type* but there is no restriction on which type this is. So, for example, an array can be used to hold a collection of **int** values or a collection of **char** values, but it cannot be used to hold a mixture of **int** and **char** values. An array can also be used to hold objects such as strings, but we will come back to look at this when we look at objects in more detail in chapter 6.

Let's look at how to use arrays in your programs. First you need to know how to create an array. Array creation is a two-stage process:

1   declare an array variable;

2   allocate memory to store the array elements.

An array variable is declared in much the same way as a simple variable except that a pair of square brackets is added after the type. For example, if an array was to hold a collection of integer variables it could be declared as follows:

```
int[] someArray;
```

Here a name has been given to the array in the same way you would name any variable. The name we have chosen is `someArray`. If the square brackets were missing in the above declaration this would just be a simple variable capable of holding a *single* integer value only. But the square brackets indicate this variable is an array allowing *many* integer values to be stored.

So, to declare an array `temperature` containing **double** values, you would write the following:

```
double[] temperature;
```

At the moment this simply defines `temperature` to be a variable that can be linked to a collection of **double** values. The memory that will eventually hold the these **double** values has not been allocated yet. This is stage two.

What information do you think would be required in order to reserve enough space in the computer's memory for all the array elements?

Well, it would be necessary to state the size of the array, that is the *maximum* number of elements required by the array. Also, since each data type requires a different amount of memory space, it is also necessary to state the type of each individual array element (this will be the same type used in stage one of the array declaration). The array type and size are then put together with a special **new** operator. For example, if we required an array of 10 integers the following would be appropriate:

```
someArray = new int[10];
```

The **new** operator creates the space in memory for an array of the given size and element type.[1] We will come back to look at this operator when looking at classes and objects in chapter 6. Once the size of the array is set it cannot be changed, so always make sure you create an array that is big enough for your purpose. Returning to the temperature example above, if you wanted the array to hold seven temperatures you would allocate memory as follows:

```
temperature = new double[7];
```

The two stages of array creation (declaring and allocating memory space for the elements) can also be combined into one step as follows:

```
double[] temperature = new double[7];
```

Let's see what effect the **new** operator has on computer memory by looking at figure 5.1.

---

[1] Of course this size should not be a negative value. A negative value will cause an error in your program.

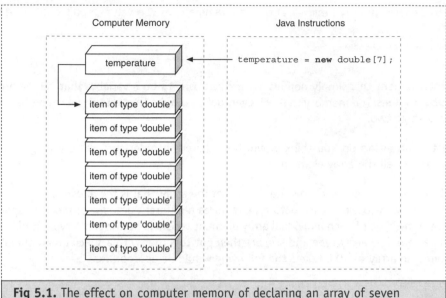

Fig 5.1. The effect on computer memory of declaring an array of seven 'double' values

As can be seen from figure 5.1, the array creation has created seven elements and linked the `temperature` variable to these seven elements. The `temperature` variable is said to hold a **reference** to the array elements. A reference is simply a location in the computer's memory (known as a memory *address*). As this array was declared to hold values of type **double**, each of the seven elements is a memory location big enough to hold a value of type **double**. In effect, the array reference, `temperature`, points to seven new variables. Each of these variables will have some initial value placed in them. If the variables are of some number type (such as **int** or **double**) the value of each will be set to zero; if the variables are of type **char** their values will be set to a special Unicode value that represents an empty character; if the variables are of **boolean** type they will each be set to **false**.

You may be wondering: what names have each of these variables been given? Well, each element in an array shares the same name as the array, so in this case each element is called `temperature`. The individual elements are then *uniquely identified* by an additional **index value**. An index value acts rather like a street number to identify houses on the same street (see figure 5.2). In much the same way as a house on a street is identified by the street name and a house number, an array element is identified by the array name and the index value.

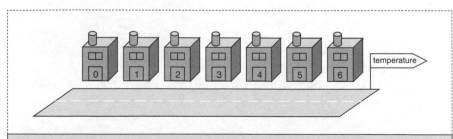

Fig 5.2. Elements in an array are identified in much the same way as houses on a street

Like a street number, these index values are always contiguous integers. Note carefully that, in Java, *array indices start from 0 and not from 1*. This index value is always enclosed in square brackets, so the first temperature in the list is identified as `temperature[0]`, the second temperature by `temperature[1]` and so on.

This means that the size of the array and the last index value are *not* the same value. In this case the size is 7 and the last index is 6. There is no such value as `temperature[7]`, for example. Remember this, as it is a common cause of error in programs! If you try and access an invalid element such as `temperature[7]`, the following program error will be generated by the system:

`java.lang.ArrayIndexOutOfBoundsException`

This type of error is called an *exception*. You will find out more about exceptions in chapter 15 but you should be aware that, very often, exceptions will result in program termination.

Usually, when an array is created, values will be added into it as the program runs. If, however, all the values of the array elements are known beforehand, then an array can be created without the use of the **new** operator by initializing the array as follows:

```
double[] temperature = {9, 11.5, 11, 8.5, 7, 9, 8.5} ;
```

The initial values are placed in braces and separated by commas. The compiler determines the length of the array by the number of initial values (in this case 7). Each value is placed into the array in order, so `temperature[0]` is set to 9, `temperature[1]` to 11.5 and so on. This is the only instance in which *all the elements* of an array can be assigned explicitly by listing out the elements in a single assignment statement. Once an array has been created, elements must be accessed *individually*.

5.3 Accessing array elements

Once an array has been created, its elements can be used like any other variable of the given type in Java. If you look back at the temperature example, initializing the values of each temperature when the array is created is actually quite unrealistic. It is much more likely that temperatures would be entered into the program as it runs. Let's look at how to achieve this.

Whether an array is initialized or not, values can be placed into the individual array elements. We know that each element in this array is a variable of type **double**. As with any variable of a primitive type, the assignment operator can be used to enter a value.

The only thing you have to remember when using the assignment operator with an array element is to specify *which* element to place the value in. For example, to allow the user of the program to enter the value of the first temperature, the following assignment could be used (again, assuming the existence of a `Scanner` object sc):

```
temperature[0] = sc.nextDouble();
```

Note again that, since array indices begin at 0, the first temperature is not at index 1 but index 0.

Array elements could also be printed on the screen. For example, the following command prints out the value of the *sixth* array element:

```
System.out.println(temperature[5]); // index 5 is the sixth element!
```

Note that an array index (such as 5) is just used to *locate* a position in the array; it is *not* the item at that position.

For example, assume that the user enters a value of 25.5 for the first temperature in the array; the following statement:

```
System.out.println("temperature for day 1 is "+ temperature[0]);
```

would then print out the message:

temperature for day 1 is 25.5

Statements like the `println` command above might seem a bit confusing at first. The message refers to "temperature for day **1**" but the temperature that is displayed is `temperature[0]`. Remember though that the temperature at index position 0 *is* the first temperature! After a while you will get used to this indexing system of Java.

As you can see from the examples above, you can use array elements in exactly the same way you can use any other kind of variable of the given type. Here are a few more examples:

```
temperature[4] = temperature[4] * 2;
```

This assignment doubles the value of the *fifth* temperature. The following `if` statement checks if the temperature for the *third* day was a hot temperature:

```
if (temperature[2] >= 18)
{
     System.out.println("it was hot today");
}
```

So far so good, but if you are just going to use array elements in the way you used regular variables, why bother with arrays at all?

The reason is that the indexing system of arrays is in fact a very powerful programming tool. The index value does not need to be a literal number such as 5 or 2 as in the examples we have just shown you; it can be *any expression that evaluates to an integer*.

More often than not an integer *variable* is used, in place of a fixed index value, to access an array element. For example, if we assume that `i` is some integer variable, then the following is a perfectly legal way of accessing an array element:

```
System.out.println(temperature[i]); // index is a variable
```

Here the array index is not a literal number (like 2 or 5) but the variable `i`. The value of `i` will determine the array index. If the value of `i` is 4 then this will display `temperature[4]`, if the value of `i` is 6 then this will display `temperature[6]`, and so on. One useful application of this is to place the array instructions within a loop (usually a **for** loop), with the loop counter being used as the array index. For example, returning to the original problem of entering all seven temperature readings, the following loop could now be used:

```
for(int i = 0; i<7; i++) // note, loop counter runs from 0 to 6
{
      System.out.println("enter max temperature for day "+(i+1));
      temperature[i] = sc.nextDouble(); // use loop counter
}
```

Note carefully the following points from this loop:

> Unlike the previous examples of **for** loop counters that started at 1, this counter starts at 0. Since the counter is meant to track the array indices, 0 is the appropriate number to start from.

> The counter goes up to, but does not include, the number of items in the array. In this case this means the counter goes up to 6 and not 7. Again this is because the array index for an array of size 7 stops at 6.

> The `println` command uses the loop counter to display the number of the given day being entered. The loop counter starts from 0, however. We would not think of the first day of the week as being day 0! In order for the message to be more meaningful for the user, therefore, we have displayed (i+1) rather than i.

Effectively the following statements are executed by this loop:

```
System.out.println("enter max temperature for day 1 ");    ⎫ 1st time round loop
temperature[0]  = sc.nextDouble();                          ⎭

System.out.println("enter max temperature for day 2 ");    ⎫ 2nd time round loop
temperature[1]  = sc.nextDouble();                          ⎭

//as above but with indices 2-5                             ⎱ 3rd–6th time round loop

System.out.println("enter max temperature for day 7 ");    ⎫ 7th time round loop
temperature[6]  = sc.nextDouble();                          ⎭
```

You should now be able to see the benefit of an array. This loop can be made more readable if we make use of a built-in feature of all arrays that returns the length of an array. It is accessed by using the word `length` after the name of the array. The two are joined by a full stop. Here is an example:

```
System.out.print("number of temperatures = ");
System.out.println(temperature.length); // returns the size of the array
```

which displays the following on to the screen:

number of temperatures = 7

Note that `length` feature returns the size of the array, not necessarily the number of items currently stored in the array (which may be fewer). This attribute can be used in place of a fixed number in the **for** loop as follows:

```
for (int i = 0; i < temperature.length, i++)
{
      // code for loop goes here
}
```

To see this technique being exploited, look at program 5.1 to see the completed TemperatureReadings program, which stores and displays the maximum daily temperatures in a week.

Program 5.1

```
import java.util.*;

public class TemperatureReadings
{
    public static void main(String[] args)
    {
        Scanner sc = new Scanner(System.in);
        // create array
        double[] temperature = new double[7];
        // enter temperatures
        for (int i = 0; i < temperature.length; i++)
        {
            System.out.println("enter max temperature for day " + (i+1));
            temperature[i] = sc.nextDouble();
        }
        // display temperatures
        System.out.println(); // blank line
        System.out.println("***TEMPERATURES ENTERED***");
        for (int i = 0; i < temperature.length; i++)
        {
            System.out.println("day "+(i+1)+" "+ temperature[i]);
        }
    }
}
```

Note how length was used to control the two **for** loops. Here is a sample test run.

enter max temperature for day 1 **12.2**

enter max temperature for day 2 **10.5**

enter max temperature for day 3 **13**

enter max temperature for day 4 **15**

enter max temperature for day 5 **13**

enter max temperature for day 6 **12.5**

enter max temperature for day 7 **12**

TEMPERATURES ENTERED

day 1 12.2

day 2 10.5

day 3 13.0

```
day 4 15.0

day 5 13.0

day 6 12.5

day 7 12.0
```

5.4 Passing arrays as parameters

In chapter 4 we looked at how methods can be used to break up a programming task into manageable chunks. Methods can receive data in the form of parameters and can send back data in the form of a return value. Arrays can be used both as parameters to methods and as return values. In the next section we will see an example of an array as a return value from a method. In this section we will look at passing arrays as parameters to a method. As an example of passing an array to a method, consider once again program 5.1, which processes temperature readings. That program contains all the processing within the `main` method. As a result, the code for this method is a little difficult to read. Let's do something about that. We will create two helper methods, `enterTemps` and `displayTemps`, to enter and display temperatures respectively. To give these helper methods access to the array they must receive it as a parameter. Here, for example, is the header for the `enterTemps` method. Notice that when a parameter is declared as an array type, the size of the array is not required but the empty square brackets are :

```
private static void enterTemps( double[] temperatureIn )
{
        // rest of method goes here
}
```

Now, although in the previous chapter we told you that a parameter just receives a copy of the original variable, this is not the case with arrays. We will explain this a little later but for now just be aware that this method will actually fill the original array. The code for the method itself is straightforward:

```
for (int i = 0; i < temperatureIn.length; i++)
{
      Scanner sc = new Scanner(System.in);
      System.out.println("enter max temperature for day " + (i+1));
      temperatureIn[i] = sc.nextDouble();
}
```

Similarly the `displayTemps` method will require the array to be sent as a parameter. Program 5.2 rewrites program 5.1 by giving the `main` method the two helper methods mentioned above. Take a look at it and then we will discuss it.

Program 5.2

```java
import java.util.*;
public class TemperatureReadings2
{
    public static void main(String[] args)
    {
        double[] temperature = new double[7];
        enterTemps(temperature); // call helper method
        displayTemps(temperature); // call helper method
    }

    // helper method to enter temperatures
    private static void enterTemps(double[] temperatureIn)
    {
        Scanner sc = new Scanner(System.in);
        for (int i = 0; i < temperatureIn.length; i++)
        {
            System.out.println("enter max temperature for day " + (i+1));
            temperatureIn[i] = sc.nextDouble();
        }
    }

    // helper method to display temperatures
    private static void displayTemps(double[] temperatureIn)
    {
        System.out.println();
        System.out.println("***TEMPERATURES ENTERED***");
        for (int i = 0; i < temperatureIn.length; i++)
        {
            System.out.println("day "+(i+1)+" "+ temperatureIn[i]);
        }
    }
}
```

Notice that when sending an array as a parameter, the array name alone is required

```java
public static void main(String[] args)
{
    double[] temperature = new double[7];
    enterTemps(temperature); // array name plugged in
    displayTemps(temperature); // array name plugged in
}
```

Now let us return to the point we made earlier. You are aware that, in the case of a simple variable type such as an **int**, it is the *value* of the variable that is copied when it is passed as a parameter. This means that if the value of a parameter is altered within a method, the original variable is unaffected outside that method. This is not the case with arrays.

As we said earlier, the enterTemps method actually fills the *original* array. How can this be? The answer is that in the case of arrays, the value sent as a parameter is not a copy of each array element but, instead, a copy of the array *reference*. In other words, the *location* of the array is sent to the receiving method not the value of the contents of the array. Now, even though the receiving parameter (temperatureIn) has a different name to the original variable in main (temperature), they are both pointing to the same place in memory so both are modifying the same array. This is illustrated in figure 5.3:

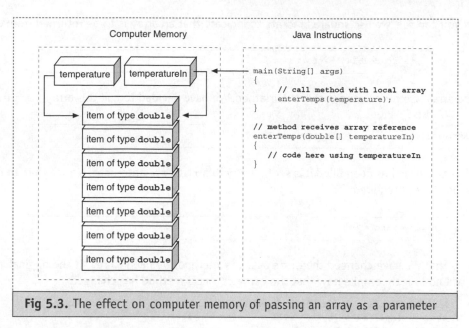

Fig 5.3. The effect on computer memory of passing an array as a parameter

Sending the array reference to a method rather than a copy of the whole array is a very efficient use of the computer's resources, especially when arrays become very large.

5.5 Returning an array from a method

A method can return an array as well as receive arrays as parameters. As an example, let us reconsider the `enterTemps` method from program 5.2. At the moment, this method accepts an array as a parameter and fills this array with temperature values. Since this method fills the *original* array sent in as a parameter, it does not need to return a value – its return type is therefore `void`:

```
private static void enterTemps(double[] temperatureIn)
{
     // code to fill the parameter, 'temperatureIn', goes here
}
```

An alternative approach would be *not* to send an array to this method but, instead, to create an array *within* this method and fill *this* array with values. This array can then be returned from the method:

```
// this method receives no parameter but returns an array of doubles
private static double[] enterTemps()
{
     Scanner sc = new Scanner(System.in);
     // create an array within this method
     double[] temperatureOut = new double[7];
     // fill up the array created in this method
     for (int i = 0; i < temperatureOut.length; i++)
     {
         System.out.println("enter max temperature for day " + (i+1));
         temperatureOut[i] = sc.nextDouble();
     }
     // send back the array created in this method
     return temperatureOut;
}
```

As you can see, we use square brackets to indicate that an array is to be returned from a method :

```
private static double[] enterTemps()
```

The array itself is created within the method. We have decided to call this array `temperatureOut`:

```
double[] temperatureOut = new double[7];
```

After the array has been filled it is sent back with a **return** statement. Notice that, to return an array, the name alone is required:

```
return temperatureOut;
```

Now that we have changed the `enterTemps` method, we need to revisit the original `main` method also. It will no longer compile now that the `enterTemps` method has changed:

```
// the original 'main' method will no loger compile!
public static void main(String[] args)
{
    double[] temperature = new double[7];
    enterTemps(temperature); // this line will now cause a compiler error
    displayTemps(temperature);
}
```

The call to `enterTemps` will no longer compile as the new `enterTemps` does not expect to be given an array as a parameter. The correct way to call the method is as follows:

```
enterTemps(); // this method requires no parameter
```

However, this method now *returns* an array. We really should do something with the array value that is returned from this method. We should use the returned array value to set the value of the original `temperature` array:

```
// just declare the 'temperature' array but do not allocate it memory yet
double[] temperature;
// 'temperature' array is now set to the return value of 'enterTemps'
temperature = enterTemps();
```

As you can see, we have not sized the `temperature` array once it has been declared. Instead the `temperature` array will be set to the size of the array returned by `enterTemps`, and it will contain all the values of the array returned by `enterTemps`. Program 5.3 presents the complete program:

Program 5.3

```java
import java.util.*;
public class TemperatureReadings3
{
 public static void main(String[] args)
 {
     double[] temperature ;
     temperature = enterTemps(); // call new version of this method
     displayTemps(temperature);
 }

 // helper method to enter temperatures returns an array
 private static double[] enterTemps()
 {
     Scanner sc = new Scanner(System.in);
     double[] temperatureOut = new double[7];
     for (int i = 0; i < temperatureOut.length; i++)
     {
         System.out.println("enter max temperature for day " + (i+1));
         temperatureOut[i] = sc.nextDouble();
     }
     return temperatureOut;
 }

 // this method is unchanged
 private static void displayTemps(double[] temperatureIn)
 {
     System.out.println();
     System.out.println("***TEMPERATURES ENTERED***");
     for (int i = 0; i < temperatureIn.length; i++)
     {
         System.out.println("day "+(i+1)+" "+ temperatureIn[i]);
     }
 }
}
```

Program 5.3 behaves in exactly the same way as program 5.2, so whether you implement `enterTemps` as in program 5.2 or as in program 5.3 is really just a matter of preference.

5.6 The enhanced 'for' loop

As you can see from the examples above, when processing an entire array a loop is required. Very often, this will be a `for` loop. With a `for` loop, the loop counter is used as the array index within the body of the loop. In the examples above, the loop counter was used not only as an array index but also to display meaningful messages to the user. For example:

```java
for (int i = 0; i < temperature.length; i++)
{
     System.out.println("day "+(i+1)+" "+ temperature[i]);
}
```

Here the loop counter was used to determine the day number to display on the screen, as well as the index of an array element. Very often, when a `for` loop is required, the *only* use made of the loop counter is as an array index to access all the elements of the array consecutively. Java 5.0 provides an enhanced version of the `for` loop especially for this purpose.

Rather than use a counter, the enhanced **for** loop consists of a variable that, upon each iteration, stores consecutive elements from the array.[2] For example, if we wished to display on the screen each value from the `temperature` array, the enhanced **for** loop could be used as follows:

```
/* the enhanced for loop iterates through elements of an array without the
   need for an array index */
for (double item : temperature) // see discussion below
{
        System.out.println(item);
}
```

In this case we have named each successive array element as `item`. The loop header is to be read as "for each `item` in the `temperature` array". For this reason the enhanced **for** loop is often referred to as the *foreach* loop. Notice that the type of the array item also has to be specified. The type of this variable is **double** as we are processing an array of **double** values. Remember that this is the type of each *individual* element within the array.

You should note that the variable `item` can be used only within the loop, we cannot make reference to it outside the loop. Within the body of the loop we can now print out an array element by referring directly to the `item` variable rather than accessing it via an index value:

```
System.out.println(item); // 'item' is an array element
```

This is a much neater solution than using a standard **for** loop, which would require control of a loop counter in the loop header, and array look up within the body of the loop.

Be aware that the enhanced **for** loop should *not* be used if you wish to modify the array items. Modifying array items with such a loop will not cause a compiler error, but it is unsafe as it may cause your program to behave unreliably. So you should use an enhanced **for** loop only when

> you wish to access the *entire* array (and not just part of the array);

> you wish to *read* the elements in the array, not *modify* them;

> you do not require the array index for additional processing.

Very often, when processing an array, it is the case that these three conditions apply. In the following sections we will make use of this enhanced **for** loop where appropriate.

5.7 Some useful array methods

Apart from the `length` feature, an array does not come with any useful built in routines. So we will develop some of our own methods for processing an array. We will use a simple integer array for this example. Here is the outline of the program we are going to write in order to do this:

---

[2] The enhanced **for** loop also works with other classes in Java, which act as alternatives to arrays. We will explore some of these classes in chapter 17.

```
import java.util.*;

public class SomeUsefulArrayMethods
{
    public static void main (String[] args)
    {
        Scanner sc = new Scanner(System.in);
        int[] someArray; // declare an integer array
        // ask user to determine size of array
        System.out.println("How many elements to store?");
        int size = sc.nextInt();
        // size array now
        someArray = new int[size];

        // call methods here
    }

    // methods to process an array here
}
```

As you can see, we have delayed the second stage of array creation here until the user tells us how many elements to store in the array. Now to some methods.

5.7.1 Array maximum

The first method we will develop will allow us to find the maximum value in an array. For example, we may have a list of scores and wish to know the highest score in this list. Finding the maximum value in an array is a much better approach than the one we took in chapter 4, where we looked at a method to find the maximum of two values and another method to find the maximum of three values. This array method can instead be used with lists of two, three, four or any other number of values. The approach we will use will be similar to the max method we developed for finding the maximum of three values. Here is the pseudocode again.

```
SET result TO first number
IF second number > result
BEGIN
    SET result TO second number
END
IF third number > result
BEGIN
    SET result TO third number
END
RETURN result
```

Here, the final result is initialized to the first value. All other values are then compared with this value to determine the largest value. Now that we have an array, we can use a loop to process this comparison, rather than have a series of many if statements. Here is a suitable algorithm:

```
SET result TO first value in array
LOOP FROM second element in array TO last element in array
BEGIN
    IF current element > result
    BEGIN
        SET result TO current element
    END
END
RETURN result
```

This method will need the array that it has to search to be sent in as a parameter. Also, this method will return the maximum item so it must have an integer return type.

```java
private static int max (int[] arrayIn)
{
    int result = arrayIn[0]; // set result to the first value in the array
    // this loops runs from the 2nd item to the last item in the array
    for (int i=1; i < arrayIn.length; i++)
    {
        if (arrayIn[i] > result)
        {
            result = arrayIn[i]; // reset result to new maximum
        }
    }
    return result;
}
```

Notice we did not use the enhanced **for** loop here, as we needed to iterate from the *second* item in the array rather than through *all* items, and the standard **for** loop gives us this additional control.

Starting from the second item in the array makes sense here as the initial maximum value has been set to be the first item in the array.

```java
int result = arrayIn[0]; // set initial maximum to first value in array
// start loop here
```

However, it would still produce the correct result if *all* the items in the array were compared to this maximum. Though this would mean that, the very first time around the loop, the first item is effectively being compared to itself, it does allow us to use the enhanced **for** loop – which is neater than the standard **for** loop:

```java
// this version of 'max' makes use of an enhanced 'for' loop
private static int max (int[] arrayIn)
{
    int result = arrayIn[0]; // set result to the first value in the array
    // this loops runs through all items in the array
    for (int currentElement: arrayIn)
    {
     if (currentElement > result)
     {
            result = currentElement; // reset result to new maximum
     }
    }
    return result;
}
```

We will stick to this version of max.

5.7.2 Array summation

The next method we will develop will be a method that calculates the total of all the values in the array. Such a method might be useful, for example, if we had a list of deposits made into a bank account and wished to know the total value of these deposits. A simple way to calculate the sum is to keep a running total and add the value of each array element to that running total. Whenever you have a running total it is important to initialize this value to zero. We can express this algorithm using pseudocode as follows:

```
SET total TO zero
LOOP FROM first element in array TO last element in array
BEGIN
    SET total TO total + value of current element
END
RETURN total
```

This method will again need the array to sum to be sent in as a parameter, and will return an integer (the value of the sum), giving us the following:

```java
private static int sum (int[] arrayIn)
{
    int total = 0;
    for (int currentElement : arrayIn)
    {
        total = total + currentElement;
    }
    return total;
}
```

Notice the use of the enhanced **for** loop here – as we need to iterate through *all* elements within the array.

5.7.3 Array membership

It is often useful to determine whether or not an array contains a particular value. For example, if the list were meant to store a unique collection of student ID numbers, this method could be used to check a new ID number before adding it to the list. A simple technique is to check each item in the list one by one, using a loop, to see if the given value is present. If the value is found the loop is exited. If the loop reaches the end without exiting then we know the item is not present. Here is the pseudocode:

```
LOOP FROM first element in array TO last element in array
BEGIN
    IF current element = item to find
    BEGIN
        EXIT loop and RETURN true
    END
END
RETURN false
```

Notice in the algorithm above that a value of **false** would be returned only if the given item is not found. If the value is found, the loop would terminate without reaching its end and a value of **true** would be returned.

Here is the Java code for this method. We need to ensure that this method receives the array to search and the item being searched for. Also the method must return a **boolean** value:

```java
private static boolean contains (int[] arrayIn, int valueIn)
{
    // enhanced 'for' loop used here
    for (int currentElement : arrayIn)
    {
        if (currentElement == valueIn)
        {
            return true; // exit loop early if value found
        }
    }
    return false; // value not present
}
```

5.7.4 **Array search**

One of the most common tasks relating to a list of values is to determine the position of an item within the list. For example, we may wish to know the position of a job waiting in a printer queue. The algorithm for this `search` method is similar to the algorithm for the `contains` method. We search through the array using a loop and compare every element in the array to the element we are looking for. This approach is often referred to as a *linear search*. Once we find the element we can return its array index. One thing we need to be careful of is to decide what to return when the value we are searching for is not in the array. A negative value such as −999 can be used for this purpose as such a value can never be a valid array index. Here is the pseudocode:

```
LOOP FROM first element in array TO last element in array
BEGIN
    IF current element = item to find
    BEGIN
        EXIT loop and RETURN current index
    END
END
RETURN -999
```

In the algorithm above a value of −999 would be returned only if the item was not found. If the item was found the loop would exit with the appropriate array index. Here is the Java code for this method. Once again we need to ensure that this method receives the array to search and the item being searched for. This method must return an integer value:

```java
private static int search (int[] arrayIn, int valueIn)
{
    // enhanced 'for' loop should not be used here!
    for (int i=0; i < arrayIn.length; i++)
    {
        if (arrayIn[i] == valueIn)
        {
            return i; // exit loop with array index
        }
    }
    return -999; // indicates value not in list
}
```

Notice, in this case, we could not use the enhanced `for` loop – as we require the method to return the index of the given item in the array, and this index is arrived at by using the standard `for` loop.

5.7.5 **The final program**

The complete program for manipulating an array is now presented below. The array methods are accessed via a menu. We have included some additional methods here for entering and displaying an array:

Program 5.4

```java
import java.util.*;

// a menu driven program to test a selection of useful array methods

public class SomeUsefulArrayMethods
{
  public static void main (String[] args)
  {
    char choice;
    Scanner sc = new Scanner(System.in);
    int[] someArray; // declare an integer array
    System.out.print("How many elements to store?: ");
    int size = sc.nextInt();
    // size the array
    someArray = new int [size];
    // menu
    do
    {
        System.out.println();
        System.out.println("[1] Enter values");
        System.out.println("[2] Array maximum");
        System.out.println("[3] Array sum");
        System.out.println("[4] Array membership");
        System.out.println("[5] Array search");
        System.out.println("[6] Display values");
        System.out.println("[7] Exit");
        System.out.print("Enter choice [1-7]: ");
        choice = sc.next().charAt(0);
        System.out.println();
        // process choice by calling helper methods
        switch(choice)
        {
            case '1': fillArray(someArray);
                      break;
            case '2': int max = max(someArray);
                      System.out.println("Maximum array value = " + max);
                      break;
            case '3': int total = sum(someArray);
                      System.out.println("Sum of array values = " + total);
                      break;
            case '4': System.out.print ("Enter value to find: ");
                      int value = sc.nextInt();
                      boolean found = contains(someArray, value);
                      if (found)
                      {
                        System.out.println(value + " is in the array");
                      }
                      else
                      {
                        System.out.println(value + " is not in the array");
                      }
                      break;
            case '5': System.out.print ("Enter value to find: ");
                      int item = sc.nextInt();
                      int index = search(someArray, item);
                      if (index == -999) // indicates value not found
                      {
                        System.out.println
                            ("This value is not in the array");
                      }
                      else
                      {
                          System.out.println
                            ("This value is at array index " + index);
                      }
                      break;
            case '6': System.out.println("Array values");
```

```
                            displayArray(someArray);
                            break;
            }
      } while (choice != '7');
      System.out.println("Goodbye");
}


// helper methods

// fills an array with values
public static void fillArray(int[] arrayIn)
{
   Scanner sc = new Scanner (System.in);
   for (int i = 0; i < arrayIn.length; i++)
   {
     System.out.print("enter value ");
     arrayIn[i] = sc.nextInt();
   }
}


// returns the total of all the values held within an array
private static int sum (int[] arrayIn)
{
    int total = 0;
    for (int currentElement : arrayIn)
    {
        total = total + currentElement;
    }
    return total;
}



// returns the maximum value in an array
private static int max (int[] arrayIn)
{
    int result = arrayIn[0];
    for (int currentElement : arrayIn)
    {
       if (currentElement > result)
     {
         result = currentElement;
     }
    }
    return result;
}


// checks whether or not an item is contained within an array
private static boolean contains (int[] arrayIn, int valueIn)
{
    for (int currentElement : arrayIn)
    {
      if (currentElement == valueIn)
      {
        return true;
      }
    }
    return false;
}

/* returns the position of an item within an array
   or -999 if the value is not present within the array */
private static int search (int[] arrayIn, int valueIn)
{
    for (int i = 0; i < arrayIn.length; i++)
    {
      if (arrayIn[i] == valueIn)
      {
        return i;
      }
    }
```

```
        return -999;
    }

    // displays the array values on the screen
    public static void displayArray(int[] arrayIn)
    {
      System.out.println();
      // standard 'for' loop used here as the array index is required
      for (int i = 0; i < arrayIn.length; i++)
      {
          System.out.println("array[" + i + "] = " + arrayIn[i]);
      }
    }
}
```

Here is a sample program run:

How many elements to store?: 5

[1] Enter values

[2] Array maximum

[3] Array sum

[4] Array membership

[5] Array search

[6] Display values

[7] Exit

Enter choice [1-7]: 1

enter value 12

enter value 3

enter value 7

enter value 6

enter value 2

[1] Enter values

[2] Array maximum

[3] Array sum

[4] Array membership

[5] Array search

[6] Display values

```
[7] Exit
Enter choice [1-7]: 2


Maximum array value = 12


[1] Enter values
[2] Array maximum
[3] Array sum
[4] Array membership
[5] Array search
[6] Display values
[7] Exit
Enter choice [1-7]: 3


Sum of array values = 30


[1] Enter values
[2] Array maximum
[3] Array sum
[4] Array membership
[5] Array search
[6] Display values
[7] Exit
Enter choice [1-7]: 4


Enter value to find: 10
10 is not in the array


[1] Enter values
[2] Array maximum
[3] Array sum
[4] Array membership
[5] Array search
```

```
[6] Display values
[7] Exit
Enter choice [1-7]: 4


Enter value to find: 7
7 is in the array


[1] Enter values
[2] Array maximum
[3] Array sum
[4] Array membership
[5] Array search
[6] Display values
[7] Exit
Enter choice [1-7]: 5


Enter value to find: 7
This value is at array index 2


[1] Enter values
[2] Array maximum
[3] Array sum
[4] Array membership
[5] Array search
[6] Display values
[7] Exit
Enter choice [1-7]: 6


Array values


array[0] = 12
array[1] = 3
array[2] = 7
```

```
array[3] = 6
array[4] = 2

[1] Enter values
[2] Sum values
[3] Find maximum value
[4] Search array
[5] Sort array
[6] Display values
[7] Exit
Enter choice [1-7]: 7


Goodbye
```

Self-test questions

1 When is it appropriate to use an array in a program?

2 What types of values can be stored in an array?

3 When is it suitable to use the enhanced **for** loop to process an array?

4 Consider the following explicit creation of an array:

```
int[] someArray = {2,5,1,9,11};
```

a) What would be the value of someArray.length ?

b) What is the value of someArray[2]?

c) What would happen if you tried to access someArray[6]?

d) Create the equivalent array by using the **new** operator and then assigning the value of each element individually.

e) Write a standard **for** loop that will double the value of every item in someArray.

f) Explain why, in this example, it would not be appropriate to use an enhanced **for** loop.

5 Assume that an array has been declared in main as follows:

```
int[] javaStudents;
```

This array is to be used to store a list of student exam marks. Now, for each of the following helper methods, write the code for the given method and the instruction in main to call this method:

a) A method, getExamMarks, that prompts the user to enter some exam marks (as integers), stores the marks in an array and then returns this array.

b) A method, increaseMarks, that accepts an array of exam marks and increases each mark by 5.

c) A method, allHavePassed, that accepts an array of exam marks and returns **true** if all marks are greater than or equal to 40, and **false** otherwise.

Programming exercises

1 Look back at program 5.3, which read in and displayed a series of temperature readings. Now design and implement another **static** method, wasHot, which displays all days that recorded temperatures of 18 degrees or over.

2 Design and implement a program that initializes an array of integers with a collection of 6 winning

lottery numbers. Allow the user to enter their 6 lottery numbers into another array. The program should compare the two arrays and tell the user if they have won the lottery or not. To win the lottery the user must have the same 6 winning lottery numbers but they might not necessarily be in the same order. Make use of methods in your program; one to allow the user to enter their lottery numbers and another to check if the user has won the lottery.

3 Design and implement a program that allows the user to enter into an array the price of 5 products in pounds sterling. The program should then copy this array into another array but convert the price of each product from pounds sterling to US dollars. The program should allow the user to enter the exchange rate of pounds to dollars, and should, when it terminates, display the contents of both arrays. Once again, make use of methods in your program to carry out these tasks.

4 Amend the program in exercise 3 above so that

a) the user is asked how many items they wish to purchase and the arrays are then sized accordingly;

b) the total cost of the order is displayed in both currencies.

5 Copy from the CD program 5.4, which manipulates an array of integers, then add additional methods to the program in order to

a) return the average from the array of integers (make use of the sum method to help you calculate the average);

b) display on the screen all those values greater than or equal to the average.

Classes and objects

Objectives:

By the end of this chapter you should be able to:

- *explain the meaning of the term **object-oriented**;*
- *explain the concept of **encapsulation**;*
- *explain the terms **class** and **object**;*
- *create objects in Java;*
- *call the methods of an object;*
- *use a number of methods of the* `String` *class;*
- *create and use arrays of objects.*

6.1 Introduction

Now at last it is time to find out what we really mean by the phrase *object-oriented*. We have mentioned it briefly already – and you have probably heard it being used in all sorts of contexts, since object-oriented development became very popular over the course of the 1990s and remains so today.

The object-oriented way of doing things is a relatively recent development in the building of software systems, and is concerned very much with the production of reusable components; it is arguable that the sophisticated graphical interfaces that are now universal would never have been developed without an object-oriented approach. Object-oriented development also lends itself to the notion of *Rapid Application Development* because it allows us to move much more smoothly between analysis and design. In addition, because of the technique of **encapsulation** or **information-hiding** that you will learn about soon, object-orientation allows us to build much more secure systems.

6.2 What is object-orientation?

Thirty or so years ago the demands on software developers were nothing compared with the demands on today's programmers. As computers became more and more powerful, the software needed to control them became more and more complex. Large, unstructured programs became increasingly difficult to develop and it quickly became clear that a **modular** approach was required, whereby programs were broken up into smaller units.

This was referred to as **structured** programming. Structured programming was the first attempt at formally modularizing program code. Now the program was no longer considered one large task, but a collection of smaller tasks – often called **procedures** or **functions** in older programming languages, but **methods** in object-oriented languages. This was the kind of thing we did in chapter 4, where we effectively used a structured approach, albeit on a rather small scale. Figure 6.1 illustrates this for a more complex situation. Here the top-level method is broken down into four tasks; the second task is broken down further into two tasks, and so on.

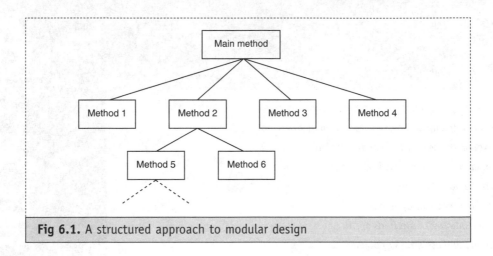

Fig 6.1. A structured approach to modular design

As an example of this approach, you can look back at program 4.8, where the `main` method called three other methods – `option1`, `option2` and `option3`.

For some time this approach to modular design dealt adequately with the increased complexity of software. But then, with the rapid microchip advances of the 1980s and the growth of the Internet in the 1990s, the demands on software developers increased again and the structured approach was found to be deficient. The reason for this is that the approach focuses on the actions (methods) but not *the things acted on* – the data. The data becomes spread throughout the system in a very unstructured way (figure 6.2).

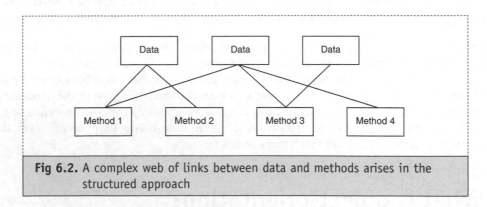

Fig 6.2. A complex web of links between data and methods arises in the structured approach

However, the *data* is central to the program's existence – so an approach such as that shown in figure 6.2 can lead to the following problems:

> data is subject to change by many methods, and data can therefore become unexpectedly corrupted, leading to unreliable programs that are difficult to debug;

> revising the data requires rewriting every method that interacts with it, leading to programs that are very difficult to maintain;

> methods and the data they act upon are not closely tied together, leading to code that is very difficult to reuse since there is a complex web of links to disentangle.

To add to the above problems, the languages used for structured programming tended also to allow us to declare *global* variables that were accessible to all the methods within a program – so it isn't hard to imagine how difficult it was to keep track of the data, and how easily errors could occur within a program.

In order to understand the object-oriented solution to this problem, let's think about another program – a program that would be suitable for a college or university for the administration of students and courses. The program would have to store information about students, such as their personal details, their marks and so on. It would have to perform tasks such as adding students, updating students' marks etc. Similarly, it would need to store information about such things as the courses on offer and the cost of the course; it would need to provide methods to update course information, add and remove courses and perform many other tasks. In some cases these methods would need information about both students and courses.

With the "old-fashioned" structured approach, all the data about students and courses would be stored as part of one big program, and once again it isn't hard to see how easy it would be to lose track of the data.

In the object-oriented approach, methods and the data they act upon are grouped together into one unit. This higher unit of organization is called an **object** (figure 6.3).

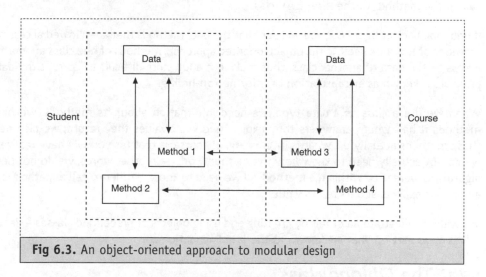

Fig 6.3. An object-oriented approach to modular design

Closely related to the idea of an object is that of a **class**. A class is the blueprint from which objects are generated. In other words, if we have six students in our university administration system, we do not need to define a student six times. We will define a student once (in a class) and then generate as many **objects** as we want from this blueprint. In one program we may have many classes, as we would probably wish to generate many kinds of objects (students, courses, lecturers etc.).

Object-oriented programming therefore consists of defining one or more classes that may interact with each other. To exploit the full power of object-orientation requires us to use an object-oriented programming language. There are many object-oriented languages such as C++, SmallTalk, Eiffel, C# and of course Java!

6.3 Classes as data types

Up till now you have been using data types such as **char**, **int** and **double**. These are simple data types that hold a single piece of information. However, you have also been using a more complex "type" – String. In Java, String is in fact a *class* – predefined for us by the people who developed the Java language. When we create new strings, we are creating objects of the String class; with an object-oriented programming language such as Java, it is possible to manipulate not just simple types, but *objects of a class*.

In this chapter you are not going to "look inside" a class, or create classes of your own. Instead we will show you how to use classes as data types – classes that have been predefined for you, either by ourselves or by the Java developers.

It should have become clear from the previous section that there are two aspects to a class:

> the data that it holds;

> the tasks it can perform.

In the next chapter you will see that the different items of data that a class holds are referred to as the **attributes** of the class; the tasks it can perform, as we have seen, are referred to as the **methods** of the class – you have seen in chapter 4 how we define class methods. However, in chapter 4, the methods were called only from within the class itself. Now we are going to see how to call the methods of *another* class. In fact you have already been doing this without quite realizing it – because you have, since the first chapter, been calling the methods of the Scanner class!

If you look back at figure 6.2, you will see that the only methods that are allowed access to the data are the methods of the class itself. In the object-oriented approach, methods of one class are normally denied direct access to the data of another class, thus making it a lot more difficult to corrupt the data. This important principle is known as **encapsulation** or **information-hiding**.

When we use a class as a data type, we need information about its methods. We need to know what methods it has, what parameters they expect, and what values they return; we also need to know what these methods actually do. What is interesting, of course, is that (as you will have realized from chapter 4) we do not actually need to know *how* the method works – in other words, we do not need to know which algorithms were used within the method. All we need to know in order to call a method is its name, the parameters it expects and its return value.

We will now illustrate all of this by creating and using objects of predefined classes – defined either by ourselves or as part of what are known as the Java Foundation classes.

6.3.1 The *Oblong* class

Let's consider a situation in which we want a program that creates and uses oblongs; maybe it is for the purposes of drawing oblongs on the screen, or for school children to use in order to practise their understanding of geometry.

We have prepared such a class (Oblong.java) for you. In the next chapter we will look inside this class and see how it was created. For now, however, you can completely ignore the program code. We have, of course, adhered to the principles discussed above and have made sure that the attributes of the class are not directly accessible. In order to use the class you do not need to know the specific names of the attributes – all you need to know is that any Oblong object can hold information about the length and the height of the oblong and that the type `double` is used for this data. An `Oblong` might also have other attributes that it uses for its own purpose, but anyone using the class doesn't need to know about this.

But of course you do need to know what the class can do – its methods – although, as we said before, you do not need to know how these methods have been implemented. What you really need to know are the **inputs** and **outputs**. A list of a method's inputs and output is often referred to as a method's **interface**. These are listed in table 6.1.

Table 6.1 The methods of the *Oblong* class			
Method	Description	Inputs	Output
`setLength`	Sets the value of the length of the oblong.	An item of type `double`	None
`setHeight`	Sets the value of the height of the oblong.	An item of type `double`	None
`getLength`	Returns the length of the oblong.	None	An item of type `double`
`getHeight`	Returns the height of the oblong.	None	An item of type `double`
`calculateArea`	Calculates and returns the area of the oblong.	None	An item of type `double`
`calculatePerimeter`	Calculates and returns the perimeter of the oblong.	None	An item of type `double`
`Oblong`	A special method called a **constructor** (see below).	Two items of data, both of type `double`, representing the length and height of the oblong respectively	Not applicable

You can see from the table that one of the available methods is a special method called a **constructor**, *which always has the same name as the class*. When you create a new object this special method is always called; its function is to reserve some space in the computer's memory just big enough to hold the required object (in our case an object of the `Oblong` class). The person developing the class doesn't have to worry about defining the constructor if this is all that he or she wants the constructor to do. However, it is very common to find that you want the constructor to do a bit more than this when a new object is created. Like any regular method, a constructor can be overloaded, so we can create constructors of our own. In the case of our `Oblong` class, the constructor has been defined so that every time a new `Oblong` object is created the length and the height are set – and they are set to the values that the user of the class sends in; so every time you create an `Oblong` you have to specify its length and its height at the same time. You will see how to do that in the program below.

6.3.2 Using the *Oblong* class

In general, when you are building applications you will need to make sure that all the necessary files are available to the compiler. If you are using the Sun Software Development Kit and compiling from the command line, then you will need all the source files to be in the same directory. In the case of most IDEs (Integrated Development Environments), the files containing the source code are made available by keeping related files together in a project. This is the case with the IDE supplied on the CD, and if you are using this compiler, then you can find out how to create projects by referring to the documentation provided for you on the disk.

The source code for the `Oblong` class is available on the CD (although you don't need to study it until the next chapter!).

Program 6.1 shows how the `Oblong` class can be used by another class, in this case a class called `OblongTester`.

Program 6.1

```java
import java.util.*;

public class OblongTester
{
 public static void main(String[] args)
 {
     Scanner sc = new Scanner(System.in);

     /* declare two variables to hold the length and height
     of the oblong as input by the user */
     double oblongLength, oblongHeight;

     // declare a reference to an Oblong object
     Oblong myOblong;

     // now get the values from the user
     System.out.print("Please enter the length of your oblong: ");
     oblongLength = sc.nextDouble();
     System.out.print("Please enter the height of your oblong: ");
     oblongHeight = sc.nextDouble();

     // create a new Oblong object
     myOblong = new Oblong(oblongLength, oblongHeight);

     /* use the various methods of the Oblong class to display
     the length, height, area and perimeter of the Oblong */
     System.out.println("Oblong length is " + myOblong.getLength());
     System.out.println("Oblong height is " + myOblong.getHeight());
     System.out.println("Oblong area is " + myOblong.calculateArea());
     System.out.println("Oblong perimeter is "
                                     + myOblong.calculatePerimeter());
 }
}
```

Let's analyse the `main` method line by line. After creating the new `Scanner` object, the method goes on to declare two variables:

```java
double oblongLength, oblongHeight;
```

As you can see, these are of type **double** and they are going to be used to hold the values that the user chooses for the length and height of the oblong.

The next line is important:

```
Oblong myOblong;
```

You can see that this line is similar to a declaration of a variable; however, as you have already seen with the String class and the Scanner class, what we are doing here is not declaring a variable of a primitive type such as **int**, but declaring the name of an *object* (myOblong) of the *class* (Oblong).

You need to be sure that you understand what this line actually does; all it does in fact is to create a variable that can hold a **reference**. As explained in the previous chapter, a reference is simply a *name* for a location in memory. At this stage we have *not* reserved space for our new Oblong object; all we have done is named a memory location myOblong, as shown in figure 6.4.

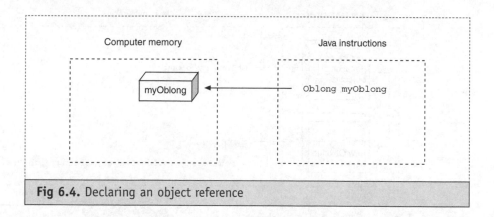

Fig 6.4. Declaring an object reference

Now of course you will be asking the question "What is going to be held in the memory location called myOblong?". We will see the answer in a moment.

Let us look at the next few lines first, though.

```
System.out.print("Please enter the length of your oblong: ");
oblongLength = sc.nextDouble();
System.out.print("Please enter the height of your oblong: ");
oblongHeight = sc.nextDouble();
```

This should be familiar to you by now; we are prompting the user to enter a value for the length of the oblong, then reading the user's chosen value from the keyboard, and then doing the same thing for the height. The values entered are stored in oblongLength and oblongHeight respectively.

Now we can return to the question of what is going to be stored in the memory location myOblong. Look at this line of code:

```
myOblong = new Oblong(oblongLength, oblongHeight);
```

This is the statement that reserves space in memory for a new Oblong object. As you saw with arrays in chapter 5, this is done by using the keyword **new**, in conjunction with the name of the class (in this case Oblong) and some parameters in the brackets. Remember what we said a while ago about a special method called a *constructor*? Well, using the class name in this way, with the keyword **new**, calls the constructor, and memory is reserved for a new Oblong object. Now, in the case of the Oblong class the people who developed it (okay, that was us!) defined their own constructor method. This method requires that two items of data, both of type **double**, get sent in as parameters. There are all sorts of ways that we can define constructors (for example, in a BankAccount class we might want to start the balance at zero when the account is created) and we shall see examples of these as we go along. In fact you have already seen another example, because you have been creating new objects of the Scanner class since chapter 1.

But wait a minute – how do we know the location in memory where the new object is stored? Well, now we have the answer to our previous question! The location of the new object is stored in the named location myOblong. This is illustrated in figure 6.5.

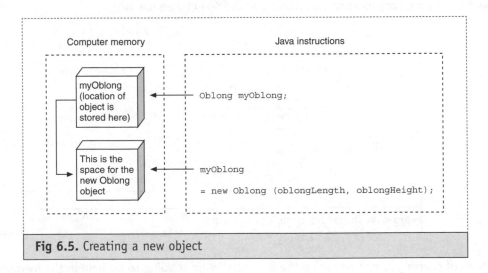

Fig 6.5. Creating a new object

As you know, we call a location that holds another location a reference. A reference "points" to another location in memory.

Now every time we want to refer to our new Oblong object we can use the variable name myOblong. You may have realized that this variable does not have to stay pointing at the Oblong we just created – for example, we could create a different oblong with the **new** keyword, and make myOblong point to that.

You should note also that if we were to declare another reference to an Oblong, like this for example:

```
Oblong anotherOblong;
```

then we could write the following instruction:

```
anotherOblong = myOblong;
```

This would mean that both myOblong and anotherOblong held exactly the same memory location, and both would refer to exactly the same Oblong object!

Two things are worth noting at this point. First, the process of creating a new object is often referred to as **instantiation**, because we are creating a new *instance* of a class. Second, you should note that, in Java, when a reference is first created it is given a special value of **null**; a **null** value indicates that no storage is allocated. We can also *assign* a **null** value to a reference at any point in the program, and test for it as in the following example:

```
Oblong myOblong;

// more code goes here

myOblong = null; // assign a null value
if(myOblong == null) // test for null value
{
        System.out.println("No storage is allocated to this object");
}
```

You should be aware of the fact that you cannot call a method of an object if no storage is allocated for the object; so watch out for this happening in your programs – it would cause a problem at run-time.

Now let's look at the next line of program 6.1:

```
System.out.println("Oblong Length is " + myOblong.getLength());
```

This line displays the length of the oblong. It uses the method of `Oblong` called `getLength`. We are *calling* a method of one class (the `getLength` method of `Oblong`) from within a method of another class (the `main` method of `OblongTester`). You can see that when we call a method from another class, we use the name of the object (in this case `myOblong`) together with the name of the method (`getLength`) separated by a full stop (often referred to as the **dot operator**); you have seen this already with the methods of the `Scanner` class.

In chapter 4, when we called the methods from within a class, we used the name of the method on its own. In actual fact, what we were doing is form of shorthand. When we write a line such as

```
demoMethod(x);
```

we are actually saying call `demoMethod`, which is a method of *this* class. In Java there exists a special keyword **this**. The keyword **this** is used within a class when we wish to refer to an object of the class itself, rather than an object of some other class. The line of code above is actually shorthand for:

```
this.demoMethod(x);
```

You will see in chapter 10 that there are occasions when we actually have to use this keyword, rather than simply allow it to be assumed.

The next three lines are similar to the first:

```
System.out.println("Oblong height is " + myOblong.getHeight());
System.out.println("Oblong area is " + myOblong.calculateArea());
System.out.println("Oblong Perimeter is "+ myOblong.calculatePerimeter());
```

We have called the `getHeight` method, the `calculateArea` method and the `calculatePerimeter` method to display the height, area and perimeter of the oblong on the screen. You might have noticed that we haven't used the `setLength` and `setHeight` methods – that is because in this program we didn't wish to change the length and height once the oblong had been created – but this is not the last you will see of our `Oblong` class – and in future programs these methods will come in useful.

Now we can move on to look at using some other classes. The first is not one of our own, but the built-in `String` class provided with all versions of Java.

6.4 Using the *String* class

You already know what a string is, and you have been using the `String` class in previous examples. Now that you are beginning to understand more about classes, we can look at the `String` class in more detail. This class is provided with many methods that you can use for manipulating strings, and we will look at some of these now.

First, there are a number of constructors. Remember that a constructor is the method that comes into action every time we create a new object. Remember also that constructors can be overloaded, so we can define lots of different constructors, which are distinguished from each other by what we place in the brackets.

The first constructor we will look at simply creates an empty string, so there is nothing to put in the brackets when we use it:

```
String str;
str = new String();
```

In fact it is more usual, when declaring and creating objects, to combine these two statements into one line:

```
String str = new String();
```

You are already familiar with doing this with the `Scanner` class:

```
Scanner sc = new Scanner(System.in);
```

Do remember, however, that this one line does two things: it names an object (`sc`) and creates space in memory for it.

Now why would anyone want to create an empty string? Well, that is a good question, and it can be asked on many occasions about other objects. The answer is that it is best, if possible, to avoid leaving a reference with a `null` value. Pointing our reference to a location as soon as we declare it will prevent us from doing silly things like creating an uninitialized object and trying to use its methods.

A more useful constructor is the one that allows us to give a value to the string at the time we create it:

```
String str = new String("Hello");
```

Now we have a string with the value "Hello". As we pointed out in the first chapter, there is an even quicker way to create this string. The assignment operator (=) is *overloaded*. You have seen that it can be used for

doubles, **ints**, **floats** and so on; each of these operations is different because, for example, the way in which **doubles** are stored in the computer's memory is different to the way in which **ints** are stored. Now this has also been extended to strings – so we can conveniently use the assignment operator to create a new string as follows:

```
String str = "Hello";
```

You should be aware that the String class is the only class that allows us to create new objects without the use of the **new** operator.

The String class has a number of interesting and useful methods, and we have listed some of them in table 6.2.

Table 6.2 Some *String* methods

Method	Description	Inputs	Output
length	Returns the length of the string	None	An item of type int
charAt	Accepts an integer and returns the character at that position in the string. Note that indexing starts from zero, not 1! You have been using this method in conjunction with the next method of the Scanner class to obtain single characters from the keyboard.	An item of type int	An item of type char
substring	Accepts two integers (for example m and n) and returns a copy of a chunk of the string. The chunk starts at position m and finishes at position n-1. Remember that indexing starts from zero. (Study the example below.)	Two items of type int	A String object
concat	Accepts a string and returns a new string which consists of the string that was sent in joined on to the end of the original string.	A String object	A String object
toUpperCase	Returns a copy of the original string, all upper case.	None	A String object
toLowerCase	Returns a copy of the original string, all lower case.	None	A String object
compareTo	Accepts a string (say myString) and compares it to the object's string. It returns zero if the strings are identical, a negative number if the object's string comes before myString in the alphabet, and a positive number if it comes later.	A String object	An item of type int

`equals`	Accepts an object (such as a `String`) and compares this to another object (such as another `String`). It returns **true** if these are identical, otherwise returns **false**.	An object of any class	A **boolean** value
`equalsIgnoreCase`	Accepts a string and compares this to the original string. It returns **true** if the strings are identical (ignoring case), otherwise returns **false**.	A `String` object	A **boolean** value
`startsWith`	Accepts a string (say `str`) and returns **true** if the original string starts with `str` and **false** if it does not (e.g. "hello world" starts with "h" or "he" or "hel" and so on).	A `String` object	A **boolean** value
`endsWith`	Accepts a string (say `str`) and returns **true** if the original string ends with `str` and **false** if it does not (e.g. "hello world" ends with "d" or "ld" or "rld" and so on).	A `String` object	A **boolean** value
`trim`	Returns a `String` object, having removed any spaces at the beginning or end.	None	A `String` object

There are many other useful methods of the `String` class which you can look up. Program 6.2 provides examples of how you can use some of the methods listed above; others are left for you to experiment with in your practical sessions.

Program 6.2

```java
import java.util.*;

public class StringTest
{
  public static void main(String[] args)
  {
    Scanner sc = new Scanner(System.in);
    // create a new string
    String str = new String();
    // get the user to enter a string
    System.out.print("Enter a string: ");
    str = sc.next();
    // display the length of the user's string
    System.out.println("The length of the string is " + str.length());
    // display the third character of the user's string
    System.out.println("The character at position 3 is " + str.charAt(2));
    // display a selected part of the user's string
    System.out.println("Characters 2 to 4 are " + str.substring(1,4));
    // display the user's string joined with another string
    System.out.println(str.concat(" was the string entered"));
    // display the user's string in upper case
    System.out.println("This is upper case: " + str.toUpperCase());
    // display the user's string in lower case
    System.out.println("This is lower case: " + str.toLowerCase());
  }
}
```

A sample run from program 6.2:

*Enter a string: **Europe***

The length of the string is 6

The character at position 3 is r

Characters 2 to 4 are uro

Europe was the string entered

This is upper case: EUROPE

This is lower case: europe

6.4.1 Comparing strings

When comparing two objects, such as `Strings`, we should do so by using a method called `equals`. We should *not* use the equality operator (`==`); this should be used for comparing primitive types only. If, for example, we had declared two strings, `firstString` and `secondString`, we would compare these in, say, an `if` statement as follows;

```
if(firstString.equals(secondString))
{
    // more code here
}
```

Using the equality operator (`==`) to compare strings is a very common mistake that is made by programmers. Doing this will not result in a compilation error, but it won't give you the result you expect! The reason for this is that all you are doing is finding out whether the objects occupy the same address space in memory – what you actually want to be doing is comparing the actual value of the string attributes of the objects.

The `String` class also has a very useful method called `compareTo`. As you can see from table 6.2 this method accepts a string (called `myString` for example) and compares it to the string value of the object itself. It returns zero if the strings are identical, a negative number if the original string comes before `myString` in the alphabet, and a positive number if it comes later.

Program 6.3 provides an example of how the `compareTo` method is used.

Program 6.3

```java
import java.util.*;

public class StringComp
{
    public static void main(String[] args)
    {
        Scanner sc = new Scanner(System.in);
        String string1, string2;
        int comparison;

        // get two strings from the user
        System.out.print("Enter a String: ");
        string1 = sc.next();
        System.out.print("Enter another String: ");
```

```
        string2 = sc.next();

        // compare the strings
        comparison = string1.compareTo(string2);
        if(comparison < 0)   // compareTo returned a negative number
        {
            System.out.println(string1 + " comes before "
                                        + string2
                                        + " in the alphabet");
        }
        else if(comparison > 0) // compareTo returned a positive number
        {
            System.out.println(string2 + " comes before "
                                        + string1
                                        + " in the alphabet");
        }
        else  // compareTo returned zero
        {
            System.out.println("The strings are identical");
        }
    }
}
```

Here is a sample run from the program:

Enter a String: **hello**

Enter another String: **goodbye**

goodbye comes before hello in the alphabet

You should note that `compareTo` is case-sensitive – upper-case letters will be considered as coming before lower-case letters (their Unicode value is lower). If you are not interested in the case of the letters, you should convert both strings to upper (or lower) case before comparing them.

If all you are interested in is whether the strings are identical, it is easier to use the `equals` method. If the case of the letters is not significant you can use `equalsIgnoreCase`.

6.5 Our own *Scanner* class for keyboard input

It might have occurred to you that using the `Scanner` class to obtain keyboard input can be a bit of a bother.

First, it is necessary to create a new `Scanner` object in every method that uses the `Scanner` class.

Second, there is no simple method such as `nextChar` for getting a single character like there is for the **int** and **double** types.

Finally, the `next` method doesn't allow us to enter strings containing spaces. In fact, there is a `nextLine` method that does return the whole string that is entered, including spaces – however, unfortunately, if the `nextLine` method is used after a `nextInt` or `nextDouble` method, then it is necessary to create a new `Scanner` object (because using the same `Scanner` object will make your program behave erratically).

To make life easier, we have created a new class which we have called `EasyScanner`. In the next chapter we will "look inside" it to see how it is written – in this chapter we will just show you how to use it. The methods of `EasyScanner` are described in table 6.3.

Table 6.3 The input methods of the *EasyScanner* class

Java type	`EasyScanner` method
`int`	`nextInt()`
`double`	`nextDouble()`
`char`	`nextChar()`
`String`	`nextString()`

To make life really easy we have written the class so that we don't have to create a new `Scanner` object in order to use it (that is taken care of in the class itself) – and we have written it so that you can simply use the name of the class itself when you call a method (you will see how to do this in the next chapter). Program 6.4 demonstrates how to use these methods.

Program 6.4

```
public class EasyScannerTester
{
    public static void main(String[] args)
    {
        System.out.print("Enter a double: ");
        double d = EasyScanner.nextDouble(); // to read a double
        System.out.println("You entered: " + d);
        System.out.println();

        System.out.print("Enter an integer: ");
        int i = EasyScanner.nextInt(); // to read an int
        System.out.println("You entered: " + i);
        System.out.println();

        System.out.print("Enter a string: ");
        String s = EasyScanner.nextString(); // to read a string
        System.out.println("You entered: " + s);
        System.out.println();

        System.out.print("Enter a character: ");
        char c = EasyScanner.nextChar(); // to read a character
        System.out.println("You entered: " + c);
        System.out.println();

    }
}
```

Here is a sample run:

Enter a double: **23.6**

You entered: 23.6

Enter an integer: **50**

You entered: 50

```
Enter a string: Hello
You entered: Hello


Enter a character: B
You entered: B
```

From now own we are going to use the `EasyScanner` for keyboard input. In the next chapter you will see that it was really quite easy to write this class, and we hope that this illustrates how very useful object-oriented programming is. We have written a simple class that can be re-used time and time again – all you have to do is make sure that `EasyScanner` is available to the compiler and you can include it in any program you wish. The source code is provided on the CD that accompanies this book – or you can simply copy it from the next chapter.

6.6 The *BankAccount* class

We have created a class called `BankAccount`, which you can copy from the CD. This could be a very useful class in the real world, for example as part of a financial control system. Once again you do not need to look at the details of how this class is coded in order to use it. You do need to know, however, that the class holds three pieces of information – the account number, the account name and the account balance. The first two of these will be `String` objects and the final one will a variable of type **double**.

The methods are listed in table 6.4.

Table 6.4 The methods of the *BankAccount* class			
Method	**Description**	**Inputs**	**Output**
BankAccount	A constructor. It accepts two strings and assigns them to the account number and account name respectively. It also sets the account balance to zero.	Two String objects	Not applicable
getAccountNumber	Returns the account number.	None	An item of type String
getAccountName	Returns the account name.	None	An item of type String
getBalance	Returns the balance.	None	An item of type **double**
deposit	Accepts an item of type **double** and adds it to the balance.	An item of type **double**	None
withdraw	Accepts an item of type **double** and subtracts it from the balance.	An item of type **double**	None

A short program which uses the `BankAccount` class is shown in program 6.5.

Program 6.5

```
public class BankAccountTester
{
  public static void main(String[] args)
  {
    BankAccount account1
                      = new BankAccount("99786754","Susan Richards");
    account1.deposit(1000);
    System.out.println("Account number: " + account1.getAccountNumber());
    System.out.println("Account name: " + account1.getAccountName());
    System.out.println("Current balance: " + account1.getBalance());
  }
}
```

The output from this program is:

Account number: 99786754

Account name: Susan Richards

Current balance: 1000.0

6.7 Arrays of objects

In chapter 5 you learnt how to create arrays of simple types such as **int** and **char**. It is perfectly possible, and often very desirable, to create arrays of objects. There, are, however, some important issues that we need to be aware of. We will illustrate this with a new version of program 6.5, the `BankAccountTester`. In program 6.6, instead of creating a single bank account, we have created several bank accounts by using an array. Take a look at the program, and then we will explain the important issues to you.

Program 6.6

```
public class BankAccountTester2
{
  public static void main(String[] args)
  {
    // create an array of references
    BankAccount[] accountList = new BankAccount[3];
    // create three new accounts, referenced by each element in the array
    accountList[0] = new BankAccount("99786754","Susan Richards");
    accountList[1] = new BankAccount("44567109","Delroy Jacobs");
    accountList[2] = new BankAccount("46376205","Sumana Khan");
    // make various deposits and withdrawals
    accountList[0].deposit(1000);
    accountList[2].deposit(150);
    accountList[0].withdraw(500);
    // print details of all three accounts
    for(BankAccount item : accountList)
    {
      System.out.println("Account number: " + item.getAccountNumber());
      System.out.println("Account name: " + item.getAccountName());
      System.out.println("Current balance: " + item.getBalance());
      System.out.println();
    }
  }
}
```

The first line of the `main` method looks no different from the statements that you saw in the last chapter that created arrays of primitive types:

```
BankAccount[] accountList = new BankAccount[3];
```

However, what is actually going on behind the scenes is slightly different. The above statement does *not* set up an array of `BankAccount` objects in memory; instead it sets up an array of *references* to such objects (see figure 6.6).

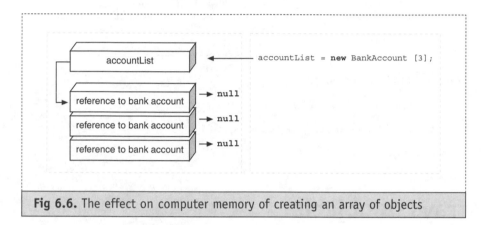

Fig 6.6. The effect on computer memory of creating an array of objects

At the moment, space has been reserved for the three `BankAccount` *references* only, *not* the three `BankAccount` objects. As we told you earlier, when a reference is initially created it points to the constant **null**, so at this point each reference in the array points to **null**.

This means that memory would still need to be reserved for individual `BankAccount` objects each time we wish to link a `BankAccount` object to the array. We can now create new `BankAccount` objects and associate them with elements in the array as we have done with these lines:

```
accountList[0] = new BankAccount("99786754","Susan Richards");
accountList[1] = new BankAccount("44567109","Delroy Jacobs");
accountList[2] = new BankAccount("46376205","Sumana Khan");
```

Three `BankAccount` objects have been created; the first one, for example, has account number of "99786754" and name "Susan Richards", and the reference at `accountList[0]` is set to point to it. This is illustrated in figure 6.7.

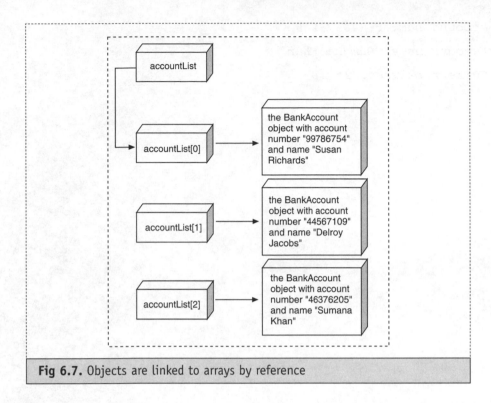

Fig 6.7. Objects are linked to arrays by reference

Once we have created these accounts, we make some deposits and withdrawals.

```
accountList[0].deposit(1000);
accountList[2].deposit(150);
accountList[0].withdraw(500);
```

Look carefully at how we do this. To call a method of a particular array element, we place the dot operator after the final bracket of the array index. This is made clear below:

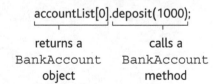

Finally, as you might expect, the output from this program is as follows:

Account number: 99786754

Account name: Susan Richards

Current balance: 500.0

Account number: 44567109

Account name: Delroy Jacobs

Current balance: 0.0

```
Account number: 46376205
Account name: Sumana Khan
Current balance: 150.0
```

Self-test questions

1 What do you understand by the term *object-oriented program development*?

2 What is meant by the term *encapsulation*?

3 Distinguish between a *class* and an *object*.

4 What is the purpose of a constructor?

5 How do you call a method of one class from a method of another class?

6 How do arrays of objects differ from arrays of primitive types?

Programming exercises

1 Implement all the programs from this chapter (make sure that the `Oblong` class and the `BankAccount` class have been copied from the CD and placed in the correct directory for your compiler to access them).

2 Adapt program 6.3 in the following ways:

a) rewrite the program so that it ignores case;

b) rewrite the program, using the `equals` method, so that all it does is to test whether the two strings are the same;

c) repeat b) using the `equalsIgnoreCase` method;

d) use the `trim` method so that the program ignores leading or trailing spaces.

3 a) Write a program that asks the user to input a string, followed by a single character, and then tests whether the string starts with that character.

b) Make your program work so that the case of the character is irrelevant.

4 Design and implement a program that performs in the following way:

❯ when the program starts two bank accounts are created, using names and numbers which are written into the code;

❯ the user is then asked to enter an account number, followed by an amount to deposit in that account;

❯ the balance of the appropriate account is then updated accordingly – or if an incorrect account number was entered a message to this effect is displayed;

> ❯ the user is then asked if he or she wishes to make more deposits;

> ❯ if the user answers 'yes', the process continues;

> ❯ if the user answers 'no', then details of both accounts (account number, account name and balance) are displayed.

CHAPTER: 07

Implementing classes

J A V A

Objectives:

By the end of this chapter you should be able to:

- *design classes using the notation of the **Unified Modeling Language (UML)**;*
- *write the Java code for a specified class;*
- *explain the difference between* `public` *and* `private` *access to attributes and methods;*
- *explain the use of the* `static` *keyword;*
- *pass objects as parameters;*
- *implement **collection classes** based on arrays.*

7.1 Introduction

This chapter is arguably the most important so far, because it is here that you are going to learn how to develop the classes that you need for your programs. You are already familiar with the concept of a class, and the idea that we can create objects that belong to a class; in the last chapter you saw how to create and use objects; you saw that we could hide or encapsulate information in a class; and you saw how we could use the methods of a class without knowing anything about how they work.

In this chapter you will look inside the classes you have studied to see how they are constructed, and how you can write classes of your own.

7.2 Implementing classes in Java

In the last chapter you saw that a class consists of:

> a set of **attributes** (the data);

> a set of **methods** that can access or change those attributes.

To help you to understand how we actually implement this in Java we are going to look at the code for the classes we used in chapter 6. We will start with the `Oblong` class.

7.2.1 The *Oblong* class

When we design a class we must, of course, consider what data the class needs to hold, and what methods are needed to access that data. The Oblong class will need to hold two items of data – the length and the height of the oblong; these will have to be real numbers, so **double** would be the appropriate type for each of these two attributes. You have already seen the methods that we provided for this class in table 6.1.

When we design classes, it is very useful to start off by using a diagrammatic notation. The usual way this is done is by making use of the notation of the **Unified Modeling Language (UML)**.[1] In this notation, a class is represented by a box divided into three sections. The first section provides the name of the class, the second section lists the attributes, and the third section lists the methods. The UML class diagram for the Oblong class is shown in figure 7.1.

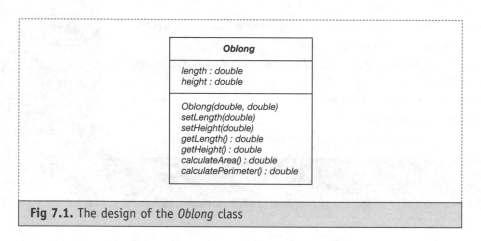

Fig 7.1. The design of the *Oblong* class

You can see that the UML notation requires us to indicate the attribute types, preceded by a colon, and in the case of the method, the parameter types in brackets, and the return types after the brackets, also preceded by a colon. Where there is no return type, nothing appears after the brackets.

As you saw in the previous chapter, we have provided our Oblong class with methods for reading and writing to the attributes – and it is conventional to begin the name of such methods with get- and set- respectively. However, it is not always the case that we choose to supply methods such as setLength and setHeight, which allow us to *change* the attributes. Sometimes we set up our class so that the only way that we can assign values to the attributes is via the constructor. This would mean that the values of the length and height could be set only at the time a new Oblong object was created, and could not be changed after that. Whether or not you want to provide a means of writing to individual attributes depends on the nature of the system you are developing and should be discussed with potential users. However, we believe that it is a good policy to provide write access to only those attributes that clearly require to be changed during the object's lifetime, and we have taken this approach throughout this book. In this case we have included "set" methods for length and height because we are going to need them in chapter 10.

Now that we have the basic design of the Oblong class we can go ahead and write the Java code for it:

[1] Simon Bennett et al., *Schaum's Outline UML (2nd edn)*, McGraw-Hill 2004.

The *Oblong* class

```java
public class Oblong
{
    // the attributes
    private double length;
    private double height;

    // the methods

    // the constructor
    public Oblong(double lengthIn, double heightIn)
    {
        length = lengthIn;
        height = heightIn;
    }

    // this method allows us to read the length attribute
    public double getLength()
    {
        return length;
    }

    // this method allows us to read the height attribute
    public double getHeight()
    {
        return height;
    }

    // this method allows us to write to the length attribute
    public void setLength(double lengthIn)
    {
        length = lengthIn;
    }

    // this method allows us to write to the height attribute
    public void setHeight(double heightIn)
    {
        height = heightIn;
    }

    // this method returns the area of the oblong
    public double calculateArea()
    {
        return length * height;
    }

    // this method returns the perimeter of the oblong
    public double calculatePerimeter()
    {
        return 2 * (length + height);
    }
}
```

Let's take a closer look at this. The first line declares the `Oblong` class. Once this is done, we declare the attributes. An `Oblong` object will need attributes to hold values for the length and the height of the oblong, and these will be of type **double**.

The declaration of the attributes in the `Oblong` class is as follows:

```java
private double length;
private double height;
```

As you can see, attributes are declared like any other variables, except that they are declared outside of any method, and they also have an additional word in front of them. In section 4.6, we talked about the *scope* of a variable. You were told there that the attributes of a class are accessible to *all* the methods – unlike *local* variables, which are accessible only to the methods in which they are declared.

As you can see, the keyword **private** has been placed before the type name. In Java, this keyword is used to restrict access to the attributes. Once they are declared as **private** (as opposed to **public**), they *cannot be accessed by methods of other classes*. The only way to get at them is via the methods of the *same* class. We talked about encapsulation (information-hiding) in the last chapter – this is how we actually achieve it in Java.

Figure 7.1 makes it clear which methods we need to define within our Oblong class. First comes the constructor. You should recall that it has the same name as the class, and, unlike any other method, it has no return type. It looks like this:

```
public Oblong(double lengthIn, double heightIn)
{
    length = lengthIn;
    height = heightIn;
}
```

The first thing to notice is that this method is declared as **public**. Unlike the attributes, we want our methods to be accessible from outside so that they can be called by methods of other classes – declaring them as **public** enables this to happen. You will recall from chapter 4 we that declared our helper methods as **private** – this of course was because we were not intending for them to be accessed by other classes.

Do you remember our saying in chapter 6 that we can create constructors of our own? Such a constructor is often termed a *user-defined*[2] constructor. We are defining it so that when a new Oblong object is created (with the keyword **new**) then not only do we get some space reserved in memory, but we also get some other stuff occurring; in this case two assignment statements are executed. The first assigns the value of the parameter lengthIn to the length attribute, and the second assigns the value of the parameter heightIn to the height attribute. Remember, the attributes are visible to all the methods of the class.

One more thing about constructors: in chapter 6 we told you that if you don't define your own constructor then a "default" constructor is provided – which does nothing more than reserve space in memory for the new object. It is called by using the constructor name (which is the same as the class name) with empty brackets. Now, once we have defined our own constructors, this default constructor is no longer automatically available. If we want it to be available then we have to re-define it explicitly. In the Oblong case we would define it as:

```
public Oblong()
{
}
```

Now let's take a look at the definition of the next method, getLength. The purpose of this method is simply to send back the value of the length attribute:

[2] Here the word *user* is referring to the person *writing* the program, not the person using it!

```
public double getLength()
{
    return length;
}
```

Once again you can see that the method has been declared as **public**, enabling it to be accessed by methods of other classes.

The next method, getHeight, behaves in the same way in respect of the height attribute.

Next comes the setLength method:

```
public void setLength(double lengthIn)
{
    length = lengthIn;
}
```

This method does not return a value, so its return type is **void**. However, it does require a parameter of type **double** that it will assign to the length attribute. The body of the method consists of a single line which assigns the value of lengthIn to the length attribute.

The next method, setHeight, behaves in the same way in respect of the height attribute.

After this comes the calculateArea method:

```
public double calculateArea()
{
    return length * height;
}
```

Once again there are no formal parameters, as this method does not need any data in order to do its job; it is of type **double** since it returns an item of this type. The actual code is just one line, namely the statement that returns the area of the oblong, calculated by multiplying the value of the length attribute by the value of the height attribute.

The calculatePerimeter method is similar and thus the definition of the Oblong class is now complete.

7.2.2 The *BankAccount* class

The UML class diagram for the BankAccount class, which we used in the previous chapter, is shown in figure 7.2.

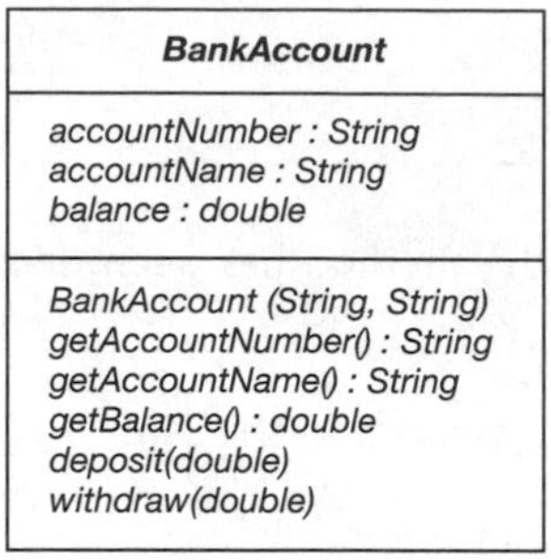

Fig 7.2. The design of *BankAccount* class

We can now inspect the code for this class:

The *BankAccount* class

```java
public class BankAccount
{
    // the attributes
    private String accountNumber;
    private String accountName;
    private double balance;

    // the methods

    // the constructor
    public BankAccount(String numberIn, String nameIn)
    {
        accountNumber = numberIn;
        accountName = nameIn;
        balance = 0;
    }

    // methods to read the attributes
    public String getAccountName()
    {
        return accountName;
    }

    public String getAccountNumber()
    {
        return accountNumber;
    }

    public double getBalance()
    {
        return balance;
    }

    // methods to deposit and withdraw money
    public void deposit(double amountIn)
    {
        balance = balance + amountIn;
    }
    public void withdraw(double amountIn)
    {
        balance = balance - amountIn;
    }
}
```

Now that we are getting the idea of how to define a class in Java, we do not need to go into so much detail in our analysis and explanation.

The first three lines declare the attributes of the class, and are as we would expect:

```
private String accountNumber;
private String accountName;
private double balance;
```

One thing to notice, however, is that `accountNumber` and `accountName` are declared as `Strings`; it is perfectly possible for the attributes of one class to be objects of another class.

Now the constructor:

```
public BankAccount(String numberIn, String nameIn)
{
    accountNumber = numberIn;
    accountName = nameIn;
    balance = 0;
}
```

You can see that when a new object of the `BankAccount` class is created, the `accountName` and `accountNumber` will be assigned the values of the parameters passed to the method. In this case, the `balance` will be assigned the value zero; this makes sense because when someone opens a new account there is a zero balance until a deposit is made.

The next three methods, `getAccountNumber`, `getAccountName` and `getBalance`, are all set up so that the values of the corresponding attributes (which of course have been declared as **private**) can be read.

After these we have the `deposit` method:

```
public void deposit(double amountIn)
{
    balance = balance + amountIn;
}
```

This method does not return a value; it is therefore declared to be of type **void**. It does however require that a value is sent in (the amount to be deposited), and therefore has one parameter – of type **double** – in the brackets. As you would expect with this method, the action consists of adding the deposit to the `balance` attribute of the `BankAccount` object.

The `withdraw` method behaves in a similar manner, but the amount is subtracted from the current balance.

7.3 The *static* keyword

You have already seen the keyword **static** in front of the names of methods or attributes in some Java classes. A word such as this (as well as the words **public** and **private**) is called a **modifier**.

Let's explore what this **static** modifier does. Consider the BankAccount class that we discussed in the previous section. Say we wanted to have an additional method which added interest, at the current rate, to the customer's balance. It would be useful to have an attribute called interestRate to hold the value of the current rate of interest. But of course the interest rate is the same for any customer – and if it changes, we want it to change for every customer in the bank; in other words for every object of the class. We can achieve this by declaring the variable as **static**. An attribute declared as **static** is a *class* attribute; any changes that are made to it are made to all the objects in the class.

It would make sense if there were a way to access this attribute without reference to a specific object; and so there is! All we have to do is to declare methods such as setInterestRate and getInterestRate as **static**. This makes a method into a *class* method; it does not refer to any specific object. We can call a class method by using the class name instead of the object name.

We have rewritten our BankAccount class as shown below, and called it BankAccount2; the new items have been emboldened. Notice that we have included three new methods as well as the new **static** attribute interestRate. The first two of these – setInterestRate and getInterestRate – are the methods that allow us to read and write to our new attribute. These have been declared as **static**. The third – addInterest – is the method that adds the interest to the customer's balance.

The modified *BankAccount* class

```java
public class BankAccount2
{
    private String accountNumber;
    private String accountName;
    private double balance;
    private static double interestRate;

    public BankAccount2(String numberIn, String nameIn)
    {
        accountNumber = numberIn;
        accountName = nameIn;
        balance = 0;
    }

    public String getAccountName()
    {
        return accountName
    }
    public String getAccountNumber()
    {
        return accountNumber;
    }
    public double getBalance()
    {
        return balance;
    }
    public void deposit(double amountIn)
    {
        balance = balance + amountIn;
    }
    public void withdraw(double amountIn)
    {
        balance = balance - amountIn;
    }
    public static void setInterestRate(double rateIn)
    {
        interestRate = rateIn;
    }
    public static double getInterestRate()
    {
```

```
            return interestRate;
        }
        public void addInterest()
        {
            balance = balance + (balance * interestRate)/100;
        }
}
```

Program 7.1 uses this modified version of the BankAccount class.

Program 7.1

```
public class BankAccountTester2
{
    public static void main(String[] args)
    {
        // create a bank account
        BankAccount2 account1 = new BankAccount2("99786754","Varinder Singh");
        // create another bank account
        BankAccount2 account2 =  new BankAccount2("99887776","Lenny Roberts");
        // make a deposit into the first account
        account1.deposit(1000);
        // make a deposit into the second account
        account2.deposit(2000);
        // set the interest rate
        BankAccount2.setInterestRate(10);
        // add interest to account 1
        account1.addInterest();
        // display the account details
        System.out.println("Account number: " + account1.getAccountNumber());
        System.out.println("Account name: " + account1.getAccountName());
        System.out.println("Interest Rate " + account1.getInterestRate());
        System.out.println("Current balance: " + account1.getBalance());
        System.out.println(); // blank line
        System.out.println("Account number: " + account2.getAccountNumber());
        System.out.println("Account name: " + account2.getAccountName());
        System.out.println("Interest Rate " + account2.getInterestRate());
        System.out.println("Current balance: " + account2.getBalance());
    }
}
```

Take a closer look at the first four lines of the main method of program 7.1. We have created two new bank accounts which we have called account1 and account2, and have assigned account numbers and names to them at the time they were created (via the constructor). We have then deposited amounts of 1000 and 2000 respectively into each of these accounts.

Now look at the next two lines:

```
BankAccount2.setInterestRate(10);
account1.addInterest();
```

The first of these lines sets the interest rate to 10. Because setInterestRate has been declared as a **static** method, we have been able to call it by using the class name BankAccount2. Because interestRate has been declared as a **static** attribute this change is effective for any object of the class. Therefore, when we add interest to this account as we do with the next line we should expect it to be calculated with an interest rate of 10, giving us a new balance of 1100.

This is exactly what we get, as can be seen from the output below:

```
Account number: 99786754

Account name: Varinder Singh

Interest rate: 10.0

Current balance: 1100.0


Account number: 99887776

Account name: Lenny Roberts

Interest rate: 10.0

Current balance: 2000.0
```

Class methods can be very useful indeed and we shall see further examples of them in this chapter. Of course, we have always declared our `main` method, and its helper methods, as **static** – because these methods belong to the class and not to a specific object.

Incidentally, it is conventional when producing UML diagrams to underline the names of class attributes and methods; you will see an example of this in our case study in chapter 11.

7.4 Initializing attributes

Looking back at the `BankAccount2` class in the previous section, some of you might have been asking yourselves what would happen if we called the `getInterestRate` method before the interest rate had been set using the `setInterestRate` method. In fact, the answer is that a value of zero would be returned. This is because, while Java does not give an initial value to local variables (which is why you get a compiler error if you try to use an uninitialized variable), Java always initializes attributes. Numerical attributes such as **int** and **double** are initialized to zero; **boolean** attributes are initialized to **false** and objects are initialized to **null**. Character attributes are given an initial Unicode value of zero.

Despite the above, it is nonetheless good programming practice always to give an initial value to your attributes, rather than leave it to the compiler. One very good reason for this is that you cannot assume that every programming language initializes variables in the same way – if you were using C++, for example, the initial value of any variable is completely a matter of chance – and you won't get a compiler error to warn you! In the `BankAccount2` class, it would have done no harm at all to have initialized the `interestRate` variable when it was declared:

```
private static double interestRate = 0;
```

In fact, one technique you could use is to give the `interestRate` attribute some special initial value (such as a negative value) to indicate to the user of this class that the interest rate had not been set. You will see another example where this technique can be used in question 1 of the programming exercises.

7.5 The *EasyScanner* class

In the previous chapter we used a class called `EasyScanner` that is going to make our lives a lot easier. We have now covered all the concepts you need in order to understand how this class works. Here it is:

The *EasyScanner* class

```java
import java.util.*;

public class EasyScanner
{
    public static int nextInt()
    {
        Scanner sc = new Scanner(System.in);
        int i = sc.nextInt();
        return i;
    }

    public static double nextDouble()
    {
        Scanner sc = new Scanner(System.in);
        double d = sc.nextDouble();
        return d;
    }

    public static String nextString()
    {
        Scanner sc = new Scanner(System.in);
        String s = sc.nextLine();
        return s;
    }

    public static char nextChar()
    {
        Scanner sc = new Scanner(System.in);
        char c = sc.next().charAt(0);
        return c;
    }
}
```

You can see that we have made every method a **static** method, so that we can simply use the class name when we call a method. You can see that the `nextString` method uses the `nextLine` method of the `Scanner` class – but as a new `Scanner` object is created each time the method is called there is no problem about using it after a `nextInt` or a `nextDouble` method as there is with `nextLine` itself.

7.6 Passing objects as parameters

In chapter 4 it was made clear that when a variable is passed to a method it is simply the *value* of that variable that is passed – and that therefore a method cannot change the value of the original variable. In chapter 5 you found out that in the case of an array it is the value of the memory location (a *reference*) that is passed and consequently the value of the original array elements can be changed by the called method.

What about objects? Let's write a little program (program 7.2) to test this out.

Program 7.2

```java
public class ParameterTest
{
  public static void main(String[] args)
  {
    // create new bank account
    BankAccount testAccount = new BankAccount("1", "Samsun Okoyo");
    test(testAccount); // send the account to the test method
    System.out.println("Account Number: " + testAccount.getAccountNumber());
    System.out.println("Account Name: " + testAccount.getAccountName());
    System.out.println("Balance: " + testAccount.getBalance());
  }

  // a method that makes a deposit in the bank account
  private static void test(BankAccount accountIn)
  {
    accountIn.deposit(2500);
  }
}
```

The output from this program is as follows:

Account Number: 1

Account Name: Samsun Okoyo

Balance: 2500.0

You can see that the deposit has successfully been made. This is because what was sent to the method was, of course, a reference to a `BankAccount` object. The object in question is located and its methods invoked in the usual way. You might think this is a very good thing, and will make life easier for you as a programmer. However, you need a word of caution here. It is very easy inadvertently to allow a method to change an object's attributes, so you need to take care – more about this in the second semester.

7.7 Collection classes

When we studied arrays in chapter 5, we used an array only as a variable within a method. However, an array can also be used as an *attribute* of a class. In declaring an array as an attribute, we can hide some of the inconveniences of the array type (such as remembering to start array indices at zero) by providing our own methods to control array access. A class that contains many items of the same type is said to be a **collection** class. In our everyday lives we can see many examples of collections:

> a train contains a collection of passengers;

> a post bag contains a collection of letters;

> a letter contains a collection of words.

As can be seen from the examples above, some collections can themselves contain other collections.

7.7.1 The *Bank* class

In chapter 6 we presented a program (program 6.5) in which three `BankAccount` objects were created and were held in an array. Now that we are able to create our own classes we can vastly improve on this approach by providing a special collection class to hold bank accounts. We will call our collection class `Bank`.

When one object itself consists of other objects, this relationship is called **aggregation**. This association, represented in UML by a diamond, is often referred to as a *part-of* relationship. For example, the association between a car object and the passengers in the car is aggregation. **Composition** (represented by a filled diamond) is a special, stronger, form of aggregation whereby the "whole" is actually dependent on the "part". For example, the association between a car and its engine is one of *composition*, as a car cannot exist without an engine. A collection class is an implementation of the aggregation relationship.

The association between the container object, `Bank`, and the contained object, `BankAccount`, is shown in the UML diagram of figure 7.3.

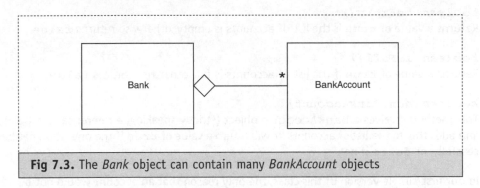

Fig 7.3. The *Bank* object can contain many *BankAccount* objects

The asterisk at the other end of the joining line indicates that the `Bank` object contains *zero or more* `BankAccount` objects. The design for the `Bank` class is now given in figure 7.4.

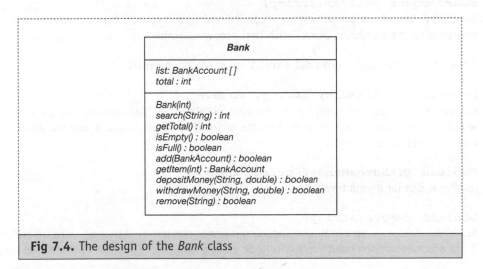

Fig 7.4. The design of the *Bank* class

As you can see, the class will have two attributes – a collection of `BankAccounts` and an integer to keep track of the number of accounts present.

There are 10 methods, which are described below. We have re-written the headers so that they are now in Java format, rather than in UML.

Bank(int)

This is the constructor. It receives an integer which will represent the maximum number of accounts allowed, and will create an array of bank accounts accordingly. You can see how, by this means, the size of the array is determined at run-time by the user of this class.

int search(String)

This is a helper method and will be declared as **private**. It accepts a String representing the account number. It then returns the array index of the account with that account number. If the account number does not exist, then a "phoney" index (−999) will be returned to indicate failure.

int getTotal()

This method simply returns the total number of accounts currently in the system.

boolean isEmpty()

Returns a value of **true** if the list of accounts is empty, otherwise returns **false**.

boolean isFull()

Returns a value of **true** if the list of accounts is full, otherwise returns **false**.

boolean add(BankAccount)

This method receives a BankAccount object (strictly speaking, a reference to a BankAccount object) and adds this to the list of accounts. It will return a value of **true** if the operation has been completed successfully, or **false** if not.

In our first simple version of this class, the only reason that an account would not be added successfully is if the list of accounts is full. Later this could be refined to ensure that an account could not be added if there is already another account with the same account number.

BankAccount getItem(String)

Receives a String representing an account number, and returns the BankAccount (strictly speaking a reference to the BankAccount) with that account number.

If the account number is not valid a **null** value will be returned.

boolean depositMoney(String, double)

Accepts a String, representing the account number of a particular account, and an amount of money which is deposited in that account. Returns **true** if the deposit was made successfully, or **false** otherwise (no such account number).

boolean withdrawMoney(String, double)

As above, but for a withdrawal.

boolean remove(String)

Accepts a String, representing an account number, and removes that account from the list. Returns **true** if the account was removed successfully, or **false** otherwise (no such account number).

The code for the Bank class is presented below. Take a careful look at it, then we will discuss it.

The *Bank* class

```java
public class Bank
{
  // attributes
  private BankAccount[] list; // to hold the accounts
  private int total; // to keep track of the number of accounts in the list

  // methods
  // the constructor
  public Bank(int sizeIn)
  {
    // size array with parameter
    list = new BankAccount[sizeIn];
    total = 0;
  }


  // helper method to find the index of a specified account
  private int search(String accountNumberIn)
  {
    for(int i = 0; i < total; i++)
    {
      BankAccount tempAccount = list[i]; // find the account at index i
      String tempNumber = tempAccount.getAccountNumber(); // get account number
      if(tempNumber.equals(accountNumberIn))
      {
        return i;
      }
    }
    return -999;
  }

  // return the total number of accounts in the list
  public int getTotal()
  {
    return total;
  }

  // check if the list is empty
  public boolean isEmpty()
  {
    if (total == 0)
    {
      return true; // list is empty
    }
    else
    {
      return false; // list is not empty
    }
  }

  // check if the list is full
  public boolean isFull()
  {
    if (total == list.length)
    {
      return true; // list is full
    }
    else
    {
      return false; // list is empty
    }
  }

  // add an item to the array
  public boolean add(BankAccount accountIn)
  {
    if (!isFull()) // check if list is full
```

```
      {
        list[total] = accountIn; // add item
        total++; // increment total
        return true; // indicate success
      }
      else
      {
        return false; // indicate failure
      }
    }

    // return an account at a particular place in the list
    public BankAccount getItem(String accountNumberIn)
    {
      int index;
      index = search(accountNumberIn);
      if(index == -999)
      {
        return null; // indicate invalid index
      }
      else
      {
        return list[index];
      }
    }

    // deposit money in a specified account
    public boolean depositMoney(String accountNumberIn, double amountIn)
    {
      int index = search(accountNumberIn);
      if(index == -999) // there was no such account number
      {
        return false; // indicate failure
      }
      else
      {
        list[index].deposit(amountIn);
        return true; // indicate success
      }
    }

    // withdraw money from a specified account
    public boolean withdrawMoney(String accountNumberIn, double amountIn)
    {
      int index = search(accountNumberIn);
      if(index == -999) // there was no such account number
      {
        return false; // indicate failure
      }
      else
      {
        list[index].withdraw(amountIn);
        return true; // indicate success
      }
    }

    // remove an account
    public boolean remove(String numberIn)
    {
        int index = search(numberIn); // find index of account
        if(index == -999) // if no such account
        {
            return false; // remove was unsuccessful
        }
        else
        {   // overwrite items by shifting other items along
            for(int i = index; i<= total-2; i++)
            {
                list[i] = list[i+1];
            }
```

```
                total--; // decrement total number of accounts
                return true; // remove was successful
            }
        }
    }
```

As you can see, we have declared two attributes – the first an array of `BankAccounts`, the second an **int** to keep track of the total.

Some of the methods require further discussion. We'll start with the constructor:

```
public Bank(int sizeIn)
{
   list = new BankAccount[sizeIn];
   total = 0;
}
```

As you can see the constructor accepts an integer value representing the maximum number of accounts allowed, and creates a new array of this size. In this way the user of the class is able to decide on this number.

The second line sets the total amount of accounts to zero – the number of accounts that will be present when the application first starts.

The next method simply returns the total. This is followed by two methods, `isEmpty` and `isFull`, which are straightforward, and simply report, respectively, on whether the list is empty or full. Notice how the `isFull` method makes use of the `length` property of the array.

Next comes the `search` method:

```
private int search(String accountNumberIn)
{
   for(int i = 0; i < total; i++)
   {
     BankAccount tempAccount = list[i]; // find the account at index i
     String tempNumber = tempAccount.getAccountNumber(); // get account number
     if(tempNumber.equals(accountNumberIn))
     {
        return i;
     }
   }
   return -999;
}
```

You have seen something like this before in chapter 5 when we searched an integer array – you can see we are using the same technique of sending back a "dummy" value if the account number is not valid. Notice that here, however, we are not searching the whole array, but are going only as far as the total number of elements that have been filled with accounts. You can also see that, because it is the account number we are searching for, each time we go round the loop, we have to first find the account, and then get its account number before making the comparison.

Now we come to the `add` method:

```
public boolean add(BankAccount accountIn)
{
   if (!isFull())
   {
      list[total] = accountIn;
      total++;
      return true;
   }
   else
   {
      return false;
   }
}
```

We check that the list is not full, and if this is the case we assign the account which it has received to the next slot in the array, with this instruction:

```
list[total] = accountIn;
```

At first sight, you might wonder why the next available index is represented by the value total. This is best illustrated by an example. Imagine that there are currently 20 accounts in the list. This means that array positions 0 to 19 will be filled. Thus, the next position to be filled will be position 20 – the same as the current total of the accounts so far.

Once we have done this, we increase the total by 1, and then return a value of **true** to indicate that the account has been added successfully. If the list had been full, a value of **false** would have been returned, as you can see from the **else** clause.

Next comes the getItem method:

```
public BankAccount getItem(String accountNumberIn)
{
   int index;
   index = search(accountNumberIn);
   if(index == -999)
   {
      return null; // indicate invalid index
   }
   else
   {
      return list[index];
   }
}
```

The method begins by calling the search method to find the index of the account in the array. As you can see, if the search method returns −999, indicating that there in no such account number in the list, then the getItem method returns a value of **null**. The user of this method will know that a **null** value indicates that the requested account does not exist.

If the account number was valid, however, the method returns the reference to the account at that position:

```
return list[index];
```

Now comes the `depositMoney` method:

```
public boolean depositMoney(String accountNumberIn, double amountIn)
{
  int index = search(accountNumberIn);
  if(index == -999) // there was no such account number
  {
    return false; // indicate failure
  }
  else
  {
    list[index].deposit(amountIn);
    return true; // indicate success
  }
}
```

Here we make use of the deposit method of `BankAccount` – but we have first to find the correct account in which to make the deposit. For this purpose we use our `search` method. Once we have obtained the position in the account, we check that it is valid by using the fact that the method will return a value of −999 if it is not. Having checked this, we return **false** if it was not valid, otherwise we use the `deposit` method of the relevant account to make the transaction. Once the deposit is made, we return a value of **true** to indicate success.

The `withdrawMoney` method is similar.

Now we come to the `remove` method, which really does need a bit of explanation. Here it is again:

```
public boolean remove(String numberIn)
{
    int index = search(numberIn); // find index of account
    if(index == -999) // if no such account
    {
        return false; // remove was unsuccessful
    }
    else
    {   // overwrite items by shifting other items along
        for(int i = index; i<= total-2; i++)
        {
            list[i] = list[i+1];
        }
        total—; // decrement total number of accounts
        return true; // remove was successful
    }
}
```

The first thing we do is to use the `search` method to obtain the position of the account that has to be removed. We use the return value of this method to ensure that the account number actually exists, and terminate the method if it does not, returning a value of **false**.

Now let's look at a strategy to remove the given item from a list. The usual approach is to shuffle the previous items in the list along so that the given item is *overwritten*. This is shown in figure 7.5, where the accounts have been identified by the name of the account holder.

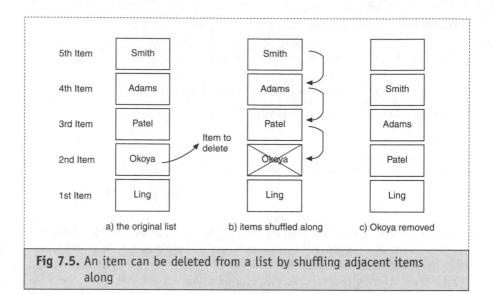

5th Item	Smith		Smith		
4th Item	Adams		Adams		Smith
3rd Item	Patel		Patel		Adams
2nd Item	Okoya		Okoya		Patel
1st Item	Ling		Ling		Ling

a) the original list   b) items shuffled along   c) Okoya removed

Fig 7.5. An item can be deleted from a list by shuffling adjacent items along

In this case the item to be removed (*Okoya*) was the second item in the list. The items to be shuffled (*Patel, Adams* and *Smith*) were the third, fourth and fifth items in the list respectively. Remembering that this list is implemented as an array, and that array indices begin at zero, the following assignments could be used to achieve this shuffling:

```
list[1] = list[2]; // overwrite Okoya with Patel
list[2] = list[3]; // overwrite Patel with Adams
list[3] = list[4]; // overwrite Adams with Smith
```

As you can see, we are repeating the same line each time, but with a different index. In other words, we keep repeating the following line:

```
list[i] = list[i + 1];
```

with a different value of `i` each time. We can achieve this with a **for** loop. The only tricky bit is to work out the start and end values of the variable `i` — and since we are using arrays (which start at 0), this makes it a little more difficult to get it right.

Clearly we don't have to bother about any items that come before the one we are deleting. In the above example we don't have to worry about *Ling*. So we start with the item we are going to delete. In our method, this was represented by the variable `index`. You should be able to see from figure 7.5 that the place to stop is one before the end – *Adams* in this example. Again since we are using arrays, which start at 0, this will not be `total − 1`, but `total − 2`. Thus we get the following **for** loop:

```
for(int i = position - 1; i<= total - 2; i++)
{
    list[i] = list[i+1];
}
```

This isn't quite the whole story. If we used this loop on the initial list to delete *Okoya*, we would be left with the array depicted in figure 7.6.

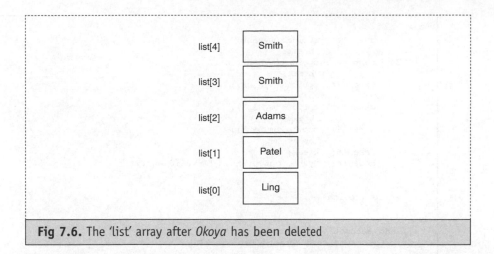

Fig 7.6. The 'list' array after *Okoya* has been deleted

As you can see, *Smith* is in two positions in the array. There is still a *Smith* in the last position of the list, as it hasn't been overwritten with anything. Although we don't really want that *Smith* in the last position, we can in fact simply ignore it – immediately after the **for** loop is finished, we reduce the total number of elements in the list by 1. Now the extra *Smith* is effectively hidden from the list.[3]

Program 7.3 is a program that uses the Bank class – notice that we are using our new EasyScanner class here.

Program 7.3

```java
public class BankProgram
{
  public static void main(String[] args)
  {
    char choice;
    int size;
    System.out.print("Maximum number of accounts? ");
    size = EasyScanner.nextInt();
    // create Bank object
    Bank myBank = new Bank(size);

    // offer menu
    do
    {
      System.out.println();
      System.out.println("1. Create new account");
      System.out.println("2. Remove an account");
      System.out.println("3. Deposit money");
      System.out.println("4. Withdraw money");
      System.out.println("5. Check account details");
      System.out.println("6. Quit");
      System.out.println();
      System.out.print("Enter choice [1-6]: ");

      // get choice
      choice = EasyScanner.nextChar();
      System.out.println();

      // process menu options
      switch (choice)
```

[3] In fact, when a new item is added into the list it will overwrite this extra *Smith* item.

```
      {
        case '1': option1(myBank);
                  break;
        case '2': option2(myBank);
                  break;
        case '3': option3(myBank);
                  break;
        case '4': option4(myBank);
                  break;
        case '5': option5(myBank);
                  break;
        case '6': break;
        default:  System.out.println("Invalid entry");
      }
    }
    while (choice != '6');
}

// add account
private static void option1(Bank bankIn)
{
    // get details from user
    System.out.print("Enter account number: ");
    String number = EasyScanner.nextString();
    System.out.print("Enter account name: ");
    String name = EasyScanner.nextString();
    // create new account
    BankAccount account = new BankAccount(number, name);
    // add account to list
    boolean ok = bankIn.add(account);
    if (!ok)
    {
        System.out.println("The list is full");
    }
    else
    {
        System.out.println("Account created");
    }
}

// remove account
private static void option2(Bank bankIn)
{
    // get account number of account to remove
    System.out.print("Enter account number: ");
    String number = EasyScanner.nextString();
    // delete item if it exists
    boolean ok = bankIn.remove(number);
    if (!ok)
    {
        System.out.println("No such account number");
    }
    else
    {
        System.out.println("Account removed");
    }
}

// deposit money in an account
private static void option3(Bank bankIn)
{
    // get details from user
    System.out.print("Enter account number: ");
    String number = EasyScanner.nextString();
    System.out.print("Enter amount to deposit: ");
    double amount = EasyScanner.nextDouble();
    boolean ok = bankIn.depositMoney(number, amount); // attempt to deposit
    if (!ok)
    {
        System.out.println("No such account number");
```

```
      }
      else
      {
         System.out.println("Money deposited");
      }
   }

   // withdraw money from an account
   private static void option4(Bank bankIn)
   {
      // get details from user
      System.out.print("Enter account number: ");
      String number = EasyScanner.nextString();
      System.out.print("Enter amount to withdraw: ");
      double amount = EasyScanner.nextDouble();
      boolean ok = bankIn.withdrawMoney(number, amount); // attempt to withdraw
      if (!ok)
      {
         System.out.println("No such account number");
      }
      else
      {
         System.out.println("Money withdrawn");
      }
   }

   // check account details
   private static void option5(Bank bankIn)
   {
      // get details from user
      System.out.print("Enter account number ");
      String number = EasyScanner.nextString();
      BankAccount account = bankIn.getItem(number);
      if (account == null)
      {
         System.out.println("No such account number");
      }
      else
      {
         System.out.println("Account number: " + account.getAccountNumber());
         System.out.println("Account name: " + account.getAccountName());
         System.out.println("Balance: " + account.getBalance());
         System.out.println();
      }
   }
}
```

You are familiar with this sort of menu-driven program, so there is not too much to say about it, except to observe that this is probably the first example of an application which, although not all that complex, could actually be thought of as the kind of application that could be used in a real business environment. Of course, in the outside world such applications are much more sophisticated than this, but they are, in principle, not too different from the sort of thing we have just done. Notice that our application involves a number of classes that we have written ourselves, and have pulled together to form a single application.

It is worth drawing attention to the way that the program makes use of some of the features of the Bank class that we incorporated into the BankProgram. In option1 (and similarly in other methods) we make use of the fact that the add method of Bank returns **true** if the new account was successfully added, and **false** otherwise:

```
boolean ok = bankIn.add(account);
if (!ok)
{
    System.out.println("The list is full");
}
else
{
    System.out.println("Account created");
}
```

In a similar way, in option5, we use the fact that the getItem method returns **null** if the account was not found:

```
BankAccount account = bankIn.getItem(number);
if (account == null)
{
    System.out.println("No such account number");
}
```

We end this chapter with an example program run from program 7.3, followed by a few ideas on how our application could be improved.

```
Maximum number of accounts? 100


1. Create new account

2. Remove an account

3. Deposit money

4. Withdraw money

5. Check account details

6. Quit


Enter choice [1-6]: 1


Enter account number: 63488965
Enter account name: Paula Wilkins
Account created


1. Create new account

2. Remove an account

3. Deposit money

4. Withdraw money
```

5. Check account details

6. Quit

Enter choice [1-6]: 1

Enter account number: 14322508

Enter account name: Sydney Isaacs

Account created

1. Create new account

2. Remove an account

3. Deposit money

4. Withdraw money

5. Check account details

6. Quit

Enter choice [1-6]: 1

Enter account number: 90871435

Enter account name: Delroy Joseph

Account created

1. Create new account

2. Remove an account

3. Deposit money

4. Withdraw money

5. Check account details

6. Quit

Enter choice [1-6]: 3

Enter account number: 90871435

Enter amount to deposit: 1500

Money deposited

1. Create new account

2. Remove an account

3. Deposit money

4. Withdraw money

5. Check account details

6. Quit

Enter choice [1-6]: **2**

Enter account number: **14322508**

Account removed

1. Create new account

2. Remove an account

3. Deposit money

4. Withdraw money

5. Check account details

6. Quit

Enter choice [1-6]: **5**

Enter account number **14322508**

No such account number

1. Create new account

2. Remove an account

3. Deposit money

4. Withdraw money

5. Check account details

6. Quit

Enter choice [1-6]: **5**

*Enter account number **90871435***

Account number: 90871435

Account name: Delroy Joseph

Balance: 1500.0

1. Create new account

2. Remove an account

3. Deposit money

4. Withdraw money

5. Check account details

6. Quit

*Enter choice [1-6]: **6***

As we pointed out there are a few improvements that could be made to our application. Two of these are identified below:

1   The final program could provide an option that allows all accounts to be displayed.

2   The add method of the Bank class could be adapted so that duplicate account numbers are not allowed.

These changes are left as practical exercises.

Finally, we should point out that for our application to be useful to any organization, it would need to be able to store the account information even after the application terminates. However, before you are able to achieve this you will have to wait until the second semester, where you will find out how to create files to hold permanent records.

Self-test questions

1   In a UML class diagram, what is placed in each of the sections **A**, **B** and **C** below?

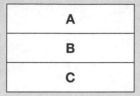

A
B
C

2   Explain the difference between **public** and **private** access to attributes and methods.

3   What is the effect of the **static** modifier when applied to:

a) an attribute

b) a method?

4   Consider the following class:

```java
public class SomeClass
{
    private int x = 10;

    public void setX(int xIn)
    {
        x = xIn;
    }

    public int getX()
    {
        return x;
    }
}
```

What would be the output from the following program?

```java
public class ImplementingClassesQ4
{
    public static void main(String[] args)
    {
        int y = 20;
        SomeClass myObject = new SomeClass();

        test(y, myObject);
        System.out.println(y);
        System.out.println(myObject.getX());
    }

    private static void test(int z, SomeClass classIn)
    {
        z = 50;
        classIn.setX(100);
    }
}
```

Programming exercises

1   The diagram below represents the design for a `Student` class such as the one that we discussed in chapter 6.

Student
studentNumber : String studentName : String markForMaths : int markForEnglish : int markForScience : int
Student(String, String) getNumber() : String getName() : String enterMarks(int, int, int) getMathsMark() : int getEnglishMark() : int getScienceMark() : int calculateAverageMark() : double

Write the code for the `Student` class. You should note that in order to ensure that a **double** is returned from the `calculateAverageMark` method you should specifically divide the total of the three marks by 3.0 and not simply by 3 (look back at chapter 1 to remind yourself why this is the case).

Another thing to think about is what you choose for the initial values of the marks. If you chose to give each mark an initial value of zero, this could be ambiguous; a mark of zero could mean that the mark simply has not been entered – or it could mean the student actually scored zero in the subject! Can you think of a better initial value?

Write a tester class to test out your `Student` class; it should create two or three students (or even better an array of students), and use the methods of the `Student` class to test whether they work according to the specification.

2   A system is being developed for use in a store that sells electrical appliances. A class called `StockItem` is required for this system. An object of the `StockItem` class will require the following attributes:

> a stock number;

> a name;

> the price of the item;

> the total number of these items currently in stock.

The first three of the above attributes will need to be set at the time a `StockItem` object is created – the total number of items in stock will be set to zero at this time. The stock number and name will not need to be changed after the item is created.

The following methods are also required:

> a method that allows the price to be re-set during the object's lifetime;

❯ a method that receives an integer and adds this to the total number of items of this type in stock;

❯ a method that returns the total value of items of this type in stock; this is calculated by multiplying the price of the item by the number of items in stock;

❯ methods to read the values of all four attributes.

The design of the `StockItem` class is shown in the following UML diagram:

StockItem
stockNumber : String name : String price : double totalStock : int
StockItem(String, String, double) setPrice(double) increaseTotalStock(int) getStockNumber() : String getName() : String getTotalStock() : int getPrice() : double calculateTotalPrice() : double

a) Write the code for the `StockItem` class.

b) Consider the following program, which uses the `StockItem` class, and in which some of the code has been replaced by comments:

```java
public class TestProg
{
    public static void main(String[] args)
    {
        String tempNumber;
        String tempName;
        double tempPrice;

        System.out.print("Enter the stock number: ");
        tempNumber = EasyScanner.nextString();
        System.out.print("Enter the name of the item: ");
        tempName = EasyScanner.nextString();
        System.out.print("Enter the price of the item: ");
        tempPrice = EasyScanner.nextDouble();

        /* Create a new item of stock using the values
           that were entered by the user */

        // Increase the total number of items in stock by 5

        // Display the stock number

        // Display the total price of all items in stock

    }
}
```

Replace the comments with appropriate code.

c) i) A further attribute, `salesTax`, is required. The value of this attribute should always be the same for each object of the class. Write the declaration for this attribute.

   ii) A class method, `setSalesTax`, is now provided for this class – it receives a **double** and sets the value of the sales tax to this value. Write a line of code that sets the sales tax for all objects of the class to 10 without referring to any particular object.

3 Implement the changes to the bank application suggested at the very end of this chapter. The source code for the `Bank` class and the `BankProgram` class is provided on the accompanying CD.

4 a) Develop a `StudentList` class to hold a collection of `Students` as described in exercise 1. The UML diagram depicting the association between a `StudentList` object and a `Student` object is shown below:

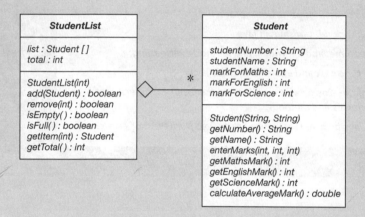

b) Develop a `StudentListTester` class to test the `StudentList` class.

5 Add some additional methods such as `nextByte` and `nextLong` to the `EasyScanner` class.

CHAPTER: 08

Extending classes with inheritance

Objectives:

By the end of this chapter you should be able to:

- explain the term **inheritance**;
- design inheritance structures using UML notation;
- implement inheritance relationships in Java;
- distinguish between **method overriding** and **method overloading**;
- explain the term **type cast** and implement this in Java;
- explain the use of the **abstract** modifier and the **final** modifier, when applied to both classes and methods;
- describe the way in which all Java classes are derived from the Object class.

8.1 Introduction

One of the greatest benefits of the object-oriented approach to software development is that it offers the opportunity for us to *reuse* classes that have already been written – either by ourselves or by someone else. Let's look at a possible scenario. Say you wanted to develop a software system and you have, during your analysis, identified the need for a class called Employee. You might be aware that a colleague in your organization has already written an Employee class; rather than having to write your own class, it would be easier to approach your colleague and ask her to let you use her Employee class.

So far so good, but what if the Employee class that you are given doesn't quite do everything that you had hoped? Perhaps your employees are part-time employees, and you want your class to have an attribute like hourlyPay, or methods like calculateWeeklyPay and setHourlyPay, and these attributes and methods do not exist in the Employee class you have been given.

You may think it would be necessary to go into the old class and start messing about with the code. But there is no need, because object-oriented programming languages provide the ability to extend existing classes by adding attributes and methods to them. This is called **inheritance**.

8.2 Defining inheritance

Inheritance is the sharing of attributes and methods among classes. We take a class, and then define other classes based on the first one. The new classes *inherit* all the attributes and methods of the first one, but also have attributes and methods of their own. Let's try to understand this by thinking about the `Employee` class.

Say our `Employee` class has two attributes, `number` and `name`, a user-defined constructor, and some basic *get-* and *set-* methods for the attributes. We now define our `PartTimeEmployee` class; this class will *inherit* these attributes and methods, but can also have attributes and methods of its own. We will give it one additional attribute, `hourlyPay`, some methods to access this attribute and one additional method, `calculateWeeklyPay`.

This is illustrated in figure 8.1 which uses the UML notation for inheritance, namely a triangle.

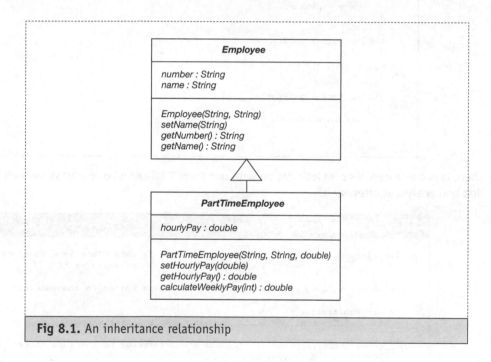

Fig 8.1. An inheritance relationship

You can see from this diagram that an inheritance relationship is a *hierarchical* relationship. The class at the top of the hierarchy – in this case the `Employee` class – is referred to as the **superclass** (or **base class**) and the `PartTimeEmployee` as the **subclass** (or **derived class**).

The inheritance relationship is also often referred to as an *is-a-kind-of* relationship; in this case a `PartTimeEmployee` *is a kind of* `Employee`.

8.3 Implementing inheritance in Java

The code for the `Employee` class is shown below:

> ### The *Employee* class
>
> ```java
> public class Employee
> {
>     private String number;
>     private String name;
>
>     public Employee(String numberIn, String nameIn)
>     {
>         number = numberIn;
>         name = nameIn;
>     }
>
>     public void setName(String nameIn)
>     {
>         name = nameIn;
>     }
>
>     public String getNumber()
>     {
>         return number;
>     }
>
>     public String getName()
>     {
>         return name;
>     }
> }
> ```

There is nothing new here, so let's get on with our `PartTimeEmployee` class. We will present the code first and analyse it afterwards.

> ### The *PartTimeEmployee* class
>
> ```java
> public class PartTimeEmployee extends Employee /* this class is a subclass
>                                                           of Employee */
> {
>     private double hourlyPay; // this attribute is unique to the subclass
>
>     // the constructor
>     public PartTimeEmployee(String numberIn, String nameIn, double hourlyPayIn)
>     {
>         super(numberIn, nameIn); // call the constuctor of the superclass
>         hourlyPay = hourlyPayIn;
>     }
>
>     // these methods are also unique to the subclass
>     public double getHourlyPay()
>     {
>         return hourlyPay;
>     }
>
>     public void setHourlyPay(double hourlyPayIn)
>     {
>         hourlyPay = hourlyPayIn;
>     }
>
>     public double calculateWeeklyPay(int noOfHoursIn)
>     {
>         return noOfHoursIn * hourlyPay;
>     }
> }
> ```

The first line of interest is the class header itself:

```
class PartTimeEmployee extends Employee
```

Here we see the use of the keyword **extends**. Using this word in this way means that the `PartTimeEmployee` class (the *subclass*) inherits all the attributes and methods of the `Employee` class (the *superclass*). So although we haven't coded them, any object of the `PartTimeEmployee` class will have, for example, an attribute called `name` and a method called `getNumber`. A `PartTimeEmployee` is now a *kind of* `Employee`.

But can you see a problem here? The attributes have been declared as **private** in the superclass so although they are now part of our `PartTimeEmployee` class, none of the `PartTimeEmployee` class methods can directly access them – the subclass has only the same access rights as any other class!

There are a number of possible ways around this:

1 We could declare the original attributes as **public** – but this would take away the whole point of encapsulation.

2 We could use the special keyword **protected** instead of **private**. The effect of this is that anything declared as **protected** is accessible to the methods of any subclasses. There are, however, two issues to think about here. The first is that you have to anticipate in advance when you want your class to be able to be inherited. The second problem is that it weakens your efforts to encapsulate information within the class, since, in Java, **protected** attributes are also accessible to any other class in the same package (you will find out much more about the meaning of the word **package** in chapter 13).

The above remarks notwithstanding, this is a perfectly acceptable approach to use, particularly in situations where you are writing a class as part of a discrete application, and you will be aware in advance that certain classes will need to be subclassed. You will see an example of this in section 8.4.

3 The other solution, and the one we will use now, is to leave the attributes as **private**, but to plan carefully in advance which `get` and `set` methods we are going to provide.

After the class header we have the following declaration:

```
private double hourlyPay;
```

This declares an attribute, `hourlyPay`, which is unique to our subclass – but remember that the attributes of the superclass, `Employee`, will be inherited, so in fact any `PartTimeEmployee` object will have *three* attributes.

Next comes the constructor. We want to be able to assign values to the number and name at the time that the object is created, just as we do with an `Employee` object; so our constructor will need to receive parameters that will be assigned to the `number` and `name` attributes.

But wait a minute! How are we going to do this? The `number` and `name` attributes have been declared as **private** in the superclass – so they aren't accessible to objects of the subclass. Luckily there is a way around this problem. We can call the constructor of the superclass by using the keyword **super**. Look how this is done:

```
public PartTimeEmployee(String numberIn, String nameIn, double hourlyPayIn)
{
    // call the constructor of the superclass
    super(numberIn, nameIn);
    hourlyPay = hourlyPayIn;
}
```

After calling the constructor of the superclass, we need to perform one more task – namely to assign the third parameter, `hourlyPayIn`, to the `hourlyPay` attribute. Notice, however, that the line that calls **super** has to be the first one.

The remaining methods of `PartTimeEmployee` are new methods specific to the subclass:

```
public double getHourlyPay()
{
    return hourlyPay;
}

public void setHourlyPay(double hourlyPayIn)
{
    hourlyPay = hourlyPayIn;
}

public double calculateWeeklyPay(int noOfHoursIn)
{
    return noOfHoursIn * hourlyPay;
}
```

The first two provide read and write access respectively to the `hourlyPay` attribute. The third one receives the number of hours worked and calculates the pay by multiplying this by the hourly rate. Program 8.1 demonstrates the use of the `PartTimeEmployee` class.

Program 8.1

```
public class PartTimeEmployeeTester
{
    public static void main(String[] args)
    {
        String number, name;
        double pay;
        int hours;
        PartTimeEmployee emp;

        // get the details from the user
        System.out.print("Employee Number? ");
        number = EasyScanner.nextString();
        System.out.print("Employee's Name? ");
        name = EasyScanner.nextString();
        System.out.print("Hourly Pay? ");
        pay = EasyScanner.nextDouble();
        System.out.print("Hours worked this week? ");
        hours = EasyScanner.nextInt();

        // create a new part-time employee
        emp = new PartTimeEmployee(number, name, pay);

        // display employee's details, including the weekly pay
        System.out.println();
        System.out.println(emp.getName());
```

```
            System.out.println(emp.getNumber());
            System.out.println(emp.calculateWeeklyPay(hours));
        }
}
```

Here is a sample test run:

Employee Number? **A103456**

Employee's Name? **Walter Wallcarpeting**

Hourly Pay? **15.50**

Hours worked this week? **20**

Walter Wallcarpeting

A103456

310.0

We can now move on to look at another inheritance example; let's choose the Oblong class that we developed in the last chapter.

8.3.1 Extending the *Oblong* class

We are going to define a new class called ExtendedOblong, which extends the Oblong class. First, let's remind ourselves of the Oblong class itself.

The *Oblong* class – a reminder

```
public class Oblong
{
    // the attributes are declared first
    private double length;
    private double height;

    // then the methods

    // the constructor
    public Oblong(double lengthIn, double heightIn)
    {
        length = lengthIn;
        height = heightIn;
    }

    // the next method allows us to read the length attribute
    public double getLength()
    {
        return length;
    }

    // the next method allows us to read the height attribute
    public double getHeight()
    {
        return height;
    }
```

```
        // the next method allows us to write to the length attribute
        public void setLength(double lengthIn)
        {
            length = lengthIn;
        }

        // the next method allows us to write to the height attribute
        public void setHeight(double heightIn)
        {
            height = heightIn;
        }

        // this method returns the area of the oblong
        public double calculateArea()
        {
            return length * height;
        }

        // this method returns the perimeter of the oblong
        public double calculatePerimeter()
        {
            return 2 * (length + height);
        }
}
```

The original `Oblong` class had the capability of reporting on the perimeter and area of the oblong. Our extended class will have the capability of sending back a string representation of itself composed of a number of symbols such as asterisks – for example:

* * * * *

* * * * *

* * * * *

Now at first glance you might think that this isn't a string at all, because it consists of several lines. But if we think of the instruction to start a new line as just another character – which for convenience we could call <NEWLINE> – then our string could be written like this.

* * * * * <NEWLINE> * * * * * <NEWLINE> * * * * *

In Java we are able to represent this <NEWLINE> character with a special character that looks like this:

`'\n'`

This is one of a number of special characters called **escape characters** – you will learn more about them in the next chapter.

Our `ExtendedOblong` class will need an additional attribute, which we will call `symbol`, to hold the character that is to be used to draw the oblong. We will also provide a `setSymbol` method, and of course we will need a method that sends back the string representation. We will call this method `draw`. The new constructor will accept values for the length and height as before, but will also receive the character to be used for drawing the oblong.

The design is shown in figure 8.2.

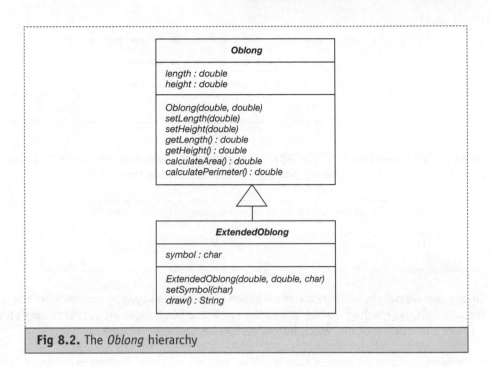

Fig 8.2. The *Oblong* hierarchy

Now for the implementation. As well as those aspects of the code that relate to inheritance, there is an additional new technique used in this class – this is the technique known as **type casting**. Take a look at the complete code first – then we can discuss this new concept along with some other important features of the class.

The *ExtendedOblong* class

```
public class ExtendedOblong extends Oblong
{
  private char symbol;

  // the constructor
  public ExtendedOblong(double lengthIn, double heightIn, char symbolIn)
  {
    super(lengthIn, heightIn);
    symbol = symbolIn;
  }

  public void setSymbol(char symbolIn)
  {
    symbol = symbolIn;
  }

  public String draw()
  {
    String s = new String(); // to hold the string representation
    int l, h;
    /* in the next two lines we type cast from double to
       integer so that we are able to count how many times we
       print the symbol */
    l = (int) getLength();
    h = (int) getHeight();
    for (int i = 1; i <= h; i++)
    {
      for (int j = 1; j <= l; j++)
      {
```

```
        s = s + symbol; // add the symbol to the string
      }
      s = s + '\n'; // add the <NEWLINE> character
    }
    return s; // return the string representation
  }
}
```

So let's take a closer look at all this. After the class header – which **extends** the Oblong class – we declare the additional attribute, symbol, and then define our constructor:

```
public ExtendedOblong(double lengthIn, doubleheightIn, char symbolIn)
{
    super(lengthIn, heightIn);
    symbol = symbolIn;
}
```

Once again we call the constructor of the superclass with the keyword **super**. After the constructor comes the setSymbol method – which allows the symbol to be changed during the oblong's lifetime – and then we have the draw method, which introduces the new concept of **type casting**:

```
public String draw()
{
    String s = new String(); // start off with an empty string
    int l, h;
    l = (int) getLength();
    h = (int) getHeight();
    for (int i = 1; i <= h; i++)
    {
      for (int j = 1; j <= l; j++)
      {
        s = s + symbol; // add a symbol to end of the string
      }
      s = s + '\n'; // add a new line to the string
    }
    return s;
}
```

Inspect the code carefully – notice that we have declared two local variables of type **int**. In order to understand the purpose of these two variables, l and h, we need to explore this business of type casting, which means forcing an item to change from one type to another.

The draw method is going to create a string of one or more rows of stars or crosses or whatever symbol is chosen. Now the dimensions of the oblong are defined as **doubles**. Clearly our draw method needs to be dealing with whole numbers of rows and columns – so we must convert the length and height of the oblong from **doubles** to **ints**. There will obviously be some loss of precision here, but that won't matter in this particular case.

As you can see from the above code, type casting is achieved by placing the new type name in brackets before the item you wish to change. This is illustrated in figure 8.3.

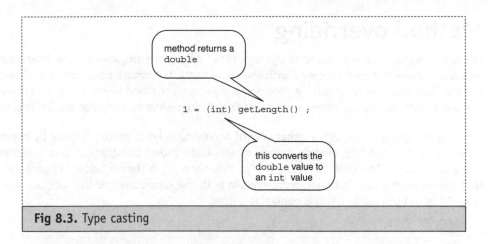

Fig 8.3. Type casting

Program 8.2 uses the `ExtendedOblong` class. It creates an oblong of length 10 and height 5, with an asterisk as the symbol; it then draws the oblong, changes the symbol to a cross, and draws it again.

Program 8.2

```
public class ExtendedOblongTester
{
    public static void main(String[] args)
    {
        ExtendedOblong extOblong = new ExtendedOblong(10,5,'*');
        System.out.println(extOblong.draw());
        extOblong.setSymbol('+');
        System.out.println(extOblong.draw());
    }
}
```

The output from program 8.2 is shown below:

```
* * * * * * * * * *

* * * * * * * * * *

* * * * * * * * * *

* * * * * * * * * *

* * * * * * * * * *


+ + + + + + + + + +

+ + + + + + + + + +

+ + + + + + + + + +

+ + + + + + + + + +

+ + + + + + + + + +
```

8.4 Method overriding

In chapter 4 you were introduced to the concept of polymorphism, which is the phenomenon whereby it is possible to have different methods with the same name, but whose behaviour is different. You saw in that chapter that one way of achieving polymorphism was by method *overloading*, which involves methods of the same class having the same name, but being distinguished by their parameter lists.

Now we are going to explore another way of achieving polymorphism, namely by **method overriding**. In order to do this we will develop a very simple class called `Customer`, and a subclass of this called `GoldCustomer`. The UML class diagram for this hierarchy is shown below in figure 8.4. You might notice that the method `dispatchGoods` appears in both the superclass and the subclass, and that its interface is identical in both classes. This is explained below.

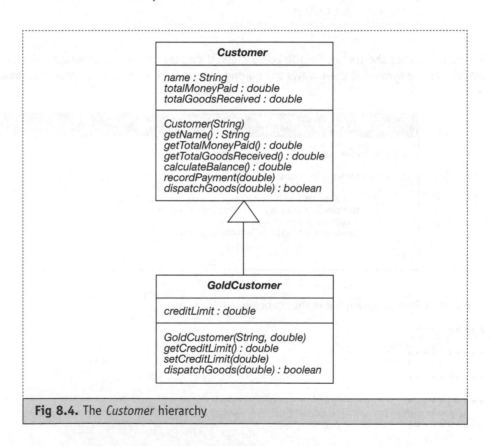

Fig 8.4. The *Customer* hierarchy

We have kept our `Customer` class very simple and given it three attributes. The first represents the customer's name. The other two, `totalMoneyPaid` and `totalGoodsRecieved`, represent the total amount of money that a customer has paid so far, and the total value of the goods that have so far been dispatched to the customer. Normally, goods would not be dispatched to a customer unless the customer had already paid for them; thus for goods of a particular value to be dispatched, the difference between `totalMoneyPaid` and `totalGoodsReceived` must be at least as much as the value of the goods.

Certain customers – known as "gold" customers – have extra privileges and are given a credit limit. Thus, in the case of such a customer, goods can be dispatched as long as the credit limit is not exceeded. You can see, then, that the behaviour of the `dispatchGoods` method is going to be different in the case of the superclass and that of the subclass. You will see in a moment how we define the method in the superclass, and then define a different version in the subclass – in other words we **override** the method in the subclass, thus achieving polymorphism. You remember that when we previously looked at method *overloading*, the different methods were distinguished by the parameter lists. In the case of method *overriding*, they are distinguished by the object with which they are associated.

So let's look at the implementation. First the `Customer` class. Note that we have made the attributes `protected`, so that they will be visible in the subclass.

The *Customer* class

```java
public class Customer
{
    protected String name;
    protected double totalMoneyPaid;   // total money paid so far by customer
    protected double totalGoodsReceived; /* value of total goods received
                                            so far by customer */
    public Customer(String nameIn)
    {
        name = nameIn;
        totalMoneyPaid = 0;
        totalGoodsReceived = 0;
    }

    public String getName()
    {
        return name;
    }

    public double getTotalMoneyPaid()
    {
        return totalMoneyPaid;
    }

    public double getTotalGoodsReceived()
    {
        return totalGoodsReceived;
    }

    public double calculateBalance()
    {
        return totalMoneyPaid - totalGoodsReceived;
    }

    // record a payment made by the customer
    public void recordPayment(double paymentIn)
    {
        totalMoneyPaid = totalMoneyPaid + paymentIn;
    }

    // dispatch goods of a particular value to the customer
    public boolean dispatchGoods(double goodsIn)
    {
        if(calculateBalance() >= goodsIn)   // customer has sufficient funds
        {
            totalGoodsReceived = totalGoodsReceived + goodsIn;
            return true; // indicate success - goods should be dispatched
        }
        else
        {
            return false; // indicate failure - goods should not be dispatched
        }
    }
}
```

This is fairly straightforward, but just take a note of the following points:

> The `calculateBalance` method returns the current balance of the customer's account – that is the difference between total amount of money paid by the customer and the total value of the goods that the customer has received so far.

> The `recordPayment` method simply records the fact that a customer has made a payment by adding the amount of the payment to the total amount that the customer has paid.

> The `dispatchGoods` method first checks that the customer has enough money in his or her account to pay for the goods that are to be dispatched. If this is the case the value of the goods being dispatched is added to the total value of the goods received so far, and a value of **true** is returned. If the customer does not have enough funds to pay for the goods (that is, the balance is less than the value of the goods) a value of **false** is returned. The return value could be used by the calling method to determine whether or not the goods should actually be sent out to the customer.

Now we can look at the `GoldCustomer` class:

The *GoldCustomer* class

```java
public class GoldCustomer extends Customer
{
    private double creditLimit;

    public GoldCustomer(String nameIn, double limitIn)
    {
        super(nameIn);
        creditLimit = limitIn;
    }

    public void setCreditLimit(double limitIn)
    {
        creditLimit = limitIn;
    }

    public double getCreditLimit()
    {
        return creditLimit;
    }

    // this method is overridden
    public boolean dispatchGoods(double goodsIn)
    {
        if((calculateBalance() + creditLimit) >= goodsIn)
        {
            totalGoodsReceived = totalGoodsReceived + goodsIn;
            return true;
        }
        else
        {
            return false;
        }
    }
}
```

As you can see, we have added an additional attribute, `creditLimit`, as required, and have provided `set-` and `get-` methods for this.

The constructor uses the keyword **super** as before to call the constructor of the superclass and then assigns the incoming parameter to the additional attribute.

Now we come to the really important part, which is the `dispatchGoods` method. Here we have a method in the subclass with exactly the same name, the same parameter list, and the same return value (in other words the same *interface*) as a method in the superclass. However, in the original method in the superclass (`Customer`), we checked whether the customer had sufficient funds with the following condition:

```
if(calculateBalance() >= goodsIn)
```

In the subclass (`GoldCustomer`) the condition has to take into account the fact that the customer is allowed a negative balance up to the limit of his or her credit; the condition therefore looks like this:

```
if((calculateBalance() + creditLimit) >= goodsIn)
```

We have *overridden* the method in the subclass. The method has the same name as the method in the superclass, but behaves differently. As we said before, in the case of method *overloading* a program knew which method was being referred to by the parameter list. In the case of method overriding, the methods are distinguished by the kind of object with which the method is associated. Consider the following lines in a program:

```
Customer firstCustomer = new Customer("Jones");
GoldCustomer secondCustomer = new GoldCustomer("Cohen", 500);
// more code here
firstCustomer.dispatchGoods(98.76);
secondCustomer.dispatchGoods(32.44);
```

In the first call to `dispatchGoods`, the version of the method as defined in `Customer` will be called, because it is associated with a `Customer` object, `firstCustomer`. In the second call to `dispatchGoods`, the version of the method as defined in `GoldCustomer` will be called, because it is associated with a `GoldCustomer` object, `secondCustomer`.

8.5 Abstract classes

Let's think again about our `Employee` class. Imagine that our business expands, and we now employ full-time employees as well as part-time employees. A full-time employee object, rather than having an hourly rate of pay, will have an annual salary. It might also need a method that calculates the monthly pay (by dividing the annual salary by 12).

Figure 8.5 shows the structure of an employee hierarchy with the two types of employee, the full-time and the part-time employee. You will see that we have included a new method in the `Employee` class, called `getStatus` – which also appears in both subclasses. We will discuss this method later.

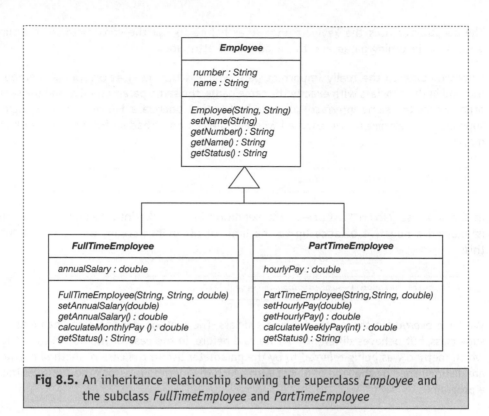

Fig 8.5. An inheritance relationship showing the superclass *Employee* and the subclass *FullTimeEmployee* and *PartTimeEmployee*

Notice how the two subclasses contain the attributes and methods appropriate to the class. If you think about this a bit more, it will occur to you that *any* employee will always be either a full-time employee or a part-time employee. There is never going to be a situation in which an individual is just a plain old employee! So users of a program that included all these classes would never find themselves creating objects of the Employee class. In fact it would be a good idea to prevent people from doing this – and, as you might have guessed, there is a way to do so, which is to declare the class as **abstract**. Once a class has been declared in this way it means that you are not allowed to create objects of that class. The Employee class simply acts a basis on which to build other classes.

The code for the Employee class appears below. If you inspect it you will notice something else interesting. Do you see that the getStatus method has also been declared **abstract**? Not only that, it also has a header but no body! Study the class for a moment and then we will tell you what this is all about.

The *Employee* class

```
public abstract class Employee // the class is declared abstract
{
    private String number;
    private String name;

    public Employee(String numberIn, String nameIn)
    {
        number = numberIn;
        name = nameIn;
    }

    public void setName(String nameIn)
```

```
        {
            name = nameIn;
        }

        public String getNumber()
        {
            return number;
        }

        public String getName()
        {
            return name;
        }

        abstract public String getStatus(); // an abstract method
}
```

The purpose of declaring a *method* as **abstract** is to force all subclasses of our class to implement this method. In this case, a `FullTimeEmployee` and a `PartTimeEmployee` – and any future subclasses of `Employee` – will have to have a method called `getStatus`; if they did not, they would not compile. The purpose of the `getStatus` method is to enable an object to report on what kind of employee it is – it will send back a `String` saying either "Full-time" or "Part-time" accordingly. Each subclass will *override* the `getStatus` method in a slightly different way.

We shall now implement the two derived classes. First the `FullTimeEmployee`:

The *FullTimeEmployee* class

```
public class FullTimeEmployee extends Employee
{
    private double annualSalary;

    public FullTimeEmployee(String numberIn,
                                        String nameIn, double salaryIn)
    {
        super(numberIn,nameIn);
        annualSalary = salaryIn;
    }

    public void setAnnualSalary(double salaryIn)
    {
        annualSalary = salaryIn;
    }

    public double getAnnualSalary()
    {
        return annualSalary;
    }

    public double calculateMonthlyPay()
    {
        return annualSalary/12;
    }

    // the abstract method is overridden
    public String getStatus()
    {
        return "Full-Time";
    }
}
```

And now the `PartTimeEmployee`:

The *PartTimeEmployee* class

```java
public class PartTimeEmployee extends Employee
{
    private double hourlyPay;

    public PartTimeEmployee(String numberIn, String nameIn, double hourlyPayIn)
    {
        super(numberIn, nameIn);
        hourlyPay = hourlyPayIn;
    }

    public void setHourlyPay(double hourlyPayIn)
    {
        hourlyPay = hourlyPayIn;
    }

    public double getHourlyPay()
    {
        return hourlyPay;
    }

    public double calculateWeeklyPay(int noOfHoursIn)
    {
        return hourlyPay * noOfHoursIn;
    }

    // the abstract method is overridden
    public String getStatus()
    {
        return "Part-Time";
    }
}
```

You may be thinking that abstract classes and abstract methods are quite interesting, but is it worth all the bother? Well, there is another really useful thing we can do with abstract classes and methods.

Say a method of some class somewhere expects to receive as a parameter an object of a particular class – an `Employee` class for example; and inside this method there is some code that calls a particular method of `Employee` – for example a method called `getStatus`. The marvellous thing about inheritance is that an object of any subclass of `Employee` is *a kind of* `Employee` and can therefore be passed as a parameter into a method that expects an `Employee` object. However, this subclass *must* have a `getStatus` method for it to be able to be passed as a parameter into a method that calls `getStatus`. By declaring the abstract method `getStatus` in the superclass we can *insist* that every subclass must have a `getStatus` method. We can tell anyone who is going to use a derivative of `Employee` to go right ahead and call a `getStatus` method because it will definitely be there – and what is more, it will behave differently for each object that it applies to.

If you think this sounds a bit complicated then an example will help. We have written a very simple class called `StatusTester`, whose sole purpose is to test out this abstract method stuff:

The *StatusTester* class

```
public class StatusTester
{
    public static void tester(Employee employeeIn)
    {
        System.out.println(employeeIn.getStatus());
    }
}
```

You can see that this class has a single method, `tester`, which receives an `Employee` object, `employeeIn`, as a parameter. It then calls the `getStatus` method of `employeeIn`. Now, because objects of the class `FullTimeEmployee` and objects of the class `PartTimeEmployee` are both kinds of `Employee`, we can pass either of them to this `tester` method. We have made this a **static** method, so it can be called by using the class name.

In program 8.3 objects of both of these types are sent to the `tester` method.

Program 8.3

```
public class RunStatusTester
{
    public static void main(String[] args)
    {
        // create a FullTimeEmployee object
        FullTimeEmployee fte = new FullTimeEmployee ("100", "Patel", 30000);
        // create a PartTimeEmployee object
        PartTimeEmployee pte = new PartTimeEmployee ("101", "Jones", 12);
        // call tester with the full-time employee
        StatusTester.tester(fte);
        // now call tester with the part-time employee
        StatusTester.tester(pte);
    }
}
```

The `tester` method will call the appropriate `getStatus` method according to the type of object it receives. Thus the output from this program will be:

Full-Time

Part-Time

8.6 The *final* modifier

You have already seen the use of the keyword **final** in chapter 1, where it was used to modify a variable and turn it into a constant. It can also be used to modify a class and a method. In the case of a class it is placed before the class declaration, like this:

```
public final class SomeClass
{
        // code goes here
}
```

This means that the class cannot be subclassed. In the case of a method it is used like this:

```
public final void someMethod()
{
    // code goes here
}
```

This means that the method cannot be overridden.

8.7 The *Object* class

One of the very useful things about inheritance is the *is-a-kind-of* relationship that we mentioned earlier. For example, when the ExtendedOblong class extended the Oblong class it became a kind of Oblong; when the PartTimeEmployee class extended the Employee class it became a kind of Employee. We have seen in section 8.6 that, in Java, if a method of some class expects to receive as a parameter an object of another class (say, for example, Vehicle), then it is quite happy to receive instead an object of a *subclass* of Vehicle – this is because that object will be *a kind of* Vehicle.

In Java, every single class that is created is in fact derived from what we might call a special "super superclass". This super superclass is called Object. So every object in Java is in fact *a kind of* Object.

This allows us to create very generic methods – methods that can receive any kind of object. It also allows us to create generic arrays – arrays of Objects.

In chapter 11 you will see an example of how we do precisely that. You will also see in chapter 17 that the Java libraries provide a number of pre-defined collection classes, all of which are generic classes designed to hold objects of the Object class.

To illustrate what we are saying, cast your mind back to the previous chapter, where we developed a collection class to hold BankAccount objects. This class had the following attribute:

```
private BankAccount[] list;
```

If we wanted to develop a generic class, we could replace this with:

```
private Object[] list;
```

Our add method would now look like this:

```
public boolean add(Object objectIn)
{
    if (!isFull())
    {
        list[total] = objectIn;
        total++;
        return true;
    }
    else
    {
        return false;
    }
}
```

This seems like a great idea, and it certainly can be very useful in some circumstances. However, there is a downside to generic classes too. Methods like `search` and `depositMoney` were methods which were relevant only to `BankAccount` objects, so we couldn't include those in a generic collection class – this sort of functionality would either have to be dealt with by the program using this class, or perhaps (as you will see in the case study in chapter 11) by creating a subclass that handles the specific functions we require.

There is another very important point about generic classes that we should mention. Consider a method like `getItem` that returned a `BankAccount`. In our new class it would look like this:

```
public Object getItem(int positionIn)
{
    if(positionIn < 1 || positionIn > total)
    {
        return null; // indicate invalid position
    }
    else
    {
        return list[positionIn - 1]; // subtract 1 to obtain the index
    }
}
```

This time the method returns an `Object`. A program that was using this method to retrieve `BankAccount` objects would need to type cast in order to convert this `Object` to a `BankAccount`. For example, if an instance of our collection class called `objectList` had been declared, we might have this line:

```
BankAccount myAccount =  (BankAccount) objectList.getItem(3);
```

In a similar way to that described in figure 8.3, we type cast from `Object` to `BankAccount` by placing the "type" name, `BankAccount`, in brackets before the item to be converted.

8.8 Wrapper classes and autoboxing

You might be wondering what you would do if you wanted to use an array of `Object`s to store a simple type such as an `int` or a `char` – or to pass such a type to a method that expects an `Object`. Java 5.0 provides a very simple means of doing this.

To understand how it works you need to know about **wrapper** classes. For every primitive type, Java provides a corresponding class – the name of the class is similar to the basic type, but begins with a capital letter – for example `Integer`, `Character`, `Float`, `Double`. They are called *wrappers* because they "wrap" a *class* around the basic *type*. So an object of the `Integer` class, for example, holds an integer value. In chapter 10 you will find that these classes also contain some other very useful methods.

Imagine we had created an array of objects as follows:

```
Object[] anArray = new Object[20];
```

One way of storing an integer value such as 37 in this array would be as follows:

```
anArray[0] = new Integer(37);
```

The constructor of the `Integer` class accepts a primitive value and creates the corresponding `Integer` object – here we have created an `Integer` object from the primitive value 37, and this is now stored in the array.

Java 5.0, however, allows us to make use of a technique known as **autoboxing**. This involves the automatic conversion of a primitive type such as an `int` to an object of the appropriate wrapper class. This allows us to do the following:

```
anArray[0] = 37;
```

One way to retrieve this value from this array and assign it to an `int` would be:

```
Integer intObject = (Integer) anArray[0];
int x = intObject.getValue();
```

Notice we need to type cast from `Object` back to `Integer`; the `Integer` class provides a `getValue` method to retrieve the primitive value form the object.

Java 5.0 also allows us to make use of a technique called **unboxing** that converts from the wrapper class back to the primitive type – so the above could be written as:

```
int x = (Integer) anArray[0];
```

8.9 A mixed list

In order to help you to understand some further important concepts connected with inheritance and polymorphism we are going to end this chapter with a final example that makes use of the `Employee` hierarchy developed earlier.

We are going to create an array – and our array is going to hold a *mixture* of different objects at the same time – some full-time employees and some part-time employees.

So, we are going to have an array that at some particular time could look like the one shown in figure 8.6.

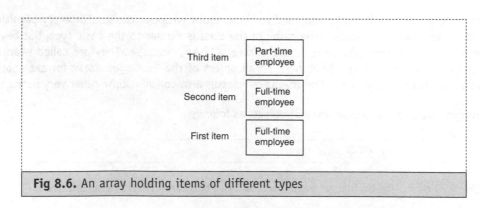

Fig 8.6. An array holding items of different types

Program 8.4 allows a user to create a list like this and test it out by displaying the details of the employee's number, name and status on the screen.

Program 8.4

```java
public class MixedListTester
{
    public static void main(String[] args)
    {
        // declare an array big enough for three employees
        Employee[] employeeList = new Employee[3];
        // declare local variables to hold values entered by user
        String num, name;
        double pay;
        char status;

        // get the user to enter the employees' details
        for(int i = 0; i < employeeList.length; i++)
        {
            System.out.print("Enter the employee number: ");
            num = EasyScanner.nextString();
            System.out.print("Enter the employee's name: ");
            name = EasyScanner.nextString();
            System.out.print("<F>ull-time or <P>art-time? ");
            status = EasyScanner.nextChar();

            if(status == 'f' || status == 'F')
            {
                System.out.print("Enter the annual salary: ");
            }
            else
            {
                System.out.print("Enter the hourly pay: ");
            }
            pay = EasyScanner.nextDouble();

            if(status == 'f' || status == 'F')
            {
                employeeList[i] = new FullTimeEmployee(num, name, pay);
            }
            else
            {
                employeeList[i] = new PartTimeEmployee(num, name, pay);
            }
            System.out.println();
        }
        for(Employee item : employeeList)
        {
            // display employee's number, name, and status
            System.out.println("Employee number: "
                                         + item.getNumber());
            System.out.println("Employee name: "
                                         + item.getName());
            System.out.println("Status: " + item.getStatus());
            System.out.println();
        }
    }
}
```

Let's take a look at what's going on here. We create an array big enough to hold three Employee objects with this line of code:

```java
Employee [] employeeList = new Employee[3];
```

Then, after declaring some local variables, we use a **for** loop to get the user to enter the details of each of the three employees. The first part of the loop therefore looks like this:

```java
for(int i = 0; i < employeeList.length; i++)
{
    System.out.print("Enter the employee number: ");
    num = EasyScanner.nextString();
    System.out.print("Enter the employee's name: ");
    name = EasyScanner.nextString();
    System.out.print("<F>ull-time or <P>art-time? ");
    status = EasyScanner.nextChar();

    if(status == 'f' || status == 'F')
    {
        System.out.print("Enter the annual salary: ");
    }
    else
    {
        System.out.print("Enter the hourly pay: ");
    }
    pay = EasyScanner.nextDouble();
```

Notice that once we have established whether the employee is full- or part-time we are able to choose the appropriate message requesting the employee's pay (annual salary for a full-time employee, hourly pay for a part-time employee).

The **for** loop continues and we create our new employee, either full-time or part-time depending on the value of the status variable:

```java
    if(status == 'f' || status == 'F')
    {
        employeeList[i] = new FullTimeEmployee(num, name, pay);
    }
    else
    {
        employeeList[i] = new PartTimeEmployee(num, name, pay);
    }
    System.out.println();
}
```

Now comes the clever bit!

```java
for(Employee item : employeeList)
{
    // display employee's number name, and status
    System.out.println("Employee number: " + item.getNumber());
    System.out.println("Employee name: " + item.getName());
    System.out.println("Status: " + item.getStatus());
    System.out.println();
}
```

We are navigating through the array and, by calling on the getNumber, getName and getStatus method of each object, we are displaying the number, name and status of each employee. And the clever thing is that the correct status is displayed, even though we didn't decide on the status of the employee until the program was run! Here is a sample test run:

Enter the employee number: **1**

Enter the employee's name: **Jones**

```
<F>ull-time or <P>art-time? f
Enter the annual salary: 30000


Enter the employee number: 2
Enter the employee's name: Agdeboye
<F>ull-time or <P>art-time? f
Enter the annual salary: 35000


Enter the employee number: 3
Enter the employee's name: Sharma
<F>ull-time or <P>art-time? p
Enter the hourly pay: 15


Employee number: 1
Employee name: Jones
Status: Full-Time

Employee number: 2
Employee name: Agdeboye
Status: Full-Time

Employee number: 3
Employee name: Sharma
Status: Part-Time
```

You will remember that the getStatus method was *overridden* in each subclass, so that when a message is sent to a FullTimeEmployee object requesting its status, the string "Full-Time" is returned, whereas in the case of a PartTimeEmployee object the string "Part-Time" is returned. As we navigate through the array the appropriate message is returned depending on the type of employee stored at each location.

Notice that there is one thing we did not do in our example – we didn't display the employee's pay; to do this we would have to use a method that was specific to one of the two employee types: getAnnualSalary in the case of a full-time employee and getHourlyPay in the case of a part-time employee. We would need, therefore, to type cast back to the appropriate employee type – we could use the getStatus method in order to determine which type of employee we are dealing with and type cast accordingly. This is left as a practical exercise.

Self-test questions

1 Explain the meaning of the term *inheritance*.

2 How is inheritance indicated in a UML class diagram?

3 Which keyword in Java is used to declare one class as a subclass of another class?

4 Distinguish between *method overriding* and *method overloading*.

5 Explain the term *type cast* and describe how type casting is implemented in Java.

6 Explain the use of the **abstract** modifier, and the **final** modifier, when applied to both classes and methods.

Programming exercises

1 Implement the `ExtendedOblong` class, together with program 8.2, the `ExtendedOblongTester`. You will, of course, need to ensure that the `Oblong` class itself is accessible to the compiler.

2 a) A class called `Vehicle` is required by a programmer who is writing software for a car dealer. An object of the class `Vehicle` will consist of a registration number, the make of the vehicle, the year of manufacture and the current value of the vehicle. The first three of these will need to be set only at the time an object is created. The current value will also be set at the time of creation, but may need to be changed during the vehicle's lifetime.

It will be necessary to have a means of reading the values of all the above data items. A method should also be provided which accepts a year as input, and returns the age of the vehicle.

The UML class diagram for `Vehicle` is shown below:

Vehicle
regNo : String make : String year : int value : double
Vehicle(String, String, int, double) getRegNo() : String getMake() : String getYear() : int getValue() : double setValue(double) calculateAge(int) : int

Write the code for the `Vehicle` class.

b) A subclass of `Vehicle` called `SecondHandVehicle` is required. The subclass will have an additional attribute, `numberOfOwners`, which will need to be set at the time a new vehicle is created, and will also need to have read access. It will also have an additional method that will report on whether or not the vehicle has had more than one previous owner. The UML class diagram for SecondHandVehicle is shown below:

SecondHandVehicle
numberOfOwners : int
SecondHandVehicle(String, String, int, double, int) *getNumberOfOwners() : int* *hasMultipleOwners() : boolean*

Write the code for the SecondHandVehicle class.

c) Write a tester class that tests all the methods of the SecondHandVehicle class.

3 Adapt program 8.4 so that it displays the employee's pay – this will be the annual salary if it was a full-time employee or the hourly pay if it was a part-time employee. You may need to re-read the whole of section 8.9 in order to do this.

4 a) Write a collection class that will hold a number of vehicle objects (as defined in exercise 2), and will provide methods to add and delete vehicles, and to return a vehicle at a particular position in the list.

b) Write a menu-driven program that uses the collection class to hold Vehicles. The menu should offer the following options:

```
1. Add a vehicle
2. Display a list of vehicle details
3. Delete a vehicle
4. Quit
```

c) Re-read section 8.9, then see if you can adapt your application so that it can keep records of second hand vehicles as well as regular vehicles. You will need to think about type casting, and also need to provide the Vehicle class with a method similar to the getStatus method of the Employee class that helps you to distinguish between new vehicles and second-hand vehicles.

CHAPTER: 09

Software quality

Objectives:

By the end of this chapter you should be able to:

- *describe each stage of the software development process;*
- *document your code so that it is easy to **maintain**;*
- *distinguish between **compile-time errors** and **run-time errors**;*
- *test a program using the strategies of **unit testing** and **integration testing**;*
- *generate test data using the strategies of **black box testing**, **white box testing** and **stress testing**;*
- *document your test results professionally using a **test log**;*
- *format your output to improve the **usability** of your programs.*

9.1 Introduction

If you buy a new computer, you will probably want that computer to be of a high quality. The features you would expect to find in a computer of high quality would be that it is fast, it has a large storage capacity, it supports the latest graphic and sound features – you may be able to think of others. Similarly, if you buy a piece of software you would want that software to be produced to a high quality. But what does it mean for software to be of a high quality? How can you measure software quality?

There are many desirable features of a piece of software. In this chapter we will concentrate on the following:

> maintainability;

> reliability;

> robustness;

> usability.

The more the software exhibits these features, the greater is the **quality** of the software. Quality is not a feature that can be bolted-on at the end of a software project. It needs to be borne in mind at every stage of software production. So, before we look at each of these quality features in turn, let us first look at how software is actually produced in industry.

9.2 Developing software

The way that software is developed has begun to change over the past decade or so – until then the method was for software developers to go through a number of phases and complete each of these before moving on to the next. It was then necessary to go back one, two or more phases to make corrections. The first phase consisted of **analysis and specification**, the process of determining what the system was required to do (analysis) and writing it down in a clear and unambiguous manner (specification). The next phase was **design**; this phase consisted of making decisions about how the system would be built in order to meet the specification. After this came **implementation**, at which point the design was turned into an actual program. This was followed by the **testing** phase. When testing was complete the system would be **installed** and a period of **operation and maintenance** followed, whereby the system was improved, and if necessary changed to meet changing requirements. This approach to software development (often called the **waterfall model**) is summarized in figure 9.1.

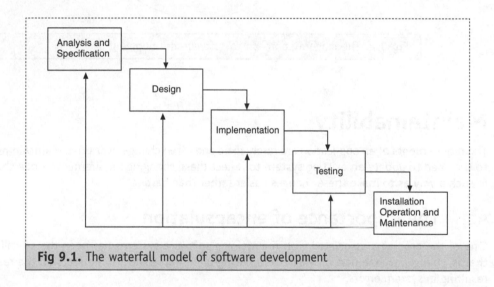

Fig 9.1. The waterfall model of software development

One problem with this approach was that it often meant that customers had to wait a very long time before they actually saw the product. Another problem was that in practice software produced in this way was actually very difficult to adapt to changing needs. Consider, for example, the infamous software problem associated with the change from 20th-century dates to 21st-century dates in the year 2000 (more commonly known as the Y2K problem).

Nowadays it is common to use the RAD approach; this stands for **rapid application development**. The RAD approach involves doing the activities described above a "little bit at a time"; in this way we build **proto-types** of the product and the potential user can be actively involved in testing them out and rebuilding until we eventually end up with the best possible product in the most satisfactory time period. The RAD process is summarized in figure 9.2.

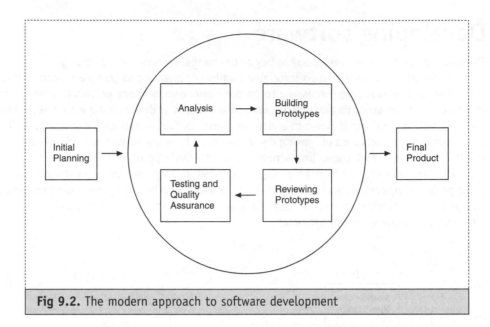

Fig 9.2. The modern approach to software development

9.3 Maintainability

The requirements of an application are rarely fixed and often change over time. **Maintaining** a system refers to the need to *update* an existing system to reflect these changing requirements. Code should be designed in such a way as to make these changes easier rather than harder.

9.3.1 The importance of encapsulation

One of the problems associated with maintaining software systems has been the so-called **ripple effect**: that is, changes to one part of the system having undesirable knock-on effects on the rest of the system, resulting in system errors.

Such effects can often be hard to detect and to trace. As we discussed in chapter 6, programs written in the old structured way can often lead to such ripple effects. The object-oriented principle of *encapsulation*, however, helps ensure that object-oriented code is easier to maintain by reducing such effects: each object should contain within it all the details it needs to do its job, and this data should be hidden inside the object so that changes made to it do not affect the rest of the system.

Java is a pure object-oriented language so programs written in Java should be easier to maintain than their structured counterparts. However, the language does not *insist* that you follow the principles of encapsulation when developing your code – that is your responsibility!

In particular, a class could be defined so that its data members are accessible to any other class – thus breaking the principles of encapsulation. Any future changes to such data would require changes to each method that accessed this data directly, resulting once again in the ripple effects you should aim to avoid. The lesson is a simple one – to ensure that your applications are easy to maintain, keep the data attributes of your classes `private`.

9.3.2 Documentation

A complete software system consists of more than just the final program. For example, most applications that you buy will come with some kind of user manual. Additional supporting materials such as these are referred to as the system's **documentation**. A comprehensive system should have documentation supporting *every* activity in the software development process. The user manual is an example of a piece of documentation that supports software installation and operation.

For a software system to be easy to maintain, the software *design* also needs to be clearly documented. Often, the people responsible for maintaining a software system are not necessarily the same people who initially developed the system. This was often the case with the Y2K problem. Many of the systems affected were decades old and the identity of the original developers was no longer known. Design documentation helps new developers understand the working of systems that they themselves may not have produced. When developing object-oriented programs, this design documentation should include:

> complete class diagrams;

> clear method definitions (parameter and return types, plus pseudocode when appropriate).

The UML notation that we have been using throughout this book is becoming a common way of expressing these design decisions. The layout of the code itself can help clarify design decisions and make code maintenance easier.

To understand how important in-code documentation like this can be, consider the two classes below: `BadReactor` and `Reactor`. Both classes keep track of the temperature within a reactor in exactly the same way except that one has been documented with care, while the other has been documented poorly. If you were asked to maintain this system so that the maximum safe temperature was to be reduced by two degrees, which class would you find easier to understand and modify?

The *BadReactor* class is very poorly documented

```
public class BadReactor
{
private int t;
public BadReactor()
{
t = 0;
}
public int getValue (){
return t;
}
public boolean increase(){
boolean b;
if (t < 10)
{t++;
 b = false;
}
else
{
t = 0;
b = true;
}
return b;
}
}
```

The *Reactor* class has been documented with care

```java
/* This class controls reactor temperature ensuring it does not go over
some maximum  */

public class Reactor
{
    public static final int MAX=10; // set maximum temperature
    private int temperature;

    public Reactor()
    {
        temperature = 0; // set initial level
    }

    public int getTemperature ()
    {    // return current level
        return temperature;
    }

    public boolean increaseTemp()
    {    /* increase temperature if safe -
        drop to zero and raise alarm if not */
        boolean alarm;
        if (temperature < MAX)
        {
            temperature ++;
            alarm = false ;
        }
        else
        {
            temperature = 0;
            alarm = true;
        }
        return alarm;
    }
}
```

Notice that the maximum temperature is fixed as a constant value in this class. This makes sense as this maximum value is fixed during the life of an object. Should this maximum value need to change in the future, all that needs to happen is for this constant value to be modified.

We have already shown you how to create constant values in chapter 1 by means of the **final** keyword. If we wish an attribute of a class to be a constant, it also makes sense to make this a **static** attribute, as its value is the same for all objects of the class:

```java
public static final int MAX=10;
```

Notice also that, since this value cannot be changed, it does no harm to make this attribute **public**.

```java
public static final int MAX=10;
```

The maximum temperature is useful information and making this attribute **public** gives easy access to this information (as we shall see later in this chapter).

When writing in-code documentation you should always include the following:

›   comments to make the meaning of your code clear;

> meaningful data names;

> constants in place of fixed literal numbers;

> consistent and clear indentation.

Look at the example programs that we have presented to you and notice how we have tried to stick to these principles throughout this book. In particular, notice the care we have taken with our indentation. We are following two simple rules all the time:

> keep braces lined up under the structure to which they belong;

> indent, by one level, all code that belongs within those braces.

For example, look back at the `increaseTemp` method of the `Reactor` class.

```
public boolean increaseTemp ()
{   /*increase temperature if safe -
    drop to zero and raise alarm if not */
    boolean alarm;
    if temperature < MAX)
    {
        temperature ++;
        alarm = false ;
    }
    else
    {
        temperature = 0;
        alarm = true;
    }
    return alarm;
}
```

matching opening and closing braces

code within braces indented

Notice how these rules are applied again with the braces of the inner **if** and **else** statements:

```
if temperature < MAX)
{
    temperature ++;
    alarm = false ;
}
```

matching opening and closing braces lined up

code within braces indented

Also, if you look back at the `Reactor` class you can see that the careful choice of variable names greatly reduces the need for comments. Always attempt to make the code as self-documenting as possible by choosing meaningful names.

9.3.3 Javadoc

Sun's Java Development Kit contains, amongst other things, full documentation (in the form of HTML files) for all the predefined Java classes. This documentation is an excellent source of information, where each class is provided with a full class description and a detailed description of every method provided by that class. For example, figure 9.3 shows some of the documentation provided for the `String` class.

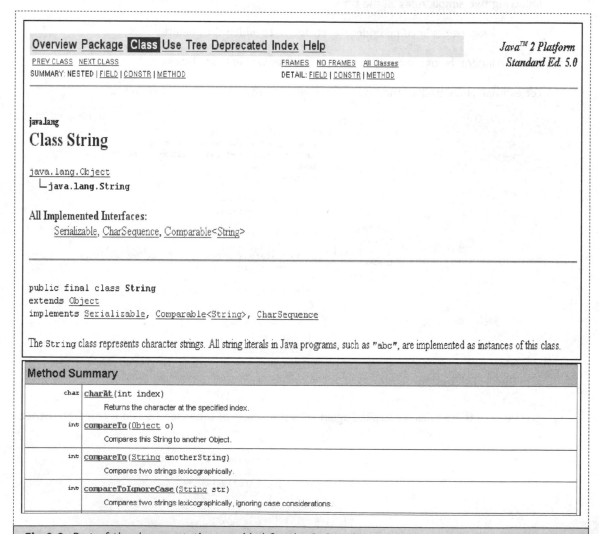

Fig 9.3. Part of the documentation provided for the String class

Sun's Java Development Kit contains a tool, `Javadoc`, that allows you to generate similar documentation for classes that you write yourself. In order to use this tool you must comment your classes in the `Javadoc` style. As we mentioned in chapter 1, `Javadoc` comments must begin with /** and end with */. So, for example, we could turn our opening comment for the `Reactor` class into a `Javadoc` comment as follows:

```
/** This class controls reactor temperature ensuring it does not go over
    some maximum
 */
public class Reactor
{
    // as before
}
```

If you wish, you may begin each new line with a leading asterisk. In fact, it is common practice to include such leading asterisks.

```
/** This class controls reactor temperature ensuring it does not go over
 *    some maximum
 */
public class Reactor
{
    // as before
}
```

Javadoc comments can also contain 'tags'. Tags are special formatting markers that allow you to record information such as the author of a piece of code. Table 9.1 gives some commonly used tags in Javadoc comments:

Table 9.1 Some Javadoc tags	
Tag	Information
@author	the name(s) of the code author(s)
@version	a version number for the code (often a date is used here)
@param	the name of a parameter and its description
@return	a description of the return value

The @author and @version tags are used in the Javadoc comment for the class itself. The @param and @return tags are used in Javadoc comments preceding each method. Below is the Reactor class amended to include some Javadoc comments.

Reactor class with Javadoc comments included

```
/** This class controls a reactors temperature
 *    ensuring it does not go over some maximum
 *    @author Charatan and Kans
 *    @version 14th August 2005
 */

public class Reactor
{
    public static final int MAX=10;
    private int temperature;

    /** Constructor initialises temperature to zero */
    public Reactor()
    {
        temperature = 0;
```

```
    }

    /** Reads the current temperature
     * @return Returns the value of the reactor's current temperature
     */
    public int getTemperature ()
    {
        return temperature;
    }

    /** Increases temperature if safe to do so
     * drop to zero and raise alarm if not
     * @return Returns true if an attempt is made to raise temperature
     *         above MAX and false otherwise
     */
    public boolean increaseTemp()
    {
        boolean alarm;
        if (temperature < MAX)
        {
            temperature ++;
            alarm = false ;
        }
        else
        {
            temperature = 0;
            alarm = true;
        }
        return alarm;
    }
}
```

Notice that the class comment must directly precede the class and method comments must directly precede the relevant method. The Javadoc HTML documentation files can then be generated either from the command line using the **javadoc** command:

javadoc Reactor.java

or invoked directly by your IDE. Figure 9.4 gives part of the documentation generated for the Reactor class:

Fig 9.4. Javadoc documentation generated for the 'Reactor' class

For professional projects it is recommended that you use this `Javadoc` method of commenting your classes. We shall return to it in our two case studies in this book.

9.4 Reliability

A **reliable** program is one that does what it is supposed to do, in other words what it is *specified* to do. When attempting to build a program, two kinds of errors could occur:

> compile-time errors;

> run-time errors.

As the name implies, **compile-time errors** occur during the process of compilation. Such errors would mean you could not run your program at all as you have not followed the rules of the language to construct a valid program. Examples of these kinds of mistakes in Java include:

> missing semi-colons;

> forgetting to close a bracket;

> being inconsistent with names and/or types;

> attempting to access a variable/object without having first initialized it.

Most Java compilers work very hard in this respect as they trap many errors that many other language compilers do not check for: ensuring that you haven't attempted to access an uninitialized variable being one example. You should become familiar with messages associated with certain kinds of errors, in order to find and fix them quickly. Often, a single mistake can cause the compiler to get confused and produce a long list of errors. Rather than attempting to fix them all, fix the first and then recompile.

Look at the program and associated error list in figure 9.5. Although there appear to be many errors, there is in fact just one. Can you spot it?

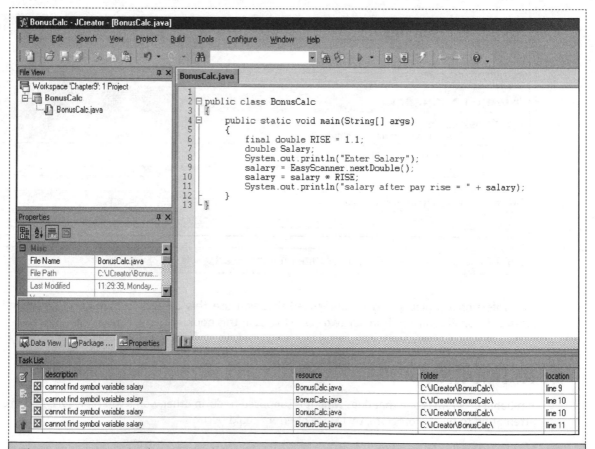

Fig 9.5. A simple mistake may result in many error messages

The only error in the code of figure 9.5 is that the variable `salary`, referenced at many points in the code, was named `Salary` (note a capital 'S') when declared.

```
double Salary; // notice capital letter
salary = EasyScanner.nextDouble(); // will result in compiler error
// more references to 'salary' here causing further compiler errors
```

All these errors can be removed by re-declaring this variable as follows:

```
double salary;
```

If you have no compilation errors then you can begin to think about testing your program in order to ensure that it does what it is supposed to do.

It is important to understand that testing can never show the *absence* of errors, only the *presence* of them. The aim therefore of any testing strategy is to uncover these errors. A program may not do what it is supposed to do either because the original requirements were not precise enough or because the programmer has made logical errors in the program, or both. Either way the final program will contain defects. This leads to two areas of testing:

> **validation** (making sure you are building the right product);

> **verification** (making sure you are building the product right).

Validation is a process of ensuring that your final system meets *the user's* requirements. This is an important process as developers often misjudge the original requirements given to them by clients. This may be because the requirements were not expressed clearly to begin with, or the clients were not sure themselves of the exact needs of the final system. Either way, validation will obviously require the interaction of the client. The RAD approach to software development, which we mentioned earlier, allows systems to be developed incrementally by means of regular validation.

Verification is a process of ensuring that the code you develop meets *your own* understanding of the user requirements. This will involve running your application in order to trap errors you may have made in program logic. A Java application typically consists of many classes working together. Testing for such errors will start with a process of **unit testing** (testing individual classes) followed by **integration testing** (testing classes that together make up an application).

9.4.1 Unit testing

Let's look at the `Reactor` class from section 9.3 as our first example. Before incorporating this class into a larger program you would want to run it in order to test if it was working reliably. This class as it stands, however, cannot be run as it has no `main` method in it.

All applications require a class with a `main` method before they can be run. Eventually, when this class is incorporated into a larger program a suitable class with a `main` method will exist, but you'll want to test this class before an entire suite of classes have been developed. One possibility would be to add a `main` method into *this* class.

While some people do take this approach, we feel it clutters up the original class and mistakes could inadvertently be typed into the original class. For this reason we prefer to take the alternative approach of writing a separate class especially to contain the `main` method. This new class then acts as the **driver** for the original class. A driver is a special program designed to do nothing except exercise a particular class. If you look back at all our previous examples, this is exactly how we tested individual classes. When testing classes in this way, *every method* of the class should be tested. Program 9.1 is an example of a driver for the `Reactor` class.

Program 9.1

```java
public class ReactorTester
{
    // define main method
    public static void main(String[] args)
    {
        char reply;
        Reactor b = new Reactor(); // generate object to test
        do
        { // test all methods
            System.out.print("current temperature is ");
            System.out.println(b.getTemperature());
            boolean error = b.increaseTemp();
            if (error) // check if increase raised an error
            {
                System.out.println("warning: alarm raised");
                System.out.println("MAXIMUM temperature: "+ Reactor.MAX);
            }
            System.out.println("temperature after increase is ");
            System.out.println(b.getTemperature());
            System.out.print("test some more (y/n)? ");
            reply = EasyScanner.nextChar();
        } while (reply != 'n'); // loop until user quits
    }
}
```

Notice how the class constant MAX was used to produce useful information in the error messages:

```java
System.out.println("MAXIMUM temperature: "+ Reactor.MAX);
```

At the moment the methods are tested in strict sequence. The usability of this driver can be improved by, for example, including a menu system to test each method. We shall return to issues that affect the usability of programs later on in this chapter.

Let's continue our discussion of unit testing by turning our attention to the `StudentList` class that we asked you to develop as an end of chapter task in chapter 7. The procedure for testing an individual class requires a bit more thought if that class *relies upon another class* that is yet to be developed. In this case the `StudentList` class requires the `Student` class to be available.

```java
public class StudentList
{
    private Student[] list; // requires access to Student class
    // more attributes and methods of StudentList written here
}
```

If you were developing the `StudentList` class, you may not have the `Student` class available to you, either because you had not yet developed it or because it was not your responsibility to develop it. It would be impossible, however, to proceed with your class development if you did not know what to expect of the classes you were relying on. The following information on the class you are relying upon is essential before you can start constructing your own class:

> the name of the class;

> the name of the methods;

> the interface (return type and parameter list) of each method.

All this information should already have been recorded in the detailed design documentation for the application you are developing (see figure 9.6).

If you need to unit test a given class that relies upon the development of another class to which you do not have access, you can develop your own **dummy** class in place of the missing class. A dummy class is one that mimics an actual class in order for testing to proceed.

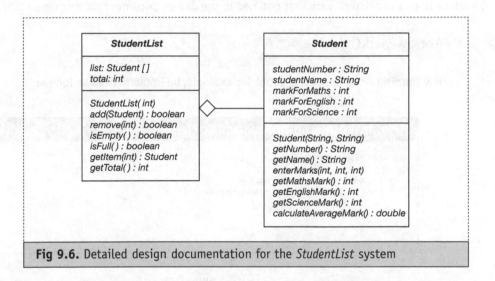

Fig 9.6. Detailed design documentation for the *StudentList* system

Such a class is often much simpler than the class it is mimicking as it only needs to include enough information to allow the given class you are testing to compile and run effectively.

In order to allow this `StudentList` class to compile, an appropriate dummy `Student` class can be developed as follows:

A dummy *Student* class

```
public class Student
{
    // no code in class
}
```

While the `StudentList` class allows `Student` objects to be stored, it does not need to call any of the methods of a `Student` class. For this reason, this dummy `Student` class contains no attributes or methods. If the `StudentList` class accessed any of the methods of the `Student` class, associated dummy methods would have to be added into the dummy `Student` class in order to allow the `StudentList` class to compile.

For example, consider the situation where there was a findStudentAverage method in the StudentList class as follows:

```java
public double findStudentAverage (int i)
{
    return student[i-1].calculateAverageMark();
}
```

Here, the findStudentAverage method of the Studentlist class is calling a method, calculateAverageMark, of the Student class. But our dummy Student class contains no methods! To get around this problem, the dummy Student class would need to be amended so that an implementation existed for the calculateAverageMark method. This implementation should have an interface that is consistent with that outlined in the design documentation of figure 9.6:

calculateAverageMark():double

So the new dummy Student class could, for example, be implemented as follows:

The amended dummy *Student* class

```java
public class Student
{
    // additional dummy method
    public double calculateAverageMark()
    {
        return 50.5;
    }
}
```

The additional dummy method in this case just returns a set mark of 50.5. In the real Student class this may have involved a complicated calculation using many individual unit marks.

Note that with this dummy class in place, a driver class with a main function still needs to be written in order to run this application. Any additional Student methods that this tester class requires (such as a constructor) will have to be added into this dummy class in the form of additional dummy methods.[1] This is left as a practical exercise at the end of this chapter.

9.4.2 Integration testing

When the individual classes in a program have been tested they can be integrated and tested together in order to ensure that the interface between classes is working correctly.

In order to test this interface the whole suite of classes needs to be recompiled together. The reason for this is that the interfaces between classes may be inconsistent. If compiler errors occur during integration then check the following:

---

[1] A particularly useful method to add into a dummy class is a toString method. Objects generated from classes that define such a method can be displayed on the screen in println commands. The toString method returns a String representation of the object attributes. See chapter 14 for more on this method.

> all methods that are called have an implementation in the receiving class;

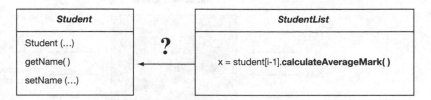

> the names of method calls match **exactly** the names of these methods in the receiving class;

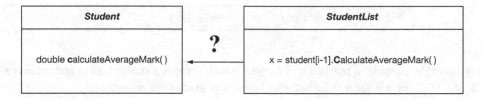

> the parameter list of a method call matches **exactly** the parameter list of these methods in the receiving class;

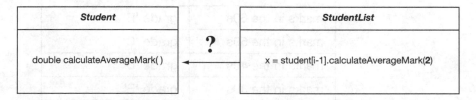

> the expected types of values returned from the method calls match the return types of these methods in the receiving class.

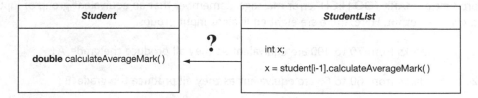

Whether you are carrying out unit testing or integration testing, the choice of test data is crucial in locating defects that may be present in the component. Two common approaches are **black box** and **white box** testing.

9.4.3 Black box testing

Black box testing is an approach to test data generation that treats the component being tested as an opaque box; that is, the details of the code are ignored (see figure 9.7). The specification is used to determine different groups of input values. A group of inputs that all produce the *same output* are regarded as equivalent. In this way inputs can be categorized into **equivalent groups**.

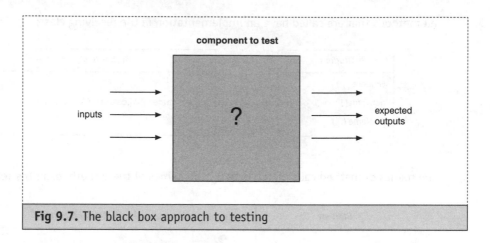

Fig 9.7. The black box approach to testing

For example, consider a method `getGrade`, which accepts a student mark and returns a student grade ('A', 'B', 'C', 'D', 'E' or 'F'). Table 9.2 illustrates how these grades are arrived at.

Table 9.2 Student grades	
marks 70 and above	grade 'A'
marks in the 60s	grade 'B'
marks in the 50s	grade 'C'
marks in the 40s	grade 'D'
marks in the 30s	grade 'E'
marks below 30	grade 'F'

Additionally a mark below 0 will produce a "MARK TOO LOW" error message, and a mark over 100 will produce a "MARK TOO HIGH" error message. Remember that an equivalent group of inputs should produce the same output. Here, there are eight equivalent input groups.

1   marks from 70 to 100 are equivalent as they all produce the grade 'A';

2   marks from 60 to 69 are equivalent as they all produce the grade 'B';

3   marks from 50 to 59 are equivalent as they all produce the grade 'C';

4   marks from 40 to 49 are equivalent as they all produce the grade 'D';

5   marks from 30 to 39 are equivalent as they all produce the grade 'E';

6   marks from 0 to 29 are equivalent as they all produce the grade, 'F';

7   marks below 0 are equivalent as they all produce a "MARK TOO LOW" error message;

8   marks above 100 are equivalent as they all produce a "MARK TOO HIGH" error message.

When testing this method you should test *at least one mark* from each equivalent group. Figure 9.8 illustrates one possible set of test data generated in this way.

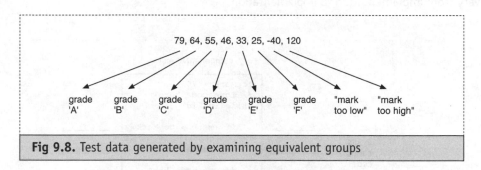

79, 64, 55, 46, 33, 25, -40, 120

grade 'A'   grade 'B'   grade 'C'   grade 'D'   grade 'E'   grade 'F'   "mark too low"   "mark too high"

Fig 9.8. Test data generated by examining equivalent groups

If a given mark from an equivalent group produces the correct result, you may be tempted to assume that all marks within that group are correct. Remember though that a sample can never *guarantee* that all test cases are correct, they can just *increase your confidence* that the code is correct.

If the code fails to produce the correct result despite having tested a sample from each equivalent group, often the error lies on the boundaries of such equivalent groups. The marks 69, 70 and 71, for example, lie around the boundary between the grade 'A' group of marks and the grade 'B' group of marks.

Therefore, in addition to taking sample test cases from each equivalent group, the boundary values in particular should be tested. In this case the following boundary values should all be tested as well as the sample from each equivalent group identified earlier:

−1, 0, 1, 29, 30, 31, 39, 40, 41, 49, 50, 51, 59, 60, 61, 69, 70, 71, 99, 100, 101

If your test cases include a sample from each equivalent group of inputs and all those values that lie on the boundary of those inputs, you are fairly likely to locate any errors that you may have in your code.

9.4.4 White box testing

White box testing is a test generation strategy that treats a software component like a transparent box into which test designers can peek while designing a test case.

Test designers can take advantage of their knowledge of the component's implementation in order to design tests that will cover all possible paths of execution through the component (see figure 9.9). You can see in figure 9.9 that a `while` loop is being used, so tests should be generated to allow the `while` loop to be executed:

> zero times;

> once;

> more than once.

Inside the loop there is a series of `if` statements; test cases should be selected so that:

> each `if` condition is executed;

> each `else` condition is executed.

Note that the test cases you use following a black box approach will be the same whatever implementation you have arrived at for your component, but the test cases produced as a result of white box testing may vary from implementation to implementation.

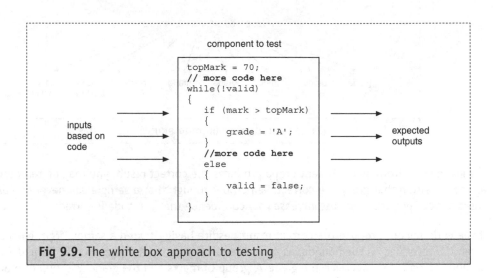

Fig 9.9. The white box approach to testing

9.4.5 **The test log**

Once a strategy is chosen, the test results should be logged in a **test log**. A test log is a document that records the testing that took place during system development.

Each test case associates an *input* with an *expected output*. The aim of the test is to find a case where the expected output is *not produced*. When such a case is found the reasons for the error have to be identified. A test log needs to record the action associated with entering a given input, the expected result of that action and then the outcome (pass or fail). If the output is not as expected, reasons for this error have to be identified and recorded in the log. Figure 9.10 illustrates a typical test log used to document the testing of the `StudentList` class.

TEST LOG			
Purpose: To test the STUDENTLIST class			
Run Number: 1	Date: 25th August 2005		
Action	Expected Output	Pass/ Fail	Reason for failure
Add student ("Ade")	message "student entered"	✓	
set mark to 69	no message expected	✓	
get grade	'B'	✓	
Add student ("Madhu")	message "student entered"	✓	
set mark to 70	no message expected	✓	
get grade	'A'	✗	Displays 'B' instead of 'A'. Due to error in if statement
other tests			

Fig 9.10. A test log is used to document the testing process

The test log indicates that an error has been identified when an incorrect grade is displayed. In such a case the reason for the error is investigated and logged. The error has been caused by an incorrect `if` statement as follows:

```
if (mark > topMark)
{
        grade = 'A';
}
```

This will not produce a PASS when the mark is *exactly* 70 (the value of `topMark`). Here is one way to fix the error:

```
if (mark > topMark-1)
{
        grade = 'A';
}
```

Now a mark of 70 would produce an 'A' grade. As soon as an error is encountered the test run is stopped while the error is fixed. When an amendment has been made to your code, *all* the test cases need to be re-executed. The reason for this is that modifications to your code could cause an error where previously there was no error. For example, if we had used real numbers to store marks, the above modification would produce a grade 'A' for a mark of 69.4 where previously it had accurately displayed this to be a grade 'B' mark.

This form of testing is known as **regression testing**. A new test log is filled in each time a program is run. Figure 9.11 illustrates test run number 2.

You may need a number of test runs before you clear all errors. Your test documentation should include *all* these test runs.

TEST LOG			
Purpose: To test the STUDENTLIST class			
Run Number: 2	Date: 25th August 2005		
Action	Expected Output	Pass/ Fail	Reason for failure
Add student ("Ade")	message "student entered"	✓	
set mark to 69	no message expected	✓	
get grade	'A'	✓	
set mark to 70	no message expected	✓	
get grade	'B'		
other tests			
:			

Fig 9.11. The testing process may involve many test runs

9.5 Robustness

A program is said to **crash** when it terminates unexpectedly. A **robust** program is one that doesn't crash even if it receives unexpected input values. For instance, if you were playing a computer game that allowed you to move falling blocks left or right using the arrow keys on your keyboard, you wouldn't want that game to suddenly stop if you hit the wrong key!

In chapter 3 we introduced you to the idea of *input validation* to deal with such unexpected values. Generally, whenever a value is received to be processed, it should be checked before processing continues, in case such a value could cause the program to crash. This is not only the case when the user enters a value, but also when a method receives a value as a parameter.

As an example, consider a car showroom that employs two sales staff. Each week, the number of cars sold for each employee is recorded and bonus payments are calculated.

A class, `SalesStaff`, has been developed for this purpose as follows:

The *SalesStaff* class

```
public class SalesStaff
{
    public static final int MAX = 2; // maximum number of staff
    private int[] staff; // to hold weekly sales figures for staff
    private double bonus;

    public SalesStaff(double bonusIn) // parameter to set bonus rate
    {
        staff = new int[MAX]; // create array
        for (int i = 0; i<staff.length;i++)
        {
            staff[i] = 0; // set figures to zero
        }
        bonus = bonusIn;
    }

    // method allows a sales figure for a given salesperson to be set
    public void setFigure(int numberIn, int valueIn)
    {    // remember array indices begin at zero
        staff[numberIn-1] = valueIn;
    }

    // method to calculate bonus
    public double getBonus(int numberIn)
    {
        return (staff[numberIn-1]*bonus);
    }
}
```

Notice once again the use of a class constant, MAX. As it stands, this class is not particularly robust. For example, look again at the `setFigure` method:

```
public void setFigure(int numberIn, int valueIn)
{
    staff[numberIn-1] = valueIn;
}
```

Can you see why this method might cause a program to crash? Well, the reason that this method could cause the program to crash is because it uses the value of one of the parameters, `numberIn`, to access an element within the array attribute, `staff`.

```
public void setFigure (int numberIn, int valueIn)
{

    staff[numberIn-1] = valueIn;

}
```

If you look back at the `SalesStaff` class you will see that this is an array with just two elements indexed, therefore, from 0 to 1. Any attempt to access an element at index 2, for example, would be an error and would cause your program to crash. To illustrate this, program 9.2 is a simple driver written to push the `SalesStaff` class to its limits.

Program 9.2

```
public class PushToLimitSalesStaff
{
 public static void main(String[] args)
 {
    int value;
    double bonus;
    char reply; // to hold user response
    System.out.println("Bonus paid for each car sold ? ");
    bonus = EasyScanner.nextDouble();
    SalesStaff cars4U = new SalesStaff(bonus); // create object
    // loop to fill up list
    int i = 0; // counter to keep track of number of items entered
    do // use 'do while' loop to control data entry
    {
        i++; // increment counter
        System.out.println ("enter sales for employee "+ i);
        value = EasyScanner.nextInt();
        cars4U.setFigure(i, value);
        System.out.println("enter more? (y,n)");
        reply = EasyScanner.nextChar();
    }while(reply=='y' || reply=='Y'); // check user response

    // display bonuses

    // to display results use a standard 'for' loop
    for(int j=1; j<=SalesStaff.MAX; j++)
    {
        System.out.print("bonus for employee " + j + " = ");
        System.out.println(cars4U.getBonus(j));
    }
 }
}
```

At the end of each repetition of the **do...while** loop, the user is asked whether they would like another repetition of the loop. This allows the user to control exactly how many values are entered. We will use this tester to add as many values as possible into the array within the `SalesStaff` object. This form of testing, where you push a component to its limits (fill up the array in this case), is referred to as **stress testing**. If you were to run this driver, the program would crash as an attempt is made to enter a third value into an array that can only hold two values (see figure 9.12).

As mentioned in chapter 5, when the program crashes it throws out the following error message explaining the reason for the crash:

```
java.lang.ArrayIndexOutOfBoundsException: 2
```

As you can see, the error message is quite descriptive: it's telling you that there is a problem with the *array index*. Also the offending array index (2) is displayed. In Java this type of error is referred to as an **exception** as it is a situation that is out of the norm. The Java system is aware of many exceptional circumstances that can occur during the life of a program and, should such an error occur, the correct exception is reported. This process of reporting an exception is known as **throwing an exception**.

In Java, one way of dealing with an exception when it is thrown is to **catch** it before it causes any damage. However, the details of how you carry this out are a bit too complex for your first semester; so we will return to it in chapter 15. For now, you should write your code so that the program does not throw such an exception in the first place. In this case you would need to ensure that an array index is valid before you use it.

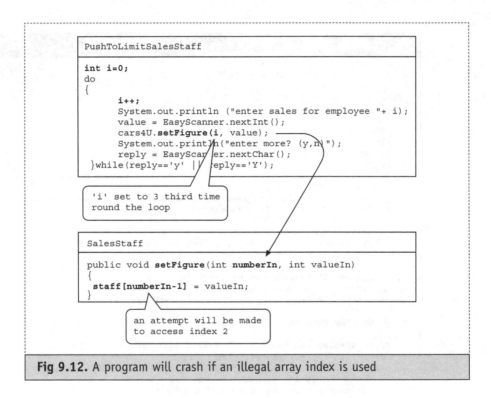

Fig 9.12. A program will crash if an illegal array index is used

It would be a good idea for the `setFigure` method to check the value of the parameter, which it could do as follows:

```
public void setFigure(int numberIn, int valueIn)
{    // check index will be valid before accessing array
    if (numberIn <= staff.length)
    {
        staff[numberIn-1] = valueIn;
    }
}
```

Now, the array access is protected inside an **if** statement. This is better as the program will no longer crash when an attempt is made to access array indices greater than 1. However, the problem is that the caller of this method would have no idea that the given sales figure was not entered.

We can get around this by sending back a **boolean** value indicating success or failure of the method as follows:

```
public boolean setFigure(int numberIn, int valueIn)
{
    if (numberIn <= staff.length)
    {
        staff[numberIn-1] = valueIn;
        return true; // method successful
    }
    else
    {
        return false; // method unsuccessful
    }
}
```

The user of this method is then free to check the value returned and take appropriate action. For example, back in the `PushToLimitSalesStaff` driver, the following amendment could be made:

```
// increment counter as before
i++;
// get input as before
System.out.println ("enter sales for employee "+ i);
value = EasyScanner.nextInt();
// store boolean return value when calling the 'setFigure' method
boolean ok = cars4U.setFigure(i, value);
// check return value to see if figure was added successfully or not
if (!ok)
{
    // some error handling here
}
else
{
    // proceed as normal here
}
```

These changes will no longer cause the `setFigure` method of `SalesStaff` to lead to a program crash and will inform the caller of any problems.

9.6 Usability

The **usability** of a program refers to the ease with which users of your application can interact with your program. A program that crashes all the time when receiving unexpected inputs is far from usable, so one way of ensuring that your program is easy to use is to make sure that it is robust. A user manual can also help make your programs easier to follow. The manual forms another important part of the documentation of your system. Such a manual could include:

> details of how to install your application;

> details of how to use your application once installed;

> a troubleshooting section where common errors that users are likely to make are identified and their solutions given.

Many applications today simply have the first of these in printed form so that the application can be installed. All additional information is then provided within the application in the form of help files. Figure 9.13, for example, illustrates the user documentation built into the JCreator IDE.

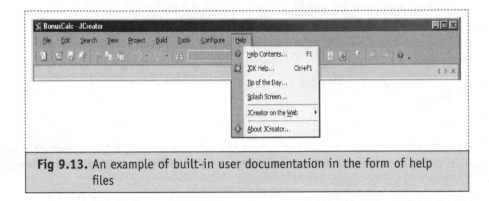

Fig 9.13. An example of built-in user documentation in the form of help files

When designing your programs, you too could think about including user advice in the form of help screens. Eventually we will see how to develop graphical interfaces such as the one given in figure 9.13. Until then, one way of adding such help files into the types of programs that we have developed so far is to include a HELP option on a menu screen. Menu-based systems offer a much more friendly way of interacting with a user than a simple series of prompts.

As an example, let's go back and look at program 9.1 (the driver for the `Reactor` class). We said at the time that this driver wasn't as user-friendly as it could be. Here is a sample test run of the driver as it was originally written to explain what we mean:

current temperature is 0

temperature after increase is 1

test some more (y/n)? **y**

current temperature is 1

temperature after increase is 2

test some more (y/n)? **y**

current temperature is 2

temperature after increase is 3

test some more (y/n)? **n**

Not very exciting, is it? Apart from the fact that this interface doesn't *look* very interesting, it's also very rigid. For example, if we wanted to add in some HELP information (to include details of what happens when an attempt is made to increase the reactor temperature above the maximum), where would we add this? Maybe we could include it at the beginning of the program, but then what if the user needs some help later on in the program? Would we have to keep offering help at every stage? By using a menu system, much of this rigidity can be removed. Here is an example of one possible menu interface for the program:

```
*** REACTOR SYSTEM ***

[1]  Get current temperature

[2]  Increase temperature

[3]  HELP

[4]  Quit


enter choice [1,2,3,4]: _
```

We've already shown you many examples of such menu-driven programs so you should be able to rewrite program 9.1 yourself to give it such an interface. With this interface the user could now, if he or she chose, increase the temperature *many* times (by repeatedly choosing option 2) and only then decide to get the current temperature (by choosing option 1). Or the user could get the temperature after each increase. The choice is left up to the user – not the program. Also, notice that a HELP option is always available.

Another issue you should think about, when considering the usability of your programs, is the number of actions a user has to carry out in order to achieve a particular task. For example, if the user chooses the 'Quit' option on a menu, adding a further pause in your program and insisting that the user then press the 'Enter' key in order to quit could be quite irritating! As another illustration of this problem let's go back to program 9.2 (the driver for the SalesStaff class). Here is a sample test run, assuming that the alterations discussed in section 9.5 have been made:

```
Bonus paid for each car sold ?

8

enter sales for employee 1

10

enter more? (y,n)

y

enter sales for employee 2

5

enter more? (y,n)

y

enter sales for employee 3

9

ERROR: too many sales figures

There are only 2 sales staff

bonus for employee 1 = 80.0

bonus for employee 2 = 40.0

press <Enter> to quit
```

This interface could do with a title and some line spaces; we'll deal with these issues in a while. For now, look at the error messages that were raised when an attempt was made to enter details of a third employee:

enter sales for employee 3

9

ERROR: too many sales figures

There are only 2 sales staff

As you can see, the error was raised *after* the sales figure (9) had been entered by the user. This entry of the last sales figure was wasted effort for the user as the figure was never used. The reason the user was asked to enter this figure was that the error was detected only after the figure was sent to the `setFigure` method:

```
i++;
System.out.println ("enter sales for employee "+ i);
// value entered before error checking
value = EasyScanner.nextInt();
// method to set figure called
boolean ok = cars4U.setFigure(i, value);
// now error checking is taking place here
if (!ok)
{
    // error messages produced here
}
}
```

The user would probably prefer the error checking to take place *before* he or she enters the sales figure. This can be achieved by checking the maximum number of employees *before* asking the user to enter a sales figure as follows:

```
i++; // increment counter
if (i<= SalesStaff. MAX)// check maximum number of employees not exceeded
{
    // get the figure
    System.out.println ("enter sales for employee "+ i);
    value = EasyScanner.nextInt();
    // can now enter the figure without further error checking
    cars4U.setFigure(i, value);
    // ask if more to enter
    System.out.println("enter more? (y,n)");
    reply = EasyScanner.nextChar();
}
// when counter is too high and cannot enter any more sales figures
else
{
    // produce error message if no more figures to enter
    System.out.print(" ERROR: there are only "+
                        SalesStaff.MAX +" sales staff");
    reply = 'n'; // to stop the loop repeating again
}
```

Notice that, when an error is detected, the variable 'reply' needs to be set to 'n' to stop the **do...while** loop repeating again. Now, here is another sample test run of program 9.2 after this amendment has been made:

Bonus paid for each car sold ?

8

```
enter sales for employee 1
10
enter more? (y,n)
y


enter sales for employee 2
5
enter more? (y,n)
y
ERROR:there are only 2 sales staff
bonus for employee 1 = 80.0
bonus for employee 2 = 40.0
```

As you can see, this time, the user did not need to enter a sales figure for a third employee. The error was raised immediately. In this case it was not necessary to check the error value returned from the setFigure method, as we ensured the values sent to this method were valid to begin with:

```
// the value of 'i' has already been checked
cars4U.setFigure(i, value);
```

Of course, developers of the SalesStaff class cannot assume that callers of the setFigure method will act as responsibly as we did here, so it is always a good idea for such methods to return error values just in case.

9.6.1 Text formatting

Look back at the test runs for the programs discussed earlier in this chapter. To make such output attractive to users, careful use of space can be extremely useful. For example, the line space between the title and the menu options of the Reactor class tester makes both the title and the options stand out.

In our example programs so far, we've shown you one way to create such space: just use an empty println() command as follows:

```
System.out.println("some output");
System.out.println(); // creates blank line on screen
System.out.println("more output here");
```

The need to add such space is so common that special formatting characters exist in Java to simplify this task. These characters can be added into strings to include such information as "add a new line" and "create a tab space". These special formatting characters are known as **escape sequences**. An escape sequence always consists of a backslash character '\' followed by a special formatting character. For example, we have already seen (in the ExtendedOblong example of chapter 8) that a new line can be forced by embedding the '\n' escape sequence into a string. Below we use '\n' escape sequence to achieve the same blank line result above (we have emboldened the escape sequence).

```
System.out.println("some output\n");
System.out.println("more output here");
```

In fact, escape sequences can be added anywhere in a string; for example, the following command achieves exactly the same result as the two output statements above by embedding the new line commands in the middle of a single string (again we have emboldened them for you).

```
System.out.println("some output\n\nmore output here");
```

Notice that in this case we needed two new-line commands, one new line to print the string over two lines, and the other line break to create a blank line between the two messages.

Table 9.3 lists some useful escape sequences.

Table 9.3 Some useful escape sequences	
\n	add a new line
\t	add a tab space
\"	add a double quote
\'	add a single quote
\\	add a backslash

Notice that an escape sequence is needed to produce a quote, an apostrophe and a backslash as these symbols could otherwise be misinterpreted within strings (for example, a double quote mark might be taken to mean the end of the string).

Careful use of such escape sequences can help in producing output that is clearer and easier to follow.

One other output problem we have come up against, with our sample programs, is the formatting of decimal output. As an illustration of this problem let's go back to program 9.2 (the driver for the SalesStaff class). Here is another sample test run, assuming that the alterations discussed in this chapter have been made:

Bonus paid for each car sold ?

5.3

enter sales for employee 1

9

enter more? (y,n)

y

enter sales for employee 2

4

enter more? (y,n)

y

ERROR:there are only 2 sales staff

bonus for employee 1 = 47.699999999999996

bonus for employee 2 = 21.2

press <Enter> to quit

Look back at the output of the bonus payments. They don't appear the way we would normally expect monetary values to be displayed do they?

Typically, monetary values have two digits after the decimal point. The first bonus payment, however, has *sixteen* digits and the second bonus payment only *one*! You can't blame the Java system for this as it has no idea that these numbers represent monetary values, or how we would like such monetary values to be displayed. Don't worry though, Java has a predefined class, DecimalFormat, that you can use to let the program know how you wish to format the display of particular decimal numbers. This class resides in the java.text package so to access it you need to add the following **import** statement to the top of your program:

```
import java.text.*;
```

Once you have access to this class you can create DecimalFormat objects in your program. These objects can then be used to format decimal numbers for you. As always, you use the **new** operator along with the object constructor to create an object. The DecimalFormat constructor has one parameter, the *format* string. This string instructs the object on how you wish to format a given decimal number. Some of the important elements of such a string are given in table 9.4.

Table 9.4 Special DecimalFormat characters

Character	Meaning
.	insert a decimal point
,	insert a comma
0	display a single digit
#	display a single digit or empty if no digit present

For example, look at the following construction of a DecimalFormat object:

```
DecimalFormat df = new DecimalFormat( "000,000.000");
```

Here the decimal format object, df, that is constructed is being informed how to format any decimal numbers that may be given to it (see figure 9.14).

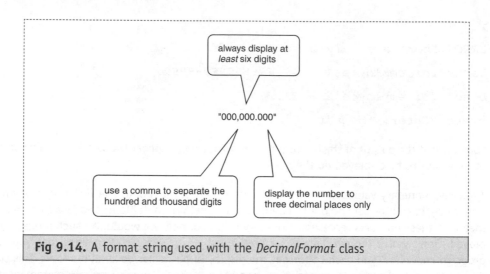

always display at *least* six digits

"000,000.000"

use a comma to separate the hundred and thousand digits

display the number to three decimal places only

Fig 9.14. A format string used with the *DecimalFormat* class

The format string `"000,000.000"` indicates that the number should be truncated to three decimal places, and a comma should be used between the hundred and thousand columns. Also, the number displayed will always have six significant digits (digits to the left of the decimal point) and three digits after.

At the moment we have just created a `DecimalFormat` object and informed it how to format a given decimal number. We haven't given it any number to format. We do this by using the `format` method of the `DecimalFormat` class. For example:

```
DecimalFormat df = new DecimalFormat( "000,000.000");
double someNumber = 12345.6789;
System.out.println("before\t" + someNumber);
System.out.println("after\t" + df.format(someNumber));
```

Since the `format` method returns the formatted number as a `String`, its returned value can be printed directly to the screen with a `System.out` command (notice also the addition of a tab space with `'\t'`). The instructions above would lead to the following values being displayed:

before   `12345.6789`

after   `012,345.679`

As you can see, not only has the number been truncated to three decimal places, but it has also been rounded up. In this case the format string insisted on having six significant digits so the formatted number has a leading zero added.

Replacing a zero in a format string with a hash (#) would mean that the digit was optional, not compulsory.

For example, look at the following piece of code:

```
DecimalFormat df = new DecimalFormat( "#00,000.000");
double someNumber = 12345.6789;
System.out.println("before\t" + someNumber);
System.out.println("after\t" + df.format(someNumber));
```

This would result in the following output:

before   12345.6789

after   12,345.679

In case you are wondering, if the decimal number that was to be formatted had *more* than six significant digits, all the extra digits would automatically be displayed. So, only use zeros for digits you insist on displaying, and use hashes for optional formatting.[2]

Bearing all this in mind, how would you format currency values? Well, such values will always have to be given to two decimal places, and they must all have at least one significant digit, so the following format string is required:

```
DecimalFormat df = new DecimalFormat("0.00");
```

Program 9.3 rewrites the `PushToLimitSalesStaff` driver by including the amendments we discussed in this chapter and improving the text formatting of output.

Program 9.3

```java
import java.text.*; // for DecimalFormat
public class PushToLimitSalesStaff
{
    public static void main(String[] args)
    {
        int value;
        double bonus;
        char reply;
        // title added
        System.out.println("\n\t\t*** BONUS CALCULATOR ***\n\n");
        // set bonus rate
        System.out.print("\t Bonus paid for each car sold ?\t");
        bonus = EasyScanner.nextDouble();
        SalesStaff cars4U = new SalesStaff(bonus);
        // get figures
        int i = 0;
        System.out.print("\n\n\t enter sales figures\n");
        do
        {
            i++;
            if (i<= SalesStaff.MAX)
            {
                System.out.print("\n\t employee "+ i + "\t");
                value = EasyScanner.nextInt();
                cars4U.setFigure(i, value);
                System.out.print("\n\t enter more? (y,n): ");
                reply = EasyScanner.nextChar();
            }
            else
            {
                System.out.println("\n\n\t ERROR:there are only " +
                                    SalesStaff.MAX + " sales staff\n");
                reply = 'n';
            }
        }while (reply == 'Y' || reply =='y');
        // display bonuses
        System.out.print("\n\n\t bonus payments\n\n");
```

[2] There are several other classes in the `java.text` package that provide useful formatting methods. The `NumberFormat` class, for example, contains a `getCurrencyInstance` method that allows you to format a given real number in the currency format of the local country.

```
        for (int j = 1; j<= SalesStaff.MAX; j++)
        {
            // notice the use of DecimalFormat class
            DecimalFormat df = new DecimalFormat( "0.00");
            System.out.print("\t employee " + j + " =\t");
            System.out.println(df.format(cars4U.getBonus(j)));
        }
    }
}
```

Here is a sample test run (we have included an actual screen shot here so that you can fully appreciate the effect of the tab and space formatting).

```
c:\ J:\Win32Apps\JCreatorLE\GE2001.exe

            *** BONUS CALCULATOR ***

    Bonus paid for each car sold ? 5.3

    enter sales figures

    employee 1      9

    enter more? (y,n): y

    employee 2      4

    enter more? (y,n): y


    ERROR:there are only 2 sales staff


    bonus payments

    employee 1 =    47.70
    employee 2 =    21.20
```

Look back at program 9.3 and compare it with this screen shot to see the effect of the various text formatting instructions.

9.6.2 Graphical user interfaces

So far in this book, we haven't talked about how to create visual, graphical interfaces of the type illustrated in figure 9.15. Figure 9.15 is the Print screen from Microsoft's *Word for Windows* application. Such interfaces are often referred to as **GUIs (Graphical User Interfaces)**. Most applications that you buy today include such an interface.

Interfaces like this are by far the friendliest and easiest for users to operate. Up until now we haven't looked at how to develop such interfaces because you had to get to know about the basics of software development in Java first. But, now we have covered these basics with you, we think you are ready! In the next chapter we show you not only how to create such interfaces but also how to use them with your existing classes.

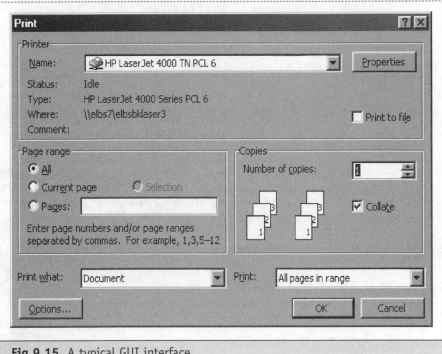

Fig 9.15. A typical GUI interface

Self-test questions

1 Describe each stage of the software development process.

2 Pythagoras's theorem states that, given a right-angled triangle with sides a and b and hypotenuse c, the following condition will always hold:

$$a^2 + b^2 = c^2$$

Consider the following program that attempts to work out the value of c^2 given the values for a and b. The program consists of a main method and two helper methods: one to square the value of a given parameter and the other to calculate the square of the hypotenuse given the values of two sides of a right-angled triangle.

```
public class QualityQ2
{
    public static void main(String[] args)
    {
        double side1, side2;
        System.out.println("Pythagoras Calculator");
        System.out.println("Enter value for side 1 of the triangle");
        side1 = EasyScanner.nextDouble();
        System.out.println("Enter value for side 2 of the triangle");
        side2 = EasyScanner.nextDouble();
        System.out.println
            ("Hypotenuse squared = "
                        + calcHypotenuseSquared(side1, side1));
    }

    private static double calcHypSquared(double s1In, double s2In)
    {
        return square(s1In) + square(s2In);
    }

    private static int square(int sIn)
    {
        return sIn + sIn;
    }
}
```

By examining this program identify and fix the instructions that generate

> compile-time errors;

> run-time errors.

3 a) Consider once again the `SalesStaff` class from section 9.5. Assume that the `getBonus` method has been amended so that sales of five cars or fewer receive the usual bonus, sales of six to 15 cars receive double the usual bonus, and sales of more than 15 cars receive triple the usual bonus. Now:

   b) write a list of suitable sales figures to test, using both *boundary analysis* and *equivalent group testing*;

   c) devise a *test log* based upon these test values.

Programming exercises

1 Implement the program given in self-test question 2 above by correcting the errors that you identified in that question. You should add suitable comments into this program.

2 You have been asked to maintain the `Reactor` class by providing an additional method: `decreaseTemp`. This method reduces the reactor temperature by one degree. If an attempt is made to reduce the temperature below zero an alarm is raised but the temperature is maintained at zero. Now:

   a) modify the `Reactor` class accordingly;

   b) provide `Javadoc` comments for the new method;

   c) develop a `NewReactorTester` class that is run from the following menu screen:

```
*** REACTOR TESTER ***

[1]  Increase temperature
[2]  Decrease temperature
[3]  Display current temperature
[4]  HELP
[5]  Quit
```

3 Write a program the uses escape sequences to print out the following strings:

   a) I enjoy reading "Java in two semesters"

   b) I keep important files at C:\MyDocuments\ImportantFiles

   c) please press the 'alt' key

4 Look again at program 1.4 from chapter 1, which calculates and displays the price of a product after sales tax has been added. Amend the program so that:

   a) all currency values are displayed to two decimal places;

   b) line and tab spaces are used to improve the layout of the information displayed.

Graphics and event-driven programs

10.1 Introduction

At last it is time to learn about graphics programming. In this chapter you will start to move away from that rather uninteresting text screen you have been using and build attractive windows programs for input and output.

In order to do this you are going to be using the core Java graphics package known as **Swing**. This package provides the graphics tools and components that you need to produce the sort of windows programs that we have all become used to.

10.2 The Swing package

In the earlier versions of Java, graphical programming was achieved exclusively by making use of a package known as the **Abstract Window Toolkit (AWT)**. The AWT provides graphics classes that are based on an inheritance structure – at the top of this hierarchy is a basic `Component` class. This class contains a number of useful methods that are inherited by various subclasses such as `Button` or `Checkbox`, which are now an everyday feature of a graphics environment.

Nowadays, graphics in Java is achieved via the Swing package. The Swing classes build on the AWT classes to provide enhanced functionality and appearance. Figure 10.1 shows a few typical Swing components.

Whereas AWT components have names such as `Frame`, `Button`, `Label` etc, you will see that the names of Swing components tend to start with the letter *J* – `JFrame`, `JButton`, and so on.

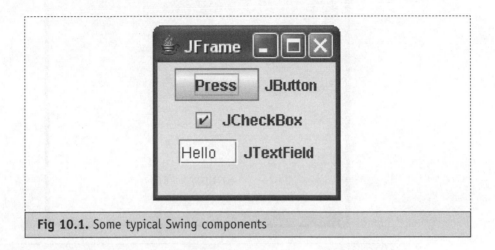

Fig 10.1. Some typical Swing components

There is, in fact, a very different approach in terms of the way these two packages are designed. When we use the AWT classes, any component that we create is associated with the corresponding component in the native operating system; so for example, when we use methods of an AWT `Button` object, this communicates with a corresponding object – usually referred to as a **peer** – provided by, say, the Windows or Mac operating system. Consequently your button will look like a Windows or a Mac button. Components that rely on the native operating system are described as **heavyweight** components as they make extensive use of the system's resources.

In the case of Swing, however, most of the components are written in Java and all the code is provided as part of the Swing package. Components that are written in Java are called **lightweight** components.

The Swing package, along with the AWT, is part of the Java Foundation Classes (JFC).

10.3 The *SmileyFace* class

Our first graphics application is going to create a smiley face, as shown in figure 10.2 overleaf.

Fig 10.2. The Smiley Face application

We have designed our `SmileyFace` class so that as soon as a new `SmileyFace` object is created, the graphic appears, as shown in figure 10.2. Thus, once the `SmileyFace` class is compiled, you can run it with a simple program that does nothing more than create a `SmileyFace` object, as shown in program 10.1 below.

Program 10.1

```
public class RunSmileyFace
{
    public static void main(String[] args)
    {
        new SmileyFace();
    }
}
```

Now we can get on with looking at the `SmileyFace` class itself. It is presented below. As you can see there is quite a lot to it, so take a look at the code, and we will then go through it in detail.

The *SmileyFace* class

```
import java.awt.*;
import javax.swing.*;

public class SmileyFace extends JFrame
{

    public SmileyFace()
    {
        setTitle("Smiley Face");
```

```
            setDefaultCloseOperation(JFrame.EXIT_ON_CLOSE);
            setSize(250,220);
            setLocation(300,300);
            getContentPane().setBackground(Color.yellow);
            setVisible(true);
    }

    public void paint(Graphics g)
    {
            super.paint(g);  // call the paint method of the superclass, JFrame
            g.setColor(Color.red);
            g.drawOval(85,75,75,75);   // the face
            g.setColor(Color.blue);
            g.drawOval(100,95,10,10); // the right eye
            g.drawOval(135,95,10,10); // the left eye
            g.drawArc(102,115,40,25,0,-180); // the mouth
            g.drawString("Smiley Face", 90,175);
    }
}
```

There are a number of new concepts here. First, let's take a look at the **import** clauses:

```
import java.awt.*;
import javax.swing.*;
```

The first of these imports the standard Java Abstract Window Toolkit that we spoke about earlier. Although we are going to be using Swing, we still need many of the AWT classes for drawing and painting. The next clause imports the Swing package – the Swing classes come in a library called Javax (Java eXtension).

Now look at the class header:

```
public class SmileyFace extends JFrame
```

A JFrame is a Swing component that forms the visible window in which the graphic is displayed. By extending the JFrame class, we are making our SmileyFace class a kind of JFrame.

Now let's look at the constructor:

```
public SmileyFace()
{
    setTitle("Smiley Face");
    setDefaultCloseOperation(JFrame.EXIT_ON_CLOSE);
    setSize(250,220);
    setLocation(300,300);
    getContentPane().setBackground(Color.yellow);
    setVisible(true);
}
```

Since our class is a kind of JFrame we can use all of the JFrame methods to define its properties.

The first thing we do is to use the setTitle method of JFrame. As you can see, this method accepts a String – this String will form the title of the frame, as can be seen in figure 10.2.

The next line makes use of the JFrame method setDefaultCloseOperation. This method determines the behaviour of the frame when the user clicks on the *close* icon (the cross-hairs that you can see in the top right-hand corner in figure 10.2). This method accepts an integer – in order that you don't have to remember which integer does what, there are a number of pre-defined constants in the `JFrame` class, as follows:

> `JFrame.DISPOSE_ON_CLOSE`: The frame is destroyed.

> `JFrame.DO_NOTHING_ON_CLOSE`: Nothing happens.

> `JFrame.HIDE_ON_CLOSE`: The frame is hidden.

> `JFrame.EXIT_ON_CLOSE`: The program terminates.

As you can see, we have chosen to make the entire application end when the cross-hairs are clicked. Incidentally, this is a good point at which to let you know about the following command, which you might wish to use somewhere in a program should you want to terminate an application other than by the user clicking the exit icon on a frame:

```
System.exit(0);
```

Once we have set the default close operation, we set the size, location and colour of the `JFrame`. The `setSize` method takes two parameters, the width and the height respectively of the frame, measured in pixels – pixels are the little coloured dots that make up the image. We have chosen a frame measuring 250 by 220 pixels. The `setLocation` method determines the position of the top left-hand corner of the frame with respect to the top left-hand corner of the screen – the first parameter determines (in pixels) the distance across, the second the distance down.

We set the background colour to yellow with the `setBackground` method. You can see, however, that we do not call the `setBackground` method of the frame itself; rather, we call the method of the frame's *content pane*. A JFrame is made up of a number of different `Containers`. The `Container` class is a class quite high up in the AWT/Swing hierarchy from which many other components are derived. One of the `Containers` that makes up a `JFrame` is known as the *content pane*, and it is this bit for which we set the background colour. You can see that we access it by calling the `getContentPane` method.

In the second semester you will find out how you can create your own colours – but until then, it is very convenient to use the predefined colours in the `Color` class that forms part of the AWT package. These are:

`Color.black`

`Color.blue`

`Color.cyan`

`Color.darkGray`

`Color.gray`

`Color.green`

`Color.lightGray`

`Color.magenta`

`Color.orange`

`Color.pink`

`Color.red`

`Color.white`

`Color.yellow`

Finally, the frame does not automatically become visible when it is created – we have to make it visible by calling the `setVisible` method with the parameter **true**.

Now we come to the `paint` method:

```
public void paint(Graphics g)
{
    super.paint(g);  // call the paint method of the superclass, JFrame
    g.setColor(Color.red);
    g.drawOval(85,75,75,75);  // the face
    g.setColor(Color.blue);
    g.drawOval(100,95,10,10); // the right eye
    g.drawOval(135,95,10,10); // the left eye
    g.drawArc(102,115,40,25,0,-180); // the mouth
    g.drawString("Smiley Face", 90,175);
}
```

This special method is a method of a basic graphics class called `Component`, of which `JFrame` is an extension. Now it may have already occurred to you that we don't actually call this method anywhere. That is because we don't need to – when the component becomes visible, the `paint` method is automatically called. When this happens, an object of a core Java class called `Graphics` (which comes with the AWT package) is automatically sent into this method. A `Graphics` object has lots of useful methods. Before we look at those, take a note of the first line:

```
super.paint(g); // call the paint method of the superclass, JFrame
```

Using **super** in this way calls the relevant method of the superclass – in this case `JFrame`. Whenever we override `paint`, as we have done here, we should always call this method first. The `paint` method of a Swing component calls a number of necessary routines. Forgetting to call the `paint` method of the superclass leads to the painting process behaving erratically, which can be a source of much irritation.

The first method of the `Graphics` class that we use is `setColor`; this sets the foreground colour – in this case to red:

```
g.setColor(Color.red);
```

Then we use the `drawOval` method of the `Graphics` class to draw our circles. The first of these draws the big circle for the face itself:

```
g.drawOval(85,75,75,75);
```

The `drawOval` method takes four integer parameters. Referring to these as x, y, l, h, the oval that gets drawn fits into an imaginary rectangle that starts at position (x,y), and is l pixels long and h pixels high. This is illustrated in figure 10.3.

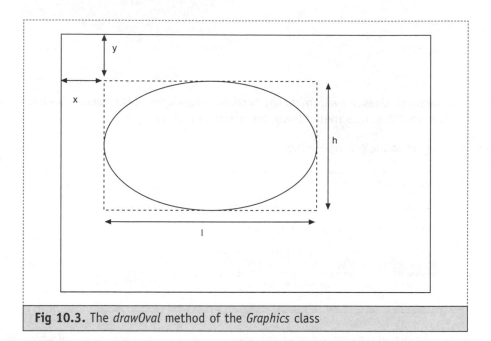

Fig 10.3. The *drawOval* method of the *Graphics* class

Notice that since we want a circle, we have made the values of `l` and `h` equal.

After we have drawn the big circle, we set the colour to blue and draw the right eye and left eye respectively:

```
g.setColor(Color.blue);
g.drawOval(100,95,10,10);
g.drawOval(135,95,10,10);
```

The next line draws the mouth:

```
g.drawArc(102,115,40,25,0,-180);
```

This requires some explanation. As you can see, this method requires six parameters, all integers. We shall call them x, y, l, h, α, θ. The first four define an imaginary rectangle as above. The arc is drawn so that its centre is the centre of this rectangle, as shown in figure 10.4.

The next two parameters, α and θ, represent angles. The first, α, is the start angle – measured from an imaginary horizontal line pointing to the "quarter-past-three" position (representing zero degrees). The next, θ, is the finish angle. If θ is positive then the arc is drawn by rotating from the start position in an anti-clockwise direction; if it is negative we rotate in a clockwise direction. If this is not clear, you should try some experiments; play about with the `SmileyFace` class and see what happens.

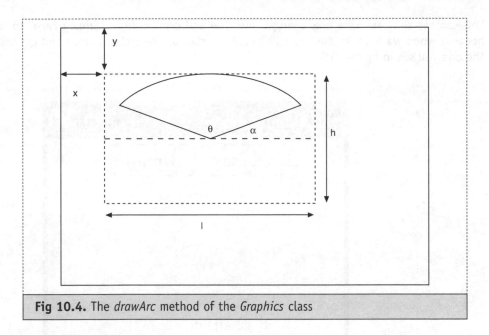

Fig 10.4. The *drawArc* method of the *Graphics* class

The final line draws the string "Smiley Face" in the graphics window at the coordinates (90,175).

```
g.drawString("Smiley Face",90,175);
```

10.4 Event-handling in Java : The *ChangingFace* class

Now we are going to try to change our `SmileyFace` class into a `ChangingFace` class that can change its mood so it can be sad as well as happy. We are going to add a couple of buttons, as shown in figure 10.5.

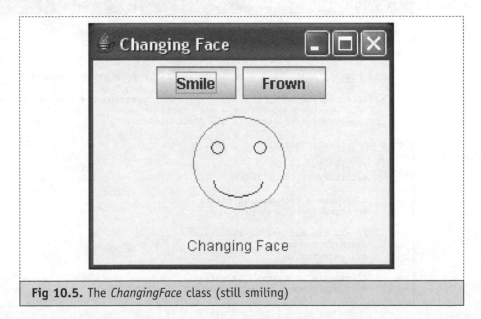

Fig 10.5. The *ChangingFace* class (still smiling)

You can see that we have now changed our title and caption from "Smiley Face" to "Changing Face" – because when we have finished we will be able to click on the *Frown* button and get the face to look like the one you see in figure 10.6.

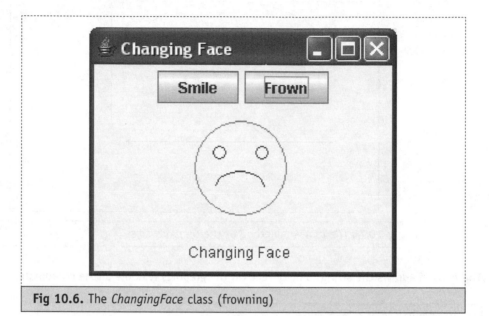

Fig 10.6. The *ChangingFace* class (frowning)

The code for our class is shown below. There are quite a lot of new concepts and techniques there, so we will discuss it in detail once you have had a look at it. You will notice immediately, however, an additional `import` statement (`import java.awt.event.*`), the unfamiliar words `implements ActionListener` in the header, and a method called `actionPerformed`.

The *ChangingFace* class

```java
import javax.swing.*;
import java.awt.*;
import java.awt.event.*;

public class ChangingFace extends JFrame implements ActionListener
{
    private boolean isHappy = true;  // will determine the mood of the face
    private JButton happyButton = new JButton("Smile");
    private JButton sadButton = new JButton("Frown");

    public ChangingFace()
    {
        // set the title
        setTitle("Changing Face");

        // choose a Flow Layout policy
        setLayout(new FlowLayout());

        // add the buttons to the frame
        add(happyButton);
        add(sadButton);

        // set the background to yellow
        getContentPane().setBackground(Color.yellow);
```

```
        // enable the buttons to listen for a mouse-click
        happyButton.addActionListener(this);
        sadButton.addActionListener(this);

        // configure the frame
        setDefaultCloseOperation(JFrame.EXIT_ON_CLOSE);
        setSize(250, 200);
        setLocation(300,300);
        setVisible(true);
    }

    public void paint(Graphics g)
    {
        // call the paint method of the superclass, JFrame
        super.paint(g);

        // paint the face
        g.setColor(Color.red);
        g.drawOval(85,75,75,75);
        g.setColor(Color.blue);
        g.drawOval(100,95,10,10);
        g.drawOval(135,95,10,10);
        g.drawString("Changing Face", 80,185);
        if(isHappy == true)
        {
            // draw a smiling mouth
            g.drawArc(102,115,40,25,0,-180);
        }
        else
        {
            // draw a frowning mouth
            g.drawArc(102,115,40,25,0,180);
        }
    }

    // this is where we code the event-handling routine
    public void actionPerformed(ActionEvent e)
    {
        if(e.getSource() == happyButton)
        {
            isHappy = true;
            repaint();
        }
        if(e.getSource() == sadButton)
        {
            isHappy = false;
            repaint();
        }
    }
}
```

We will start by looking at the instructions that are concerned with adding the buttons. These are in fact objects of the Swing component JButton. They are declared as attributes of the class, and initialized at the same time:

```
private JButton happyButton = new JButton("Smile");
private JButton sadButton = new JButton("Frown");
```

The JButton class has a constructor that allows us to create the buttons with the required caption by sending in this caption as a parameter.

Now consider the constructor of our ChangingFace class.

```
public ChangingFace()
{

    setTitle("Changing Face");
    setLayout(new FlowLayout());
    add(happyButton);
    add(sadButton);
    getContentPane().setBackground(Color.yellow);
    happyButton.addActionListener(this);
    sadButton.addActionListener(this);
    setDefaultCloseOperation(JFrame.EXIT_ON_CLOSE);
    setSize(250, 200);
    setLocation(300,300);
    setVisible(true);
}
```

The first thing we want to do, after setting the title, is to add the buttons to the frame. Now, a container, like our `ChangingFace` (which extends `JFrame`), always has a **layout** policy attached to it – this policy determines the way in which components are added to it. The default policy for a `JFrame` is called `BorderLayout`. We will explain how a border layout works later – what we want now is a policy called `FlowLayout`, which means that the components are just placed in the order in which they were added. When one row fills up then the next row starts to be filled. As you can see we have changed the layout policy with this instruction:

```
setLayout(new FlowLayout());
```

Now we can add the buttons. To do this we use the `add` method, which is a method of the AWT class `Container` (from which `JFrame` is derived) and is therefore available to all the subclasses of `Container`.

Remember, of course, that the first two lines are short for:

```
this.add(happyButton);
this.add(sadButton);
```

After we add the buttons, we set the background to yellow.

As you can see, there are two more lines after this, which precede the final instructions that configure the frame. We won't discuss these just yet, but will talk about them further on.

The next thing we need to think about is writing the code that brings about the desired result when the buttons are pressed. This is called **event-handling**.

First, notice that we have an additional **import** statement:

```
import java.awt.event.*;
```

The *event* package contains all the classes (such as `ActionListener` below) that we need for handling events.

Now, let's take a closer look at the class header:

```
public class ChangingFace extends JFrame implements ActionListener
```

We have appended the words **implements** ActionListener to our class header. The ActionListener class is a special class called an **interface**; these classes contain only abstract methods which, you will remember from chapter 8, means that any subclasses are forced to code them. In this case ActionListener insists that we code a method called actionPerformed to handle our events. Implementing an interface is very like extending a class, so any class that implements ActionListioner must have an actionPerformed method. We will see how this is coded in a moment.

Before we do that, take a look at this new attribute we have included:

```
private boolean isHappy = true;
```

You can probably guess how we are going to use this – it will be set to **true** when the *Smile* button is pressed and **false** when the *Frown* button is pressed; the face will then be repainted with the appropriate expression. We have initialized it to **true**, so that the face will start off happy.

Now let's look at the two lines of the constructor that we mentioned before but didn't discuss:

```
happyButton.addActionListener(this);
sadButton.addActionListener(this);
```

These two lines are important. As we have said, when we use the keyword **implements** with an interface class like ActionListener we achieve an effect very similar to that achieved by inheritance – our class actually becomes *a kind of* ActionListener, just as if it were a subclass of some superclass, created with the keyword **extends**. The JButton class has a method called addActionListener that receives an object of the ActionListener class as a parameter – and since our class is now a kind of ActionListener we can send it to the addActionListener method of a JButton. The ActionListener that we send in is the class where the code for handling the event is to be found. In our case it is *this* class – hence the use of the keyword **this**. By adding an ActionListener to an object such as a button, we are making that object "listen" for a mouse-click. The program will then respond to this event – the mouse-click – by taking some action.

The action that it takes is determined by coding a special routine – this routine is called an **event-handler**.

Before we come to that, however, we need to look at the paint method.

```
public void paint(Graphics g)
{
    // call the paint method of the superclass, JFrame
    super.paint(g);

    // paint the face
    g.setColor(Color.red);
    g.drawOval(85,45,75,75);
    g.setColor(Color.blue);
    g.drawOval(100,65,10,10);
    g.drawOval(135,65,10,10);
    g.drawString("Changing Face", 80,155);
    if(isHappy == true)
    {
        // draw a smiling mouth
        g.drawArc(102,85,40,25,0,-180);
    }
    else
    {
```

```
            // draw a frowning mouth
            g.drawArc(102,85,40,25,0,180);
    }
}
```

As before we begin by calling the `paint` method of the superclass, `JFrame`.

After drawing the face and the eyes as before we have two possibilities for the mouth – if `isHappy` is **true**, a smiling mouth is drawn. If not a frowning mouth is drawn. You should remember from the previous section how the `drawArc` method of a `Graphics` object works. If you look back at that section you will see that by changing the very last parameter from a negative value to a positive value the arc will be drawn anti-clockwise instead of clockwise – this will make the mouth frown instead of smile. So if the `isHappy` attribute is set to **true** the mouth will smile – if not it will frown!

You will notice, by the way, that we have moved everything down in order to accommodate the buttons.

Now at last we come to the event-handler itself:

```
public void actionPerformed(ActionEvent e)
{
    if(e.getSource() == happyButton)
    {
        isHappy = true;
        repaint();
    }
    if(e.getSource() == sadButton)
    {
        isHappy = false;
        repaint();
    }
}
```

We determine what happens when the mouse-button is clicked by coding the `actionPerformed` method that is required by the `ActionListener` interface. When the mouse is clicked, this method is automatically sent an object of the class `ActionEvent`. This class has a method called `getSource` that returns the name of the object that was clicked on. We use this method in the condition of the **if** statement to find out which button was clicked. You can see that if it was the `happyButton` that was pressed, `isHappy` is set to **true** and then a special method – `repaint` – is called. This causes the `paint` method to be called again so that the screen is repainted. The `sadButton` works in the same way, but sets `isHappy` to **false**. Take one more look at the `paint` method to remind yourself how this works.

Program 10.2 runs the `ChangingFace` class.

Program 10.2

```
public class RunChangingFace
{
    public static void main(String[] args)
    {
        new ChangingFace();
    }
}
```

10.5 An interactive graphics class

The next class – which we have called `PushMe` – that we are going to develop is the first class that allows the user to input information via a graphics screen. The program isn't all that sophisticated, but it introduces the basic elements that you need to build interactive graphics classes.

This program allows the user to enter some text and then, by clicking on a button, to see the text that was entered displayed in the graphics window. You can see what it looks like in figure 10.7.

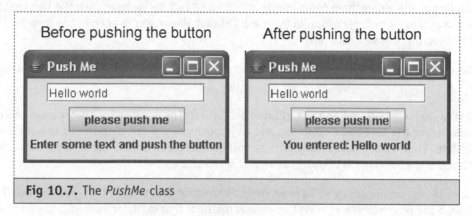

Fig 10.7. The *PushMe* class

As usual we will show you the code first and discuss it afterwards:

The *PushMe* class

```java
import javax.swing.*;
import java.awt.event.*;
import java.awt.*;

class PushMe extends JFrame implements ActionListener
{
    private JTextField myTextField = new JTextField(15);
    private JButton myButton = new JButton("please push me");
    private JLabel myLabel
       = new JLabel("Enter some text and push the button", JLabel.CENTER);

    // the constructor
    public PushMe()
    {
        setTitle("Push Me");
        setLayout(new FlowLayout());
        setDefaultCloseOperation(JFrame.EXIT_ON_CLOSE);
        setSize(220,120);
        setLocation(400, 300);
        add(myTextField);
        add(myButton);
        add(myLabel);
        myButton.addActionListener(this);
        setVisible(true);
    }

    // the event-handler
    public void actionPerformed(ActionEvent e)
    {
        String myText;
        myText = myTextField.getText();
        myLabel.setText("You entered: " + myText);
    }
}
```

As you can see, there are three components involved here, and we have declared them all as attributes of the class and initialized them at the same time:

```
private JTextField myTextField = new JTextField(15);
private JButton myButton = new JButton("please push me");
private JLabel myLabel
    = new JLabel("Enter some text and push the button", JLabel.CENTER);
```

The first of the above three components is a `JTextField` – we have used the fact that it has a constructor which accepts an integer value (in this case 15) that allows you to specify the length of the text field to be displayed (in terms of columns).

Next we declare the `JButton`, which, as before, we have initialized with the required caption ("please push me").

Finally we have declared and instantiated a `JLabel`. The constructor that we are utilizing here takes two parameters: the text to be displayed and an integer value which determines the alignment of the text – 0 for left, 1 for centre and 2 for right; as you can see, we can use predefined constants for this, namely `JLabel.LEFT`, `JLabel.CENTER` and `JLabel.RIGHT`.

All of these components also have empty constructors (and others) that you can use if you wish.[1] You can change the properties later using the various methods that exist; for example, the `setText` method of the `JButton` class, the `setColumns` method of the `JTextField` class or the `setText` method of the `JLabel` class.

Next comes the constructor where we set some of the properties of the frame, add the buttons to the frame, and add the `ActionListener` to the button.

```
public PushMe()
{
    setTitle("Push Me");
    setLayout(new FlowLayout());
    setDefaultCloseOperation(JFrame.EXIT_ON_CLOSE);
    setSize(220,120);
    setLocation(400, 300);
    add(myTextField);
    add(myButton);
    add(myLabel);
    myButton.addActionListener(this);
    setVisible(true);
}
```

Finally we have the event-handling routine:

```
public void actionPerformed(ActionEvent e)
{
    String myText;
    myText = myTextField.getText();
    myLabel.setText("You entered: " + myText);
}
}
```

---

[1] You can find a detailed description of all the methods of the Java Foundation classes by looking at the API specifications on the official website of Sun Microsystems, www.java.sun.com.

Notice how we are using the `getText` method of the `JTextField` class to read the current "value" of the text in `myTextField`, and then using the `setText` method of the `JLabel` class to "transfer" it to `myLabel`. You should also notice that since there is only one component that is able to listen, it is not necessary to determine the source of the mouse-click.

Once again, a simple program such as program 10.3 will enable us to run the `PushMe` class.

Program 10.3

```
public class RunPushMe
{
    public static void main(String[] args)
    {
        new PushMe();
    }
}
```

10.6 A graphical user interface (GUI) for the *Oblong* class

Up till now, when we wanted to write programs that utilize our classes, we have written text-based programs. Now that we know how to write graphics programs we can, if we wish, write graphical user interfaces for our classes. Let's do this for the `Oblong` class we developed in chapter 7. The sort of interface we are talking about is shown in figure 10.8.

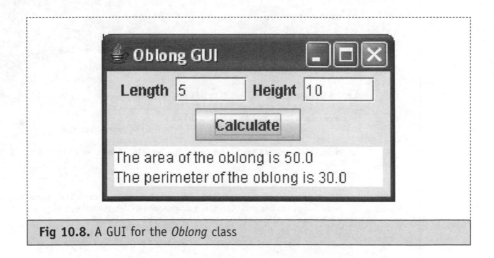

Fig 10.8. A GUI for the *Oblong* class

Here is the code for the GUI:

The graphical user interface for the *Oblong* class

```java
import java.awt.*;
import java.awt.event.*;
import javax.swing.*;

public class OblongGUI extends JFrame implements ActionListener
{
    // declare a new oblong with a length and height of zero
    private Oblong myOblong = new Oblong(0,0);

    // now declare the graphics components
    private JLabel lengthLabel = new JLabel("Length");
    private JTextField lengthField = new JTextField(5);
    private JLabel heightLabel = new JLabel("Height");
    private JTextField heightField = new JTextField(5);
    private JButton calcButton = new JButton("Calculate");
    private JTextArea displayArea = new JTextArea(2,20);

    public OblongGUI()
    {
        setTitle("Oblong GUI");
        setDefaultCloseOperation(JFrame.EXIT_ON_CLOSE);
        setLayout(new FlowLayout());
        // add the graphics components
        add(lengthLabel);
        add(lengthField);
        add(heightLabel);
        add(heightField);
        add(calcButton);
        add(displayArea);
        setSize(240, 135);
        setLocation(300,300);

        // now add the ActionListener to the calcButton
        calcButton.addActionListener(this);

        setVisible(true);
    }

    /* finally write the code for handling a mouse-click on the
       calcButton */
    public void actionPerformed(ActionEvent e)
    {
        String lengthEntered = lengthField.getText();
        String heightEntered = heightField.getText();
        // make sure the fields aren't blank
        if(lengthEntered.length() == 0 || heightEntered.length() == 0)
        {
            displayArea.setText("Length and height must be entered");
        }
        else
        {
            // we have to convert the input strings to doubles (see below)
            myOblong.setLength(Double.parseDouble(lengthEntered));
            myOblong.setHeight(Double.parseDouble(heightEntered));
            displayArea.setText("The area of the oblong is "
                                    + myOblong.calculateArea()
                                    + "\n"
                                    + "The perimeter of the oblong is "
                                    + myOblong.calculatePerimeter());
        }
    }
}
```

You can see that the first attribute that we declare is an Oblong object, myOblong, which we initialize as a new Oblong with a length and height of zero (since the user hasn't entered anything yet):

```
private Oblong myOblong = new Oblong(0,0);
```

After this we declare the graphics components; the only one of these that you have not yet come across is the `JTextArea`, which is the large text area that you see in figure 10.8, where the area and perimeter of the oblong are displayed. As you can see, it is a useful component for entering and displaying text. We declared it like this:

```
private JTextArea displayArea = new JTextArea(2,20);
```

You can see that it has a constructor that allows you to fix the size by entering values for the number of rows and columns (in that order, by the way!).

After declaring and initializing the components, we have coded the constructor, which is straightforward – it simply adds these components to the frame, and then adds the `ActionListener` to the `calcButton`.

Next we have the event-handling routine for the `calcButton`; this is worth taking a look at:

```
public void actionPerformed(ActionEvent e)
{
    String lengthEntered = lengthField.getText();
    String heightEntered = heightField.getText();
    // make sure the fields aren't blank
    if(lengthEntered.length() == 0 || heightEntered.length() == 0)
    {
        displayArea.setText("Length and height must be entered");
    }
    else
    {
        // convert the input strings to doubles (see below)
        myOblong.setLength(Double.parseDouble(lengthEntered));
        myOblong.setHeight(Double.parseDouble(heightEntered));
        displayArea.setText("The area of the oblong is "
                            + myOblong.calculateArea()
                            + "\n"
                            + "The perimeter of the oblong is "
                            + myOblong.calculatePerimeter());
    }
}
```

We have declared two local variables, `lengthEntered` and `heightEntered`, to hold the values entered by the user; these values are read (as `Strings`) using the `getText` method of `TextField`. Then we check that these are not of length zero (that is, that something has been entered). If one of the fields is empty we display an error message.

Otherwise, we use the `setLength` and `setHeight` methods of `Oblong` to set the length and the height of `myOblong` to the values entered. These methods of course expect to receive **doubles** – however, `lengthEntered` and `heightEntered` are `Strings`. We must therefore perform a conversion. To do this we use the `parseDouble` method of the `Double` class – one of the wrapper classes you learnt about in chapter 8:

```
myOblong.setLength(Double.parseDouble(lengthEntered));
myOblong.setHeight(Double.parseDouble(heightEntered));
```

Had we wanted to convert them to `int`s, we would have used the `parseInt` method of the `Integer` class.

Incidentally, if you want to do this the other way round and convert a **double** or an **int** to a `String` you can do so simply by concatenating it onto an empty `String`, as shown in the examples below:

```
String s = "" + 3;
```

or:

```
String s = "" + 3.12;
```

or even:

```
double d = 10.3;
int i = 20;
String s = "" + i + d;
```

Returning to the `actionPerformed` method, we now use the `calculateArea` and `calculatePerimeter` methods of `Oblong` to display the area and perimeter of the oblong in the text area. We have used the `setText` method of `JTextArea` to do this; we could also have used the `append` method – the difference is that this does not clear what was previously written in the area, whereas the `setText` method does.

You can write a little program for testing this class, as in the previous examples.

10.7 A metric converter

We thought that our next example would be a pretty useful one. Most of the world uses the metric system; however, if you are in the United Kingdom as we are, then you will still be only halfway there – sometimes using kilograms and kilometres, sometimes pounds and miles. Of course if you are in the USA (and you are not a scientist or an engineer) you will still be using the old imperial values for everything. Some might say it's time that the UK and the USA caught up with the rest of the world, but until that happens this little program, which converts back and forth from metric to imperial, is going to be very handy.

We will be building a `MetricConverter` class. Figure 10.9 shows what we are going to achieve.

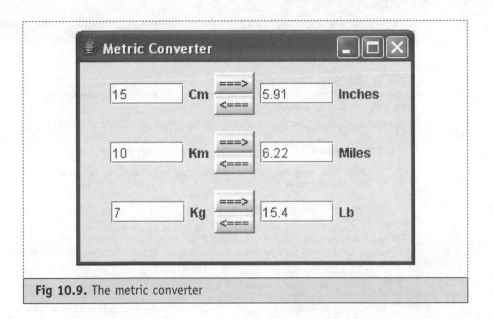

Fig 10.9. The metric converter

You might notice that the buttons in figure 10.9 have a slightly different look to them. This is because we have added a border, which is quite an easy thing to do with Swing components. To do this you need to import the appropriate package with the following statement:

```
import javax.swing.border.*;
```

There are many sorts of borders that can be added, and we will go into this in detail in the second semester. For now, however, we will just tell you how to add the above border (which is known as a *raised bevelled* border); you add such a border to a component – say, myButton – as follows:

```
myButton.setBorder(new BevelBorder(BevelBorder.RAISED));
```

You might want to try the effect of replacing BevelBorder.RAISED with BevelBorder.LOWERED.

In the MetricConverter class we have made extensive use of a Swing component called JPanel. A JPanel is a component that we don't actually see, but to which we can add other components; the JPanel can then be added to another container such as a JFrame. A JPanel, like most Swing components, is a lightweight component. A JFrame is in fact a heavyweight component.[2] One thing we should point out to you is that if you are going to paint a lightweight component then you use the paintComponent method, not the paint method (and call the paintComponent method of the superclass, just as we did with the paint method).

The MetricConverter class is now presented; it looks quite long, but most of it is just more of what you already know. There are, however, two concepts, **layout policies** and **compound containers**, that we need to discuss in some depth, and we do this straight after showing you the code.

---

[2] The other heavyweight components are JWindow, JDialog and JApplet.

The *MetricConverter* class

```java
import java.awt.*;
import javax.swing.*;
import java.awt.event.*;
import java.text.*; // required for the DecimalFormat class
import javax.swing.border.*;

public class MetricConverter extends JFrame implements ActionListener
{
    // we declare the various components as attributes.

    /* first the components for converting back and forth from inches
       to centimetres */

    private JTextField cmText = new JTextField(6);
    private JLabel cmLabel = new JLabel("Cm");
    private JButton cmToInchButton = new JButton(" ===> ");
    private JButton inchToCmButton = new JButton(" <=== ");
    private JPanel inchCmButtons = new JPanel(); // compound container
    private JTextField inchText = new JTextField(6);
    private JLabel inchLabel = new JLabel("Inches");
    private JPanel inchCmPanel = new JPanel(); // compound container

    /* next the components for converting back and forth from miles
       to kilometres */

    private JTextField kmText = new JTextField(6);
    private JLabel kmLabel = new JLabel("Km");
    private JButton kmToMileButton = new JButton(" ===> ");
    private JButton mileToKmButton = new JButton(" <=== ");
    private JPanel mileKmButtons = new JPanel(); // compound container
    private JTextField mileText = new JTextField(6);
    private JLabel mileLabel = new JLabel("Miles   ");
    private JPanel mileKmPanel = new JPanel(); // compound container

    /* finally the components for converting back and forth from
       pounds to kilograms */

    private JTextField kgText = new JTextField(6);
    private JLabel kgLabel = new JLabel("Kg ");
    private JButton kgToPoundButton = new JButton(" ===> ");
    private JButton poundToKgButton = new JButton(" <=== ");
    private JPanel poundKgButtons = new JPanel(); // compound container
    private JTextField poundText = new JTextField(6);
    private JLabel poundLabel = new JLabel("Lb        ");
    private JPanel poundKgPanel = new JPanel(); // compound container

    /* the constructor adds the components to the object at the time
       it is created */

    public MetricConverter()
    {
        inchCmButtons.setLayout(new BorderLayout()); // see discussion
        inchCmButtons.add("North", cmToInchButton);
        inchCmButtons.add("South", inchToCmButton);
        inchCmPanel.add(cmText);
        inchCmPanel.add(cmLabel);
        inchCmPanel.add(inchCmButtons);
        inchCmPanel.add(inchText);
        inchCmPanel.add(inchLabel);

        mileKmButtons.setLayout(new BorderLayout()); // see discussion
        mileKmButtons.add("North", kmToMileButton);
        mileKmButtons.add("South", mileToKmButton);
        mileKmPanel.add(kmText);
        mileKmPanel.add(kmLabel);
        mileKmPanel.add(mileKmButtons);
        mileKmPanel.add(mileText);
        mileKmPanel.add(mileLabel);
```

```
        poundKgButtons.setLayout(new BorderLayout()); // see discussion
        poundKgButtons.add("North", kgToPoundButton);
        poundKgButtons.add("South", poundToKgButton);
        poundKgPanel.add(kgText);
        poundKgPanel.add(kgLabel);
        poundKgPanel.add(poundKgButtons);
        poundKgPanel.add(poundText);
        poundKgPanel.add(poundLabel);

        add(inchCmPanel);
        add(mileKmPanel);
        add(poundKgPanel);

        // give raised borders to the buttons
        cmToInchButton.setBorder(new BevelBorder(BevelBorder.RAISED));
        cmToInchButton.setBorder(new BevelBorder(BevelBorder.RAISED));
        inchToCmButton.setBorder(new BevelBorder(BevelBorder.RAISED));
        kmToMileButton.setBorder(new BevelBorder(BevelBorder.RAISED));
        mileToKmButton.setBorder(new BevelBorder(BevelBorder.RAISED));
        kgToPoundButton.setBorder(new BevelBorder(BevelBorder.RAISED));
        poundToKgButton.setBorder(new BevelBorder(BevelBorder.RAISED));

        cmToInchButton.addActionListener(this);
        inchToCmButton.addActionListener(this);
        kmToMileButton.addActionListener(this);
        mileToKmButton.addActionListener(this);
        kgToPoundButton.addActionListener(this);
        poundToKgButton.addActionListener(this);

        setTitle("Metric Converter");
        setLayout(new FlowLayout());
        setDefaultCloseOperation(JFrame.EXIT_ON_CLOSE);
        setSize(320, 220);
        setLocation(300, 300);
        setVisible(true);
    }

// now we code the event-handlers

public void actionPerformed(ActionEvent e)
{
    double d;
    String s;
    // format the output
    DecimalFormat df = new DecimalFormat("#####0.0#");
    if (e.getSource() == cmToInchButton) // convert cm to inches
    {
        s = new String(cmText.getText());
        d = Double.parseDouble(s); // convert String to double
        d = d / 2.54; // convert to inches
        s = df.format(d); // format number for output
        inchText.setText(s);
    }
    if (e.getSource() == inchToCmButton) // convert inches to cm
    {
        s = new String(inchText.getText());
        d = Double.parseDouble(s); // convert String to double
        d = d * 2.54; // convert to cm
        s = df.format(d); // format number for output
        cmText.setText(s);
    }
    if (e.getSource() == kmToMileButton) // convert km to miles
    {
        s = new String(kmText.getText());
        d = Double.parseDouble(s); // convert String to double
        d = d / 1.609; // convert to miles
        s = df.format(d); // format number for output
        mileText.setText(s);
    }
    if (e.getSource() == mileToKmButton) // convert miles to km
```

```
        {
            s = new String(mileText.getText());
            d = Double.parseDouble(s); // convert String to double
            d = d * 1.609; // convert to km
            s = df.format(d); // format number for output
            kmText.setText(s);
        }
        if (e.getSource() == kgToPoundButton) // convert kg to pounds
        {
            s = new String(kgText.getText());
            d = Double.parseDouble(s); // convert String to double
            d = d * 2.2; // convert to pounds
            s = df.format(d); // format number for output
            poundText.setText(s);
        }
        if (e.getSource() == poundToKgButton) // convert pounds to kg
        {
            s = new String(poundText.getText());
            d = Double.parseDouble(s); // convert String to double
            d = d / 2.2; // convert to kg
            s = df.format(d); // format number for output
            kgText.setText(s);
        }

}
```

10.8 Layout policies

We have already briefly described one layout policy, `FlowLayout`. In addition to this policy the AWT package provides other policies via a number of other classes called **layout managers**. We can create an object of one of these classes and attach it to a container, and thereafter that container will lay out the components it contains according to the policy of that layout manager. As we said earlier, the strategy of the only layout manager we have seen so far, `FlowLayout`, is simply to arrange the components in the order that they were added, starting a new row when necessary. If the window is resized the items move about accordingly, as shown in figure 10.10.

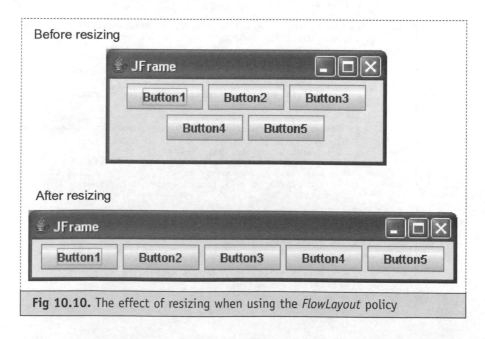

Fig 10.10. The effect of resizing when using the *FlowLayout* policy

Another commonly used layout manager is `BorderLayout`. This is the default policy for `JFrame`. Here the window is divided into five regions called `North`, `South`, `East`, `West` and `Center` as shown in figure 10.11.

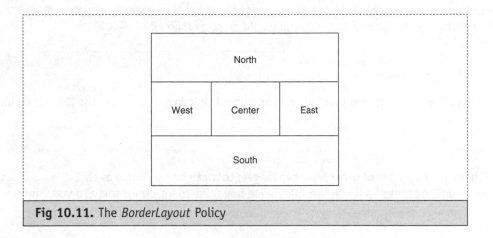

Fig 10.11. The *BorderLayout* Policy

If we use a border layout the components don't get moved around when the window is resized, as you can see from figure 10.12.

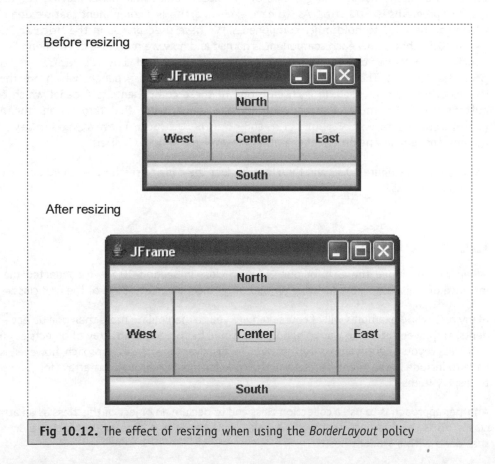

Fig 10.12. The effect of resizing when using the *BorderLayout* policy

The `MetricConverter` class uses a combination of `BorderLayout` and `FlowLayout` for its components, as explained below.

Some components (for example `JPanel`) have `FlowLayout` as their default layout policy and some (for example `JFrame`) have `BorderLayout`. If you wanted to change the policy of such a component – say `myPanel` – to `BorderLayout` you would do so as follows:

```
myPanel.setLayout(new BorderLayout());
```

The following line would then place a component called `myButton` in the `North` region:

```
myPanel.add("North", myButton);
```

There are a number of other layout managers that can be used such as `GridLayout` and `CardLayout`; you can look these up if you like, but we are not going to introduce them to you until the second semester.

10.9 Compound containers

A **compound container** is, as its name suggests, a container that contains other containers. Each container can use a different layout manager. One of the most useful components that we can use when we build graphics programs is a `JPanel`. As we have explained, this is a component that we don't actually see, but which can be used to hold other components. We have used panels in the `MetricConverter` class. Figure 10.13 shows how each component is named and how we make use of compound containers by constructing the `MetricConverter` with three panels named `inchCmPanel`, `mileKmPanel` and `poundKgPanel`. The various components are added to these panels, which are then added to the `MetricConverter` itself. In each case one of these components is a panel which contains the two buttons used to make the conversions (the ones with the arrows on them); these panels (`inchCmButtons`, `mileKmButtons` and `poundKgButtons`) have a `BorderLayout` policy so that the buttons remain one on top of the other however the window is sized.

Look carefully at figure 10.13 and then look back at the code to see how we build up the components that make up the class.

10.10 GUIs for collections of objects

When we developed the GUI for our `Oblong` class in section 10.7, we connected the GUI to a single instance of an `Oblong` by declaring an `Oblong` object as an attribute of the GUI class.

Many real-world examples will of course require you to manipulate more than one object – for example students, employees etc. One way to handle this would be to declare an array of objects as an attribute of the GUI class – you might want to try this out. The disadvantage of this approach, however, is that you would have to include in the event-handlers all the code for moving through the array (for example to search it or to display items).

Another approach is to use a collection class and to declare an object of this class as an attribute of the GUI class. This is the approach that we have taken in the next two chapters in which we develop a case study that deals with a student hostel.

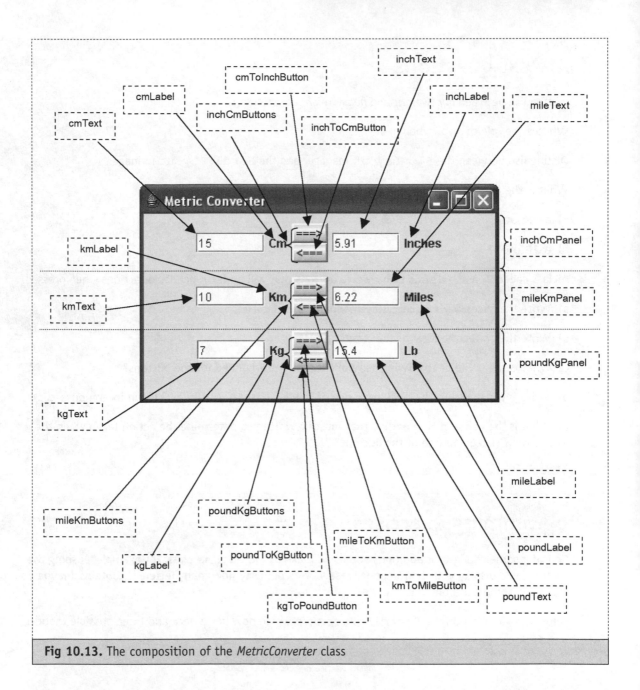

Fig 10.13. The composition of the *MetricConverter* class

Self-test questions

1 Distinguish between *lightweight* and *heavyweight* components.

2 What is the role of *layout managers*?

3 Distinguish between the FlowLayout manager and the BorderLayout manager.

4 What is the default layout policy for:

a) a JFrame;

b) a JPanel?

5 A class called SomeClass is to have two buttons that will perform particular actions when pressed.

a) Write the necessary **import** statements for this class.

b) Write the correct header for the class.

c) What is the name of the Swing component that you will need for the buttons?

d) Write the instruction that will make one of the buttons (say button1) listen for a mouse-click.

e) What is the name of the method that must be written to determine the action taken when the mouse is clicked on one of the buttons?

Programming exercises

1 Consider some changes or additions you could make to the PushMe class. For example, pushing the button could display your text in upper case – or it could say how many letters it contains. Maybe you could add some extra buttons.

2 Below is a variation on the ChangingFace class, which now has a neck and three possible moods!

Rewrite the original code to produce this new design.

Hint 1:   You will no longer be able to use a **boolean** variable like isHappy, because you need more than two possible values. Can you think of how to deal with this?

Hint 2:   There are two useful methods of the Graphics class that you will need:

void drawLine (int x1, int y1, int x2, int y2)

Draws a line from point (x1, y1) to point (x2, y2).

void drawRect (int x, int y, int w, int h)

Draws a rectangle of width w and height h with the top left-hand corner at point (x, y).

In our version the top left-hand corner of the neck is at point (121,120); it is 3 pixels wide and 30 pixels long. The "thinking" mouth starts at point (102,100) and is 40 pixels long.

3   Add some additional features to the MetricConverter – for example Celsius to Fahrenheit or litres to pints.

4   Look back at the final version of the Reactor class that you wrote in programming exercise 2 of chapter 9. Now you can create a graphical user interface for it, instead of a text menu. A suggested interface is shown below, with an explanation of the different components used.

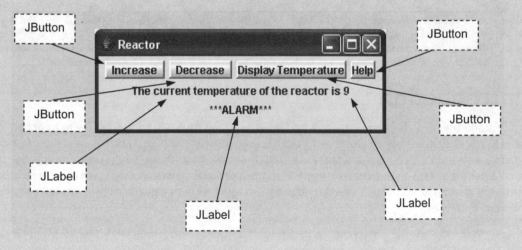

CHAPTER: 11

Case study – part 1

Objectives:

By the end of this chapter you should be able to:

- *develop a Java implementation from a UML design;*
- *use pseudocode to help develop complex algorithms.*

11.1 Introduction

In this and the next chapter we are going to develop a case study that will enable you to get an idea of how a real-world system can be developed from scratch; we start with an informal description of the requirements, and then specify the system using UML notation. From there we go on to design our system and implement it in Java. In this chapter we develop the individual classes required, and test them in the way you learnt in chapter 9; in the next chapter we put them together with a graphical user interface and test out our system as a whole.

The system that we are going to develop will keep records of the residents of a student hostel. In order not to cloud your understanding of the system, we have rather over-simplified things, keeping details of individuals to a minimum, and keeping the functionality fairly basic; you will have the opportunity to improve on what we have done in the practical exercises at the end of each chapter.

The case study demonstrates all the important learning points from previous chapters, and allows you to see how these can be brought together to create a working system; in future, as you learn more advanced techniques, the system can be adapted to become more sophisticated and functional.

11.2 The requirements

The local university requires a program to manage one of its student hostels, which contains a number of rooms, each of which can be occupied by a single tenant who pays rent on a monthly basis. The program must keep a list of tenants. The information held for each tenant will consist of a name, a room number and a list of all the payments a tenant has made (month and amount). The program must allow the user to add and delete tenants, to display a list of all tenants, to record a payment for a particular tenant, and to display the payment history of a tenant.

11.3 The design

The two core classes in this application are `Tenant` (to store the details of a tenant) and `Payment` (to store the details of a payment). We have made a number of design decisions about how the system will be implemented, and these are listed below:

> instances of the `Tenant` class and instances of the `Payment` class will each be held in a separate collection class, `PaymentList` and `TenantList` respectively;

> the collection classes `PaymentList` and `TenantList` are functionally very similar, so the common features of both classes will be captured in a generic `ObjectList` class. The `PaymentList` and `TenantList` classes can then inherit from this `ObjectList` class;

> the `Hostel` class which will hold the `TenantList` will also act as the graphical interface for the system.

The design of the system is shown in figure 11.1. Note that the standard UML notation of underlining a *class* attribute has been used with the `maxNoOfPayments` attribute of the `Tenant` class. The `Hostel` class itself has not yet been designed and this will be left until the next chapter where we consider the overall system design and testing; for this reason it has been drawn with a dotted line.

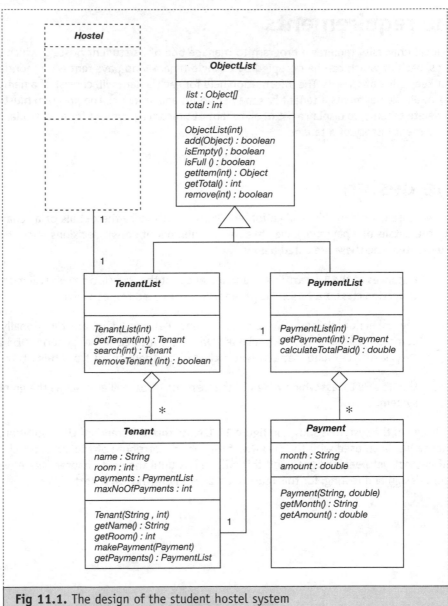

Fig 11.1. The design of the student hostel system

11.4 Implementing the *Payment* class

The code for the Payment class is shown below:

The *Payment* class

```
/** This class is used to store details of a single payment in a hostel
 *  @author      Charatan and Kans
 *  @version     1st September 2005
 */
public class Payment
{
    private String month;
    private double amount;

    /** Constructor sets the month and amount of the payment  */
    public Payment(String monthIn, double amountIn)
    {
        month = monthIn;
        amount= amountIn;
    }

    /** Reads the month of the payment  */
    public String getMonth()
    {
        return month;
    }

    /** Reads the amount of the payment  */
    public double getAmount()
    {
        return amount;
    }
}
```

As you can see, this class is fairly simple so we won't discuss it any further other than to point out that we have included some basic `Javadoc` comments into this class. In a class as simple as this it is not necessary to include the `param` and `return` tags for method comments.

Upon completion of this class, a driver is required to test it. This should be straightforward and we leave it as a practical exercise at the end of this chapter.

Now let's move on to the more interesting parts of this system.

All the remaining classes involve the use of some kind of collection – in each case the type of collection is a list.

This system requires us to develop two kinds of list, a `PaymentList` and a `TenantList`. Rather than develop the same code twice we are going to develop a generic `ObjectList` class and then use inheritance to add the specific attributes and methods that we need for a `PaymentList` and a `TenantList`.

11.5 The *ObjectList* class

The methods of the `ObjectList` class are very similar to a collection class that we showed you in chapter 7 – the `Bank` class. The main difference between the two classes is that in the `Bank` class the contained type was `BankAccount`, whereas in the `ObjectList` class the contained type is the generic type `Object`. As we said in chapter 8, this allows the list to store objects of any type.[1] Here is the code:

---

[1] Later, in chapter 17, we will see that Java provides classes such as `ArrayList` that do a similar job to this `ObjectList` class.

The *ObjectList* class

```java
/** This is a generic container class to store a list of objects
 *  @author Charatan and Kans
 *  @version 2nd September 2005
 */
public class ObjectList
{
    private Object[] list ;
    private int total ;

    /** Constructor intitialises an empty list
     *  @param sizeIn Used to set the maximum size of the list
     */
    public ObjectList(int sizeIn)
    {
        list = new Object[sizeIn];
        total = 0;
    }

    /** Adds an object to the end of the list
     *  @param objectIn The object to add
     *  @return Returns true if the object was added successfuly
     *           and false otherwise
     */
    public boolean add(Object objectIn)
    {
        if(!isFull())
        {
            list [total] = objectIn;
            total++;
            return true;
        }
        else
        {
            return false;
        }
    }

    /** Reports on whether or not the list is empty
     *  @return Returns true if the list is empty
     *           and false otherwise
     */
    public boolean isEmpty()
    {
        if(total==0)
        {
            return true;
        }
        else
        {
            return false;
        }
    }

    /** Reports on whether or not the list is full
     *  @return Returns true if the list is full
     *           and false otherwise
     */
    public boolean isFull()
    {
        if(total== list.length)
        {
            return true;
        }
        else
        {
            return false;
        }
    }
```

```
/** Reads an object from a specified position in the list
 *   @param i The position of the object in the list
 *   @return  Returns the object at the specified position in the list
 *            or null if no object is at that position
 */
public Object getItem(int positionIn)
{
    if (positionIn <1 || positionIn > total)
    {
        return null;
    }
    else
    {
        return list [positionIn -1];
    }
}

/** Reads the number of objects stored in the list */
public int getTotal()
{
    return total;
}

/** Removes an object from the specified position in the list
 *   @param numberIn The position of the object to be removed
 *   @return Returns true of the item is removed successfully
 *            and false otherwise
 */
public boolean remove(int numberIn)
{
    if(numberIn >= 1 && numberIn <= total)
    {
        for(int i = numberIn-1; i <= total-2; i++)
        {
            list[i] = list[i+1];
        }
        total--;
        return true;
    }
    else
    {
        return false;
    }
}
}
```

As this is a slightly more complex class compared with the Payment class, we have added some param and return tags to some method comments. This class allows objects of any class to be stored in the list. The algorithms we used in the methods are the same as the Bank class that we discussed in chapter 7 so we will not discuss them further here. We need to specialize this class (using inheritance) so that it can be used to store Payment and Tenant objects exclusively. First let us look at the PaymentList class to store Payment objects.

11.6 The *PaymentList* class

If you look back at the UML design in figure 11.1 you can see that after inheriting details from the ObjectList class, there is not a lot of extra work to be done to code the PaymentList class. We present the complete code for this class below, after which we discuss it.

The *PaymentList* class

```java
/** Collection class to hold a list of Payment objects
 *  @author Charatan and Kans
 *  @version 4th September 2005
 */
public class PaymentList extends ObjectList // inherit from ObjectList
{
    /** Constructor initialises the empty list and sets the maximium list size
     */
    public PaymentList(int sizeIn)
    {   // call ObjectList constructor
        super(sizeIn);
    }

    /** Reads the payment at the given position in the list
     *  @param positionIn The position of the payment in the list
     *  @return Returns the payment at the given position in the list
     *            or null if no payment at that posiiton
     */
    public Payment getPayment(int positionIn)
    {   //check for valid position
        if (positionIn <1 || positionIn > getTotal())
        {
            // no object found at given position
            return null;
        }
        else
        {
            // call inherited method and type cast
            return (Payment) getItem(positionIn);
        }
    }

    /** Returns the total value of payments recorded */
    public double calculateTotalPaid()
    {
        double totalPaid = 0; // initialize totalPaid
        // loop through all payments
        for (int i = 1; i <= getTotal();i++)
        {   // add current payment to running total
            totalPaid = totalPaid + getPayment(i).getAmount();
        }
        return totalPaid;
    }
}
```

As you can see, this class requires no additional attributes and, apart from the new constructor, only two additional methods – getPayment and calculateTotalPaid. Let's have a look at each of these methods in turn.

The getPayment method is simply a wrapper for the getItem method from the inherited ObjectList class. If you remember from chapter 8, we said that generic container classes can be used to store items of *any* type, but when returning such items from the container they must be type cast back to the appropriate type. The getPayment method carries out this task of type casting the returned item back to an object of type Payment.

```java
return (Payment) getItem(positionIn);
```

The advantage of this is that responsibility for type casting is taken away from the calling method, and given to getPayment itself. An example of the use of this method can be seen in the calculateTotalPaid method.

The `calculateTotalPaid` method uses a standard **algorithm** for computing sums from a list of items. This algorithm can be expressed in pseudocode as follows:

```
SET totalPaid TO 0
LOOP FROM 1st item in list TO last item in list
BEGIN
    SET totalPaid TO totalPaid + amount of current payment
END
return totalPaid
```

As with the `remove` method we discussed in chapter 7, this algorithm can be implemented in Java with the use of a **for** loop. Notice how the position of the last item in the list is determined by the `getTotal` method; remember that we do not have access to the `total` attribute, since this was declared as **private** in the superclass.

```
double totalPaid = 0;
for (int i=1; i<= getTotal();i++)
{
    totalPaid = totalPaid + getPayment(i).getAmount();
}
return totalPaid;
```

The body of the loop takes the amount associated with the current payment and adds it to the running total. As you can see, the `getPayment` method is used to return the current payment and the `getAmount` method is used to find out the amount associated with that payment.

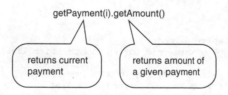

Before we move on, it is important to test this `PaymentList` class in order to ensure that it is functioning correctly. Program 11.1 provides a menu-driven interface for this test driver. Notice the careful use of the new line, '\n' and tab, '\t', escape sequences to improve the display of information on the screen.

Program 11.1

```
public class PaymentListTester
{
    public static void main(String[] args)
    {
        char choice;
        int total;
        PaymentList pl; // declare PaymentList object to test
        // get size of list
        System.out.print("\nMaximum number of payments? ");
        total = EasyInEasyScanner.getIntnextInt();
        pl = new PaymentList(total); // create object to test
        // menu
        do
```

```java
        {
            // display options
            System.out.println("\n[1] Add a payment");
            System.out.println("[2] List all payments");
            System.out.println("[3] Get number of payments made");
            System.out.println("[4] Get total payments made");
            System.out.println("[5] Quit");
            System.out.print("\nEnter a choice [1,2,3,4,5]: ");
            // get choice
            choice = EasyInEasyScanner.getCharnextChar()();
            // process choice
            switch(choice)
            {
                case '1': option1(pl); break;
                case '2': option2(pl); break;
                case '3': option3(pl); break;
                case '4': option4(pl); break;
                case '5': System.out.print("\n\nBYE"); break;
                default: System.out.print("\n1-5 only");
            }
        } while (choice != '5');
    }


    // static helper methods
    // add payment
    private static void option1(PaymentList listIn)
    {   if (!listInpl.isFull())// only add if list has space
        {
            System.out.print("\nenter month:\t");
            String month = EasyScanner.nextString();
            System.out.print("enter amount:\t");
            double amount = EasyScanner.nextDouble();
            listIn.add(new Payment (month, amount));;
        }
        else // error message if list is full
        {
            System.out.println("\n!!!SORRY, LIST IS FULL!!!");
        }
    }


    // display payments
    private static void option2(PaymentList listIn)
    {
        System.out.print("\nMONTH \tAMOUNT\n");// header
        // loop through payments in list
        for (int i = 1; i <= listIn.getTotal();i++)
        {
            Payment p = listIn.getPayment(i);
            System.out.print(p.getMonth());
            System.out.println("\t" + p.getAmount());
        }
    }


    // get total number of payments
    private static void option3(PaymentList listIn)
    {
        System.out.print("\ntotal number payments made: ");
        System.out.println(listIn.getTotal());
    }


    // get total of payments made
    private static void option4(PaymentList listIn)
    {
        System.out.print("\ntotal sum of payments made: ");
        System.out.println(listIn.calculateTotalPaid());
    }
}
```

There is nothing particularly new here so let's look at a sample test run of this driver program:

Maximum number of payments? 2

[1] Add a payment

[2] List all payments

[3] Get number of payments made

[4] Get total payments made

[5] Quit

Enter a choice [1,2,3,4,5]: **1**

enter month: Jan

enter amount: 240

[1] Add a payment

[2] List all payments

[3] Get number of payments made

[4] Get total payments made

[5] Quit

Enter a choice [1,2,3,4,5]: **1**

enter month: Feb

enter amount: 225

[1] Add a payment

[2] List all payments

[3] Get number of payments made

[4] Get total payments made

[5] Quit

Enter a choice [1,2,3,4,5]: **2**

```
MONTH AMOUNT

Jan 240.0

Feb 225.0


[1] Add a payment

[2] List all payments

[3] Get number of payments made

[4] Get total payments made

[5] Quit

Enter a choice [1,2,3,4,5]: 3

total number payments made: 2


[1] Add a payment

[2] List all payments

[3] Get number of payments made

[4] Get total payments made

[5] Quit


Enter a choice [1,2,3,4,5]: 4


total sum of payments made: 465.0


[1] Add a payment

[2] List all payments

[3] Get number of payments made

[4] Get total payments made

[5] Quit

Enter a choice [1,2,3,4,5]: 1


!!!SORRY, LIST IS FULL!!!


[1] Add a payment

[2] List all payments
```

```
[3] Get number of payments made

[4] Get total payments made

[5] Quit


Enter a choice [1,2,3,4,5]: 5


BYE
```

Although some aspects of the interface could be improved, the PaymentList class appears to be functioning properly. In order to be more confident, more rigorous testing would need to be carried out. For now though, this amount of testing is sufficient so we will move on to the Tenant class.

11.7 Implementing the *Tenant* class

As you can see from the UML diagram of figure 11.1, the Tenant class contains four attributes: name, room, payments, maxNoOfPayments.

The first two of these represent the name and the room of the tenant respectively. The third attribute, payments, is to be implemented as a PaymentList object and the last attribute, maxNoOfPayments, is to be implemented as a **static** class attribute. The maxNoOfPayments attribute will also be implemented as a *constant* as we are assuming that tenants make a *fixed* number of payments in a year (twelve – one for each month). As we discussed in chapter 9, it makes sense to declare class constants as **public**. Below is the code for the Tenant class.

The *Tenant* class

```java
/** Class used to record the details of a tenant
 *  @author Charatan and Kans
 *  @version 5th September 2005
 */
public class Tenant
{
    private String name;
    private int room;
    private PaymentList payments;
    public static final int maxNoOfPayments = 12;

    /** Constructor initialises the name and room number of the tenant
     *  and sets the payments made to the empty list
     */
    Tenant(String nameIn, int roomIn)
    {
        name = new String(nameIn);
        room = roomIn;
        payments = new PaymentList(maxNoOfPayments);
    }

    /** Reads the name of the tenant */
    public String getName()
    {
        return name;
    }
```

```
    /** Reads the room number of the tenant */
    public int getRoom()
    {
        return room;
    }

    /** Records a payment for the tenant */
    public void makePayment(Payment paymentIn)
    {
        payments.add(paymentIn); // call PaymentList method
    }

    /** Reads the payments made by the tenant */
    public PaymentList getPayments()
    {
        return payments;
    }
}
```

As there is nothing very new in this class, we don't really need to discuss it any further other than to point out that the `payments` attribute, being of type `PaymentList`, can respond to any of the `PaymentList` methods we discussed in section 11.6. The `makePayment` method illustrates this by calling the `add` method of `PaymentList`.

```
public void makePayment(Payment paymentIn)
{
    payments.add(paymentIn); // add method of PaymentList called
}
```

The implementation of a driver to test this class will be very similar to program 11.1 and is left as a practical exercise at the end of this chapter.

11.8 Implementing the *TenantList* class

The `TenantList` class, like the `PaymentList` class of section 11.6, inherits from the generic `ObjectList` class. As you can see from figure 11.1, the `TenantList` class requires no new attributes and, apart from the constructor, has only three new methods:

>   getTenant;

>   search;

>   removeTenant.

The `getTenant` method behaves in much the same way as the `getPayment` method of the `PaymentList` class. That is, it acts as a wrapper for the `getItem` method of the generic `ObjectList` class and type casts the returned item back to an object of the correct type, which in this case is an object of type `Tenant`.

```
public Tenant getTenant(int positionIn)
{   // call inherited method and type cast
    return (Tenant)getItem(positionIn);
}
```

The search method is unique to the `TenantList` class. Here is a reminder of its interface:

search (int): Tenant

The integer parameter represents the room number of the tenant that this method is searching for. The tenant returned is the tenant living in that particular room; if no tenant is found in that room then **null** is returned.

We have already met an algorithm for searching an array in section 5.7.4 of this book. That algorithm dealt with searching an *entire* array and this was adapted in section 7.7.1 where we searched a *partially filled* array. This is an example of searching a partially filled array so the code is similar to that in the `Bank` example of section 7.7.1. In the previous algorithms we returned a dummy value of −999 to indicate an unsuccessful search. In this case, however, we must return a value of **null**:

```
public Tenant search(int roomIn)
{
    for(int i=1;i<=getTotal();i++)
    {   // find tenant with given room number
        if(getTenant(i).getRoom() == roomIn)
        {
            return getTenant(i);
        }
    }
    return null; // no tenant found with given room number
}
```

Notice that to check the room number of a particular tenant we call the `getTenant` method to identify the tenant, and then the `getRoom` method to identify this tenant's room number:

```
if(getTenant(i).getRoom() == roomIn)
{
        return getTenant(i);
}
```

Finally, let's look at the `removeTenant` method. The interface for this method is given as follows:

removeTenant(int): boolean

Here the integer parameter represents the room number of the tenant that is to be removed from the list and the **boolean** return value indicates whether or not such a tenant has been removed successfully. From this interface we get the following method header:

```
public boolean removeTenant (int roomIn)
{
    // code for methods goes here
}
```

Most of the work of this method is going to be carried out by the `remove` method of the `ObjectList` class. The job of the `removeTenant` method is to determine which tenant to delete before calling the `remove` method. It is very similar to the `remove` method we looked at in the `Bank` example of section

7.7.1. In that case we looked for the bank account with the given account number whereas in this case we are looking for a tenant in a given room number:

```java
for(int i=1;i<=getTotal();i++)
{ // remove tenant with given room number
    if(getTenant(i).getRoom() == roomIn)
    {
        remove(i); // call remove method of ObjectList
        return true; // indicate success
    }
}
return false; // indicate failure
```

The complete code for the `TenantList` class is now presented below.

The *TenantList* class

```java
/** Collection class to hold a list of tenants
 *   @author Charatan and Kans
 *   @version 6th September 2005
 */
public class TenantList extends ObjectList
{

    /** Constructor initialises the empty list and sets the maximimum
     *   list size
     */
    public TenantList(int sizeIn)
    {
        super(sizeIn); // call ObjectList constructor
    }

    /** Reads the tenant at the given position in the list
     *   @param positionIn The position of the tenant in the list
     *   @return Returns the tenant at the given position in the list
     *           or null if no tenant at that posiiton
     */
    public Tenant getTenant(int positionIn)
    {
        if (positionIn<1 || positionIn>getTotal())//check for valid position
        {
            return null; // no object found at given position
        }
        else
        {
            // call inherited method and type cast
            return (Tenant) getItem(positionIn);
        }
    }

    /** Searches for the tenant in the given room number
     *   @param roomIn The room number to search for
     *   @return Returns the tenant in the given room
     *           or null if no tenant in the given room
     */
    public Tenant search(int roomIn)
    {
        for(int i = 1;i <= getTotal();i++)
        {   // find tenant with given room number
            if(getTenant(i).getRoom() == roomIn)
            {
                return getTenant(i);
            }
        }
        return null; // no tenant found with given room number
    }
}
```

```
/** Removes the tenant in the given room number
 *   @param roomIn The room number to of the tenant to remove
 *   @return Returns true if the tenant is removed successfully
 *           or false otherwise
 */
public boolean removeTenant(int roomIn)
{
    for(int i = 1;i <= getTotal();i++)
    {   // remove tenant with given room number
        if(getTenant(i).getRoom() == roomIn)
        {
            remove(i);
            return true;
        }
    }
    return false; // no tenant found with given room number
}
}
```

Program 11.2 is a driver to test the `TenantList` class. Once again, notice the use of escape sequences to help format output on the screen.

Program 11.2

```
public  class TenantListTester
{
    public static void main(String[] args)
    {   // declare variables
        char choice;
        int total;
        TenantList tl;
        // get size of list
        System.out.print("\nHow many tenants will there be ? ");
        total = EasyScanner.nextInt();
        tl = new TenantList(total); // create list
        // menu
        do
        {   // display options
            System.out.println("\n[1] Add a tenant");
            System.out.println("[2] List all tenants");
            System.out.println("[3] Add a payment");
            System.out.println("[4] List payments");
            System.out.println("[5] Remove a tenant");
            System.out.println("[6] Quit");
            System.out.print("\nEnter a choice [1,2,3,4,5,6]: ");
            choice = EasyScanner.nextChar();// get choice
            // process choice
            switch(choice)
            {
                case '1':option1(tl); break;
                case '2':option2(tl); break;
                case '3':option3(tl); break;
                case '4':option4(tl); break;
                case '5':option5(tl); break;
                case '6':System.out.print("\n\nBYE"); break;
                default: System.out.print("\n1-5 only");
            }
        } while (choice != '6');
    }

    private static void option1(TenantList listIn)
    {
        if (!listIn.isFull())// add only if list is not full
        {
            System.out.print("\nenter name:\t");
```

```java
            String name = EasyScanner.nextString();
            System.out.print("enter room:\t");
            int room = EasyScanner.nextInt();
            listIn.add(new Tenant (name, room));
        }
        else // error message if list is full
        {
            System.out.println("\n!!!SORRY, LIST IS FULL!!! \n");
        }
    }

    private static void option2(TenantList listIn)
    {
        System.out.print("\nNAME \tROOM\n");// header
        // loop through tenants in list
        for (int i =1; i <= listIn.getTotal();i++)
        {
            Tenant t = listIn.getTenant(i);
            System.out.print(t.getName());
            System.out.println("\t" + t.getRoom());
        }
    }

    private static void option3(TenantList listIn)
    {
        // get room number of tenant
        System.out.print("\nenter room number of tenant:\t");
        int room = EasyScanner.nextInt();
        // find relevant tenant
        Tenant t = listIn.search(room);
        if (t != null) // check tenant exists before adding payment
        {
            System.out.print("\nenter month:\t");
            String month = EasyScanner.nextString();
            System.out.print("enter amount:\t");
            double amount = EasyScanner.nextDouble();
            Payment p = new Payment (month, amount);
            t.makePayment(p);
        }
        else // no tenant with given room number found
        {
            System.out.print("\n!!!NO TENANT IN THIS ROOM!!! \n");
        }
    }

    private static void option4(TenantList listIn)
    {
        // get room number of tenant
        System.out.print("\nenter room number of tenant:\t");
        int room = EasyScanner.nextInt();
        // find relevant tenant
        Tenant t = listIn.search(room);
        if (t != null)// check such a tenant exists before displaying
        {
            PaymentList pl = t.getPayments();
            System.out.print("\nMONTH \tAMOUNT\n");// header
            // loop through payments in list
            for (int i =1; i <= pl.getTotal();i++)
            {
                Payment p = pl.getPayment(i);
                System.out.print(p.getMonth());
                System.out.println("\t" + p.getAmount());
            }
            // display total amount paid
            System.out.print("\nTOTAL PAID:\t");
            System.out.println(pl.calculateTotalPaid());
        }
        else // no tenant with given room number found
        {
            System.out.print("\n!!!NO TENANT IN THIS ROOM!!! \n");
```

```
            }
        }

        private static void option5(TenantList listIn)
        {
            // get room number of tenant
            System.out.print("\nenter room number of tenant:\t");
            int room = EasyScanner.nextInt();
            // check tenant exists
            Tenant t = listIn.search(room);
            if (t != null)// only remove if tenant exists
            {
                listIn.removeTenant(room);
            }
            else // no tenant in given room
            {
                System.out.print("\n!!! NO TENANT IN THIS ROOM!!! \n");
            }
        }
    }
```

By now, such a menu system should be familiar to you. We just draw your attention to the validation that we have added to some of these menu options.

Option 1 allows the user to add a tenant to the list. We have ensured that a tenant is added only if the list is currently *not full*.

```
if (!listIn.isFull())// only add if list is not full
{
    // code to get tenant details and add
}
else // error message if list is full
{
    System.out.println("\n!!!SORRY, LIST IS FULL!!! \n");
}
```

Notice we haven't carried out any error checking on the rooms at this stage. Responsibility for ensuring that tenants do not occupy the same room has not been given to the TenantList class so should not be tested here. This job will be given to the Hostel class that we will develop in the next chapter.

Option 3 allows the user to record the payment for a tenant in a given room. We have ensured that a tenant actually exists in that room before recording the payment.

```
int room = EasyScanner.nextInt();
// find relevant tenant
Tenant t = listIn.search(room);
// check tenant exists before adding payment
if (t != null)
{
    // code to get and record payment goes here
}
else // no tenant with given room number found
{
    System.out.print("\n!!!NO TENANT IN THIS ROOM!!! \n");
}
```

Options 4 and 5 include similar validation as both require a tenant to exist in a given room before further action can be taken. Below is a sample test run of program 11.2.

How many tenants will there be ? **2**

[1] Add a tenant

[2] List all tenants

[3] Add a payment

[4] List payments

[5] Remove a tenant

[6] Quit

Enter a choice [1,2,3,4,5,6]: **1**

enter name: **Bart**

enter room: **3**

[1] Add a tenant

[2] List all tenants

[3] Add a payment

[4] List payments

[5] Remove a tenant

[6] Quit

Enter a choice [1,2,3,4,5,6]: **1**

enter name: **Louise**

enter room: **1**

[1] Add a tenant

[2] List all tenants

[3] Add a payment

[4] List payments

[5] Remove a tenant

[6] Quit

Enter a choice [1,2,3,4,5,6]: **2**

```
NAME ROOM
Bart 3
Louise 1


[1] Add a tenant
[2] List all tenants
[3] Add a payment
[4] List payments
[5] Remove a tenant
[6] Quit


Enter a choice [1,2,3,4,5,6]: 1
!!!SORRY, LIST IS FULL!!!


[1] Add a tenant
[2] List all tenants
[3] Add a payment
[4] List payments
[5] Remove a tenant
[6] Quit


Enter a choice [1,2,3,4,5,6]: 3


enter room number of tenant: 5


!!!NO TENANT IN THIS ROOM!!!


[1] Add a tenant
[2] List all tenants
[3] Add a payment
[4] List payments
[5] Remove a tenant
[6] Quit
```

Enter a choice [1,2,3,4,5,6]: 3

enter room number of tenant: 3

enter month: Jan
enter amount: 240

[1] Add a tenant

[2] List all tenants

[3] Add a payment

[4] List payments

[5] Remove a tenant

[6] Quit

Enter a choice [1,2,3,4,5,6]: 3

enter room number of tenant: 3

enter month: Feb
enter amount: 225

[1] Add a tenant

[2] List all tenants

[3] Add a payment

[4] List payments

[5] Remove a tenant

[6] Quit

Enter a choice [1,2,3,4,5,6]: 4

enter room number of tenant: 2

!!!NO TENANT IN THIS ROOM!!!

[1] Add a tenant

[2] List all tenants

[3] Add a payment

[4] List payments

[5] Remove a tenant

[6] Quit

Enter a choice [1,2,3,4,5,6]: **4**

enter room number of tenant: **3**

MONTH AMOUNT

Jan 240.0

Feb 225.0

TOTAL PAID: 465.0

[1] Add a tenant

[2] List all tenants

[3] Add a payment

[4] List payments

[5] Remove a tenant

[6] Quit

Enter a choice [1,2,3,4,5,6]: **5**

enter room number of tenant: **7**

!!! NO TENANT IN THIS ROOM!!!

[1] Add a tenant

[2] List all tenants

[3] Add a payment

[4] List payments

[5] Remove a tenant

[6] Quit

```
Enter a choice [1,2,3,4,5,6]: 5


enter room number of tenant: 3


[1] Add a tenant

[2] List all tenants

[3] Add a payment

[4] List payments

[5] Remove a tenant

[6] Quit


Enter a choice [1,2,3,4,5,6]: 2


NAME  ROOM

Louise 1


[1] Add a tenant

[2] List all tenants

[3] Add a payment

[4] List payments

[5] Remove a tenant

[6] Quit

Enter a choice [1,2,3,4,5,6]: 6


BYE
```

Self-test questions

1 Describe the class associations given in the UML design of figure 11.1.

2 Why was a generic `ObjectList` class developed in this case study?

3 How are class attributes recorded in a UML diagram?

4 How might you improve the application developed in this case study?

Programming exercises

1 Test the `Payment` class of section 11.4 by implementing a suitable driver class.

2 Amend the driver from exercise 1 above, so that instead of the user entering a month directly, another menu is displayed with the 12 months listed as follows:

```
[1]   January
[2]   February
[3]   March
[4]   April
[5]   May
[6]   June
[7]   July
[8]   August
[9]   September
[10]  October
[11]  November
[12]  December

enter month [1 to 12]:
```

3 Test the `Tenant` class of section 11.7 by implementing a suitable driver class.

4 Implement and run program 11.2 to test the amended `TenantList` class developed in exercise 3 above.

5 Amend program 11.2 so that all monetary values are displayed to two decimal places. (Hint: Look back at the `DecimalFormat` class discussed in chapter 9.)

6 Make any changes to the `Hostel` case study that you considered in self-test question 4.

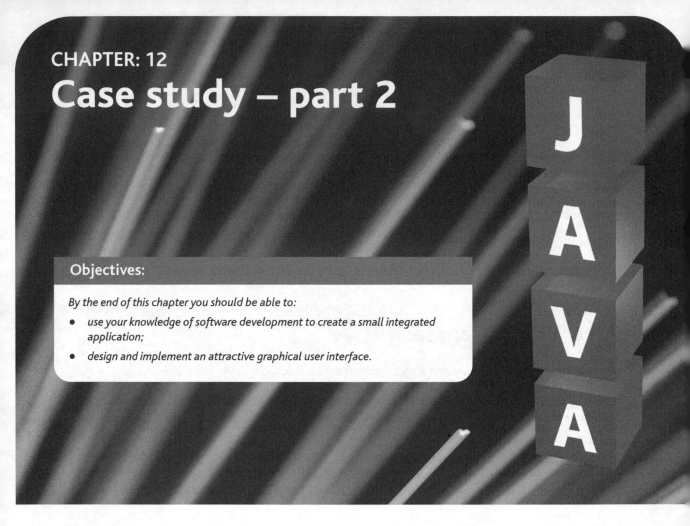

CHAPTER: 12

Case study – part 2

Objectives:

By the end of this chapter you should be able to:

- *use your knowledge of software development to create a small integrated application;*
- *design and implement an attractive graphical user interface.*

12.1 Introduction

All that remains for us to do to complete our case study is to design, implement and test the `Hostel` class which will not only keep track of the tenants but will also act as the graphical user interface for the system.

12.2 Keeping permanent records

In practice, an application such as the *Student Hostel System* would not be much use if we had no way of keeping permanent records – in other words, of saving a file to disk. However, reading and writing files is something that you will not learn until your second semester (chapter 20). So, in the meantime, in order to make it possible to keep a permanent record of your data, we have created a special class for you to use; we have called this class `TenantFileHandler`. This class (along with the rest of the files from this case study) can be found on the accompanying CD.

The `TenantFileHandler` class has two **static** methods: the first, `saveRecords`, needs to be sent two parameters, an integer value indicating the number of rooms in the hostel, and a `TenantList`, which is a reference to the list to be saved; the second, `readRecords`, requires only a reference to a `TenantList` so that it knows where to store the information that is read from the file.

The `readRecords` method will be called when the application is first loaded (so this method call will therefore be coded into the constructor), and the `saveRecords` method will be called when we finish the application (and will therefore be coded into the event-handler of a "Save and Quit" button). We will also provide the option of exiting without saving, just in case, for any reason, the user should want to abandon any changes.

12.3 Design of the GUI

There will be two aspects to the design of the graphical interface. Firstly we need to design the visual side of things; then we need to design the algorithms for our event-handling routines so that the buttons do the jobs we want them to, like adding or displaying tenants.

Let's start with the visual design. We need to choose which graphics components we are going to use and how to lay them out. One way to do this is to make a preliminary sketch such as the one shown in figure 12.1. We have named our components so that it is obvious what kind of component we are talking about; for example, `nameField` is a `JTextField`, `addButton` is a `JButton` and `displayArea1` is a `JTextArea`.

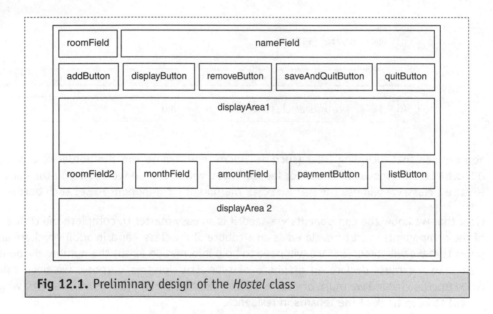

Fig 12.1. Preliminary design of the *Hostel* class

We are going to use a simple `FlowLayout` policy, so to get our components where we want them we will have to play about with the size of the components and the size of the frame. You can see from the design that we have not included any labels to mark the purpose of components. For example the `roomField` has no associated label to indicate that a room number is to be entered into this field. Instead we will give such components a *titled border* indicating their purpose. As the name suggests, this is a facility in Swing to give a component a particular style of border that includes a title. We will examine this and other types of border in detail in chapter 19, but introduce its use here in this case study. To help you see what we are aiming at, we have, with figure 12.2, "cheated" and let you look ahead at the end result. This shows the effect of running our `Hostel` interface in a 550 × 450 frame.

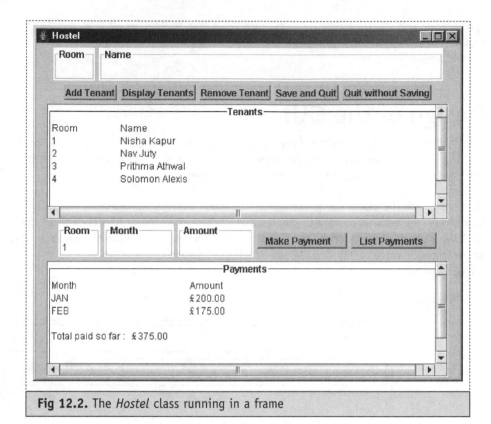

Fig 12.2. The *Hostel* class running in a frame

You can see that including titles (such as "Room" and "Name") in the border of a component such as a `JTextField` removes the need for labels. As you will see when we show you the complete code for the `Hostel` class, we will use the `setBorder` method of a component to set such borders.

Now that we know the components we need, it is an easy matter to complete the UML class diagram. Each of the components must be declared as an attribute of the class – and, in addition, there are two more attributes that we will need. First we will need to hold information about the number of rooms available in the hostel, so we must declare an attribute of type **int** for this purpose; we have called our attribute `noOfRooms`. Second we must, of course, declare an attribute of type `TenantList` (which we have called `list`) to keep track of the tenants in residence.

We are going to need only two methods: a constructor to add the components and read the data from the file, and an `actionPerformed` method for the event-handling routines.

The class design is shown in figure 12.3.

Hostel
noOfRooms : int *list : TenantList* *roomField : JTextField* *nameField : JTextField* *addButton : JButton* *displayButton : JButton* *removeButton : JButton* *saveAndQuitButton : JButton* *quitButton : JButton* *displayArea1 : JTextArea* *roomField2 : JTextField* *monthField : JTextField* *amountField : JTextField* *paymentButton : JButton* *listButton : JButton* *displayArea2 : JTextArea*
Hostel(int) *actionPerformed(ActionEvent)*

Fig 12.3. The UML design of the *Hostel* Class

12.4 Designing the event-handlers

As you can see, there are seven buttons that need to be coded so that they respond in the correct way when pressed. Our code for the `actionPerformed` method will therefore take the following form:

```
public void actionPerformed(ActionEvent e)
{
    if(e.getSource() == addButton)
    {
        // code for add button goes here
    }

    if(e.getSource() == displayButton)
    {
        // code for display button goes here
    }

    if(e.getSource() == removeButton)
    {
        // code for remove button goes here
    }

    if(e.getSource() == paymentButton)
    {
        // code for payment button goes here
    }

    if(e.getSource() == listButton)
    {
        // code for list button goes here
    }

    if(e.getSource() == saveAndQuitButton)
    {
        // code for saveAndQuit button goes here
    }
    if(e.getSource() == quitButton)
    {
        // code for quit button goes here
    }
}
```

We have summarized below the task that each button must perform, and then gone on to design our algorithms using pseudocode:

The addButton

The purpose of this button is to add a new `Tenant` to the list. The values entered in `roomField` and `nameField` must be validated; first of all, they must not be blank; second, the room number must not be greater than the number of rooms available (or less than 1!); finally, the room must not be occupied. If all this is okay, then the new tenant is added (we will make use of the `add` method of `TenantList` to do this) and a message should be displayed in `displayArea1`. We can express this in pseudocode as follows:

```
read roomField
read nameField
IF roomField blank OR nameField blank
    display blank field error in displayArea1
ELSE IF roomField value <1 OR roomField value >noOfRooms
    display invalid room number error in displayArea1
ELSE IF tenant found in room
    display room occupied error in displayArea1
ELSE
BEGIN
    add tenant
    blank roomField
    blank nameField
    display message to confirm success in displayArea1
END
```

The displayButton

Pressing this button will display the full list of tenants (room number and name) in `displayArea1`.

If all the rooms are vacant a suitable message should be displayed; otherwise the list of tenants' rooms and names should appear under appropriate headings as can be seen in figure 12.2. This can be expressed in pseudocode as follows:

```
IF list is empty
    display rooms empty error in displayArea1
ELSE
BEGIN
    display header in displayArea1
    LOOP FROM first item TO last item in list
    BEGIN
        append tenant room and name to displayArea1
    END
END
```

The removeButton

Clicking on this button will remove the tenant whose room number has been entered in `roomField`.

As with the `addButton`, the room number entered must be validated; if the number is a valid one then the tenant is removed from the list (we will make use of the `remove` method of `TenantList` to do this) and a confirmation message is displayed. The pseudocode for this event-handler is given as follows:

```
read roomField
IF roomField blank
    display blank field error in displayArea1
ELSE IF roomField value < 1 OR roomField value > noOfRooms
    display invalid room number error in displayArea1
ELSE IF no tenant found in room
    display room empty error in displayArea1
ELSE
BEGIN
    remove tenant from list
    display message to confirm success in displayArea1
END
```

The paymentButton

This button records payments made by an individual tenant whose room number is entered in roomField2. The values entered in roomField2, monthField and amountField must be validated to ensure that none of the fields is blank, that the room number is a valid one and, if so, that it is currently occupied.

If everything is okay then a new payment record is added to that tenant's list of payments (we will make use of the makePayment method of PaymentList to do this) and a confirmation message is displayed in displayArea2. This design is expressed in pseudocode as follows:

```
read roomField2
read monthField
read amountField
IF roomField2 blank OR monthField blank OR amountField blank
    display fields empty error in displayArea2
ELSE IF roomField2 value<1 OR roomField2 value>noOfRooms
    display invalid room number error in displayArea2
ELSE IF no tenant found in room
    display room empty error in displayArea2
ELSE
BEGIN
    create payment from amountField value and monthField value
    add payment into list
    display message to confirm success in displayArea2
END
```

The listButton

Pressing this button causes a list of payments (month and amount) made by the tenant whose room number is entered in roomField2 to be displayed in displayArea2.

After validating the values entered, each record in the tenant's payment list is displayed. Finally, the total amount paid by that tenant is displayed (we will make use of the calculateTotalPaid method of PaymentList to do this). The pseudocode is given as follows:

```
read roomField2
IF roomField2 blank
display room field empty error in displayArea2
ELSE IF roomField2 value<1 OR roomField2 value>noOfRooms
    display invalid room number error in displayArea2
ELSE IF no tenant found in room
    display room empty error in displayArea2
ELSE
BEGIN
    find tenant in given room
    get payments of tenant
    IF payments = 0
        display no payments error in displayArea2
    ELSE
    BEGIN
        display header in displayArea2
        LOOP FROM first payment TO last payment
        BEGIN
            append amount and month to displayArea2
        END
        display total paid in displayArea2
        blank monthField
        blank amountField
    END
END
```

The *saveAndQuitButton*

Pressing this button causes all the records to be saved to a file (here we make use of the `saveRecords` method of the `TenantFileHandler` class that we talked about in section 12.2); it then closes the frame, terminating the program.

It contains only two lines of code and we have therefore not written pseudocode for it.

The *quitButton*

Pressing this button terminates the program without saving the changes.

12.5 Implementation

The complete code for the `Hostel` class now appears below. When you come to reading the code, you should notice that we have utilized the `NumberFormat` class (which is to be found in the `java.text` package) to print the amounts in the local currency. Also note the use of the `parseInt` method of the `Integer` class to convert the room values, entered as text, into integer values and the use of the `setBorder` method to set the border of a component (as discussed in section 12.3).

Study the code and the comments carefully and compare it with the pseudocode to make sure you understand it.

The *Hostel* class

```java
import java.awt.*;
import java.awt.event.*;
import java.text.*;
import javax.swing.*;
import javax.swing.border.*;

/** GUI for the Hostel application
  * @author Charatan and Kans
  * @version 7th September 2005
  */
public class Hostel extends JFrame implements ActionListener
{
    // the attributes
    private  int noOfRooms;
    private  TenantList list;
    private  JButton addButton = new JButton("Add Tenant");
    private  JButton displayButton = new JButton("Display Tenants");
    private  JButton removeButton = new JButton("Remove Tenant");
    private  JTextField roomField = new JTextField(4);
    private  JTextField nameField = new JTextField(39);
    private  JButton saveAndQuitButton = new JButton("Save and Quit");
    private  JButton quitButton = new JButton("Quit without Saving");
    private  JTextArea displayArea1 = new JTextArea(8,45);
    private  JTextArea displayArea2 = new JTextArea(8,45);
    private  JTextField roomField2 = new JTextField(4);
    private  JTextField monthField = new JTextField(7);
    private  JTextField amountField = new JTextField(8);
    private JButton paymentButton = new JButton("   Make Payment       ");
    private  JButton listButton = new JButton("   List Payments       ");

    //the constructor
    public Hostel (int numberIn)
    {
        // initialse the number of rooms and the TenantList
        noOfRooms = numberIn;
        list = new TenantList(noOfRooms);

        // set layout policy to FlowLayout
        setLayout(new FlowLayout());
        // allow program to end when cross-hairs are clicked
        setDefaultCloseOperation(JFrame.EXIT_ON_CLOSE);
        // set appearance of JFrame
        setTitle("Hostel");
        setSize(550, 450);
        setLocation(400,100);
        getContentPane().setBackground(Color.cyan);
        // create a border style to be used for the JButtons
        BevelBorder raisedBevel = new BevelBorder(BevelBorder.RAISED);
        // add components
        add(roomField);
        /* The setBorder method is used to give a a component a titled
           border. This version of the method accepts an appropriate
           TitleBoarder object */
        roomField.setBorder(new TitledBorder("Room"));
        // repeat this process for the nameField
        add(nameField);
        nameField.setBorder(new TitledBorder("Name"));
        //   JButtons are added, their background colours and borders set
        add(addButton);
        addButton.setBackground(Color.green);
        addButton.setBorder(raisedBevel);
        add(displayButton);
        displayButton.setBorder(raisedBevel);
        displayButton.setBackground(Color.green);
        add(removeButton);
        removeButton.setBackground(Color.green);
        removeButton.setBorder(raisedBevel);
        add(saveAndQuitButton);
```

```
        saveAndQuitButton.setBackground(Color.green);
        saveAndQuitButton.setBorder(raisedBevel);
        add(quitButton);
        quitButton.setBackground(Color.green);
        quitButton.setBorder(raisedBevel);
        /* By default the title of a component will be left justified.
           To choose another justification (in this case to centre the
           title) another version of the constructor is required.
           This takes a border style (we chose black line),
           the title (we chose "Tenants"),
           the justification (we chose Centre)
           and the title position (we chose Top) */
        displayArea1.setBorder
            (new TitledBorder(new LineBorder(Color.black),
                "Tenants",TitledBorder.CENTER,TitledBorder.TOP));
        // A JScrollPane created for displayArea1 (see discussion below)
        JScrollPane p1 = new JScrollPane(displayArea1);
        add(p1);
        // the remaining components are added in a similar way
        add(roomField2);
        roomField2.setBorder(new TitledBorder("Room"));
        add(monthField);
        monthField.setBorder(new TitledBorder("Month"));
        add(amountField);
        amountField.setBorder(new TitledBorder("Amount"));
        add(paymentButton);
        paymentButton.setBackground(Color.green);
        paymentButton.setBorder(raisedBevel);
        add(listButton);
        listButton.setBorder(raisedBevel);
        listButton.setBackground(Color.green);
        displayArea2.setBorder
            (new TitledBorder(new LineBorder(Color.black),
                "Payments",TitledBorder.CENTER,TitledBorder.TOP));
        // see discussion below about ScrollPanes
        JScrollPane p2 = new JScrollPane(displayArea2);
        add(p2);
        // listeners given to buttons
        addButton.addActionListener(this);
        displayButton.addActionListener(this);
        paymentButton.addActionListener(this);
        listButton.addActionListener(this);
        removeButton.addActionListener(this);
        listButton.addActionListener(this);
        saveAndQuitButton.addActionListener(this);
        quitButton.addActionListener(this);
        // read records from file into the list
        TenantFileHandler.readRecords(list);
        // make GUI visible
        setVisible(true);
    }

    // the event handlers
    public void actionPerformed(ActionEvent e)
    {
        if(e.getSource() == addButton)
        {
            String roomEntered = roomField.getText();
            String nameEntered = nameField.getText();
            if(roomEntered.length()==0 || nameEntered.length()==0)
            {
                displayArea1.setText
                    ("Room number and name must be entered");
            }
            else if(Integer.parseInt(roomEntered)< 1
                            ||
                Integer.parseInt(roomEntered)>noOfRooms)
            {
                displayArea1.setText
                    ("There are only " + noOfRooms + " rooms");
```

```
                    }
                    else if(list.search(Integer.parseInt(roomEntered)) != null)
                    {
                        displayArea1.setText("Room number "
                                            + Integer.parseInt(roomEntered)
                                            + " is occupied");
                    }
                    else
                    {
                        Tenant t =
                            new Tenant(nameEntered,Integer.parseInt(roomEntered));
                    list.add(t);
                    roomField.setText("");
                    nameField.setText("");
                    displayArea1.setText("New tenant in room "
                                        + roomEntered
                                        + " successfully added");
                }
            }

        if(e.getSource() == displayButton)
        {
            int i;
            if(list.isEmpty())
            {
                displayArea1.setText("All rooms are empty");
            }
            else
            {
                displayArea1.setText("Room" + "\t" + "Name" + "\n");
                for(i = 1; i <= list.getTotal(); i++)
                {
                    displayArea1.append(list.getTenant(i).getRoom()
                    + "\t"
                    + list.getTenant(i).getName() + "\n");
                }
            }
        }

        if(e.getSource() == removeButton)
        {
            String roomEntered = roomField.getText();
            if(roomEntered.length()==0)
            {
                displayArea1.setText("Room number must be entered");
            }
            else if(Integer.parseInt(roomEntered) < 1
                            || Integer.parseInt(roomEntered)>noOfRooms)
            {
                displayArea1.setText("Invalid room number");
            }
            else if(list.search(Integer.parseInt(roomEntered)) == null)
            {
                displayArea1.setText
                    ("Room number " + roomEntered + " is empty");
            }
            else
            {
                list.removeTenant(Integer.parseInt(roomEntered));
                displayArea1.setText("Tenant removed from room "
                                    + Integer.parseInt(roomEntered));
            }
        }

        if(e.getSource() == paymentButton)
        {
            String roomEntered = roomField2.getText();
            String monthEntered =  monthField.getText();
            String amountEntered = amountField.getText();
            if(roomEntered.length()==0 || monthEntered.length()==0
```

```
                                        || amountEntered.length()==0)
    {
        displayArea2.setText
            ("Room number, month and amount must all be entered");
    }
    else if(Integer.parseInt(roomEntered) < 1
                        || Integer.parseInt(roomEntered)>noOfRooms)
    {
        displayArea2.setText("Invalid room number");
    }
    else if(list.search(Integer.parseInt(roomEntered)) == null)
    {
        displayArea2.setText
            ("Room number " + roomEntered + " is empty");
    }
    else
    {
        Payment p = new Payment
            (monthEntered,Double.valueOf(amountEntered).doubleValue());
        list.search(Integer.parseInt(roomEntered)).makePayment(p);
        displayArea2.setText("Payment recorded");
    }
}

if(e.getSource() == listButton)
{
    int i;
    String roomEntered = roomField2.getText();
    if(roomEntered.length()==0)
    {
        displayArea2.setText("Room number must be entered");
    }
    else if(Integer.parseInt(roomEntered) < 1
                        || Integer.parseInt(roomEntered) > noOfRooms)
    {
        displayArea2.setText("Invalid room number");
    }
    else if(list.search(Integer.parseInt(roomEntered)) == null)
    {
        displayArea2.setText("Room number "
                + Integer.parseInt(roomEntered)+ " is empty");
    }
    else
    {
        Tenant t = list.search(Integer.parseInt(roomEntered));
        PaymentList p = t.getPayments();
        if(t.getPayments().getTotal() == 0)
        {
            displayArea2.setText
            ("No payments made for this tenant");
        }
        else
        { /* The NumberFormat class is similar to the
             DecimalFormat class that we used previously. The
             getCurrencyInstance method of this class reads the
             system values to find out which country we are in,
             then uses the correct currency symbol */
            NumberFormat nf = NumberFormat.getCurrencyInstance();
            String s;
            displayArea2.setText
                ("Month" + "\t\t" + "Amount" + "\n");
            for(i = 1; i <= p.getTotal(); i++)
            {
                s =  nf.format(p.getPayment(i).getAmount());
                displayArea2.append("" + p.getPayment(i).getMonth()
                                    + "\t\t"  + s  + "\n");
            }
            displayArea2.append("\n"
                    + "Total paid so far :    "
                    + nf.format(p.calculateTotalPaid()));
```

```
                        monthField.setText("");
                        amountField.setText("");
                    }
                }
            }
            if(e.getSource() == saveAndQuitButton)
            {
                TenantFileHandler.saveRecords(noOfRooms,list);
                System.exit(0);
            }
            if(e.getSource() == quitButton)
            {
                System.exit(0);
            }
        }
    }
```

Before we complete our look at the `Hostel` application we just draw your attention to a few new features. First, as discussed in section 12.3, we have given titled borders to some of our components by calling a component's `setBorder` method. For example, to give the `roomField` component a titled border we used the following:

```
roomField.setBorder(new TitledBorder("Room"));
```

You can see that the parameter to this method is a `TitledBorder` object, and the constructor for this object receives the title to be set (in this case "Room"). The default position of the title is the top left-hand corner of the component. For different positions, other forms of the `TitledBorder` constructor can be used (look at the code for an example of a centre justified title). We will look at border styles in more detail in chapter 19.

As well as titled borders we have also made use of **Scroll Panes** in this GUI. A scroll pane allows *scroll bars* to be added to visual components such as text areas. This is useful if the component sometimes needs to display more information than is possible in its visible area. In the case of our `Hostel` GUI, we have two text areas: `displayArea1` and `displayArea2`. The former is used to display the details of all tenants while the latter is used to display the details of all payments. When the number of tenants or payments becomes large, a standard text area of a fixed size may not be sufficient to display all this information. So we have added scroll bars to these text areas by converting them to scroll panes. We do this by simply calling the `JScrollPane` constructor as follows:

```
// creates a scroll pane from displayArea1
JScrollPane p1 = new JScrollPane(displayArea1);
```

It is then the scroll pane (`p1`) that is added to the frame not the text area (`displayArea1`):

```
// add scroll pane to frame not the original text area
add(p1);
```

We will come across scroll panes again in the second semester.

The code needed to run the `Hostel` class now appears below as program 12.1. This program creates a hostel with five rooms; in the end of chapter exercises you will be given the opportunity to adapt this program so that the number of rooms can be entered by the user.

Program 12.1

```
public class RunHostel
{
    public static void main(String[] args)
    {
        // assume only 5 rooms available
        new Hostel(5);
    }
}
```

Before concluding this case study we shall consider how to test the application to ensure that it conforms to the original specification.

12.6 Testing the system

If you look back at the `Hostel` class you can see that much of the event-handling code is related to the validation of data entered from the graphical interface. Much of the testing for such a system will, therefore, be geared around ensuring such validation is effective. This is a form of *white box* testing as we are looking at the implementation to determine this validation; it is not made explicit in the specification.

Amongst the types of validation we need to test is the display of suitable error messages when input text fields are left blank, or when inappropriate data has been entered into these text fields. Of course, as well as input validation, we also need to test the basic functionality of the system. The specification can be used to determine suitable test data in this case and so a form of *black box* testing will also be appropriate.

Figure 12.4 is one possible test log that may be developed for the purpose of testing the `Hostel` class. As we will be running this program in the UK, we have defined the expected currency output to be displayed with a pound symbol (£); obviously you should replace this currency symbol with that of your own country. We include a few sample screen shots produced from running program 12.1 against this test log in figures 12.5–12.8. We will leave the complete task of running program 12.1 against the test log as a programming exercise at the end of this chapter.

TEST LOG			
Purpose: To test the HOSTEL class			
Run Number:	Date:		
Action	Expected Output	Pass/	Reason for
		Fail	Failure
Display tenants	"Empty list" message		
Add tenant: Patel, Room Number blank	"Blank field" message		
Add tenant: blank, Room Number 1	"Blank field" message		
Add tenant: Patel, Room Number 1	Confirmation message		
Add tenant: Jones, Room Number 6	Error message: There are only 5 rooms		
Add tenant: Jones, Room Number 1	Error Message: Room 1 is occupied		
Add tenant: Jones, Room Number 2	Confirmation Message		
Display tenants	ROOM NAME 1 Patel 2 Jones		
List payments, Room Number 1	"Empty list" message		
Make payment: Room blank, Month January, Amount 100	"Blank field" message		
Make Payment: Room 1, Month blank, Amount 100	"Blank field" message		
Make payment: Room 1, Month January, Amount blank	"Blank field" message		
Make payment: Room 1, Month January, Amount 100	Confirmation message		
Make payment: Room 1, Month February, Amount 200	Confirmation message		
List payments: Room Number blank	"Blank field" message		
List payments, Room Number 1	MONTH AMOUNT January £100 February £200 Total paid so far £300		
List payments: Room Number 2	"Empty list" message		
List payments: Room Number 5	"Room Empty" message		
Remove tenant: Room Number blank	"Blank field" message		
Remove tenant: Room Number 1	Confirmation Message		
Display tenants	2 Jones		
List payments: Room Number 1	"Room Empty" message		

Fig 12.4. A test log to ensure the reliability of the *Hostel* class

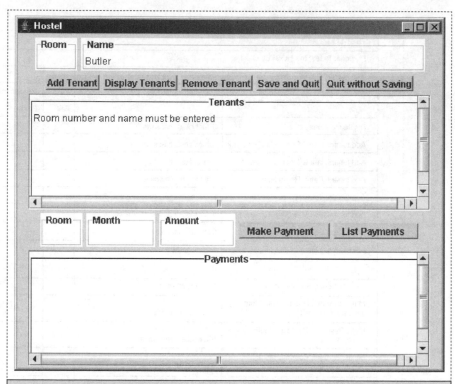

Fig 12.5. Error messages are produced in *displayArea1*. In this case an attempt is made to add a tenant without filling in the *roomField*

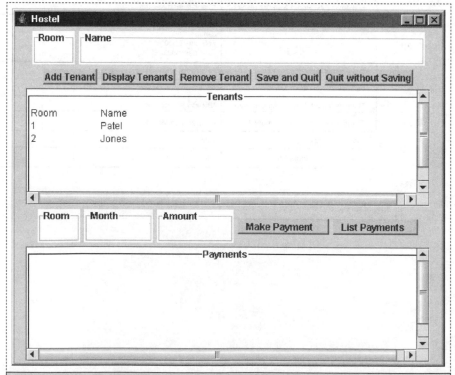

Fig 12.6. The *displayArea1* is also used to display a list of tenants entered

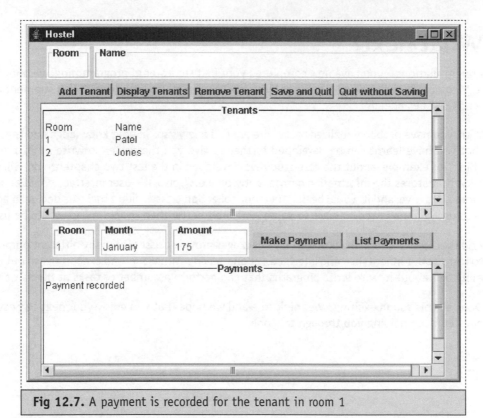

Fig 12.7. A payment is recorded for the tenant in room 1

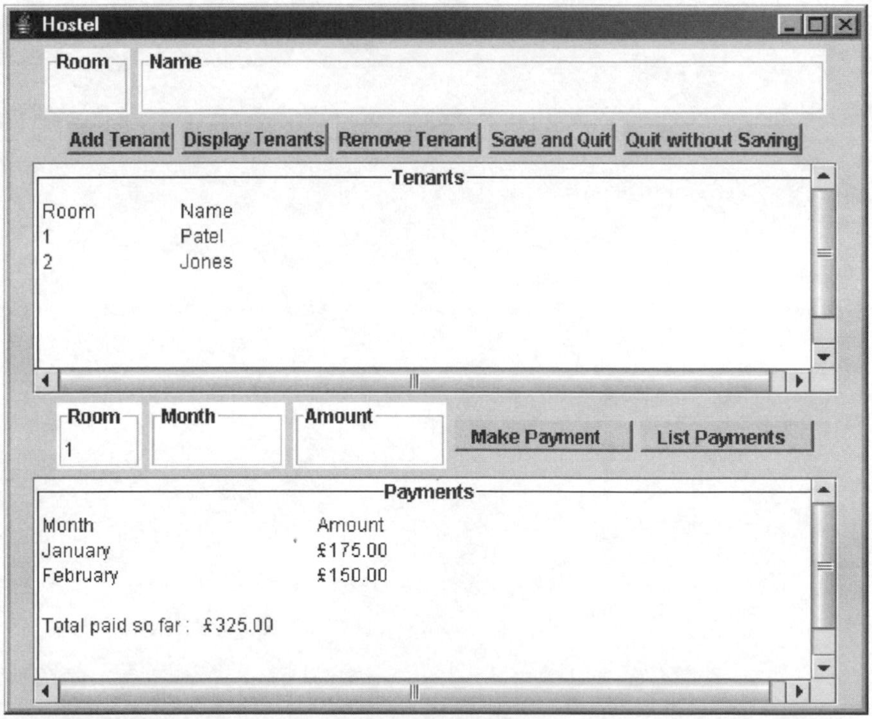

Fig 12.8. Details of the payments for room 1 are displayed in *displayArea2* when the *listButton* is pressed

12.7 What next?

Congratulations – you have now completed your first semester of programming; we hope you have enjoyed it. Many of you will be going on to at least one more semester of software development and programming – so what lies ahead?

Well, you have probably realized that there are still a few gaps in your knowledge and that some of the stuff that you have learnt can be developed further to give you the power to write multi-functional programs. Think, for example, about the case study we developed in the last two chapters; you will need to write the code that stores the information permanently on a disk; also, the user interface could be made to look a bit more attractive; and it would be helpful if our collection classes didn't make us decide in advance how many records we are allowed to have, so something a bit better than simple arrays would be useful.

And there is lots more; the standard Java packages provide classes for many different purposes; there is more to learn about inheritance and interfaces; about dealing with errors and exceptions; about network programming and about how to write programs that can perform a number of tasks at the same time.

Does all this sound exciting? We think so – and we hope that you enjoy your next semester as much as we have enjoyed helping you through this one.

Programming exercises

You will need to copy the entire suite of classes that make up the student hostel system from the accompanying CD.

1 Run program 12.1 against the test log given in figure 12.4.

2 Rewrite program 12.1 so that instead of fixing the number of rooms to 5, the user is asked how many rooms the hostel is to have.

3 Modify the `Hostel` class by adding a `search` button. Clicking on the button should display the name of the tenant in the room entered in the `roomField` text box. The name is to be displayed in `displayArea1`. If no tenant is present in the given room, an error message should be displayed in `displayArea1`.

4 Make any additions to the `Hostel` class that you feel would enhance the final application. For example you might want to include additional validation to ensure that negative money values are never accepted for payments.

Semester Two

Packages

Objectives:

By the end of this chapter you should be able to:

- *identify the role of **packages** in organizing classes;*
- *create and deploy your own packages in Java;*
- *access classes residing in your own packages;*
- *explain how the **classpath** environment variable is used to locate class files;*
- *identify the core packages in the **Java API**.*

13.1 Introduction

Welcome back to the second semester of our programming course. We spent the first semester laying the foundations you would need to develop programs in Java. During that time you came a long way. You learnt about the idea of variables, control structures, methods and arrays, and then went on to develop your own classes and extend these classes using inheritance. Finally you developed applications consisting of many classes working closely together and interacting with users via attractive graphical interfaces. Along the way you also learnt about the UML notation and issues affecting software quality. At the beginning of that semester you probably didn't expect to come as far as you have. Well, the second semester might look equally challenging but, with some help from us along the way, you can look forward to new and more advanced challenges.

The first thing we are going to do this semester is to take a more in-depth look at Java's package concept.

13.2 Understanding packages

A **package**, in Java, is a *named collection* of *related classes*. Of course, you have already come across the idea of a package in your first semester. To draw some geometric shapes you used the `Graphics` class which resides in the `awt` package. To format text you used classes in the `text` package. To produce attractive GUIs you used classes such as `JButton` and `JLabel` from the `swing` package. Giving meaningful names to a set of related classes in this way makes it easy for programmers to locate these classes when required.

Packages can themselves contain other packages. For example, as well as containing related visual component classes, the `awt` package also contains the `event` package, since this group of classes is still logically related to Java's Abstract Window Toolkit.

The package name actually corresponds to the *name of the directory* (or folder as some operating systems call it) in which all the given classes reside. All predefined Java packages themselves reside in a global Java directory, named simply `java`. This directory is not itself a package but a store for other packages. Figure 13.1 illustrates this hierarchy of packages.

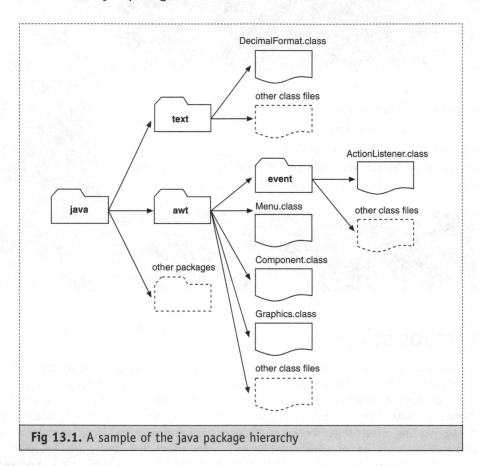

Fig 13.1. A sample of the java package hierarchy

As you can see from figure 13.1, packages contain class files (that is the compiled Java byte code), not source files (the original Java instructions). This means the location of the original Java source files is unimportant here. They may be in the same directory as the class files, in another directory or, as in the case of the predefined Java packages, they may even no longer be available!

13.3 Accessing classes in packages

Suppose you are writing the code for a new class. Can you recall how you can give it access to a class contained within a package? Just referencing the class won't work. For example, let's assume a class you are writing needs a `DecimalFormat` object. The following will not compile:

```
public class SomeClass
{
    private DecimalFormat someFormatObject; // a problem here
}
```

This won't compile because the compiler won't be able to find a class called DecimalFormat. One way to tell the compiler where this class file resides is, as you already know, to add an **import** statement above the class. This class is in the text package so the following would be appropriate:

```
import java.text.*; // allows compiler to find the DecimalFormat.class file

public class SomeClass
{
    private DecimalFormat someFormatObject; // now this will compile
}
```

As we mentioned in chapter 1, the asterisk allows you to have access to *all* class files in the given package. Can you see how the **import** statement matches the directory structure we illustrated in figure 13.1? Effectively the compiler is being told to look for classes in the text directory (package), which in turn is in the java directory (whose location is already known to the Java run-time system). The location of a file is often referred to as the **path** to that file. In the Windows operating systems this path would be expressed as follows:

java\text\

In other operating systems forward slashes may be used instead of backward slashes. The Java **import** statement simply expresses this path but uses dots instead of backward or forward slashes. Note that there can only ever be one '.*' in an **import** statement and the '.*' must follow a package name. However, you can have as many **import** statements as you require. Here are some examples of valid and invalid **import** statements:

```
import java.*.*;        // illegal as contains more than one '.*'
import java.*;          // illegal as 'java' is not a package
import java.text.*;     // fine, allows access to classes in text package
import java.awt.event.*; // fine, allows access to classes in event package
```

If you want, you could list a *specific* class file instead of accessing all the files in a package as follows:

```
import java.text.DecimalFormat; // access to the DecimalFormat class only
```

However, as there is no overhead in allowing access to all files in a package, we will use the asterisk notation in this book.

It is actually possible to access classes from within packages *without* the need for an **import** statement. To do this, references to any such classes must be appended onto the package name itself. Returning to the DecimalFormat example, we could have removed the **import** statement and referred to the package directly in the class as follows:

```
public class SomeClass
{
     /* appending the class name onto the package name avoids the need to
        import the given package */

     private java.text.DecimalFormat someFormatObject;
}
```

The package plus class name is in fact the proper name for this class. An **import** statement just provides us with a convenient shorthand so that we do not always have to include the package name with the class name. As you can imagine, having to append the class name onto the package name every time we use a class from a package would be very cumbersome, so the **import** statement is preferable. There are times, however, when the long name is necessary.

The long class name can be useful when the class name on its own clashes with the name of another class. For example, let us assume we have developed our own class called `Graphics` – perhaps as part of a game application. Giving this name to the class is not a great idea as there already is a `Graphics` class in the awt package, but it is possible to choose this name if we wish. Now, let us assume that the constructor for this class takes two integer coordinates. We might require both our `Graphics` class in a program and the `Graphics` class in the awt package:

```
import java.awt.*; // for the awt Graphics class
import javax.swing.*; // for swing components

// something wrong in this class!

public class Game extends JPanel // this class can do some drawing
{
     // some code here

     // call constructor of our Graphics class
     Graphics moveCar  = new Graphics (20, 40);
     // more code here

     public void paint (Graphics g) // this is the awt Graphics class
     {
         // call methods of awt Graphics class here
     }
}
```

As you can see, we are referencing two `Graphics` classes here: our own `Graphics` class:

```
Graphics moveCar  = new Graphics (20, 40);
```

and the awt `Graphics` class in the `paint` method:

```
public void paint (Graphics g)
{
     // call methods of awt Graphics class here
}
```

Not surprisingly, this will result in a compiler error! When the compiler tries to find a class it initially looks in the *current folder* before it looks in any package folders. Assuming our own `Graphics` class is in the same folder as this `Game` class, it will decide that this is the `Graphics` class we are interested in. So, when we come to call the methods of the `awt Graphics` class (such as `drawOval`) the compiler will complain, as our `Graphics` class has no such methods in it!

To resolve this name clash, we can use the extended package name to differentiate between the two classes.

```
public void paint   (java.awt.Graphics g)
{
        // call methods of awt Graphics class here
}
```

Now we no longer have a name clash with our class and the complier can process references to both classes.

13.4 Developing your own packages

You might be surprised to know that all the classes that you have developed so far already reside in a *single* package. This may seem strange as you didn't instruct the compiler to add your classes to any package. In fact, what actually happens is that if you don't specifically ask your classes to be put in a package, then they all get added to some large unnamed package.

In order to locate and deploy your class files easily, and avoid any name clashes in the future, it might be a good idea to use named packages to organize your classes.

As an example, let's go back to our *Hostel* application from chapters 11 and 12 and create a unique package in which to put our class files – we will call this package `hostelApp`.[1] To instruct the compiler that you wish to add the classes that make up this application into a package called `hostelApp`, simply add the following **package** command at the top of each of the original source files:

```
package hostelApp;
```

This line instructs the compiler that the class file created from this source file must be put in a package called `hostelApp`. Here, for example, is the `Payment` class with this **package** line added:

```
package hostelApp; // add this line to the top of the source file

public class Payment
{
    // as before
}
```

When you compile this class, your Java IDE should create a directory called `hostelApp` for you and place the `Payment` class in this directory.[2] This directory in turn will be kept in a location known by your system. On our machine, which uses a Windows operating system, the location known by the system is called `myProjects`, which is itself in a directory called `jCreator` (which is in the root directory on our hard drive). Figure 13.2 illustrates the directory structure that will exist in this case.

---

[1] We will stick to the standard Java convention of beginning package names with a lower-case letter.
[2] If your development environment doesn't do this for you, you will have to manually create such a directory and move your class file into it.

Fig 13.2. The directory structure of the *hostelApp* package

All the classes that make up this *Hostel* application (such as `Tenant`, `Hostel` and so on) will need to be amended in a similar way:

1   add the following line to the top of each source file

```
package hostelApp;
```

2   ensure that the compiled class files are placed in the `hostelApp` directory.

Now the last step. We need to import this package into programs like any other package. If you had developed the `hostelApp` package in this way, and written program 12.1 (the driver for the hostel application) as normal (outside of a package), the program would no longer compile:

Program 12.1 will not compile now!

```
public class RunHostel
{
    public static void main(String[] args)
    {
        new Hostel(5); // something wrong here!
    }
}
```

The instruction that makes reference to the `Hostel` class will cause an error because that class no longer resides in the same directory as every other class file, but instead resides in its own package directory – `hostelApp`. The obvious answer is to import that package into this file. Program 13.1 amends program 12.1 accordingly:

Program 13.1

```
import hostelApp.*; // import classes from our package

public class RunHostel
{
    public static void main(String[] args)
    {
        new Hostel(5); // now this line will compile
    }
}
```

13.5 Package scope

Up until now we have declared all our classes to be **public**. This has meant they have been visible to all other classes. When we come to adding our classes into our own packages, this becomes particularly important. This is because *classes can be made visible outside of their package only if they are declared as* **public**. Unless they are declared as **public**, classes by default have what is known as **package** scope. This means that they are visible *only to other classes within the same package*.

Not all classes in the package need be declared as **public**. Some classes may be part of the implementation only and the developer may not wish them to be made available to the client. These classes can have **package** scope instead of **public** scope. In this way, packages provide an extra layer of security for your classes.

In the case of our hostel application, we might choose to make only the Hostel class **public**, and keep all the other files required in this application hidden within the package by giving them package scope. To give a class package scope, just remove the **public** modifier from in front of the class declaration. For example, returning to the Payment class, we can give this package scope as follows:

```
package hostelApp; // this class is added into the package

class Payment // this class has package scope
{
    // as before
}
```

Now, when the hostelApp package is imported into another class, this other class has access only to the Hostel class; not to classes like Payment which are hidden in the package with package scope. This is demonstrated in the code fragment below:

```
import hostelApp.*; // this imports only the public classes in the package
public class SomeOtherClass
{
    Payment p = new Payment(  ); /* will not compile as Payment is hidden in
                                    the hostelApp package */
}
```

If you begin to develop your own packages and have trouble importing them, it could be that you have to modify the **classpath** variable.

The classpath is a special **environment variable**. Environment variables provide your operating system with information such as the location of important files in your system. The special environment variable related to the location of Java packages is the classpath variable.

13.6 Setting the classpath environment variable

The details of how the classpath environment variable is set will differ from one operating system to another. In Windows, for example, you place an instruction such as the one below in the autoexec.bat file using an application like Microsoft NotePad.

> SET CLASSPATH = C:\jCreator\myProjects

If you are working in a UNIX environment you would use the setenv command. Check with your tutor the exact method to use. Note that the classpath is not the location of *classes* in packages, but the location of *packages* themselves. It would be wrong to set the classpath as follows:

> SET CLASSPATH = C:\ jCreator\myProjects\hostelApp

This is because the hostelApp folder does not contain a package – it *is* a package! It is possible to set more than one location in your classpath, if necessary, by separating these locations by a semi-colon. For example:

> SET CLASSPATH=C:\java\lib; C:\jCreator\myProjects

Here the classpath has been set to look in the lib folder for packages, as well as the myProjects folder.

13.7 Running applications from the command line

Way back in chapter 1, we discussed the process of compiling and running Java programs. If you remember, we said that if are working within a Java IDE you will have simple icons to click in order to carry out these procedures. If, however, you are working from a command line, like a DOS prompt for example, you would use the **javac** command (followed by the name of the source file) to compile a source file and **java** (followed by the name of a class) to run an application.

When you run a class that resides in a package you must amend this slightly. As an example let's once again consider the *Hostel* application. When you run an application you must run the class that contains the main method. Program 13.1 provided such a class for running the *Hostel* application. We called this class RunHostel. This class file was *not* part of a package, so it can be run simply from the command line as follows:

> java RunHostel

Notice that the .class extension is not added to the name of the class. When you type the **java** command you are in fact running the java.exe program, which is an implementation of the Java Virtual Machine. This command will run the given class assuming the classpath has been set appropriately. If the classpath had not been previously set we could specify it as part of this command. For example if the classpath were C:\jCreator\myProjects then we could write

> java -cp C:\jCreator\myProjects RunHostel

Note that the parameter cp, indicating the classpath, is prefixed with a minus sign. Now let's assume that we provided a similar class, with a main method, as part of the hostelApp package. This class will be identical to RunHostel, but we will send in a different number of rooms to the Hostel constructor. It is called RunHostelFromPackage. The code is presented in program 13.2 below.

Program 13.2

```
package hostelApp; // add this class to our package

public class RunHostelFromPackage
{
    public static void main(String[] args)
    {
        new Hostel(10);
    }
}
```

Notice that, to add this class to the `hostelApp` package, we had to include the **package** `hostelApp` line to the top of the class. Now, to run this class from the command line we could try the following:

java RunHostelFromPackage

Unfortunately this won't work as the Java interpreter won't be able to find a class of the given name. In order to run a class that is contained within a package you must append the class name onto the name of the package. So, in this case you can run this class by using the following command:

java hostelApp.RunHostelFromPackage

Note that even if this class had the same name as the original program, `RunHostel`, the package name would have allowed the correct class file to have been found and executed.

Before we move on, let's just stop and have a look at the parameter that we always give to `main` methods:

```
public static void main(String[] args)
```

As you know, this means that `main` is given an array of `String` objects as a parameter. How are these `String` objects passed on to `main`? Up until now we have not discussed them at all. Well, values for these strings can be passed to `main` when you run the given class from the command line. Often, as in our previous program, there is no need to pass any such strings and this array of strings is effectively empty. Sometimes, however, it is useful to send in such parameters. They are sent to `main` from the command line by listing the strings, one after the other after the name of the class as follows:

java ClassName firstString secondString otherStrings

As you can see, the strings are separated by spaces. Any number of strings can be sent in this way. For example if a program were called `ProcessNames`, two names could be sent to it as follows:

java ProcessNames Aaron Quentin

Notice that, were the strings to contain spaces, they must be enclosed in quotes:

java ProcessNames "Aaron Kans" "Quentin Charatan"

These strings will be placed into main's array parameter (args), with the first string being at args[0], the second at args[1] and so on. The number of strings sent to main is variable. The main method can always determine the number of strings sent by checking the length of the array (args.length). Program 13.3 is a simple implementation of the ProcessNames class.

Program 13.3

```
public class ProcessNames
{
    public static void main(String[] args)
    {
        if (args.length != 0)// check some arguments have been sent
        {
            // loop through all elements in the 'args' array
            for (int i = 0; i<args.length; i++)
            {
                // access individual strings in array
                System.out.println("hello " + args[i]);
            }
        }
    }
}
```

We can run this program from the command line as follows:

java ProcessNames "Batman and Robin" Superman

Notice "Batman and Robin" needed to be surrounded by quotes as it has spaces in it, whereas Superman does not. Running this program would produce the obvious result:

```
hello Batman and Robin
hello Superman
```

13.8 Deploying your packages

A very common way of making your packages available to clients is to convert them to JAR files. A JAR file (short for Java Archive) has the extension .jar and is simply a compressed file. Most IDEs provide a means of creating JAR files; however, very often the file created is simply a flat file containing the relevant .class files. If this is all you want then that is fine. However, in most cases you want your client to be able to import the package into an application, and in order to do this the JAR file must have a *structure*. Let's take as an example the hostelApp package from section 13.4. If we were to call our JAR file hostel.jar, then the structure of the file would have to be as shown in figure 13.3.

Fig 13.3. The correct structure of a JAR file

If, in a Windows environment, the `hostel.jar` file were placed in the folder `C:\jCreator\myProjects`, then the correct classpath statement would be:

> **SET CLASSPATH = C:\jCreator\myProjects\hostel.jar**

As you can see, the JAR file acts as the directory in which the package resides.

A JAR file such as the one above can by created using any compression software, such as WinZip, and then changing the extension to `.jar`. However, the usual way to create such a file is to use the `jar.exe` application – this is provided with the SUN software development kit and also with most standard IDEs. Assuming that the `hostelApp` folder that contains the required `.class` files is in the same directory as the `jar.exe` application (or that the system path is appropriately set to provide access to it) then the correct statement to create the above package is:

> **jar cvf hostel.jar hostelApp**

As you can see there are various switches that are used with the `jar` program. The ones used above have the following effect:

c: create a new JAR file;
v: provide full (verbose) output to report on progress;
f: provide a name for the JAR file.

After these switches comes the name of the output file – `hostel.jar` in our case. Finally we must list the files we wish to be included. In the above example we require a properly structured file, so we just have to include the name of the directory where the files reside, `hostelApp`.

13.8.1 Creating "executable" JAR files

If you are working in a graphics environment, and there is a JVM (Java Virtual Machine) installed on your computer, then it is possible to create a JAR file that will run the program by double-clicking on its icon. In this case, we must include a file called a manifest file (which normally has the extension `.mf`). The manifest file can list all the files in the package, but if we want the JAR file to be executable it must contain information about which class in the package is the one with the `main` method. If this class is part of the package it would need to be included in the package directory (as with the `RunHostelFromPackage` example in section 13.7). Alternatively it could be in the directory that contains the package, in which case the package would be specified in the **import** statement.

If we assume that the `main` class is called `RunHostel`, our manifest file would look like this:

```
Manifest-Version: 1.0

Main-Class: RunHostel
```

In the first section we have to specify a version number for the manifest file, which would normally be 1.0. In the next section we identify the `main` class.

Now, assuming that we are currently in a directory containing the manifest file (which we have called `manifest.mf`), the file `RunHostel.class`, and the directory `hostelApp` (containing the files in the package) we could create the executable file with the following line:

jar cvfm RunHostel.jar manifest.mf RunHostel.class hostelApp

The additional "m" switch after the "c", "v" and "f" switches indicates that we wish to include the manifest file stated. You can see that after providing the name of the manifest file we have listed what to include – the file `RunHostel.class` and the directory `hostelApp`. Now double-clicking on the resulting JAR file's icon will run the application.

If you are using a Windows operating system there is another way you could provide an icon that will run your application, without creating a JAR file. You can create a shortcut to the file `javaw.exe`, the JVM specifically designed to run in a Windows graphical environment. You can then set the shortcut's properties so that the `main` class is added as a parameter. Figure 13.4 shows an example of this – it assumes that the required classes are in the directory `C:\Hostel`; note that we have included the classpath here as described in section 13.7.

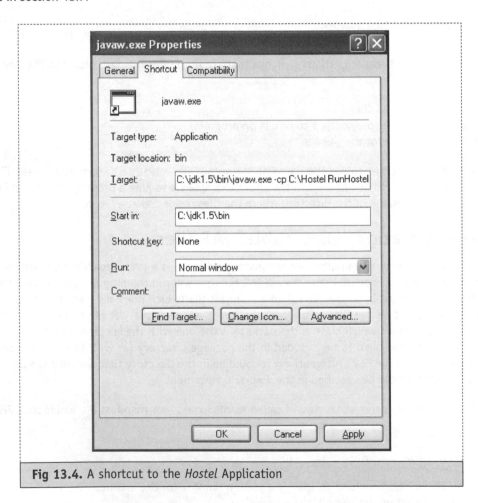

Fig 13.4. A shortcut to the *Hostel* Application

13.9 An overview of the core Java API packages

Before we end this chapter, we will provide a brief overview of the core predefined Java packages, sometimes referred to as the **Java API** (Application Program Interface). It is important to become familiar with these packages, and the classes provided within them, to avoid any unnecessary duplication of work on your part. For example, you wouldn't want to bother defining a `DecimalFormat` class when one is already available to you, would you? Details of all these packages can be found at the Sun website: www.java.sun.com.

Table 13.1 provides a list of the core Java packages with some information about the family of classes they provide.

Table 13.1 Core packages in the Java API	
Package Name	**Description**
`java.awt`	Contains classes such as `Graphics` that allow simple shapes to be drawn, as well as classes such as `Color` and `Font` for controlling the appearance of colours and fonts. We have already looked at some of the classes from this package in chapter 10 and will look at a few more in chapter 19. Many of the other classes in this package have now been superseded by classes in the `swing` package.
`java.awt.event`	Contains classes and interfaces such as `ActionListener` and `MouseListener` for handling events triggered by visual components. We have met some of these interfaces in chapter 10, and will look at others in chapter 14.
`java.io`	Contains classes such as `BufferedReader` and `File` for system input and output through data streams, and files. We will examine this package in chapter 20.
`java.lang`	Contains the key Java classes such as `System`, `Object` and `String`. Consequently, this package is implicitly imported into every Java program.
`java.net`	Contains classes such as `Socket` and `ServerSocket` for implementing networking applications. We will look at some of these classes in chapter 23.
`java.sql`	Contains classes such as `DriverManager` and `Connection` for communicating with databases. We will look at some of these classes in chapter 23.
`javax.swing`	An extension to the standard Java API, provides classes such as `JButton` and `JLabel` for managing visual components that aim to be more platform independent than their AWT counterparts. We have had a look at some classes from this package in chapter 10 and we will look at more classes from this package in chapters 18 and 19.
`java.text`	Contains classes such as `DecimalFormat` for formatting of information. We already met this class in chapter 8.
`java.util`	Contains many utility classes, such as `Random`, and collection classes such as `HashMap` and `ArrayList`. We will examine some of the classes from this package in chapter 17.

As you can see, we will be exploring many of these packages in more depth throughout this semester.

Self-test questions

1   What role do *packages* have in the development of classes?

2   Identify valid and invalid **import** statements amongst the following list:

```
import java.*;
import java.swing.*;
import java.awt.JButton;
import javax.swing.JButton;
import javax.swing.JButton.*;
import java.text.*.*;
import javax.swing.*;
```

2   What does it mean for a class to have *package scope*?

3   Consider the following outline of a class, used in a computer game, that makes reference to the
    JButton class:

```
public class GameController
{
     private JButton myButton;
     // more code here
}
```

At the moment the line referencing the JButton class will not compile.

a) Identify three different techniques to allow this class with a JButton attribute to compile.

b) Amend this GameController class so that it is added into a package called gameApp, but it is
    visible only to other classes in this package.

4   Look back at figure 13.2 which illustrates the directory structure of our hostelApp package. Now
    assume that this directory structure changes so that we keep all our packages in a directory called
    javaBook, as follows:

a) How could this change be accommodated by modifying the classpath only?

b) If the classpath is not altered, how else could this change be accommodated?

Programming exercises

1 Make the changes discussed in this chapter so that the *Hostel* application is now part of a package called `hostelApp`.

2 At the moment program 13.2 (`RunHostelFromPackage`) fixes the number of rooms the hostel can handle:

```
public class RunHostelFromPackage
{
   public static void main(String[] args)
   {
      new Hostel(10); // rooms fixed to 10
   }
}
```

a) Amend this class so that the number could be sent in as a command line parameter. If no value has been sent in via the command line, the program should size the hostel with a default value of 10 rooms.

b) Write the command to run this application from the command line to create a hostel with 25 rooms.

3 The `lang` package contains a class called `Math`, which has a **static** method called `random` designed to generate random numbers. There is also a random number class, `Random`, in the `util` package. Browse your Java documentation to find out more about these random number generation techniques. Then write a program that generates five lottery numbers from 1 to 50 using:

a) the **static** random method of the `Math` class in the `lang` package;

b) the random number class, `Random`, in the `util` package.

CHAPTER: 14

Abstraction, inheritance and interfaces

Objectives:

By the end of this chapter you should be able to:

- explain the terms **abstraction** and **abstract data type**;
- explain the difference between **dynamic (run-time) binding** and **static (compile-time) binding**;
- create your own interfaces in Java;
- make use of **adapters** in programs;
- explain the purpose of **inner classes** and use these classes appropriately;
- explain the purpose of the `toString` method.

14.1 Introduction

In your first semester you were introduced to a number of important concepts in connection with object-oriented development. In this chapter we will pull together some of those ideas and provide you with a better understanding of the object-oriented way of doing things.

The chapter begins by exploring the idea of **abstraction** and **abstract data types**. It then goes on to examine in more depth the concepts of inheritance and polymorphism that you learnt about in the first semester and relates these to this whole notion of abstraction. We then look more closely at abstract classes and methods, and give you the chance to increase your understanding of interfaces by means of some useful and interesting examples.

14.2 Abstraction

The concept of **abstraction** is an important theme in object-oriented development; it is the idea of focusing on what an object does, without worrying about the detail of how it does it. It is therefore particularly relevant at the analysis stage when we are trying to determine exactly what it is that we want our system to do. The more abstract our specification, the more likely we are to build a system that is flexible and maintainable, because we do not tie ourselves down to one particular design.

A class template is often referred to as an **abstract data type**, because normally all that is available to the user of such a type is the method descriptions (inputs, output and behaviour) as opposed to information about the data (attributes). Object-oriented programming languages differ from earlier languages in that the principal data types that they manipulate are abstract data types (objects of a class) rather than the simple (primitive) types such as `int` and `char`.

Central to all this is the idea that we can broadly define a class, specifying its fundamental behaviour, and concentrating on the important details that make the class what it is. Part of the process of analysis involves *abstracting* the relevant details of a system and discarding irrelevant details. For example, if we are analysing a system that is concerned with keeping student records, we do not need to worry about cleaning the class-rooms or serving the coffee in the breaks – important as these activities might be, they are not relevant to our system.

It is possible at the analysis stage to describe classes in very general terms simply by describing their methods together with their inputs and outputs. We do not worry about how these methods perform their duties until we start to think about the design and implementation of our system.

A very useful technique in all of this, and crucial to the object-oriented way of doing things, is the technique of defining a class in terms of what we already know and making it possible to extend these definitions later.

We have already come across a number of techniques that help us to achieve this: inheritance, polymorphism, abstract classes and interfaces. We will now explore these in more detail.

14.3 Run-time versus compile-time binding

Cast your mind back to section 8.9. In this section we developed a program that created an array which held a mixture of `FullTimeEmployees` and `PartTimeEmployees`, both of which had inherited a `getStatus` method from the `Employee` class, and each of which had overridden this method in a different way. Here is a reminder of the program.

Program 8.4 – A reminder

```
public class MixedListTester
{
    public static void main(String[] args)
    {
        // declare an array big enough for three employees
        Employee[] employeeList = new Employee[3];
        // declare local variables to hold values entered by user
        String num, name;
        double pay;
        char status;

        // get the user to enter the employees' details
        for(int i = 0; i < employeeList.length; i++)
        {
            System.out.print("Enter the employee number: ");
            num = EasyScanner.nextString();
            System.out.print("Enter the employee's name: ");
            name = EasyScanner.nextString();
            System.out.print("<F>ull-time or <P>art-time? ");
            status = EasyScanner.nextChar();

            if(status == 'f' || status == 'F')
            {
```

```
                        System.out.print("Enter the annual salary: ");
                }
                else
                {
                        System.out.print("Enter the hourly pay: ");
                }
                pay = EasyScanner.nextDouble();

                if(status == 'f' || status == 'F')
                {
                        employeeList[i] = new FullTimeEmployee(num, name, pay);
                }
                else
                {
                        employeeList[i] = new PartTimeEmployee(num, name, pay);
                }
                System.out.println();
        }
        for(int i = 0; i < employeeList.length; i++)
        {
                // display employee's number, name, and status
                System.out.println("Employee number: "
                                        + employeeList[i].getNumber());
                System.out.println("Employee name: "
                                        + employeeList[i].getName());
                System.out.println("Status: " + employeeList[i].getStatus());
                System.out.println();
        }
    }
}
```

We do not know until the program is run whether each particular element in the array is going to hold a `FullTimeEmployee` or a `PartTimeEmployee` – and yet when the `getStatus` method is called, the correct version is executed.

How does this work? When the program is compiled it is not known whether, on each iteration of the loop, the employee will be full-time or part-time; this is decided by the user each time the program is *run*. The technique which makes it possible for this decision to be made is known as **run-time binding** or **dynamic binding**. Let's investigate this a bit more.

First let's consider what would happen in the case of a language that did not use run-time binding, but instead used **compile-time** or **static binding**. In this case, when the code for a class was compiled, the code for each of its methods would simply be compiled alongside it; the compiler would ensure that every time an object of that class received a message to invoke that method, the control of the program would jump to the place where the code for the method was stored – the instructions in that method would then be executed, and the program control would then return to the place where it left off.

But as you can see, that wouldn't work in a case like the `MixedListTester` (program 8.4) where we don't know until run-time what sort of object we are dealing with. In our final loop we had the following line:

```
System.out.println("Status: " + employeeList[i].getStatus());
```

Where should the program jump to? The compiler can't write the instruction to jump to a particular place, because there is more than one possible place for it to go; it could jump to the place where the instructions for the `getStatus` method of the `FullTimeEmployee` class is located – or it could jump to the place where the `getStatus` method of the `PartTimeEmployee` class is located. This decision is made not at the time the program is compiled, but at the time it is run. So what has to happen is that every time a new object is created, it must hold information about where its methods are stored; in this way the decision about which actual method is called can be postponed until run-time. This is the technique that constitutes run-time binding.

So Java normally uses dynamic (run-time) binding. However, as you can probably tell, dynamic binding involves a bit more processing and a bit more storage space than does static binding, so it might be sensible not to use it unless it's necessary; and of course it is necessary only if a method might be overridden. Therefore, if you know that a method is not going to be overridden, you can use the **final** modifier with a method, meaning that this method cannot be overridden; if you do that, then static binding will be used.

Before moving on, let's make sure you understand the difference between method *overriding* and method *overloading*. Both are forms of *polymorphism*, a concept you came across in the first semester. Overriding, which we have just used, involves redefining a superclass method in a subclass. Overloading on the other hand, when applied to methods, means having many methods with the same name, distinguished from one another by the parameter list. We saw several examples of this in the first semester – one of the most frequent uses is to provide a number of different constructors for a single class.

14.4 Abstract classes and interfaces

You should recall from chapter 8 that the superclass `Employee` is declared as **abstract**, meaning that you are not permitted to create instances of this class; also, one of its methods, `getStatus`, is an abstract method, meaning that only the header is defined here – every subclass must have its own version of the method.

Now it is possible to have a class in which *all* methods are abstract; such a class is called an **interface**. You have already come across one interface, `ActionListener`, which is provided as part of the `java.awt.event` package; but it is perfectly possible to create our own interfaces.

Let's consider an example to illustrate the use of interfaces. Imagine that we are producing a program that could be used by different organizations; we would like to place the organization's logo somewhere on the screen. It would be useful if we could produce a class that we could customize later with a particular logo – that way the class is re-usable, because we just have to attach the right logo at the time.

Now we can think back to our earlier discussion about abstraction, and see how the notion of interfaces helps us out here. What is it that would make a class *attachable*? Let's think about this in very abstract terms – in other words let's try to identify the essence of the thing that makes something attachable, and ignore everything else. Well, it would seem that the obvious answer to our question is that it would need to have an *attach* method! Having such a method would make our class attachable – whatever else it has is its own business, but we want to make sure it has this particular method. Interfaces allow us to do this. To see what we mean let's define an `Attachable` interface:

The *Attachable* interface

```
import javax.swing.*;

public interface Attachable
{
     public void attach(JFrame frameIn, int xPos, int yPos);
}
```

Do you see what we've done here? We have defined an interface, Attachable, with a single method attach. You can see that to do this we used the keyword Interface instead of the keyword Class. The method is abstract so it is not actually defined here – that is left to the particular class that implements Attachable. Incidentally, we do not have to use the **abstract** modifier here because all interface methods are abstract by definition.

Implementing an interface is very much like inheriting a class; the class that implements Attachable, for example, becomes a *kind of* Attachable – and it will of course "inherit" and redefine the attach method.

Notice that we have defined our method header to accept three parameters – the JFrame that the logo should attach itself to (hence the need to import the Swing package), and two coordinates to enable the user of the class to decide where it is to be attached.

Let's look at an example; say we wanted any class that had anything to do with our books to bear a *Charatan and Kans* logo. A CAndKLogo class must be *attachable* so it could look like this:

The *CAndKLogo* class

```
import java.awt.*;
import javax.swing.*;

public class CAndKLogo implements Attachable
{
    public void attach(JFrame frameIn, int xPos, int yPos)
    {
        Graphics g = frameIn.getContentPane().getGraphics();
        g.setFont(new Font("Serif", Font.BOLD,15));
        g.setColor(Color.red);
        g.fillRect(xPos,yPos,125,20);
        g.setColor(Color.yellow);
        g.drawString("Charatan & Kans", xPos + 3, yPos + 15);
    }
}
```

We have seen before the use of the word **implements**, which is used with interfaces and has a similar effect to **extends**, which is used with classes. You can see that the class now defines its own version of the attach method, as required by the Attachable interface – if it did not do this, then of course it would not compile.

The method itself consists of code for drawing stuff on the frame. The first line looks like this:

```
Graphics g = frameIn.getContentPane().getGraphics();
```

When we have used Graphics objects in the past, we have done so within a component's paint (or paintComponent) method – a Graphics object is automatically sent to this method, and contains the information about the component that is needed by other methods such as drawString or setColor. In this case we need to generate a Graphics object which will contain this information with respect to the component in question (which is received as a parameter to the attach method). We do this with the getGraphics method of Component – we refer to this process as *getting the graphics context*. Notice that it is in fact the JFrame's content pane whose graphics context we require. Once we have done this, we use various methods of the Graphics class to produce our logo, using the coordinates that were received as parameters to position it in the right place. One such method is setFont:

```
g.setFont(new Font("Serif", Font.BOLD,15));
```

You can see here that we have created our own font and then set the component's font to this new font. You will find more about creating fonts in chapter 19.

Now this logo – or indeed any other `Attachable` – can be attached to a `JFrame`. This is done in the example that follows, which we have called `LogoFrame`.

The *LogoFrame* class

```
import java.awt.*;
import javax.swing.*;

public class LogoFrame extends JFrame
{
    // the attributes - an attachable object and its co-ordinates
    private Attachable logo;
    private int xPos;
    private int yPos;

    // the constructor
    public LogoFrame(Attachable logoIn, int xIn, int yIn)
    {
        setTitle("Logo Frame");
        logo = logoIn;
        xPos = xIn;
        yPos = yIn;
        setDefaultCloseOperation(JFrame.DISPOSE_ON_CLOSE);
        setSize(250,250);
        setLocation(200,200);
        setVisible(true);
    }

    // the paint method
    public void paint(Graphics g)
    {
        super.paint(g);
        // call the attach method of the attachable object
        logo.attach(this, xPos, yPos);
    }
}
```

You can see that this class has three attributes – an `Attachable` object, and two integers representing the position of that object. Of course this class could have other attributes and do other things – indeed in practice it certainly would do; but all we are interested in is how to get a logo attached to it.

Now let's take a closer look at the constructor.

```
    public LogoFrame(Attachable logoIn, int xIn, int yIn)
    {
        setTitle("Logo Frame");
        logo = logoIn;
        xPos = xIn;
        yPos = yIn;
        setDefaultCloseOperation(JFrame.DISPOSE_ON_CLOSE);
        setSize(250,250);
        setLocation(200,200);
        setVisible(true);
    }
```

The nice thing about this is that the particular `Attachable` object to be added doesn't have to be specified here – it is passed in as a parameter. But because it is `Attachable` we know that it will have an `attach` method – and we are therefore able to use it to paint the component:

```
public void paint(Graphics g)
{
    super.paint(g);
    // call the attach method of the attachable object
    logo.attach(this, xPos, yPos);
}
```

Program 14.1 creates a `LogoFrame`; the *Charatan and Kans* logo is added at coordinates (10,5), roughly in the top left-hand corner.

Program 14.1

```
public class LogoTester
{
    public static void main(String[] args)
    {
        new LogoFrame(new CAndKLogo(), 3, 5);
    }
}
```

The result of running this program can be seen in figure 14.1.

Fig 14.1. The *Charatan and Kans* logo

Of course, it would now be a simple matter to change our logo; all we would have to do is send in a different logo as a parameter. Even our arch-rivals *Bharatan and Bans* could devise a logo that could be added very easily, as shown in program 14.2, which in this case displays it in the right-hand corner (coordinates (110,5)).

Program 14.2

```java
public class LogoTester2
{
    public static void main(String[] args)
    {
        new LogoFrame(new BAndBLogo(), 110, 5);
    }
}
```

The result of displaying their logo is shown in figure 14.2.

Fig 14.2. The *Bharatan and Bans* logo

You will no doubt agree that their logo isn't nearly as good as ours! However, just in case you want to see how *not* to do it, here is the code for their logo:

The *BAndBLogo* class

```java
import java.awt.*;
import javax.swing.*;

public class BAndBLogo implements Attachable
{
    public void attach(JFrame frameIn, int xPos, int yPos)
    {
        Graphics g = frameIn.getContentPane().getGraphics();
        g.setFont(new Font("SanSerif", Font.ITALIC +Font.BOLD,15));
        g.setColor(Color.blue);
        g.fillRect(xPos,yPos,125,20);
        g.setColor(Color.yellow);
        g.drawString("Bharatan & Bans",xPos + 3, yPos + 15);
    }
}
```

14.5 More on interfaces

We are now going to develop a program that makes use of two more interfaces that are provided with the AWT. It is a program with which you can amuse your friends. Figure 14.3 shows how it looks when it runs. We have called it – rather unimaginatively – the RedCircle program; a red circle always moves away from the cursor so you can never click on it, despite being told to do so! And if in desperation you start to click the mouse, the words "Keep Trying" flash onto the screen!

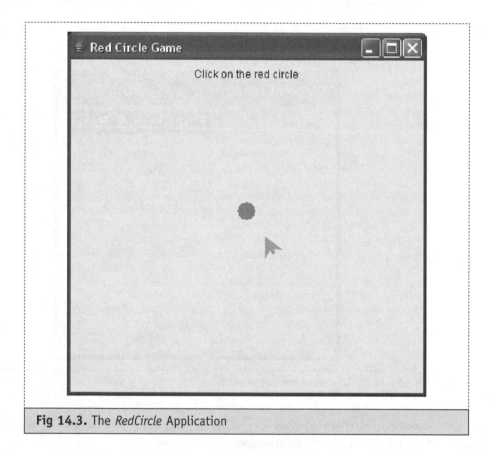

Fig 14.3. The *RedCircle* Application

As well as being a bit of fun it also introduces something new, namely the way to program a response to different mouse events like moving and dragging as well as just clicking. As we have said, this will involve using two new interface classes instead of the single ActionListener interface that we have used before.

Here is the code for the class:

The *RedCircle* class

```java
import java.awt.*;
import javax.swing.*;
import java.awt.event.*;

public class RedCircle extends JFrame
                       implements MouseMotionListener, MouseListener
```

```
{
        private int xPos;
        private int yPos;
        private int width;
        private int height;
        private boolean mouseDown;

    // the constructor
    public RedCircle(int widthIn, int heightIn)
    {
        setTitle("Red Circle Game");
        addMouseMotionListener(this);
        addMouseListener(this);
        width = widthIn;
        height = heightIn;
        xPos = width/2 -20;
        yPos = height/2 - 20;
        setSize(width, height);
        setLocation(300,300);
        setVisible(true);
    }

    // the paint method
    public void paint(Graphics g)
    {
        super.paint(g);
        g.clearRect(0,0, width, height);
        g.drawString("Click on the red circle", width/2 - 60, 50);
        g.setColor(Color.red);
        g.fillOval(xPos,yPos,20,20);

        if(mouseDown)
        {
            g.drawString("Keep trying!!!", width/2 - 40, height - 10);
        }
    }

    /* The next two methods define what happens when the mouse is
    moved or dragged. They are part of the MouseMotionListener
    interface. The red circle always stays 50 pixels above and
    50 pixels to the left of the cursor*/

    public void mouseMoved(MouseEvent e)
    {
        xPos = e.getX() - 50;
        yPos = e.getY() - 50;
        repaint();
    }

    public void mouseDragged(MouseEvent e)
    {
        xPos = e.getX() - 50;
        yPos = e.getY() - 50;
        repaint();
    }

    /* The next two methods define what happens when the mouse
    button is pressed or released. They are part of the
    MouseListener interface*/

    public void mousePressed(MouseEvent e)
    {
        mouseDown = true;
        repaint();
    }

    public void mouseReleased(MouseEvent e)
    {
        mouseDown = false;
        repaint();
```

```
    }

    /* The MouseListener interface also insists that we implement
    the next three methods. We are not actually going to use them
    here, so we have just left them blank */

    public void mouseClicked(MouseEvent e)
    {
    }

    public void mouseEntered(MouseEvent e)
    {
    }

    public void mouseExited(MouseEvent e)
    {
    }
}
```

The class itself is an extension of JFrame. You can see that here we are implementing *two* interface classes, MouseListener and MouseMotionListener; notice that the syntax is to separate them by a comma. You will notice that while we are not allowed to *extend* more than one class, it is perfectly possible to *implement* as many interfaces as we wish.

```
public class RedCircle extends JFrame implements MouseMotionListener, MouseListener
```

Both of these interfaces will of course have abstract methods which we then have to implement. The first one, MouseMotionListener, has two such methods which are described in table 14.1.

Table 14.1 The methods of *MouseMotionListener*	
mouseMoved	Specifies the behaviour that occurs when the mouse is moved when no button is depressed.
mouseDragged	Specifies the behaviour that occurs when the mouse is moved with the left-hand button depressed.

The second interface, MouseListener, has five methods which are described in table 14.2.

Table 14.2 The methods of *MouseListener*	
`mousePressed`	Specifies the behaviour that occurs when the left-hand button is pressed.
`mouseReleased`	Specifies the behaviour that occurs when the left-hand button is released.
`mouseClicked`	Specifies the behaviour that occurs when the left-hand button is clicked on a component.
`mouseEntered`	Specifies the behaviour that occurs when the cursor enters a component.
`mouseExited`	Specifies the behaviour that occurs when the cursor leaves a component.

The last three of the methods in table 14.2 are not used in this application so we have just left them blank.

The declaration of the attributes is shown below; the first two integer attributes xPos and yPos will be used to keep track of the position of the red circle. The next two attributes, width and height, will be used to hold the width and the height of the frame that the program runs in. We have allowed this to be determined at run-time, by allowing the constructor to accept these values from the program that creates the RedCircle object. The other attribute, mouseDown, is a **boolean** variable and will be set to **true** while the left-hand button of the mouse is depressed, and **false** once it is released. The default value for a **boolean** attribute is **false**, which is in fact what we require to start off with.

```
private int xPos;
private int yPos;
private int width;
private int height;
private boolean mouseDown;
```

Next we have the constructor:

```
public RedCircle(int widthIn, int heightIn)
{
    setTitle("Red Circle Game");
    addMouseMotionListener(this);
    addMouseListener(this);
    width = widthIn;
    height = heightIn;
    xPos = width/2 - 20;
    yPos = height/2 - 20;
    setSize(width, height);
    setLocation(300,300);
    setVisible(true);
}
```

The first thing the constructor does, after setting the title, is to add the two listeners to the frame itself; remember that writing the method names without attaching them to an object is actually attaching them to **this** object, and is short for:

```
this.addMouseMotionListener(this);
this.addMouseListener(this);
```

The next thing it does is to assign the values received to width and height respectively.

The next thing we do is to get the circle to appear in the centre of the window when the frame first becomes visible. So we halve the width and height of the frame to find the central point of the window; to get the centre of the circle dead in the middle we subtract 20 (the radius of the circle) from the width and the height – remind yourself of the drawOval method in chapter 10 to understand why we have done this. The values calculated in this way are assigned to xPos and yPos.

As soon as the frame becomes visible, the paint method is called, and this is the one that we have coded next:

```java
public void paint(Graphics g)
{
    super.paint(g);
    g.clearRect(0,0, width, height);
    g.drawString("Click on the red circle", width/2 - 60, 50);
    g.setColor(Color.red);
    g.fillOval(xPos,yPos,20,20);
    if(mouseDown)
    {
        g.drawString("Keep trying!!!", width/2 - 40, height - 10);
    }
}
```

You will see soon that the paint method is called every time the mouse is moved. The first thing that is done (after calling the paint method of the superclass) is that the clearRect method is called to clear the entire frame. After drawing the initial string that tells the user to click on the circle, we set the colour to red, and then draw the circle, this time using fillOval instead of drawOval to get a solid circle. The circle is drawn at position (xPos, yPos). Remember, this method gets called every time the program encounters a repaint command, and as we shall see in a moment this happens every time the mouse moves; and each time the screen gets repainted, xPos and yPos will have changed.

After the circle is drawn, the status of the mouse-button is tested by checking the value of mouseDown; as we said earlier, this attribute is going to be set to **true** if the left mouse-button is down, and **false** if not. If it is **true** the words "Keep Trying!!!" are drawn on the screen. We have tried to organize things so that this is drawn centred near the bottom of the window; you can see that we have used the dimensions of the frame to do this – we have set the x-coordinate to be half the frame width minus 40. The value of 40 is what we have estimated to be half the number of pixels taken up by the phrase "Keep Trying!!!". There are actually more accurate ways of doing this using font metrics, but we want to keep things simple at the moment, so we just had a go to see what it looks like, then tried again till we got it right! Similarly we have set the y-coordinate to be 10 pixels higher than the bottom of the window, and, as you will see when you run the program, this looks pretty good.

Now we come to the event-handling routines. This time, as we have mentioned, we are not using the ActionListener interface but are using two new interface classes, MouseMotionListener and MouseListener. The first method we implement, mouseMoved, is one of the two abstract methods of MouseMotionListener:

```java
public void mouseMoved(MouseEvent e)
{
    xPos = e.getX() - 50;
    yPos = e.getY() - 50;
    repaint();
}
```

This method is continually invoked while the mouse is moving; each time it is invoked xPos and yPos are assigned new values. The value assigned to each of them is always the value of the current coordinate of the cursor minus 50. After every assignment the window is repainted; thus, as the cursor moves, the circle moves too – always staying just north-west of it. Notice that the method is automatically sent an object of the MouseEvent class and that we use the getX and getY methods of this class to obtain the current coordinates of the cursor.

The other method of the MouseMotionListener interface, mouseDragged, determines what happens when the mouse is moved with the button held down (dragged). We have coded it in exactly the same way, so that dragging the mouse has the same effect as above.

The next two methods are declared in the MouseListener interface and determine what happens when the mouse-button is pressed and released. You can see that we have defined them so that when the button is pressed, the mouseDown attribute is set to **true** and the window is repainted; when the button is released it is set to **false**, and the window is repainted once again.

```
public void mousePressed(MouseEvent e)
{
    mouseDown = true;
    repaint();
}

public void mouseReleased(MouseEvent e)
{
    mouseDown = false;
    repaint();
}
```

The MouseListener interface also insists that we implement the mouseClicked, mouseEntered and mouseExited methods. We are not actually going to use these here, so as you can see from the code we have just left them blank.

Program 14.3 runs the class in a 400 × 400 frame.

Program 14.3

```
public class RunRedCircle
{
    public static void main(String[] args)
    {
        new RedCircle(400, 400);
    }
}
```

14.6 Adapters and inner classes

As you can see from the above example, using an interface means that we have to code all the interface methods, even those we are not interested in – for example in the RedCircle class we have had to code the methods mouseClicked, mouseEntered, mouseExited of the MouseListener interface which are not relevant to our particular application.

There is a way around this, which is to use an **adapter**. An adapter is a special class that acts as an intermediary between our class and the interface, making it unnecessary to code all the methods because the class can be extended in the normal way using inheritance. An adapter is provided for every interface that comes with the standard Java packages. For example, the adapter equivalent for `MouseListener` is called `MouseAdapter`. Although we don't have access to the source code for this class, we could guess that it looks like this:

```
class MouseAdapter implements MouseListener
{
    public void mousePressed(MouseEvent e)
    {
    }

    public void mouseReleased(MouseEvent e)
    {
    }

    public void mouseClicked(MouseEvent e)
    {
    }

    public void mouseEntered(MouseEvent e)
    {
    }

    public void mouseExited(MouseEvent e)
    {
    }
}
```

You might be wondering why we do not use adapters all the time. The reason is that very often the class that we want to extend is already extending another class. As we have mentioned before, in Java a class is allowed to inherit from one superclass only. Inheriting from more than one superclass is known as **multiple inheritance**. There is good reason for languages not allowing this, and you will find more about it in chapter 24. In the case of the `RedCircle` class, this class already extends `JFrame`; it cannot therefore also extend `MouseAdapter`.

There is a way, however, that we could use this adapter in the `RedCircle` class. Consider the following line in the constructor, which adds the `MouseListener` to the `JFrame`:

```
addMouseListener(this);
```

As you know, the parameter indicates the class where the program can find the instructions for processing the event (in this case a `MouseEvent`). In the `RedCircle` class this code will be found in the class itself, hence the use of the keyword **this**. Another option would be to write a class, called, for example, `RedCircleAdapter`, for this express purpose; this class would extend `MouseAdapter` and would code the `mousePressed` and `mouseReleased` methods. The above line would then have to be changed to:

```
addMouseListener(new RedCircleAdapter());
```

Of course, it might occur to you that the `RedCircleAdapter` class is not something that is ever going to be used for any other program, and it seems rather odd to write a separate class for such a narrow purpose. In cases like this, we can write what we call an **inner class** – which, as its name suggests, is a class written within another class. The way we have done this with the `RedCircle` class is shown below.

The *RedCircleWithAdapter* class

```java
import java.awt.*;
import javax.swing.*;
import java.awt.event.*;

public class RedCircleWithAdapter extends JFrame
                                  implements MouseMotionListener
{
    private int xPos;
    private int yPos;
    private int width;
    private int height;
    private boolean mouseDown;

    //inner class
    class RedCircleAdapter extends MouseAdapter
    {
        public void mousePressed(MouseEvent e)
        {
            mouseDown = true;
            repaint();
        }

        public void mouseReleased(MouseEvent e)
        {
            mouseDown = false;
            repaint();
        }
    }

    // the constructor
    public RedCircleWithAdapter(int widthIn, int heightIn)
    {
        setTitle("Red Circle Game");
        addMouseMotionListener(this);
        addMouseListener(new RedCircleAdapter());
        width = widthIn;
        height = heightIn;
        xPos = widthIn/2 -20;
        yPos = heightIn/2 - 20;
        setSize(width, height);
        setLocation(300,300);
        setVisible(true);
    }

    // the paint method
    public void paint(Graphics g)
    {
        super.paint(g);
        g.clearRect(0,0,width, height);
        g.drawString("Click on the red circle", width/2 - 60, 50);
        g.setColor(Color.red);
        g.fillOval(xPos,yPos,20,20);

        if(mouseDown)
        {
            g.drawString("Keep trying!!!", width/2 - 40, height - 10);
        }
    }

    public void mouseMoved(MouseEvent e)
    {
        xPos = e.getX() - 50;
        yPos = e.getY() - 50;

        repaint();
    }

    public void mouseDragged(MouseEvent e)
```

```
        {
            xPos = e.getX() - 50;
            yPos = e.getY() - 50;
            repaint();
        }
    }
```

The inner class, `RedCircleAdapter`, has been emboldened for clarity. Notice how it is possible to refer to attributes of the outer class (in this case `mouseDown`) in the inner class.

14.7 The *toString* method

In chapter 8 you found out that, in Java, every class is inherited from a "super superclass" called `Object`. In other words every object of every class is a kind of `Object`. The `Object` class has a method called `toString` that returns a `String`, and which can be overridden by subclasses of `Object` – in other words by any other class. Methods of other classes can be set up to use this method – some classes in the standard Java packages have methods (for example `print` and `println`) which take an `Object` object as a parameter and use its `toString` method; we could also write such methods in our own classes.

An example will show you how useful this can be for the purposes of testing. Let's look at our `BankAccount` class, which we developed in chapter 7. We will add a `toString` method as defined below, thus overriding the `toString` method of the `Object` class which `BankAccount`, like all other classes, inherits:

```
public String toString()
{
    return "Account Number: "
        + accountNumber
        + "Name: "
        + accountName
        + "Balance: "
        + balance
        + "\n";
}
```

Now look at program 14.4:

Program 14.4

```
public class RunAccount
{
    public static void main(String[] args)
    {
        BankAccount account1 = new BankAccount("001", "Sarah Patel");
        BankAccount account2 = new BankAccount("002", "Robinder Grewel");
        System.out.println(account1);
        System.out.println(account2);
    }
}
```

Do you see that in each case the parameter to the `println` method is just the name of the object? This is possible because, as we indicated earlier, there is a version of `println` provided that accepts an object and outputs the return value of the object's `toString` method. Since we have overridden the `toString` method in our `BankAccount` class as shown, the output from this program will be:

Account Number: 001

Account Name: Sarah Patel

Current Balance: 0.0

Account Number: 002

Account Name: Robinder Grewel

Current Balance: 0.0

Self-test questions

1 Explain the terms *abstraction* and *abstract data type*.

2 What is the difference between *dynamic (run-time) binding* and *static (compile-time) binding*?

3 a) Explain the difference between an *interface* and an *adapter* in Java.

   b) Consider the following interface:

```
public interface SomeInterface
{
    public void method1();
    public int method2();
}
```

   Write an adapter, `SomeAdapter`, that could be used as an alternative to this interface.

4 Explain the purpose of *inner classes* and describe how they are used.

5 Write an appropriate `toString` method for the `Oblong` class that we developed in chapter 7.

Programming exercises

1 Implement the `RedCircle` application from section 14.5.

2 a) Write an interface, `Checkable`, that has one method, `check`, which receives no parameters and returns a `boolean`. This interface will be used to check the integrity of different objects.

   b) Adapt the `BankAccount` class that we originally developed in chapter 7 so that it implements the `Checkable` interface. A valid `BankAccount` number will be defined as having seven digits, and the `check` method will therefore be overridden to reflect this.

   c) Write a short program to test the new `BankAccount` class, by providing a method that receives a `Checkable` object.

   d) Use the above program for a different `Checkable` object that also implements the `Checkable` interface. An example could be the `Oblong` class in which the length and height are validated as being non-negative integers.

3 Design and implement a program that allows the user to draw a rectangle by dragging the mouse. You should look at the `RedCircle` class to get some ideas for this – you will need to think about how you determine the start position of the rectangle, and how you will calculate its width and height.

4 Consider the following class:

```
import java.awt.*;
import java.awt.event.*;
import javax.swing.*;

public class SomeGraphicsClass extends JFrame implements MouseListener
{
    private JButton aButton = new JButton("Press here");

    public SomeGraphicsClass()
    {
        setTitle("Question 4");
        setLayout(new FlowLayout());
        add(aButton);
        aButton.addMouseListener(this);
        setSize(250, 200);
    }

    public void mousePressed(MouseEvent e)
    {
    }

    public void mouseReleased(MouseEvent e)
    {
    }

    public void mouseEntered(MouseEvent e)
    {
    }

    public void mouseExited(MouseEvent e)
    {
    }

    public void mouseClicked(MouseEvent e)
    {

    }
}
```

Write the code for a class called `ExtendedGraphicsClass` that is a subclass of `SomeGraphicsClass`. The class will have one additional attribute, a `JLabel`, initially displaying the text "The mouse has not been pressed yet". The constructor must be overridden to enable this attribute to be added to the `JFrame` along with the `JButton`. It must also contain an instruction to make the frame visible.

The class will also override the methods `mousePressed` and `mouseReleased` so that, as shown below, the label will display the text "The mouse button has been pressed" when the mouse button is pressed, and "The mouse button has been released" when the mouse button is released.

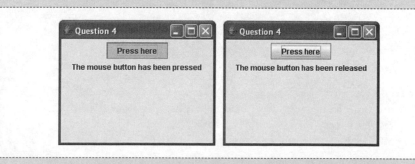

5 Experiment with the other methods of the `MouseListener` interface (`mouseEntered` and `mouseExited`) that you have not yet used.

For example, the simple little application shown below adds a button to a frame using a flow layout. The button is yellow, but turns red when the cursor moves over it. In this example we simply sized the button by adding some blank text, and then called its `setFocusPainted` method with a parameter of **false** in order to remove the highlighting around the text.

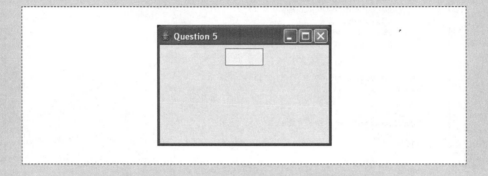

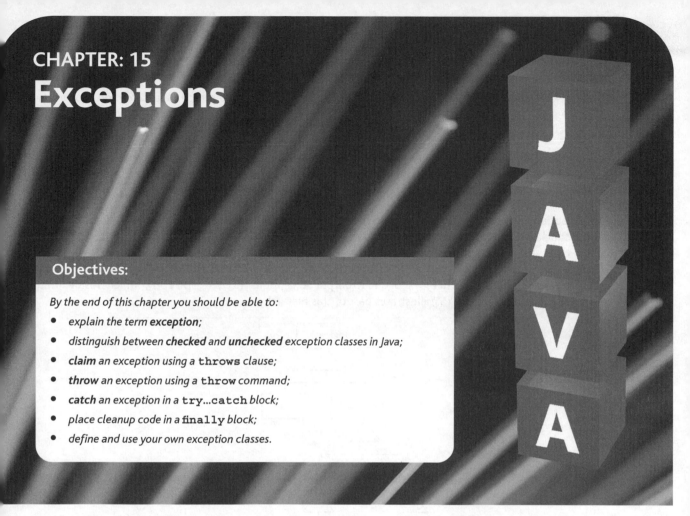

CHAPTER: 15

Exceptions

Objectives:

By the end of this chapter you should be able to:

- *explain the term **exception**;*
- *distinguish between **checked** and **unchecked** exception classes in Java;*
- ***claim** an exception using a `throws` clause;*
- ***throw** an exception using a `throw` command;*
- ***catch** an exception in a `try...catch` block;*
- *place cleanup code in a `finally` block;*
- *define and use your own exception classes.*

15.1 Introduction

One way in which to write a program is to assume that everything proceeds smoothly and as expected – users input values at the correct time and of the correct format, files are never corrupt, array indices are always valid and so on. Of course this view of the world is very rarely accurate. In reality, unexpected situations arise that could compromise the correct functioning of your program.

We said in chapter 9 that you should aim to write programs that are robust; that is, programs that continue to function even if unexpected situations should arise. So far we have tried to achieve this by carefully constructed `if` statements that send back error flags when appropriate. However, in some circumstances, these forms of protection against undesirable situations prove inadequate. In such cases the *exception handling* facility of Java must be used.

15.2 Pre-defined exception classes in Java

An **exception** is an event that occurs during the life of a program which could cause that program to behave unreliably. You can see that the events we described in the introduction fall into this category. For example, accessing an array with an invalid index could cause that program to terminate.

Each type of event that could lead to an exception is associated with a pre-defined *exception class* in Java. When a given event occurs, the Java run-time environment determines which exception has occurred and an object of the given exception class is generated. This process is known as **throwing** an exception.

These exception classes have been named to reflect the nature of the exception. For example, when an array is accessed with an illegal index an object of the `ArrayIndexOutOfBoundsException` class is thrown.

All exception classes inherit from the base class `Throwable` which is found in the `java.lang` package. These subclasses of `Throwable` are found in various packages and are then further categorized depending upon the type of exception. For example, the exception associated with a given file not being found (`FileNotFoundException`) and the exception associated with an end of file having been reached (`EOFException`) are both types of input/output exceptions (`IOException`), which reside in the `java.io` package. Figure 15.1 illustrates part of this hierarchy.

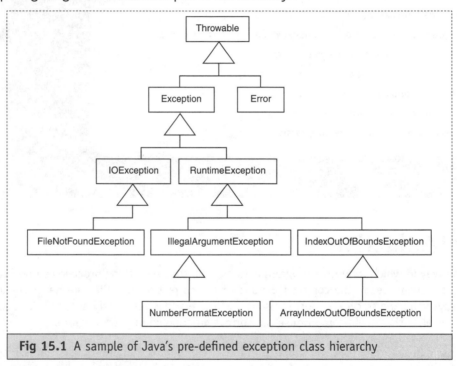

Fig 15.1 A sample of Java's pre-defined exception class hierarchy

As you can see from figure 15.1, there are two immediate subclasses of `Throwable`: `Exception` and `Error`. The `Error` class describes internal system errors that are very unlikely ever to occur (so called "hard" errors). For example, one subclass of `Error` is `VirtualMachineError` where some error in the JVM has been detected. There is little that can be done in the way of recovery from such errors other than to end the program as gracefully as possible. All other exceptions are subclasses of the `Exception` class and it is these exceptions that programmers deal with in their programs. The `Exception` class is further subdivided. The two most important subdivisions are shown in figure 15.1, `IOException` and `RuntimeException`.

The `RuntimeException` class deals with errors that arise from the logic of a program. For example, a program that converts a string into a number, when the string contains non-numeric characters (`NumberFormatException`) or accesses an array using an illegal index (`ArrayIndexOutOfBoundsException`).

The IOException class deals with external errors that could affect the program during input and output. Such errors could include, for example, the keyboard locking, or an external file being corrupted.

Since nearly every Java instruction could result in a RuntimeException error, the Java compiler does not flag such instructions as potentially error-prone. Consequently these types of errors are known as **unchecked** exceptions.[1] It is left to the programmer to ensure that code is written in such a way as to avoid such exceptions. For example, checking an array index before looking up a value in an array with that index. Should such an exception arise, it will be due to a program error and will not become apparent until run-time.

The Java compiler *does*, however, flag up those instructions that may generate all other types of exception (such as IOException errors) since the programmer has no means of avoiding such errors arising. For example, an instruction to read from a file may cause an exception because the file is corrupt. No amount of program code can prevent this file from being corrupt. The compiler will not only flag such an instruction as potentially error-prone, it will also specify the exact exception that could be thrown. Consequently, these kinds of errors are known as **checked exceptions**. Programmers have to include code to inform the compiler of how they will deal with checked exceptions generated by a particular instruction, before the compiler will allow the program to compile successfully.

15.3 Handling exceptions

Consider a simple program that allows the user to enter an aptitude test mark at the keyboard; the program then informs the user if he or she has passed the test and been allowed on a given course. We could use the nextInt method (from either our EasyScanner class, or the original Scanner class) to allow the user to enter this mark. However, in order to show you how exceptions can be dealt with in your programs, we will not take this approach – instead we will devise our own class, TestException, that will contain a class method called getInteger. Before we do that, here is the outline of the main application:

```java
public class AptitudeTest
{
      public static void main (String[] args)
      {       int score;
              System.out.print("Enter aptitude test score: ");
              score = TestException.getInteger(); // calling class method
              // test score here
      }
}
```

Now let's look at an outline for the TestException class.

```java
public class TestException
{
      // this method is declared 'static' as it is a class method
      public static int getInteger()
      {
              // code for method goes here
      }
}
```

---

[1] Exceptions derived from Error are also unchecked.

The getInteger method must allow the user to enter an integer at the keyboard and then return that integer. There are many ways we could try and read an integer from the keyboard. As we have said, rather than make use of the nextInt method in the Scanner class, the approach we will take here will be to use a rather low-level method called read in the System.in object. So far we have used the System.out object to display information on the screen, but we have not explored the System.in object. This object is an object of the InputStream class that you will find out more about in chapter 20.

You will remember from chapter 1 that each character on the keyboard is represented by a Unicode number. For countries in which the standard western alphabet is used, the lower case letters 'a' through to 'z' are represented by the Unicode values 97 through to 122 inclusive. Special characters also have Unicode values. For example, the carriage return character has a Unicode value 13. The InputStream class provides a read method that is a bit like the next method of the Scanner class, except that it treats the String as a series of Unicode numbers. Each number is considered to be of type **byte**, so that the String itself is an array of bytes. Figure 15.2 illustrates the effect of the read method when someone enters the word "hello" at the keyboard.

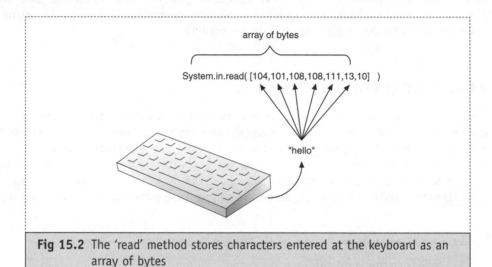

Fig 15.2 The 'read' method stores characters entered at the keyboard as an array of bytes

Notice that the array of bytes is not returned as a value. Instead they are placed into the parameter. Also note that the newline character is given a Unicode value of 10.

The getInteger method will first have to take this array of bytes and convert it into a string. Luckily a version of the String constructor returns a String object from an array of bytes. We then remove any trailing spaces at the end of the String, this can be done with the String method trim as follows:

```
byte [] buffer = new byte[512]; // declare a large byte array
System.in.read(buffer); // characters entered stored in array
String s = new String (buffer); // make string from byte array
s = s.trim(); // trim string
```

Now, finally, we have to convert this string into an integer. We can use the parseInt method of the Integer class to allow us to do this:

```
int num = Integer.parseInt(s); // converts string to an 'int'
```

Our `TestException` class now looks like this:

```
// this is a first attempt, it will not compile!
public class TestException
{
      public static int getInteger()
      {
              byte [] buffer = new byte[512];
              System.in.read(buffer);
              String s = new String (buffer);
              s = s.trim();
              int num = Integer.parseInt(s);
              return num; // send back the integer value
      }
}
```

Unfortunately, as things stand, this class will *not* compile. The cause of the error is in the `getInteger` method, in particular the way we used the `read` method of `System.in`. Whenever this method is used, the Java compiler *insists* that we be very careful. To understand this better take a look at the header for this `read` method, taken from the Java language specification, in particular the part we have emboldened:

```
public int read (byte[] b) throws IOException
```

Up until now you have not seen a method header of this form. The words **throws** `IOException` are the new bits in this method header. In Java this is known as a method **claiming an exception**.

15.3.1 Claiming an exception

The term **claiming an exception** refers to a given method having been marked to indicate that it will pass on an exception object that it might generate. So the term **throws** `IOException` means that the method *could* cause an input/output exception in your program. The type of error that could take place while data is being read includes the loss of a network connection or a file being corrupted, for example.

Remember, when an exception occurs, an exception object is created. This is an unwanted object that could cause your program to fail or behave unpredictably, and so should be dealt with and not ignored. Rather than dealing with this exception object *within* the `read` method, the Java people decided it would be better if callers of this method dealt with the exception object in whatever way they felt was suitable. In effect, they *passed the error* on to the caller of the method (see figure 15.3).

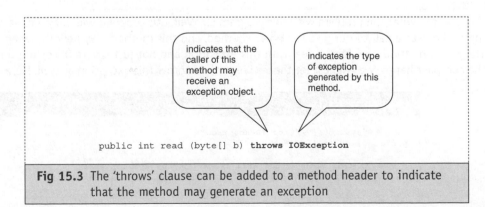

Fig 15.3 The 'throws' clause can be added to a method header to indicate that the method may generate an exception

As the type of exception generated (IOException) is not a subclass of RuntimeException, it is an example of a *checked exception*. In other words, the compiler *insists* that if the read method is used, the programmer deals with this exception in some way, and does not just ignore it as we did originally. That is why we had a compiler error initially. There are always two ways to deal with an exception:

1   deal with the exception within the method;

2   pass on the exception out of the method.

The developers of the read method decided to pass on the exception, so now our getInteger method has to decide what to do with this exception. In a while we will show you how to deal with an exception within a method, but for now we will just make our getInteger method pass on the exception too. We do this by simply adding a **throws** clause to our method:

```
import java.io.* // for IOException class
public class TestException
{
    // adding this throws clause will allow this method to compile
    public static int getInteger() throws IOException
    {
            // as before
    }
}
```

Notice that, as the IOException class is in the io package, we now need the following **import** statement at the top of this class:

```
import java.io.* // for IOException class
```

Now that the getInteger method has claimed the IOException, it *will* compile as we have not just *ignored* the exception, we have made a *conscious decision* to pass the exception on to any method that calls this getInteger method. Now, let's look at the AptitudeTest class again.

```
// something wrong here!
public class AptitudeTest
{
    public static void main (String[] args)
    {
            int score;
            System.out.print("Enter aptitude test score: ");
            score = TestException.getInteger(); // calling class method
            // test score here
    }
}
```

Can you see what the problem with this program is? Well, this program will not compile now as the main method makes a call to our getInteger method, and this method may now throw an IOException! The main method now has to deal with this exception and not just ignore it. For the time being, to keep the compiler happy, we will just let the main method throw this exception as well. Here is the code:

Program 15.1

```
import java.io.*; // for IOException
public class AptitudeTest
{
    // this main method will throw out any IOExceptions
    public static void main (String[] args) throws IOException
    {
            int score;
```

```
            System.out.print("Enter aptitude test score: ");
            // the 'getInteger' method may throw an IOException
            score = TestException.getInteger();
            if (score >= 50)
            {
                System.out.println("You have a place on the course!");
            }
            else
            {
                System.out.println("Sorry, you failed your test");
            }
        }
    }
```

Dealing with the exception in the way we have is not a very good idea. We have effectively continually passed on the exception object until it gets thrown out of our program to the operating system. This may cause the program to terminate when such an exception occurs. Before we deal with this problem let us show you a test run. Take a look at it as something very interesting happens.

Enter aptitude test score: **12w**

java.lang.NumberFormatException: 12w

> *at java.lang.Integer.parseInt(Integer.java:418)*

> *at java.lang.Integer.parseInt(Integer.java:458)*

> *at TestException.getInteger(TestException.java:10)*

> *at AptitudeTest.main(AptitudeTest.java:11)*

As you can see, when asked to enter an integer, the user inadvertently added a character into the number (**12w**). This has led to an exception being generated and thrown out of our program. Again looking at the output generated, you can see that when an exception is generated in this way the Java system gives you quite a lot of information. This information includes the name of the method that threw the exception, the class that the method belongs to, the line numbers in the source files where the error arose, and the type of exception that was thrown. Such information is referred to as the **stack trace** of the exception.

Look at the name of the exception that is thrown. It's not the one we were worried about, IOException, but NumberFormatException. This exception is raised when trying to convert a string into a number when the string contains non-numeric characters, as we were trying to do in this case within our getInteger method:

```
public static int getInteger() throws IOException
{
    // some code here
    int num = Integer.parseInt(s); /* will cause a NumberFormatException,
                                       if string s, contains non-numeric
                                       characters*/
}
```

Why didn't the compiler warn us about this when we first used the parseInt method in our implementation of getInteger? Well, the reason is that the exception that could arise (NumberFormatException) is a subclass of RuntimeException and so is unchecked!

Notice that run-time exceptions do not need to be claimed in method headers in order for them to be thrown. For example, although the following is valid in Java, it is not *necessary* to claim the `NumberFormatException` in the header.

```
/* multiple exceptions can be claimed in the method header as follows by
   seperating exception names with commas. However run-time exceptions
   do not need to be claimed in this way */
public static int getInteger() throws IOException, NumberFormatException
{
     // some code here
}
```

The way we have dealt with exceptions so far has not been very effective. As you can see from the test run of program 15.1, continually throwing exceptions up to the calling method does not really solve the problem. It may keep the compiler happy, but eventually it means exception objects will escape from your programs and cause them to terminate. Instead, it is better at some point to handle an exception object rather than throw it. In Java this is known as **catching an exception**.

15.3.2 Catching an exception

One route for an exception object is *out* of the current method and *up to* the calling method. That's the approach we used in the previous section. Another way out for an exception object, however, is into a `catch` block. Once an exception object is trapped in a `catch` block, and that block ends, the exception object is effectively terminated. In order to trap the exception object in a `catch` block you must surround the code that could generate the exception in a `try` block. The syntax for using a `try` and `catch` block is as follows:

```
try
{
    // code that could generate an exception
}
catch (Exception e) // type of exception must be specified as a parameter
{
    // action to be taken when an exception occurs
}
// other instructions could be placed here
```

There are a few things to note before we show you this `try`...`catch` idea in action. First, any number of lines could be within the `try` block, and more than one of them could cause an exception. If none of them causes an exception the `catch` block is missed and the lines following the `catch` block are executed. If any one of them causes an exception the program will leave the `try` block and look for a `catch` block that deals with that exception.

Once such a `catch` clause is found, the statements within it will be executed and the program will then *continue* with any statements that follow the `catch` clause – it will *not* return to the code in the `try` clause. Look carefully at the syntax for the `catch` block:

```
catch (Exception e)
{
    // action to be taken when an exception occurs
}
```

This looks very similar to a method header. You can see that the **catch** block header has one parameter: an object, which we called e, of type Exception. Since *all* exceptions are subclasses of the Exception class, this will catch *any* exception that should arise. However, it is better to replace this exception class with the *specific* class that you are catching so that you can be certain *which* exception you have caught. As there may be more than one exception generated within a method, there may be more than one **catch** block below a **try** block – each dealing with a different exception. When an exception is thrown in a **try** block, the **catch** blocks are inspected in order – the first matching **catch** block is the one that will handle the exception.

Within the **catch** block, programmers can, if they choose, interrogate the exception object using some Exception methods, some of which are listed in table 15.1.

Table 15.1 Some methods of the *Exception* class	
Method	Description
printStackTrace	prints (onto the console) a stack trace of the exception
toString	returns a detailed error message
getMessage	returns a summary error message

With this information in mind we can deal with the exceptions in the previous section in a different way. All we have to decide is where to catch the exception object. For now we will leave the getInteger method as it is, and catch offending exception objects in the main method of program 15.2.

Program 15.2

```java
import java.io.*;
public class AptitudeTest2
{
    public static void main (String[] args)
    {
        try
        {
            int score;
            System.out.print("Enter aptitude test score: ");
            // getInteger may throw IOException or NumberFomatException
            score = TestException.getInteger();
            if (score >= 50)
            {
                System.out.println("You have a place on the course!");
            }
            else
            {
                System.out.println("Sorry, you failed your test");
            }
        }
        // if something does goes wrong!
        catch (NumberFormatException e)
        {
            System.out.println("You entered an invalid number!");
        }
        catch (IOException e)
        {
            System.out.println(e); // calls toString method
        }
        // even if no exception thrown/caught, this line will be executed
        System.out.println("Goodbye");
    }
}
```

Notice that by catching an offending exception object there is no need to pass that object out of the method by raising that exception in the method header. Since we catch the `IOException` here, the `throws IOException` clause can be removed from the header of `main`. In program 15.2 we have chosen to print out an error message if an `IOException` is raised (by implicitly calling the `toString` method), whereas we have chosen to print our own message if a `NumberFormatException` is raised. Now look at a sample test run of program 15.2:

Enter aptitude test score: **12w**

You entered an invalid number!

Goodbye

As you can see the user once again entered an invalid integer, but this time the program did not terminate. Instead the exception was handled with a clear message to the user, after which the program continued to operate normally.

15.4 The 'finally' clause

From the previous sections you can see that three courses of action may now take place in a **try** block:

1   the instructions within the **try** block are all executed successfully;

2   an exception occurs within the **try** block; the **try** block is exited and a matching **catch** block is found for this exception;

3   an exception occurs within the **try** block; the **try** block is exited but no matching **catch** block is found for this exception; so the exception is thrown from the method.

It may be the case that, no matter which of these courses of action take place, you wish to execute some additional instructions before the method terminates. Often such a scenario arises when you wish to carry out some cleanup code, such as closing a file or a network connection that you have opened in the **try** block. The **finally** clause allows us to do this. The syntax for the **finally** clause is as follows:

```
try
{
    // code that could generate an exception
}
catch (Exception e) /* if one or more 'catch' clauses are
                       specified, they must be given before the 'finally'
                       clause */
{
    // action to be taken when an exception occurs
}
finally
{
    // cleanup code goes here
}
  // other instructions could be placed here
```

Notice that when **catch** clauses are specified, the **finally** clause must come directly *after* such clauses. If no such **catch** clauses are specified, the **finally** clause must follow directly after the **try** clause. Now, when the code in the **try** block is executed the following three courses of action can take place:

1   the instructions within the **try** block are all executed successfully; if there are any **catch** blocks specified they are skipped and the code in the **finally** block is executed;

2   an exception occurs within the **try** block; the **try** block is exited and a matching **catch** block is found for this exception, after which the code in the **finally** block is executed;

3   an exception occurs within the **try** block; the **try** block is exited but no matching **catch** block is found for this exception; so the code in the **finally** block is executed – after which the exception is thrown from the given method.

Program 15.3 is a simple demonstration of how the **finally** clause works under these three scenarios:

Program 15.3

```java
public class TestTryCatchFinally
{
    public static void main(String[] args)
    {
        try
        {
                System.out.println("START TRY\n");
                String[] colours = {"RED","BLUE","GREEN"}; // initialize array
                System.out.print("Which colour? (1,2,3): ");
                String pos = EasyScanner.nextString();
                // next line could throw NumberFormatException
                int i = Integer.parseInt(pos);
                // next line could throw ArrayIndexOutOfBoundsException
                System.out.println(colours[i-1]);
                System.out.println("\nEND TRY\n");
        }
        // include a catch only for ArrayIndexOutOfBoundsException
        catch(ArrayIndexOutOfBoundsException e)
        {
                System.out.println("\nENTER CATCH\n");
                System.out.println(e);

        }
        // this code will always be executed
         finally
        {
                System.out.println("\nENTER FINALLY\n");
                System.out.println("Goodbye\n");
        }
    }
}
```

This code should be fairly self-explanatory. Just notice that we have provided a **catch** block for the ArrayIndexOutOfBoundsException but we have not provided a **catch** block for the NumberFormatException, so such an exception would be thrown from main should it arise. Also, notice that we displayed messages to indicate when we are in each of the **try**, **catch** and **finally** blocks.

Here is one test run:

START TRY

Which colour? (1,2,3): **2**
BLUE

END TRY

ENTER FINALLY

Goodbye

Here the user enters a valid colour number, so the **try** block completes successfully. The **catch** block is skipped and the **finally** block is executed.

Here is another test run:

START TRY

Which colour? (1,2,3): **4**

ENTER CATCH

java.lang.ArrayIndexOutOfBoundsException: 3

ENTER FINALLY

Goodbye

Here the user enters an invalid colour number, the **try** block does not complete as an ArrayIndexOutOfBoundsException is thrown. A matching **catch** block is found for this exception and executed. Upon completion of this **catch** block the program continues with the code in the **finally** block.

Here is the last test run:

START TRY

Which colour? (1,2,3): **2c**

```
ENTER FINALLY

Goodbye

Exception in thread "main" java.lang.NumberFormatException:
For input string: "2c"
        at java.lang.NumberFormatException.forInputString
                            (NumberFormatException.java:48)
        at java.lang.Integer.parseInt(Integer.java:456)
        at java.lang.Integer.parseInt(Integer.java:497)
        at TestTryCatchFinally.main(TestTryCatchFinally.java:11)
```

In this case, the user entered an invalid number causing a `NumberFormatException` – so the **try** block did not complete successfully. However, there is no **catch** block provided for this exception. Without a **finally** clause this would have led to program termination *immediately* as the exception escapes from `main`. We have a **finally** clause, however, so this is executed *before* the program terminates with the offending exception.

These three test runs match the three scenarios we identified for **try...catch...finally** blocks earlier. You will notice from the three test runs above that, if the instructions inside the **finally** clause were written as normal below the **catch** clause (without putting them into a **finally** block), the first two test runs would have produced exactly the same result. This is because code following a **catch** block is always executed if no exception is thrown, or if an exception is thrown and a matching **catch** clause is found and executed. Only in scenario three, when an exception is thrown and no matching **catch** is found (perhaps because no **catch** clauses were specified), does the **finally** clause really make a difference to program flow.

You may well come across the third scenario when developing your programs, so the **finally** clause should be used here for cleanup code. Using the **finally** clause in scenarios one and two is optional.

15.5 Exceptions in GUI applications

In the previous section we showed you how the `parseInt` method could potentially result in a `NumberFormatException` being thrown. If this were not handled at some point, the exception object would escape out of your program and cause the program to terminate. However, this isn't the first time that you used the `parseInt` method. You often had to use it when implementing GUI applications. In such applications all user input is initially considered a string, and in order to retrieve integer values from these strings you used the `parseInt` method (and to retrieve decimal values you used `parseDouble`). At the time, you never considered handling these exceptions, and your applications never seemed to terminate as a result of invalid data entry. For example, do you remember the `Hostel` case study of chapters 11 and 12? Figure 15.4 illustrates a sample screen shot when a user enters an invalid room number.

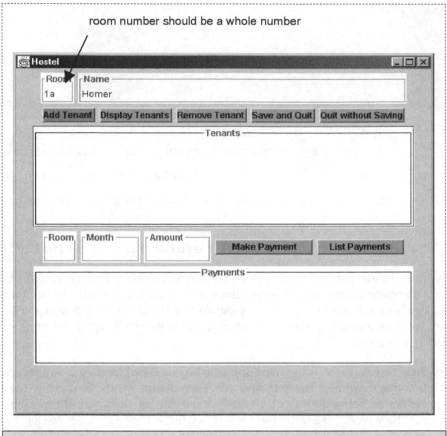

room number should be a whole number

Fig 15.4 A sample screen shot from the 'Hostel' case study illustrating an invalid room number having been entered

When such an event occurred within a GUI application, the application seemed to continue operating regardless. After our discussion on exceptions this might seem surprising as the text entered is being processed by a `parseInt` method. To remind you, here is a fragment from the event-handler:

```
if(e.getSource() == addButton)
{
        // some code here
        String roomEntered = roomField.getText(); // read text entered
        // the parseInt method could cause an exception!
        if(Integer.parseInt(roomEntered)< 1
                        || Integer.parseInt(roomEntered)>noOfRooms)
        {
            displayArea1.setText("There are only " + noOfRooms + " rooms");
        }
        // some code here
}
```

In fact, when an invalid number is entered as illustrated in figure 15.4, a `NumberFormatException` occurs but

> you will not see details of the exception in your graphics screen since they will always be displayed on your black console window (which may be hidden during the running of your application);

> exceptions do not terminate GUI applications; however, they may make them behave unpredictably.

So, if you uncover your black console screen you will see a list of exceptions that have been thrown during the running of your GUI applications – you may be surprised to see how many are actually thrown when you thought your program was operating correctly.

Often, graphical programs will continue to operate normally in the face of exceptions. To ensure this is the case you should still add exception handling code into your GUI applications. For example, we could amend the event-handler above as follows:

```
if(e.getSource() == addButton)
{
    try
    {
        // previous add button code goes here
    }
    // if any lines throw NumberFormatException this handler is activated
    catch (NumberFormatException nfe)
    {
        // display error message and clear original text in room field
        displayArea1.setText("Invalid room number" + nfe.getMessage()
                                        + "\nEnter whole numbers only!");
        roomField.setText("");
    }
}
```

Notice we had to pick a different name for our exception object. We chose `nfe` (for **N**umber**F**ormat**E**xception) rather than just `e` as before, as we already have an object called `e` in this event-handler. Now if we run the application again, with the same input as depicted in figure 15.4 we get the response given in figure 15.5 overleaf.

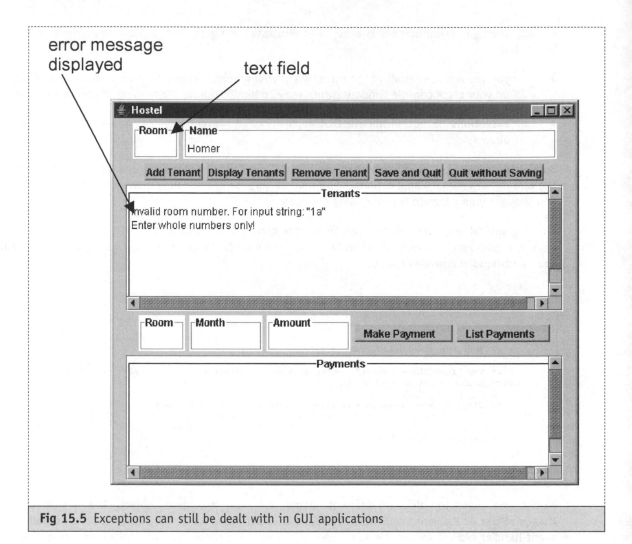

error message
displayed

text field

Fig 15.5 Exceptions can still be dealt with in GUI applications

15.6 Using exceptions in your own classes

So far we have mainly been dealing with how to handle exceptions that are thrown by predefined Java methods, such as `read` and `parseInt`. Up until now, the methods you have been writing yourself have not had to deal with exceptions unless they themselves used a Java method that throws an exception.

We have managed to avoid the need for exceptions by using **if** statements to monitor abnormal situations, and to send back boolean error values when appropriate, to warn users of our methods that something went wrong. In this way, exceptions never arose. As an example, think back to the `Bank` class of chapter 7. Some important parts of this class are presented again below.

The *Bank* class – a reminder

```java
public class Bank
{
  // attributes
  private BankAccount[] list;
  private int total;

   // the constructor
  public Bank(int sizeIn)
  {
    // size array with parameter
    list = new BankAccount[sizeIn];
    total = 0;
  }


  // add an item to the array
  public boolean add(BankAccount accountIn)
  {
    if (!isFull()) // check if list is full
    {
      list[total] = accountIn;
      total++;
      return true; // indicate success
    }
    else
    {
      return false; // indicate failure
    }
  }


  // return an account at a particular place in the list
  public BankAccount getItem(String accountNumberIn)
  {
    int index;
    index = search(accountNumberIn);
    if(index == -999) // check for error
    {
      return null; // indicate failure
    }
    else
    {
      return list[index]; // everything ok
    }
  }


  // deposit money in a specified account
  public boolean depositMoney(String accountNumberIn, double amountIn)
  {
    int index = search(accountNumberIn);
    if(index == -999) // check for error
    {
      return false; // indicate failure
    }
    else
    {
      list[index].deposit(amountIn);
      return true; // indicate success
    }
  }


  // withdraw money from a specified account
  public boolean withdrawMoney(String accountNumberIn, double amountIn)
  {
    int index = search(accountNumberIn);
    if(index == -999) // check for error
    {
      return false; // indicate failure
    }
```

```
        else
        {
           list[index].withdraw(amountIn);
           return true; // indicate success
        }
     }

     // remove an account
     public boolean remove(String numberIn)
     {
        int index = search(numberIn);
        if(index == -999) // check for error
        {
           return false; // indicate failure
        }
        else
        {
           for(int i = index; i<= total-2; i++)
           {
               list[i] = list[i+1];
           }
           total--;
           return true; // indicate successful
        }
     }

  // search for an account
  private int search(String accountNumberIn)
  {
     for(int i = 0; i < total; i++)
     {
        BankAccount tempAccount = list[i];
        String tempNumber = tempAccount.getAccountNumber();
        if(tempNumber.equals(accountNumberIn))
        {
            return i;
        }
     }
     return -999; // when item is not found
  }

  // other methods go here
}
```

As you can see, the methods given above may not necessarily always be able to carry out their intended tasks successfully. For example, the `add` method would not be able to add a bank account to the list if the list were full. Similarly, the `depositMoney` method could not deposit money into a given bank account if that bank account number did not exist in the list. In each case, failure was indicated by returning some error value back to the caller. The `add` and `depositMoney` methods both return a **boolean** value of **false** to indicate failure. The `getItem` method, on the other hand, returns a **null** value to indicate failure whereas the **private** `search` method returns a value of −999.

Within the methods themselves, **if...else** statements are used to prevent errors such as accessing an array with an invalid array index. Look again, for example, at the `depositMoney` method.

```
public boolean depositMoney(String accountNumberIn, double amountIn)
{
    int index = search(accountNumberIn);
    if(index == -999) // check for error
    {
      return false; // indicate failure
    }
    else
    {
      list[index].deposit(amountIn);
      return true; // indicate success
    }
}
```

The **if...else** statement checks that a valid array index has been returned by the search method, thus preventing an ArrayIndexOutOfBoundsException from being thrown. Sometimes the technique of avoidance and reporting of errors in **return** values does not work. In such cases exception-handling techniques can be used. As an example of this, consider the Bank constructor once again:

```
public Bank(int sizeIn)
{
    list = new BankAccount[sizeIn];
    total = 0;
}
```

What could potentially go wrong with a call to this constructor?

Well, the array is sized depending upon the value sent in as a parameter. That value can be any integer. A negative value would not be a valid array size, however, and this would cause an exception in your program. The name of the exception that is thrown can always be tested by writing a small **try ... catch** block in a main method. Program 15.4 is one such simple tester program which uses an array of integers:

Program 15.4

```
/* the purpose of this class is just to test which exception is thrown
   when a negative array size is entered */

public class TrapException
{
  public static void main(String[] args)
  {
    try
    {
      // here write the code you are testing
      System.out.println("Enter size");
      int size = EasyScanner.nextInt();
      int[] list = new int[size];
    }
    catch (Exception e) // this will catch any exception that is thrown
    {
      System.out.println(e); // will display the name of the exception
    }
  }
}
```

Notice that since all exceptions are of type `Exception`, the **catch** clause above will catch any exception that occurs. When testing your applications it might be a good idea to place the instructions inside `main` in such a **try … catch** block. Here is a sample test run:

```
Enter size

-5

java.lang.NegativeArraySizeException:
```

As you can see, this results in a `NegativeArraySizeException`. Returning to the `Bank` constructor, we could check if the parameter was negative within the constructor, but then how do we report back that an error has occurred? Usually we would make use of the return value, but constructors have no return value! The only way to report back errors from constructors is to make use of exceptions.

15.7 Throwing exceptions

In a way, the `Bank` constructor is already making use of exceptions to indicate that an error has occurred. It returns a `NegativeArraySizeException` to report the error. The issue that we have to deal with is – how do we inform users of this class that such an exception may be thrown?

One way of indicating that a method may throw an exception is to add the exception to the method header in a **throws** clause. As a first attempt we could amend the `Bank` constructor as follows:

```
// try this?
public Bank(int sizeIn) throws NegativeArraySizeException
{
    list = new BankAccount[sizeIn];
    total = 0;
}
```

However, it is not usually considered good programming practice for methods to claim unchecked exceptions in this way as it places no requirements on users of this method to acknowledge the exception. Another problem with claiming this particular exception is that the underlying implementation (an array) is revealed in the name of the exception. If in future a decision was made to replace the array representation with another representation, this exception name will not be valid.

Both of these problems could be solved by throwing a general exception (of type `Exception`), rather than a specific exception (like `NegativeArraySizeIndex` for example). A general exception will be checked by the compiler, forcing the caller to deal with this exception and not ignore it, and the exception name does not reveal the underlying representation. Here's how the header for the constructor would be amended if this were the chosen strategy:

```
public Bank(int sizeIn) throws Exception
{
    // some code here
}
```

Unfortunately this approach does require some modifications to the actual body of the method. While the Java system will automatically detect and throw a specific exception object (of type `NegativeArrayIndexException` for example), there is no event that will lead to a general exception object (of type `Exception`) being thrown. In order to throw a general exception object you must:

> detect the situation when such an exception should be thrown and then;

> write an instruction explicitly to throw the exception using the **throw** command;

> use the **new** command to generate an object of type Exception.

In the case of the constructor, the exception object will be thrown when the array size is less than zero. Here is the amended constructor:

```
public Bank (int sizeIn) throws Exception
{
    if (sizeIn < 0) // throw exception object under this condition
    {
        throw new Exception ("cannot set a negative size");
    }
    else
    {
        list = new BankAccount[sizeIn];
        total = 0;
    }
}
```

Notice that when you explicitly throw an exception object you may also pass along a message as a parameter as we did in this case:

```
throw new Exception ("cannot set a negative size");
```

This message can be retrieved by the receiver of this exception object by calling its getMessage method. As an example of this let us amend the Bank tester class from chapter 7 (BankProgram) to check for this exception:

```
public class BankProgram
{
    public static void main(String[] args)
    {
        try
        {
            // some code here
            System.out.print("Maximum number of accounts? ");
            size = EasyScanner.nextInt();
            // call Bank constructor
            Bank myBank = new Bank(size); // may throw checked Exception

            // rest of code here
        }
        catch (Exception e)
        {
            System.out.println(e.getMessage());
        }
    }
    // other static methods here as before
}
```

Notice how throwing a checked exception object, from the Bank constructor, forced us in the BankProgram tester class to deal with the error – it could not be ignored. Here is a sample test run of the amended BankProgram class:

Maximum number of accounts?   -5

cannot set a negative size

Notice also how the error message no longer reveals the underlying array representation. This approach of throwing general exceptions, while adequate, also has its drawbacks:

> the name of the exception does not explain the source of the problem; the `getMessage` method must be used to determine that;

> the `catch` clause we used to deal with the resulting exception object will catch *any* exception that is thrown, as all exceptions are derived from the exception class, but we may wish to handle other exceptions in a different way to the constructor exception.

If these issues affect your application you will have to create your own exception classes rather than throwing general exceptions.

15.8 Creating your own exception classes

You can create your own exception class by inheriting from any predefined exception class. Generally speaking, if you wish your exception class to be unchecked then it should inherit from `RuntimeException` (or one of its subclasses), whereas if you wish your exception to be checked you can inherit from the general `Exception` class.

In the case of the `Bank` class we have decided to make the exception thrown by the constructor checked, so we will define our exception class by inheriting from the general `Exception` class. Remember, the problem that arose was the possibility of a negative size, so we will call this exception class `NegativeSizeException`. Look at the code first and then we will discuss it.

The NegativeSizeException class

```
public class NegativeSizeException extends Exception
{
  public  NegativeSizeException () // constructor without parameter
  {
    super("cannot set a negative size");
  }

  public NegativeSizeException (String message)// constructor with parameter
  {
    super (message);
  }
}
```

As well as inheriting from some exception class, user-defined exception classes should have two constructors defined within them. One should take no parameter and simply call the constructor of the superclass with a message of your choosing:

```
public  NegativeSizeException ()
{
    super("cannot set a negative size"); // calls Exception constructor
}
```

The other constructor should allow a user-defined message to be supplied with the exception object:

```
public NegativeSizeException (String message)
{
    super (message); // message supplied as parameter
}
```

The `Bank` constructor can now be implemented as follows:

```
public Bank (int sizeIn) throws NegativeSizeException
{
    if (sizeIn < 0) // throw exception object under this condition
    {
        throw new NegativeSizeException();
    }
    else
    {
        list = new BankAccount[sizeIn];
        total = 0;
    }
}
```

Now here is an outline of the amended tester:

```
public class BankProgram
{
    public static void main(String[] args)
    {
        try
        {
            // some code here
            System.out.print("Maximum number of accounts? ");
            size = EasyScanner.nextInt();
            // Bank constructor may throw NegativeSizeException
            Bank myBank = new Bank(size);
            // rest of code here
        }
        catch (NegativeSizeException e) // to deal with Bank error
        {
            System.out.println(e.getMessage());
            System.out.println("due to error in Bank constructor");
        }
        catch (Exception e) // to catch all other errors
        {
            System.out.println("Some unforseen error");
            e.printStackTrace(); // print stack trace to determine cause
        }
    }
    // other static methods here as before
}
```

Notice how we added a general **catch** Exception clause to catch any exceptions that we might not yet have considered. We have printed the stack trace in this error-handler to determine the exact cause of this unexpected error:

```
catch (Exception e)
{
    System.out.println("Some unforseen error");
    e.printStackTrace();
}
```

During testing this is always a good strategy. However, you need to ensure that the general `catch` `Exception` clause is the *last* `catch` clause you specify. For example, something like the following will not compile:

```
// this will not compile!
try
{
    // some code here
}
catch (Exception e) // catches all exceptions
{
    // some code here
}
catch (NegativeSizeException e) // will never be reached now!
{
    // some code here
}
```

The above will not compile as the first general `catch` clause (`catch` Exception) will catch *all* exception types (including NegativeSizeException). So any `catch` clauses below (such as catch NegativeSizeException) will never be reached. To write unreachable code in Java causes a compiler error.

15.9 Re-throwing exceptions

Ordinarily, when an exception is caught in a `catch` block, that exception has been dealt with. It is, however, possible to throw an exception from *within* a `catch` block. For example, let us consider the Bank constructor again. Here, an `if` statement was used to determine when to throw an exception object:

```
public Bank (int sizeIn) throws NegativeSizeException
{
    if (sizeIn < 0) // throw exception object under this condition
    {
        throw new NegativeSizeException();
    }
    else
    {
        list = new BankAccount[sizeIn];
        total = 0;
    }
}
```

We could, instead, have allowed the original NegativeArraySizeException to be thrown and then throw our own NegativeSizeException in a `catch` block as follows:

```
public Bank (int sizeIn) throws NegativeSizeException
{
    try // check for exceptions
    {
        list = new BankAccount[sizeIn];
        total = 0;
    }
    catch (NegativeArraySizeException e) // allow this to be caught
    {
        throw new  NegativeSizeException ();// now throw our own exception
    }
}
```

This technique might be useful if the condition required for the `if` statement were difficult to formulate, or where there were several points in a method where an exception could be thrown. In the latter case all these possible points of error could be included in a single `try` block.

15.10 Documenting exceptions

We finish off this chapter by looking at how to document methods that may throw exceptions, using the `Javadoc` tool we described in chapter 9. The `@throws` tag should be used to document the name of any exceptions that may be thrown by a method. Here for example, is the `Bank` constructor, documented with `Javadoc` comments:

```
/** Creates an empty collection of bank accounts
 *  and fixes the maximum size of this collection
 *
 *  @param  sizeIn                   The maximum size of the collection
 *                                   of bank accounts
 *  @throws NegativeSizeException    If the collection is sized
 *                                   with a negative value
 */

public Bank (int sizeIn) throws NegativeSizeException
{
    // as before
}
```

Generally speaking, when documenting methods in this way, it is good practice to document *all* exceptions that a method may throw (be they checked or unchecked). Multiple `@throws` tags can be used to list multiple exceptions.

Self-test questions

1 What is an *exception*?

2 Distinguish between *checked* and *unchecked* exceptions and then identify which of the following exceptions are checked, and which are unchecked:

> ❯ FileNotFoundException;

> ❯ NegativeArraySizeException;

> ❯ NumberFormatException;

> ❯ IOException;

> ❯ Exception;

> ❯ ArrayIndexOutOfBoundsException;

> ❯ RuntimeException.

3 Explain the following terms:

a) *throwing* an exception;

b) *claiming* an exception;

c) *catching* an exception.

4 What is the purpose of a **finally** clause?

5 Look at the program below and then answer the questions that follow:

```java
public class ExceptionsQ5
{
        public static void main(String[] args)
        {
                int[] someArray = {12,9,3,11};
                int position = getPosition();
                display (someArray, position);
                System.out.println("End of program" );
        }
        private static int getPosition()
        {
                System.out.println("Enter array position to display");
                String positionEntered = EasyScanner.nextString();
                return Integer.parseInt(positionEntered);
        }
          private static void display (int[] arrayIn, int posIn)
          {
                System.out.println("Item at this position is: " +
                                                arrayIn[posIn]);
          }
}
```

a) Will this result in any compiler errors?

b) Which methods could throw exceptions?

c) Identify the names of the exceptions that could be thrown and the circumstances under which they could be thrown.

6 When would it be appropriate to define your own exception class?

Programming exercises

1 Implement the program given in question 5 above. Now:

a) Re-write `main` so that it catches any exceptions it may now throw by displaying a message on the screen indicating the exception thrown.

b) At the moment, the "End of program" message may not always be executed. Add an appropriate **finally** clause so that this message is always executed at the end of the program.

c) Add an additional **catch** clause in `main` to catch any unaccounted-for exceptions (within this **catch** clause print out the stack trace of the exception).

d) Create your own exception class `InvalidPositionException` (make this a checked exception).

e) Re-write the display method so that it throws the `InvalidPositionException` from a **catch** block.

f) Re-write `main` to take account of this amended display method.

g) Document these exceptions using appropriate `Javadoc` comments.

2 The `Scanner` class has methods `nextInt` and `nextDouble` for reading an **int** and a **double** value from the keyboard respectively. Both of these methods throw an exception if an appropriate numerical value is not entered.

a) Write a tester program to find out the name of this exception.

b) Develop a new version of the `EasyScanner` class, say `EasyScannerPlus`, so that instead of throwing exceptions the methods `nextInt` and `nextDouble` repeatedly display an error message and allow for data re-entry.

c) Write a tester programme to test out the methods of your `EasyScannerPlus` class.

3 Look back at the `Hostel` case study of chapters 11 and 12 and make use of exceptions where appropriate. Amend the `Javadoc` documentation for this application to include information on any exceptions you may have included.

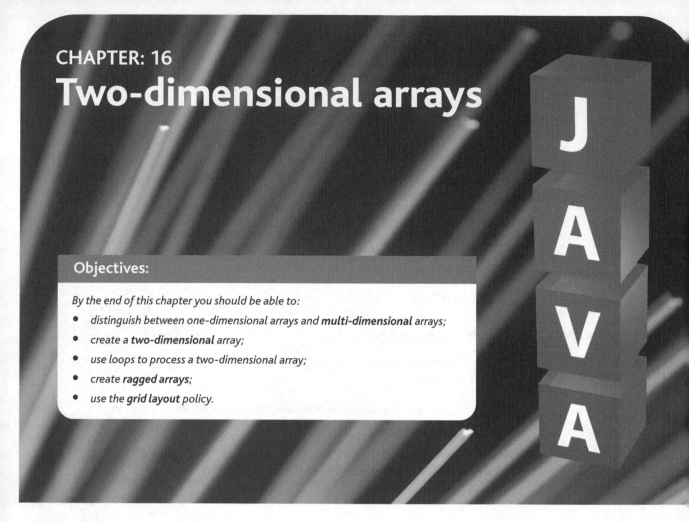

CHAPTER: 16

Two-dimensional arrays

Objectives:

By the end of this chapter you should be able to:

- *distinguish between one-dimensional arrays and **multi-dimensional** arrays;*
- *create a **two-dimensional** array;*
- *use loops to process a two-dimensional array;*
- *create **ragged arrays**;*
- *use the **grid layout** policy.*

16.1 Introduction

Do you remember the temperature-reading example we used in chapter 5? There we used an array to hold seven temperature readings (one for each day of the week):

```
double[] temperature; // declare array reference
temperature = new double[7]; // create array of 7 double values
```

Creating an array allowed us to use loops when processing these values, rather than having to repeat the same bit of code seven times – once for each different temperature variable. Now consider the situation where temperatures were required for the four weeks of a month. We could create four arrays as follows:

```
double[] temperature1 = new double [7]; // to hold week 1 temperatures
double[] temperature2 = new double [7]; // to hold week 2 temperatures
double[] temperature3 = new double [7]; // to hold week 3 temperatures
double[] temperature4 = new double [7]; // to hold week 4 temperatures
```

How would the temperatures for these four months be entered? The obvious solution would be to write four loops, one to process each array. Luckily there is a simpler approach – create a **multi-dimensional** array.

A multi-dimensional array is an array that has *more than one* index. So far, the arrays that we have shown you have had only one index – for this reason they are very often referred to as **one-dimensional** arrays. However, an array may have as many indices as is necessary (up to the limit of the memory on your machine). Usually, no more than two indices will ever need to be used. An array with two indices is called a **two-dimensional** array.

16.2 Creating a two-dimensional array

To create a two-dimensional (2D) array, simply provide the size of both indices. In this example we have four lots of seven temperatures:

```
double [][] temperature ; // declares a 2D array
temperature = new double [4][7]; // creates memory for a 4 by 7 array
```

Whereas you would think of a one-dimensional array as a list, you would probably visualize a two-dimensional array as a table (although actually it is implemented in Java as an array of arrays). The name of each item in a two-dimensional array is the array name, plus the row and column index (see figure 16.1).

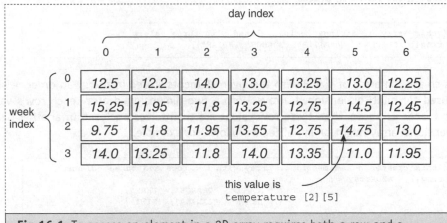

Fig 16.1 To access an element in a 2D array requires both a row and a column index

Here we have decided to view the first index as the week index and the second index as the day index. Note again that both indices begin at zero. With a two-dimensional array, nested loops are commonly used to process each element – one loop for each array index. As it is normal to think of days and weeks beginning at one and not zero, in the following code fragment we've started our day and week counters at 1, and then taken 1 off these counters to get back to the appropriate array index:

```
// the outer loop controls the week row
for (int week = 1; week <= temperature.length; week++)
{
        // the inner loop controls the day column
        for (int day = 1; day <=temperature[0].length; day++)
        {
                System.out.println("enter temperetaure for week " + week
                                    + " and day " + day);
                /* as array indices start at zero not 1, we must take one
                   off the loop counters */
                temperature[week-1][day-1] = EasyScanner.nextDouble();
        }
}
```

Notice that in a two-dimensional array, the `length` attribute returns the length of the *first* index (this is what we have visualized as the number of rows):

```
// here, the length attribute returns 4 (the number of rows)
for (int week = 1; week <= temperature.length; week++)
```

The number of columns is determined by obtaining the length of a particular row. In the example below we have chosen the first row but we could have chosen any row here:

```
// the length of a row returns the number of columns (7 in this case)
for (int day = 1; day <= temperature[0].length; day++)
```

16.3 Initializing two-dimensional arrays

As with one-dimensional arrays, it is possible to declare and initialize a multi-dimensional array with a collection of values all in one line. With a one-dimensional array we separated these values by commas and enclosed these values in braces:

```
// this array of strings is initialized with three values
String[] a1DArray = {"APPLE", ORANGE", "PEAR"};
```

This creates an array of size 3 with the given elements stored in the given order. A similar technique can be used for multi-dimensioned arrays. With a two-dimensioned array each row's values are surrounded with braces as above, then these row values are themselves enclosed in another pair of braces. A two-dimensional array might be initialized as follows, for example:

```
// this creates a 2 dimensional array with two rows and three columns
String[][] a2DArray = {
                        {"APPLE", "ORANGE", "PEAR"},
                        {"LEMON", "BANANA", "KIWI"}
                };
```

This instruction creates the same array as the following group of instructions:

```
String[][] a2DArray = new String[2][3]; // size array
// initilaize values
a2DArray[0][0] = "APPLE";
a2DArray[0][1] = "ORANGE";
a2DArray[0][2] = "PEAR";
a2DArray[1][0] = "LEMON";
a2DArray[1][1] = "BANANA";
a2DArray[1][2] = "KIWI";
```

16.4 Ragged arrays

In the examples of two-dimensional arrays discussed so far, each row of the array had the same number of columns. Each row of the `temperature` array, for example, had 7 columns and each row of `a2DArray` had 3 columns. However, it is not necessary for every row to have the same number of columns. A two-dimensional array with a variable number of columns is called a **ragged array**. For example, let's return to `a2DArray` and initialize it with a variable number of columns for each row:

```
// this creates a 2 dimensional array with a variable number of columns
String[][] a2DArray = new String[][]
                {
                        {"APPLE, "ORANGE" }, // two columns
                        {"LEMON", "BANANA", "KIWI", "LIME"} // four columns
                };
```

Figure 16.2 illustrates the array created after this initialization:

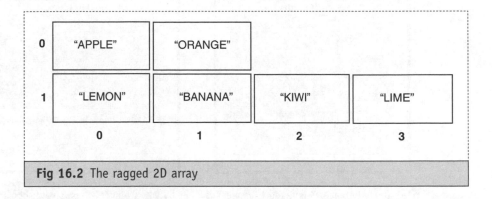

0	"APPLE"	"ORANGE"		
1	"LEMON"	"BANANA"	"KIWI"	"LIME"
	0	1	2	3

Fig 16.2 The ragged 2D array

To declare such an array without initialization, we need to specify the number of rows first and leave the number of columns unspecified. In the example above we have two rows:

```
// columns left unspecified
String[][] a2DArray = new String[2][];
```

Now, for each row we can fix the appropriate size of the associated column. In the example above the first row has 2 columns, the second row 4 columns:

```
a2DArray[0] = new String[2]; // number of columns in first row
a2DArray[1] = new String[4]; // number of columns in second row
```

You can see clearly from these instructions that Java implements a two-dimensional array as an array of arrays. When processing ragged arrays you must be careful not to use a fixed number to control the number of columns. The actual number of columns can always be retrieved by calling the `length` attribute of each row. For example:

```
int numberOfColumnsInFirstRow = a2DArray[0].length;
int numberOfColumnsInSecondRow = a2DArray[1].length;
```

Let's look at a complete application now that makes use of two-dimensional arrays.

16.5 The *NoughtsAndCrosses* class

Noughts and crosses (or Tic-Tac-Toe as its known in the USA) is a traditional two-player game for children and involves a three by three grid of squares. Players win a game when they get a line of noughts or crosses. Figure 16.3 provides some screen shots of this game being played.

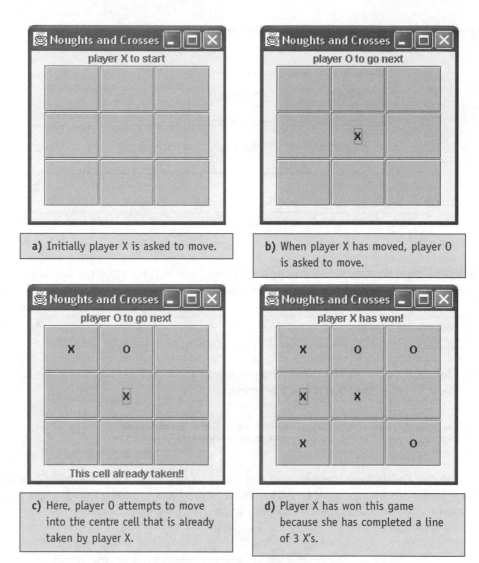

a) Initially player X is asked to move.

b) When player X has moved, player O is asked to move.

c) Here, player O attempts to move into the centre cell that is already taken by player X.

d) Player X has won this game because she has completed a line of 3 X's.

Fig 16.3 Some sample screen shots from a game of noughts and crosses

As you can see from figure 16.3, the game consists of a board with nine squares. Each of these squares is, in fact, a button from the Swing package. The layout suggests that a two-dimensional array of buttons would be a good way to implement this board, so that's exactly what we'll do. An array of visual components is perfectly valid. We would create this array in the obvious way:

```
JButton [][] cell; // declare 'cell' to be a 2D array of buttons
cell = new JButton [3][3]; // create memory for a 3 by 3 array of buttons
```

Of course we could create this array in one line if we choose:

```
JButton [][] cell = new JButton [3][3];
```

Unlike the array we used in section 16.2, this array is an array of objects. To add a JButton object into this array we have to use the JButton constructor to create the button. In this game, the button's caption indicates a particular player (X or O) is occupying that given cell. Initially no cell will be occupied, so a blank caption is required. For example, to add a button into the first position in the 2D array we have the following:

```
cell[0][0] = new JButton();
```

Each button also needs to respond to a mouse-click and therefore requires an ActionListener to be added to it. For example:

```
cell[0][0].addActionListener(this);
```

Finally, to achieve the desired layout we will add each button to a JPanel. Assuming this panel is called board, we get the following:

```
board.add(cell[0][0]);
```

We will discuss the layout policy of this panel later. Obviously, we need to create nine new buttons, add nine ActionListeners and add each of these nine buttons to the board. Rather than repeat the above lines nine times, we use nested loops as follows:

```
for (int r = 0; r<3; r++) // row index
{
    for (int c = 0; c < 3; c++) // column index
    {
        cell[r][c] = new JButton(); // create new button
        cell[r][c].addActionListener(this); // add listener
        board.add(cell[r][c]); // add to board
    }
}
```

As you can see, using a 2D array of buttons (rather than creating nine individual buttons) allowed us to use loops to reduce the coding effort. This array will also be useful when processing the mouse-click events from each button. Rather than having to have nine if statements to capture the appropriate mouse-click event, we can now just use a single if statement and place that if statement within a pair of nested loops:

```
public void actionPerformed(ActionEvent e)
{
    for (int r = 0; r<3; r++)
    {
        for (int c = 0; c < 3; c++)
        {
            if (e.getSource()== cell[r][c])
            {
                // code to process event here
            }
        }
    }
}
```

The code for this NoughtsAndCrosses class is now presented below. Examine it carefully, and then we will discuss it in more detail.

The *NoughtsAndCrosses* class

```java
import javax.swing.*;
import java.awt.*;
import java.awt.event.*;

public class NoughtsAndCrosses extends JFrame implements ActionListener
{
    private boolean gameOver; // to keep track of the game status
    private String player; // to keep track of the current player
    private JPanel board = new JPanel(); // to hold the nine cells
    private JButton [][]cell= new JButton [3][3]; // the cells
    // these next label provides a border around the cells
    private JLabel blank = new JLabel("         ");
    // the next two labels are centre alligned
    private JLabel error = new JLabel(" ", JLabel.CENTER);
    private JLabel info = new JLabel ("player X to start", JLabel.CENTER);

    // the constructor
    public NoughtsAndCrosses()
    {
      gameOver = false;
      player = "X"; // player X to start the game
      setDefaultCloseOperation(JFrame.EXIT_ON_CLOSE);
      setTitle("Noughts and Crosses");
      setSize(230, 230);
      setLocation(300, 100);
      getContentPane().setBackground(Color.yellow);
      board.setLayout(new GridLayout(3,3)); // discussed later
      // creates and adds nine buttons to the board
      for (int r = 0; r < 3; r++)
      {
        for (int c = 0; c < 3; c++)
        {
          cell[r][c] = new JButton();
          cell[r][c].addActionListener(this);
          board.add(cell[r][c]);
        }
      }
      // positions the items on the screen
      add("Center", board);
      add ("West", blank);
      add("East", blank);
      add("North", info);
      add("South", error);
      setVisible(true);
    }

    public void actionPerformed(ActionEvent e)
    {
      if (!gameOver)// process mouse click only if game is not over
      {
       for (int r = 0; r < 3; r++)
       {
         for (int c = 0; c < 3; c++)
         {
           if (e.getSource()== cell[r][c])
           {
             processEvent(r,c); // call helper method to process event
           }
         }
       }
      }
    }

    // helper method to process a given button press
    private void processEvent(int rowIn, int colIn)
    {
      // check no attempt made to move into an occupied cell
```

```
          if (cell[rowIn][colIn].getText().equals("X") ||
                      cell[rowIn][colIn].getText().equals("O"))
      {
         error.setText("This cell already taken!!");
      }
      else
      {
         // clear any error messages
         error.setText(" ");
         // change button caption to current player
         cell[rowIn][colIn].setText(player);
         // check whether this moves results in game over
         if (hasWon(rowIn, colIn))// process game over
         {
            info.setText("  player " + player + " has won!");
            gameOver = true;
         }
         else // process game not over
         {
            // change player
            if (player.equals("X"))
            {
                player = "O";
            }
            else
            {
                player = "X";
            }
            info.setText("player "+player+" to go next");
         }
      }
  }
}


   // helper method to check if game over
   private boolean hasWon(int rowIn, int colIn)
   {
       boolean won;
       // check current row
       won = true;
       for(int c = 0; c < 3; c++)
       {
           if (!cell[rowIn][c].getText().equals(player))
           {
              won = false;
           }
       }
       if (!won)
       {
       // check current column
           won = true;
           for(int r = 0; r < 3; r++)
           {
              if (!cell[r][colIn].getText().equals(player))
              {
                won = false;
              }
           }
       }
       if (!won)
       {
           // check left diagonal
           won = true;
           for(int num = 0; num < 3; num++)
           {
              if (!cell[num][num].getText().equals(player))
              {
                won = false;
              }
           }
       }
```

```
              if (!won)
              {
                  // check right diagonal
                  won = true;
                  for(int c = 0; c < 3; c++)
                  {
                      if (!cell[2-c][c].getText().equals(player))
                      {
                          won = false;
                      }
                  }
              }
              return won;
      }
}
```

First of all, let's go back and consider the `board` panel. We are using this panel to hold the nine buttons and we would like the buttons to appear as a three by three grid. An easy way to achieve this is to give the panel a **grid layout**. This is a layout policy that we have not discussed yet. A grid layout policy allows you to specify the number of rows and columns for the items you wish to add. In this case we require three rows and three columns of buttons so we specify the layout as follows:

```
board.setLayout(new GridLayout(3,3));
```

This layout policy ensures that once three buttons are added to the panel, the next three would be on the next row, and the last three on the final row. Now, let's go back and examine the `actionPerformed` method in a bit more detail. You can see that this method calls a helper method, `processEvent`, which processes a mouse-click event for a given button. This method receives the button's row and column indices as parameters. Initially, the caption of the given button is checked to ensure that the player has not moved into an occupied square. A square is occupied when its caption is set to "X" or "O". Like other visual components such as a `JLabel`, a `JButton` has a `getText` method that returns its caption.

```
if (cell[rowIn][colIn].getText().equals("X") ||
                  cell[rowIn][colIn].getText().equals("O"))
{       // 'error' label used to display error messages
        error.setText("This cell already taken!!");
}
```

If the cell is not taken the move is allowed to go ahead. This involves clearing any error messages that may have been displayed and re-setting the cell's caption to the current player. The `setText` method of a `JButton` sets its caption to the given sign:

```
error.setText(""); // clears the text of a JLabel
cell[rowIn][colIn].setText(player); // sets the caption of a JButton
```

Two possibilities now arise; either the player has won the game, in which case a congratulatory message is displayed, or the game has not been won and the current player changes to the next player:

```
if (hasWon(rowIn, colIn))// calls another helper method
{
        // code to set congratulatory message and gameOver status
}
else
{
        // code to change player and inform them of their go
}
```

Again, this method calls another helper method, hasWon, to determine whether or not a player has won the game. Notice that this helper method is sent the row and column index of the cell currently selected. The row and column index of the current move will help determine whether or not the player has won the game by selecting this cell. There are four ways in which a player can win a game:

> the player completes a row;

> the player completes a column;

> the player completes the left diagonal;

> the player completes the right diagonal.

Figure 16.4 illustrates a player having won a game by completing a row. Here the last move was at 'rowIn' position 1, and 'colIn' position 2.

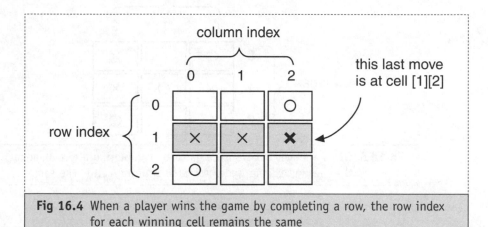

Fig 16.4 When a player wins the game by completing a row, the row index for each winning cell remains the same

In order to check this row we must check the captions of cell[1][0], cell[1][1] and cell[1][2] and see if they are all set to the current player ("X"). If at least one caption is not set to the current player, then the player has not won this game by completing a row. As you can see, in order to do this, the original row position (1 in this case) of each button remains the same, while the column position changes. This can be achieved by fixing the row number to the current row (rowIn) and using a loop to check every column in that row:

```
won = true; // assume the player has won
for(int c = 0; c < 3; c++) // move through the columns
{
        // keep the row fixed at 'rowIn'
        if (!cell[rowIn][c].getText().equals(player)) // check caption
        {
            won = false; // indicate failure to win
        }
}
```

At the end of this loop, if the value of 'won' is **true** the player has won, otherwise other possibilities for winning must be checked. If a player wins a game by completing a column, then the column index will be fixed to the current column (colIn):

```
won = true;
for(int r = 0; r < 3; r++)
{
        // column index remains fixed
        if (!cell[r][colIn].getText().equals(player))
        {
            won = false;
        }
}
```

The final two possibilities for winning a game are if the player completes a left or right diagonal. Figure 16.5 illustrates a player winning by completing a left diagonal.

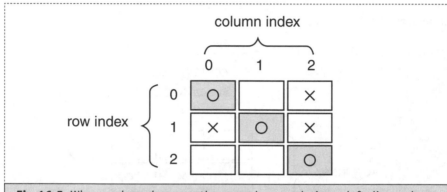

Fig 16.5 When a player has won the game by completing a left diagonal, the row and column index for each winning cell is the same

You can see from figure 16.5 that to check the left diagonal we need to check `cell[0][0]`, `cell[1][1]` and `cell[2][2]`. Of course, if the player's current move is not in one of these cells, it is not necessary to check this left diagonal. However, here we will check the left (and right) diagonal regardless.

If you look at the row and column index of each cell in the left diagonal, you can see that both values are identical to each other. These values move from 0 to 2. Once again, a loop can be used to check this for us:

```
won = true;
for(int num = 0; num < 3; num++)
{
        // keep row and column index the same
        if (!cell[num][num].getText().equals(player))
        {
            won = false;
        }
}
```

Finally, when checking the right diagonal, the cells to check are `cell[2][0]`, `cell[1][1]` and `cell[0][2]`. You can see that the column index moves from 0 to 2: this can be controlled by a **for** loop. The row index, however, moves down from 2 to 0. This row index can be arrived at by subtracting the column index from 2.

```
won = true;
for(int c = 0; c < 3; c++)
{
     // row index calculated by subtracting the column index from 2
     if (!cell[2-c][c].getText().equals(player))
     {
         won = false;
     }
}
```

Program 16.1 now runs this game.

Program 16.1

```
public class RunNoughtsAndCrosses
{
  public static void main (String[] args)
  {
    new NoughtsAndCrosses();
  }
}
```

Self-test questions

1 Consider the following array declaration, to store a collection of student grades.

```
char [][] grades = new char[4][20];
```

Grades are recorded for 4 tutorial groups, and each tutorial group consists of 20 students.

a) How many dimensions does this array have?

b) What is the value of `grades.length`?

c) What is the value of `grades[0].length`?

d) Write the instruction to record the grade 'B' for the first student in the first tutorial group.

2 Consider the following scenarios and, for each, declare the appropriate array:

a) `goals`: an array to hold the number of goals each team in a league scores in each game of a season. The league consist of 20 teams and a season consists of 38 games.

b) `seats`: an array to record whether or not a seat in a theatre is booked or not. There are 70 rows of seats in the theatre and each row has 20 seats.

3 Consider an application that records the punctuality of trains on a certain route.

a) Declare a 2D array, `late`, to hold the number of times a train on this route was late for each day of the week, and for each week of the year.

b) Write a fragment of code that adds up the total number of days in the year when a train was late more than twice in a given day.

4 a) Distinguish between a regular 2D array and a *ragged* array.

b) Write instructions to create a ragged 2D array of integers, called `triangle`, that has the following form:

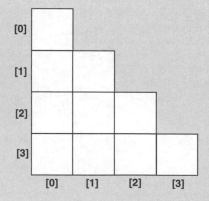

c) Write a fragment of code to find the largest number in the `triangle` array.

5 Describe the *grid layout* policy.

Programming exercises

1 From the accompanying CD, copy the `NoughtsAndCrosses` class. Now

a) amend the constructor so that the size of the grid is sent in as a parameter;

b) amend the `actionPerformed` and `hasWon` methods to take into account the variable grid size.

2 Look back at the application discussed in self-test question 3. The UML diagram below gives the complete design for an appropriate `CheckTrain` class:

CheckTrain
late: int[][]
CheckTrain()   *recordLate(int, int)*   *totalLate() : int*   *getLate(int, int) : int*   *wasLate(int, int) : boolean*

The methods of this class are described below:

`CheckTrain()`
Constructor, sets the number of times the train was late on each day of the year to zero.

`recordLate(int, int)`
Accepts a day and a week number, and increments the number of times the train was late on that day of the week. Throws an `InvalidDateException` when an invalid day or week number is submitted.

`totalLate() : int`
Returns the total number of times the train was late.

`getLate(int, int) : int`
Returns the number of times the train was late on the given day and week number. Throws an `InvalidDateException` when an invalid day or week number is submitted.

`wasLate(int, int) : boolean`
Returns **`true`** if the train was late on the given day and week number, and **`false`** otherwise. Throws an `InvalidDateException` when an invalid day or week number is submitted

a) Implement the `CheckTrain` class. You will also need to implement a checked `InvalidDateException` class.

b) Write a tester for the `CheckTrain` class.

3   Consider a scenario in which a university allows lecturers to borrow equipment. The equipment is available for use 5 days a week and for 7 periods during each day. When the equipment is booked for use, the details of the booking (room number and lecturer name) are recorded. When no booking is recorded, the equipment is available for use.

a) Create a `Booking` class defined in the UML diagram below:

Booking
room : String name : String
Booking(String, String) getRoom() : String getName() : String

b) Now a `TimeTable` class is defined to process these bookings. Its UML diagram is given below:

TimeTable
times: Booking[][]
TimeTable(int, int) makeBooking(int, int, Booking) : boolean deleteBooking(int, int) : boolean isFree(int, int) : boolean getBooking(int, int) : Booking numberOfDays() : int numberOfPeriods() : int

As you can see, the attribute of this class is a two-dimensional array of `Booking` objects. The methods of this class are defined below:

TimeTable(int, int)
Constructor accepts the number of days per week and number of periods per day and sizes the timetable accordingly. Throws a `TimeTableException` if the number of days per week exceeds 7, and if either of the parameters are negative.

makeBooking(int, int, Booking) : boolean
Accepts the booking details for a particular day and period and, as long as this slot is not previously booked, updates the timetable accordingly. Returns **true** if the booking was recorded successfully and **false** if the slot was previously booked. Throws a `TimeTableException` if the day or period number is invalid.

deleteBooking(int, int) : boolean
Deletes the booking details for a particular day and period. Returns **false** if the given slot was not previously booked, and **true** if the slot was deleted successfully. Throws a `TimeTableException` if the day or period number is invalid.

isFree(int, int) : boolean
Accepts a day and period number and returns **true** if the given slot is free, and **false** otherwise.

Throws a `TimeTableException` if the day or period number is invalid.

getBooking(int, int) : Booking
Accepts a day and period number and returns the booking for the given slot or `null` if no booking is made for the given slot. Throws a `TimeTableException` if the day or period number is invalid.

numberOfDays() : int
Returns the number of days associated with this timetable.

numberOfPeriods() : int
Returns the number of periods associated with this timetable.

Implement this class in Java. You will also need to implement a checked `TimeTableException` class.

c) Write a suitable tester for this class.

d) Develop a GUI for this application, with the timetable displayed as a grid of `JTextAreas`. For example:

You should use the grid layout policy to achieve this timetable layout.

CHAPTER: 17

The Java Collections Framework

Objectives:

By the end of this chapter you should be able to:

- *use the* `ArrayList` *class to store a **list** of objects;*
- *use the* `HashSet` *class to store a **set** of objects;*
- *use the* `HashMap` *class to store objects in a **map**;*
- *fix the type of elements within a collection using the **generics** mechanism;*
- *use an* `Iterator` *object to scan through a collection;*
- *create objects of your own classes, and use them in conjunction with Java's collection classes.*

17.1 Introduction

An array is a very useful type in Java but it has its restrictions:

> once an array is created it must be sized, and this size is fixed;

> it contains no useful pre-defined methods.

Think back to the `Bank` class of chapter 7. We used an array to implement this class. In doing so we had to put an upper limit to the size of this collection of accounts. Sometimes, however, an upper limit is not known. Just creating a very big array is very wasteful of memory – and what happens if even this very big array proves to be too small? Another problem is that to carry out any interesting processing (like searching the array) required us to write complex algorithms.

One solution to the first problem would be to create a reasonable sized array and, when the array is full, copy this array into a slightly bigger array and use this new array and continue doing this every time the array gets full. A solution to the second problem would be to do as we did with the `ObjectList` class in chapter 11 – that is wrap the array in a generic collection class and provide useful array methods (like searching) in this collection class.

Luckily we do not need to go to such lengths; the Java people have already done this for us. They've developed a group of generic collection classes that grow as more elements are added to them, and these classes provide lots of useful methods. This group of collection classes are referred to as the **Java Collections Framework**. These classes are all found in the `java.util` package so to access them we require the following **import** statement:

```
import java.util.*;
```

The collection classes themselves are organized around several collection interfaces that define different types of collections that we might be interested in using. Three important interfaces from this group are:

> `List`;

> `Set`;

> `Map`.

We will now examine these interfaces and some of the classes provided in the Java Collections Framework (JCF) which implement these interfaces.

17.2 The *List* interface and the *ArrayList* class

The `List` interface specifies the methods required to process an *ordered list* of objects. Such a list may contain duplicates. Examples of a list of objects include jobs waiting for a printer, emergency calls waiting for an ambulance and the names of players that have won the Wimbledon tennis tournament over the last 10 years. In each case ordering is important, and repetition may also be required. We often think of such a collection as a *sequence* of objects.

There are two implementations provided for the `List` interface in the JCF. They are `ArrayList` and `LinkedList`. Here we will look at the `ArrayList` class.

The `ArrayList` class is very similar to the `ObjectList` class that we developed in chapter 11. Like the `ObjectList` class, classes from the JCF (such as `ArrayList`) are *generic* collection class. This means they can be used to store objects of *any* type.[1]

Let's use an `ArrayList` to store a queue of jobs waiting for a printer, and let us represent these jobs by a series of Job ID `String`s. The `ArrayList` constructor creates an empty list. Take a look at it and then we will discuss it, as it introduces a new concept:

```
// creates an ArrayList object -'printQ'
ArrayList<String> printQ = new ArrayList<String>();
```

Creating an object by calling a constructor is nothing new, but what is that stuff in angled brackets after the class name `ArrayList`? Well, the stuff in angled brackets is a new feature introduced in Java 5.0 that allows us to *fix* the type of objects stored in a particular collection object. This feature is called **generics**.

---

[1] As we discussed before in chapter 8, generic collections cannot store primitive types like **int** and **double**. If primitive types are required then objects of the appropriate wrapper class (`Integer`, `Double` and so on) must be used. However, as discussed in chapter 8, *autoboxing* and *unboxing* (introduced in Java 5.0) automate the process of moving from a primitive type to its associated wrapper.

17.2.1 Generics

The **generics** mechanism allows us to send one or more types to a class (or interface) as a parameter. For this reason generics are also sometimes referred to as *parameterized types*. All the collection classes within the JCF have been modified, since Java 5.0, to allow us to make use of the generics mechanism to fix the type of elements within a collection.

In the case of the `printQ` object, we want each element within this collection to be of type `String`. To make use of generics to fix a collection's element type, *angled brackets* are used to specify this type during object creation as follows:

```
// this will make 'printQ' a list that holds String objects only
ArrayList<String> printQ = new ArrayList<String>();
```

You can see that it is easy to use the idea of generics to fix the type of the items within the collection. We just append the collection type with the type of the elements to be held in angled brackets.

Prior to Java 5.0, and the introduction of generics, we would have created the `printQ` object in the usual way:

```
// this is the old way of creating a 'printQ' object
ArrayList printQ = new ArrayList ();
```

This would have created a generic collection object, much like the creation of an `ObjectList` object from chapter 11. The objects stored in such a collection would all be of the generic `Object` type. While this allows such collection classes to be generic, there are several drawbacks with this old approach:

> As we saw in chapters 8 and 11, each time we retrieve items from such a collection, we must always remember to type cast back from `Object` to the actual type of the element.

> The compiler does not insist that the elements stored in the collection are of a consistent type. So, for example, the first item in the collection may be an object of type `String` and the second an object of some other class like `Oblong`.

> Because the type of objects in the collection cannot be guaranteed to be anything other than the generic type `Object`, type casting to a specific type upon retrieval may not succeed. For example, we may assume the collection contain `String` objects, and type cast back to a `String` when we retrieve an item. But there is no guarantee that the object is *actually* a `String`. If it is not a `String` this will throw an unchecked `ClassCastException` at run-time.

Fixing the type of elements within a collection using the generics mechanism has the following benefits:

> it allows the compiler to check that items added into the collection are always of the correct type;

> it removes the need for type casting when we retrieve items from the collection;

> it avoids the possibility of `ClassCastExceptions`.

Of course, the generics mechanism can be used to fix *any* object type for the elements within a collection. For example, say we wished create a list of `JButtons` we could do so as follows:

```
// this will make 'someButtons' a list of JButtons
ArrayList<JButton> someButtons = new ArrayList <JButton> ();
```

If, on the other hand, we wished to create a list of integers, we could do so like this:

```
// this will make 'someNumbers' a list of Integers
ArrayList <Integer> someNumbers = new ArrayList <Integer> ();
```

Notice that the `Integer` class must be used here, not the primitive **int** type. When using the collection classes within the JCF, we will always use the generics mechanism to fix the type of elements within the collection.

You should be aware that the type of any object created using this generics mechanism is now the class name *plus* the stuff in angled brackets. So, for example, if we were to write a method that received a list of strings, we would specify it as follows:

```
// this method receives an ArrayList<String> object
public void someMethod (ArrayList<String> printQIn)
{
      // some code here
}
```

17.2.2 Using the interface type instead of the implementation type

In order to create the object `printQ`, we have used the `ArrayList` class to implement the `List` interface. What if, at some point, we decide to change to the `LinkedList` implementation? Or some other implementation that might be available in the future? If we did this, then all references to the type of this object (such as in the method header of the previous section) would have to be modified to give the new class name.

There is an alternative approach. It is actually considered better programming practice to declare collection objects to be the type of the interface (`List` in this case) rather than the type of the class that implements this collection. So this would be a better way to create our `printQ` object:

```
// the type is given as 'List' not 'ArrayList'
List<String> printQ = new ArrayList<String>();
```

Notice that the interface type still needs to be marked as being a list of `String` objects using the generics mechanism. A method that receives a `printQ` object would now be declared as follows:

```
// this method receives a List<String> object
public void someMethod (List<String> printQIn)
{
      // some code here
}
```

The advantage of this approach is that we can change our choice of implementation in the future (maybe by using `LinkedList` or some other class that might be available that implements the `List` interface), without having to change the type of the object (which will always remain as `List`). This is the approach that we will take.

Now, let us look at some `List` methods.

17.2.3 *List* methods

The `List` interface defines two `add` methods for inserting into a list, one that inserts the item at the end of the list and one that inserts the item at a specified position in the list. Like arrays, `ArrayList` positions begin at zero. We wish to use the `add` method that adds items to the end of the list as we are modelling a queue here. This `add` method requires one parameter, the object to be added into the list:

```
printQ.add("myLetter.doc");
printQ.add("myFoto.jpg");
printQ.add("results.xls");
printQ.add("chapter.doc");
```

Notice that, since we have marked this list as containing `String` objects only, an attempt to add an object of any other type will result in a compiler error:

```
// will not compile as 'printQ' can hold Strings only!
printQ.add(new Oblong(10, 20));
```

All the Java collection types have a `toString` method defined, so we can display the entire list to the screen:

```
System.out.println(printQ); // implicitly calling the toString method
```

When the list is displayed, the values in the list are separated by commas and enclosed in square brackets. So this `println` instruction would display the following list:

[myLetter.doc, myFoto.jpg, results.xls, chapter.doc]

As you can see, the items in the list are kept in the order in which they were inserted using the `add` method above.

As we said earlier, the `add` method is overloaded to allow an item to be inserted into the list at a particular position. When the item is inserted into that position, the item previously at that particular position and all items behind it shuffle along by one place (i.e. they have their indices incremented by one). This `add` method requires two parameters, the position into which the object should be inserted, and the object itself. For example, let's insert a high priority job at the front of the queue (position zero):

```
printQ.add(0, "importantMemo.doc"); // inserts into front of the queue
```

Notice that the index is provided first, then the object. The index must be a valid index within the current list or it may be the index of the back of the queue. An invalid index throws an unchecked `IndexOutOfBoundsException`.

Displaying this list confirms that the given job ("importantMemo.doc"), has been added to the front of the queue, and all other items shuffled by one place:

[importantMemo.doc, myLetter.doc, myFoto.jpg, results.xls, chapter.doc]

If we wish to overwrite an item in the list, rather than insert a new item into the list, we can use the `set` method. The `set` method requires two parameters, the index of the item being overwritten and the new object to be inserted at that position. Let us change the name of the last job from "chapter.doc" to "newChapter.doc". This is the fifth item in the list so its index is 4:

```
printQ.set(4, "newChapter.doc");
```

If the index used in the `set` method is invalid an `IndexOutOfBoundsException` is thrown once again. Displaying the new list now gives us the following:

[importantMemo.doc, myLetter.doc, myFoto.jpg, results.xls, newChapter.doc]

Lists provide a `size` method to return the number of items in the list, so we could have renamed the last job in the queue in the following way also:

```
printQ.set(printQ.size()-1, "newChapter.doc"); // last position is size-1
```

The `indexOf` method returns the index of the first occurrence of a given object within the list. It returns −1 if the object is not in the list. For example, the following checks the index position of the job "`myFoto.jpg`" in the list:

```
int index = printQ.indexOf("myFoto.jpg"); // check index of job
if (index != -1) // check object is in list
{
        System.out.println("myFoto.jpg is at index position: " + index);
}
else // when job is not in list
{
        System.out.println("myFoto.jpg not in list");
}
```

This would display the following from our list:

myFoto.jpg is at index position: 2

Items can be removed either by specifying an index or an object. When an item is removed, items behind this item shuffle to the left (i.e. they have their indices decremented by one). As an example, let us remove the "`myFoto.jpg`" job. If we used its index, the following is required:

```
printQ.remove(2);
```

Once again, an `IndexOutOfBoundsException` would be thrown if this was not a valid index. This method returns the object that has been removed, which could be checked if necessary. Displaying the list would confirm the item has indeed been removed:

[importantMemo.doc, myLetter.doc, results.xls, newChapter.doc]

Alternatively, we could have removed the item by referring to it directly rather than by its index:[2]

```
printQ.remove("myFoto.jpg");
```

This method returns a **boolean** value to confirm that the item was in the list initially, which again could be checked if necessary.

Do you remember, from chapter 7, the complicated procedure for removing an item from an array? With a `List` we just use the `remove` method.

Behind the scenes you can guess how this `remove` method works. It looks in the list for the given `String` object ("`myFoto.jpg`"). It uses the `equals` method of the `String` class to identify a match. Once it finds such a match it shuffles items along in much the same way as our `remove` method from chapter 7.

---

[2] If there were more than one occurrence of the object, the first occurrence would be deleted.

Of course, as we have already said, these collection classes can be used to store objects of *any* type – not just `Strings`. For methods like `remove` to work properly, the contained object must have a properly defined `equals` method. We will return to this later in the chapter, when we look at how to use objects of our own classes in conjunction with the classes in the JCF.

The `get` method allows a particular item to be retrieved from the list via its index position. The following displays the job at the head of the queue:

```
// the first item is at position 0
System.out.println("First job is " + printQ.get(0));
```

This would display the following:

First job is importantMemo.doc

The `contains` method can be used to check whether or not a particular item is present in the list:

```
if (printQ.contains("poem.doc")) // check if value is in list
{
      System.out.println("poem.doc is in the list");
}
else
{
      System.out.println("poem.doc is not in the list");
}
```

Finally, the `isEmpty` method reports on whether or not the list contains any items:

```
if (printQ.isEmpty()) // returns true when list is empty
{
      System.out.println("Print queue is empty");
}
else
{
      System.out.println("Print queue is not empty");
}
```

17.3 Using the enhanced 'for' loop with collection classes

In chapter 5 we showed you how the enhanced **for** loop can be used to iterate through an entire array. The use of this loop is not restricted to arrays, it can also be used with the `List` (and `Set`) implementations provided in the JCF. For example, here an enhanced **for** loop is used to iterate through the `printQ` list to find and display those jobs that end with a ".doc" extension:

```
for (String item: printQ) // iterate through all items in the 'printQ'list
{
      if (item.endsWith(".doc"))// check the extension of the job ID
      {
          System.out.println(item); // display this item
      }
}
```

Notice that the type of each item in the `printQ` list is `String`. Within the loop we use the `String` method `endsWith` to check if the given job ID ends with `String` ".doc". Assuming we had the following `printQ`:

[importantMemo.doc, myLetter.doc, results.xls, newChapter.doc]

the enhanced **for** loop above would produce the following output:

importantMemo.doc

myLetter.doc

newChapter.doc

If we do not wish to iterate through the *entire* list, or if we wish to *modify* the items within a list as we iterate through them, then (as we have said before) the enhanced **for** loop should not be used.

For example, if we wished to display the items in the printQ that are behind the head of the queue, the enhanced **for** loop is not appropriate as we are not processing the *entire* printQ. Instead the following standard **for** loop could be used:

```
// remember second item in list is at index 1!
for (int pos = 1; pos < printQ.size(); pos++)
{
        System.out.println(printQ.get(pos)); // retrieve item in printQ
}
```

Notice how the size method is used to determine the last index in the loop header. Within the loop, the get method is used to look up an item at the given index.

Again, if we assume we have the following printQ:

[importantMemo.doc, myLetter.doc, results.xls, newChapter.doc]

the **for** loop above would produce the following output:

myLetter.doc

results.xls

newChapter.doc

17.4 The *Set* interface and the *HashSet* class

The Set interface defines the methods required to process a collection of objects in which there is no repetition, and ordering is unimportant. Let's consider the following collections and consider if they are suitable for a set:

> a queue of people waiting to see a doctor;

> a list of number one records for each of the 52 weeks of a particular year;

> car registration numbers allocated parking permits.

The queue of people waiting to see a doctor cannot be considered to be a set as ordering is important here. Order may also be important when recording the list of number one records in a year. It would also be necessary to allow for repetition – as a record may be number one for more than one week. So a set is not a good choice for this collection. The collection of car registration numbers can be considered a set, however, as there will be no duplicates and ordering is unimportant.

Java provides two implementations of this `Set` interface: `HashSet` and `TreeSet`. Here we will look at the `HashSet` class. The constructor creates an empty set. We will use the set to store a collection of vehicle registration numbers (as `Strings`):

```
// creates an empty set of String objects
Set<String> regNums = new HashSet<String>();
```

Again, notice that we have used the generics mechanism to indicate that this is a set of `String` objects, and we have given the type of this object as the interface `Set<String>`. Now let us look at some `Set` methods.

17.4.1 *Set* methods

Once a set is created the methods specified in the `Set` interface can be used. The `add` method allows us to insert objects into the set, so let us add a few registration numbers:

```
regNums.add("V53PLS");
regNums.add("X85ADZ");
regNums.add("L22SBG");
regNums.add("W79TRV");
```

We can display the entire set as follows:

```
System.out.println(regNums); // implicitly calling the toString method
```

The set is displayed in the same format as a list, in square brackets and separated by commas:[3]

[W79TRV, X85ADZ, V53PLS, L22SBG]

Notice that, unlike lists, the order in which the items are displayed is not determined by the order in which the items were added. Instead, the set is displayed in the order in which the items are stored internally (and over which we have no control). This will not be a problem as ordering is unimportant in a set:

As with a list, the `size` method returns the number of items in the set:

```
System.out.println("Number of items in set: " + regNums.size() );
```

This would print the following onto the screen:

Number of items in set: 4

If we try to add an item that is already in the set, the set remains unchanged. Let us assume the four items above have been added into the set and we now try and add a registration number that is already in the set:

```
regNums.add("X85ADZ");   // this number is already in the set
System.out.println(regNums);
```

When this set is displayed, "X85ADZ" appears only once:

[W79TRV, X85ADZ, V53PLS, L22SBG]

The `add` method returns a **boolean** value to indicate whether or not the given item was successfully added. This value can be checked if required:

---

[3] Unfortunately this is not consistent with the mathematical notation for sets with which you are probably familiar – enclosing values in curly brackets. We will return to this in the end of chapter exercises.

```
boolean ok = regNums.add("X85ADZ"); // store boolean return value
if (!ok) //check if add method returned a value of false
{
        System.out.println("item already in the set!");
}
```

The `remove` method deletes an item from the set if it is present. Again, assuming that the four items given above are in the set, we can delete one item as follows:

```
regNums.remove("X85ADZ");
```

If we now display the set, the given registration will have been removed:

[W79TRV, V53PLS, L22SBG]

As with the `add` method, the `remove` method returns a **boolean** value of **false** if the given item to remove was not actually in the set.

The `Set` interface also includes `contains` and `isEmpty` methods that work in exactly the same way as their `List` counterparts.

17.4.2 Iterating through the elements of a set

The enhanced **for** loop can be used to iterate through all the elements of a set. Let us look at an example.

In the UK the first letter of the registration number was at one time used to determine the time period when the vehicle came to market. A registration beginning with 'S', for example, denoted a vehicle that came to market between August 1998 and February 1999, while a registration beginning with 'T' denoted a vehicle that came to market between March 1999 and August 1999. The following enhanced **for** loop will allow us to iterate through the collection of registration numbers and display all registrations after 'T'.

```
for (String item: regNums) // iterate through all items in 'regNums'
{
        if (item.charAt(0) > 'T') // check first letter of registration
        {
            System.out.println(item); // display this registration
        }
}
```

Again, notice that the type of every element within our `regNums` set is `String`. Within the loop we use the `String` method `charAt` to check the first letter of registration. Assuming we have the following set of registration numbers:

[W79TRV, V53PLS, L22SBG]

the enhanced **for** loop above would produce the following result:

W79TRV

V53PLS

Let us consider a slightly different scenario now. Instead of simply displaying registration numbers after 'T', we now wish to modify the original `regNums` set so that registrations prior or equal to 'T' are removed. We could try using an enhanced **for** loop again:

```
// this will compile but is not safe!
for (String item: regNums) // iterate through all items in 'regNums'
{
      if (item.charAt(0) <= 'T') // check first letter of registration
      {
         regNums.remove(item); // remove this registration
      }
}
```

Here we are once again iterating over the elements of the regNums set. But this time, within the loop, we are attempting to *remove* the given element from the set. As we said in chapter 5, enhanced **for** loops should *not* be used to modify or remove elements from the original collection. To do so would not give a compiler error but it may cause your program to behave unpredictably. If we cannot use an enhanced **for** loop here, how else can we iterate over the elements in a set? Unlike an array, values in the set cannot be retrieved by an index value. Instead, to access the items in a set, the iterator method can be used to obtain an **iterator** object.

17.4.3 *Iterator* objects

An Iterator object allows the items in a collection to be retrieved by providing three methods defined in the Iterator interface (see table 17.1).

Table 17.1 Methods of the *Iterator* interface			
Method	Description	Inputs	Outputs
hasNext	Returns **true** if there are more elements in the collection to retrieve and **false** otherwise.	None	An item of type **boolean**.
next	Retrieves one element from the collection.	None	An item of the given element type.
remove	Removes from the collection the element that is currently retrieved.	None	None

To obtain an Iterator object from the regNums set, the iterator method could be called as follows:

```
// the 'iterator' method retrieves an Iterator object from a set
Iterator<String> elements = regNums.iterator();
```

Here we have called the iterator method and stored the item returned by this method in a variable we have called elements. The generics mechanism has been used here to indicate that the Iterator object will be used to iterate over String objects only:[4]

```
Iterator<String> elements = regNums.iterator();
```

---

[4] If the type had been given simply as Iterator, instead of Iterator<String>, the elements in the collection would be treated by the iterator object to be of the generic Object type, rather than the specific String type.

Once an `Iterator` object has been created, a **while** loop can be used to iterate through the collection, with the `hasNext` method the test of the loop. The body of the loop can then retrieve items with the `next` method and, if required, delete items with the `remove` method. Let us see how this would work with the `regNums` set.

```
/* an Iterator object can be used with a 'while' loop if we wish to
   iterate over a set and modify its contents */

// first create an Iterator object as discussed before
Iterator<String> elements = regNums.iterator();
// repeatedly retrieve items as long as there are items to be retrieved
while (elements.hasNext())
{
    String item = elements.next(); // retrieve next element from set
    if (item.charAt(0) <= 'T') // check first letter of registration
    {
        elements.remove(); // call Iterator method to remove registration
    }
}
```

Within the loop we call the `next` method of our `Iterator` object to retrieve the `next` item within the collection. Since we have specified the `Iterator` object to retrieve `String` objects, we know that this method will return a `String`. We have stored this `String` object in a variable we have called `item`:

```
// the String returned from the Iterator object is stored in a variable
String item = elements.next();
```

It is always a good idea to store the object returned by the `next` method in a variable, as the `next` method should be called only *once* within the loop. Storing the result in a variable allows us to refer to this object as many times as we like. In this case we refer to the object only once, in the test of the **if** statement:

```
if (item.charAt(0)<= 'T') // check the first character in this String
```

If the registration number needs to be removed from the set, we may do so now safely – by calling the remove method of our `Iterator` object:

```
elements.remove(); // call Iterator method to remove current item
```

17.5 The *Map* interface and the *HashMap* class

The `Map` interface defines the methods required to process a collection consisting of *pairs* of objects. Rather than looking up an item via an index value, the first object of the pair is used. The first object in the pair is considered a **key**, and the second its associated **value**. Ordering is unimportant in maps, and keys are unique.

It is often useful to think of a map as a *look-up* table, with the key object the item used to look up (access) an associated value in the table. For example, the password of users of a network can be looked up by entering their username. Table 17.2 gives an example of such a look-up table:

Table 17.2 A look-up table for users of a network	
Username	Password
lauraHaliwell	monkey
sunaGuven	television
bobbyMann	elephant
lucyLane	monkey
bernardAnderson	velvet

We can look up the password of a user by looking up their user name in table 17.2. The password of *lauraHaliwell*, for example, is *monkey*, whereas the password of *bobbyMann* is *elephant*. Notice that it is important we make usernames the key of the look-up table and *not* passwords. This is because usernames are unique – no two users can have the same username. However, passwords are not unique. Two or more users may have the same password. Indeed, in table 17.2, two users (*lauraHaliwell* and *lucyLane*) do have the same password (*monkey*).

Let us implement this kind of look-up table using a `Map`. As with the previous interfaces, there are two implementations provided for the `Map` interface: `HashMap` and `TreeMap`. Here we will look at the `HashMap` class. The constructor creates the empty map:

```
Map<String, String> users = new HashMap<String, String>();
```

As before the type of the collection is given as the interface: `Map`. Notice that to use the generics mechanism to fix the types used in a `Map` object, we must provide *two* types in the angled brackets. The first type will be the type of the key and the second the type of its associated value. In this case, *both* are `String` objects, but in general each may be of any object type.

To add a user's name and password to this map we use the `put` method as follows. The `put` method requires two parameters, the key object and the value object:

```
users.put("lauraHaliwell", "popcorn");
```

Note that the `put` method treats the first parameter as a key item and the second parameter as its associated value. Really, we should be a bit more careful before we add user IDs and passwords into this map – only user IDs that are not already taken should be added. If we did not check this, we would end up overwriting a previous user's password. The `containsKey` method allows us to check this. This method accepts an object and returns **true** if the object is a key in the map and **false** otherwise:

```
if (users.containsKey("lauraHaliwell")) // check if ID taken
{
    System.out.println("user ID already taken");
}
else // ok to use this ID
{
    users.put("lauraHaliwell", "popcorn");
}
```

Notice we do not need to check that the password is unique as multiple users can have the same password. If we did require unique passwords the `containsValue` method could be used in the same way we used the `containsKey` method above.

Later a user might wish to change his or her password. The put method overrides the value associated with a key if that key is already present in the map. The following changes the password associated with "lauraHaliwell" to "popcorn":

```
users.put("lauraHaliwell", "popcorn");
```

The put method returns the value that was overwritten, or null if there was no value before, and this can be checked if necessary.

Later, a user might be asked to enter his or her ID and password before being able to access company resources. The get method can be used to check whether or not the correct password has been entered. The get method accepts an object and searches for that object among the keys of the map. If it is found, the associated value object is returned. If it is not found the null value is returned:

```
System.out.print("enter user ID ");
String idIn = EasyScanner.nextString();
System.out.print("enter password ");
String passwordIn = EasyScanner.nextString();
// retrieve the actual password for this user
String password = users.get(idIn);
// password will be 'null' if the user name was invalid
if (password != null)
{
        if ( passwordIn.equals(password))// check password is correct
        {
                // allow access to company resources here
        }
        else // invalid password
        {
                System.out.println ("INVALID PASSWORD!");
        }
}
else // no such user
{
        System.out.println ("INVALID USERNAME!");
}
```

As you can see, once the user has entered what they believe to be their username and password, the actual password for the given user is retrieved using the get method.

We know the password retrieved will be of type String as we created our Map by specifying that both the keys and values of the Map object would be Strings. We can then check whether this password equals the password entered by calling the equals method of the String class:

```
if ( passwordIn.equals(password))
```

We have to be careful when we use the equals method to compare two objects in the way that we have done here. In this case, we are comparing the password entered by the user with the password obtained by the get method. However, the get method might have returned a null value instead of a password (if the key entered was invalid). The equals method of the String class does not return false when comparing a String with a null value, instead it throws a NullPointerException. So, to avoid this exception, we must check the value returned by the get method is not null *before* we use the equals method:

```
// check password returned is not 'null' before calling 'equals' method
if (password!= null)
{
        if ( passwordIn.equals(password))// now it is safe to call 'equals'
        {
                // allow access to company resources
        }
        else
        {
                System.out.println ("INVALID PASSWORD!");
        }
}
```

Note that the **null** value is always checked with primitive comparison operators (== for equality and != for inequality).

Like all the other Java collection classes, the HashMap class provides a toString method so that the items in the map can be displayed:

```
System.out.print(users); // implicitly calls 'toString' method
```

Key and value pairs are displayed in braces. Let us assume we have added two more users: "bobbyMann" and "sunaGuven", with passwords `"elephant"` and `"television"` respectively. Displaying the map would produce the following output:

{lauraHaliwell=popcorn, sunaGuven=television, bobbyMann=elephant}

As with a set, the order in which the items are displayed is not determined by the order in which they were added but upon how they have been stored internally.

In order to scan the items in the map, the keySet method can be used to return the set of keys.

```
// the keySet method returns the keys of the map as a set object
Set<String> theKeys = users.keySet();
```

Again notice that we know this set of keys returned by the keySet method will be a set of String objects, so we mark the type of this set accordingly.

The set of keys can then be processed in the ways discussed in section 17.2: using either an enhanced **for** loop or by making use of the iterator method of sets.

For example, we might wish to display the contents of the map in our own way, rather than the format given to us by the toString method. An enhanced **for** loop can be used to iterate through the keys of the map; within the loop we can look up the associated password using the get method:

```
for(String item: theKeys)// iterate through the set of keys
{
        String password = users.get(item); // retrieve password value
        System.out.println(item + "\t" + password); // format output
}
```

This would display the map in the following table format:

lauraHaliwell   popcorn

sunaGuven   television

bobbyMann   elephant

As with the other collections, a map provides a `remove` method. In the case of map, a key value is given to the method. If the key is present in the map both the key and value pair are removed:

```
// this removes the given key and its associated value
users.remove("lauraHaliwell");
```

Displaying the map now shows the user's ID and password have been removed:

{sunaGuven=television, bobbyMann=elephant }

The `remove` method returns the value of the object that has been removed, or **null** if the key was not present. This value can be checked if necessary to confirm that the given key was in the map.

Finally, the map collection provides `size` and `isEmpty` methods that behave in exactly the same way as the `size` and `isEmpty` methods for sets and lists.

17.6 Using your own classes with Java's collection classes

In the examples above, we stuck to the pre-defined `String` type for the type of objects used in the collection classes of Java. However, objects of any class can be used inside these collections – including objects of your own classes. Care needs to be taken, however, when using your own classes. As an example, let us consider an application to store a collection of books that a person may own. Figure 17.1 gives the UML design for a `Book` class:

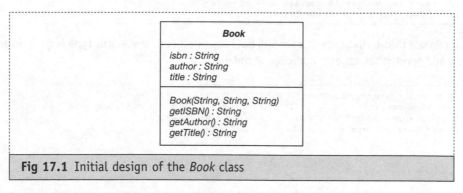

Fig 17.1 Initial design of the *Book* class

This class consists of an ISBN number, an author and a title. An ISBN number is a unique International Standard Book Number that is allocated to each new book title. Before we deal with a *collection* of books, here is the initial implementation of the `Book` class.

The *Book* class

```
public class Book
{
  private String isbn;
  private String title;
  private String author;

  public Book(String isbnIn, String titleIn, String authorIn)
  {
    isbn = isbnIn;
    title = titleIn;
    author = authorIn;
  }

  public String getISBN()
  {
    return isbn;
  }

  public String getTitle()
  {
    return title;
  }

  public String getAuthor()
  {
    return author;
  }
}
```

There is nothing new here so let's move on to see how objects of this class can be stored in the Java collection classes. To begin with, let's create a list to contain `Book` objects:

```
// create empty list to contain Book objects
List<Book> books = new ArrayList<Book>();
```

You can see that to indicate this list will hold `Book` objects, the `Book` type is given in angled brackets. Now let's add some book objects and display the list:

```
// create two Book objects
Book b1 = new Book("0123234521", "G Costanza", "Where's the luck?");
Book b2 = new Book("0823477542", "J Marr", "Half Empty");
// add Book objects to list
books.add(b1);
books.add(b2);
System.out.println(books); // implicitly call toString method of List
```

As things stand this will display the following list on the screen:

```
[Book@6800d6e5, Book@681cd6e5]
```

This isn't exactly what we require! What is going on here and what is the strange information displayed in the list? Well, when Java collections are displayed on the screen by calling their `toString` method, each object in the collection is displayed by calling its own `toString` method. The `Book` has no `toString` method defined so the default `toString` method inherited from the `Object` class is called. All this method does is retrieve the class name of the object (`Book`), and the memory address of the object.

If you wish to use objects of your own classes as objects in Java's collection classes, and you wish to call the `toString` method of the collection class, a meaningful `toString` method should be defined in your class.

17.6.1 Defining a *toString* method

Here is one possible `toString` method we could provide for our `Book` class:

```
public String toString()
{
    return "(" + isbn +", "+ author + ", " + title +")\n";
}
```

We create a single `String` by joining the ISBN, author and title `Strings`. To improve the look of this `String` we have separated the attributes by commas and have enclosed it in round brackets, plus we have added a new-line character at the end. Now if we print out the list we get the following:

```
[(0123234521, G Costanza, Where's the luck?)
, (0823477542, J Marr, Half Empty)
]
```

While you might wish to improve this `String` representation of a book further (maybe by adding more formatting), this is acceptable for testing purposes.

17.6.2 Defining an *equals* method

Another issue arises if we wish to use methods such as `contains` and `remove`. Methods such as these call the `equals` method of the contained object to determine whether or not a given object is in the collection. The `Book` class does not define its own `equals` method so again the inherited `equals` method of the `Object` class is called. This method is inadequate as it simply compares the memory address of two objects rather than the attributes of two objects. For example, the following would display **false** on the screen when we would want it to display **true**:

```
// check a book that is in the list
boolean check = books.contains
                        (new Book("0823477542", "J Marr", "Half Empty"));
// display result
System.out.println(check);
```

To use objects of your own classes effectively, a meaningful `equals` method should be defined. One possible interpretation of two books being equal is simply that their ISBNs are equal, so the following `equals` method could be added to the `Book` class:

```
public boolean equals (Object objIn) // equals method must have this header
{
    Book bookIn = (Book) objIn; // type cast to a Book
    // check isbn
    return    isbn.equals(bookIn.isbn);
}
```

Notice that the `equals` method must accept an item of type `Object`. The body of the method then needs to type cast this item back to the required type (`Book` in this case).

If you are using lists, these are the only two additional methods you need to provide in your class. Also, if you are using objects of your own classes only as *values* of a map, then again these are the only two additional methods you need to provide. If, however, you are using objects of your classes as keys of a map or as the items of a set, then you need to include an additional method in your classes: `hashCode`.

17.6.3 Defining a *hashCode* method

To understand how to define your own hashCode method you need to understand how the HashSet and HashMap implementations work. Both of these Java classes have been implemented using an array. Unlike the ArrayList class however (which has also been implemented using an array), the position of the items in the HashSet and HashMap arrays is not determined by the order in which they were added. Instead, the position into which items are added into these arrays is determined by their hashCode method.

The hashCode method returns an integer value from an object. This integer value determines where in the array the given object is stored. Objects that are equal (as determined by the object's equals method) should produce identical hashCode numbers and, ideally, objects that are not equal should return different hashCode numbers.

The reason for using hashCode numbers is that they considerably reduce the time it takes to search a given array for a given item. If items were stored consecutively, then a search of the array would require *every* item in the array being checked using the equals method, until a match was found. This would become very inefficient when the collection becomes very large. So, instead, the HashSet and HashMap classes make use of the hashCode method, so that when a search is required for an item, say x, that item's hashCode number is computed and this value is used to look up other items in the array. Then, only objects with the same hashCode number are compared to x using their equals method.

If you are using objects of your own classes, and you have not provided a hashCode method, the inherited hashCode method from the Object class is called. This does not behave in the way we would wish. It generates the hashCode number from the memory address of the object, so two "equal" objects could have different hashCode values. Program 17.1 demonstrates this.

Program 16.2

```java
public class TestHashCode
{
  public static void main (String[] args)
  {
    // create two "equal" books
    Book book1 = new Book("0823477542", "J Marr", "Half Empty");
    Book book2 = new Book("0823477542", "J Marr", "Half Empty");
    // check their hashCode numbers
    System.out.println(book1.hashCode());
    System.out.println(book2.hashCode());
  }
}
```

This would produce the following hashCode numbers for the two "equal" books:

1745955844

1748315140

As you can see, the hashCode numbers do not match – even though the objects are "equal". This means that if we were searching for the given book in a HashSet or in the keys of a HashMap, the book would not be found, as only objects with identical hashCode values are checked. Also, we cannot ensure that objects in the HashSet or the keys of the HashMap will be unique, as two (or more) identical books (with different hashCode values) would both be stored in the underlying array at different array positions.

We need to define our own hashCode method for the Book class so that objects of this class can be used effectively with the HashSet and HashMap classes.

Luckily, all of Java's predefined classes (such as `String`) have a meaningful `hashCode` method defined. These `hashCode` methods return equal `hashCode` numbers for "equal" objects.

So one way of defining the `hashCode` number for an object of your class would be to add together the `hashCode` numbers generated by all the attributes to determine object equality. For `Book` equality we checked the ISBN only. This ISBN is a `String`, so all we need to do is to return the `hashCode` number of this `String`:

```
// this is a suitable hashCode method for our Book class
public int hashCode()
{
        // derive hash code by returning hash code of ISBN string
        return isbn.hashCode();
}
```

If you have more than one attribute that plays a role in determining object equality, then add each such attribute's `hashCode` number (assuming the attribute is not of primitive type) to determine your object's `hashCode` number.

If primitive attributes also play a part in object equality, they too can simply be added into your `hashCode` formula by generating an integer value from each primitive attribute. Here is a simple set of guidelines for generating an integer value from the primitive types (although much more sophisticated algorithms exist than these!):

> **byte, short, int, long**: leave as they are;

> **float, double**: type cast to an integer;

> **char**: use its Unicode value;

> **boolean**: use an **if...else** statement to allocate 1 if the attribute is **true** and 0 if it is **false**.

17.7 Developing a collection class for *Book* objects

In the previous section we amended the `Book` class by supplying it with a `toString` method, an `equals` method and a `hashCode` method. If you look at the documentation of any class in the Java API you will see that it also possess these three methods. When developing classes professionally you should always include these methods. That way, objects of these classes can be used with any collection type.

Now we have a suitable `Book` class we can store objects of this class in one of the Java collection classes. Which collection shall we use? There is no ordering required on the collection of books so we do not really need a list here. We could store these books in a set, but since each book has a unique ISBN it makes more sense to use a map and have ISBNs as the keys to the map, with `Book` objects themselves as the values of the map.

We will use this collection to help us develop our own class, `Library`, which keeps track of the books that a person may own. Figure 17.2 gives its UML design:

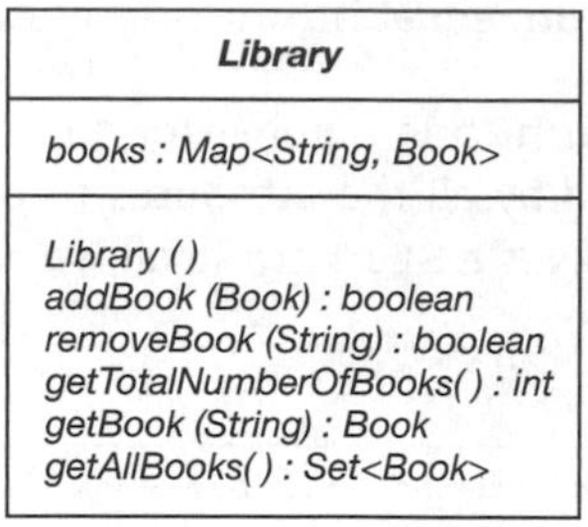

Fig 17.2 UML design for the *Library* class

Notice that the keys of the map are specified to be `String` objects (to represent ISBNs), and the values of the map are specified as `Book` objects.

Here is the implementation of the `Library` class. Take a look at it and then we will discuss it.

The *Library* class

```java
import java.util.*;

public class Library
{
    Map <String, Book> books; // declare map collection

    // create empty map
    public Library()
    {
      books = new HashMap<String, Book>();
    }

    // add the given book into the collection
    public boolean addBook(Book bookIn)
    {
      String keyIn = bookIn.getISBN(); // isbn will be key of map
      if (books.containsKey(keyIn)) // check if isbn already in use
      {
        return false; // indicate error
      }
      else // ok to add this book
      {
        books.put(keyIn, bookIn); // add key and book pair into map
        return true;
      }
    }

    // remove the book with the given isbn
    public boolean removeBook(String isbnIn)
    {
      if (books.remove(isbnIn) != null) // check if item was removed
      {
        return true;
      }
      else // when item is not removed
      {
        return false;
      }
    }
}
```

```
        // return the number of books in the collection
        public int getTotalNumberOfBooks()
        {
          return books.size();
        }

        // return the book with the given isbn or null if no such book
        public Book getBook (String isbnIn)
        {
          return books.get(isbnIn);
        }

        // return the set of books in the collection
        public Set<Book> getAllBooks ()
        {
          Set<Book> bookSet = new HashSet<Book>(); // to store the set of books
          Set<String> theKeys = books.keySet(); // get the set of keys
          // iterate through the keys and put each value in the bookSet
          for (String isbn : theKeys)
          {
            Book theBook =  books.get(isbn);
            bookSet.add(theBook);
          }
          return bookSet; // return the set of books
        }
    }
```

Most of this class should be self-explanatory. Just consider how complicated some of these methods would have been if we had used an array instead of a map!

We just draw your attention to the `getAllBooks` method. The UML diagram indicates that this method should return a *set* of books. An alternative approach could have been to return the map itself, but it would be more useful for this method to return a set of objects, as a set is easier to scan than a map. It is fine to use a set as there is no repetition of books.

```
public Set<Book> getAllBooks ()
{
    // code to create this set goes here
}
```

There is no map method that returns the set of *values* in the map, so a suitable set needs to be created in this method:

```
Set<Book> bookSet = new HashSet<Book>();
```

This set is empty initially and we must fill it with book objects. In order to access these values we use the `keySet` method that returns the set of keys. Remember the keys are `String` objects:

```
Set<String> theKeys = books.keySet();
```

An enhanced **for** loop can now be used to iterate over these ISBNs:

```
for (String isbn : theKeys)
{
        Book theBook =  books.get(isbn);
        bookSet.add(theBook);
}
```

You can see that the ISBN number is used to retrieve the associated `Book` object by calling the `get` method of maps. The given book is then added to the set of books.

Finally, after this loop is complete and the set of books has been created, we can return this set from the method:

```
return bookSet;
```

That completes our discussion of the `Library` class. We leave the task of creating a tester for this class to the end of chapter exercises.

Self-test questions

1 Distinguish between the following types of collection in the Java Collections Framework:

> `List`;

> `Set`;

> `Map`.

2 Consider the following instruction:

```
Map <String, Student> javaStudents = new HashMap<String, Student>();
```

a) Why is the type of this object given as `Map` and not `HashMap`?

b) What is the purpose of the stuff in angled brackets?

c) Assuming the object `javaStudents` has been created as above, why would the following line cause a compiler error?

```
javaStudents.put("U0012345", "Fadi");
```

3 Consider again the `StockItem` class from chapter 7. Here is the UML diagram:

StockItem
stockNumber : String name : String price : double totalStock : int
StockItem(String, String, double) setPrice(double) increaseTotalStock(int) getStockNumber() : String getName() : String getTotalStock() : int getPrice() : double calculateTotalPrice() : double

a) Define an appropriate `toString` method for this class.

b) Define an appropriate `equals` method for this class.

c) Define an appropriate `hashCode` method for this class.

4 In section 17.4 a set called `regNums` was created to store a collection of car registration numbers. Several registration numbers were added and then the set displayed, using the pre-defined `toSring` method, as follows:

`[W79TRV, X85ADZ, V53PLS, L22SBG]`

a) In mathematics, sets are not listed with square brackets in this way. Instead braces are used as follows:

```
{W79TRV, X85ADZ, V53PLS, L22SBG}
```

Write a fragment of code, which makes use of the enhanced **for** loop, to produce the more familiar set notation given above for the regNums set.

b) Write a fragment of code, which makes use of the iterator method, to remove all registration numbers ending in 'S'.

Programming exercises

1 In this chapter we looked at an example of a printer queue. A *queue* is a collection where the first item added into the queue is the first item removed from the queue. Consequently, a queue is often referred to as a *first in first out* (FIFO) collection.

A *stack*, on the other hand, is a *last in first out* (LIFO) collection – much like a stack of plates, where the last plate added to the stack is the first plate removed from the stack. The method to add an item onto a stack is often called *push*. The method to remove an item from a stack is often called *pop*.

Below, we give the UML design for a NameStack class, which stores a stack of names.

NameStack
stack : List<String>
NameStack( ) push(String) pop( ) : String size( ) : int isEmpty( ) : Boolean toString( ) : String

A description of each NameStack method is given below:

NameStack()
Initializes the stack of names to be empty.

push(String)
Adds the given name onto the top of the stack.

pop() : String
Removes and returns the name at the top of the stack. Throws a NameStackException if an attempt is made to pop an item from an empty stack.

size() : int
Returns the number of names in the stack.

isEmpty() : boolean
Returns **true** if the stack is empty and **false** otherwise.

`toString() : String`
Returns a `String` representation of the stack of names.

a) Why was `List<String>` an appropriate collection to use here?

b) Implement the `NameStack` class. You will also need to implement a `NameStackException` class.

c) Test the `NameStack` class with a suitable tester.

2　Consider an application that keeps track of the registration numbers of all cars that have a permit to use a company car park. It also keeps track of the registration numbers of the cars actually in the car park at any one time. While there is no limit to the number of cars that can have permits to park in the car park, the capacity of the car park is limited. Below we give the UML design for the `CarRegister` class:

CarRegister
permit : Set<String> *parked : Set<String>* *capacity : int*
CarRegister(int) *givePermit (String) : boolean* *recordParking(String) : boolean* *recordExit (String) : boolean* *isParked(String) : boolean* *isFull( ) : boolean* *numberParked() : int* *getPermit() : Set<String>* *getParked() : Set<String>* *getCapacity() : int*

A description of each `CarRegister` method is given below:

`CarRegister(int)`
Initializes the `permit` and `parked` sets to be empty and sets the capacity of the car park with the given parameter. Throws a `CarRegisterException` if the given parameter is negative.

`givePermit(String) : boolean`
Records the registration of a car given a permit to park. Returns **false** if the car has already been given a permit and **true** otherwise.

`recordParking(String) : boolean`
Records the registration of a car entering the car park. Returns **false** if the car park is full, or the car has no permit to enter the car park, and **true** otherwise.

`recordExit (String) : boolean`
Records the registration of a car leaving the car park. Returns **false** if the car was not initially registered as being parked and **true** otherwise.

`isParked(String) : boolean`
Returns **true** if the car with the given registration is recorded as being parked in the car park and **false** otherwise.

isFull() : boolean
Returns **true** if the car park is full and **false** otherwise.

numberParked() : int
Returns the number of cars currently in the car park.

getPermit() : Set<String>
Returns the set of car registrations allocated permits.

getParked() : Set<String>
Returns the set of registration numbers of cars in the car park.

getCapacity() : int
Returns the maximum capacity of the car park.

a) Why was Set<String> an appropriate collection to use here?

b) Implement the CarRegister class. You will also need to implement a CarRegisterException class.

c) Test the CarRegister class with a suitable tester.

3 Copy, from the accompanying CD, the Book and Library classes and then implement a tester for the Library class.

4 In chapter 7 we introduced a BankAccount class and a collection class to hold bank accounts called Bank. The Bank class was implemented using an array.

a) Which of Java's collection classes would be a more appropriate to use instead of an array to implement the Bank class?

b) What modifications would be need to be made to the BankAccount class before objects of this class could be used in the collection type identified in part (a) of this question?

c) Make the changes to the BankAccount class that you identified in part (b) of this question.

d) Re-write the Bank class to make use of the collection type identified in part (a) of this question rather than an array.

e) Produce a tester for this Bank class based on the original tester from chapter 7.

CHAPTER: 18
Advanced graphics programming

J
A
V
A

Objectives:

By the end of this chapter you should be able to:

- *create pull-down and pop-up menus;*
- *create **dialogue windows**, **radio buttons** and **combo boxes**;*
- *use the* JFileChooser *class to access the computer's file system;*
- *use a **slider** to alter a value.*

18.1 Introduction

In chapter 10 you learnt how to make use of some of the basic components of the Swing package. In this chapter you are going to learn how to utilize many more of these components, so that you can add features like menus, dialogues and radio buttons to your graphical interfaces.

There is a wealth of classes available in the Swing package, and all we are attempting to do here is to introduce you to some of these classes to show you what is available, and to familiarize you with some of their methods. For that reason, the examples you will find here are very simple ones, designed simply to give you the basic idea of what it is possible to do with Swing. For a full description of the classes available, we strongly recommend that you visit the excellent Sun website (www.java.sun.com) and look at the API (Application Programming Interface) specifications, where all the Java classes and their methods are comprehensively described.

18.2 Making choices

One of the most common ways for an application to interact with the user is to provide a number of choices – just as we did with the text-based menus that we introduced you to in the first semester. With graphical applications, there are a number of ways of doing this, and in this section we present you with some of the ways that this can be done – we will show you how to create pull-down menus, pop-up menus, dialogue windows, radio buttons and combo boxes.

18.2.1 Pull-down menus

A pull-down menu is a very common way to offer choices to the user of a program. Such a menu is shown in figure 18.1. This is a very simple example; the program displays a flag consisting of three horizontal stripes. The colour of each stripe can be changed by means of the pull-down menus on the top bar.

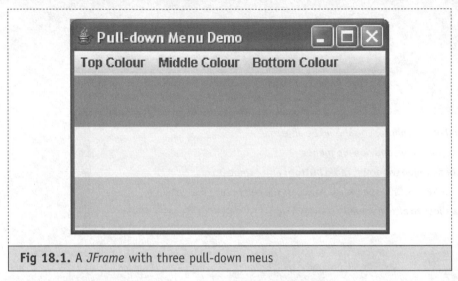

Fig 18.1. A *JFrame* with three pull-down meus

As an example, figure 18.2 shows the choices offered by the first menu:

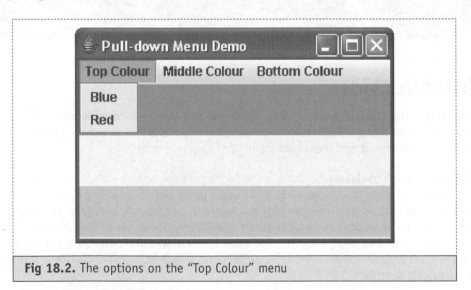

Fig 18.2. The options on the "Top Colour" menu

The code for the `Flag` class is presented below:

The *Flag* class

```
import java.awt.*;
import java.awt.event.*;
import javax.swing.*;

public class Flag extends JFrame implements ActionListener
{
```

```java
// declare and create three panels, one for each stripe
private JPanel topPanel = new JPanel();
private JPanel middlePanel = new JPanel();
private JPanel bottomPanel = new JPanel();

// declare and create the top menu bar
private JMenuBar bar = new JMenuBar();

// declare and create the three menus
private JMenu topStripeMenu = new JMenu("Top Colour");
private JMenu middleStripeMenu = new JMenu("Middle Colour");
private JMenu bottomStripeMenu = new JMenu("Bottom Colour");

// declare and create each menu item
private JMenuItem blueStripe = new JMenuItem("Blue");
private JMenuItem redStripe = new JMenuItem("Red");
private JMenuItem whiteStripe = new JMenuItem("White");
private JMenuItem yellowStripe = new JMenuItem("Yellow");
private JMenuItem greenStripe = new JMenuItem("Green");
private JMenuItem blackStripe = new JMenuItem("Black");

// the constructor
public Flag()
{
  setTitle("Pull-down Menu Demo"); // set the title of the frame

  // set each stripe to an initial colour
  topPanel.setBackground(Color.red);
  middlePanel.setBackground(Color.yellow);
  bottomPanel.setBackground(Color.green);

  // add menu items to the top stripe menu
  topStripeMenu.add(blueStripe);
  topStripeMenu.add(redStripe);

  // add menu items to the middle stripe menu
  middleStripeMenu.add(whiteStripe);
  middleStripeMenu.add(yellowStripe);

  // add menu items to the bottom stripe menu
  bottomStripeMenu.add(greenStripe);
  bottomStripeMenu.add(blackStripe);

  // add the menus to the menu bar
  bar.add(topStripeMenu);
  bar.add(middleStripeMenu);
  bar.add(bottomStripeMenu);

  // add the menu bar to the frame
  setJMenuBar(bar);

  // add listerners to each menu item
  blueStripe.addActionListener(this);
  redStripe.addActionListener(this);
  whiteStripe.addActionListener(this);
  yellowStripe.addActionListener(this);
  greenStripe.addActionListener(this);
  blackStripe.addActionListener(this);

  // select a GridLayout
  setLayout(new GridLayout(3,1));

  // add the panels to the frame
  add(topPanel);
  add(middlePanel);
  add(bottomPanel);

  // choose settings for the frame and make it visible
  setDefaultCloseOperation(JFrame.EXIT_ON_CLOSE);
  setSize(300,200);
```

```
      setVisible(true);
   }

   // the event handler
   public void actionPerformed(ActionEvent e)
   {
      if (e.getSource() == blueStripe)
      {
         topPanel.setBackground(Color.blue); // set top stripe to blue
      }
      if (e.getSource() == redStripe)
      {
         topPanel.setBackground(Color.red); // set top stripe to red
      }
      if (e.getSource() == whiteStripe)
      {
         middlePanel.setBackground(Color.white); // set middle stripe to white
      }
      if (e.getSource() == yellowStripe)
      {
         middlePanel.setBackground(Color.yellow); // set middle stripe to yellow
      }
      if (e.getSource() == greenStripe)
      {
         bottomPanel.setBackground(Color.green); // set bottom stripe to green
      }
      if (e.getSource() == blackStripe)
      {
         bottomPanel.setBackground(Color.black); // set bottom stripe to black
      }
   }
}
```

If you take a look at the attributes you will see that there are three aspects to creating a menu – there is the menu bar at the top and then the different menus – and each of these has its own list of menu items:

```
// the top menu bar
private JMenuBar bar = new JMenuBar();

// the three menus
private JMenu topStripeMenu = new JMenu("Top Colour");
private JMenu middleStripeMenu = new JMenu("Middle Colour");
private JMenu bottomStripeMenu = new JMenu("Bottom Colour");

// the menu items
private JMenuItem blueStripe = new JMenuItem("Blue");
private JMenuItem redStripe = new JMenuItem("Red");
private JMenuItem whiteStripe = new JMenuItem("White");
private JMenuItem yellowStripe = new JMenuItem("Yellow");
private JMenuItem greenStripe = new JMenuItem("Green");
private JMenuItem blackStripe = new JMenuItem("Black");
```

Figure 18.3 clarifies how each of these items is used to create the menu.

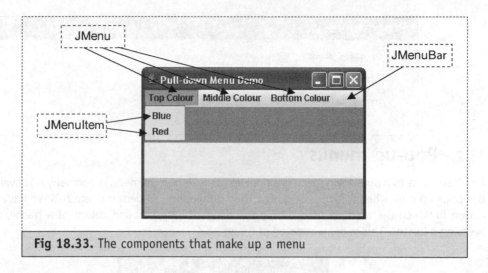

Fig 18.33. The components that make up a menu

Now we can look at the constructor. We start by assigning an initial colour to each stripe. After that we add the individual menu items to the menus:

```
// add menu items to the top stripe menu
topStripeMenu.add(blueStripe);
topStripeMenu.add(redStripe);

// add menu items to the middle stripe menu
middleStripeMenu.add(whiteStripe);
middleStripeMenu.add(yellowStripe);

// add menu items to the bottom stripe menu
bottomStripeMenu.add(greenStripe);
bottomStripeMenu.add(blackStripe);
```

Next these menus are added to the menu bar:

```
bar.add(topStripeMenu);
bar.add(middleStripeMenu);
bar.add(bottomStripeMenu);
```

We now use the `setJMenuBar` method of `JFrame` to add the menu bar to the frame:

```
setJMenuBar(bar);
```

All the rest of the constructor is straightforward and does not require further explanation. Notice how we have used a grid layout to get the stripes where we want them.

The `actionPerformed` method is also straightforward – we set the colour of a particular stripe according to the menu item that was selected. For example, the following sets the middle stripe to yellow:

```
if (e.getSource() == yellowStripe)
{
  middlePanel.setBackground(Color.yellow);
}
```

The flag can now be created with program 18.1:

Program 18.1

```
public class RunFlag
{
   public static void main(String[] args)
   {
      new Flag();
   }
}
```

18.2.2 Pop-up menus

An alternative to a pull-down menu is a pop-up menu. A pop-up menu is normally not available all the time, but pops up only when it is necessary, and then disappears. To demonstrate this we have created an application in which the menu is used simply to change the background colour of a frame, and is invoked by pressing a button. This is demonstrated in figure 18.4.

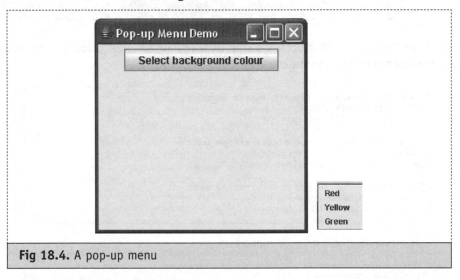

Fig 18.4. A pop-up menu

Here is the code for the PopupDemo class:

The PopupDemo class

```
import java.awt.*;
import java.awt.event.*;
import javax.swing.*;

public class PopupDemo extends JFrame implements ActionListener
{
   // declare and create the button
   private JButton button = new JButton("Select background colour");

   // declare and create the pop-up menu
   private JPopupMenu popup = new JPopupMenu();

   // declare and create the menu items
   private JMenuItem red = new JMenuItem("Red");
   private JMenuItem yellow = new JMenuItem("Yellow");
   private JMenuItem green = new JMenuItem("Green");

   // the constructor
   public PopupDemo()
   {
      setTitle("Pop-up Menu Demo"); // set the title of the frame
```

```
                  // add the menu items to the menu
                  popup.add(red);
                  popup.add(yellow);
                  popup.add(green);

                  // set the location of the pop-up menu
                  popup.setLocation(260,180);

                  // add ActionListeners to the menu items and to the button
                  red.addActionListener(this);
                  yellow.addActionListener(this);
                  green.addActionListener(this);
                  button.addActionListener(this);

                  // choose a flow layout, then add the button to the frame
                  setLayout(new FlowLayout());
                  add(button);

                  // remove the highlighting around the button text
                  button.setFocusPainted(false);

                  // choose settings for the frame and make it visible
                  setDefaultCloseOperation(JFrame.EXIT_ON_CLOSE);
                  setSize(250,250);
                  setVisible(true);
              }

              // the event-handler
              public void actionPerformed(ActionEvent e)
              {
                  if (e.getSource() == button)
                  {
                      popup.setVisible(true); // show the pop-up menu
                  }
                  if (e.getSource() == red)
                  {
                      getContentPane().setBackground(Color.red); // set background to red
                      popup.setVisible(false); // hide the pop-up menu
                  }
                  if (e.getSource() == yellow)
                  {
                      getContentPane().setBackground(Color.yellow); // set background to yellow
                      popup.setVisible(false); // hide the pop-up menu
                  }
                  if (e.getSource() == green)
                  {
                      getContentPane().setBackground(Color.green); // set background to green
                      popup.setVisible(false); // hide the pop-up menu
                  }
              }
          }
```

There is nothing here that is especially new; you have come across all the concepts before, so all we really have to draw your attention to is the line of code that declares and creates a new pop-up menu:

```
    private JPopupMenu popup = new JPopupMenu();
```

The menu items are added to this menu in the constructor:

```
      popup.add(red);
      popup.add(yellow);
      popup.add(green);
```

Notice how, in the `actionPerformed` method, the menu is made visible when the button is pressed, and then is hidden once the background colour has been selected.

Although this is unconnected to the concept of menus, we should also draw your attention to the use of the `setFocusPainted` method which we have used here for the first time – calling this method with a parameter of **false** removes the highlighting around the text of the button when it is in focus:

```
button.setFocusPainted(false);
```

18.2.3 The *JDialog* class and the *JRadioButton* class

An alternative to a pop-up menu is a dialogue window. The Swing class that we use to produce such a window is the `JDialog` class. As with a pop-up menu, its purpose is to provide a means of communication between the user and the program. It is useful for those occasions when we do not want a part of a frame or window permanently devoted to this communication because it is only needed at particular times.

A `JDialog` object allows us to add any components we wish to it, so that we can provide the interface of our choice. In our example we are going to use radio buttons to change the background colour of a frame, just as we did with the pop-up menu. We could, if we had wished, have used buttons instead. For other applications we could have added other components such as text boxes – a good example of this would be a dialogue that asked the user to enter his or her password; once this is done the dialogue window can be disposed.

The application is shown in figure 18.5.

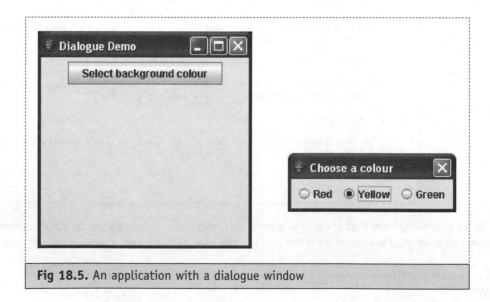

Fig 18.5. An application with a dialogue window

The code for this class, `DialogDemo` is shown below.

The *DialogDemo* class

```java
import java.awt.*;
import java.awt.event.*;
import javax.swing.*;

public class DialogDemo extends JFrame implements ActionListener
{
  // declare and create the button
  private JButton button = new JButton("Select background colour");

  // declare and create the dialogue window
  private JDialog dialog = new JDialog();

  // declare and create a group for the radio buttons
  private ButtonGroup group = new ButtonGroup();

  // declare and create the radio buttons
  private JRadioButton red = new JRadioButton("Red");
  private JRadioButton yellow = new JRadioButton("Yellow");
  private JRadioButton green = new JRadioButton("Green");

  // the constructor
  public DialogDemo()
  {
    setTitle("Dialogue Demo"); // set the title of the frame

    // add the radio buttons to the group
    group.add(red);
    group.add(yellow);
    group.add(green);

    // set the layout policy of the dialogue window to flow layout
    dialog.setLayout(new FlowLayout());

    // set title of dialogue
    dialog.setTitle("Choose a colour");

    // add the radio buttons to the dialogue window
    dialog.add(red);
    dialog.add(yellow);
    dialog.add(green);

    // get the dialogue window to size itself
    dialog.pack();

    // set the location of the dialogue window
    dialog.setLocation(550,400);

    // add ActionListeners to the button and to the radio buttons
    button.addActionListener(this);
    red.addActionListener(this);
    yellow.addActionListener(this);
    green.addActionListener(this);

    // set the policy of the frame to flow layout
    setLayout(new FlowLayout());

    // add the button to the frame
    add(button);

    // remove the highlighting around the button text
    button.setFocusPainted(false);

    // configure the frame
    setDefaultCloseOperation(JFrame.EXIT_ON_CLOSE);
    setSize(250,250);
```

```
        setLocation(250,250);
        setVisible(true);
    }

    // the event handler
    public void actionPerformed(ActionEvent e)
    {
        if (e.getSource() == button)
        {
            dialog.setVisible(true); // make the dialogue window visible
        }

        // select correct action for each radio button
        if (e.getSource() == red)
        {
            getContentPane().setBackground(Color.red); // set background to red
        }
        if (e.getSource() == yellow)
        {
            getContentPane().setBackground(Color.yellow); // set background to yellow
        }
        if (e.getSource() == green)
        {
            getContentPane().setBackground(Color.green); // set background to green
        }
    }
}
```

By now you are familiar with much of this code. We will draw your attention to the specific instructions relating to the dialogue window and to the radio buttons. In fact, the `JDialog` class is very similar to `JFrame`, both being derived from the AWT `Window` class. As you can see, we have created the `JDialog` object with the following constructor:

```
private JDialog dialog = new JDialog();
```

As with a `JFrame`, the `JDialog` has a default border layout policy, which, for simplicity, we have changed to a flow layout. The components are added to the dialogue box as follows.

```
dialog.add(red);
dialog.add(yellow);
dialog.add(green);
```

Notice also how we have used the container method `pack`, which, when there is a flow layout policy, makes the container adjust its size in order to lay the components out in the most compact manner:

```
dialog.pack();
```

With regard to the radio buttons, it is possible for the buttons to act independently, or, alternatively, as a group. In this case we require them to behave as a group, because we want only one to be able to be selected at any one time. You can see that in order to do this, we have created an object `ButtonGroup`:

```
private ButtonGroup group = new ButtonGroup();
```

We add each button to the group as follows, so that they act together:

```
group.add(red);
group.add(yellow);
group.add(green);
```

18.2.4 **Modal and non-modal dialogues**

An object of the JDialog class can be **modal** or **non-modal**; in the above example, the Dialog constructor that we used – the empty constructor – creates a non-modal dialogue. This means that any listening components on the originating frame are still enabled and we can therefore interact with the frame even while the dialogue is visible. In our simple example, the only other listening component is the "close" icon; with the non-modal dialogue, we can still close the frame while the dialogue is visible.

A modal dialogue on the other hand works in such a way as to "freeze" any interaction with the parent frame until the dialogue is disposed of. To create a modal dialogue you can use a different constructor, which takes two parameters. The first is a reference to the originating frame. The second is a **boolean** parameter; if this parameter is **true** a modal dialogue will be created, if **false** a non-modal dialogue will be created.

Thus, in our example we could have created a modal dialogue with the following line:

```
private JDialog dialog = new JDialog(this, true);
```

This would make it impossible to close the frame while the dialogue window is visible.

You should also note that there is a constructor of JDialog which takes just one parameter, a reference to the originating frame. This constructor is useful in the case where the code for the frame resides in a different class to that of the dialogue; you will see an example of this in the case study in chapter 21.

18.2.5 **The *JComboBox* class**

The component known as a *combo box* – provided in Swing by the JComboBox class – should be familiar to everyone, as it is the most common means of providing a choice from a list of options. We have created once again a very simple class (ComboBoxDemo) to demonstrate this – a combo box provides the choice of background colour for the frame. This is shown in figure 18.6.

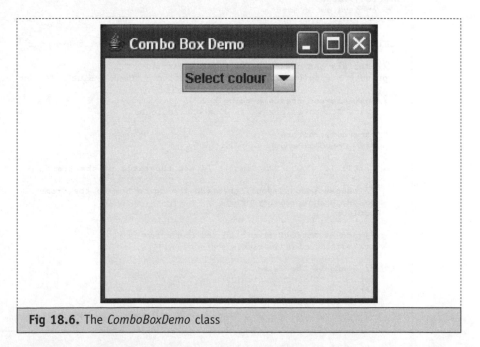

Fig 18.6. The *ComboBoxDemo* class

The choices are revealed when the down arrow is clicked, as can be seen in figure 18.7.

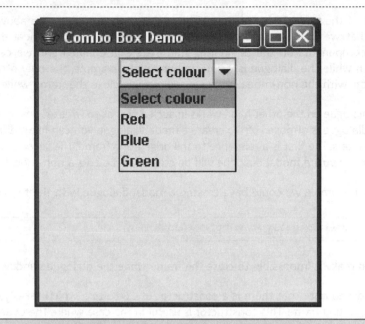

Fig 18.7. The *ComboBoxDemo* class – showing the options

Here is the code for our `ComboBoxDemo` class.

The *ComboBoxDemo* class

```java
import java.awt.*;
import java.awt.event.*;
import javax.swing.*;

public class ComboBoxDemo extends JFrame implements ActionListener
{
  // declare and create an array of strings
  private String[] colours = {"Select colour","Red", "Blue", "Green"};

  // declare and create a combo box
  private JComboBox box = new JComboBox(colours);

  // the constructor
  public ComboBoxDemo()
  {
     setTitle("Combo Box Demo"); // set the title of the frame

    // choose a flow layout, then add the combo box to the frame
    setLayout(new FlowLayout());
    add(box);

    // add an ActionListener to the combo box
    box.addActionListener(this);

    // configure the frame
    setDefaultCloseOperation(JFrame.EXIT_ON_CLOSE);
    setSize(250,250);
    setVisible(true);
  }
```

```
public void actionPerformed(ActionEvent e)
{
    // determine which item is selected
    String item = (String) box.getSelectedItem();
    if (item.equals("Red"))
    {
        getContentPane().setBackground(Color.red); // set background to red
    }
    if (item.equals("Blue"))
    {
        getContentPane().setBackground(Color.blue); // set background to blue
    }
    if (item.equals("Green"))
    {
        getContentPane().setBackground(Color.green); // set background to green
    }
    // set selcted item to the first option so that "select colour" is displayed
    box.setSelectedIndex(0);
}
}
```

Once again we will draw your attention to only a few points. First, notice that the `JComboBox` is created with a constructor that accepts an array of objects – normally `String`s – that defines the choices. In the above class we defined the array of strings, `colours`, and then used this as the parameter:

```
private String[] colours = {"Select colour","Red", "Blue", "Green"};
private JComboBox box = new JComboBox(colours);
```

As is very common when using the combo box, the first option, "Select colour" is not actually an option but is there simply to direct the user.

An `ActionListener` is added to the combo box in the constructor:

```
box.addActionListener(this);
```

Note how, in the `actionPerformed` method we use the `getSelectedItem` method of `JComboBox` to determine which item was selected. This method returns the selected item, an `Object`, which in this case must be type cast back to a `String`.

```
String item = (String) box.getSelectedItem();
```

Finally, note the last line of the `actionPerformed` method:

```
box.setSelectedIndex(0);
```

The `setSelectedIndex` method of `JComboBox` sets the selected item to the one indicated. In this case we require the selected item to be "Select colour", so that after the selection is made the user sees this displayed again. This is the first item in the list – index 0 of the array.

18.3 The *JFileChooser* class

A JFileChooser object interacts with your computer's operating system to enable you to search directories and select files. To illustrate the use of this class we will develop a class called FileHandler that will produce a frame containing a menu bar consisting of a couple of menu options. As well as the menu bar, it provides a text area, as shown in figure 18.8.

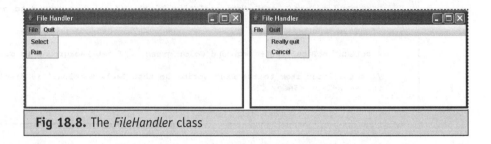

Fig 18.8. The *FileHandler* class

Choosing the *Select* option from the *File* menu will cause a dialogue window to appear as shown in figure 18.9.

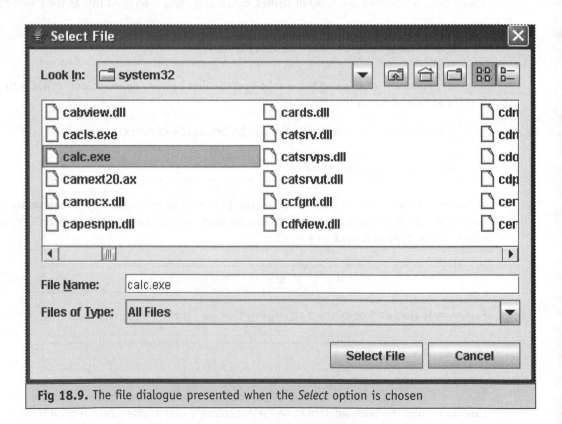

Fig 18.9. The file dialogue presented when the *Select* option is chosen

You can see that in figure 18.9 we have chosen the file called *calc.exe*, which is the calculator program that comes with the Windows operating system. Once we select this file a message appears in our text area, telling us the name of the file chosen. This is illustrated in figure 18.10.

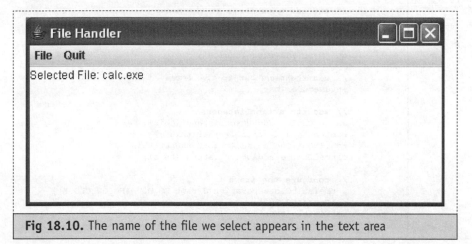

Fig 18.10. The name of the file we select appears in the text area

If the file we have chosen is an executable file, then selecting the *Run* option of the *File* menu will run the program, in this case the Windows calculator. When we get to the next chapter, we will learn more about handling files, and will be able to add an option to our menu which will allow us to look inside a file.

Once again, there is not a huge amount of new material here – there is the code for creating the `JFileChooser` object, and there is the running of the executable itself. We will discuss these after you have inspected the code for the `FileHandler` class.

The *FileHandler* class

```java
import java.awt.event.*;
import java.io.*;
import javax.swing.*;

public class FileHandler extends JFrame implements ActionListener
{
    // the attributes

    // declare a TextArea
    private JTextArea viewArea = new JTextArea(10,55);

    // declare the menu components
    private JMenuBar bar = new JMenuBar();
    private JMenu fileMenu = new JMenu("File");
    private JMenu quitMenu = new JMenu("Quit");
    private JMenuItem selectChoice = new JMenuItem("Select");
    private JMenuItem runChoice = new JMenuItem("Run");
    private JMenuItem reallyQuitChoice = new JMenuItem("Really quit");
    private JMenuItem cancelChoice = new JMenuItem("Cancel");

    // declare an attribute to hold the chosen file
    private File chosenFile;

    // the constructor
    public FileHandler()
    {
        setTitle("File Handler"); // set title of the frame

        add(viewArea); // add the text area
```

```java
        // add the menus to the menu bar
        bar.add(fileMenu);
        bar.add(quitMenu);

        // add the menu items to the menus
        fileMenu.add(selectChoice);
        fileMenu.add(runChoice);
        quitMenu.add(reallyQuitChoice);
        quitMenu.add(cancelChoice);

        // add the menu bar to the frame
        setJMenuBar(bar);

        // add the ActionListeners
        selectChoice.addActionListener(this);
        runChoice.addActionListener(this);
        reallyQuitChoice.addActionListener(this);
        cancelChoice.addActionListener(this);

        // configure the frame
        setDefaultCloseOperation(JFrame.DO_NOTHING_ON_CLOSE);
        setSize(450,200);
        setVisible(true);
    }

    // the event handler
    public void actionPerformed(ActionEvent e)
    {
        if(e.getSource() == selectChoice)
        {
            // create a new JFileChooser object
            JFileChooser chooser = new JFileChooser();

            // show the dialogue
            chooser.showDialog(this, "Select File");

            // determine which file has been selected
            chosenFile = chooser.getSelectedFile();

            // display the name of the chosen file
            viewArea.append("Selected File: " + chosenFile.getName()+ '\n');
        }

        if(e.getSource() == runChoice)
        {
            // create a RunTime object
            Runtime rt = Runtime.getRuntime();
            try
            {
                // run the file
                rt.exec(chosenFile.getPath());
            }

            // if the file name is null
            catch(NullPointerException npe)
            {
                viewArea.append("No file selected\n");
            }

            // if the file cannot be executed
            catch(IOException ioe)
            {
                viewArea.append("Not an executable file\n");
            }
        }
        if(e.getSource() == reallyQuitChoice)
        {
            System.exit(0);
        }
```

```
                    if(e.getSource() == cancelChoice)
                    {
                        viewArea.append("Quit option cancelled\n");
                    }
                }
            }
```

First of all, you will notice that we have declared the following attribute:

```
    private File chosenFile;
```

An object of the `File` class (which resides in the `java.io` package) will hold a representation of a file. Once we have selected a file, its details will be held in this attribute.

Now, let's take a look at the `actionPerformed` method. First there is the option associated with choosing the menu item that lets us select a file:

```
if(e.getSource() == selectChoice)
{
    JFileChooser chooser = new JFileChooser();
    chooser.showDialog(this, "Select File");
    chosenFile = chooser.getSelectedFile();
    viewArea.append("Selected File: " + chosenFile.getName()+ '\n');
}
```

After creating the `JFileChooser` object, we call the `showDialog` method to make the dialogue window visible. This requires two parameters. The first is a reference to the originating component (in our case **this** frame); the second is the text required on the *accept* button, in this case "Select File", as you saw in figure 18.9. Once the user has selected the file, the `getSelectedFile` method is called to return the file selected; this is then assigned to the `chosenFile` attribute. After this we use the `getName` method of the `File` class to display the name of the file in the text area. If we had wanted the full path name to be displayed we could have used `getPath` instead of `getName`.

Here is the code for the `runChoice` option, which loads and runs the selected file.

```
if(e.getSource() == runChoice)
{
    Runtime rt = Runtime.getRuntime(); // create a RunTime object
    try
    {
            rt.exec(chosenFile.getPath()); // run the file
    }

    // if the file name is null
    catch(NullPointerException npe)
    {
            viewArea.append("No file selected\n");
    }

    // if the file cannot be executed
    catch(IOException ioe)
    {
            viewArea.append("Not an executable file\n");
    }
}
```

As you can see we are making use of a standard Java class called `Runtime`. We create an object of this class and then assign it the return value of the `getRuntime` method, which is a **static** method of the `Runtime` class. The object returned by this method contains information about the Java application that is currently running. Being armed with information about the current application, the `Runtime` object is able to execute a command – specific to the particular operating system – as a separate process in the computer's memory. It does this with its `exec` method, which executes the command that is sent in as a parameter. You can see from the above that we are sending in the full path name of the selected file (by using the `getPath` method of `File`). If the file is an executable file then it will be loaded and run.

You can see that two exceptions have been handled. The first is a `NullPointerException`, which would be thrown if the file name sent into the `exec` method were **null** – that is if no file had been selected. The second is `IOException`. This would occur it the file was not executable.

All that is now required is a program such as program 18.2 to create an instance of the `FileHandler` class.

Program 18.2

```java
public class RunFileHandler
{
        public static void main(String[] args)
        {
            new FileHandler();
        }
}
```

18.4 The *JSlider* class

A `JSlider` allows us to control the value of a variable by moving a sliding bar – a *slider* – which is used to vary a value of an integer within a particular range.

The `JSlider` class has a method called `getValue` which returns an integer representing the distance that the bar has been moved. An example should make it clear how this works; in figure 18.11 we have placed a slider at the top of a frame, and added a label to show the current value returned by `getValue`. When you run the program you will see that the default value of the range is 0 to 100.

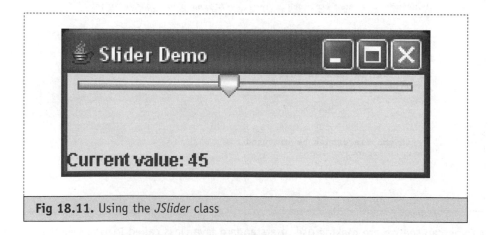

Fig 18.11. Using the *JSlider* class

Here is the code for this `SliderDemo` class:

The *SliderDemo* class

```java
import javax.swing.*;
import javax.swing.event.*;

public class SliderDemo extends JFrame implements ChangeListener
{
    // declare and initialize a horizontal slider
    private JSlider bar = new JSlider(JSlider.HORIZONTAL);

    // declare and initialize a label
    private JLabel valueLabel = new JLabel();

    // the constructor
    public SliderDemo ()
    {
        setTitle("Slider Demo"); // set the title of the frame

        // set the slider to its minimum value
        bar.setValue(0);
        // add the slider to the top of the frame
        add("North", bar);
        // set the initial text for the label
        valueLabel.setText("Current value: 0");

        // add the label to the frame
        add("South", valueLabel);

        // add the listener to the slider
        bar.addChangeListener(this);

        // configure the frame
        setDefaultCloseOperation(JFrame.EXIT_ON_CLOSE);
        setSize(250,100);
        setLocation(300,300);
        setVisible(true);
    }

    // the event-handler
    public void stateChanged(ChangeEvent e)
    {
        // report on the current position of the bar
        valueLabel.setText("Current value: " + bar.getValue());
    }
}
```

Much of the code is self-explanatory. There are a few things to point out here, however. First, notice that we have maintained the `BorderLayout` policy for the frame and added the slider to the `North` sector. Second, you should observe that the constructor allows us to decide upon the orientation of the slider with a predefined integer parameter that can be either `JSlider.HORIZONTAL` or `JSlider.VERTICAL`. Third, you should note that the interface that we need to implement in this case is `ChangeListener` (provided in the `javax.swing.event` library). The method that handles the event is `stateChanged`, which receives a `ChangeEvent` object; notice how we report on the movement of the bar by using the `getValue` method:

```java
public void stateChanged(ChangeEvent e)
{
    valueLabel.setText("Current value: " + bar.getValue());
}
```

Program 18.3 runs the `SliderDemo` class. If you run the program, you will see that the minimum and maximum values of the slider default to 0 and 100. If you require alternative limits there is an appropriate constructor provided – this takes two integer parameters, representing the minimum and maximum respectively.

Program 18.3

```
public class RunSliderDemo
{
  public static void main(String[] args)
  {
    new SliderDemo();
  }
}
```

Self-test questions

1 Identify as many different ways as you can whereby a user can be offered choices in a graphical application.

2 Explain how a `JMenuBar`, a `JMenu` and a `JMenuItem` are used to construct a pull-down menu.

3 What is the difference between a *modal* and a *non-modal* dialogue?

4 In what circumstances might a *pop-up* menu be preferable to a *pull-down* menu?

5 What advantage does a `JDialog` have over a `JPopupMenu`?

6 Explain how a number of *radio buttons* can be made to work together.

7 Distinguish between the `getName` and the `getPath` methods of the `File` class.

8 Explain how to determine which item has been selected from a `JComboBox`.

9 Write a fragment of code that will invoke the Windows Notepad program (`notepad.exe`), assuming that this is located in the directory `C:\Windows`.

10 What is the default range of a `JSlider`?

Programming exercises

1 Implement the programs from this chapter, and adapt them as you wish.

2 Adapt the `DialogDemo` class of section 18.2.3 so that it uses a modal dialogue instead of a non-modal dialogue.

3 Create a graphical user interface for the `Library` class that we created in chapter 17.

4 Adapter the `SliderDemo` from section 18.4 so that instead of printing an integer value, it draws an expanding square as the slider is moved. This is demonstrated in the following diagram:

5 Look back at programming exercise 3 from chapter 14, where you wrote a program that allowed the user to draw a rectangle by dragging the mouse. Adapt this program so that the user has the choice of drawing other shapes such as ovals and straight lines.

6 In programming exercise 3(d) of chapter 16 you wrote a graphical interface for a timetable application. Improve on this interface by providing combo boxes for the *day* and *period* options.

CHAPTER: 19

Enhancing the user interface

J
A
V
A

Objectives:

By the end of this chapter you should be able to:

- *use a variety of Swing components;*
- *add **borders** and **icons** to components;*
- *create **message boxes** and **input boxes**;*
- *create your own colours and fonts;*
- *use the* `CardLayout` *manager;*
- *explain some of the principles behind the creation of good user interfaces.*

19.1 Introduction

The means by which a user communicates with a program is referred to as the **user interface** or **human–computer interface**. You have already discovered that using the Swing package enables you to produce very professional and attractive user interfaces. In this chapter we are going to introduce you to some more features of Swing so that you can enhance your user interfaces even further. We will also show you how you can improve your interfaces by creating your own colours and fonts, and we also introduce some additional layout managers. Finally, we provide some guidelines for good interface design.

19.2 The *Border* interface

As you saw in chapter 10, a very useful feature of Swing is the ability to add a variety of attractive borders to any component. All the basic components such as the `JButton` and the `JLabel` are derived from `JComponent`, and inherit its `setBorder` method, which can be used to add the border of your choice.

In the `javax.swing.border` package is a `Border` interface. In this package there are eight standard border classes that implement this interface. These are:

> `BevelBorder;`

> `SoftBevelBorder;`

> LineBorder;

> EtchedBorder;

> TitledBorder;

> MatteBorder;

> CompoundBorder;

> EmptyBorder.

Figure 19.1 shows examples of these borders.

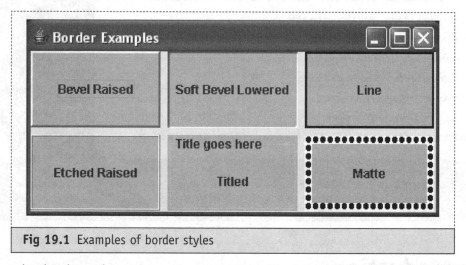

Fig 19.1 Examples of border styles

Each of these border classes has one or more constructors. The following fragment of code, with explanatory comments, shows the constructors that were invoked to produce the borders shown above:

```java
// BevelBorder
/* the constructor takes an integer parameter, the value of which can be
   BevelBorder.RAISED or BevelBorder.LOWERED. There are other
   constructors that allow for the selection of highlight and shadow
   colours */
BevelBorder bevel = new BevelBorder(BevelBorder.RAISED);

// SoftBevelBorder - similar to BevelBorder
SoftBevelBorder soft = new SoftBevelBorder(SoftBevelBorder.LOWERED);

// LineBorder
/* the first parameter to the constructor defines the colour of the
   line; the second defines the thickness of the line. There is also
   a constructor that accepts one parameter for the colour only, the
   thickness defaulting to 1 */
LineBorder line = new LineBorder(Color.black, 2);

// EtchedBorder - similar to BevelBorder
EtchedBorder etched = new EtchedBorder(EtchedBorder.RAISED);

// TitledBorder
/* the String parameter determines the title. A number of other
   constructors exist to allow for positioning of the title. */
TitledBorder titled = new TitledBorder("Title goes here");

// MatteBorder
```

```
/* the parameter determines the icon used to form the border - see next
   section. There are other constructors that allow adjustment of the
   insets, and a simple coloured line border. */
MatteBorder matte = new MatteBorder(new ImageIcon("Circle.gif"));
```

Once created, a border can then be added to a component called, for example, `myLabel` with the following line of code:

```
myLabel.setBorder(bevel);
```

If you want to create more complex border combinations, you can use the `CompoundBorder` class in conjunction with the `EmptyBorder` class (which allows the insertion of empty space around components).

19.3 Combining text and graphics with the *Icon* interface

In the Swing package there is a very useful interface – the `Icon` interface. Any class that implements this interface can be passed into the `setIcon` method that is defined for many of the basic Swing components such as `JButton` or `JLabel`.

To demonstrate how this works we are going to define a simple class called `SquareIcon`, which will produce an icon consisting of a red square, the size of which can be passed into the constructor. Here is the code for the class:

The *SquareIcon* class

```
import javax.swing.*;
import java.awt.*;

public class SquareIcon implements Icon
{
    private int size;

    public SquareIcon(int sizeIn)
    {
        size = sizeIn;
    }

    // all the following methods are required by the Icon interface
    public void paintIcon(Component c, Graphics g, int x, int y)
    {
        g.setColor(Color.red);
        g.fillRect(x, y, size, size);
    }

    public int getIconWidth()
    {
        return size;
    }

    public int getIconHeight()
    {
        return size;
    }
}
```

There is a need for only one attribute, which will hold the width (and height) of the square. The constructor sets the value of this to whatever is sent in. The `paintIcon` method, which we are required to implement, is called automatically when the icon is created, and is automatically sent four attributes:

```
public void paintIcon(Component c, Graphics g, int x, int y)
{
        g.setColor(Color.red);
        g.fillRect(x, y, size, size);
}
```

Methods of the first parameter can be used to find out information (such as the foreground or background colour) of the component on which the icon is painted. The second parameter is the graphics context, and the final two are the coordinates at which the icon should be painted. These will have been calculated to take into account any borders that exist on the component.

The `getWidth` and `getHeight` methods have to be implemented at the insistence of the `Icon` interface.

The `IconDemo` class shown below creates a `SquareIcon` and adds this, together with some text, to a `JButton`.

The *IconDemo* class

```
import javax.swing.*;
import java.awt.*;
import java.awt.event.*;

public class IconDemo extends JFrame implements ActionListener
// adds an icon and text to a component
{
    private JButton button = new JButton();
    private SquareIcon icon = new SquareIcon(30);

    public IconDemo()
    {
        button.setMargin(new Insets(0,0,0,0));
        button.setIcon(icon);            // adds the icon to the button
        button.setText(" Quit  ");   // adds the text to the button
        add(button);
        button.addActionListener(this);

        // configure the frame
        setDefaultCloseOperation(JFrame.EXIT_ON_CLOSE);
        setSize(180,100);
        setVisible(true);
    }
    public void actionPerformed(ActionEvent e)
    {
        System.exit(0);
    }
}
```

You can see that we have used, respectively, the `setIcon` and `setText` methods of `JButton` (inherited from `JComponent`) to add our icon and then some text to the button.[1] Prior to this we called the `setMargin` method to set all the insets to zero; this has the effect of making the icon and text fill the whole button.

As usual, the application can be run with a program such as program 19.1.

---

[1] There is also a version of the `JButton` constructor that accepts the desired icon and text as parameters.

Program 19.1

```
public class RunIconTest
{
   public static void main(String[] args)
   {
        new IconDemo()
   }
}
```

The result of running this program is shown in figure 19.2

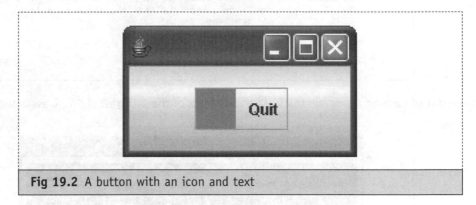

Fig 19.2 A button with an icon and text

19.4 The *ImageIcon* class

A very useful class that is defined in the Swing package, and which implements the `Icon` interface, is the `ImageIcon` class. This class allows you to create an icon from a file in `.gif` or `.jpg` format. We took a file called "Quit.gif", which consists of a red circle on a white background, and then, in our `IconDemo` class, replaced this line:

```
private SquareIcon icon = new SquareIcon(30);
```

with this one:

```
private ImageIcon icon = new ImageIcon("Quit.gif");
```

The result is shown in figure 19.3.

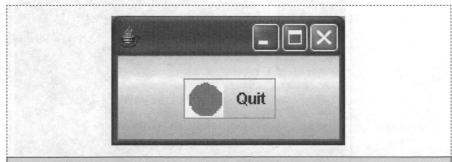

Fig 19.3 A button with an icon and text: in this case, the icon was created from a file

If you want to add an image from a file to a `JFrame`, then you can use the `ImageIcon` class to add the image to a `JLabel` which can then be added to the frame. This is illustrated in the `ImageHolder` class below:

The *ImageHolder* class

```java
import javax.swing.*;

public class ImageHolder extends JFrame
{
    public ImageHolder()
    {
        ImageIcon image = new ImageIcon("Cover.jpg"); // create the image
        JLabel label = new JLabel(image); // add the image to a label
        add(label); // add the label to the frame
        setSize(250,340);
        setVisible(true);
    }
}
```

The result of running a program that creates an object of the `ImageHolder` class is shown in figure 19.4.

Fig 19.4   Displaying an image from a file

In this case we arranged for the frame to be big enough initially to hold the image; however if you reduce the size of the frame you will see that eventually you only get to see part of the image. What would be useful here is for some scrollbars to be available so that we could move the image about within the frame. To do this we can use the `JScrollPane` class as shown below:

The *ImageHolderWithScrollPane* class

```java
import javax.swing.*;

public class ImageHolderWithScrollPane extends JFrame
{
    public ImageHolderWithScrollPane()
    {
        ImageIcon image = new ImageIcon("Cover.jpg"); // create the image
        JLabel label = new JLabel(image); // add the image to a label
        JScrollPane pane = new JScrollPane(label); /* add the label to a
                                                       scrollpane*/
        add(pane); // add the scrollpane to the frame
        setSize(250,340);
        setVisible(true);
    }
}
```

You will now find that when the size of the frame is reduced, scrollbars appear as shown in figure 19.5.

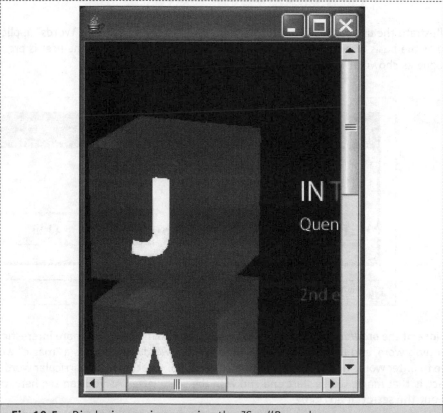

Fig 19.5 Displaying an image using the *JScrollPane* class

19.5 Creating message boxes and input boxes

In the Swing package there is a very useful class called JOptionPane. By making use of this class we can provide dialogue boxes of four possible types. These are described in table 19.1; examples of each can be seen in the application that we will describe shortly.

Table 19.1 The *JOptionPane* dialogue types	
Option	Displays a list of buttons to enable the user to choose an option; see figure 19.6.
Input	Allows the user to enter data via a text field or list. Also provides an "OK" and a "Cancel" button; see figure 19.7.
Message	Displays a message and an "OK" button; see figures 19.8 and 19.9.
Confirm	Asks the user a question and provides "Yes" and "No" buttons for the answer; see figure 19.10.

To illustrate the use of these dialogues, we are going to create a "Magic Words" application, which could be used as the basis of a children's game. When the program first starts, the user is presented with an **option** dialogue as shown in figure 19.6.

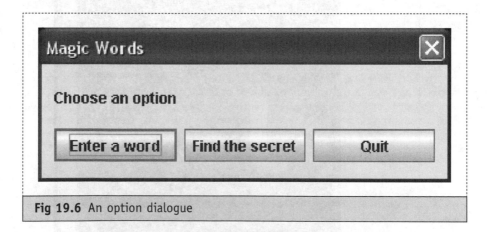

Fig 19.6 An option dialogue

The idea of the program (which you could easily adapt to make it a lot more interesting) is to allow the user to enter a word, and then be told whether or not the word entered was a "magic" word. The user can continue to enter words and try to work out the "secret" of what makes a particular word magical – the answer, in fact, is that magic words start and end with the same letter. As you can see here, the user can choose to find out the secret at any time.

If the user chooses to enter a word, the **input** dialogue shown in figure 19.7 appears:

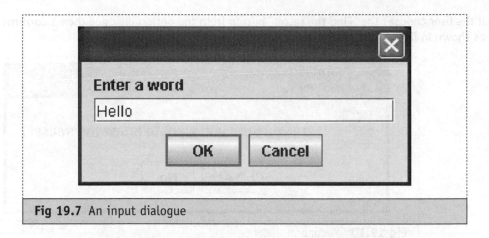

Fig 19.7 An input dialogue

Once the "OK" button is pressed a **message** dialogue appears, informing the user whether or not the word entered was a magic word (figure 19.8).

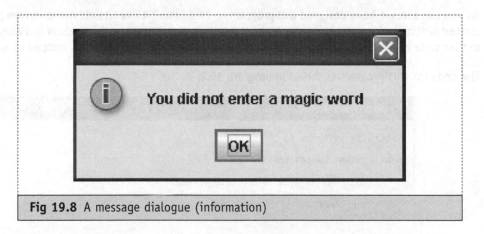

Fig 19.8 A message dialogue (information)

There are different types of message dialogue – the one shown in figure 19.8 is an information message dialogue. If no text had been entered, a different sort of dialogue – showing an error message – would appear as shown in figure 19.9.

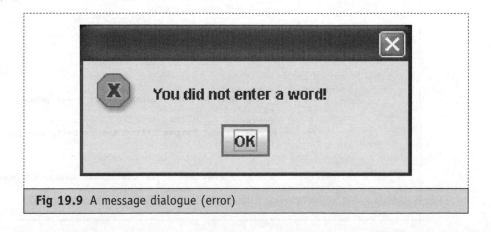

Fig 19.9 A message dialogue (error)

If the user chooses the "Find the secret" button from the option dialogue then a **confirm** dialogue appears as shown in figure 19.10.

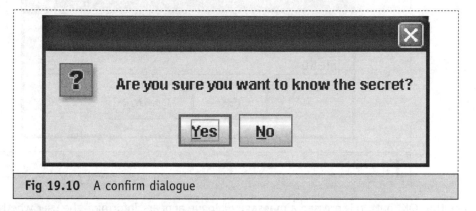

Fig 19.10   A confirm dialogue

Choosing the "Yes" button causes another information message box to appear, revealing the secret.

As you can see, we have designed this program to be a little bit like the old menu-driven programs that you started writing before you knew much about graphics. The `JOptionPane` class has allowed us to create a similar style of program but using graphical message boxes and input boxes instead of a text screen.

The code for this program is shown in program 19.2.

Program 19.2

```java
import javax.swing.*;

public class MagicWords
{
    public static void main(String[] args)
    {
      int result;
      do
      {
          // declare an array of strings to represent the choices
          String[] choice = {"Enter a word", "Find the secret", "Quit"};
          /* create an option dialogue; the showOptionDialog method
             returns an integer */
          result = JOptionPane.showOptionDialog
                              (null,
                               "Choose an option",
                               "Magic Words",
                               JOptionPane.DEFAULT_OPTION,
                               JOptionPane.PLAIN_MESSAGE,
                               null,
                               choice,
                               "Enter a word");
          switch(result)
          {
              case 0 : // the first button, "Enter a word", was pushed
                       enterWord();
                       break;
              case 1 : // the second button, "Find the secret", was pushed
                       findSecret();
                       break;
          }
      }while(result != 2); // continue until the "Quit" button is pushed
      System.exit(0);
    }
```

```java
    // helper methods

private static void enterWord()
{
        char first, last;
        String word, message;
        /* create an input dialogue; the showInputDialog method
           returns a string */
        word = JOptionPane.showInputDialog
                                    (null, "Enter a word",
                                     null,
                                     JOptionPane.PLAIN_MESSAGE);
        if(word != null) // the cross-hairs were not clicked on
        {
            if(word.length() != 0)
            {
                word = word.toUpperCase();
                first = word.charAt(0);
                last = word.charAt(word.length() - 1);
                if(first == last)
                {
                    message = "You entered a magic word";
                }
                else
                {
                    message = "You did not enter a magic word";
                }
                // create a message dialogue, giving information
                JOptionPane.showMessageDialog
                                    (null, message,
                                     null,
                                     JOptionPane.INFORMATION_MESSAGE);
            }
            else
            {
                // create a message dialogue, showing an error
                message = "You did not enter a word!";
                JOptionPane.showMessageDialog
                                    (null, message,
                                     null,
                                     JOptionPane.ERROR_MESSAGE);
            }
        }
    }

    private static void findSecret()
    {
        /* create a confirm dialogue; the showConfirmDialog method
           returns an integer */
        int answer;
        answer = JOptionPane.showConfirmDialog
                            (null,
                             "Are you sure you want to know the secret?",
                             null,
                             JOptionPane.YES_NO_OPTION,
                             JOptionPane.QUESTION_MESSAGE);
        if(answer == JOptionPane.YES_OPTION)
        {
            /* the message dialog defaults to an information
               message if the following constructor is used */
            JOptionPane.showMessageDialog
             (null,
              "A magic word starts and ends with the same letter");
        }
    }
}
```

As you can see, we have used the approach that we took in early chapters whereby a **do...while** loop controls the menu and a **switch** statement is used to process the user's choice. Our program is really more for demonstration purposes than anything else, and more commonly the JOptionPane class will be used as part of a more complex graphical application.

Let's take a look at some of the features of JOptionPane that we have used in the above program.

We have used four **static** methods of JOptionPane to create our dialogues; each of these methods has more than one version, but we will concentrate on the one we have used here – the others simply take a different combination of parameters.

We have begun by declaring an array of Strings, choice, to represent our three options:

```
String[] choice = {"Enter a word", "Find the secret", "Quit"};
```

The first thing that we have done within our **do...while** loop is to create an option dialogue (as shown in figure 19.6), for which purpose we use the showOptionDialog method:

```
result = JOptionPane.showOptionDialog
                        (null,
                         "Choose an option",
                         "Magic Words",
                         JOptionPane.DEFAULT_OPTION,
                         JOptionPane.PLAIN_MESSAGE,
                         null,
                         choice,
                         "Enter a word");
```

You can see that the version of this method that we have used takes eight parameters. The first of these is the parent component (that is the component such as a JFrame or JPanel from which the dialogue was generated). In our program the dialogue was not generated from any other component, so this parameter is **null**.

The second parameter is a String – this determines the question or instruction that will appear in the dialogue – in our case "Choose an option'.

The third parameter, also a String, determines the title.

The fourth parameter is an integer that will determine which buttons will appear on the dialogue box. Predefined constants exist for this purpose. The one we have used here is JOptionPane.DEFAULT_OPTION, which provides different defaults for the different types of dialogues. In the case of an option dialogue, the default is to provide no buttons other than those that determine our choices. However, as you will see below, for other types of dialogues we can choose other options such as JOptionPane.OK_OPTION, JOptionPane.YES_NO_OPTION, or finally, JOptionPane.YES_NO_CANCEL_OPTION.

The fifth parameter determines the icon that is displayed on the box. The possible options are shown in table 19.2.

Table 19.2 Message types available in the *JOptionPane* class	
JOptionPane.PLAIN_MESSAGE	No icon is displayed
JOptionPane.INFORMATION_MESSAGE	An information icon is displayed (see figure 19.8)
JOptionPane.ERROR_MESSAGE	An error icon is displayed (see figure 19.9)
JOptionPane.QUESTION_MESSAGE	A question icon is displayed (see figure 19.10)
JOptionPane.WARNING_MESSAGE	A warning icon is displayed

The sixth parameter can be an Icon of your choice – **null** in our case.

The seventh parameter is the array of Strings that represents our list of options.

The final parameter determines the option that is initially highlighted.

The showOptionDialog method returns an integer, which we have assigned to result. The value of this integer represents the option selected – 0 for the first, 1 for the second and so on. In our case, pushing the "Quit" button will cause a value of 2 to be returned, and this is used to terminate the **do...while** loop. A return value of 0 causes the enterMarks method to be called. Let's take a closer look at this.

After declaring some variables, we create an input dialogue (figure 19.7) by calling the showInputDialog method of JOptionPane:

```
word = JOptionPane.showInputDialog
              (null, "Enter a word", null, JOptionPane.PLAIN_MESSAGE);
```

The version of this method that we have used here returns the string that was entered, and takes four parameters representing, respectively, the parent component, the message, the title and the message type.

The next bit of this method tests for a **null** return value (caused by closing the dialogue with the cross-hairs) and then, if all is well, goes on to determine whether or not a magic word was entered. It then assigns either the string "You entered a magic word" or the string "You did not enter a magic word" to a String variable, message. If no word was entered it assigns the string "You did not enter a word" to message.

If a word was entered, the showMessageDialogue method of JOptionPane is called:

```
JOptionPane.showMessageDialog
              (null, message, null, JOptionPane.INFORMATION_MESSAGE);
```

This method has the same parameter list as above; you can see that we have used message as the second parameter, and have chosen an information message as the message type. You can see the result in figure 19.8.

If no word was entered we again create a message box, but this time it is an error message (figure 19.9).

If the user had selected the "Find the secret" from the original option dialogue, this would have caused the helper method findSecret to be called. This method calls the showConfirmDialog method of JOptionPane:

```
answer = JOptionPane.showConfirmDialog (null,
                        "Are you sure you want to know the secret?",
                        null,
                        JOptionPane.YES_NO_OPTION,
                        JOptionPane.QUESTION_MESSAGE);
```

The first three parameters here are the same as above, as is the final one. The one before the last represents the option type required.

The method returns an integer that is assigned to a variable called `answer`. The possible return values are shown in table 19.3.

Table 19.3 Possible return values from the *showConfirmDialog* method	
JOptionPane.YES_OPTION	The "Yes" button was pressed
JOptionPane.NO_OPTION	The "No" button was pressed
JOptionPane.CANCEL_OPTION	The "Cancel" button was pressed
JOptionPane.OK_OPTION	The "OK" button was pressed
JOptionPane.CLOSED_OPTION	The dialogue was closed by clicking on the cross-hairs

You can see from the code that if the "Yes" button were pressed, then an information message box is created, explaining the secret of a magic word.

19.6 Creating new colours

Those of you who have studied some elementary physics will know that there are three primary colours, red, green and blue;[2] all other colours can be obtained by mixing these in different proportions.

Mixing red, green and blue in equal intensity produces white light; the colour we know as black is in fact the absence of all three. Mixing equal amounts of red and green (and no blue) produces yellow light; red and blue produce a mauvish colour called magenta; and mixing blue and green produces cyan, a sort of turquoise.

Residing in the AWT package is a class called `Color`. We have already been using the pre-defined attributes of this class such as `red`, `green`, `blue`, `lightGray` and so on. However, it is perfectly possible to create our own colours. A new colour is created by mixing any of the primary colours, which can be added in different degrees of intensity. This intensity for each colour can range from a minimum of zero to a maximum of 255. So there are 256 possible intensities for each primary colour, and the total number of different colours available to us is therefore $256 \times 256 \times 256$, or 16,777,216. To create our new colour we simply use the constructor of the `Color` class, which accepts three integer parameters, representing the intensity of red, green and blue respectively.

[2] Don't confuse this with the mixing of coloured paints, where the rules are different. In the case of mixing coloured lights (as on a computer monitor) we are dealing with reflection of light – in the case of paints we are dealing with absorption, so the primary colours, and the rules for mixing, are different. For paints the primary colours are red, blue and yellow.

The `ColourTester` class tests out a few new colours that we have created as well as demonstrating the principles we mentioned earlier about mixing the primary colours.

The *ColourTester* class

```java
import java.awt.*;
import javax.swing.*;

public class ColourTester extends JFrame
{
    public ColourTester()
    {
        // configure the frame
        setDefaultCloseOperation(JFrame.EXIT_ON_CLOSE);
        setSize(150,160);
        setVisible(true);
    }

    public void paint(Graphics g)
    {
        super.paint(g); // call the paint method of the superclass

        // create six new colours of our own
        Color magenta = new Color(255,0,255);
        Color cyan = new Color(0,255,255);
        Color black = new Color(0,0,0);
        Color purple = new Color(210,100,210);
        Color orange = new Color(250,150,0);
        Color brown =  new Color(200,150,150);

        // draw a string in each of the new colours
        g.setColor(magenta);
        g.drawString("This is magenta", 10,40);
        g.setColor(cyan);
        g.drawString("This is cyan", 10,60);
        g.setColor(black);
        g.drawString("This is black", 10,80);
        g.setColor(purple);
        g.drawString("This is purple", 10,100);
        g.setColor(orange);
        g.drawString("This is orange", 10,120);
        g.setColor(brown);
        g.drawString("This is brown", 10,140);
    }
}
```

Figure 19.11 overleaf shows the result (in monochrome here, of course) of running a program that creates an object of this class.

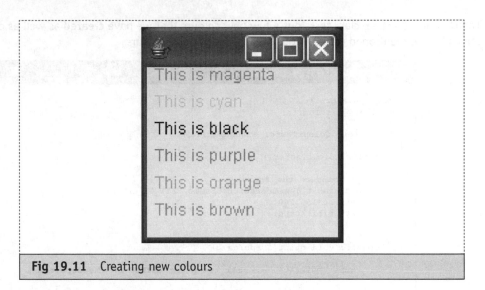

Fig 19.11   Creating new colours

19.7 Creating new fonts

Creating our own fonts is a similar process to that of creating colours, this time making use of the Font class which again resides in the AWT package. You saw an example of this in section 14.4, where you saw that the Font constructor takes three attributes – two strings representing a font name and a style respectively, and an integer representing the font size.

The possible font names are "Serif", "SansSerif", "Monospaced", "Dialog" and "DialogInput". The possible styles are Font.PLAIN, Font.BOLD and Font.ITALIC; the last two of these can be combined by using the plus sign. The FontTester class below shows examples of the different options.

The *FontTester* class

```java
import java.awt.*;
import javax.swing.*;

public class FontTester extends JFrame
{
    public FontTester()
    {
        setDefaultCloseOperation(JFrame.EXIT_ON_CLOSE);
        setSize(260,260);
        setVisible(true);
    }

    public void paint(Graphics g)
    {
        super.paint(g); // call the paint method of the superclass

        // create seven new fonts of our own
        Font font1 = new Font("SansSerif",Font.PLAIN,16);
        Font font2 = new Font("Serif",Font.PLAIN,20);
        Font font3 = new Font("Monospaced",Font.PLAIN,30);
        Font font4 = new Font("Dialog",Font.BOLD,20);
        Font font5 = new Font("DialogInput",Font.BOLD,20);
        Font font6 = new Font("Serif",Font.ITALIC,30);
```

```
        Font font7 = new Font("Serif",Font.ITALIC + Font.BOLD,16);

        // draw a string in each of the new fonts
        g.setFont(font1);
        g.drawString("This is font1", 10,47);
        g.setFont(font2);
        g.drawString("This is font2", 10,75);
        g.setFont(font3);
        g.drawString("This is font3", 10,105);
        g.setFont(font4);
        g.drawString("This is font4", 10,135);
        g.setFont(font5);
        g.drawString("This is font5", 10,165);
        g.setFont(font6);
        g.drawString("This is font6", 10,200);
        g.setFont(font7);
        g.drawString("This is font7", 10,230);
    }
}
```

Figure 19.12 shows the result of creating an object of this class.

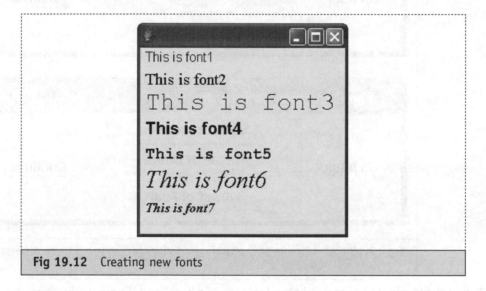

Fig 19.12   Creating new fonts

19.8 More layout policies

In chapter 10 you learnt about two layout policies – FlowLayout and BorderLayout. The GridLayout manager was introduced to you in chapter 16. Another very useful layout manager is CardLayout. The components in a container that implements a CardLayout policy are arranged like cards in a pack. The CardLayout class provides five methods that allow you to display each "card" in turn – these are first, next, previous, last and random. There is also a show method, which allows you to display a particular card by reference to a unique string assigned when the cards are added to a container (normally a JPanel). This layout policy is particularly useful when you want to break up a screen into different sections, so that the sections can be shown one at a time. The example that follows (figure 19.13) provides a possible start-up screen for a game – the screen is divided into three "cards" that allow players to choose their level, then the character they want to be, and finally the imaginary location for the game scenario. Buttons on either side allow the user to go back to a previous screen or to continue.

Fig 19.13 An example of the *CardLayout* manager, showing three different screens

The code for this class is shown below (only the "Go back" and "Continue" buttons have been made functional):

The *Cards* class

```
import javax.swing.*;
import java.awt.*;
import java.awt.event.*;

class Cards extends JFrame implements ActionListener
{
        // create a CardLayout object
        private CardLayout cardLayout = new CardLayout();

        // create a panel to hold the cards
        private JPanel centrePanel = new JPanel();

        // create the buttons for selecting the next and previous cards
        private JButton nextButton = new JButton("Continue");
        private JButton previousButton = new JButton(" Go back ");
```

```
// create the cards
private JPanel firstCard = new JPanel();
private JPanel secondCard = new JPanel();
private JPanel thirdCard = new JPanel();

// the constructor
public Cards()
{
    // add labels and buttons to the cards
    firstCard.add(new JLabel("Choose your level"));
    firstCard.add(new JButton(" Novice "));
    firstCard.add(new JButton("Regular"));
    firstCard.add(new JButton(" Expert "));
    firstCard.add(new JButton("      Elite      "));
    secondCard.add(new JLabel("Select a character"));
    secondCard.add(new JButton("Zorrkk"));
    secondCard.add(new JButton("Kluggg"));
    secondCard.add(new JButton("Grrogg"));
    secondCard.add(new JButton("Skrank"));
    thirdCard.add(new JLabel("Select a location"));
    thirdCard.add(new JButton("Castle of Doom"));
    thirdCard.add(new JButton(" Forest of Fear "));

    previousButton.setBackground(Color.yellow);
    nextButton.setBackground(Color.yellow);

    // add the buttons and the centre panel to the frame
    add("West", previousButton);
    add("Center", centrePanel);
    add("East", nextButton);

    // set the layout of the centre panel to a CardLayout
    centrePanel.setLayout(cardLayout);

    // add the cards to the centre panel
    centrePanel.add(firstCard,"level");
    centrePanel.add(secondCard,"character");
    centrePanel.add(thirdCard,"location");

    // add Actionlisteners to the buttons
    nextButton.addActionListener(this);
    previousButton.addActionListener(this);

    // configure the frame
    setTitle("The Dungeons of Schpiltz");
    setSize(360,125);
    setLocation(300,300);
    setVisible(true);
}

// the event handler
public void actionPerformed(ActionEvent e)
{
    if(e.getSource() == nextButton)
    {
        cardLayout.next(centrePanel); // show the next card
    }
    else if(e.getSource() == previousButton)
    {
        cardLayout.previous(centrePanel); // show the previous card
    }
}
}
```

The only things that we need to draw to your attention to are the ones that are to do with the `CardLayout` class. You can see that we have created a `CardLayout` object as an attribute:

```
private CardLayout cardLayout = new CardLayout();
```

We have also created a panel called `centrePanel` that is the component to which this layout is going to be attached:

```
private JPanel centrePanel = new JPanel();
```

The three different screens that you see in figure 19.13 – in other words the "cards" – are created as `JPanel`s:

```
private JPanel firstCard = new JPanel();
private JPanel secondCard = new JPanel();
private JPanel thirdCard = new JPanel();
```

In the constructor, various buttons and labels are added to these cards, and the `centrePanel` is added to the main panel along with the buttons for going back and continuing.

When all that is done we set the layout of the centre panel using the `cardLayout` object that we defined previously:

```
centrePanel.setLayout(cardLayout);
```

Next we add the cards to the centre panel, and assign each one a unique string as described earlier:

```
centrePanel.add(firstCard,"level");
centrePanel.add(secondCard,"character");
centrePanel.add(thirdCard,"location");
```

Finally we add our `ActionListener`s to the two control buttons and configure the frame.

The `actionPerformed` method then makes use of the `next` and `previous` methods of `CardLayout`:

```
public void actionPerformed(ActionEvent e)
{
    if(e.getSource() == nextButton)
    {
        cardLayout.next(centrePanel);
    }
    else if(e.getSource() == previousButton)
    {
        cardLayout.previous(centrePanel);
    }
}
```

You can see that these two methods require that the component to which the cards are attached be sent in as a parameter. If we had wanted to use the `show` method here it would have taken the following form:

```
cardLayout.show(centrePanel, "location");
```

That would display the third card.

The layout managers that you have come across so far should be enough for much of the programming that you will be doing. However, those of you who will be required to produce really professional interfaces may want to have even more control over the way things look. For this purpose the `GridBagLayout` manager is an ideal layout manager. However, this is a complex layout manager, and we are not going to go into its use here – those of you who wish to know about this manager should consult a Java reference text.

19.9 Guidelines for creating good user interfaces

Nowadays users expect to access their programs via attractive graphical interfaces, using mice, pull-down or pop-up menus, icons and so on. A great deal has been written about the human–computer interface, and there has been much research on the subject. Here we summarize a few of these ideas in order to furnish you with some simple guidelines to help you when you are creating user interfaces for your applications:

> The first rule is to keep it simple. Resist the temptation to show off your programming skills by making your interface too flashy or overly complex. The usual result of this is to put the user off the program.

> Don't use too many colours on one screen; the psychological effect of this can be to make the user feel bombarded by too much at one time.

> Try not to mix too many fonts. Although the idea of having a number of different fonts might sound tempting at first, the effect of this is recognized as having a negative effect on the eye.

> Think carefully about how the user might navigate through the program – don't bury menu options or different screens in large numbers of layers. Always provide a simple route back to the main program menu or screen – and apart from that provide just one way back and one way forward.

> Think carefully about who is going to be using the program. Will it be an expert user or a novice user? What sort of language are you using, and is it appropriate for the type of user in question? For example a dialogue window that says "Sorry, but the file you have requested does not exist" is likely to be far more helpful to the average user than "File I/O error".

> Think carefully about the needs of users with disabilities. For example, people with visual impairments require such things as strongly contrasting colours for background and foreground; also such users are likely to benefit greatly from sound prompts. However, a program that actually *relied* on sound prompts would be useless to a deaf person. There is now UK and EU legislation that needs to be adhered to when creating computer programs that might be used for people with special needs – any professional developer needs to be familiar with the laws in this area.

Self-test questions

1 Write fragments of code to create each of the `JOptionPane`s shown below:

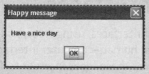

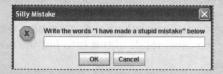

2 Explain the principle behind the creation of colours on a monitor.

3 For what kind of situation is the `CardLayout` manager useful?

4 Explain some of the principles behind the creation of good user interfaces.

5 What issues would you take into account in regard to interface design when considering the needs of users with disabilities?

Programming exercises

1 Look back at section 19.2 in which examples of the different border styles were presented. Experiment with other style combinations by using the various constructors and methods that you learnt about in that section.

2 Making good use of the `JOptionPane` class (section 19.5), design and implement a program that would help primary school children to test their arithmetic.

3 Adapt the library application you developed in programming exercise 3 of the last chapter by adding a password facility. You can use the `JPasswordField` class, which extends `JTextField`. To hide the input you should use the `setEchoChar` method, which takes as a parameter the character that echoes on the screen when each key is pressed (traditionally a star).

CHAPTER: 20

Working with files

Objectives:

By the end of this chapter you should be able to:

- *explain the principles of **input** and **output** and identify a number of different input and output devices;*
- *explain the concept of an **I/O stream**;*
- *describe the basic file-handling techniques used in the Java language;*
- *distinguish between **text**, **binary** and **object** encoding of data;*
- *distinguish between **serial** access files and **random** access files;*
- *create and access files in Java using all the above encoding and access methods.*

20.1 Introduction

When we developed our case study in chapters 11 and 12 it became apparent that in reality an application such as that one wouldn't be much use unless we had some way of storing our data permanently – even when the program has been terminated and the computer has been switched off. You will remember in those chapters, because you had not yet learnt how to do this, we provided a special class called `TenantFileHandler` that enabled you to keep permanent records on disk.

Now it is time to learn how to do this yourself. As you are no doubt already aware, a named block of externally stored data is called a **file**.

When we are taking an object-oriented approach, as we have been doing, we tend not to separate the data from the behaviour; however, when it comes to storing information in files then of course it is only the data that we are interested in storing. When referring to data alone it is customary to use the terms **record** and **field**. A record refers to a single data instance – for example a person, a stock-item, a student and so on; a **field** refers to what in the object-oriented world we would normally call an attribute – a name, a stock-number, an exam mark etc.

In this chapter we will learn how to create files, and write information to them, and to read the information back when we need it. We start by looking at this process in the overall context of input and output, or I/O as it is often called; you will then go on to learn a number of different techniques for keeping permanent copies of your data.

20.2 Input and output

Any computer system must provide a means of allowing information to come in from the outside world (**input**) and, once it has been processed, to be sent out again (**output**). The whole question of input and output, particularly where files are concerned, can sometimes seem rather complex, especially from the point of view of the programmer.

As with all aspects of a computer system, the processes of input and output are handled by the computer hardware working in conjunction with the system software – that is, the operating system (Windows XP or Unix for example). The particular application program that is running at the time normally deals with input and output by communicating with the operating system, and getting it to perform these tasks in conjunction with the hardware.

All this involves some very real complexity and involves a lot of low-level details that a programmer is not usually concerned with; for example, the way in which the system writes to external media such as disks, or the way it reconciles the differences between the speed of the processor with the speed of the disk-drive.

20.3 Input and output devices

The most common way of getting data input from the outside world is via the keyboard; and the most common way of displaying output data is on the screen. Therefore, most systems are normally set up so that the *standard* input and output devices are the keyboard and the screen respectively. However, there are many other devices that are concerned with input and output: magnetic and optical disks for permanent storage of data; network interface cards and modems for communicating with other computers; and printers for producing hard copies.

We should bear in mind that the process, in one sense, is always the same, no matter what the input or output device. All the data that is processed by the computer's central processing unit in response to program instructions is stored in the computer's main memory or RAM (Random Access Memory). Input is the transfer of data from some external device to main memory whereas output is the transfer of data from main memory to an external device. In order for input or output to take place, it is necessary for a channel of communication to be established between the device and the computer's memory. Such a channel is referred to as a **stream**. The operating system will have established a **standard input stream** and a **standard output stream**, which will normally be the keyboard and screen respectively. In addition to this, there is usually a **standard error stream** where error messages can be displayed; this is normally also set to the screen. All of these default settings for the standard streams can be changed either via the operating system or from within the program itself.

In chapter 15 you saw that the `System` class has two attributes called `in` and `out` – it also has an additional attribute called `err`; these objects are already set up to provide access to the standard input, output and error streams. The attribute `in` is an object of a class called `InputStream`. This class provides some low-level methods to deal with basic input – they are low-level because they deal with sequences of bytes, rather than characters. A higher-level class, `InputStreamReader` can be wrapped around this class to deal with character input; `InputStreamReader` objects can subsequently be wrapped by another class, `BufferedReader`, which handles input in the form of strings.

This rather complex way of reading from the keyboard is how things were done before Java 5.0 provided the `Scanner` class. Program 20.1 illustrates how you would get keyboard input in this manner.

Program 20.1

```java
import java.io.*;
public class KeyBoardInput
{
    public static void main(String[] args)
    {
        InputStreamReader input = new InputStreamReader(System.in);
        BufferedReader reader = new BufferedReader(input);

        try
        {
            System.out.print("Enter a string: ");
            String test = reader.readLine();
            System.out.print("You entered: " + test);
        }

        catch(IOException e)
        {
            e.printStackTrace();
        }

    }
}
```

You can see that the `readLine` method of `BufferedReader` is used to get a string of characters from the keyboard; as you would expect, the method reads characters from the keyboard until the user presses the return key. It throws an `IOException` if an error (such as a keyboard lock) occurs during the process, and this has to be handled.

In this chapter, instead of dealing with input and output to the standard streams, we are going to be dealing with the input and output of data to external disk drives in the form of files – but, as you will see, the principles are the same.

20.4 File-handling

The output process, which consists of transferring data from memory to a file, is usually referred to as **writing**; the input process, which consists of transferring data from a file to memory, is referred to as **reading**. Both of these involve some low-level detail to do with the way in which data is stored physically on the disk. As programmers we do not want to have to worry more than is necessary about this process – which, of course, will differ from one machine to the next and from one operating system to the next. Fortunately, Java makes it quite easy for us to deal with these processes. As we shall see, Java provides low-level classes which create **file streams** – input or output streams that handle communication between main memory and a named file on a disk. It also provides higher-level classes which we can "wrap around" the low-level objects, enabling us to use methods that relate more closely to our logical way of thinking about data. In this way we are shielded from having to know too much detail about the way our particular system stores and retrieves data to or from a file.

As we shall see, this whole process enables us to read and write data in terms of units that we understand – for example, in the form of strings, lines of text, or basic types such integers or characters; Java even allows us to store and retrieve whole objects.

20.4.1 **Encoding**

Java supports three different ways of **encoding** data – that is, representing data on a disk. These are **text**, **binary** and **object**.

Text encoding means that the data on the disk is stored as characters in the form used by the external system – most commonly ASCII. Java, as we know, uses the Unicode character set, so some conversion takes place in the process, but fortunately the programmer does not have to worry about that. As an example, consider saving the number 107 to a text file – it will be saved as the character '1' in ASCII code (or whatever is used by the system) followed by the character '0', followed by the character '7'. A text file is therefore readable by a text editor (such as Windows Notepad).

Binary encoding, on the other hand, means that the data is stored in the same format as the internal representation of the data used by the program to store data in memory. So the number 107 would be saved as the binary number 1101011. A binary file could not be read properly by a text editor as we shall see in section 20.6.

Finally, object-encoding is a powerful mechanism provided by Java whereby a whole object can be input or output with a single command.

You are probably asking yourself which is the best method to use when you start to write applications that read and write to files. Well, if your files are going to be read and written by the same application, then it really makes very little difference how they are encoded! Just use the method that seems the easiest for the type of data you are storing. However, do bear in mind that if you wanted your files to be read by a text editor then you must, of course, use the text encoding method.

20.4.2 **Access**

The final thing that you need to consider before we show you how to write files in Java is the way in which files are accessed. There are two ways in which this can take place – **serial** access and **random** access. In the first (and more common) method, each item of data is read (or written) in turn. The operating system provides what is know as a **file pointer**, which is really just a location in memory that keeps track of where we have got to in the process of reading or writing to a file.

Another way to access data in a file is to go directly to the record you want – this is known as random access, and is a bit like going straight to the clip you want on a DVD; whereas serial access is like using a video tape, where you have to work your way through the entire tape to get to the bit you want. Java provides a class (`RandomAccessFile`) that we can use for random access. We will start, however, with serial access.

20.5 **Reading and writing to text files**

In this and the following section we are going to use as an example a very simple class called `Car`; the code for this class is given below, and the source code is provided on the accompanying CD:

The *Car* class

```java
public class Car
{
    private String registration;
    private String make;
    private double price;

    public Car(String registrationIn, String makeIn, double priceIn)
    {
        registration = registrationIn;
        make = makeIn;
        price = priceIn;
    }

    public String getRegistration()
    {
        return registration;
    }

    public String getMake()
    {
        return make;
    }

    public double getPrice()
    {
        return price;
    }
}
```

Program 20.2 below is a very simple menu-driven program that manipulates a list of cars, held in memory as a `List`; it provides the facility to add new cars to the list, to remove cars from the list and to display the details of all the cars in the list. As it is a demonstration program only, we have not bothered with such things as input validation, or checking if the list is empty before we try to remove an item.

The difference between this and other similar programs that we have discussed before, is that the list is kept as a permanent record – as we mentioned before, we did a similar thing in our case study in chapter 12, but there the process was hidden from you.

The program is designed so that reading and writing to the file takes place as follows: when the quit option is selected, the list is written as a permanent text file called `Cars.txt`; each time the program is run, this file is read into the list.

The program is presented below; notice that we have provided two helper methods, `writeList` and `readList` for the purpose of accessing the file; as we shall explain, the `writeList` method also deals with creating the file for the first time.

Program 20.2

```java
import java.util.*;      // required for List and ArrayList
import java.io.*;        // required for handling the IOExceptions

public class TextFileTester
{
    public static void main(String[] args)
    {
        char choice;
        // create an empty list to hold Cars
        List<Car> carList = new ArrayList<Car>();
        // read the list from file when the program starts
        readList(carList);
```

```java
        // menu options
        do
        {
            System.out.println("\nText File Tester");
            System.out.println("1. Add a car");
            System.out.println("2. Remove a car");
            System.out.println("3. List all cars");
            System.out.println("4. Quit\n");
            choice = EasyScanner.nextChar();
            System.out.println();
            switch(choice)
            {
                case '1' : addCar(carList);
                            break;
                case '2' : removeCar(carList);
                            break;
                case '3' : listAll(carList);
                            break;
                case '4' : writeList(carList); // write to the file
                            break;
                default   : System.out.print
                            ("\nPlease choose a number from 1 - 4 only\n ");
            }
        }while(choice != '4');
    }

    // method for adding a new car to the list
    private static void addCar(List<Car> carListIn)
    {
        String tempReg;
        String tempMake;
        double tempPrice;

        System.out.print("Please enter the registration number: ");
        tempReg = EasyScanner.nextString();
        System.out.print("Please enter the make: ");
        tempMake = EasyScanner.nextString();
        System.out.print("Please enter the price: ");
        tempPrice = EasyScanner.nextDouble();
        carListIn.add(new Car(tempReg, tempMake, tempPrice));
    }

    /* method for removing a car from the list - in a real
       application this would need to include some validation */
    private static void removeCar(List<Car> carListIn)
    {
        int pos;
        System.out.print("Enter the position of the car to be removed: ");
        pos = EasyScanner.nextInt();
        carListIn.remove(pos - 1);
    }

    // method for listing details of all cars in the list
    private static void listAll(List<Car> carListIn)
    {
        for(Car item : carListIn)
        {
            System.out.println(item.getRegistration()
                                + " "
                                + item.getMake()
                                + " "
                                + item.getPrice());
        }
    }

    // method for writing the file
    private static void writeList(List<Car> carListIn)
    {
        try
```

```
        {
            /* create a FileWriter object, carFile, that handles the
               low-level details of writing the list to a file
               which we have called "Cars.txt" */
            FileWriter carFile = new FileWriter("Cars.txt");
            /* now create a PrintWriter object to wrap around carFile;
               this allows us to user high-level functions such as
               println */
            PrintWriter carWriter = new PrintWriter(carFile);
            // write each element of the list to the file
            for(Car item : carListIn)
            {
                carWriter.println(item.getRegistration());
                carWriter.println(item.getMake());
                /* println can accept a double, then write it as a
                   text string */
                carWriter.println(item.getPrice());
            }
            /* close the file so that it is no longer accessible to
               the program */
            carWriter.close();
        }

        // handle the exception thrown by the FileWriter methods
        catch(IOException e)
        {
            System.out.println("There was a problem writing the file");
        }
    }

    // method for reading the file
    private static void readList(List<Car> carListIn)
    {
        String tempReg;
        String tempMake;
        String tempStringPrice;
        double tempDoublePrice;
        try
        {
            /* create a FileReader object, carFile, that handles the low-
               level details of reading the list from the "Cars.txt" file */
            FileReader carFile = new FileReader("Cars.txt");
            /* now create a BufferedReader object to wrap around carFile;
               this allows us to user high-level functions such as
               readLine */
            BufferedReader carStream = new BufferedReader(carFile);
            // read the first line of the file
            tempReg = carStream.readLine();
            /* read the rest of the first record, then all the rest of the
               records until the end of the file is reached */
            while(tempReg != null)  // a null string indicates end of file
            {
                tempMake = carStream.readLine();
                tempStringPrice = carStream.readLine();
                /* as this is a text file we have to convert the price
                   to double */
                tempDoublePrice = Double.parseDouble(tempStringPrice);
                carListIn.add
                        (new Car(tempReg, tempMake, tempDoublePrice));
                tempReg = carStream.readLine();
            }
            /* close the file so that it is no longer accessible to
               the program */
            carStream.close();
        }

        /* handle the exception that is thrown by the FileReader
           constructor if the file is not found */
        catch(FileNotFoundException e)
        {
```

```
                    System.out.println("\nNo file was read");
            }

            // handle the exception thrown by the FileReader methods
            catch(IOException e)
            {
                System.out.println("\nThere was a problem reading the file");
            }
        }
    }
```

It is only the `writeList` and `readList` methods that we need to analyse here – none of the other methods involves anything new. Let's start with `writeList`. The first thing to notice is that, after declaring a `Car` object, we enclose everything in a **try** block. This is because all the methods (including the constructor) of the `FileWriter` class that we are going to use throw `IOExceptions` in situations in which the file cannot be written (for example if the disk is full).

The first thing we need to do (within the **try** block) is to open a file in which to keep our records. To do this we use the class called `FileWriter`; this is one of the classes we talked about earlier that provide the low-level communication between the program and the file. By opening a file we establish a *stream* through which we can output data to the file. We create a `FileWriter` object, `carFile`, giving it the name of the file to which we want to write the data:

```
FileWriter carFile = new FileWriter("Cars.txt");
```

In this case we have called the file `Cars.txt`.[1] Creating the new `FileWriter` object causes the file to be opened in output mode – meaning that it is ready to receive data; if no file of this name exists then one will be created. Opening the file in this way (in output mode) means that any data that we write to the file will wipe out what was previously there. That is what we need for this particular application, because we are simply going to write the entire list when the program terminates. Sometimes, however, it is necessary to open a file in **append** mode; in this mode any data written to the file would be written after the existing data. To do this we would simply have used another constructor, which takes an additional (boolean) parameter indicating whether or not we require append mode:

```
FileWriter carFile = new FileWriter("Cars.txt", true);
```

The next thing we do is create an object, `carWriter`, of the `PrintWriter` class, sending it the `carFile` object as a parameter.

```
PrintWriter carWriter = new PrintWriter(carFile);
```

This object can now communicate with our file via the `carFile` object; `PrintWriter` objects have higher level methods than `FileWriter` objects (for example `print` and `println`) that enable us to write whole strings like we do when we output to the screen.

Now we are ready to write each `Car` in the list to our file – we can use a `for` loop for this:

```
for(Car item : carListIn)
{
    carWriter.println(item.getRegistration());
    carWriter.println(item.getMake());
    carWriter.println(item.getPrice());
}
```

[1] As we have not supplied an absolute pathname, the file will be saved in the current directory.

On each iteration we use the println method of our PrintWriter object, carWriter, to write the registration number, the make and the price of the car to the file; println converts the price to a String before writing it. Notice also that the println method inserts a newline character at the end of the string that it prints; if we did not want the newline character to be inserted, we would use the print method instead.

Now that we have finished with the file it is most important that we *close* it. Closing the file achieves two things. First, it ensures that a special character, the end-of-file marker,[2] is written at the end of the file. This enables us to detect when the end of the file has been reached when we are reading it – more about this when we explore the readList method. Second, closing the file means that it is no longer accessible by the program, and is therefore not susceptible to being written to in error. We close the file by calling the close method of PrintWriter:

```
carWriter.close();
```

Finally we have to handle any IOExceptions that may be thrown by the FileWriter methods:

```
catch(IOException e)
{
        System.out.println("There was a problem writing the file");
}
```

In a moment we will explore the code for reading the file. But bear in mind that if we were to run our program and add a few records, and then quit the program we would have saved the data to a text-file called Cars.txt, so we should be able to read this file with a text editor. When we did this, we created three cars, and then looked inside the file using Windows Notepad. Figure 20.1 shows the result.

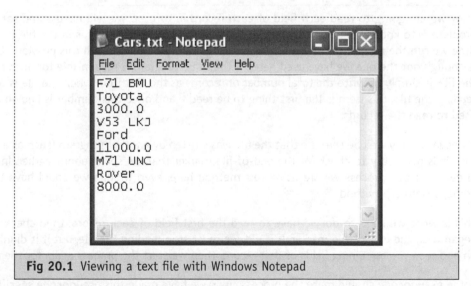

Fig 20.1 Viewing a text file with Windows Notepad

As we have written each field using the println statement, each one, as you can see, starts on a new line. If our aim were to view the file with a text editor as we have just done, then this might not be the most suitable format – we might, for example, have wanted to have one record per line; we could also have printed some headings if we had wished. However, it is actually our intention to make our program read the entire file into our list when the program starts – and as we shall now see, one field per line makes reading the text file nice and easy. So let's take a look at our readList method.

[2] Most systems use ASCII character 26 as the end-of-file marker.

First, we need to declare some variables to hold the value of each field as we progressively read through the file. Remembering that this is a text file we declare three `Strings`:

```
String tempReg;
String tempMake;
String tempStringPrice;
```

But the last of these will have to be converted to a **double** before we store it in the list so we also need a variable to hold this value once it is converted:

```
double tempDoublePrice;
```

Now, as before, we put everything into a **try** block, as we are going to have to deal with the exceptions that may be thrown by the various methods we will be using.

The first thing we need to do is to open the file that we wish to read; we create an object – `carFile` – of the class `FileReader` which deals with the low-level details involved in the process of reading a file. The name of the file, `Cars.txt`, that we wish to read is sent in as a parameter to the constructor; this file is then opened in read mode.

```
FileReader carFile = new FileReader("Cars.txt");
```

Now, in order that we can use some higher-level read methods, we wrap up our `carFile` object in an object of a class called `BufferedReader`. We have called this new object `carStream`.

```
BufferedReader carStream = new BufferedReader(carFile);
```

Now we are going to read each field of each record in turn, so we will need some sort of loop. The only problem is to know when to stop – this is because the number of records in the file can be different each time we run the program. There are different ways in which to approach this problem. One very good way (although not the one we have used here), if the same program is responsible for both reading and writing the file, is simply to write the total number of records as the first item when the file is written. Then, when reading the file, this item is the first thing to be read – and once this number is known a **for** loop can be used to read the records.

However, it may well be the case that the file was written by another program (such as a text editor). In this case it is necessary to check for the end-of-file marker that we spoke about earlier. In order to help you understand this process we are using this method here, even though we could have used the first (and perhaps simpler) method.

This is what we have to do: we have to read the first field of each record, then check whether that field began with the end-of-file marker. If it did, we must stop reading the file, but if it didn't we have to carry on and read the remaining fields of that record. Then we start the process again for the next record.

Some pseudocode should make the process clear; we have made this pseudocode specific to our particular example:

```
BEGIN
     READ the registration number field of the first record
     LOOP While the field just read does not contain the end-of-file marker
     BEGIN
          READ the make field of the next record
          READ the price field of the next record
          CONVERT the price to a double
          Create a new car with details just read and add it to the list
```

```
                READ the registration number field of the next record
        END
END
```

The code for this is shown below:

```
tempReg = carStream.readLine();
while(tempReg != null)   // a null string indicates end of file
{
        tempMake = carStream.readLine();
        tempStringPrice = carStream.readLine();
        tempDoublePrice = Double.parseDouble(tempStringPrice);
        carListIn.add (new Car(tempReg, tempMake, tempDoublePrice));
        tempReg = carStream.readLine();
}
```

Notice that we are using the `readLine` method of `BufferedReader` to read each record. This method reads a line of text from the file; a line is considered anything that is terminated by the newline character. The method returns that line as a `String` (which does not include the newline character). However, if the line read consists of the end-of-file marker, then `readLine` returns a **null**, making it very easy for us to check if the end of the file has been reached. In section 20.7 you will be able to contrast this method of `BufferedReader` with the `read` method, which reads a single character only.

Once we have finished with the file, we mustn't forget to close it!

```
carStream.close();
```

Finally, we must handle any exceptions that may be thrown by the methods of `FileReader`; first, the constructor throws a `FileNotFound` exception if the file is not found:

```
catch(FileNotFoundException e)
{
        System.out.println("\nNo file was read");
}
```

All the other methods may throw `IOExceptions`:

```
catch(IOException e)
{
        System.out.println("\nThere was a problem reading the file");
}
```

20.6 Reading and writing to binary files

In many ways, it makes little difference whether we store our data in text format or binary format; but it is, of course, important to know the sort of file that we are dealing with when we are reading it. For example, in the previous section you saw that we needed to convert a `String` to a **double** when it came to handling the price of a car. However, it is important for you to be familiar with the ways of handling both types of file, so now we will show you how to read and write data to a binary file using exactly the same example as before.

The only difference in our program will be the `writeList` and `readList` methods. First let's look at the code for the new `writeList` method:

```java
private static void writeList(List<Car> carListIn)
{
    Car tempCar;
    try
    {
        FileOutputStream carFile = new FileOutputStream("Cars.bin");
        DataOutputStream carWriter = new DataOutputStream(carFile);
        for(Car item : carListIn)
        {
            carWriter.writeUTF(item.getRegistration());
            carWriter.writeUTF(item.getMake());
            carWriter.writeDouble(item.getPrice());
        }
        carWriter.close();
    }
    catch(IOException e)
    {
        System.out.println("There was a problem writing the file");
    }
}
```

You can see that the process is similar to the one we used to write a text file, but here the two classes that we are using are `FileOutputStream` and `DataOutputStream` which deal with the low-level and high-level processes respectively. The `DataOutputStream` class provides methods such as `writeDouble`, `writeInt` and `writeChar` for writing all the basic scalar types, as well a method called `writeUTF` for writing strings. UTF stands for *Unicode Transformation Format*, and the method is so-called because it converts the Unicode characters (which are used in Java) to the more commonly used ASCII format when it writes the string to a file.

Before moving on to the `readList` method it is worth reminding ourselves that a file written in this way – that is, a binary file – cannot be read by a text editor. And to prove the point, figure 20.2 shows the result of trying to read such a file in Windows Notepad.

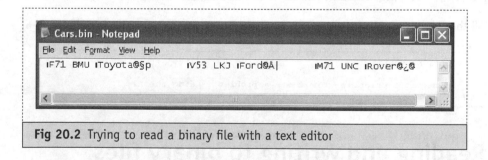

Fig 20.2 Trying to read a binary file with a text editor

So now we can look at the `readList` method:

```java
private static void readList(List<Car> carListIn)
{
    String tempReg;
    String tempMake;
    double tempPrice;
    boolean endOfFile = false;
    try
    {

        FileInputStream carFile = new FileInputStream("Cars.bin");
        DataInputStream carStream = new DataInputStream(carFile);
        while(endOfFile == false)
        {
            try
            {
                tempReg = carStream.readUTF();
                tempMake = carStream.readUTF();
                tempPrice = carStream.readDouble();
                carListIn.add(new Car(tempReg, tempMake, tempPrice));
            }
            catch(EOFException e)
            {
                endOfFile = true;
            }
        }
        carStream.close();
    }
    catch(FileNotFoundException e)
    {
        System.out.println("\nThere are currently no records");
    }

    catch(IOException e)
    {
        System.out.println("There was a problem reading the file");
    }

}
```

You can see that the two classes we use for reading binary files are `FileInputStream` for low-level access and `DataInputStream` for the higher-level functions; they have equivalent methods to the those we saw previously when writing to files.

The most important thing to observe in this method is the way we test whether we have reached the end of the file. In the case of a binary file we can do this by making use of the fact that the `DataInputStream` methods throw `EOFExceptions` when an end of file marker has been detected during a read operation. So all we have to do is declare a **boolean** variable, `endOfFile`, which we initially set to **false**, and we use this as the termination condition in the **while** loop. Then we enclose our read operations in a **try** block, and, when an exception is thrown, `fileNotFound` is set to **true** within the **catch** block, causing the **while** loop to terminate.

20.7 Reading a text file character by character

As you will have realized by now, there are many ways in which we can deal with handling files, and the methods we choose will depend largely on what it is we want to achieve.

In this section we will show you how to read a text file character by character – this is a useful technique if we do not know anything about the structure of the file. The way we have done this is to add a new option to the `FileHandler` class that we developed in section 18.3. We have added a *Display contents* option to the *File* menu. To demonstrate this we created a file called `Poem.txt` with a text editor, and when we selected it and displayed its contents we got the result shown in figure 20.3.

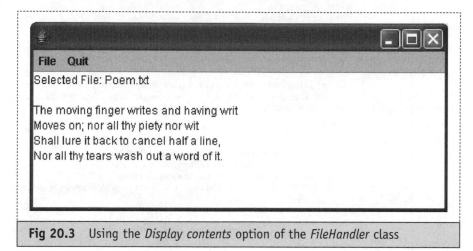

Fig 20.3   Using the *Display contents* option of the *FileHandler* class

The technique that we used to do this was to read each character of the file, display it in the viewing area, then move on to the next character. We have designed the program to stop either when the end of the file has been reached or when a stipulated maximum number of characters has been read. We put this last condition in as a safeguard in case the user should try to display a very large file by mistake.

Here is the code for the event-handler for the new menu option, which we called `displayContentsChoice`:

```
if(e.getSource() == displayContentsChoice)
{
    try
    {
        final int MAX = 1000;
        FileReader testFile = new FileReader(chosenFile.getName());
        BufferedReader textStream = new BufferedReader(testFile);
        int ch; // to hold the integer (Unicode) value of the character
        char c; // to hold the character when type cast from integer
        int counter = 0; // to count the number of characters read so far
        ch = textStream.read(); // read the first character from the file
        c = (char) ch; // type cast from integer to character
        viewArea.append("\n");
        /* continue through the file until either the end of the file is
           reached (in which case -1 is returned) or the maximum number
           of characters stipulated have been read*/
        while( ch != -1 && counter <= MAX)
        {
            counter++; // increment the counter
            viewArea.append("" + c); // display the character
            ch = textStream.read(); // read the next character
            c = (char) ch;
        }
        textStream.close();
        viewArea.append("\n");
    }

    catch(IOException ioe)
    {
        if(chosenFile == null)   // no file selected
        {
            viewArea.append("No file selected\n");
```

```
        }
        else
        {
            viewArea.append("There was a problem reading the file\n");
        }
    }
}
```

The main thing to notice here is that we are using the read method of BufferedReader; this method reads a single character from the file and returns an integer, the Unicode value of the character read. If the character read was the end-of-file marker then it returns −1, making it an easy matter for us to check whether the end of the file has been reached. In the above example, as explained earlier, we stop reading the file if we have reached the end or if more than the maximum number of characters allowed has been read; here we have set that maximum to 1000. You can see that in the above method, after each read operation, we type cast the integer to a character, which we then display in the view area.

20.8 Object serialization

If you are going to be dealing with files that will be accessed only within a Java program, then one of the easiest ways to do this is to make use of two classes called ObjectInputStream and ObjectOutputStream. These classes have methods called, respectively, readObject and writeObject that enable us to read and write whole objects from and to files. The process of converting an object into a stream of data suitable for storage on a disk is called **serialization**.

Any class whose objects are to be read and written using the above methods must implement the interface Serializable. This is a type of interface that we have not actually come across before – it is known as a **marker** and in fact contains no methods. Its purpose is simply to make an "announcement" to anyone using the class; namely that objects of this class can be read and written as whole objects. In designing a class we can, then, choose not to make our class Serializable – we might want to do this for security reasons (for example, to stop whole objects being transportable over the World Wide Web) or to avoid errors in a distributed environment where the code for the class was not present on every machine.

In the case of our Car class, we therefore need to declare it in the following way before we could use it in a program that handles whole objects:

```
public class Car implements Serializable
```

Note that the Serializable interface resides within the java.io package, so this package needs to be imported for us to access it.

Now we can re-write the writeList and readList methods of program 20.2 so that we manipulate whole objects. First the writeList method:

```
private static void writeList(List<Car> carListIn)
{
    try
    {
        FileOutputStream carFile = new FileOutputStream("Cars.obf");
        ObjectOutputStream carStream = new ObjectOutputStream(carFile);

        for(Car item : carListIn)
        {
            carStream.writeObject(item);
        }
```

```
                carStream.close();
        }
        catch(IOException e)
        {
            System.out.println("There was a problem writing the file");
        }
    }
```

You can see how easy this is – you just need one line to save a whole object to a file by using the `writeObject` method of `ObjectOutputStream`.

Now the `readList` method:

```java
private static void readList(List<Car> carListIn)
{
        boolean endOfFile = false;
        Car tempCar;
        try
        {
            // create a FileInputStream object, carFile
            FileInputStream carFile = new FileInputStream("Cars.obf");
            // create an ObjectInputStream object to wrap around carFile
            ObjectInputStream carStream = new ObjectInputStream(carFile);
            // read the first (whole) object with the readObject method
            tempCar =  (Car) carStream.readObject();
            while(endOfFile != true)
            {
                try
                 {
                     carListIn.add(tempCar);
                    // read the next (whole) object
                    tempCar = (Car) carStream.readObject();
                }
                /* use the fact that readObject throws an EOFException to
                    check whether the end of the file has been reached */
                catch(EOFException  e)
                {
                    endOfFile = true;
                }
            }
            carStream.close();
        }

        catch(FileNotFoundException e)
        {
            System.out.println("\nNo file was read");
        }

        catch(ClassNotFoundException e) // thrown by readObject
        {
            System.out.println
                    ("\nTrying to read an object of an unknown class");
        }

        catch(StreamCorruptedException e) // thrown by the constructor
        {
            System.out.println("\nUnreadable file format");
        }

        catch(IOException e)
        {
            System.out.println("There was a problem reading the file");
        }
    }
```

Again you can see how easy this is – a whole object is read with the readObject method.

We should draw your attention to a few of the exception handling routines we have used here – first notice that we have once again made use of the fact that readObject throws an EOFException to check for the end of the file. Second, notice that readObject also throws a ClassNotFoundException, which indicates that the object just read does not correspond to any class known to the program. Finally, the constructor throws a StreamCorruptedException, which indicates that the input stream given to it was not produced by an ObjectOutputStream object – underlining the fact that reading and writing whole objects are complementary techniques that are specific to Java programs.

One final thing to note – if an attribute of a Serializable class is itself an object of another class, then that class too must be Serializable in order for us to be able to read and write whole objects as we have just done. You will probably have noticed that in the case of the Car class, one of its attributes is a String – fortunately the String class does indeed implement the Serializable interface, which is why we had no problem using it in this way in our example.

Before moving on, it is worth noting that all the Java collection classes such as HashMap and ArrayList are themselves Serializable.

20.9 Random access files

All the programs that we have looked at so far in this chapter have made use of serial access. For small applications this will probably be all you need – however, if you were to be writing applications that handled very large data files it would be desirable to use random access methods. Fortunately Java provides us with this facility.

The class that we need is called RandomAccessFile. This enables us to open a file for random access. Random access files can be opened in either read–write mode or in read-only mode; the constructor therefore takes, in addition to the name of the file, an additional String parameter which can be either "rw" or "r", indicating the mode in which the file is to be opened.

In addition to methods similar to those of the DataOutputStream class (such as writeUTF, readDouble and so on), RandomAccessFile has a method called seek. This takes one attribute, of type long, which indicates how many bytes to move the file-pointer before starting a read or write operation.

So now we have the question of how far to move the pointer – we need to be able to calculate the size of each record. If we are dealing only with primitive types, this is an easy matter. These types all take up a fixed amount of storage space, as shown in table 20.1 overleaf.

Table 20.1 Size of the primitive types	
byte	1 byte
short	2 bytes
char	2 bytes
int	4 bytes
long	8 bytes
float	4 bytes
double	8 bytes
boolean	1 bit[3]

The difficulty comes when a record contains Strings, as is commonly the case. The size of a String object varies according to how many characters it contains. What we have to do is to restrict the length of each string to a given amount; let's take the Car class as an example. The data elements of any Car object consist of two Strings and a **double**. We will make the decision that the two String attributes – registration number and make – will be restricted to 10 characters only. Now, any String variable will always take up one byte for each character, plus two extra bytes (at the beginning) to hold an integer representing the length of the String. So now we can calculate the maximum amount of storage space we need for a car as follows:

```
registration (String)    12 bytes
make (String)            12 bytes
price (double)            8 bytes
TOTAL                    32 bytes
```

This still leaves us with one problem – what if one of the String attributes entered is actually *less* than 10? The best way to deal with this is to pad the string out with spaces so that it always contains *exactly* 10 characters. This means that the size of every Car object will always be exactly 32 bytes – you will see how we have done this when you study program 20.3. This program uses a rather different approach to the one we have used so far in this chapter. Two options (as well as a *Quit* option) are provided. The first, the option to add a car, simply adds the car to the end of the file. The second, to display the details of a car, asks the user for the position of the car in the file then reads this record directly from the file. You can see that there is now no need for a List in which to store the cars.

Study the program carefully – then we will discuss it.

---

[3] Allow for 1 byte when calculating storage space.

Program 20.3

```java
import java.io.*;

public class RandomFileTester
{
  private static final int CAR_SIZE = 32; // each record will be 32 bytes
  public static void main(String[] args)
  {
    char choice;
    do
    {
        System.out.println("\nRandom File Tester");
        System.out.println("1. Add a car");
        System.out.println("2. Display a car");
        System.out.println("3. Quit\n");
        choice = EasyScanner.nextChar();
        System.out.println();
        switch(choice)
        {
            case '1' : addCar();
                       break;
            case '2' : displayCar();
                       break;
            case '3' : break;
            default  : System.out.print("\nChoose 1 - 3 only please\n ");
        }
    }while(choice != '3');
  }

  private static void addCar()
  {
    String tempReg;
    String tempMake;
    double tempPrice;
    System.out.print("Please enter the registration number: ");
    tempReg = EasyScanner.nextString();
    //limit the registration number to 10 characters
    if(tempReg.length() > 10)
    {
        System.out.print("Ten characters only - please re-enter: ");
        tempReg = EasyScanner.nextString();
    }
    // pad the string with spaces to make it exactly 10 characters long
    for(int i = tempReg.length() + 1 ; i <= 10 ; i++)
    {
        tempReg = tempReg.concat(" ");
    }

    // get the make of the car from the user
    System.out.print("Please enter the make: ");
    tempMake = EasyScanner.nextString();

    // limit the make number to 10 characters
    if(tempMake.length() > 10)
    {
        System.out.print("Ten characters only - please re-enter: ");
        tempMake = EasyScanner.nextString();
    }
     // pad the string with spaces to make it exactly 10 characters long
    for(int i = tempMake.length() + 1; i <= 10; i++)
    {
        tempMake = tempMake.concat(" ");
    }

    // get the price of the car from the user
    System.out.print("Please enter the price: ");
    tempPrice = EasyScanner.nextDouble();
```

```java
        // write the record to the file
        writeRecord(new Car(tempReg, tempMake, tempPrice));
    }

    private static void displayCar()
    {
        int pos;
        // get the position of the item to be read from the user
        System.out.print("Enter the car's position in the list: ");
        pos = EasyScanner.nextInt(); // read the record requested from file
        Car tempCar = readRecord(pos);
        if(tempCar != null)
        {
            System.out.println(tempCar.getRegistration().trim()
                                    + " "
                                    + tempCar.getMake().trim()
                                    + " "
                                    + tempCar.getPrice());
        }
        else
        {
            System.out.println("Invalid postion") ;
        }
    }

    private static void writeRecord(Car tempCar)
    {
      try
      {
          // open a RandomAccessFile in read-write mode
          RandomAccessFile carFile = new RandomAccessFile("Cars.rand", "rw");
          // move the pointer to the end of the file
          carFile.seek(carFile.length());
          // write the three fields of the record to the file
          carFile.writeUTF(tempCar.getRegistration());
          carFile.writeUTF(tempCar.getMake());
          carFile.writeDouble(tempCar.getPrice());
          // close the file
          carFile.close();
      }
      catch(IOException e)
      {
          System.out.println("There was a problem writing the file");
      }
    }

    private static Car readRecord(int pos)
    {
        String tempReg;
        String tempMake;
        double tempPrice;
        Car tempCar = null; /* a null value will be returned if there was a
                               problem reading the record */
        try
        {
            // open a RandomAccessFile in read-only mode
            RandomAccessFile carFile = new RandomAccessFile("Cars.rand","r");
            // move the pointer to the start of the required record
            carFile.seek((pos-1) * CAR_SIZE);
            // read the three fields of the record from the file
            tempReg = carFile.readUTF();
            tempMake = carFile.readUTF();
            tempPrice = carFile.readDouble();
            // close the file
            carFile.close();
            // use the data just read to create a new Car object
            tempCar = new Car(tempReg, tempMake, tempPrice);
        }
        catch(FileNotFoundException e)
        {
```

```
            System.out.println("\nNo file was read");
        }

        catch(IOException e)
        {
            System.out.println("There was a problem reading the file");
        }
        // return the record that was read
        return tempCar;
    }
}
```

You can see that in the addCar method we have called writeRecord with a Car object as a parameter. Let's take a closer look at the writeRecord method. First the line to open the file in read-write mode:

```
RandomAccessFile carFile = new RandomAccessFile("Cars.rand", "rw");
```

Now the instruction to move the file pointer:

```
carFile.seek(carFile.length());
```

You can see how we use the seek method to move the pointer a specific number of bytes; here the correct number of bytes is the size of the file (as we want to write the new record at the end of the file), so we use the length method of RandomAccessFile to determine this number.

Now we can move on to look at the readRecord method. You can see that this is called from within the displayCar method, with an integer parameter, representing the position of the required record in the file.

The file is opened in read-only mode:

```
RandomAccessFile carFile = new RandomAccessFile("Cars.rand","r");
```

Then the seek method of RandomAccessFile is invoked as follows:

```
carFile.seek((pos-1) * CAR_SIZE);
```

You can see that the number of bytes through which to move the pointer has been calculated by multiplying the size of the record by one less than the position. This is because in order to read the first record we don't move the pointer at all; in order to read the second record we must move it 1×32 bytes; for the third record 2×32 bytes; and so on.

The final thing to note about program 20.3 is that in the displayCar method we have used the trim method of String to get rid of the extra spaces that we used to pad out the first two fields of the record.

Here is a test run from the program (starting off with an empty file):

Random File Tester
1. Add a car
2. View a car
3. Quit

1

Please enter the registration number: **R54 HJK**
Please enter the make: **Vauxhall**
Please enter the price: **7000**

Random File Tester
1. Add a car
2. View a car
3. Quit

1

Please enter the registration number: **T87 EFU**
Please enter the make: **Nissan**
Please enter the price: **9000**

Random File Tester
1. Add a car
2. View a car
3. Quit

2

Enter the car's position in the list: **2**
T87 EFU Nissan 9000.0

Self-test questions

1 Explain the principles of *input* and *output* and identify different input and output devices.

2 What is meant by the term *input/output stream?*

3 Distinguish between *text*, *binary* and *object encoding* of data.

4 What is the difference between *serial access* files and *random access* files?

5 Explain the purpose of the `Serializable` interface.

6 Calculate the number of bytes required to store an object of a class, the attributes of which are declared as follows:

```
private int x;
private char c;
private String s;
```

You can assume that the `String` attribute will always consists of exactly 20 characters.

Programming exercises

You will need to have access to the Car *class, the source code for which is available on the CD – or you can simply copy it from this chapter. The source code for programs 20.2 and 20.3 is also on the CD.*

1 Run program 20.2 then adapt it so that it handles binary files, as described in section 20.6.

2 Add the *Display Contents* option to the `FileHandler` class from chapter 18, as described in section 20.7.

3 Run program 20.3.

4 Adapt program 20.2 so that it uses object encoding, as explained in section 20.8 (don't forget that the `Car` class must implement the `Serializable` interface).

5 Adapt the `Library` application of chapter 17 so that it keeps permanent records.

CHAPTER: 21

Advanced Case Study

Objectives:

By the end of this chapter you should be able to:

- *specify system requirements by developing a **use case model**;*
- *annotate a **composition** association on a UML diagram;*
- *specify **enumerated types** in UML and implement them in Java;*
- *develop test cases from **behaviour specifications** found in the use case model;*
- *use the* JTabbedPane *class to create an attractive user interface;*
- *add **tool tips** to Swing components;*
- *add **short cut keys** to Swing menu items.*

21.1 Introduction

You have covered quite a few advanced topics now in this second semester. In this chapter we are going to take stock of what you have learnt by developing an application that draws upon all these topics. We will make use of Java's package notation for bundling together related classes; we will implement interfaces; we will catch and throw exceptions; we will make use of the collection classes in the `java.util` package and we will store objects to file. We will also make use of many Swing components to develop an attractive graphical interface.

As with the case study we presented to you in the first semester, we will discuss the development of this application from the initial stage of requirements analysis, through to final implementation and testing stages. Along the way we will look at a few new concepts.

21.2 System overview

The application that we will develop will keep track of planes using a particular airport. So as not to over-complicate things, we will make a few assumptions:

> there will be no concept of *gates* for arrival and departure – passengers will be met at a runway on arrival and be sent to a runway on departure;

> planes entering airport airspace and requesting to land are either called in to land on a free runway, or are told to join a queue of circling planes until a runway becomes available;

> once a plane departs from the airport it is removed from the system.

21.3 Requirements analysis and specification

Many techniques are used to uncover system requirements. Amongst others, these include interviewing the client, sending out questionnaires to the client, reviewing any documentation if a current system already exists and observing people carrying out their work. A common way to document these requirements in UML is to develop a **use case model**. A use case model consists of **use case diagrams** and **behaviour specifications**.

A *use case diagram* is a simple way of recording the *roles* of different users within a system and the services that they require the system to deliver. The users (people or other systems) of a system are referred to as **actors** in use case diagrams and are drawn as simple stick characters. The roles these actors play in the system are used to annotate the stick character. The services they require are the so-called *use cases*. For example, in an ATM application an actor may be a customer and one of the use cases (services) required would be to withdraw cash. A very simple use case diagram for our application is given in figure 21.1.

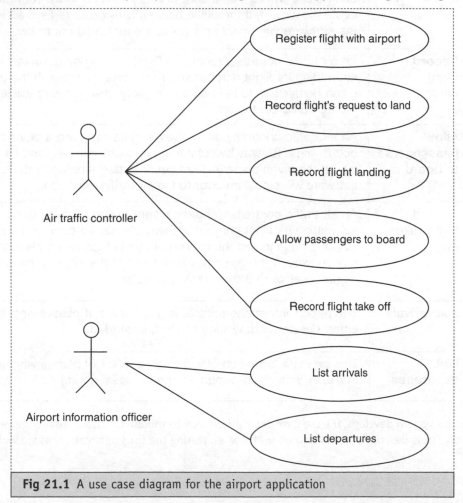

Fig 21.1 A use case diagram for the airport application

Figure 21.1 depicts the actors in this application (air traffic controllers and information officers) and the services these actors require (registering a flight, listing arrivals and so on). Once a list of use cases has been identified, *behaviour specifications* are used to record their required functionality. A simple way of recording behaviour specifications is to give a simple textual description for each use case. Table 21.1 contains behaviour specifications for each use case given in figure 21.1. Note that the descriptions are always given from the users' point of view.

Table 21.1 Behaviour specifications for the airport application	
Register flight with airport	An air traffic controller registers an incoming flight with the airport by submitting its unique flight number, and its city of origin. If the flight number is already registered by the airport, the software will signal an error to the air traffic controller.
Record flight's request to land	An air traffic controller records an incoming flight entering airport airspace, and requesting to land, by submitting its flight number. As long as the plane has previously registered with the airport, the air traffic controller is given an unoccupied runway number on which the plane will have permission to land. If all runways are occupied however, this permission is denied and the air traffic controller is informed to instruct the plane to circle the airport. If the plane has not previously registered with the airport, the software will signal an error to the air traffic controller.
Record flight landing	An air traffic controller records a flight landing on a runway at the airport by submitting its flight number and the runway number. If the plane was not given permission to land on that runway, the software will signal an error to the air traffic controller.
Allow passengers to board	An air traffic controller allows passengers to board a plane currently occupying a runway by submitting its flight number, and its destination city. If the given plane has not yet recorded landing at the airport, the software will signal an error to the air traffic controller.
Record flight take off	An air traffic controller records a flight taking off from the airport by submitting its flight number. If there are planes circling the airport, the first plane to have joined the circling queue is then given permission to land on that runway. If the given plane was not at the airport, the software will signal an error to the air traffic controller.
List arrivals	The airport information officer is given a list of planes whose status is either due-to-land, waiting-to-land, or landed.
List departures	The airport information officer is given a list of planes whose status is currently waiting-to-depart (taking on passengers).

As the system develops, the use case descriptions may be modified as detailed requirements become uncovered. These descriptions will also be useful when testing the final application, as we will see later.

21.4 **Design**

The detailed design for this application is now presented in figure 21.2. It introduces some new UML notation. Have a look at it and then we will discuss it.

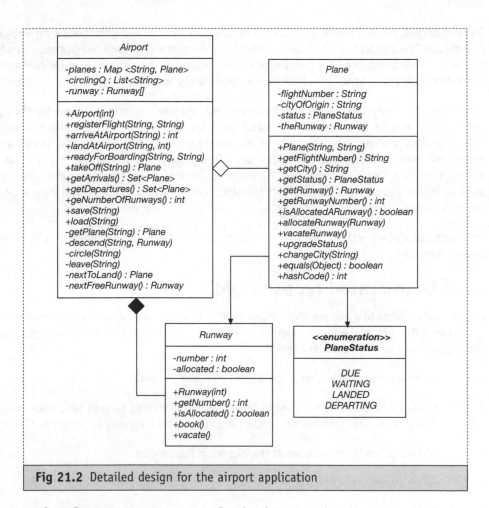

Fig 21.2 Detailed design for the airport application

As you can see from figure 21.2, an `Airport` class has been introduced to represent the functionality of the system as a whole. UML allows us to identify those parts of a class that should have **private** scope and those that should have **public** scope by using a minus sign (−) to indicate **private** scope and a plus sign (+) to indicate **public** scope. You can see that the **public** methods of the `Airport` class correspond closely to the use cases identified during requirements analysis and specification. The **private** methods of the `Airport` class are there simply to help implement the functionality of the class.

The requirements made clear that there would be *many* planes to process in this system. Since the airport exists regardless of the number of planes at the airport, the relationship between the `Airport` and `Plane` class is one of containment, as indicated with a hollow diamond. It made sense to consider the collection classes in the `java.util` package at this point. As we record planes in the system, and process these planes, we will always be using a plane's flight number as a way of identifying an individual plane. A `Map` is the obvious collection to choose here, with flight numbers the *keys* of the `Map` and the planes associated with these flight numbers as *values* of the `Map`.

The one drawback with a Map, however, is that it is not ordered on input. When considering which plane in a circling queue of planes to land, ordering is important, as the first to join the queue should be the first to land. So we have also introduced a List to hold the flight numbers of circling planes. Notice that the contained Plane type requires equals and hashCode methods to work effectively with these collection classes.

The airport will also consist of a number of runways. In fact the airport cannot exist without this collection of runways. The airport is said to be *composed of* a number of runways as opposed to *containing* a number of planes. Notice that the UML notation for **composition** is the same as that for containment, except that the diamond is filled rather than hollow. We use an array to hold this collection of Runway objects.

Turning to the contained classes, the Runway class provides methods to allow for the runway number to be retrieved, and for a runway to be booked and vacated. The Plane class also has access to a Runway object, to allow a plane to be able to book and vacate runways. You can see that as well as each plane being associated with a runway, the plane also has a flight number, a city and a status associated with it. The arrows from the Plane class to the PlaneStatus and Runway classes indicate the direction of the association. In this case a Plane object can send messages to a Runway and PlaneStatus object, but not vice versa.

The status of a plane is described in the PlaneStatus diagram. This diagram is the UML notation for an *enumerated type*.

21.4.1 Enumerated types in UML

A type that consists of a few possible values, each with a meaningful name, is referred to as an **enumerated type**. The status of a plane is one example of an enumerated type. This status changes depending upon the plane's progress to and from the airport:

> when a plane registers with the airport, it is *due* to land;

> when a plane arrives in the airport's airspace, it is *waiting* to land (this plane may be told to come in and land, or it may have to circle the airport until a runway becomes available);

> when a plane touches down at the airport, it has *landed*;

> when a plane starts boarding new passengers, it is *departing* the airport.

You can see from the design of the system that such a type is captured in UML by marking this type with <<enumeration>> as follows:

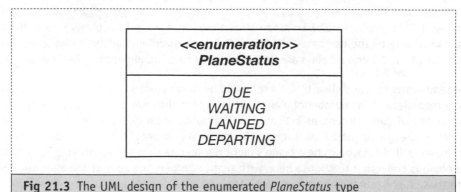

Fig 21.3 The UML design of the enumerated *PlaneStatus* type

We need to mark this UML diagram with <<enumeration>> so that it is not confused with a normal UML class diagram. With a normal UML class diagram, attributes and methods are listed in the lower portion. With an enumerated type diagram, the possible values of this type are given in the lower portion of the diagram, with each value being given a meaningful name. An attribute that is allocated a `PlaneStatus` type, such as `status` in the `Plane` class, can have any one of these values.

This completes our design analysis, so now let's turn our attention to the Java implementation.

21.5 Implementation

Since we are developing an application involving several classes, it makes sense to bundle these classes together into a single package. We will call this package `airportSys`. This means that all our classes will begin with the following **package** statement:

```
package airportSys;
```

This will allow our entire suite of classes to be imported into another application with the following **import** statement:

```
import airportSys.*;
```

It is a good idea to hide implementation level exceptions (such as `ArrayIndexOutOfBounds Exception`) from users of the application and, instead, always throw some general application exception. In order to be able to do this, we define our own general `AirportException` class.

The *AirportException* class

```
package airportSys; // add to package

/**
 * Application Specific Exception
 *
 * @author Charatan and Kans
 * @version 1st September 2005
 */
public class AirportException extends Exception
{
  /**
   * Default Constructor
   */
  public AirportException ()
  {
    super("Error: Airport System Violation");
  }

  /**
   * Constructor that accepts an error message
   */
  public AirportException (String msg)
  {
    super(msg);
  }
}
```

Notice that, as with all the classes we shall develop here, we have added `Javadoc` comments into the class definition. Now let's consider the remaining classes. First of all, we will look at the implementation of the enumerated `PlaneStatus` type.

21.5.1 Implementing enumerated types in Java

Prior to Java 5.0, there was no enumerated type mechanism in the language. Very often developers used a class containing integer constants. Here is an example of how this might have been done for `PlaneStatus`:

```
// this is the old way of implementing PlaneStatus
public class PlaneStatus
{
        // declare integer constants with appropriate names
        public static final int DUE = 0;
        public static final int WAITING = 1;
        public static final int LANDED = 2;
        public static final int DEPARTING = 3;
}
```

However, with this approach it is not possible to declare variables of type `PlaneStatus`. Instead integers have to be used. For example:

```
int status; // this variable is of type integer
status = PlaneStatus.DUE; // class constants can be used to assign values
```

Another problem with this approach is that there is nothing to stop us assigning *any* **int** value to this variable:

```
// this would be ok but makes no sense!
status = 100;
```

Also, when this variable is displayed on the screen the integer value would be displayed, instead of a meaningful name:

```
// assign a value to the variable
status = PlaneStatus.DEPARTING;
// this would display the value 3
System.out.println(status);
```

There are ways to get around these restrictions, but they are messy to implement in Java. Fortunately, a simple enumerated type mechanism has now been added to Java 5.0.

In order to define an enumerated type such as `PlaneStatus`, the **enum** keyword has been introduced. The `PlaneStatus` type can now be implemented simply as follows:

```
// this is the new way of defining enumerated types in Java
public enum PlaneStatus
{
        DUE, WAITING, LANDED, DEPARTING
}
```

You can see how easy it is to define an enumerated type. When defining such a type, do not use the **class** keyword, use the **enum** keyword instead. The different values for this type are then given within the braces, separated by commas.

These values create class constants, with the given names, as before. However, the type of each class constant is `PlaneStatus` now, not **int**, and variables can now be declared of this type. For example, here we declare a variable of the `PlaneStatus` type and assign it one of these class constant values:

```
PlaneStatus status; // declare PlaneStatus variable
status = PlaneStatus.DEPARTING; // assign variable a class constant
```

The variable `status` can take no other values, apart from those defined in the enumerated `PlaneStatus` type. Each enumerated type you define will also have an appropriate `toString` method generated for it, so values can be displayed on the screen:

```
System.out.println("Value = " + status);
```

Assuming we created this variable as above, this would display the following:

Value = DEPARTING

As well as a `toString` method, a few other methods are generated for you as well, and the **switch** statement can be used in conjunction with enumerated type variables. We will see examples of these features when we look at the code for the other classes in this application.

Of course, we must remember to add this `PlaneStatus` type into our `airportSys` package:

The PlaneStatus type

```
package airportSys; // add to package

/**
 * Enumerated plane status type.
 *
 * @author Charatan and Kans
 * @version 1st September 2005
 */
public enum PlaneStatus
{
        DUE, WAITING, LANDED, DEPARTING
}
```

21.5.2 The *Runway* class

Here is the code for the Runway class, take a look at it and then we will discuss it.

The *Runway* class

```java
package airportSys; // add class to package
import java.io.*;  // for Serializable interface

/**
 * This class is used to store details of a single runway.
 *
 * @author Charatan and Kans
 * @version 1st September 2005
 */
public class Runway implements Serializable
{
  // attributes
  private int number;
  private boolean allocated;

  /**
   * Constructor sets the runway number
   * @param      numberIn          Used to set the runway number
   * @throws     AirportException     When the runway number is less than 1
   */
  public Runway (int numberIn) throws AirportException
  {
    if (numberIn <1)
    {
      throw new AirportException ("invalid runway number "+numberIn);
    }
    number = numberIn;
    allocated = false; // runway vacant intially
  }

  /**
   * Returns the runway number
   */
  public int getNumber()
  {
    return number;
  }

  /**
   * Checks if the runway has been allocated
   * @return    Returns true if the runway has been allocated
   *            and false otherwise
   */
  public boolean isAllocated()
  {
    return allocated;
  }

  /**
   * Records the runway as being booked
   */
  public void book()
  {
    allocated = true;
  }

  /**
   * Records the runway as being vacant
   */
  public void vacate()
  {
    allocated = false;
  }

}
```

There is not much that needs to be said about this class. As we may wish to save and load objects from our system, we have to remember to indicate that this class is `Serializable`.

```
public class Runway implements Serializable
```

Notice that we have defined this as a **public** class so that it is accessible outside of the package. We did this as a runway is a generally useful concept in many applications; declaring this class **public** allows it to be re-used outside of the `airportSys` package. In fact, we have declared most of our classes **public** for this reason.

21.5.3 The *Plane* class

Here is the code for the `Plane` class. Have a close look at it and then we will discuss it.

The *Plane* class

```java
package airportSys;
import java.io.*;

/**
 * This class stores the details of a single plane
 *
 * @author Charatan and Kans
 * @version 2nd September 2005
 */
public class Plane implements Serializable
{

  // attributes
  private String flightNumber;
  private String city;
  private PlaneStatus status;
  private Runway theRunway;


  /**
   * Constructor sets initial flight details of plane
   * @param    flightIn       The plane's flight number
   * @param    cityOfOrigin   The plane's city of origin
   */
  public Plane(String flightIn, String cityOfOrigin)
  {
    flightNumber = flightIn;
    city = cityOfOrigin;
    status = PlaneStatus.DUE; // initial plane status set to DUE
    theRunway = null; // indicates no runway allocated
  }

  /**
   * Returns the plane's flight number
   */
  public String getFlightNumber()
  {
    return flightNumber;
  }
  /**
   * Returns the city asscoiated with the flight
   */
  public String getCity()
  {
    return city;
  }

  /**
   * Returns the current status of the plane
```

```java
     */
    public PlaneStatus getStatus()
    {
      return   status;
    }

    /**
     * Returns the runway allocated to this plane
     * or null if no runway allocated
     */
    public Runway getRunway()
    {
      return   theRunway;
    }

    /**
     * Returns the runway number allocated to this plane
     * @throws     AirportException if no runway allocated
     */
    public int getRunwayNumber()throws AirportException
    {
      if (theRunway == null)
      {
        throw new AirportException
                  ("flight "+flightNumber+" has not been allocated a runway");
      }
      return theRunway.getNumber();
    }

    /**
     * Checks if the plane is allocated a runway
     * @return     Returns true if the plane has been allocated a runway
     *             and false otherwise
     */
    public boolean isAllocatedARunway()
    {
      return theRunway != null;
    }

    /**
     * Allocates the given runway to the plane
     * @throws     AirportException if runway parameter is null or
     *             runway already allocated
     */
    public void allocateRunway(Runway runwayIn)throws AirportException
    {
      if (runwayIn == null) // check runway has been sent
      {
        throw new AirportException ("no runway to allocate");
      }
      if (runwayIn.isAllocated()) // check if runway already allocated
      {
          throw new AirportException ("runway already allocate");
      }
      theRunway = runwayIn;
      theRunway.book();
    }

    /**
     * De-allocates the current runway
     * @throws     AirportException if no runway allocated
     */
    public void vacateRunway() throws AirportException
    {
      if (theRunway == null)
      {
        throw new AirportException ("no runway allocated");
      }
      theRunway.vacate();
    }
```

```
/**
 * Upgrades the status of the plane.
 * @throws AirportException when trying to upgrade a DEPARTING status
 */
public void upgradeStatus() throws AirportException
{
  switch(status)
  {
    case DUE: status = PlaneStatus.WAITING; break;
    case WAITING: status = PlaneStatus.LANDED; break;
    case LANDED: status = PlaneStatus.DEPARTING; break;
    case DEPARTING: throw new AirportException
                         ("Cannot upgrade DEPARTING status");
  }
}

/**
 * Changes the city associated with the plane
 */
public void changeCity (String destination)
{
  city = destination;
}

/**
 * Checks whether the plane is equal to the given object
 */
public boolean equals(Object objIn)
{
    if (objIn!=null)
    {
            Plane p = (Plane)objIn;
            return p.flightNumber.equals(flightNumber);
    }
    else
    {
            return false;
    }
}

/**
 * Returns a hashcode value
 */
public int hashCode()
{
    return flightNumber.hashCode();
}
}
```

Again, most of the points we raised with the Runway class are relevant to this Plane class. It needs to be Serializable and it is declared **public**.

Since Plane objects will be used in collection classes we have provided this class with an equals and a hashCode method. You can see that both of these methods make use of the plane's flight number.

In addition you should look at the way in which we dealt with the status attribute. During class design we declared this attribute to be of the enumerated PlaneStatus type, so it has been implemented as follows:

```
private PlaneStatus status;
```

We can then assign this attribute values from the enumerated `PlaneStatus` type. For example, in the constructor, we initialize the status of a plane to `DUE`:

```
public Plane(String flightNumberIn, String cityOfOrigin)
{
    flightNumber = flightNumberIn;
    city = cityOfOrigin;
    status = PlaneStatus.DUE;
    theRunway = null;
}
```

The `getStatus` method returns the value of the `status` attribute, so the appropriate return type is `PlaneStatus`:

```
public PlaneStatus getStatus()
{
  return  status;
}
```

The `upgradeStatus` method is interesting as it demonstrates how the **switch** statement can be used with enumerated type variables such as `status`:

```
public void upgradeStatus() throws AirportException
{
  switch(status) // this is an enumerated type variable
  {
    // 'case' statements can check the different enumerated values
    case DUE: status = PlaneStatus.WAITING; break;
    case WAITING: status = PlaneStatus.LANDED; break;
    case LANDED: status = PlaneStatus.DEPARTING; break;
    case DEPARTING: throw new AirportException
                    ("Cannot upgrade DEPARTING status");
  }
}
```

Here we are upgrading the status of a plane as it makes its way to, and eventually from, the airport. Notice that the value of the `status` attribute is checked in the **case** statements, but this value is *not* appended onto the `PlaneStatus` class name. For example:

```
// just use a status name here
case DUE: status = PlaneStatus.WAITING; break;
```

However, in all other circumstances, such as assigning to the `status` attribute, the enumerated value *does* have to be appended onto the `PlaneStatus` class name:

```
// use class + status name here
case DUE: status = PlaneStatus.WAITING; break;
```

You can see that we should not be upgrading the status of a plane if its current status is `DEPARTING`, so an exception is thrown in this case:

```
case DEPARTING: throw new AirportException
                    ("Cannot upgrade DEPARTING status");
```

Before we leave this class, also notice that by adding a runway attribute, `theRunway`, into the `Plane` class we can send messages to (access methods of) a `Runway` object, for example:

```
public void allocateRunway(Runway runwayIn)throws AirportException
{
    // some code here
    theRunway.book(); // 'book' is a 'Runway' method
}
```

21.5.4 The *Airport* class

The `Airport` class encapsulates the functionality of the system. It does not include the interface to the application. As we have done throughout this book, the interface of an application is kept separate from its functionality. That way, we can modify the way we choose to implement the functionality without needing to modify the interface, and vice versa. Examine it closely, being sure to read the comments, and then we will discuss it.

The *Airport* class

```java
package airportSys;
import java.util.*;
import java.io.*; // for IOException

/**
 * Class to provide the functionality of the airport system
 *
 * @author Charatan and Kans
 * @version 4th September 2005
 */
public class Airport
{
    // attributes
    private Map<String, Plane> planes;  // registered planes
    private List<String> circlingQ; // flight numbers of circling planes
    private Runway []runway; // runways allocated to the airport


    /**
     * Constructor creates an empty collection of planes,
     * and allocates runways to the airport
     * @param     numIn The number of runways
     * @throws    AirportException with a negative runway number
     */
    public Airport (int numIn) throws AirportException
    {
        try
        {
            // intialize runways
            runway = new Runway [numIn];
            for (int i = 0; i<numIn; i++)
            {
                runway[i] = new Runway (i+1);
            }
            // no planes allocated to airport
            planes = new HashMap<String, Plane>();
            circlingQ = new ArrayList<String>();
        }
        catch (Exception e)
        {
            throw new AirportException("Invalid Runway Number");
        }
    }

    /**
     * Registers a plane with the airport
     * @param     flightIn The plane's flight number
     * @param     cityOfOrigin The plane's city of origin
     * @throws    AirportException if flight number already registered.
     */
    public void registerFlight (String flightIn, String cityOfOrigin)
                                        throws AirportException
    {
        if (planes.containsKey(flightIn))
        {
            throw new AirportException
                        ("flight "+flightIn+" already registered");
```

```
        }
        Plane newPlane = new Plane (flightIn, cityOfOrigin);
        planes.put(flightIn, newPlane);
    }

    /**
     * Records a plane arriving at the airport
     * @param    flightIn The plane's flight number
     * @throws   AirportException if plane not previously registered
     *              or if plane already arrived at airport
     */
    public int arriveAtAirport (String flightIn) throws AirportException
    {
        Runway vacantRunway = nextFreeRunway(); // get next free runway
        if (vacantRunway != null) // check if runway available
        {
            descend(flightIn, vacantRunway); // allow plane to descend on runway
            return vacantRunway.getNumber(); // return booked runway number
        }
        else // no runway available
        {
            circle(flightIn); // plane must join circling queue
            return 0; // indicates no runway available to land
        }
    }


    /**
     * Records a plane landing on a runway
     * @param    flightIn The plane's flight number
     * @param    runwayNumberIn The runway number the plane is landing on
     * @throws   AirportException if plane not previously registered
     *              or if the runway is not allocated to this plane
     *              or if plane has not yet signalled its arrival at the airport
     *              or if plane is already recorded as having landed.
     */
    public void landAtAirport (String flightIn, int runwayNumberIn)
                                                throws AirportException
    {
      Plane thisPlane = getPlane(flightIn); // throws exception if invalid
      if (thisPlane.getRunwayNumber()!= runwayNumberIn)
      {
        throw new AirportException
                    ("flight "+flightIn+" should not be on this runway");
      }
      if (thisPlane.getStatus() == PlaneStatus.DUE)
      {
        throw new AirportException
                    ("flight "+flightIn+" not signalled its arrival");
      }
      if (thisPlane.getStatus().compareTo(PlaneStatus.WAITING)>0)
      {
        throw new AirportException ("flight "+flightIn+" already landed");
      }
      thisPlane.upgradeStatus(); // upgrade status from WAITING to LANDED
    }

    /**
     * Records a plane boarding for take off
     * @param    flightIn The plane's flight number
     * @param    destination The city of destination
     * @throws   AirportException if plane not previously registered
     *              or if plane not yet recorded as landed
     *              or if plane already recorded as ready for take off
     */
    public void readyForBoarding(String flightIn, String destination)
                                                throws AirportException
    {
      Plane thisPlane = getPlane(flightIn); // throws exception if invalid
      if (thisPlane.getStatus().compareTo(PlaneStatus.LANDED)<0)
```

```
      {
          throw new AirportException ("flight "+flightIn+" not landed");
      }
      if (thisPlane.getStatus() == PlaneStatus.DEPARTING)
      {
          throw new AirportException
                        ("flight "+flightIn+" already registered to depart");
      }
      thisPlane.upgradeStatus(); // upgrade status from LANDED to DEPARTING
      thisPlane.changeCity(destination); // change city to destination city
  }


  /**
   * Records a plane taking off from the aiprort
   * @param    flightIn The plane's flight number
   * @throws   AirportException if plane not previously registered
   *           or if plane not yet recorded as landed
   *           or if the plane not previously recorded as ready for take off
   */
  public Plane takeOff (String flightIn) throws AirportException
  {
      leave(flightIn); // remove from plane register
      Plane nextFlight = nextToLand(); // return next circling plane to land
      if (nextFlight != null) // check circling flight exists
      {
          // allocate runway to circling plane
          Runway vacantRunway = nextFreeRunway();
          descend(nextFlight.getFlightNumber(), vacantRunway);
          return nextFlight;
      }
      else // no circling planes
      {
          return null;
      }
  }


  /**
   * Returns the set of planes due for arrival
   */
  public Set<Plane> getArrivals()
  {
      Set<Plane> planesOut = new HashSet<Plane>(); // create empty set
      Set<String> items = planes.keySet(); // get all flight numbers
      for(String thisFlight: items) // check status of all
      {
          Plane thisPlane = planes.get(thisFlight);
          if (thisPlane.getStatus() != PlaneStatus.DEPARTING)
          {
              planesOut.add(thisPlane); // add to set
          }
      }
      return planesOut;
  }


  /**
   * Returns the set of planes due for departure
   */
  public Set<Plane> getDepartures()
  {
      Set<Plane> planesOut = new HashSet<Plane>(); // create empty set
      Set<String> items = planes.keySet();
      for(String thisFlight: items)
      {
          Plane thisPlane = planes.get(thisFlight);
          if (thisPlane.getStatus() == PlaneStatus.DEPARTING)
          {
              planesOut.add(thisPlane); // add to set
          }
      }
      return planesOut;
```

```
   }

   /**
    * Returns the number of runways
    */
   public int getNumberOfRunways()
   {
       return runway.length;
   }


   /**
    * Saves airport object to file
    * @param    fileIn The name of the file
    * @throws   IOException if problems with opening and saving to given file
    */
   public void save(String fileIn)throws IOException
   {
       FileOutputStream fileOut = new FileOutputStream(fileIn);
       ObjectOutputStream objOut = new ObjectOutputStream (fileOut);
       objOut.writeObject(planes);
       objOut.writeObject(circlingQ);
       objOut.writeObject(runway);
       objOut.close();
   }


   /**
    * Loads airport object from file
    * @param    fileName The name of the file
    * @throws   IOException if problems with opening and loading given file
    * @throws   ClassNotFoundException if objects in file not of right type
    */
   public void load (String fileName)
                       throws IOException, ClassNotFoundException
   {
       FileInputStream fileInput = new FileInputStream(fileName);
       ObjectInputStream objInput = new ObjectInputStream (fileInput);
       planes = (Map<String, Plane>) objInput.readObject();
       circlingQ = (List<String>) objInput.readObject();
       runway = (Runway[])objInput.readObject();
       objInput.close();
   }

   // helper methods

   /**
    *   Returns next free runway or null if no free runway
    */
   private Runway nextFreeRunway()
   {
       for (int i = 0; i < runway.length; i++)
       {
         if (!runway[i].isAllocated())
         {
           return runway[i];
         }
       }
       return null;
   }

   /**
    * Returns the registered plane with the given flight number
    * @throws   AirportException if flight number not yet registered.
    */
   private Plane getPlane(String flightIn) throws AirportException
   {
       if (!planes.containsKey(flightIn))
       {
         throw new AirportException
                         ("flight "+flightIn+" has not yet registered");
```

```
        }
        return planes.get(flightIn);
    }

/**
 * Records a plane descending on a runway
 * @param    flightIn The plane's flight number
 * @param    runwayIn The runway the plane will be landing on
 * @throws   AirportException if plane not previously registered
 *                or if plane already arrived at airport
 *                or if plane already allocated a runway
 */
private void descend (String flightIn, Runway runwayIn)
                                        throws AirportException
{
  Plane thisPlane = getPlane(flightIn); // throws exception if invalid
  if (thisPlane.getStatus().compareTo(PlaneStatus.WAITING) > 0)
  {
      throw new AirportException ("flight "+flightIn+
          " already at airport has status of "
                                  +thisPlane.getStatusName());
  }
  if (thisPlane.isAllocatedARunway())
  {
    throw new AirportException ("flight "+flightIn+
      " has already been allocated runway "+thisPlane.getRunwayNumber());
  }
  thisPlane.allocateRunway(runwayIn);
  if (thisPlane.getStatus() == PlaneStatus.DUE)
  {
      thisPlane.upgradeStatus();// upgrade status from DUE to WAITING
  }
}

/**
 * Records a plane joining the planes circling the airport
 * @param    flightIn The plane's flight number
 * @throws   AirportException if plane not previously registered
 *                or if plane already arrived
 */
private void circle (String flightIn) throws AirportException
{
  Plane thisPlane = getPlane(flightIn); // throws exception if invalid
  if (thisPlane.getStatus() != PlaneStatus.DUE)
  {
    throw new AirportException ("flight "+flightIn+" already at airport");
  }
  thisPlane.upgradeStatus(); // updraged status from DUE to WAITING
  circlingQ.add(flightIn);
}

/**
 * Records a plane taking off from the airport
 * @param    flightIn The plane's flight number
 * @throws   AirportException if plane not plane not previously registered
 *                or if plane not yet recorded as landed
 *                or if the plane not previously recorded as ready for take off
 */
private void leave (String flightIn) throws AirportException
{
  Plane thisPlane = getPlane(flightIn); // throws exception if invalid
  // throw exceptions if plane is not ready to leave airport
  if (thisPlane.getStatus().compareTo(PlaneStatus.LANDED)<0)
  {
    throw new AirportException ("flight "+flightIn+" not yet landed");
  }
  if (thisPlane.getStatus() == PlaneStatus.LANDED)
  {
      throw new AirportException
                        ("flight "+flightIn+" must register to board");
```

```
      }
      // process plane leaving airport
      thisPlane.vacateRunway(); // runway now free
      planes.remove(flightIn); // remove plane from list
   }

   /**
    * Locates next circling plane to land
    * @return Returns the next circling plane to land
    *          or null if no planes
    */
   private Plane nextToLand()throws AirportException
   {
      if (!circlingQ.isEmpty()) // check circling plane exists
      {
         String flight =  circlingQ.get(0);
         circlingQ.remove(flight);
         return getPlane(flight); // could throw exception if not in list
      }
      else // no circling plane
      {
         return null;
      }
   }

}
```

There is not a lot that is new here, but we draw your attention to a few implementation issues.

First, in the constructor you can see that we catch a general exception, in case something goes wrong when allocating the array, and throw our application-specific exception when this occurs:

```
public Airport (int numIn) throws AirportException
{
    try
    {
        // array exceptions may be thrown here
        runway = new Runway [numIn];
        for (int i = 0; i < numIn; i++)
        {
           runway[i] = new Runway (i+1);
        }
        // code to initialize other collections here

    }
    catch (Exception e)// catch array exceptions
    {
        // re-throw AirportException
        throw new AirportException("Invalid Runway Number");
    }
}
```

Most of the other **public** methods simply check for a list of exceptions, and then upgrade the plane's status as it makes its way to and eventually from the airport.

Here, for example, is the method that records a plane that has previously landed at the airport, being ready to board new passengers for a new destination:

```
/**
 * Records a plane ready for boarding new passengers
 * @param     flightIn The plane's flight number
 * @param     destination The city of destination
 * @throws    AirportException if plane not previously registered
 *            or if plane not yet recorded as landed
 *            or if plane already recorded as ready for boarding
 */
public void readyForBoarding(String flightIn, String destination)
                                          throws AirportException
{
    Plane thisPlane = getPlane(flightIn); // may throw AirportException
    // check for other exceptions
    if (thisPlane.getStatus().compareTo(PlaneStatus.LANDED)<0)
    {
        throw new AirportException ("flight "+flightIn+" not landed");
    }
    if (thisPlane.getStatus() == PlaneStatus.DEPARTING)
    {
        throw new AirportException
                    ("flight "+flightIn+" already registered to depart");
    }
    thisPlane.upgradeStatus(); // upgrade status from LANDED to DEPARTING
    thisPlane.changeCity(destination); // change city to destination city
}
```

The first thing we need to do in this method is to check whether or not an `AirportException` needs to be thrown. The `Javadoc` comments make clear that there are three situations in which we need to throw such an exception.

First, an exception needs to be thrown if the given flight number has not been registered with the airport. At some point we also need to retrieve the `Plane` object from this flight number. Calling the helper method `getPlane` will do both of these things for us, as it throws an `AirportException` if the flight is not registered.

```
// retrieves plane or throws AirportException if flight is not registered
Plane thisPlane = getPlane(flightIn);
```

To check for the remaining exceptions we need to check that the plane currently has the appropriate status to start taking on passengers. The `getStatus` method of a plane returns the status of a plane for us. We know from the previous section that this method returns a value of the enumerated type `PlaneStatus`.

As well as having a `toString` method generated for you when you declare an enumerated type such as `PlaneStatus`, a `compareTo` method (to allow for comparison of two enumerated values) is also generated. This method works in exactly the same way as the `compareTo` method you met when looking at `String` methods. That is, it returns 0 when the two values are equal, a number less than 0 when the first value is less than the second value and a number greater than 0 when the first value is greater than the second value. One enumerated type value is considered *less than* another if it is listed before that value in the original type definition. So, in our example, `DUE` is *less than* `WAITING`, which is *less than* `LANDED` and so on. If a plane has a status that is less than `LANDED` it has not yet landed, so cannot be ready to board passengers – an `AirportException` is thrown:

```
// use 'compareTo' method to compare two status values
if (thisPlane.getStatus().compareTo(PlaneStatus.LANDED)<0)
{
        throw new AirportException ("flight "+flightIn+" not yet landed");
}
```

We also need to throw an `AirportException` if the plane already has a status of `BOARDING`. Although the `compareTo` method can be used to check for equality as well, with most classes it is common to use an `equals` method to do this. An `equals` method is generated for any enumerated type, such as `PlaneStatus`, that you define. However, because of the way enumerated types are implemented in Java, the simple equality operator (`==`) can also be used to check for equality:

```
// equality operator can be used to check if 2 enumerated values are equal
if (thisPlane.getStatus()== PlaneStatus.DEPARTING)
{
        throw new AirportException
                        ("flight "+flightIn+" already registered to depart");
}
```

Having checked for exceptions, we can now indicate that this plane is ready for boarding by upgrading its status (from `LANDED` to `DEPARTING`), and by recording the flights new destination city:

```
// we have cleared all the exceptions so we can update flight details now
thisPlane.upgradeStatus(); // upgrades status from LANDED to DEPARTING
thisPlane.changeCity(destination); // changes city to destination city
```

The inequality operator (`!=`) can be used with enumerated types, to check for inequality of two enumerated type values. An example of this can be seen in the implementation of the `arrivals` method:

```
/**
 * Returns the set of planes due for arrival
 */
public Set<Plane> getArrivals()
{
    Set<Plane> planesOut = new HashSet<Plane>(); // create empty set
    Set<String> items = planes.keySet(); // get all flight numbers
    for(String thisFlight: items) // check status of all
    {
      Plane thisPlane = planes.get(thisFlight);
      if (thisPlane.getStatus() != PlaneStatus.DEPARTING)
      {
            planesOut.add(thisPlane); // add to set
      }
    }
    return planesOut;
}
```

Here we create an empty set of planes. We then add planes into this set if they do not have a status of `DEPARTING`:

```
// use inequality operator to check if status does not equal some value
if (thisPlane.getStatus() != PlaneStatus.DEPARTING)
{
        planesOut.add(thisPlane);
}
```

Before we leave this section, let us take a look at the save and load methods that allow us to save and load the attributes in our application. We have three attributes here, planes (the Map of registered planes), circlingQ (the List of flight numbers of the planes circling the airport) and runway (the array of runways).

Since we have declared our Plane and Runway classes to be Serializable, and because enumerated types such as PlaneStatus and collection classes such as Map and List are already Serializable, it is a simple matter to write these objects to a file, and read them from a file.

```
/**
 * Saves attributes to file
 *
 * @param      fileIn The name of the file
 * @throws     IOException if problems with opening and saving to given file
 */
public void save(String fileIn)throws IOException
{
    FileOutputStream fileOut = new FileOutputStream(fileIn);
    ObjectOutputStream objOut = new ObjectOutputStream (fileOut);
    // write three attributes to file
    objOut.writeObject(planes);
    objOut.writeObject(circlingQ);
    objOut.writeObject(runway);
    // close file
    objOut.close();
}

/**
 * Loads attributes from file
 * @param      fileName The name of the file
 * @throws     IOException if problems with opening and loading given file
 * @throws     ClassNotFoundException if objects in file not of right type
 */
public void load (String fileName)
                        throws IOException, ClassNotFoundException
{
    FileInputStream fileInput = new FileInputStream(fileName);
    ObjectInputStream objInput = new ObjectInputStream (fileInput);
    // read three attributes from file
    planes = (Map<String, Plane>) objInput.readObject();
    circlingQ = (List<String>) objInput.readObject();
    runway = (Runway[])objInput.readObject();
    // close file
    objInput.close();
}
```

Notice that when we load the attributes from file, we must indicate their type. The collection class types need to be marked using the generics mechanism:

```
// indicate the type of each collection using genrics mechanism
planes = (Map<String, Plane>) objInput.readObject();
circlingQ = (List<String>) objInput.readObject();
```

There is nothing particularly new in the remaining methods. Take a look at the comments provided to follow their implementation.

21.6 Testing

In chapter 9 we discussed various testing strategies. These included unit testing and integration testing. We have left unit testing to you as a practical task, but we will spend a little time here considering integration testing. A useful technique to devise test cases during integration testing is to review the behaviour specifications of use cases, derived during requirements analysis.

Remember, a use case describes some useful service that the system performs. The behaviour specifications capture this service from the point of view of the user. When testing the system you take the place of the user, and you should ensure that the behaviour specification is observed.

Often, there are several routes through a single use case. For example, when registering a plane, either the plane could be successfully registered, or an error is indicated. Different routes through a single use case are known as different **scenarios**. During integration you should take the place of the user and make sure that you test *each* scenario for *each* use case. Not surprisingly, this is often known as **scenario testing**. As an example, reconsider the "*Record flight's request to land*" use case:

An air traffic controller records an incoming flight entering airport airspace, and requesting to land at the airport, by submitting its flight number. As long as the plane has previously registered with the airport, the air traffic controller is given an unoccupied runway number on which the plane will have permission to land. If all runways are occupied however, this permission is denied and the air traffic controller is informed to instruct the plane to circle the airport. If the plane has not previously registered with the airport an error is signalled.

From this description three scenarios can be identified:

Scenario 1
An air traffic controller records an incoming plane entering airport airspace and requesting to land at the airport, by submitting its flight number, and is given an unoccupied runway number on which the plane will have permission to land.

Scenario 2
An air traffic controller records an incoming plane entering airport airspace and requesting to land at the airport, by submitting its flight number. The air traffic controller is informed to instruct the plane to circle the airport as all runways are occupied.

Scenario 3
An air traffic controller records an incoming plane entering airport airspace and requesting to land at the airport, by submitting its flight number. An error is signalled as the plane has not previously registered with the airport.

Similar scenarios can be extracted for each use case. During testing we should walk through each scenario, checking whether the outcomes are as expected.

21.7 Design of the GUI

Figure 21.4 illustrates the interface design we have chosen for the *Airport* application. The type of Swing components used have been labelled.

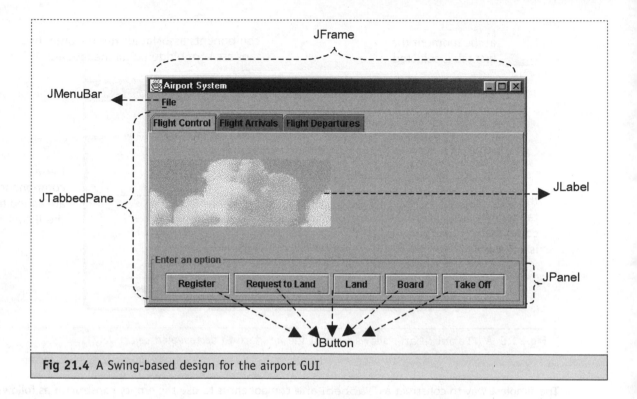

Fig 21.4 A Swing-based design for the airport GUI

Notice that we have used a label (JLabel) to hold a GIF image here:

```
JLabel jlblPicture = new JLabel(); // create JLabel component
jlblPicture.setIcon(new ImageIcon ("clouds.gif")); // add image
```

As you can see from figure 21.4, most of the Swing components we use (such as JFrame and JLabel) have already been introduced to you. However, the JTabbedPane is a Swing component that we have not yet looked at.

21.8 The *JTabbedPane* class

The JTabbedPane class provides a very useful Swing component for organizing the user interface. You can think of a JTabbedPane component as a collection of overlapping tabbed "cards", on which you place other user interface components.[1] A particular card is revealed by clicking on its **tab**. This allows certain parts of the interface to be kept hidden until required, thus reducing screen clutter.

A JTabbedPane component can consist of any number of tabbed cards. Each card is actually a *single* component of your choice. If you use a container component such as a JPanel, you can effectively associate many components with a single tab (see figure 21.5).

---

[1] A similar effect can be achieved by using the CardLayout manager discussed in chapter 19, but the JTabbedPane involves considerably less coding effort and provides a more sophisticated interface.

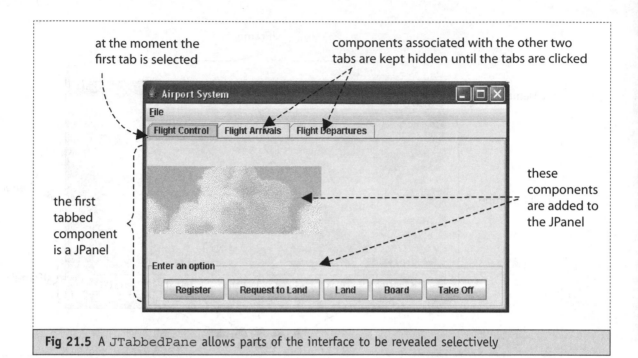

at the moment the
first tab is selected

components associated with the other two
tabs are kept hidden until the tabs are clicked

the first
tabbed
component
is a JPanel

these
components
are added to
the JPanel

Fig 21.5 A `JTabbedPane` allows parts of the interface to be revealed selectively

The simplest way to construct a `JTabbedPane` component is to use the empty constructor as follows:

```
JTabbedPane tabs = new JTabbedPane();
```

We can now add tabbed components to the `JtabbedPane`.[2] When adding a tabbed component to a `JTabbedPane`, you call the `addTab` method. The method requires two parameters – the first is the title that will appear on the tab and the second the component to add. The "Flight Control" tab can be created as follows:

```
// create a JPanel component
JPanel controlPanel = new JPanel();

// other components can be added to this panel either now or later

// add this panel to the JTabbedPane component and give the tab a title
tabs.addTab("Flight Control", controlPanel);
```

The "Flight Arrivals" and "Flight Departures" tabs both consist of a text area for displaying plane details. Figure 21.6 shows the airport GUI after selecting the "Flight Arrivals" tab.

---

[2] By default, the tabs you add will appear at the top of the `JTabbedPane` (as in figure 21.4). A version of the `JTabbedPane` constructor allows you to choose whether they appear at the top, the bottom, the left or the right.

Fig 21.6 Both "Flight Arrivals" and "Flight Departures" consist of a text area

In this case, we do not need to associate a tab with a JPanel, as the tab will only reveal a single component: the text area. Our text areas require scroll panes, however. To add scroll bars to a JTextArea, the JTextArea component has to be added to a JScrollPane component. The JScrollPane is then added to the JTabbedPane as follows:

```
// create text area
JTextArea jtaArrivals = new JTextArea(30,20);
// add text area to scroll pane
JScrollPane jspArrivals = new JScrollPane(jtaArrivals);
// add scroll pane to JTabbedPane component
tabs.addTab("Flight Arrivals", jspArrivals);
```

Notice that we have begun the name of Swing components with a summary of the type of component, so the name of the JTextArea component begins with 'jta' and so on.

21.9 The *AirportFrame* class

The GUI for the airport application is contained within a JFrame. The JFrame will need the Airport object to be one of its attributes so that it can be modified. The outline of this class is given below:

The *AirportFrame* class

```
package airportSys; // add to package
import java.awt.*; // for Layout managers and Color
import java.awt.event.*; // for ActionListener interface
import javax.swing.*; // for Swing components
import javax.swing.border.*; // for Swing borders
import java.io.*; // for File input, output
import java.util.*; // for Set class

/**
 * Class to provide GUI for Airport application
 *
 * @author Charatan and Kans
```

```
* @version 5th September 2005
*/
public class AirportFrame extends JFrame implements ActionListener
{
        //attributes
        private Airport myAirport; // reference to Airport object
      // code to declare graphical components here
  }

  /**
   * Constructor initializes Airport object and arranges the GUI components
   * @param  numIn The number of runways
   */
  public AirportFrame(int numIn)
  {
        try // check for Exceptions
        {
          myAirport = new Airport (numIn); // send number of runways
        }
        catch (AirportException ae)
        {
            ae.printStackTrace(); // display error to console
            JOptionPane.showMessageDialog  (this,"AIRPORT SYSTEM VIOLATION",
                                "Error", JOptionPane.ERROR_MESSAGE);
            System.exit(1); // indicates exit with error
        }
        // rest of code left to complete
  }

  /**
   * Process button presses and update arrivals and departures information
   */
  public void actionPerformed (ActionEvent e)
  {
        // code to respond to button clicks and menu selections here
        listArrivals(); // update arrivals tab
        listDepartures(); // update departures tab
  }

  private void listArrivals()
  {
        // code to display arrivals information in arrivals text area
  }

  private void listDepartures()
  {
        // code to display departures information in departures text area
  }
}
```

As you can see, the outline of this class follows a familiar pattern. Adding the detail should be a simple matter and we leave this to you as a practical task. Our implementation can also be copied from the accompanying CD. We will just draw your attention to one or two Swing features that we have decided to incorporate into our implementation that will be new to you.

First, we have added **tool tips** to our buttons. A tool tip is an informative description of the purpose of a GUI component. This informative description is revealed when the user places the cursor over the component. Figure 21.7 shows the tool tip that is revealed when the cursor is placed over the "Land" button:

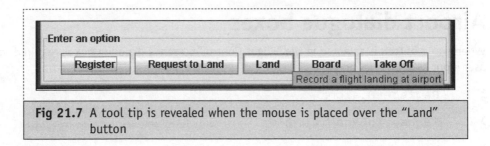

Fig 21.7 A tool tip is revealed when the mouse is placed over the "Land" button

Adding a tool tip to a Swing component is easy; just use the `setToolTipText` method:

```
// create Swing component
JButton jbtnLand = new JButton ("Land");
// add tool tip text
jbtnLand.setToolTipText("Record a flight landing at the airport");
```

We have also created **short cut** key access to our File menu. Ordinarily, a graphical component is selected by clicking on it with a mouse. Sometimes it is convenient to provide keyboard access to such items (this might be useful, for example, when the user does not have access to a working mouse). In the case of our GUI, the file menu can be selected with a mouse or by pressing the ALT and F keys simultaneously (ALT-F). It is clear that this is an alternative method of accessing the "File" menu by the fact that the 'F' of "File" is underlined (see figure 21.8).

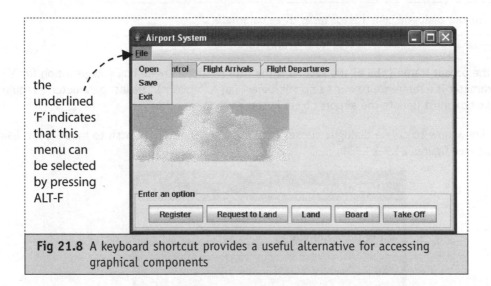

Fig 21.8 A keyboard shortcut provides a useful alternative for accessing graphical components

Again, creating keyboard short cuts for Swing components is straightforward, just use the `setMnemonic` method:

```
// create Swing component
JMenu fileMenu = new JMenu("File");
// add keyboard shortcut
fileMenu.setMnemonic('F');
```

21.10 Airport dialogue boxes

Whenever a button is selected in the "Flight Control" screen, a dialogue box is required to get and process user input. We have defined five dialogue classes for this purpose:

> `RegisterDialog;`

> `RequestToLandDialog;`

> `LandingDialog;`

> `BoardingDialog;`

> and `TakeOffDialog.`

The button responses are coded in the `actionPerfomed` method of the `AirportFrame` class. Here, for example, is how we generate a `RegisterDialog` in response to the selection of the "Register" button:

```
public void actionPerformed (ActionEvent e)
{
    if (e.getSource()==jbtnRegister) // "Register" Button selected
    {
        // generate Register Dialogue Box
        new RegisterDialog(this,"Registration form", myAirport);
    }
    // more processing here
}
```

As you can see, our dialogue constructor takes three parameters:

```
new RegisterDialog(this,"Registration form", myAirport);
```

The first is the parent frame (**this**) the second is the title of the dialogue box ("Registration form") and the final parameter is a reference to our `Airport` object (`myAirport`). The last parameter is required as each dialogue box must update the airport object in some way or another.

You already know how to create dialogue classes from chapter 19. You may wish to model your dialogue boxes on ours (see figures 21.9–21.13)

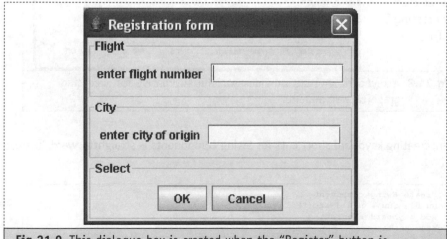

Fig 21.9 This dialogue box is created when the "Register" button is selected

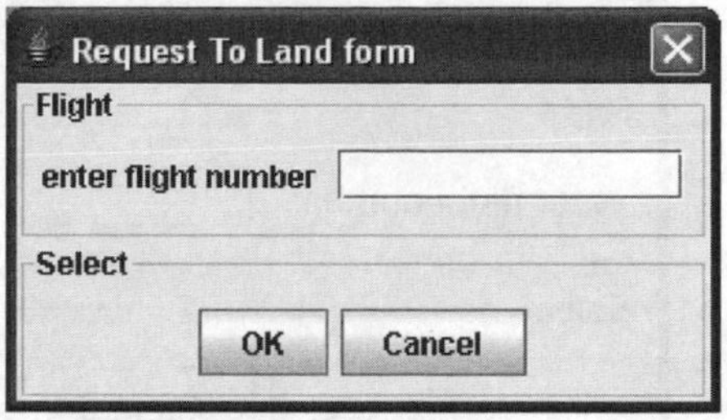

Fig 21.10 This dialogue box is created when the "Request to Land" button is selected

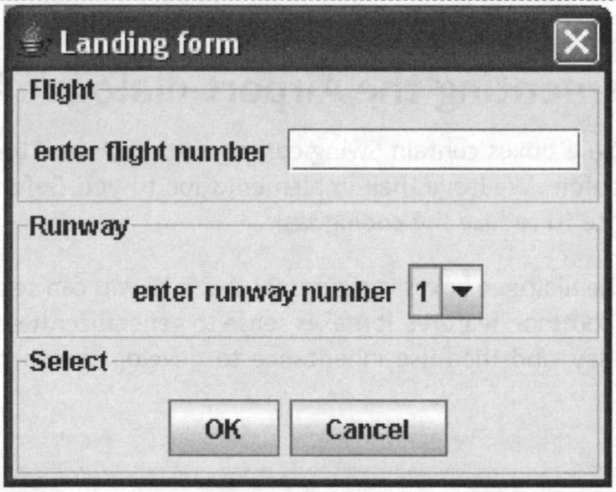

Fig 21.11 This dialogue box is created when the "Land" button is selected

Fig 21.12 This dialogue box is created when the "Board" button is selected

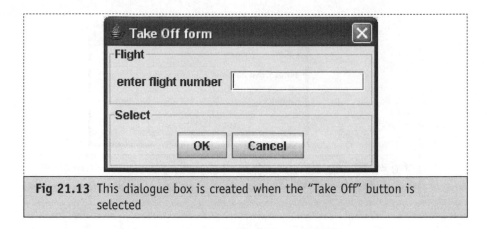

Fig 21.13 This dialogue box is created when the "Take Off" button is selected

21.10.1 Implementing the Airport dialogue boxes

The `Airport` dialogue boxes contain Swing components such as `JPanel`, `JLabel`, and `JTextField`, that you have met before. We leave their implementation to you. Before we do that, you may wish to consider using inheritance to reduce the coding task.

If you look back at the dialogue boxes in figures 21.9–21.13 you can see that, although no two are identical, they all share many common features. It makes sense to generalize these common features into a base class, `AirportDialog` say, and then use inheritance to develop the specialized dialogue classes (see figure 21.14).

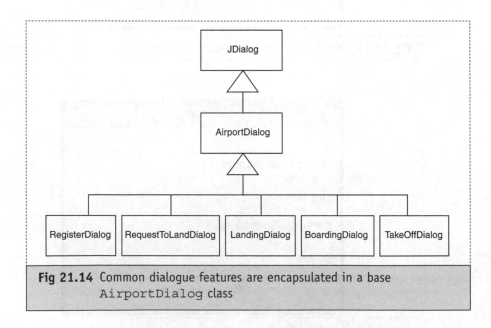

Fig 21.14 Common dialogue features are encapsulated in a base `AirportDialog` class

As an example of the visual components that are common to all the `Airport` dialogue boxes, look back at the "Request To Land" dialogue box, and the "Take Off" dialogue boxes. These dialogue boxes contain only visual components that are common to all dialogue boxes (see figure 21.15)

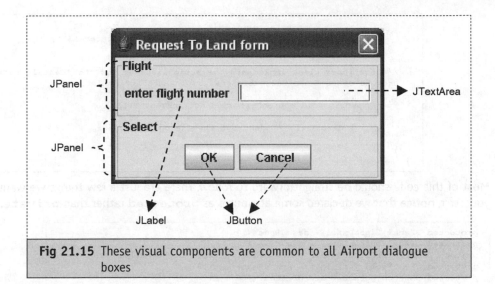

Fig 21.15 These visual components are common to all Airport dialogue boxes

Here is the code for the `AirportDialog` base class. Take a look at it and then we will discuss it.

The *AirportDialog* class

```java
package airportSys;

import java.awt.*;
import java.awt.event.*;
import javax.swing.*;
import javax.swing.border.*;

/**
 *  This is an abstract class for a general Airport dialog
 *
 *  @author Charatan and Kans
 *  @version 6th September 2005
 */
abstract class AirportDialog extends JDialog implements ActionListener
{
   // notice we have given some attributes 'protected' access
   protected JPanel flightPanel = new JPanel();
   protected JPanel buttonPanel = new JPanel();
   private JLabel jlbFlightNumber = new JLabel ("enter flight number ");
   protected JTextField jtfFlight = new JtextField(12);
   protected JButton jbtnOk = new JButton ("OK");
   private JButton jbtnCancel = new JButton ("Cancel");
   protected Airport associatedAirport; // airport object

   public AirportDialog(JFrame frameIn, String titleIn, Airport airportIn)
   {
       super(frameIn, true); // associate dialog with parent frame
       associatedAirport = airportIn; // make link to airport object
       // position dialog and set title
       setLocation(100,200);
       setTitle(titleIn);
       // add visual components
       flightPanel.add(jlbFlightNumber);
       flightPanel.add(jtfFlight);
       flightPanel.setBorder(new TitledBorder("Flight"));
       buttonPanel.add(jbtnOk);
       buttonPanel.add(jbtnCancel);
       buttonPanel.setBorder(new TitledBorder("Select"));
       // we will disuss the next two actionListener lines after this code
```

```
        jbtnOk.addActionListener(this);
        jbtnCancel.addActionListener(new CancelButtonListener());
    }

    // this inner class implements the actionlistener for the 'Cancel' button
    private class CancelButtonListener implements ActionListener
    {
        public void actionPerformed(ActionEvent event)
        {
            dispose(); // destroys the dialog box
        }
    }
}
```

Most of this code should be straightforward to follow. There are just a few things we want to point out to you. First, notice that we declared some attributes as **protected** rather than **private**:

```
protected JPanel flightPanel = new JPanel();
protected JPanel buttonPanel = new JPanel();
private JLabel jlbFlightNumber = new JLabel ("enter flight number ");
protected JTextField jtfFlight = new JtextField(12);
protected JButton jbtnOk = new JButton ("OK");
private JButton jbtnCancel = new JButton ("Cancel");
protected Airport associatedAirport;
```

The use of the **protected** modifier, as opposed to **public** or **private**, was explained in chapter 8. An attribute that is declared as **protected** can be accessed by a method of a subclass, or by any class within the same package.

In chapter 8 we told you that declaring attributes as **protected** has two drawbacks. First, it is not always possible to anticipate in advance that a class will be subclassed; second, **protected** access weakens encapsulation, because access is given to all classes within the package, not just the subclasses. For these reasons we have mostly chosen not to use **protected**, but rather to plan carefully when deciding on which attributes are to have get- and set- methods. On this occasion, however, we have relaxed our rule and used **protected**, because neither of the above problems actually applies: we do know in this case that other classes will need to inherit from this class – and because this class is not declared as **public** within our package, we do not need to worry about weakening encapsulation. The advantage of doing this is, of course, that we are able to cut out a considerable amount of additional coding by accessing these attributes directly in subclasses. Notice that the Airport object is a **protected** attribute here as all dialogues will require access to this attribute.

One last thing we need to tell you about the AirportDialog class is the way we dealt with the event-handling code. There are two buttons in this class, the 'Cancel' button and the 'OK' button, which require event-handling code.

The behaviour of the 'OK' button will vary from dialogue box to dialogue box, so that will be left for each inherited class to define, in an actionPerformed method.[3] The behaviour of the 'Cancel' button will be the same for all dialogue boxes, however – to simply dispose of the dialogue. So it is appropriate to implement the behaviour for this button in this base class. However, we have a small problem here. If we define an actionPerformed method in the base class (for the 'Cancel' button) and an actionPerformed method in an inherited class (for the 'OK' button), the inherited class method will always override the base class method! For that reason we have defined an inner class (see section 14.6), CancelButtonListener, which contains its own actionPerformed method:

[3] In fact, each sub-class *must* implement this method as this base class (AirportDialog) claims to implement the ActionPerformed interface.

```
abstract class AirportDialog extends JDialog implements ActionListener
{
    // some code here

    // this actionlistener will be implemented in the inherited classes
    jbtnOk.addActionListener(this);
    /* this action listener will be the same for all classes so it is
       implemented once here in the base class, in an inner class below */
    jbtnCancel.addActionListener(new CancelButtonListener());

    // inner class contains actionPerformed method for the 'Cancel' button
    private class CancelButtonListener implements ActionListener
    {
        public void actionPerformed(ActionEvent event)
        {
            dispose(); // destroys the dialog box
        }
    }
}
```

Finally, program 21.1 imports the `airportSys` package and runs the application with four runways:

Program 21.1

```
import airportSys.*; // import all the classes from this package

public class RunAirport
{
    public static void main (String[] args)
    {
        new AirportFrame(4); // generate GUI with 4 runways
    }
}
```

Self-test questions

1 In section 21.6 we developed scenarios for the use case "*Register flight arrival*". Develop scenarios for all the other use cases in table 21.1.

2 How can **private** and **public** scope be denoted in UML diagrams?

3 What is the difference between *containment* and *composition* in UML?

4 Consider an enumerated type, Light. This type can have one of three values: RED, AMBER and GREEN. It will be used to display a message to students, indicating whether or not a lecturer is available to be seen.

    a) Specify this type in UML.

    b) Implement this type in Java.

    c) Declare a Light variable, doorLight;

    d) Write a **switch** statement that checks doorLight and displays "I am away" when doorLight is RED, "I am busy" when doorLight is AMBER and "I am free" when doorLight is GREEN.

5 Identify the benefits offered by the JTabbedPane component.

6 How can the tool tip "*This button stops the game*" be added to a JButton called jbStop?

7 How can a JMenu item called viewMenu be allocated a short cut key "V"?

Programming exercises

1 Implement all the classes required for the airport application. You may wish to consider using JOptionPane dialogues to provide information and error messages such as those given below:

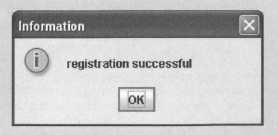
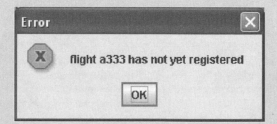

2 Develop tester programs for the Runway, Plane and Airport classes.

Multi-threaded programs

Objectives:

By the end of this chapter you should be able to:

- *explain how concurrency is achieved by means of **time-slicing**;*
- *distinguish between **threads** and **processes**;*
- *implement threads in Java;*
- *explain the difference between **asynchronous** and **synchronized** thread execution;*
- *explain the terms **critical section** and **mutual exclusion**, and describe how Java programs can be made to implement these concepts;*
- *explain how **busy waiting** can be avoided in Java programs;*
- *provide a **state transition diagram** to illustrate the thread life-cycle;*
- *produce animated applications.*

22.1 Introduction

In this chapter you are going to learn how to make a program effectively perform more than one task at the same time – this is known as **multi-tasking**, and Java provides mechanisms for achieving this within a single program.

22.2 Concurrent processes

If you have been using computers for only a few years, then you will probably think nothing of the fact that your computer can appear to be doing two or more things at the same time. For example, a large file could be downloading from the web, while you are listening to music and typing a letter into your word processor. However, those of us who were using desktop computers in the 1980s don't take this for granted! We can remember the days of having to wait for our document to be printed before we could get on with anything else – the idea of even having two applications like a spreadsheet and a database loaded at the same time on a personal computer would have been pretty exciting!

At first sight it does seem rather extraordinary that a computer with only one central processing unit (CPU) can perform more than one task at any one time. The way it achieves this is by some form of **time-slicing**; in other words it does a little bit of one task, then a little bit of the next and so on – and it does this so quickly it appears that it is all happening at the same time.

A running program is usually referred to as a **process**; two or more processes that run at the same time are called **concurrent** processes. Normally, when processes run concurrently each has its own area in memory where its program code and data are kept, and each process's memory space is protected from any other process. All this is dealt with by the operating system; modern operating systems such as Windows and Unix have a process management component whose job it is to handle all this.

22.3 Threads

We have just introduced the idea of a number of programs – or processes – operating concurrently. There are, however, times when we want a *single* program to perform two or more tasks at the same time. Whereas two concurrent programs are known as processes, each separate task performed by a single program is known as **thread**. A thread is often referred to as a **lightweight process**, because it takes less of the system's resources to manage threads than it does to manage processes. The reason for this is that threads do not have completely separate areas of memory; they can share code and data areas. Managing threads, which also work on a time-slicing principle, is the job of the JVM working in conjunction with the operating system.

In all the programs we have developed so far, we have always waited for one task to complete before another one starts. So now let's develop a program where this is not the case.

What we are going to try to achieve with this program is a simple counter as shown in figure 22.1.

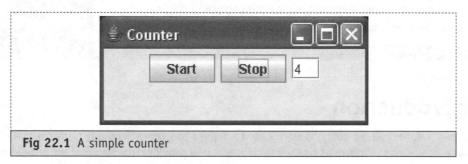

Fig 22.1 A simple counter

The intention is that when we press the "Start" button the numbers 1 to 10 will keep flashing by in the window; pressing the "Stop" button should stop this process and clicking on the crosshairs should terminate the application. Intuitively you might think that the way to do this would be to have a loop that keeps flashing the numbers, and which is controlled by some **boolean** variable, so that the loop continues while the variable is set to **true**, and stops when it is set to **false**.

This is what we have tried in our first attempt, which we have called CounterVersionOne. We should warn you, though, that it doesn't do the job, and could make your system hang up.

The *CounterVersionOne* class

```
/* this class doesn't do what we intend! in fact, it could make your
   system hang up, so we don't recommend you try it!*/

import java.awt.*;
import java.awt.event.*;
import javax.swing.*;

public class CounterVersionOne extends JFrame implements ActionListener
{
  private JButton startButton = new JButton("Start");
  private JButton stopButton = new JButton("Stop");
  private JTextField counterWindow = new JTextField(2);
  private boolean go;   /*  it is intended that this variable should
                            control the loop */

  public CounterVersionOne()
  {
      setTitle("Counter");
      add(startButton);
      add(stopButton);
      add(counterWindow);
      startButton.addActionListener(this);
      stopButton.addActionListener(this);

      setDefaultCloseOperation(JFrame.EXIT_ON_CLOSE);
      setLayout(new FlowLayout());
      setSize(250,100);
      setLocation(300,300);
      setVisible(true);
  }

  private void startCounterRunning()
  {
      // continuously display the numbers 1 to 10
      int count = 1;
      while(go)
      {
          counterWindow.setText("" + count);
          count++;
          if(count > 10) // reset the counter if it has gone over 10
          {
              count=1;
          }
      }
  }

  public void actionPerformed(ActionEvent e)
  {
      if(e.getSource() == startButton)
      {
          go = true;
          startCounterRunning();
      }
      else if(e.getSource() == stopButton)
      /* this doesn't actually work, because the startCounterRunning
         method is still executing! */
      {
          go = false;
      }
  }
}
```

It is quite easy to see how this program is intended to work. Pressing the "Start" button sets a **boolean** attribute, go, to **true** and then calls the startCounterRunning, method, which looks like this:

```
private void startCounterRunning()
{
        int count = 1;
        while(go)
        {
            counterWindow.setText("" + count);
            count++;
            if(count > 10)
            {
                count=1;
            }
        }
}
```

You can see that this method involves a **while** loop that is controlled by the value of the go attribute; while it is **true** the loop continuously displays the numbers 1 to 10 in the text window.

Pressing the "Stop" button sets the value of go to **false**, with the intention that the loop will terminate. However, if you create an object of this class, as in program 22.1, you will find that pressing the "Stop" button has no effect, and pressing the crosshairs won't terminate the application! In fact it is likely that your whole system will hang up.

Program 22.1

```
public class RunCounterVersionOne
{
    public static void main(String[] args)
    {
        new CounterVersionOne();
    }
}
```

Can you see what's wrong here? The answer is that there is only one *thread of control*. The program, as always, starts with the first line of the main method and carries on to the end of this method; in this case this involves simply creating a CounterVersionOne object. If the mouse is clicked on the "Start" button then, as we have seen, the loop is started. But because there is only a single thread, this is all that can happen. The whole program is now tied up in this loop; it doesn't matter how often you click on the "Stop" button, the program will never get the chance to process this event, because it is busy executing the loop.

What we need is to set up a separate thread that can busy itself with the loop, while another thread carries on with the rest of the program. Luckily Java provides us with a Thread class that allows us to do exactly that.

22.4 The *Thread* class

The Thread class provides a number of different methods that allow us to create and handle threads in our Java programs. The Thread class implements an interface called Runnable; this provides a method called run, which must be implemented. The code for this method determines the action that takes place when the thread is started.

One of the simplest ways to create a thread is to extend the Thread class. Let's do this with our previous example, and create a class called CounterThread; this is shown below.

The *CounterThread* class

```
import javax.swing.*;

public class CounterThread extends Thread
{
    private JTextField counterWindow;   /* this is the window where the
                                           numbers are displayed */
    private boolean go = true; // this variable controls the loop

    /* the text window where the numbers are displayed is sent in as a
       parameter to the constructor */
    public CounterThread(JTextField windowIn)
    {
        counterWindow = windowIn;
    }

    public void run()
    {
        int count = 1;
        while(go)
        {
            counterWindow.setText("" + count);

            /* Some additional code is going to go here later to
               improve our program */

            count++;
            if(count > 10) // reset the counter if it has gone over 10
            {
                count=1;
            }
        }
    }

    // this method will stop the numbers being displayed
    public void finish()
    {
        go = false;
    }
}
```

You can see that the business of displaying the numbers in the text window is now the responsibility of this class, and the instructions are placed within the run method. This method needs to know where to display the output, so the JTextField object has been passed into the constructor and assigned to an attribute of the class, making it accessible to the run method. You will see shortly that, in fact, we do not actually call this run method directly.

We have also provided a finish method that sets go back to **false**, and therefore terminates the thread.

Now we can write our new class, which we have called CounterVersionTwo:

The *CounterVersionTwo* class

```java
import java.awt.*;
import java.awt.event.*;
import javax.swing.*;

public class CounterVersionTwo extends JFrame implements ActionListener
{
  private JButton startButton = new JButton("Start");
  private JButton stopButton = new JButton("Stop");
  private JTextField counterWindow = new JTextField(2);
  private CounterThread thread;

  public CounterVersionTwo()
  {
      setTitle("Counter");
      add(startButton);
      add(stopButton);
      add(counterWindow);

      startButton.addActionListener(this);
      stopButton.addActionListener(this);

      setDefaultCloseOperation(JFrame.EXIT_ON_CLOSE);
      setLayout(new FlowLayout());
      setSize(250,100);
      setLocation(300,300);
      setVisible(true);
  }


  public void actionPerformed(ActionEvent e)
  {
     if(e.getSource() == startButton)
     {
         //create a new thread
         thread = new CounterThread(counterWindow);
         // start the thread
         thread.start();
     }
     else if(e.getSource() == stopButton)
     {
        // stop the thread
        thread.finish();
     }
  }
}
```

You can see that pressing the "Start" button creates a new thread and starts it running by calling the object's start method, which automatically calls the run method; as we mentioned above, the run method should not be called directly, but should always be called by invoking start. Pressing the "Stop" button calls the thread's finish method.

If you create an object of this class you will see that it now does what we wanted. Pressing "Start" will, as before, cause the numbers to rush by in the display window. You might notice, however, that the way they are displayed is a little erratic; pressing "Stop" does indeed stop the thread – but you might notice that the program does not always respond immediately, but instead continues to display the numbers for a little while before actually stopping. The reason for this slightly erratic behaviour is explained in the section that follows, which also shows how we can improve matters.

22.5 Thread execution and scheduling

As we explained earlier, concurrency, with a single processor, is achieved by some form of time-slicing. Each process or thread is given a little bit of time – referred to as a **quantum** – on the CPU, then the next process or thread takes its turn and so on.

Now, as you can imagine, there are some very complex issues to consider here. For example, what happens if a process that currently has the CPU cannot continue because it is waiting for some input, or perhaps is waiting for an external device like a printer to become available? When new processes come into existence, when do they get their turn? Should all processes get an equal amount of time on the CPU or should there be some way of prioritizing?

The answers to these questions are not within the domain of this book. However, it is important to understand that the responsibility for organizing all this lies with the operating system; in the case of multi-threaded Java programs this takes place in conjunction with the JVM. Different systems use different **scheduling algorithms** for deciding the order in which concurrent threads or processes are allowed CPU time. This is hidden from the user, and from the programmer. In the case of an application such as our counter program, all we can be sure about is the fact that one thread has to complete a quantum on the CPU before another thread gets its turn – we cannot, however, predict the amount of time that will be allocated to each thread; hence the slightly unpredictable behaviour that we have seen.

Fortunately, however, we are not totally at the mercy of the operating system and the JVM. The `Thread` class provides some very useful methods, one of which is a method called `sleep`. This method forces a thread to give up the CPU for a specified amount of time, even if it hasn't completed its quantum. The time interval, in milliseconds, is passed in as a parameter. During this time, other threads can be given the CPU. The `sleep` method could throw an `InterruptedException` and must be enclosed in a **try...catch** block.

So in our `CounterThread` example above, we could rewrite our `run` method as shown below – the additional code is emboldened:

```
public void run()
{
    int count = 1;
    while(go)
    {
        counterWindow.setText("" + count);
        try
        {
            sleep(1); //force the thread to sleep for 1 msec
        }
        catch(InterruptedException e)
        {
        }
        count++;
        if(count > 10)
        {
            count = 1;
        }
    }
}
```

You can see that now, on every iteration of the loop, we force the thread to sleep for 1 millisecond; this gives any other thread the chance to get a turn on the CPU. So when we run this program in a frame, the "Stop" button responds straight away. This is because, after each number is displayed, the thread rests for a millisecond and the main thread has a chance to get the CPU, so events like mouse-clicks can be processed.

The other advantage of using the `sleep` method here is that the cycle can now be timed; you can try altering the sleep time to, say, 500 milliseconds or 1 second, and watch the numbers being displayed accordingly. You might want to adapt this program so that the interval is passed in as a parameter.

In many programs that involve more than one thread you will find it necessary to force a thread to stop after one or more iterations to allow other events to be processed (rather than relying on the unpredictable scheduling of the operating system). If you do not want the thread to wait a specific period of time before resuming, then you can use the `yield` method rather than `sleep`; `yield` does not require any parameters.

22.6 An alternative implementation

Very often it is not possible to extend the `Thread` class, because the class we are writing needs to extend another class such as a `JPanel` or `JFrame`. The `Thread` class provides an alternative constructor that takes as a parameter a `Runnable` object where it expects to find the code for the `run` method.

So, the alternative approach involves creating a class that implements the `Runnable` interface, and then declaring a separate `Thread` object, either within this class or as a separate class. Study the following version of our `CounterThread`:

The *AlternativeCounter* class

```
import javax.swing.*;

public class AlternativeCounter implements Runnable
{
    private JTextField counterWindow;
    private boolean go = true;

    // a thread object is now created as an attribute of the class
    private Thread cThread = new Thread(this);

    public AlternativeCounter(JTextField windowIn)
    {
        counterWindow = windowIn;
    }

    public void run()
    {
        int count = 1;
        while(go)
        {
            counterWindow.setText("" + count);
            count++;
            try
                {
                    // the sleep method of the thread object is called
                    cThread.sleep(1);
                }
            catch(InterruptedException e)
                {
                }
            if(count > 10)
            {
                count = 1;
            }
        }
    }

    // a separate method is now required to start the thread
```

```
    public void begin()
    {
        cThread.start();
    }

    public void finish()
    {
        go = false;
    }
}
```

As can be seen from the comments, there are three changes that have been made.

First, a new `Thread` object is created as an attribute. As we explained before, the object where the `run` method is to be found is passed as a parameter; in the above example, it is **this** object itself that we must pass in.

Second, in the `run` method, we previously called the `sleep` method of **this** object. We can no longer do this, of course, because the `AlternativeCounter` class does not extend the `Thread` class. Instead, we call the `sleep` method of the thread object, `cThread`.

Finally, we have had to create a new method, `begin`, which calls the `start` method of `cThread`. Again, we have had to do this because our `AlternativeCounter` class is not an extension of `Thread`, and therefore does not have a `start` method of its own.

In order to make use of this new class we have had to rewrite `CounterVersionTwo`; we have named the new version of this class `CounterVersionThree`:

The *CounterVersionThree* class

```
import java.awt.*;
import java.awt.event.*;
import javax.swing.*;

public class CounterVersionThree extends JFrame implements ActionListener
{
    private JButton startButton = new JButton("Start");
    private JButton stopButton = new JButton("Stop");
    private JTextField counterWindow = new JTextField(2);

    /* we are now using the AlternativeCounter class instead of the
       CounterThread class that we used in version two */
    private AlternativeCounter aCounter;

    public CounterVersionThree()
    {
        setTitle("Counter");
        add(startButton);
        add(stopButton);
        add(counterWindow);

        startButton.addActionListener(this);
        stopButton.addActionListener(this);

        setLayout(new FlowLayout());
        setDefaultCloseOperation(JFrame.EXIT_ON_CLOSE);
        setSize(250,100);
        setLocation(300,300);
        setVisible(true);
    }

    public void actionPerformed(ActionEvent e)
```

```
    {
        if(e.getSource() == startButton)
        {
            aCounter = new AlternativeCounter(counterWindow);
            /* this time we have to use the object's begin method; it does
               not have a start method as it is not an extension of Thread */
            aCounter.begin();
        }
        else if(e.getSource() == stopButton)
        {
            aCounter.finish();
        }
    }
}
```

You can see the only real difference in this version is that we now have to call the `begin` method of the `AlternativeCounter` object, instead of the `start` method as we were able to do in version two.

22.7 Synchronizing threads

In section 22.5 we explained that under normal circumstances the behaviour of two or more threads executing concurrently is not co-ordinated, and we are not able to predict which threads will be allocated CPU time at any given moment. Unco-ordinated behaviour like this is referred to as is **asynchronous** behaviour.

It is, however, often the case that we require two or more concurrently executing threads or processes to be co-ordinated – and if they were not, we could find we had some serious problems. There are many examples of this. One of the most common is that of a **producer–consumer** relationship, whereby one process is continually producing information that is required by another process. A very simple example of this is a program that copies a file from one place to another. One process is responsible for reading the data, another for writing the data. Since the two processes are likely to be operating at different speeds, this would normally be implemented by providing a *buffer*, that is a space in memory where the data that has been read is queued while it waits for the write process to access it and then remove it from the queue.

It should be fairly obvious that it could be pretty disastrous if the read process and the write process tried to access the buffer at the same time – both the data and the indices could easily be corrupted. In a situation like this we would need to treat the parts of the program that access the buffer as **critical sections** – that is, sections that can be accessed only by one process at a time.

Implementing critical sections is known as **mutual exclusion**, and fortunately Java provides a mechanism for the implementation of mutual exclusion in multi-threaded programs. In this book we are not going to go into any detail about how this is implemented, because the whole subject of concurrent programming is a vast one, and is best left to texts that deal with that topic. What we intend to do here is simply to explain the mechanisms that are available in Java for co-ordinating the behaviour of threads.

Java provides for the creation of a **monitor**, that is a class whose methods can be accessed by only one thread at a time. This entails the use of the modifier `synchronized` in the method header. For instance, a `Buffer` class in the above example might have a read method declared as:

```
public synchronized Object read()
{
    .....
}
```

Because it is `synchronized`, as soon as some object invokes this method a **lock** is placed on it; this means that no other object can access it until it has finished executing. This can, however, cause a problem known as **busy waiting**. This means that the method that is being executed by a particular thread has to go round in a loop until some condition is met, and as a consequence the CPU time is used just to keep the thread going round and round in this loop until it times out – not very efficient! As an example of this, consider the `read` and `write` methods that we talked about in the example above. The `read` method would not be able to place any data in the buffer if the buffer were full – it would have to loop until some data was removed by the `write` method; conversely, the `write` method would not be able to obtain any data if the buffer were empty – it would have to wait for the `read` method to place some data there.

Java provides methods to help us avoid busy waiting situations. The `Object` class has a method called `wait`, which suspends the execution of a thread (taking it away from the CPU) until it receives a message from another thread telling it to wake up. The object methods `notify` and `notifyAll` are used for the purpose of waking up other threads. Sensible use of these methods allow programmers to avoid busy waiting situations.

22.8 Thread states

A very useful way to summarize what you have learnt about threads is by means of a **state transition diagram**. Such a diagram shows the various states that an object can be in, and the allowed means of getting from one state to another – the **transitions**. The state transition diagram for a thread is shown in figure 22.2.

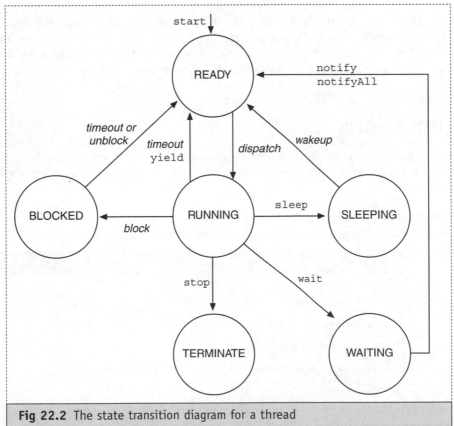

Fig 22.2 The state transition diagram for a thread

As we have said, much of the thread's life-cycle is under the control of the operating system and the JVM; however, as you have seen, some transitions are also under the control of the programmer. In figure 22.2 the transitions that are controlled by the operating system and the JVM are italicized; those that the programmer can control are in plain font.

As you have seen, a thread is brought into existence by invoking its `start` method. At this point it goes into the **ready** state. This means it is waiting to be allocated time on the CPU; this decision is the responsibility of the operating system and JVM. Once it is **dispatched** (that is given CPU time), it is said to be in the **running** state. Once a thread is running, a number of things can happen to it:

> It can simply timeout and go back to the **ready** state; you have seen that it is possible for the programmer to force this to happen by ensuring that its `yield` method is invoked.

> The programmer can also arrange for the `sleep` method to be called, causing the thread to go into the **sleeping** state for a given period of time. When this time period has elapsed the thread wakes up and goes back to the ready state.

> The programmer can use the `wait` method to force the thread to go into the **waiting** state until a certain condition is met. Once the condition is met, the thread will be informed of this fact by a `notify` or `notifyAll` method, and will return to the ready state.

> A thread can become **blocked**; this is normally because it is waiting for some input, or waiting for an output device to become available. The thread will return to the ready state when either the normal timeout period has elapsed or the input/output operation is completed.

> When the `run` method finishes the thread is terminated. It is actually possible to use the `stop` method of `Thread` for this purpose, but it can be very dangerous to stop a thread in the middle of its execution; it could, for example, be in the middle of writing to a file. It is far better to use a control variable instead, so that the thread terminates naturally.

22.9 Animations

One of the more practical ways of utilizing threads is to produce animations. Clearly, an application that uses animated graphics is going to consist of some sort of continuous loop that displays a serious of different images.

Let's start off by animating our familiar `SmileyFace` program. The following class, when instantiated, produces a face that changes its expression from smile to frown once a second:

The *AnimatedFace* class

```java
import java.awt.*;
import javax.swing.*;

public class AnimatedFace extends JFrame implements Runnable
{
    private boolean isHappy;

    // a separate thread is required to run the animation
    private Thread thread1;

    public AnimatedFace()
    {
```

```
            isHappy = true;

            setDefaultCloseOperation(JFrame.EXIT_ON_CLOSE);
            setSize(250,250);
            setLocation(300,300);
            getContentPane().setBackground(Color.yellow);
            setVisible(true);

            // create a new thread
            thread1 = new Thread(this);
            // start the thread
            thread1.start();
        }

        public void run()
        {
            while(true)  // a continuous loop
            {
                // on each iteration of the loop the mood is changed.....
                if(isHappy == true)
                {
                    isHappy = false;
                }
                else
                {
                    isHappy = true;
                }
                // ..... and the face is repainted
                repaint();
                try
                {
                    thread1.sleep(1000);
                }
                catch(InterruptedException e)
                {
                }
            }
        }

        public void paint(Graphics g)
        {
            super.paint(g);
            g.setColor(Color.red);
            g.drawOval(85,75,75,75);   // the face
            g.setColor(Color.blue);
            g.drawOval(100,95,10,10); // the right eye
            g.drawOval(135,95,10,10); // the left eye
            g.drawString("Animated Face", 82,175);
            if(isHappy == true)
            {
                // draw a smiling mouth
                g.drawArc(102,115,40,25,0,-180);
            }
            else
            {
                // draw a frowning mouth
                g.drawArc(102,115,40,25,0,180);
            }
        }
    }
```

As you can see, this time we have done everything in one class, the constructor of which creates and starts the thread. The `run` method consists of a loop that goes on for ever until the thread is destroyed. On each iteration of the loop the mood is changed, the face is repainted, and the thread is forced to sleep for one second.

Program 22.2 runs the `AnimatedFace` as usual.

Program 22.2

```
public class RunAnimatedFace
{
        public static void main(String[] args)
        {
            new AnimatedFace();
        }
}
```

22.9.1 Animation using a series of images

The traditional way of producing animations in film has been to display a continuous series of images, which, to the eye, gives the impression of movement. In this section we are going to use that technique here to create an animated application.

Our animation is going to depict an old-style vinyl record going round on a turn-table; it is not, perhaps, the most imaginative animation ever, but we have no doubt that you will be able to be far more artistic and produce some spectacular animations of your own! There are eight images involved here, as shown in figure 22.3.

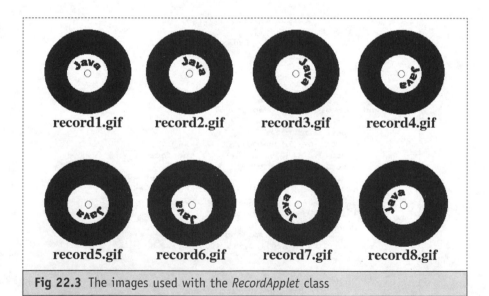

Fig 22.3 The images used with the *RecordApplet* class

The code for the class is presented below.

The *Record* class

```java
import java.awt.*;
import javax.swing.*;

public class Record extends JFrame implements Runnable
{
    // declare some constants
    public static final String fileName = "record";
    public static final int numberOfImages = 8;
    public static final int sleepTime = 100;

    private JLabel label = new JLabel();
    private ImageIcon image;
    private Thread animationThread;

    public Record()
    {
        // create a new thread
        animationThread = new Thread(this);

        // add the label to the frame and centre the image
        add("Center",label);
        label.setHorizontalAlignment(JLabel.CENTER);

        // configure the frame
        setTitle("Revolving Record");
        setDefaultCloseOperation(JFrame.EXIT_ON_CLOSE);
        getContentPane().setBackground(Color.white);
        setSize(300,300);
        setVisible(true);

        // start the thread
        animationThread.start();
    }

    public void run()
    {
        int currentImage = 0;
        String strImage;
        while(true)
        {
            strImage = fileName + (currentImage+1) + ".gif";
            image = new ImageIcon(strImage);

            label.setIcon(image);

            try
            {
                animationThread.sleep(sleepTime);
            }
            catch(InterruptedException e)
            {
            }
            currentImage++;
            if(currentImage == numberOfImages)
            {
                currentImage = 0;
            }
        }
    }
}
```

As you can see, we have declared a number of attributes, so we will start by looking at these:

```
public static final String fileName = "record";
public static final int numberOfImages = 8;
public static final int sleepTime = 100;

private JLabel label = new JLabel();
private ImageIcon image;
private Thread animationThread;
```

The first three of these are constants that we will use later on. Once we have declared them, we declare a JLabel, which will later be added to the frame. This JLabel will hold a series of images in turn, and so for this purpose we declare an ImageIcon. Finally we declare a Thread.

Now let's look at the constructor:

```
animationThread = new Thread(this);
add("Center",label);
label.setHorizontalAlignment(JLabel.CENTER);
setTitle("Revolving Record");
setDefaultCloseOperation(JFrame.EXIT_ON_CLOSE);
getContentPane().setBackground(Color.white);
setSize(300,300);
setVisible(true);
animationThread.start();
```

Most of this is really self-explanatory. We create a new thread, we add the label to the centre of the frame, and set its alignment to JLabel.CENTER; we then configure the frame and finally we start the thread.

Now the run method:

```
public void run()
{
        int currentImage = 0;
        String strImage;
        while(true)
        {
                strImage = fileName + (currentImage + 1) + ".gif";
                image = new ImageIcon(strImage);
                label.setIcon(image);
                try
                {
                    animationThread.sleep(sleepTime);
                }
                catch(InterruptedException e)
                {
                }
                currentImage++;
                if(currentImage == numberOfImages)
                {
                        currentImage = 0;
                }
        }
}
```

The body of this method consists of an infinite loop. On each iteration we use an integer variable, currentImage, to construct the name of the image – "record1.gif", "record2.gif" and so on – and then set the label's icon to this image. After each new image is displayed, the thread is made to sleep for a given period. The value of currentImage is then incremented, and set back to zero once all eight images have been displayed.

22.10 The *Timer* class

Now that you understand the concept of multi-threaded programs, we can introduce you to the Timer class. This class conveniently provides a facility for scheduling threads. The way a Timer object works is to generate ActionEvents at fixed intervals. We therefore have to associate a Timer object with an ActionListener object. Whenever it generates an ActionEvent, the instructions in the actionPerformed method associated with the Timer's ActionListener are executed. We will illustrate this by adapting our Record class – it will behave exactly as before, but now we will use a Timer. The code for our new class, RecordVersion2 is shown below:

The *RecordVersion2* class

```java
import java.awt.*;
import java.awt.event.*;
import javax.swing.*;

public class RecordVersion2 extends JFrame implements ActionListener
{
    public static final String fileName = "record";
    public static final int numberOfImages = 8;
    public static final int sleepTime = 100;

    private ImageIcon image;
    private JLabel label = new JLabel();
    private int currentImage = 0;

    // declare a Timer
    private Timer animationTimer;

    public RecordVersion2()
    {
        // create a new Timer object
        animationTimer = new Timer(sleepTime, this);

        // add the label to the frame and centre the image

        add(label);
        label.setHorizontalAlignment(JLabel.CENTER);
        label.setIcon(new ImageIcon ("record1.gif"));

        // configure the frame
        setTitle("Revolving Record");
        setDefaultCloseOperation(JFrame.EXIT_ON_CLOSE);
        getContentPane().setBackground(Color.white);
        setSize(300,300);
        setVisible(true);

        // start the Timer
        animationTimer.start();
    }

    // the instructions for the Timer
    public void actionPerformed(ActionEvent e)
    {
        String strImage = fileName + (currentImage+1) + ".gif";
        image = new ImageIcon(strImage);
        label.setIcon(image);
        currentImage++;
        if(currentImage == numberOfImages)
        {
            currentImage = 0;
        }
    }
}
```

You can see that we have declared an object of the `Timer` class, `animationTimer`, as an attribute, and have instantiated it in the constructor:

```
animationTimer = new Timer(sleepTime, this);
```

The constructor of the `Timer` requires two parameters – an integer representing the interval during which it must wait before performing the action again, and a reference to an `ActionListener` where it will expect to find an `actionPerformed` method containing the instructions it is to perform each time the given interval elapses. Our `RecordVersion2` class is an `ActionListener` because it implements the `ActionListener` interface. The final instruction in the constructor starts the `Timer`:

```
animationTimer.start();
```

As you can see from the code, the instructions that were previously part of the thread's `run` method in our original version are now placed in the `actionPerformed` method – there is no need to make them part of a loop, because this is taken care of by the `Timer` itself.

Before finishing with timers, we will do one more thing – we will adapt our class by adding a "Stop" and "Start" button to it. Figure 22.4 shows how it is going to look.

Fig 22.4 The new version of the *Record* class

In this case the `actionPerformed` method is going to have to deal with the buttons – that is, it will ensure that the timer is started when the "Start" button is pressed and stopped when the "Stop" button is pressed. Therefore the `actionPerformed` method associated with the timer cannot be declared as part of this class; we need to write a separate class for this purpose. The easiest way to do this is to write an inner class, because that will enable us to access the attributes. You can see how we do that below – we have called the inner class `TimerListener` – notice how we create a new object of this class when we create the `Timer` object in the constructor.

The *RecordVersion3* class

```java
import java.awt.*;
import java.awt.event.*;
import javax.swing.*;

public class RecordVersion3 extends JFrame implements ActionListener
{

    public static final String fileName = "record";
    public static final int numberOfImages = 8;
    public static final int sleepTime = 10;

    private ImageIcon image;
    private JLabel label = new JLabel();
    private JButton startButton = new JButton("Start");
    private JButton stopButton = new JButton("Stop");
    private int currentImage = 0;
    private Timer animationTimer;

        // define an inner class to hold the timer instructions
        class TimerListener implements ActionListener
        {
          public void actionPerformed(ActionEvent e)
          {
                String strImage = fileName + (currentImage + 1) + ".gif";
                image = new ImageIcon(strImage);
                label.setIcon(image);
                currentImage++;
                if(currentImage == numberOfImages)
                {
                    currentImage = 0;
                }
          }
        }

    public RecordVersion3()
    {
        // create a new Timer object
        animationTimer = new Timer(sleepTime, new TimerListener());

        setDefaultCloseOperation(JFrame.EXIT_ON_CLOSE);
        setLayout(new FlowLayout());
        // add the buttons and label to the frame and centre the image
        add(startButton);
        add(stopButton);
        add(label);
        label.setHorizontalAlignment(JLabel.CENTER);
        label.setIcon(new ImageIcon ("record1.gif"));

        startButton.addActionListener(this);
        stopButton.addActionListener(this);

        // configure the frame
        setTitle("Revolving Record");
        getContentPane().setBackground(Color.white);
        setSize(300,300);
        setVisible(true);
    }

    public void actionPerformed(ActionEvent e)
    {
        if(e.getSource() == startButton)
        {
                animationTimer.start(); // start the timer
        }
        else
        {
                animationTimer.stop(); // stop the timer
        }
    }
}
```

Self-test questions

1 Explain how concurrency is achieved by means of *time-slicing*.

2 Distinguish between *threads* and *processes*.

3 What is the difference between *asynchronous* and *synchronized* thread execution?

4 What is meant by the terms *critical section* and *mutual exclusion*? How are Java programs made to implement these concepts?

5 Explain how *busy waiting* can be avoided in Java programs.

6 The class below has had its `run` method replaced by a comment.

```
class Threads6 extends JFrame implements Runnable
{
        private JLabel label = new JLabel("Hello");
        private Thread thread1;

        public Threads6()
        {

                label.setHorizontalAlignment(JLabel.CENTER);
                add(label);
                thread1 = new Thread(this);
                setTitle("Question 6");
                setDefaultCloseOperation(JFrame.EXIT_ON_CLOSE);
                setSize(200,100);
                setVisible(true);

                thread1.start();
        }

        public void run()
        {
            // code goes here
        }
}
```

a) Replace the comment with code so that when an object of the class is created it will produce a frame containing a label whose caption changes once every second from "Hello" to "Goodbye". This is shown below:

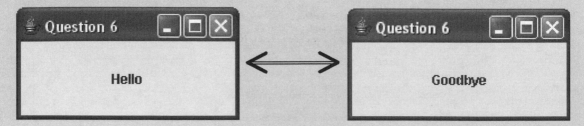

b) Adapt the code so that the interval between changes can be determined at the time the object is created.

Programming exercises

1 Design some experiments that will help you to observe the behaviour of threads. A suggestion is to provide a `Thread` class with an id number that can be allocated at the time an object is created; the `run` method could simply print out this id a given number of times. A program could then be written to create and run a number of threads concurrently so that the output can be studied. You could vary the number of times the threads loop before terminating and see if there is any observable difference.

2 Implement the programs from this chapter. The images that you need for the `Record` class are on the CD or they can be downloaded from the website. Try to design some animations of your own.

3 Modify the `CounterVersionTwo` class (with the `sleep` method implemented) so that:

a) the sleep interval is passed in as a parameter from the main program;

b) two separate counters run concurrently as shown below; each counter could be made to operate with a different sleep interval.

CHAPTER: 23

Java in a network environment

Objectives:

By the end of this chapter you should be able to:

- *describe the **client–server** model;*
- *explain the difference between an **application** and an **applet**;*
- *explain the purpose of the* `init`, `start`, `stop` *and* `destroy` *methods;*
- *implement Java applets using the* `JApplet` *class;*
- *describe **Java Database Connectivity (JDBC)** technology;*
- *write a Java program that accesses a remote database and executes SQL queries on that database;*
- *explain the function of the Java* `Socket` *and* `ServerSocket` *classes;*
- *write a simple client–server application using sockets.*

23.1 Introduction

In this chapter we are going to explore some of the ways in which Java can be used to write programs that communicate over a network. We will be restricting ourselves to programs that involve some sort of data transfer, as opposed to programs which are themselves distributed over a network and which need to call the methods of remote objects. There is in fact a Java mechanism for the latter situation – *Remote Method Invocation (RMI)*. We will not be dealing with RMI here, however, because there are many theoretical issues involved and the subject is better placed in a book that deals primarily with networking.

Network programs rely very much on the concept of a **client** and a **server**. A server program provides some sort of service for other programs – clients – normally located on a different machine. The service it provides could be one of many things – it could send some files to the client; it could send web pages to the client; it could read some data from the local machine and send that across, maybe having done some processing first; it could perform a complex calculation; it could print some material on a local printer. The possibilities are endless.

It should be noted that the distinction between a client and server can become blurred: a program acting as a client in one situation could also act as a server in another, and vice versa. It is also important to note that it is often the case that a machine, rather than a program, is referred to as a server. This usually happens when a machine is dedicated to running a particular server program – typically a file server – and does very little else. Strictly speaking we should refer to the machine that a server runs on as the **host**.

Communication between a client and a server could be over a local area network, a wide area network, or over the Internet. Server programs that offer a service via the Internet have to obey a particular set of rules or protocols to ensure that the client and server are "speaking the same language". Common examples are **File Transfer Protocol (FTP)** for servers that send files, and **Hypertext Transfer Protocol (HTTP)** for services that send web pages to a client.

In this chapter we are going to explore three types of program:

> first we will look at applets – programs that are downloaded from a remote site to run on the local machine under the control of a browser;

> second we will show you how to communicate with a database server operating either locally or on a remote machine in order to store and retrieve data from the database;

> finally we will look at the notion of sockets – special programs that allow data to pass between two programs running on different computers.

23.2 Applets

An **applet** is a Java program that can be downloaded from the World Wide Web and run in a browser such as Internet Explorer or Netscape. The fact that Java runs on a virtual machine and is therefore platform independent means that the type of operating system running on the client machine is unimportant.

As you know, applications, as opposed to applets, are made runnable by providing a class that contains a `main` method. The `main` method provides the overall means of controlling the program. However, an applet, as we have said, runs in a browser. Control of the applet thus becomes the responsibility of the browser and there is no need for a `main` method – if there were a `main` method in the class, it would simply be ignored when the applet ran.

You will have observed that in this book, apart from the earlier very simple text-based programs, we have organized things in such a way that the `main` method is never included in the functional class, but instead is placed in a separate "driver" class. In the case of the graphical applications that we have developed, we have provided a class whose `main` method does nothing more than create an instance of a class that extends a `JFrame`.

23.2.1 Running an applet in a browser

In order to run an applet in a browser (or in one of the applet viewers provided with most Java IDEs), we need to include an instruction in a web page that tells the browser to load the applet and run it. Web pages are written in a special language known as **Hypertext Markup Language (HTML)**, or one of its associated languages such as **Extensible Markup Language (XML)**. HTML code is interpreted by browsers such as Netscape and Internet Explorer to produce the formatted text and graphics that we are used to seeing.

We are not going to go into any detail here about how to write HTML or XML; we will talk only about the commands you need in order to get your applets running. Commands in HTML are called **tags** and are enclosed in angle brackets. The tag that we are interested in here is the one that tells the browser to load and run a Java class. This uses the key word *applet*, as we shall see in a moment.

Cast your mind back to the `ChangingFace` class from chapter 10. We are going to make two changes, which are described below:

> the class will extend JApplet instead of JFrame;

> the constructor will be replaced with a special method called init (short for *initialize*), and the code that we originally had in the constructor will now be placed in this special init method.

The ChangingFaceApplet class is shown below:

The *ChangingFaceApplet* class

```java
import javax.swing.*;
import java.awt.*;
import java.awt.event.*;

public class ChangingFaceApplet extends JApplet implements ActionListener
{
  private boolean isHappy = true;   // will determine the mood of the face
  private JButton happyButton = new JButton("Smile");
  private JButton sadButton = new JButton("Frown");

  public void init() // initialization routines are placed in thsi method
  {
      // use a flow layout
      setLayout(new FlowLayout());

      // add the buttons to the panel
      add(happyButton);
      add(sadButton);

      // set the background to yellow
      getContentPane().setBackground(Color.yellow);   // changed

      // make the buttons transparent
      happyButton.setOpaque(false);
      sadButton.setOpaque(false);

      // enable the buttons to listen for a mouse-click
      happyButton.addActionListener(this);
      sadButton.addActionListener(this);
  }

  public void paint(Graphics g)   // changed
  {
      // call the paint method of the superclass, JApplet
      super.paint(g);   // changed
      g.setColor(Color.red);
      g.drawOval(85,45,75,75);
      g.setColor(Color.blue);
      g.drawOval(100,65,10,10);
      g.drawOval(135,65,10,10);
      g.drawString("Changing Face", 80,155);
      if(isHappy == true)
      {
          // draw a smiling mouth
          g.drawArc(102,85,40,25,0,-180);
      }
      else
      {
          // draw a frowning mouth
          g.drawArc(102,85,40,25,0,180);
      }
  }
```

```
// this is where we code the event-handling routine
public void actionPerformed(ActionEvent e)
{
    if(e.getSource() == happyButton)
    {
        isHappy = true;
        repaint();
    }
    if(e.getSource() == sadButton)
    {
        isHappy = false;
        repaint();
    }
}
}
```

We have provided below the bare minimum HTML code that will load and run this class in a browser; it doesn't add any headings, or attempt to produce a pretty webpage – those of you who know HTML or XML will be able to add those features if you wish:

```
<HTML>
<APPLET CODE = "ChangingFaceApplet.class" WIDTH = "250" HEIGHT = "175" >
</APPLET>
</HTML>
```

As some of you might know, HTML tags often have an opening and a closing version, the latter starting with a forward slash (/). The relevant text is contained within these tags. So in our example the HTML tags tell the browser that the text contained represents an HTML page. The text within the APPLET tags provides the information about the applet that needs to be loaded; this is done with special words (called *attributes* just to confuse us!) which are part of the tag. In this case we provide the name of the class (with the CODE attribute) and the dimensions of the applet window (with the attributes WIDTH and HEIGHT). Figure 23.1 overleaf shows the ChangingFace class running in a browser.

Of course, it is necessary to have the correct file (in this case ChangingFaceApplet.class) in the same directory as the HTML file; alternatively it is possible to make absolute references to directories in the HTML code, but you should look at books on HTML in order to find out more about this. Do notice, however, that it is the compiled byte code that you need (that is, the file with the .class extension), and not the Java source code.

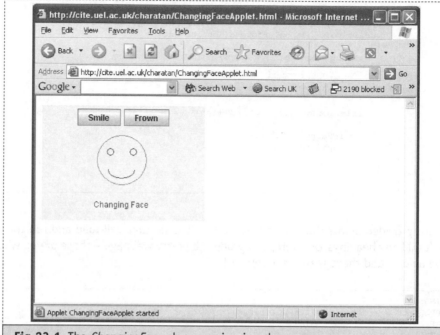

Fig 23.1 The *ChangingFace* class running in a browser

23.3.2 Special applet methods

In addition to the `init` method there are three other special applet methods that you can code if you wish; `start`, `stop` and `destroy`. Together with the `paint` method these are automatically called in a special order which is explained in table 23.1 below.

Table 23.1 The special applet methods (working with the `paint` method)	
Method	**Invocation**
`init`	Invoked the first time the applet is loaded (or reloaded) by a browser
`start`	Invoked after `init` when the applet is first loaded (or reloaded) and then invoked each time the applet is made visible again by returning to the page
`paint`	Invoked immediately after `start`
`stop`	Invoked when the applet is hidden (by pointing the browser at a different page)
`destroy`	Invoked after `stop` when the applet is abandoned (by closing the browser)

23.2.3 Guidelines for creating applets

As you have seen, when creating applets, as opposed to applications, there are a few differences that you need to be aware of. These are summarized below:

1   Ensure that your class extends the `JApplet` class.

2   Place any initialization routines, such as setting initial values, in an `init` or a `start` method rather than in a constructor.

3   Do not include a `main` method, as any code in the `main` method is ignored by the browser.

4   Make sure that any input and output goes through the Swing interface – the user will not normally see the text console when using a browser.

5   Do not include any buttons or other controls that attempt to terminate the program – applets terminate when the page is closed in the browser.

6   Always declare your class as **public**.

23.3 Accessing remote databases

It is not an uncommon occurrence that we need to develop an application that requires the use of data that is held on a database which is stored either locally or on a remote site. Java is able to access such a database by means of a technology called **Java Database Connectivity (JDBC)**; manufacturers of database management systems provide JDBC drivers by means of which Java programs can access their databases. A driver is a piece of software that enables communication between two programs, or between a software program and a piece of hardware, by translating the output of one program into a form understood by the other one.

To make life even easier for us, the Java foundation classes contain a package known as `java.sql`. This package provides the means by which our Java programs can contain commands written in standard SQL (Structured Query Language), which is the well-established means of writing database instructions. In this chapter we are not going to teach you SQL, but will assume you are familiar with some basic commands. The example we are going to use is for a MySQL database. MySQL, a shareware product, has proved to be very popular with developers over recent years, and its popularity continues to grow; more information can be obtained from www.mysql.org. The developers of MySQL provide a driver known as Connector/J (formerly known as mm.mysql), which can be downloaded. It needs to be unzipped and its contents stored to a folder to which the classpath has been set. The driver itself is called `Driver.class` and, once the package is unzipped, will reside in the hierarchy `org.gjt.mm.mysql` – so you can see that the classpath must be set to the folder that contains the `org` directory.

For our example we have set up a little database called *ElectricalStore* that contains a table called *products*. This table is described below (table 23.2); it is assumed that you are familiar with relational databases and the data types available.

Table 23.2 The *Products* table		
Field	Data type	Length
SerialNumber	char	(7)
Make	char	(10)
Description	char	(20)
Price	decimal	(10, 2)

We have populated this database, and, in order to query it, we have developed a class called `ProductQuery`. This class, once an instance of it is created, executes just one SQL statement:

```
select * from products;
```

Those of you who are familiar with SQL will know that this query retrieves all the fields from all the records in the *products* table. The information obtained is then displayed in a text area as you can see from figure 23.2.

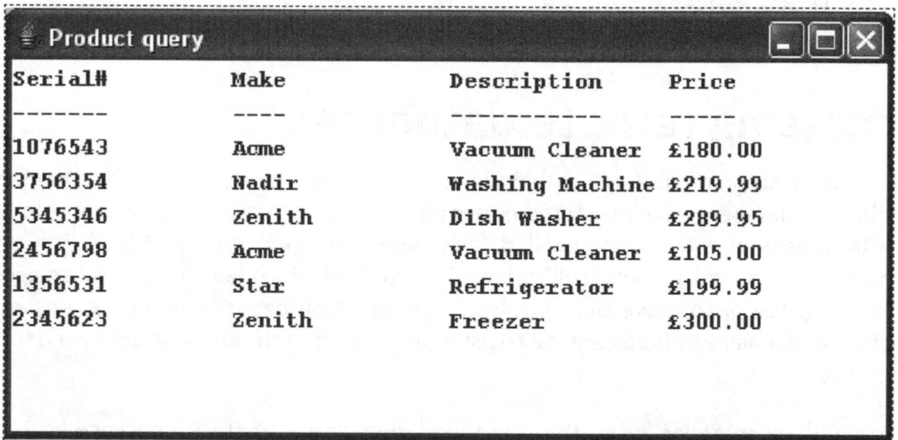

Fig 23.2 Displaying the information from the *ElectricalStore* database

Take a look at the `ProductQuery` class below, and then we will go through it with you.

The *ProductQuery* class

```java
import java.sql.*;
import javax.swing.*;
import java.awt.*;

public class ProductQuery extends JFrame
{
    // the attributes
    public static final String driver = "org.gjt.mm.mysql.Driver";
    public static final String url
                    = "jdbc:mysql://localhost/ElectricalStore";
    public static final String username = "U1098765";
    public static final String password = "scott";

    private Connection con;
    private Statement st;
    private ResultSet result;
    private JTextArea display = new JTextArea(25,25);
```

```java
        // the constructor
    public ProductQuery()
    {
            // configure the frame and text area
            setTitle("Product query");
            add("Center",display);
            setSize(520,250);
            setVisible(true);
            display.setTabSize(16);
            display.setFont(new Font("DialogInput", Font.BOLD, 14));

            try
            {
                    // load the MySQL jdbc driver
                    Class.forName(driver);
            }
            catch(ClassNotFoundException e)
            {
                display.setText("Driver not found");
            }

            try
            {
                // connect to the database
                con = DriverManager.getConnection(url, username, password);

                // create an SQL statement
                st = con.createStatement();

                // execute an SQL query
                result = st.executeQuery("select * from products");

                // create a heading
                display.setText("Serial#" + "\t" + "Make" + "\t" +
                                    "Description" + "\t" + "Price" + "\n");
                display.append("——-" + "\t" + "—" + "\t" +
                                    "————-" + "\t" + "—-" + "\n");

                // display results
                while(result.next()) // move to next record
                {
                        // retrieve and display first field
                        display.append(result.getString(1) + "\t");
                        // retrieve and display second field
                        display.append(result.getString(2) + "\t");
                        // retrieve and display third field
                        display.append(result.getString(3)+ "\t");
                        // retrieve and display fourth field
                        display.append("£" + result.getString(4)+ "\n");
                }
            }

            catch(SQLException e) // handle the SQLException
            {
                    e.printStackTrace();
            }
        }
    }
```

You can see that we have declared some `String` constants as attributes – these will be explained later, when they are used. After these, we have declared a `Connection` object, a `Statement` object and a `ResultSet` object, none of which you have previously encountered. These are part of the `java.sql` package, and we will explain them in a moment. The final attribute declaration is a `JTextArea` object, `display`, which will be used to display the results.

The first thing we do in the constructor, after configuring the frame and the text area, is to load the driver:

```
try
{
        Class.forName(driver);
}
catch(ClassNotFoundException e)
{
        display.setText("Driver not found");
}
```

You can see we are using a method of a Java class called `Class`. Objects of the `Class` class are constructed by the Java Virtual Machine and they hold representations of all the running classes. The **static** method `forName` loads a class into memory, and returns a representation of that class. The class is located by a string representing its file name. In this case the string, `driver`, was defined as an attribute:

```
public static final String driver = "org.gjt.mm.mysql.Driver";
```

You can see we have given a full path reference to the MySQL driver. Notice that the `forName` method throws a checked exception, `ClassNotFoundException`, if the class is not found, so we have had to enclose it in a **try...catch** block.

Once the driver is loaded we establish a connection to the database as follows:

```
con = DriverManager.getConnection(url, username, password);
```

The class `DriverManager` is located in the `java.sql` package, along with `Connection`, `Statement` and `ResultSet`. The `getConnection` method of `DriverManager` establishes a connection with the database referred to by the parameter `url`, which was defined in the attribute declarations as:

```
public static final String url
                    = "jdbc:mysql://localhost/ElectricalStore";
```

This is the correct format for the MySQL database called *ElectricalStore* residing on the local machine. Other databases will require a slightly different format, the details of which can be found in the documentation for that product. Note that *localhost* is the way in which operating systems refer to the local machine – it is in fact an alias for **IP (Internet Protocol) address** 127.0.0.1, the normal loopback IP. If the database were located on another machine on the network, then this would be replaced by its name or IP address.[1] As you can see, the `getConnection` method receives, in addition to the **url (uniform resource locator)**, the user name and password; if this is not required, there is a version of `getConnection` that accepts the url only.

The method returns a `Connection` object, which we have assigned to the attribute `con`. A `Connection` object created in this way has a number of methods that allow communication with the database. One of these methods is called `createStatement`, and it is the next one we use:

```
st = con.createStatement();
```

As you saw, we declared a `Statement` object, `st`, as an attribute and this is now assigned the return value of the `createStatement` method. A `Statement` object is used for executing SQL statements and returning their results; in the next line we use its `executeQuery` method:

```
result = st.executeQuery("select * from products");
```

---

[1] The system administrator will, of course, have had to set up the correct permissions for the database.

The data returned by executing the query is assigned to a `ResultSet` object, `result`. A `ResultSet` object holds a tabular representation of the data, and a pointer is maintained to allow us to navigate through the records. The `next` method moves the pointer to the next record, returning **false** if there are no more records. The individual fields are returned with methods such as `getString`, `getDouble` and `getInt`. You can see how we have used these methods in the `ProductQuery` class:

```
while(result.next())
{
        display.append(result.getString(1) + "\t");
        display.append(result.getString(2) + "\t");
        display.append(result.getString(3)+ "\t");
        display.append("£" + result.getString(4)+ "\n");
}
```

The version of `getString` that we have used here takes an integer representing the position of the field – in our example 1 is the *SerialNumber*, 2 is *Make* and so on. There is also a version of `getString` that accepts the name of the field. So, for example, we could have used, for the second field:

```
display.append(result.getString("Make") + "\t");
```

Since all we are doing is displaying the data we used `getString` for the last field, even though it holds numeric data – this saved us the trouble of doing any formatting on it. If we had wished to do any processing with this data, we could have used the `getDouble` method to retrieve it as a **double** rather than a `String`.

You should note that all the above methods may throw `SQLExceptions`, hence the use of the **try...catch** block.

23.3.1 Connecting to Microsoft databases

The Microsoft Foundation has its own technology for database connectivity, known as **Open Database Connectivity (ODBC)**. The latest Java versions include what is called a JDBC-to-ODBC bridge driver to enable a Java program to interact with a Microsoft database such as Access. In order to do this it is necessary to configure the database using the Windows ODBC Data Source Administrator tool; this is accessed via the control panel. This allows you to assign a name to a particular database; this name can then be used in the Java program. If for example we created an Access database similar to the one in the previous example, and we then assigned the name *ElectricalStore* to it using the ODBC tool, the correct format for the url string would be:

`"jdbc:odbc:ElectricalStore"`

We would have had to previously load the appropriate driver, which, as we said, is packaged with Java. Its full path name is:

`"sun.jdbc.odbc.JdbcOdbcDriver"`

23.4 Sockets

In chapter 20 you were introduced to the idea of a *stream* – a channel of communication between the computer's main memory and some external device such as a disk. In that chapter you were shown how Java provides high-level classes that hide the programmer from the low-level details of how data is stored on a disk or other device. Just as the external storage of data is a complicated business, so too is the transmission of data across a network.

A **socket** is a software mechanism that is able to hide the programmer from the detail of how data is actually transmitted, in a not dissimilar way to that in which the high-level file handling classes protect the programmer from the details of external storage. Sockets were originally developed for the Unix operating system and they enabled the programmer to treat a network connection as just another stream to which data can be written and from which it can be read. Sockets have since been developed for other operating systems such as Windows, and fortunately for Java.

In order to understand sockets it is also necessary to understand the concept of a **port**. A machine on a network is referred to by its IP (Internet Protocol) address. However, any particular server can perform a number of different functions, and therefore needs to be able to distinguish between different types of request, such as email requests, file transfer requests, requests for web pages and so on. This is accomplished by assigning each type of request a special number known as a *port*. Many ports numbers are now internationally recognized, and so all computers will agree on their meaning. For example, a request on port 80 will always be expected to be an HTTP request; port 23 is reserved for Telnet[2] requests; port 21 is for FTP (File Transfer Protocol) requests. A client program can therefore assume that server programs will be using these ports for those particular services.

All sockets must be capable of doing the following:

> connect to a remote machine;

> send data;

> receive data;

> close a connection.

A socket which is to be used for a server must additionally be able to:

> bind to a port (that is to associate the server with a port number);

> listen for incoming data;

> accept connections from a remote server on the bound port.

The Java `Socket` class has methods that correspond to the first four of the above; the `ServerSocket` class provides methods for the last three.

23.5 A simple server application

The server we are going to build is going to offer a very simple service to a client; it will wait to receive two integers, and then it will send back the sum of those two integers. Clearly this would not in reality be a very useful server – a real-world server would be offering a far more complex service – perhaps performing some very complicated processing, or retrieving data from a database running on the same machine, or maybe printing on a printer local to the server. However, our simple addition server demonstrates the principles of a client–server protocol very nicely.

---

[2] Telnet is a special protocol used for interactive remote command-line sessions.

The application will display a frame containing a text area in which it reports on its behaviour – it will tell us when it is waiting for a connection, when a connection has been established with a client, when the numbers to be added have been received, and when the information has been sent back to the client.

The `AdditionServer` class is presented below – have a look at it and then we'll take you through it.

The *AdditionServer* class

```java
import java.net.*;
import java.io.*;
import javax.swing.*;

public class AdditionServer extends JFrame
{

    private JTextArea textWindow = new JTextArea();
    private int port;

    // the constructor
    public AdditionServer(int portIn)
    {
        port = portIn;
        setTitle("Addition Server");
        add("Center",textWindow);
        setDefaultCloseOperation(JFrame.EXIT_ON_CLOSE);
        setSize(400, 300);
        setVisible(true);
        startServer();
    }

    private void startServer()
    {
        // declare a "general" socket and a server socket
        Socket connection;
        ServerSocket listenSocket;

        // declare low level and high level objects for input
        InputStream inStream;
        DataInputStream inDataStream;

        // declare low level and high level objects for output
        OutputStream outStream;
        DataOutputStream outDataStream;

        // declare other variables
        String client;
        int first, second, sum;
        boolean connected;

        while(true)
        {
            try
            {
                // create a server socket
                listenSocket = new ServerSocket (port);
                textWindow.append("Listening on port " + port + "\n");

                // listen for a connection from the client
                connection = listenSocket.accept();
                connected = true;

                // create an input stream from the client
                inStream = connection.getInputStream();
                inDataStream = new DataInputStream(inStream);

                // create an output stream to the client
                outStream = connection.getOutputStream ();
                outDataStream = new DataOutputStream(outStream);
```

```
                    // wait for a string from the client
                    client = inDataStream.readUTF();
                    textWindow.append("Connection established with "
                                                    + client + "\n");
                    while(connected)
                     {
                            // read an integer from the client
                            first = inDataStream.readInt();
                            textWindow.append("First number received: "
                                                        + first + "\n");
                            // read an integer from the client
                            second = inDataStream.readInt();
                            textWindow.append("Second number received: "
                                                        + second + "\n");

                            sum = first + second;
                            textWindow.append("Sum returned: "
                                                        + sum + "\n");

                            // send the sum to the client
                            outDataStream.writeInt(sum);
                     }
                 }

                 catch (IOException e)
                 {
                     connected = false;
                 }
            }
        }
    }
```

You can see that we have declared a text area as an attribute, as well as an integer to hold the port number that the server is to bind to. As you can see, this is accepted by the constructor and assigned to this attribute; thus the port is selected by the user of this class. The rest of the constructor is concerned with configuring the frame and then calling a **private** method `startServer`.

The `startServer` method begins by declaring a number of variables:

```
// declare a "general" socket and a server socket
Socket connection;
ServerSocket listenSocket;

// declare low level and high level objects for input
InputStream inStream;
DataInputStream inDataStream;

// declare low level and high level objects for output
OutputStream outStream;
DataOutputStream outDataStream;

// declare other variables
String client;
int first, second, sum;
boolean connected;
```

The first two variables are, respectively, a `Server` and a `ServerSocket`. As this is a server application it requires both the general functionality of the `Socket` class and the specialist functionality of the `ServerSocket` class.

Next we declare the objects that we will need to establish an input stream with the client. We have come across the classes `InputStream` and `DataInputStream` before, in chapter 20. The former allows communication at a low level in the form of bytes; the latter allows the high-level communication in the form of strings, integers, characters and so on with which we are familiar.

After this we declare objects of OutputStream and DataOutputStream that we will need to establish the output stream. Finally we make some other declarations that we will need later on.

Now we start an infinite loop. The idea is that the server will accept a connection request from a client, and when that client is finished making requests it will be ready to receive connections from other clients; this will continue until the server is terminated.

From now everything is placed in a **try** block because the constructor of the ServerSocket class, and its accept method may both throw IOExceptions.

The first two instructions in the **try** block look like this:

```
listenSocket = new ServerSocket(port);
textWindow.append("Listening on port " + port + "\n");
```

We are creating a new ServerSocket object and binding it to a particular port. Next we call the accept method of the ServerSocket class to listen for a client requesting a connection on that port.

```
connection = listenSocket.accept();
connected = true;
```

The accept method returns an object of the Socket class, which we assign to the connection variable that we declared earlier. We then set the **boolean** variable, connected, to **true**.

The server is now listening for requests from clients on that port. This information is displayed in the text window as shown in figure 23.3.

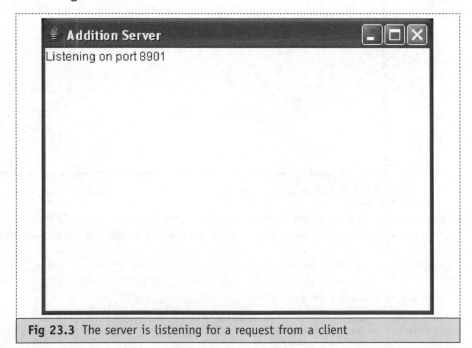

Fig 23.3 The server is listening for a request from a client

The next thing we do is call the `getInputStream` method of the `Socket` object, `connection`. This returns an object of the `InputStream` class, thus providing a stream from client to server. We then wrap this low-level `InputStream` object with a high-level `DataInputStream` object, in the same way as we did when handling files in chapter 20:

```
inStream = connection.getInputStream();
inDataStream = new DataInputStream(inStream);
```

We then create an output stream in the same way:

```
outStream = connection.getOutputStream ();
outDataStream = new DataOutputStream(outStream);
```

As you will see shortly, we have designed our client to send its IP address to the server once it is connected. So our next instructions to the server are to wait to receive a string on the input stream, and then to display a message as shown in figure 23.4:

```
client = inDataStream.readUTF();
textWindow.append("Connection established with " + client + "\n" );
```

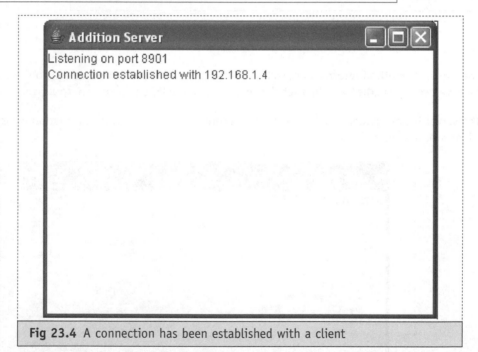

Fig 23.4 A connection has been established with a client

Once a connection has been established we want the server to perform the addition calculation for the client as many times as the client requires. Thus we provide a **while** loop that continues until the connection is lost:

```
while(connected)
{
    // read an integer from the client
    first = inDataStream.readInt();
    textWindow.append("First number received: " + first + "\n");
    // read an integer from the client
    second = inDataStream.readInt();
    textWindow.append("Second number received: " + second + "\n");
    sum = first + second;
```

```
        textWindow.append("Sum returned: " + sum + "\n");
        // send the sum to the client
        outDataStream.writeInt (sum);
    }
```

You can see that we read two integers from the input stream, displaying them each time. We then calculate and display the sum which we send back to the client on the output stream. Figure 23.5 shows an example of this:

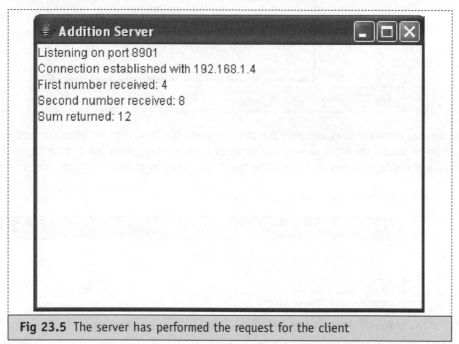

Fig 23.5 The server has performed the request for the client

The accept method of `ServerSocket` throws an `IOException` when the connection is lost. Therefore we have coded the **catch** block so that the connected variable that controls the inner **while** loop is set to **false**, so that when the client closes the connection the server will no longer expect to receive integers, but will return to the top of the outer **while** loop, and wait for another connection request:

```
catch (IOException e)
{
        connected = false;
}
```

We can run our server with program 23.1, which in this example will bind the server to port 8901:

Program 23.1

```
public class RunAdditionServer
{
    public static void main (String[] args)
    {
        new AdditionServer(8901);
    }
}
```

Now we can go on and build a client application that will communicate with the server.

23.6 A simple client application

Our `AdditionClient` is shown in figure 23.6.

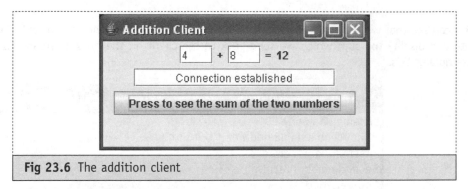

Fig 23.6 The addition client

You can see from the diagram how the client is going to work. The connection is established as soon as the application starts; then the user is free to enter numbers and press the button to send the numbers to the server and display the result. The middle text box is used to display messages regarding the connection.

Here is the code for the `AdditionClient`:

> ### The *AdditionClient* class
>
> ```java
> import java.net.*;
> import java.io.*;
> import javax.swing.*;
> import java.awt.*;
> import java.awt.event.*;
>
> public class AdditionClient extends JFrame implements ActionListener
> {
>     // declare the visual components
>     private JTextField firstNumber = new JTextField(3);
>     private JLabel plus = new JLabel("+");
>     private JTextField secondNumber = new JTextField(3);
>     private JLabel equals = new JLabel("=");
>     private JLabel sum = new JLabel();
>     private JTextField msg = new JTextField(20);
>     private JButton addButton
>             = new JButton("Press to see the sum of the two numbers");
>
>     // declare low level and high level objects for input
>     private InputStream inStream;
>     private DataInputStream inDataStream;
>
>     // declare low level and high level objects for output
>     private OutputStream outStream;
>     private DataOutputStream outDataStream;
>
>     // declare a socket
>     private Socket connection;
>
>     // declare attributes to hold details of remote machine and port
>     private String remoteMachine;
>     private int port;
>
>     // constructor
>     public AdditionClient(String remoteMachineIn, int portIn)
>     {
>         remoteMachine = remoteMachineIn;
>         port = portIn;
> ```

```java
        // add the visual components
        add(firstNumber);
        add(plus);
        add(secondNumber);
        add(equals);
        add(sum);
        add(msg);
        add(addButton);

        // configure the frame
        setLayout(new FlowLayout());
        setTitle("Addition Client");
        msg.setHorizontalAlignment(JLabel.CENTER);
        addButton.addActionListener(this);
        setDefaultCloseOperation(JFrame.EXIT_ON_CLOSE);
        setSize(300, 150);
        setLocation(300,300);
        setVisible(true);

        // start the helper method that starts the client
        startClient();
    }

private void startClient()
{
    try
    {
        // attempt to create a connection to the server
        connection = new Socket(remoteMachine, port);
        msg.setText("Connection established");

        // create an input stream from the server
        inStream = connection.getInputStream();
        inDataStream = new DataInputStream(inStream);

        // create an output stream to the server
        outStream = connection.getOutputStream();
        outDataStream = new DataOutputStream(outStream);

        // send the host IP to the server
         outDataStream.writeUTF(connection.getLocalAddress().getHostAddress());
    }
    catch (UnknownHostException e)
    {
            msg.setText("Unknown host");
    }
    catch (IOException except)
    {
        msg.setText("Network Exception");
    }
}

public void actionPerformed(ActionEvent e)
{
    try
    {
        // send the two integers to the server
        outDataStream.writeInt(Integer.parseInt(firstNumber.getText()));
        outDataStream.writeInt(Integer.parseInt(secondNumber.getText()));

        // read and display the result sent back from the server
        int result = inDataStream.readInt();
        sum.setText("" + result);
    }
    catch(IOException ie)
    {
        ie.printStackTrace();
    }
}
}
```

We have declared a number of attributes, mostly concerned with the graphics components and with the input and output streams. We have also declared an object of the `Socket` class, and we have additionally declared a string, `remoteMachine`, and an integer, `port`. Both of these will be initialized via the constructor in order to allow the user of the class to specify the remote machine on which the server is running and the port on which it is listening.

Thus the constructor accepts a `String` and an **int**, which it assigns to `remoteMachine` and `port` respectively. The rest of the constructor is concerned with adding components to the frame and configuring it. Finally the constructor calls the **private** method `startClient`.

The `startClient` method itself begins with a **try** block. This is necessary because the constructor of the `Socket` class potentially throws two exceptions. It is called like this:

```
connection = new Socket(remoteMachine, port);
```

Creating a new `Socket` in this way broadcasts a message requesting a response from the remote machine specified (either by its network name or its IP address), listening on the port in question. If the connection is established, and no exception is therefore thrown, the constructor goes on to display the message "Connection established" in the message area, and then to initialize the input and output streams. It finishes with this instruction:

```
outDataStream.writeUTF(connection.getLocalAddress().getHostAddress());
```

You will recall that we programmed the server so that the first thing it did after the connection was established was to wait for a string from the client. Here you can see how the client sends its address to the server on the output stream. It calls the `getLocalAddress` method of the `Socket` class. This returns an object of the `InetAddress` class. The `InetAddress` class holds a representation of an IP address and enables us to obtain the host name, or the IP address (as a `String`), with the methods `getHostName` and `getHostAddress` respectively.

Now we have to catch the exceptions that can be thrown by the constructor. If the host we are trying to connect to is unknown then an `UnknownHostException` is thrown:

```
catch (UnknownHostException e)
{
        msg.setText("Unknown host");
}
```

You can see that in this case an appropriate message is placed in the message area. If there is another network error (perhaps no server is running on the specified host), then an `IOException` is thrown:

```
catch (IOException except)
{
        msg.setText("Network Exception");
}
```

The `actionPerformed` method determines what happens when we press the button that gets the server to perform the addition for us:

```
public void actionPerformed(ActionEvent e)
{
    try
    {
        outDataStream.writeInt(Integer.parseInt(firstNumber.getText()));
        outDataStream.writeInt(Integer.parseInt(secondNumber.getText()));

        int result = inDataStream.readInt();
        sum.setText("" + result);
    }
    catch(IOException ie)
    {
        ie.printStackTrace();
    }
}
```

This is straightforward: we send the two numbers to the server and read the response. We enclose everything in a **try...catch** block so that the exceptions thrown by the readInt and writeInt methods are handled.

The socket example here is clearly rather elementary. Java provides a very wide range of possibilities for communication via sockets, for example secure sockets and sockets for multicasting. This is beyond the scope of this book, but it is hoped that we have given you a flavour for what is available so that those of you who want to develop your skills in this area are able to move forward.

In question 6 of the programming exercises that follow we have shown you our version of a socket-based chat application – we have provided some hints so that you can try this for yourself.

Self-test questions

1   Explain the principles of *client–server* architecture.

2   What is the difference between an *applet* and an *application* in Java?

3   Explain the purpose of the following methods of the `JApplet` class:

> `init`;

> `start`;

> `stop`;

> `destroy`.

4   Explain the technology known as **Java Database Connectivity (JDBC)**.

5   Explain the function and purpose of the Java `Socket` and `ServerSocket` classes.

Programming exercises

1   Implement the applets that we developed in this chapter. You should find that your IDE provides an applet viewer in which to test and run the applets. However, you may then wish to run these in a browser and eventually to upload them to a remote website. Make sure that the `.class` file is in the same directory as the HTML file that loads the applet.

2   Look back at the `MetricConverter` class in chapter 10 and the `RedCircle` class that we developed in chapter 14. Convert these to applets so that you can run them in a browser.

3   If you have a database program such as MySQL, then implement the `ProductQuery` class – either by adapting it for your own database, or creating the *ElectricalStore* database.

4   If you have a Microsoft database system such as Access, then try to adapt the `ProductQuery` class to interact with this database. You should read section 23.3.1 carefully and make sure you configure your database using the Windows ODBC Data Source Administrator tool.

5   Write a server application that tells jokes to the client, and lets the client respond. A good example would be a classic "Knock Knock" joke. The client would receive the message "Knock Knock" from the server, and would be expected to reply "Who's there?" and so on. You could adapt the program so that a different joke is told each time a client connects (that is, if you actually know that many "Knock Knock" jokes).

6   The application shown below is a client–server chat application, which you can try to implement. We have given you some hints below.

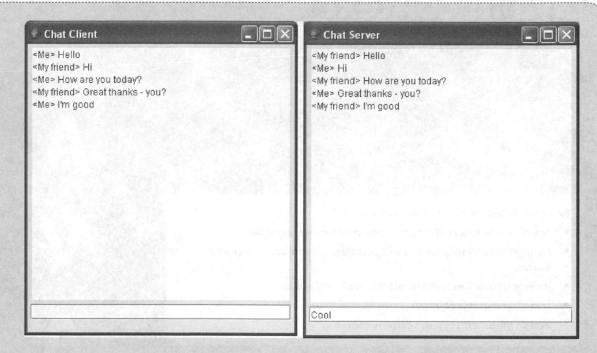

Here are the hints:

❯ Both the client and the server have to be able to listen for connections, and at the same time be capable of sending messages entered by the user. They will therefore need to be multi-threaded. The main thread will allow the user to enter messages which it will send to the remote program. The other thread will listen for messages from the remote program and display them in the text area.

❯ When the thread is created it will need to receive a reference to the text area where the messages are to be displayed, and a reference to the socket connection. It will need to create an input stream which must be associated with this connection. Its run method must be written so that the thread continuously waits for messages on the input stream and then displays them in the text area. Both the client and the server classes will need to create an object of this thread and start the thread running.

❯ In the above example, rather than having a button that has to be pressed, the message is sent and echoed in the text area when the <Enter> key is pressed. To achieve this the class must implement the KeyListener interface. This has methods keyPressed, keyReleased and keyTyped; they receive an object of the KeyEvent class, one of whose methods is keyChar, which returns the character that was pressed. This can be used to see if it was the <Enter> key ('\n') that was pressed.

In fact, the only difference between the client and the server is the fact that initially the server waits for the client to initiate a connection – once the connection is established the behaviour is the same.

You can see that in the above example, the local user is referred to as <Me> and the remote user as <My friend>. You could improve on this by sending the name of the user to the remote program which it can in turn send to the thread that it creates.

Good luck with your version!

CHAPTER: 24

Java in context

Objectives:

By the end of this chapter you should be able to:

- *provide a brief history of the development of the Java language;*
- *identify the potential problems with **pointers**, **multiple inheritance** and **aliases**;*
- *develop* `clone` *methods to avoid the problem of aliases;*
- *identify **immutable objects**;*
- *explain the benefits of Java's **garbage collector**.*

24.1 Introduction

Originally named *Oak*, Java was developed in 1991 by Sun Microsystems. At the time, the intention was to use it to program consumer devices such as video recorders, mobile phones and televisions. The expectation was that these devices would soon need to communicate with each other. As it turned out, however, this concept didn't take off until later. Instead, it was the growth of the Internet through the World Wide Web that was to be the real launch pad for the language.

The original motivation behind its development explains many of its characteristics. In particular, the **size** and **reliability** of the language became very important.

24.2 Language size

Generally, the processor power of a system controlling a consumer device is very small compared with that of a PC; so the language used to develop such systems should be fairly compact. Consequently, the Java language is relatively small and compact when compared with other traditional languages. At the time Java was being developed, C++ was a very popular programming language. For this reason the developers of Java decided to stick to conventional C++ syntax as much as possible. Consequently Java syntax is very similar to C++ syntax.

Just because the Java language is relatively small, however, does not mean that it is not as powerful as some other languages. Instead, the Java developers were careful to remove certain language features that they felt led to common program errors. These include the ability for a programmer to create **pointers** and the ability for a programmer to develop **multiple inheritance** hierarchies.

24.2.1 Pointers

A pointer, in programming terms, is a variable containing an address in memory. Of course Java programmers can do something very similar to this – they can create *references*. Figure 24.1 repeats an example we showed you in chapter 6.

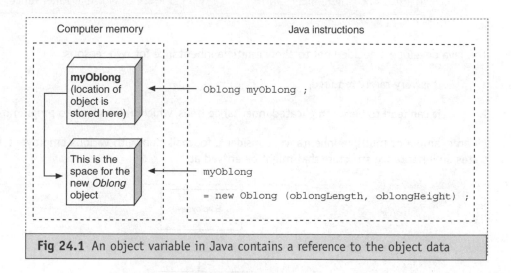

Fig 24.1 An object variable in Java contains a reference to the object data

In figure 24.1, the variable `myOblong` contains a reference (address in memory) of an `Oblong` object. The difference between a *reference* and a *pointer* is that the *programmer* does not have control over which address in memory is used – the *system* takes care of this. Of course, internally, the system creates a pointer and controls its location. In a language like C++ the programmer can directly manipulate this pointer (move it along and back in memory). This was seen as giving the programmer greater control. However, if this ability is abused, critical areas of memory can easily be corrupted. For this reason the Java language developers did not allow users to manipulate pointers directly.

24.2.2 Multiple inheritance

Inheritance is an important feature of object-oriented languages. Many object-oriented languages, such as C++ and Eiffel, allow an extended form of inheritance known as multiple inheritance. When programming in Java, a class can only ever inherit from at most one superclass. Multiple inheritance allows a class to inherit from more than one superclass (see figures 24.2 and 24.3).

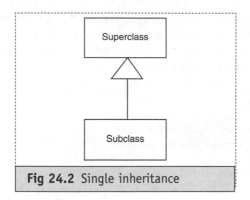

Fig 24.2 Single inheritance

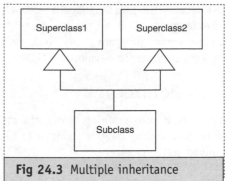

Fig 24.3 Multiple inheritance

The Java developers decided not to allow multiple inheritance for two reasons:

> it is very rarely required;

> it can lead to very complicated inheritance trees, which in turn lead to programming errors.

As an example of multiple inheritance, consider a football club with various employees. Figure 24.4 illustrates an inheritance structure that might be arrived at.

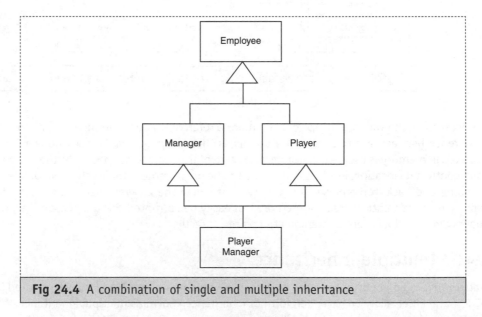

Fig 24.4 A combination of single and multiple inheritance

Here, a `PlayerManager` inherits from both `Player` and `Manager`, both of which in turn inherit from `Employee`! As you can see this is starting to get a little messy. Things become even more complicated when we consider method overriding. If both `Player` and `Manager` have a method called `payBonus`, which method should be called for `PlayerManager` – or should it be overridden?

Although Java disallows multiple inheritance it does offer a type of multiple inheritance – interfaces. As we have seen in previous chapters, a class can inherit from only one base class in Java but can implement many interfaces.

24.3 **Language reliability**

The Java language developers placed a lot of emphasis on ensuring that programs developed in Java would be reliable. One way in which they did this was to provide the extensive exception handling techniques that we covered in chapter 15. Another way reliability was improved was to remove the ability for programmers to directly manipulate pointers as we discussed earlier in this chapter. Errors arising from pointer manipulation in other languages are very common. A related problem, however, is still prevalent in Java but can be avoided to a large extent. This is the problem of **aliasing**.

24.3.1 **Aliasing**

Aliasing occurs when the *same* memory location is accessed by variables with *different* names. As an example, we could create an object, oblong1, of the Oblong class as follows:

```
Oblong oblong1 = new Oblong (10, 20);
```

We could then declare a new variable, oblong2, which could reference the same object:

```
Oblong oblong2 = oblong1;
```

Here oblong1 is simply a different name for object1 – in other words an **alias**. The effect of creating an alias is illustrated in figure 24.5.

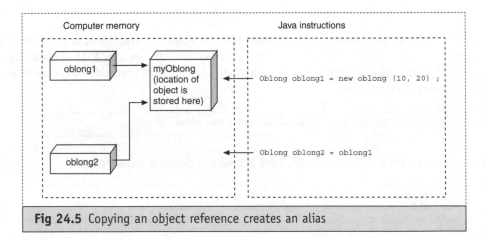

Fig 24.5 Copying an object reference creates an alias

In practice a programmer would normally create an alias only with good reason. For example, in chapter 7, when we deleted bank accounts from a list, we were able to make good use of aliasing by assigning an object reference to a different object with a statement like:

```
list[i] = list[i+1];
```

After this instruction, list[i] is pointing to the same object as list[i+1]. In this case that was the intention. However, a potential problem with a language that allows aliasing is that it could lead to errors arising inadvertently. Consider for example a Customer class that keeps track of just two bank accounts. Here is the outline of that class:

```
public class Customer
{
        // two private attributes to hold bank account details
        private BankAccount account1;
        private BankAccount account2;

        // more code here

        // two access methods
        public BankAccount getFirstAccount()
        {
                return account1;
        }

        public BankAccount getSecondAccount()
        {
                return account2;
        }
}
```

Consider the methods `getFirstAccount` and `getSecondAccount`. In each case we have sent back a reference to a **private** attribute, which is itself an object. We did this to allow users of this class to interrogate details about the two bank accounts, with statements such as:

```
BankAccount tempAccount = someCustomer.getFirstAccount();
System.out.println("balance of first account = "+tempAccount.getBalance());
```

Let us assume that this produced the following output:

balance of first account = 250.0

This is fine, but the `tempAccount` object, that we have just created, is now an alias for the **private** `BankAccount` object in the `Customer` class. It can be used to manipulate this **private** `BankAccount` object without going through any `Customer` methods. To demonstrate this let us withdraw money from the alias:

```
tempAccount.withdraw(100); // withdraw 100 from alias
```

Now let us go back and examine the bank account in the `Customer` class:

```
double balance = someCustomer.getFirstAccount().getBalance();
System.out.println("balance of first account = " + balance);
```

In this case we have retrieved the first bank account, and its balance in one instruction. We then display this balance, giving the following output:

balance of first account = 150.0

The balance of this internal account has been reduced by 100 without the `Customer` class having any control over this! From this example you can see how dangerous aliases can be.

There are a few examples in this book where we have returned references to **private** objects, but we have been careful not to take advantage of this by manipulating **private** attributes in this way. However, the important point is that they *could* be manipulated in that way. In order to make classes extra secure (for example, in the development of safety-critical systems), aliasing should be avoided.

The problem of aliases arises when a copy of an object's *data* is required but instead a copy of the object's *reference* is returned. These two types of copies are sometime referred to as *deep copy* (for a copy of an object's data) and *shallow copy* (for a copy of an object's reference). By sending back a shallow copy, the original object can be manipulated, whereas a deep copy would not cause any harm to the original object.

In order to provide such a deep copy, a class should define a method that returns an exact copy of the object data. Such a method exists in the `Object` class, but this should be overridden in any user-defined class. The method is called `clone`. We want to send back copies of `BankAccount` objects, so we need to include a `clone` method in the original `BankAccount` class.

24.3.2 Overriding the *clone* method

You have seen examples of overriding `Object` methods before. In chapter 17, for instance, we overrode the `toString` and `hashCode` methods in the `Object` class. There is one important difference, however, between the `clone` method and other `Object` methods such as `hashCode` and `toString`. The `clone` method is declared as **protected** in the `Object` class, whereas methods such as `hashCode` and `toString` are declared as **public**.

Methods which are **protected** can only be called from within the same package (`Object` is in the `java.lang` package), or *within* subclasses. Methods which are **protected** are *not* part of the external interface of a class.

So if we wish to provide a `clone` method for any class, we are *forced* to override the `clone` method from `Object`. When we override this method we must make it **public** and not **protected**. When overriding methods you are able to give them wider access modifiers but not less – so a **protected** method can be overridden to be **public**, but not vice versa. The return type of the `clone` method is always `Object`:

```
// clone methods you write must have this interface
public Object clone() // must be a public method
{
      // code goes here
}
```

There were sound security reasons for the Java developers forcing you to override the `clone` method if you wish objects of your classes to be cloned, rather than allow objects of *all* classes to use the `clone` method in the `Object` class. For example, you might be developing a class in which you did not want objects of that class to be cloned.

However, we *do* want to provide the original `BankAccount` class with a `clone` method. Such a method would allow the `Customer` class to send back clones of `BankAccount` objects, rather than aliases as it is currently doing. Here is outline of the `BankAccount` class with one possible implementation of such a method:

```
class BankAccount
{
      // private attributes as before
      private String accountNumber;
      private String accountName;
      private double balance;
      // previous methods go here
      // now provide a clone method
      public Object clone()
      {
        // call contsructor to create a new object identical to this object
        BankAccount copyOfThisAccount = new BankAccount
                              (accountNumber, accountName);
```

```
        /* after this the balance of the two bank accounts might not be the
           same, so copy the balance as well */
        copyOfThisAccount.balance = balance;
        // finally, send back this copy
        return copyOfThisAccount;
    }
}
```

Notice that in order to set the balance of the copied bank account we have directly accessed the **private** balance attribute of the copy:

```
copyOfThisAccount.balance = balance;
```

This is perfectly legal as we are in a BankAccount class, so all BankAccount objects created within this class can access their **private** attributes. Now, whenever we need to copy a BankAccount object we just call the clone method. For example:

```
// create the original object
BankAccount ourAccount = new BankAccount ("98765432", "Charatan and Kans");
// now make a copy using the clone method, notice a type cast is required
BankAccount tempAccount = (BankAccount) ourAccount.clone();
// other instructions here
```

The clone method sends back an exact copy of the original account, not a copy of the reference (see figure 24.6).

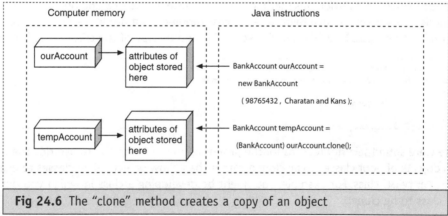

Fig 24.6 The "clone" method creates a copy of an object

Now, whatever we do to the copied object will leave the original object unaffected, and vice versa.

In a similar way, we can ensure that classes that contain BankAccount objects do not inadvertently send back references (and hence aliases) to these objects:

```
class Customer
{
    // as before here

    // next two methods now send back clones, not aliases
    public BankAccount getFirstAccount()
    {
        return (BankAccount)account1.clone();
    }

    public BankAccount getSecondAccount()
    {
```

```
          return (BankAccount)account2.clone();
     }
}
```

Now, in our earlier example, the problem is removed because of the use of the clone method in the Customer class, as illustrated in the fragment below:

```
Customer someCustomer = new Customer();

// some code to update someCutomer here


/* now a temporary variable is created to read details of first account but
   this is not an alias it is a clone */
BankAccount tempAccount = someCustomer.getFirstaccount();
System.out.println("balance of first account = " +
                                        tempAccount.getBalance();
// assume the balance is displayed as 500

temp.withdraw(100); /* because temp is a clone the private BankAccount
                       attribute account1 is unaffected */
System.out.println("balance of first account = " +
                        someCustomer.getFirstAccount().getBalance());
// the balance of the customer's first account will be still be 500
```

24.3.3 Immutable objects

We said methods that return references to objects actually create aliases and that this can be dangerous. However, these aliases are not *always* dangerous. Consider the following features of the original BankAccount class:

```
class BankAccount
{
     private String accountNumber;

     // other attributes and methods here

     public String getAccountNumber()
     {
        return accountNumber;
     }
}
```

In this case the getAccountNumber method returns a reference to a **private** String object (accountNumber). This is an alias for the **private** String attribute. However, this alias causes no harm as there are no String methods that allow a String object to be altered. So, this alias cannot be used to alter the **private** String object.

Objects which have no methods to alter their state are known as **immutable objects**. String objects are immutable objects. Objects of classes that you develop may also be immutable depending on the methods you have provided. If such objects are immutable, you do not have to worry about creating aliases of these objects and do not need to provide them with clone methods. For example, let's go back to the Library application (consisting of a collection of Book objects) that we developed in chapter 17. Rather than show you the code, figure 24.7 shows you the UML design for the Library and Book classes.

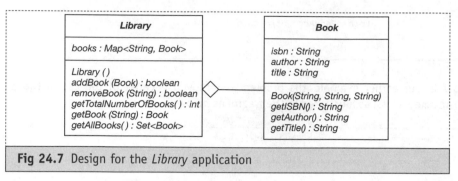

Fig 24.7 Design for the *Library* application

As you can see, the Library class contains a collection of Book objects. These Book objects are part of the **private** books attribute in the Library class. However the getBook method returns a reference to one of these Book objects and so sends back an alias. This is not a problem, however, because if you look at the design of the Book class the only methods provided are get methods. In other words, there are no Book methods that can alter the attributes of the Book object once the Book object has been created. A Book object is an immutable object.

24.3.4 Using the *clone* method of the "Object" class

Although the clone method in the Object class is not made available as part of your class's external interface, it can be used *within* classes that you develop. In particular, you might wish to use it within a clone method that you write yourself, as it does carry out the task of copying an object for you – albeit with some restrictions.

The clone method from the Object class copies the *memory contents* allocated to the object attributes. This is sometimes referred to as a *bit-wise copy*. This means that it makes exact copies of attributes that are of primitive type, and it makes copies of references for attributes that are objects. Of course, a copy of a reference gives you an alias – but if the object in question is immutable, this is not a problem. This means that:

> if a class's attributes are all of primitive type, then make your clone method just call the clone method of Object;

> if a class's attributes include objects, and these objects are *all* immutable, then again make your clone method just call the clone method of Object;

> if a class's attributes include any objects which are *not* immutable, then you *cannot* rely upon the clone method of Object to make a sensible copy and so you must write your own instructions for providing a clone.

Bearing these points in mind, let us revisit the clone method for our BankAccount class.

```
class BankAccount
{
        // attributes
        private String accountNumber;
        private String accountName;
        private double balance;

        public Object clone()
        {
           // code goes here
        }
```

```
        // other code here
}
```

To make a copy of a `BankAccount` object we need a new bank account with an identical account number, name and balance. The `balance` attribute is of type **double**, so a bit-wise copy would be fine here. The account name and number are both `String` objects; since Strings are immutable a bit-wise copy is fine here also. This means the *entire* object can be safely copied using the `clone` method of `Object`. Here is a first attempt at using this method within our own `clone` method – it will not compile!:

```
// this attempt to clone a BankAccount will not compile
public Object clone()
{
        // call 'clone' method of superclass Object
        return  super.clone();

}
```

This will not compile at the moment because the `clone` method of `Object` checks whether developers of this class really want to allow cloning to go ahead.

To indicate that developers do want cloning to go ahead, they have to mark their class as implementing the `Cloneable` interface. This interface, much like `Serializable`, contains no methods. It is just used to mark a class with some extra information. So, in order to call the `clone` method of `Object`, we need to mark the `BankAccount` class as follows:

```
// marking this class Cloneable allows us to call clone method of Object
public class BankAccount implements Cloneable
{
        // code here can use 'super.clone()'
}
```

There is one last thing we need to do in order to use the `clone` method of the `Object` class. This method throws a checked `CloneNotSupportedException` if the calling class does not implement the `Cloneable` interface. Of course we know our class does implement this interface, but as this is a checked exception, we still need to provide a **try...catch** around the call to `super.clone()` to keep the compiler happy. Here is the modified `BankAccount` class:

```
// mark that objects of this class can be cloned
public class BankAccount implements Cloneable
{
        // attributes as before
        private String accountNumber;
        private String accountName;
        private double balance;


        // this method allows BankAccount objects to be cloned
        public Object clone()
        {
          try
          {
              return super.clone(); // call 'clone' from Object
          }
          catch (CloneNotSupportedException e) // will never be thrown!
          {
              return null;
          }
        }

        // other code here
}
```

Whether or not you use `super.clone()` in your implementation of the `clone` method, it is always a good idea to mark your class `Cloneable`, so it is clear that objects from your class can be cloned.

24.3.5 Garbage collection

When an object is created using the **new** operator, a request is being made to grab an area of free computer memory to store the object's attributes. Because this memory is requested during the running of a program, not during compilation, the compiler cannot guarantee that enough memory exists to meet this request. Memory could become exhausted for two related reasons:

> continual requests to grab memory are made when no more free memory exists;

> memory that is no longer needed is not released back to the system.

These problems are common to all programming languages and the danger of memory exhaustion is a real one for large programs, or programs running in a small memory space. Java allows both of the reasons listed above to be dealt with effectively and thus ensures that programs do not crash unexpectedly.

First, exception-handling techniques can be used to monitor for memory exhaustion and code can be written to ensure the program terminates gracefully. More importantly, Java has a built-in **garbage collection** facility to release unused memory. This is a facility that regularly trawls through memory looking for locations used by the program, freeing any locations that are no longer in use.

For example consider program 24.1 below.

Program 24.1

```
public class Tester
{
  public static void main(String[] args)
  {
      char ans;
      Oblong object; // reference to object created here
      do
      {
        System.out.print("Enter length: ");
        double length = EasyScanner.nextDouble();
        System.out.print("Enter height: ");
        double height = EasyScanner.nextDouble();
        // new object created each time we go around the loop
        object = new Oblong(length, height);
        System.out.println("area = "+ object.calculateArea());
        System.out.println("perimeter = "+ object.calculatePermeter());
        System.out.print("Do you want another go? ");
        ans = EasyScanner.nextChar();
      } while (ans == 'y' || ans == 'Y');
  }
}
```

Here, a new object is created each time we go around the loop. The memory used for the previous object is no longer required. In a language like C++ the memory occupied by old objects would not be destroyed unless the programmer added instructions to do so. So if the programmer forgot to do this, and this happened on a large scale in your C++ program, the available memory space could easily be exhausted. The Java system, however, regularly checks for such unused objects in memory and destroys them.

Although automatic garbage collection does make extra demands on the system (slowing it down while it takes place), this extra demand is considered by many to be worthwhile by removing a heavy burden on programmers. In fact, Microsoft's new language, C# (pronounced "C Sharp"), also includes a garbage collection facility.

24.4 The role of Java

While Java began life as a language to program consumer devices, it has now evolved into a standard application programming language and competes with other languages such as C++.

Java retains much of the C++ syntax and this has helped its growth in popularity as C++ programmers have found it relatively easy to move over to Java. Unsafe and unsound C++ features, such as pointers and multiple inheritance, have been removed from the language. In addition, robust exception-handling features have been incorporated into Java to help ensure the reliability of Java programs.

Where system efficiency is the most important criterion for a software project, languages like C++ still play an important role as the JVM model can place an overhead on the speed of the final system. Also, while Java's garbage collector certainly improves the robustness of Java programs, it can compromise program efficiency. However, with the growth of the Internet, system reliability, robustness and cross-platform capability are becoming increasingly important. Java offers all these attributes and so its future certainly looks very secure.

24.5 What next?

This chapter marks the end of our Java coverage for your second semester in programming. Although you have covered a lot of material, there is still more that you can explore. For example, there are some packages that we have not had space to discuss here. Table 24.1 lists a few you might wish to study further.

Table 24.1 Some additional Java packages	
Package name	**Description**
`java.beans`	Contains classes such as `Beans`, that relate to the development of re-useable visual components within a rapid application development environment.
`java.math`	Contains classes such as `BigInteger` and `BigDecimal` that do not have upper and lower limits on their number ranges, and so allow for extremely rigorous calculations.
`java.rmi`	Contains classes such as `RMISecurityManager` for dealing with remote method calling within a distributed environment.
`javax.xml.parsers`	Contains classes such as `DocumentBuilder` that allow you to *parse* an XML document. To *parse* a document means to check that it is valid and then to take some action.

You might find out more about packages such as these in advanced modules on your course. In the meantime, don't forget you can get further information on the Java language at the Sun website www.java.sun.com/docs.

Now that you have completed two semesters of programming we are pretty certain that you will have come to realize what an exciting and rewarding an activity it can be. So whether you are going on to a career in software engineering, or some other field in computing – or even if you are just going to enjoy programming for its own sake, we wish you the very best of luck for the future.

Self-test questions

1 Distinguish between a *pointer* and a *reference*.

2 What does the term *multiple inheritance* mean and why does Java disallow it?

3 Consider the following class:

The *Critical* class

```java
public class Critical
{
  private int value;

  public Critical (int valueIn)
    {
      value = valueIn;
    }
  public void setValue(int valueIn)
    {
       value = valueIn;
    }
  public int getValue ()
    {
      return value;
    }
}
```

a) Explain why `Critical` objects are not immutable.

b) Write fragments of code to create `Critical` objects and demonstrate the problem of aliases.

c) Develop a `clone` method in the `Critical` class (make use of the `clone` method of `Object` here).

d) Write fragments of code to demonstrate the use of this `clone` method.

4 Look back at the classes from the two case studies of chapters 11 and 21.

a) Which methods in these classes return aliases?

b) Which aliases could be dangerous?

c) How can these aliases be avoided?

5 What are the advantages and disadvantages of a *garbage collection* facility in a programming language?

Programming exercises

1 Implement the `Critical` class of self-test question 3 and then write a tester program to demonstrate the problem of aliases.

2 Amend the `Critical` class by adding a `clone` method as discussed in self-test question 3(c) and then amend the tester program you developed in the previous programming exercise to demonstrate the use of this `clone` method.

3 Implement the changes you identified in self-test question 4, in order to remove the aliases that might have been present in the classes from the two case studies.

4 Review all the classes that you have developed so far and identify any problems with aliases. Provide appropriate `clone` methods to avoid these aliases.

Index